Handbook of Fiscal Federalism

Edited by

Ehtisham Ahmad

Advisor, International Monetary Fund, USA

Giorgio Brosio

Professor of Economics, University of Turin, Italy

Edward Elgar

Cheltenham, UK • Northampton, MA, USA

Published by
Edward Elgar Publishing Limited
Glensanda House
Montpellier Parade
Cheltenham
Glos GL50 1UA
UK

Edward Elgar Publishing, Inc.
136 West Street
Suite 202
Northampton
Massachusetts 01060
USA

A catalogue record for this book
is available from the British Library

ISBN-13: 978 1 84542 008 6
ISBN-10: 1 84542 008 X

Typeset by Cambrian Typesetters, Camberley, Surrey
Printed and bound in Great Britain by MPG Books Ltd, Bodmin, Cornwall

Contents

v

PART III   IMPLEMENTING MULTILEVEL FISCAL SYSTEMS

PART IV   EMERGING ISSUES

Contributors

Ehtisham Ahmad, International Monetary Fund, Washington, DC, USA.

Junaid Ahmad, World Bank, Washington, DC, USA.

Maria Albino-War, International Monetary Fund, Washington, DC, USA.

Maria Flavia Ambrosanio, Catholic University of Milan, Italy.

Pranab Bardhan, University of California, Berkeley, USA.

Richard M. Bird, University of Toronto, Canada.

Robin Boadway, Queen's University, Kingston, Canada.

Massimo Bordignon, Catholic University of Milan, Italy.

Albert Breton, University of Toronto, Canada.

Giorgio Brosio, University of Turin, Italy.

Roger D. Congleton, George Mason University, Fairfax, VA, USA.

Bernard Dafflon, University of Fribourg, Germany.

Silvana Dalmazzone, University of Turin, Italy.

Shantayanan Devarajan, World Bank, Washington, DC, USA.

Robert D. Ebel, World Bank and Urban Institute, Washington, DC, USA.

Reiner Eichenberger, University of Zurich, Switzerland.

Bruno S. Frey, University of Zurich, Switzerland.

Brian Galligan, University of Melbourne, Australia.

Stuti Khemani, World Bank, Washington, DC, USA.

Ben Lockwood, University of Warwick, UK.

Govinda Rao, National Institute of Public Finance and Policy, New Delhi, India.

Federico Revelli, University of Turin, Italy.

Pierre Salmon, University of Bourgogne, Laboratoire d'Économie et de Gestion, Dijon, France.

Bob Searle, Commonwealth Grants Commission, Canberra, Australia.

Anwar Shah, World Bank, Washington, DC, USA.

Shekhar Shah, World Bank, Washington, DC, USA.

Raju Singh, International Monetary Fund, Washington, DC, USA.

Paul Bernd Spahn, University of Frankfurt, Germany.

John D. Wilson, Department of Economics, Michigan State University, East Lansing, MI, USA.

Foreword

Editing a handbook is an opportunity and at the same time a challenge for the editors. It requires a reconsideration of the entire field with the aim of selecting the main areas that have to be covered and of searching for recent and promising avenues of research. It requires a fine balance between completeness and innovative features and between distinct normative and positive approaches to the field. While taking cognizance of the policy debate in countries, we have avoided country-specific case studies. At the same time, the book should be of use to academics as well as to policy makers.

We are fortunate that many of the leading experts in the field agreed to prepare chapters for the Handbook – including some that have made seminal contributions to the literature. In many cases, the chapters presented take the debate further than has been the case. We express our gratitude to all of the contributors.

Preparation of the volume was enormously facilitated by a seminar held at the Centro Studi per il Federalismo in Moncalieri in August 2004. Overlaps and gaps between the initial draft contributions were considerably reduced as a result, including the commissioning of new chapters, while the consistency of the whole volume was substantially increased. The seminar also gave the authors the opportunity of finalizing their individual contributions with a view to the overall consistency of the Handbook. We are grateful for the financial and operational support offered for the organization of the seminar by the Centro Studi per il Federalismo.

We are very grateful, in particular, to Professor Umberto Morelli, Director of the Centro, and to Paolo Caraffini and Patrizia Ieluzzi. Amy Deigh provided invaluable help in the final editing phase of volume.

Finally we would like to express our thanks to Mahnaz and Olga for putting up with the disruptions that the preparation of this volume has caused.

Introduction: fiscal federalism – a review of developments in the literature and policy

Ehtisham Ahmad and Giorgio Brosio

Motivation

This Handbook addresses fiscal relations between different levels of government under the general rubric of 'fiscal federalism'. While the study of federal systems is an important part of the volume, it also covers other forms of intergovernmental relations. This ranges from unitary states, regional systems, to more decentralized operations, including community-level organizations, and federal systems through to supranational constructs (such as the European Union: EU). The volume seeks to provide a review of the latest literature on the broad subject of fiscal federalism, and also to guide practitioners and policy makers seeking informed policy options.

In the case of intergovernmental relations, the recent evolution of theory has been rapid and substantial. The traditional, largely normative, approach was based on the assumption of a benevolent government. Much of the recent literature drops this assumption and takes governments and politicians and officials as self-interested players. Thus, the normative approach has largely given way to a political economy approach. The latter emphasizes the importance of institutional arrangements, including the legal, political and administrative aspects, and information flows to ensure that there are appropriate incentives and sanctions to generate good governance. The volume, thus, has a combination of analytical and policy-oriented contributions.

The diffusion of federal or decentralized arrangements across the world, including changes in supranational arrangements, has been equally rapid. There have been reactions to excessive centralization in some unitary states, such as Indonesia, that have led to demands for greater responsibilities or resources for regional or local government, if not federalism. In unitary states such as Spain and Italy, quasi-federal constructs have been adopted. While this volume does not include country studies, the choice of the chapters and their content reflects the trends and policy questions that are apparent across the globe.

In countries with an established and strong legal framework, new institutional approaches, such as the diffusion of asymmetric arrangements, have emerged. There are also new relationships between governments, such as contractual agreements. The Handbook provides an account of this evolution.

1

Clearly, intergovernmental fiscal relations pose different challenges according to the distinct economic and societal characteristics of each country. In developing countries, decentralization has been promoted by some multilateral agencies and bilateral donors as an instrument for improving service delivery in sectors that are crucial for the alleviation of poverty. Poverty reduction is a new and crucial task for decentralized systems. It is not exclusively a developing-country issue, but mirrors the policy debates in industrial countries where poverty reduction has shifted from local governments to higher-level programmes, usually at the central level, for social security for the aged and disabled and unemployment insurance for the unemployed. Successful decentralization that leads to improvements in public service delivery and poverty reduction requires substantial reforms to improve governance, such as transparency of government operations and the provision of information. Consequently, these practical considerations require an adaptation of the theory, as shown in the chapters of this volume dealing with the design of intergovernmental systems. However, in all countries the decentralization process poses a challenge for maintaining sustainable macroeconomic conditions.

The evolution of federal and decentralized systems has been paralleled by the emergence of new issues, such as environmental protection, the sharing of natural resources among levels of government, corruption and the impact of federalism and decentralization on national unity. The Handbook also provides chapters on these topics.

The Handbook is structured as follows. Part I deals with the different approaches to fiscal federalism. Ben Lockwood examines the political economy aspects. Chapters by Pierre Salmon and Albert Breton address the vertical and horizontal aspects of federalism and competition. Federico Revelli examines issues related to spatial interactions across governments. We then have three chapters on aspects of contractual approaches to decentralization. Roger Congleton's addresses asymmetric federalism, and Reiner Eichenberger and Bruno Frey review the literature on 'functional, overlapping and competing jurisdictions' (FOCJ) to which they have made seminal contributions. Paul Bernd Spahn then reviews the important and growing area of contract federalism.

Part II deals with decentralization and development, with a review of the issues and literature by Pranab Bardhan. Govinda Rao addresses the process of decentralization in countries that have been subject to central or development planning. Partly based on their work in the World Bank's World Development Report on Service Delivery, Junaid Ahmad, Shantayanan Devarajan, Stuti Khemani and Shehkar Shah address the interactions between decentralization and service delivery.

Part III is devoted to the design and implementation of multilevel systems. Bernard Dafflon provides a comprehensive discussion of the expenditure assignments issue. Flavia Ambrosanio and Massimo Bordignon provide the equivalent discussion on revenue assignments and administrative constraints. As tax competition is an important determinant of revenue assignments, we next have a survey of this area by John Wilson. Given expenditure and revenue assignments, we next address the need for transfers to subnational governments. Robin Boadway examines the equity and efficiency considerations that could underpin the design of transfer systems. Ehtisham Ahmad and Bob Searle address how transfer systems might be implemented. The increasingly important issues of governance and management of the public finances, including the overall macroeconomic considerations, are surveyed by Ehtisham Ahmad, Maria Albino-War and Raju Singh.

Part IV is devoted to important emerging issues and contains an eclectic collection. In many countries, the control over natural resources poses considerable challenges to national unity, and price and quantity variability threatens the smooth management of the economy, particularly at the subnational level. Giorgio Brosio examines this issue, the scope for possible assignments of natural resource revenues to subnational governments, and the pros and cons of more generalized sharing of natural resources.

Environmental issues are also increasingly at the fore of the policy and analytical discussion, and Silvana Dalmazzone provides an example of how such matters might be analysed – focusing largely on the mechanisms needed at different levels of government to control pollution.

Anwar Shah reviews the possible links between corruption and decentralization – surveying a growing and somewhat contentious literature. Richard Bird and Robert Ebel address the issues involved in keeping countries together in the face of sharp ethnic and cultural divides which permeate many societies.

Finally, we present a political scientist's approach to fiscal federalism with Brian Galligan's chapter on institutions and decentralized governments.

The evolution of the literature has led to substantive changes in the approaches to fiscal federalism, and in the coverage of associated issues. The editors' choices have been challenging, the aim of this Handbook is to cover the literature, and to provide the reader with new avenues for exploring the field in terms of both the analytical approaches and policy relevance. Further elaboration of these issues and chapter summaries follow.

Approaches to fiscal federalism

The genesis of fiscal federalism and the normative perspective
Federal systems have been in existence at least since the American Revolution and independence. The text drafted by the convention at Philadelphia in 1787 provides the first example of a modern federal constitution (see Madison et al. 1788). As is frequently the case with most theories, the literature on fiscal

federalism has been strongly influenced by the geo-political context in which it originated; namely, the federal systems of North America. This has led to problems relating to its extension to other cases, especially to the nation states of Europe and Asia. A simple example refers to the assignment problem. Fiscal federalism theory (see, for example, Musgrave 1961; Olson 1969) dictates that responsibilities should be assigned according to the equivalence principle, or that the jurisdiction responsible for a given public policy should coincide with the geographic coverage of the impact of these policies on households and the relevant electorate. This presupposes that subnational jurisdictions can be created, merged or modified at practically zero cost.

The creation of new government units has been a common practice in North America, where there is still a possibility of extending the coverage of public services, incorporating new territory to create new jurisdictions. This is generally not possible for most Asian or European local governments – the main units for the operation of decentralized systems. Cities with the same rank in terms of their political or spatial hierarchy – for example, district, province, or regional capitals – tend to have a huge variance in terms of size of area, of population, and of wealth and economic specialization. On the basis of the equivalence principle, it would be hard to deny to the smallest or weakest jurisdictions at a given level the powers that theory considers appropriate for the biggest and most capable ones.

The past half-century or so has seen a significant pressure and move towards decentralization or federalization all over the world. The decentralization process has rendered the study of fiscal federalism more relevant in a policy context, and there has been a parallel development of economic method and analysis in tandem with most of the institutional changes that have taken place. For example, a frequent occurrence has been the creation of regions through the insertion of a new level of administration between the centre and local governments. Regional systems do not fit well within the mainstream theory of fiscal federalism, which has focused largely on choices between federal and unitary systems. Regional systems have developed very different institutions, and it is hard to portray a universal type.

More than forty years have elapsed since economists formally addressed the theory of fiscal federalism and the working of subnational government units. Richard Musgrave's definition of fiscal federalism as a system whose purpose 'is to permit different groups living in various states to express different preferences for public services; and this, inevitably, leads to differences in the levels of taxation and public services' appeared in 1959 (Musgrave 1959, p. 179). The Tiebout (1956) model also provided an underpinning of the literature for several decades. Mancur Olson's seminal contribution to this literature – namely, the principle of equivalence – was published in 1969. Wallace Oates (1972) presented the first systematization three years later.

The early literature on fiscal federalism was characterized by a strong normative flavour, which pervaded economic discipline at the time. Since, by hypothesis, governments are run by benevolent policy makers intending to maximize the welfare of their communities, government failures cannot derive from the deviant behaviour of rulers or governing elites intent on pursuing their personal interest, but only from lack of expertise and knowledge. For example, spillovers generated by local government operations could be addressed by earmarked grants administered by the central government. Thus the central government would ensure full internalization of spillovers, while decentralization will accomplish preference matching. In fact neither conclusion is warranted. Central governments may be able to vary policies to meet local preferences, but may not be able to ensure internalization of spillovers generated by local governments (Breton 1965).

When applied to bottom-up processes of federalization, such as the European Union, fiscal federalism theory has not been up to the challenge, because of missing political economy considerations. Defence and foreign policy have not been reassigned to the European level, contrary to every dictate of the theory, simply because European governments and citizens are strongly attached to vestiges of national identity and security.

Political economy approaches versus benevolent policy makers?
As stated by Ben Lockwood in Chapter 1, assuming benevolent policy makers amounts to modelling government as a black box, in which meaningful political institutions are absent. Benevolent rulers could be replaced by personally motivated policy-makers and associated institutions. The political economy literature, for instance, has developed the interplay of a national legislature and a set of locally elected policy makers. Modelling of politics and institutions is still relatively simplified and partial. A substantive advance has been to introduce accountability as an issue – which did not exist as a problem in a framework based on a premise of benevolent policy makers. Positive approaches assume that with interested policy makers, measures will be needed to address the absence of accountability in its various forms.

Chapter 1 provides a comprehensive review of the literature on decentralization based on the political economy approach. Lockwood models the behaviour of governments, whether at the national or local levels, taking into account actual institutions and processes, such as elections and legislatures. The chapter starts with a large component of this literature, the legislative models. The legislature, whose representatives have conflicting interests over regional public goods provision, makes the decisions on centralized functions. The results are then compared with those of a decentralized system. The analysis shows that with decentralization there is better matching to preferences, implying a larger consumer surplus than with a centralized government. This holds both in the case where citizens have identical preferences within each region, and also in the case where there is non-homogeneity of preferences in the regions.

A second important result concerns accountability. There are at least two meanings of this concept. The first relates to whether institutions allow politicians or officials to misuse public funds for their own purposes. The second refers to the distortions exerted by lobbies on resource allocation. There are three reasons why a decentralized government reduces rent diversion. The first is simply a scale effect. In a centralized setting, the size of total rent is higher, thus creating more inducements for diversion. The second reason is the reduction in the probability that voters will be pivotal in determining the outcome of the national election. In turn, this reduces the inducement for elected officials to implement the imperfect contract they have with their electors. A third reason is enhanced competition, which is dealt with at length in the following chapters by Salmon, Breton and Revelli.

Some or most of the results on the political economy of decentralization could be reversed if lobbies function in a decentralized system. James Madison had warned against capture by 'factions' at the local level in the *Federalist Papers*. The results of modern political economy models are less conclusive, but there is a prevalence of views that centralized government can reduce the distorting power of the lobbies, provided that specific conditions are met. These include provision that the national legislature be elected according to proportional representation, circulation of more accurate and timely information on the sources and uses of public funds, and managed or restricted organization of lobbies at the central level.

Thus, the support in the political economy context for decentralization remains a qualified one.

Decentralization and competition
Competition has generally been recognized as one of the biggest merits of decentralized government. The argument has originally been advanced in the *Federalist Papers* where it was argued that the federal entity created by the (American) constitution would introduce a vertical separation of powers that would complement a horizontal separation. Since Montesquieu (1914), separation of powers in the public sphere essentially refers to competition, and that citizens would have more alternatives for fulfilling their aspirations. When they perceive themselves to be disadvantaged by a decision of the executive, they can turn to the judiciary to overturn the decision, or for compensation, and vice versa, or they can address issues to the legislative power. In a decentralized setting, they also have the alternative of addressing either the central and/or their local government, or of voting with their feet. This is reflected in the traditional Tiebout (1956) approach to decentralized

government – competition is driven by mobility of citizens/consumers of public services. Citizens and consumers move their residence to those jurisdictions that provide them with the quantity and quality of services that they are looking for at the lowest cost, especially in terms of taxation.

In turn, competition ensures the matching of provision of services with local preferences, and inefficiency is minimized. Although this process of competition has been labelled 'voting with one's feet', there is actually no politics in this model.

Once we recognize that governments are not run by benevolent policy makers, but by interested individuals, not only is politics introduced explicitly in the model, but also other forms of competition appear, which do not require mobility of voters. Local politicians need consensus to accede to, or to stay in, power. Citizens exploit this quest for consensus to force local governments – that is, politicians – to compete to stay in office.

There is a plurality of ways in which governments can compete, as shown by Pierre Salmon (Chapter 2), who reviews the literature on horizontal competition. This literature contains important early contributions by Salmon himself, and the chapter deals with both mobility-induced competition and other types of competition.

Salmon does not question the assumption of costless mobility, as is occasionally done by others, but critically examines some of the results reached by the mobility literature. To take an example, one of the most common and politically significant conclusions of this literature is that mobility, whose effects epitomize globalization, deprives governments of autonomous choices. To be more specific, a tenet of this literature is that in a mobile world all taxes are benefit taxes and thus redistribution by government is no longer possible. Salmon's answer is that that is not necessarily the case, because individuals and firms have heterogeneous wants and preferences. In fact, redistribution can be Pareto optimal. According to Salmon, space is highly heterogeneous, meaning that various jurisdictions have different endowments of natural resources and of collective capital. In other words, there are locational rents which attenuate the constraint that all taxes have to be benefit taxes. Part or all of these rents can be used for redistribution to mobile poor.

Information is a crucial base for promoting competition. There are various components of this kind of competition. For example, voters can compare performances and can oust elected officials when not satisfied by the outcome of policies. Elected officials can also try to secure re-election by attracting, with targeted policies such as subsidized housing, groups of individuals from other jurisdictions who are likely to vote for them. Laboratory federalism has its roots in this literature, as does 'yardstick competition'.

Vertical competition takes places, furthermore, between central and subnational governments and can be viewed, as explained by Albert Breton

(Chapter 3), as a mechanism for the efficient assignment of functions among levels of government. Breton's chapter is quintessentially positive. His judgement is that the criteria elaborated by the theory for the assignment of responsibilities between layers of government have a very limited capacity to explain the real world of assignments. As an example, when an external shock takes place – let us imagine a technological innovation that increases the advantages of scale in relation to governments' policies – this should instantaneously lead to a reassignment of responsibilities (Breton calls these 'powers'). In fact, what happens in most cases is simply reorganization of activities. Reassignment is driven, particularly in countries with effective mechanisms of checks and balances, by vertical competition between layers of government. A basic assumption is that politicians maximize expected consent. If this is the case 'given tax prices . . . politicians will endeavour to supply goods and services (including redistribution and regulation) to their citizens in quantities and qualities that match as closely as possible what these citizens desire'.

As is the case with markets, competition between governments maximizes consumer surplus. In Breton's words, intergovernmental vertical competition 'will forge Wicksellian connections' – that is, the link between the quantity of a particular good or service supplied by governments and the tax/price – 'as tight as possible so as to be granted the (expected) consent (vote) of citizens'. In other words, vertical competition generates assignments of policy responsibilities that reflect the comparative advantage of different tiers of governments.

Obviously, there are important constraints to its proper working. Institutions are extremely important. First, the structure of federal systems should be taken into account. Classical, two-tiered, federations are prone to competition between federal and state governments, but they reduce competition at the lower level, that is, between states and localities. The nature of the second chamber, in particular its mode of selection – popular vote or appointment by subnational government – can also be crucial in determining the extent of vertical competition.

Breton shows how distinct provisions of constitutions can shape competition, sometimes favouring the central government over subnational units, such as in the case of the 'commerce clause' inserted in the American constitution, or the recognition by the Canadian constitution of the distinct legal system of the Province of Quebec based on civil law. This is because laws designed by the federal government and concerning property and civil rights often require complementary legislation by provincial legislatures. Obviously, constitutional courts, including their composition and the length of tenure of judges, are a crucial element in shaping vertical competition. Finally, asymmetric arrangements would be hard to explain without recourse to vertical competition. They are a main, although neglected, feature of intergovernmental arrangements. This issue is taken up further in Congleton's chapter.

In general, governments create a host of spatial interactions, forming an intricate web of relations, consisting of spillover of policies, of imitation effects, and of competitive behaviour. Local governments interact not only with the central government, but also among themselves. In fact, there are possibly more horizontal than vertical interactions. Federico Revelli (Chapter 4) deals with all these interactions and provides a comprehensive survey of the literature. Governments can interact with one another along three main channels: preferences, constraints and expectations.

In the presence of a direct preference interaction, the benefits of local public services provided in a jurisdiction spillover into neighbouring localities. This could be the case, for example, of public transport, education, training and environmental protection. Empirically, one should observe either positive or negative correlations among public expenditures as a result of the spillover, depending on the patterns of complementarity or substitutability. However, the empirical literature that investigates the size and direction of such spillovers is rather thin and does not provide definite results. Revelli feels that this could be caused by some other form of interaction taking place on the revenue side of budget.

Thus we immediately come across the second channel of interaction: the fiscal policy of a jurisdiction influences the size of a 'resource' in nearby localities and affects the budget constraint of other governments. Models of tax competition represent the classical example of the interaction of such indirect constraints. Tax competition theory yields two main empirical predictions. First, the desired tax rate in a jurisdiction depends on the tax rates set in nearby jurisdictions. Second, the tax base that locates in a jurisdiction is affected by the tax rate in that jurisdiction, as well as by those in neighbouring jurisdictions.

Finally, in the presence of expectations interaction, an action chosen by a government affects the expectations of the electorates of other jurisdictions. In the presence of an informational spillover from nearby jurisdictions, voters evaluate the performance of their own government relative to other governments, as dealt with in more detail in Salmon's chapter. In reality, each local jurisdiction interacts possibly with a large number of other jurisdictions and in most instances the influence of jurisdictions' policies will be reciprocal.

Revelli's chapter explores the empirical implications of the three forms of interaction sketched above, illustrates the main problems encountered by the empirical literature, and also draws implications for further research. Among the main problems Revelli mentions is the possibility that alternative theoretical models generate similar empirical predictions in terms of spatial reaction functions. Consequently, the estimation of a reduced-form interjurisdictional policy reaction function may not by itself allow sensible choices among competing theoretical hypotheses of spatial interaction, such as tax competition, expenditure spillovers and yardstick competition. Second, it is essential to avoid mistaking the presence of correlated shocks – a fairly common phenomenon when dealing with local government data – as evidence of actual strategic interaction by policy makers. For example, a reduction in the tax rates of a jurisdiction could be erroneously interpreted as a response to an analogous move in neighbouring jurisdictions, while in fact it might be generated by an increase in central transfers that affects each jurisdiction.

Contractual, and contractarian, dimensions of intergovernmental relations
Normative approaches to intergovernmental relations are characterized by a separation of functions, as in classical federations, and/or by hierarchy, as in unitary states. They have also relied on the assumption of the spatial uniformity of functional arrangements across governments at the same level. Separation and hierarchy do not exclude contractual relations, and these in turn generate asymmetric arrangements. In practice, the increasing use of intergovernmental contracts and reliance on asymmetric arrangements around the world are emerging as characteristics of present-day intergovernmental systems. This popularity is, on the one hand, a sign of the increased sophistication of intergovernmental relations, and on the other, possibly, of the increased political legitimacy of subnational governments. It would have been almost unimaginable in a traditional unitary state that municipalities could bargain with the central government and force it to come to formal agreements with them. This is, however, the real world and it has advantages, as shown in successive chapters by Roger Congleton, Reiner Eichenberger and Bruno Frey, and Paul Bernd Spahn.

Chapter 5, by Roger Congleton, is a close complement to Breton's treatment of vertical competition. In fact, Breton's final section suggested that competition would be conducive to different assignments for most subnational units. In other words, asymmetry is a consequence of vertical competition. Under asymmetric federalism or decentralization, government units at the same level have different allocative and regulatory powers. This is a common feature of federal and decentralized systems, although it has frequently been neglected. Congleton's chapter provides an explanation of why asymmetric arrangements arise and of their implications for political competition and service provision. Congleton's approach is based on bargaining between local governments and the centre. Symmetries emerge at the end of this process because subnational governments want to minimize the political risks of being associated with the central government in specific policies, or because they want to maximize their economic advantages. Congleton considers many cases.

The first, a rather frequent occurrence in history, is the case where the state is formed through the merging of existing provinces, cities and other forms of semiautonomous governments, as in the case of the United States, or the Netherlands. These units perceive mutual advantages from merging into a unique unity, such as scale economies and lower decision costs. Without the creation of the new state each distinct unit would need to bargain with each of the other ones to get the same results. There are also, however, political risks. A region could be excluded from the majority that governs the state and it could, as a consequence, suffer a net loss. More specifically, it would have to pay more than it would receive. Of course, there are institutions that reduce this risk, such as qualified majorities. Asymmetric assignment may be a better alternative: '[u]nder menu federalism, member states choose which services they will have produced centrally in much the same way that consumers select services from large firms in the marketplace'.

The second, opposite, case is that of over-centralization. Here the central government plays a pervasive role. For distinct reasons, some local governments perceive that the current level of service provision is underprovided in some sectors and that they could derive advantages if the responsibility for these sectors were devolved to them. An example could be public transportation. Local management could extend the transport network, reducing travel time and making the locality more attractive to individuals and firms. This would expand the tax base. Consequently, the same local units would be willing to pay compensation to the central government if powers were devolved to them.

The arguments developed by Congleton have many implications. First, asymmetric federalism or decentralization can emerge under a number of plausible circumstances. Second, bargaining between central and local governments determines the degree of centralization. Third, asymmetry is an efficiency-enhancing mechanism, provided that there are enough checks and balances at the local level to force local governments to promote the interests of their community.

Finally, most of the conclusions reached in Congleton's chapter match closely those of Breton. Assignment of responsibilities derives not from principles but from bargaining and competition between governments.

Chapter 6, by Reiner Eichenberger and Bruno Frey, presents the 'FOCJ' model, which the authors have proposed in the literature. It is a view of an ideal model of the spatial organization of the public sector, where the links between government units and territories are increasingly attenuated, if not severed. Their model, of which the real world offers an increasing number of (albeit partial) applications, refers to a federal/decentralized system whose constituent units have four distinctive characteristics. They are functional (F), or more precisely mono-functional; they are responsible for a single policy and their size is determined according to the spatial impact of the policy for which they are responsible. As a consequence they have to overlap (O), meaning that several functional jurisdictions operate on the same territory. Created by citizens' initiative they introduce competition (C) in the public sector, but they have enforcement powers, implying that they are real jurisdictions (J). In fact, what is needed is a constitutional provision sanctioning the right of citizens to create new jurisdictions. The FOCJ model rests basically on the distinction between provision and production, and on the increased possibilities of introducing competition even in monopolistic sectors, as shown by the privatization of natural monopolies such as telecommunications. As an example, a citizen of Bogotá may be part of mono-functional district that provides primary education to residents of the city. At the same time he/she will pay taxes to another jurisdiction that provides health care for a much larger area. A third jurisdiction will take care of road maintenance and has its headquarters located in a distant Colombian department. All these government units may make agreements with similar units located in the same country or in another one, as happens, for example, in the European Union.

Eichenberger and Frey's FOCJ idea has been widely discussed. The chapter included in this volume also provides an attempt to apply FOCJ to developing countries. Since FOCJ requires limited and flexible institutional arrangements, it is particularly suited, according to the authors, to developing countries, considering the weaknesses of their legal institutions. It represents a challenging suggestion that has to cope, however, with possibly low levels of citizen political participation in many countries.

In Chapter 7, Paul Bernd Spahn deals with a crucial innovation in intergovernmental relations: namely, substitution of rules and hierarchical commands by contracts. Since contracting is by definition consensual, it can take place, within the public sector, only among autonomous bodies with no hierarchical links. The use of contracts to order intergovernmental arrangements reflects the autonomy of decentralized governments, as well as the lack of information and sanctions available to a central government to enforce hierarchical arrangements.

Spahn compares the American and the German constitutions. The American constitution is based on the separation of responsibilities and functions between the federal and state governments. Initially, this represented a form of dual federalism, with the federal government operating almost completely independent from the states. However, growing interdependence between the federal government and the states has increased possibilities of conflict and opportunities for cooperation. Contracts can help to prevent conflict and generate cooperation.

The German constitution promotes concurrency of functions, typical of a corporatist tradition. In general, the federal government dictates policies and the states (*Länder*) execute them. However, the use of regulation and commands is resented by entities subject to these, and reduces accountability and transparency. Spahn argues that contracts can and should be used even in corporatist federal systems. In fact, they have been sponsored and popularized in Europe by the European Union, whose institutions, such as the bicameral system and the separation of legislation and execution, have shades of many of the German characteristics. The use of contracts has wide implications. For example, at the institutional level the most important is asymmetry of assign-ments. At the fiscal management level it increases the need for and importance of performance budgeting and of accrual accounting at the subnational level, and desirable as it might be, this might not be feasible in many countries, as argued by Ahmad, Albino-War and Singh later in the volume.

Contracts require not only autonomous government but also a well-structured, 'third party' to facilitate their execution. They require an appropri-ate legal framework, with easy recourse to the courts and sanctions. In most countries, the specific legislation of contracts between public entities is miss-ing as is an efficient judiciary for solving disputes. These requirements are problematic for many developing countries, although contracting has the same potential as in industrialized countries, as Eichenberger and Frey suggest in their chapter.

Decentralization in developing countries

Federalism and decentralization were traditionally found in rich countries with fully-fledged democratic systems. Latin America was an exception to this pattern, but federations come and go according to the shifting from democra-tic to autocratic rule. Federalization was promoted by Britain to provide a post-colonial framework to countries that had been created, particularly in the large and diverse countries (such as India and Nigeria) and also some smaller ones (such as the United Arab Emirates). Federations did not survive in some cases (British West Indies, Rhodesia and Nyasaland), or were subject to extreme stresses as in Nigeria. But they survived, even prospered, in other parts of the world (particularly in India).

The last two decades have witnessed the spread of decentralized governance in the developing world. New federations are being created. Some formerly unitary states, such as China, have gradually been transformed into effective multilevel systems, with lower levels of government enjoying a considerable degree of autonomy. Special legal arrangements were instituted for the return-ing colonies of Hong Kong and Macau. In Indonesia, a unitary constitution continues. However the reaction to decades of centralized rule has led to a formal incorporation of decentralization in laws enacted in 2000, and more recently to asymmetric arrangements for the natural resource region of Aceh.

These changing political and economic conditions require an adaptation of institutions and of the tools for their analysis as shown by Pranab Bardhan (Chapter 8). Decentralization is called to serve different objectives, such as poverty alleviation and improved service delivery. But problems remain and the evidence on improved service delivery and poverty reduction is inconclusive. Bardhan's chapter focuses on two logically related topics: (a) how decentralization improves policy outcomes in developing countries, and can thus generate growth and poverty alleviation; and (b) how the fiscal federalism literature has to be modified to provide a solid theoretical ground for policy making in this context.

There is no question that special characteristics of developing countries represent a challenge for decentralization and that the theory has to be modified to take these into account, in order to realize the presumed advantages of decentralized government. Bardhan argues that subnational units can derive limited benefit from mobility of individuals and firms, since they are greatly constrained by costs and social norms, such as exclusion of outsiders by tightly knit communities. High agency costs might accompany decentralization, given the potentially weak monitoring of bureaucrats and politicians. This enhances the likelihood that there will be elite capture, or that the benefits of public spending will be largely appropriated by the well-to-do or well-connected, particularly in highly unequal societies. Moreover, the traditional fiscal federalism literature stresses the efficiency advantages of decentralization at the expense of equity considerations. For example, it assigns redistribution to the central level. In the context of poorer countries, the trade-off between efficiency and equity needs to be modified. More equality, or enhanced poverty reduction thorough local action, may generate more growth. It may also improve political accountability, since poverty reduction should lead to increased literacy and thus to a greater likelihood of popular control.

The benefits of decentralization are not obvious. Potentially, they can be substantial, but require appropriate policy making and a properly designed legal and institutional framework. This cautious evaluation is substantiated by Bardhan's survey of the literature. As expected, in most cases decentralization leads to increased devolution of resources to subnational governments. This may lead to an increased allocation of resources to sectors, such as education and health, that are strategic for alleviation of poverty. However, there is no convincing evidence that this has brought substantial improvements in the actual delivery of services, particularly to the disadvantaged groups in society. Some funds may be diverted by political and bureaucrat slack. These conclusions are also shared by the authors of the World Bank's World Development Report (WDR), on service delivery (see World Bank 2003), Junaid Ahmad, Shantayanan Devarajan, Stuti Khemani and Shehkar Shah. Chapters 8 and 10 both make policy suggestions about the appropriate legal and fiscal framework that is needed to turn decentralization into an effective instrument for improving governance.

Effective service delivery is often the basic argument for decentralization that is increasingly stressed by multilateral agencies, such as the World Bank and the United Nations Development Programme, and bilateral donors. Chapter 10, by Junaid Ahmad et al., examines the nexus between decentralization and improved service delivery, and is partly based on their work for the WDR. Their argument is that the attempts to bolster aggregate spending in the key areas have not had a significant impact, partly because the central government is unable to ensure that the funding actually reaches target groups, and possibly because central decision making might not match local preferences. The authors examine the administrative, fiscal and political aspects of decentralization and its linkages with improved service delivery, and review in greater detail the evidence on issues raised earlier, for example, in the chapter by Bardhan.

While central governments could conceivably vary service delivery to match local preferences, for example, by contracting out implementation and actual provision, this chapter argues that it is preferable for local governments to undertake this provision, as it would eventually lead to a better match of political power and incentives to ensure effective delivery, although the existence of 'elite capture' is acknowledged. The authors also recognize that the ideal sequencing of decentralization requires that the devolution of functions should come first, to be followed by financing and administration, but that this order might not be practicable in each case. There is some discussion of medium-term economic frameworks (MTEFs), a policy instrument favoured by the World Bank to provide a better intertemporal framework for decision making. However, MTEFs are resource intensive and few developing countries manage to implement these at the central level due to capacity constraints – but the detailed discussion of public financial management issues at the subnational level, including accounting, reporting and audit is left to another chapter (Ahmad, Albino-War and Singh). In this context, the advocacy for local government borrowing is tempered with the caveats that sequencing is important, and certain preconditions must be met before the borrowing would become 'productive'. However, Junaid Ahmad et al. argue that 'decentralization is not a one-off policy change; it is an ongoing process where the end point of accountable and efficient local governments may well take many decades to achieve'. In this framework, it would be difficult to know when to adjust objectives for greater decentralization – since any failures could be attributed to not having stayed the course. This is at variance with the more cautious approach taken by Bardhan.

Decentralization is taking place in industrial, developing and transition countries. Difficulties are magnified in developing countries with a centrally planned tradition, as in the case of China, Vietnam and, to a lesser extent, India. The continuing role of the central planners presents further challenges to decentralization. These challenges are analysed by Govinda Rao in Chapter 9. There is no doubt that Soviet-type central planning is the negation of federalism and that milder forms of planning also distort the operations of decentralized units. Central planning pertained largely to a past epoch, but has implications for the design of policy at the present time, and the chapter provides useful insights on the impact of excessive government intervention in the economy with decentralized jurisdictions. For example, an excessive emphasis on physical investment can lead to distortions in the allocation of resources, at the expense, for example, of maintenance of the existing capital stock. Investment plans that exceed available savings can lead, as in the case of India, to cuts in the amount of resources transferred from the central to subnational governments, inducing them to introduce, *faute de mieux*, highly distorting taxes, given the distribution of revenue-raising powers under the constitution. Even horizontal equity may suffer from excesses in investment.

Another negative feature of central planning is that it engenders a lack of transparency. In principle, the rationale of many decisions that concern subnational government is based on 'scientific method' and a wide national consensus. Thus transparency should be a major concern in this framework. In reality this is not, generally, the case where the central planners take the major decisions, as this distorts prices and signals for decision making. There is often a rigidity about transfers, and political influences make it difficult to adjust regional allocations and the lack of transparency induces inefficiencies in spending.

In countries moving from central planning to the market, there is generally a substantial reform agenda to make decentralization work.

Design and reform of intergovernmental fiscal relations
We turn next to the design issues that face policy makers in countries with multilevels of administration or government. This includes the assignment of spending functions for each level of government, and requirements for own-source revenues. Given administrative constraints, it is likely that the major or more complex revenue sources will be assigned to or controlled by the centre. The possibility of vertical, as well as horizontal, imbalances across the same level of government feeds into the design of transfer systems. In all cases, the requirements for greater transparency and accountability and maintaining macroeconomic stability, place constraints on the way that public funds are budgeted, and spending reported and accounted for. Thus, governance issues are critical and are increasingly the focus of attention within countries, as well as of donors anxious to see that aid funds are used effectively.

Assigning responsibilities to subnational governments, assigning revenues to all levels of government, and supplementing local revenue with central government transfers are the basic ingredients of government operations in any multilevel system. These are at the same time the core of fiscal federalism theory.

We discuss each of these elements sequentially.

Expenditure assignments

The assignment of expenditure responsibility is a crucial element of any inter-governmental system, since it determines at the same time the number of levels of government and the number of units within each level. As mentioned above, the problem cannot be solved in isolation. Local governments have coexisted with central authority in most countries, and the size and functions of local government have been determined by time, space, history and politics. However, economic considerations are important and cannot be neglected by policy makers. In Chapter 11, Bernard Dafflon assesses expenditure assignments in this framework.

According to the theory, once expenditures are assigned properly, the number of layers of government and the number of units comprising each layer should be automatically determined. Unfortunately, reality is more complex than the theory makes it out to be.

Characteristics particular to each country determine the number of layers and only partly explain the constitutional assignment of responsibilities. Within such a constrained framework, only 'reassignment at the margin of evolving functions and resources to existing political units' appears feasible. The chapter has a normative flavour, since it tries to single out the criteria that should guide the proposed marginal changes in existing assignments. However, the criteria neither derive solely from the economist's basket of tools, nor should they be imposed through a top-down decision making process.

Rather, Dafflon proposes a 'decentralization matrix', where a number of criteria for reassignment are listed as rows, and layers of government to which functions are attributable as columns. The matrix should be created with the contribution of all the stakeholders sitting at the negotiating table. This echoes the working of the constituent assembly proposed by Breton and Scott (1978), although it might be noted that Breton has successively moved towards a strictly positive approach to the assignment issue, as seen in his chapter in this volume. The initial list provided by Dafflon can be lengthened to bring into consideration the interests, the concerns and the hindsight of the various stakeholders.

There is also some flexibility concerning the number of columns, which relates to layers of government. Cooperation between distinct layers, and within the same layer, is becoming an increasingly popular (both in principle and de facto) characteristic of intergovernmental relations. As we have seen, its importance is also stressed in this volume by Eichenberger and Frey and by Spahn.

Revenue assignments

On the revenue side, the increase in mobility of persons, firms, and in general factors generates stimuli to competition but also some constraints, as shown in the chapter by Flavia Ambrosanio and Massimo Bordignon, and in the complementary chapter by John Wilson.

In Chapter 12, Ambrosanio and Bordignon deal with the main normative and positive components of the assignment of revenue. Various instruments are available, the most important of which are clearly taxes. The authors' main argument is that there is always a case for financing local governments with own-source taxes. Even in improbable cases, where all decentralized government units are identical in terms of the preferences and the economic conditions of their inhabitants and where no mobility exists, local taxes instead of revenue shares provided by the central government would still be preferable in order to generate incentives for greater subnational accountability. Local taxation would, in fact, introduce a limited amount of yardstick competition between local governments. As these limiting conditions are gradually lifted, the role of local taxes is enhanced. This is clearly the case when, for example, preferences differ among local governments about the desired level of local goods.

At the same time, lifting the restricting conditions reduces the choice of tax instruments. Consider the mobility of individuals and firms. If we take a Brennan and Buchanan (1980) approach, and assume that local politicians are totally rapacious and exploitative, then most mobile tax bases (for example, on income taxes or sales taxes, such as value-added tax: VAT) could be assigned to local governments. But there are a number of arguments against assignment of mobile tax bases to local governments that are reviewed in the chapter. When the Brennan and Buchanan assumption is dropped and politicians can be constrained by citizens and when localities (greatly) differ in their fiscal capacities, taxes cannot remain the only source of financing, unless society is ready to accept a (great) deal of inequality in the level of local service provision. Thus, the tax assignment must be designed jointly with a transfer system.

An interesting point is made by the authors with reference to dynamic issues. They point out that local taxation could play an important role in curbing expectations of soft budget constraints. This is because the threat by the central government not to intervene *ex post* to solve difficulties faced by local governments may simply be not credible *ex ante*, if the local governments do not have sufficient autonomy in determining their own revenues in order to take care of unpredictable events.

The chapter also presents a review of the arguments referring to the choice of distinct tax instruments and of the merits and demerits of alternative systems of revenue sharing between central and subnational governments.

The final section of the chapter is devoted to tax administration issues. While local administration clearly enhances the autonomy and accountability of decentralized government units, it would be important not to duplicate administration, or impose additional compliance burdens on the taxpayer for essentially the same tax bases. It is also important to be cognizant of administrative capacity limitations at the subnational level as well as of possible economies of scale in tax administration. These issues will affect the assignment, design and administration of the main taxes such as income taxes and VAT.

In Chapter 13, Wilson deals with tax competition. This is a topic that is receiving increasing attention in the literature and that lies at the crossroads of intergovernmental models of competition analysed by Salmon and Revelli and the tax assignment discussion by Ambrosanio and Bordignon.

The traditional literature posited that tax competition would almost inevitably lead to an inefficient level of local spending, because local tax rates were geared to attract tax bases from other jurisdictions. However, this literature concentrated solely on horizontal tax competition. Recent developments also address vertical competition and show that within this combined framework, tax competition is not necessarily welfare decreasing. This is the case when central government is assumed to maximize total welfare of the country and can use transfers to eliminate inefficiencies. Where central transfers cannot be provided, because of institutional limits, then competition leads to a welfare reduction. To appreciate the arguments, consider two distinct cases. The first is that of a very small country with even smaller regions that levy a tax on capital. If capital is mobile and there are no regional, that is, horizontal, externalities, then if one region raises its tax rates, capital will immediately fly to the rest of the world, not to other regions. No region would benefit from the move while the entire country will suffer from a decline in the supply of capital. There would thus be only a vertical externality, implying a lower than optimal level of public spending.

The second case is that of a big country, with a substantial weight in the world economy. In this case there would be no vertical externalities, but only horizontal ones, since the tax base for the whole country is fixed. In this case, horizontal externalities would lead to a lower than optimal level of public goods.

The relative size of horizontal and vertical externalities is also determined by the relative size of the different levels of government. Wilson's analysis provides interesting insights concerning global tax strategies. It shows, for example, that allocating more tax powers in Europe to the EU (supranational level), could increase the welfare of European citizens by making the EU more competitive relative to the United States.

The tax competition limits to revenue assignments makes this area a fruitful avenue for further research and policy development.

Transfer systems

In most countries, equity, and particularly horizontal or spatial equity, plays an

important role in shaping intergovernmental arrangements. In classical federations, individual states were assumed to be self-sufficient. In unitary states,
ad hoc grants were paid in exceptional cases to local governments in financial
distress, but equalizing fiscal capacities was not considered to be a normal task
of the central government. However, equalization or untied transfers are now
an integral part of most intergovernmental systems. The magnitude of overall
transfers, including both equalization transfers and special-purpose grants to
meet central or donor objectives, generates problems for financing, requires
transparency and proper institutions for allocation and finally consideration of
their efficiency aspects, as illustrated in the chapter by Robin Boadway, and in
that by Ehtisham Ahmad and Bob Searle.

Needs for public services and taxing capacities differ across various areas
within a country, but it is often the case that poorer regions have greater needs
as well as relatively limited resources. In the absence of central government
intervention to provide transfers to the less well-endowed areas and/or to those
with greater needs, households otherwise in identical circumstances will be
treated differently according to the area of residence. The principle of horizontal equity would be violated. Efficiency in the allocation of resources
would also be imperilled by movements of population to areas that are fiscally
able to provide better services or to impose lower taxes. This is because these
movements are not based on differences of productivity. In Chapter 14, Robin
Boadway provides a thoughtful illustration of the equity and efficiency rationale for intergovernmental transfers.

While the grounds for establishing equalization transfers are clear, the
degree of equalization to be introduced into the system is subject to controversy. First, in general, people have different views about equity. Second,
satisfying horizontal equity may conflict with welfare maximization applied at
the level of the whole country. This is the case, for example, when there are
economies of scale in the production of local services. The principle of horizontal equity would imply that the central government should compensate
with transfers the higher costs of smaller jurisdictions. In this case, the welfare
maximization at national level would have to be sacrificed, because transfers
would be paid not only to people in greater need, but also to those who might
be less needy but happen to live in small and/or high-cost localities. Another
difficulty arises when subnational governments choose different expenditure
and tax policies which will result in equals being treated unequally. The
central government could obviously correct these situations, but at the expense
of local autonomy, which is a cornerstone of decentralized government.

There are two additional reasons mentioned in the chapter to establish
equalization transfers. One is the implementation of national minimum standards, in areas such as education and health, which is the typical core of the
functions, assigned to subnational governments in federal or otherwise highly

decentralized systems, but is also at the same time crucial for determining the well-being of the entire population. The second reason is that transfers can serve to absorb temporary shocks in subnational governments' fiscal capacity. While there are arguments for the central government to intervene with transfers to absorb these shocks, there are similarly valid arguments for suggesting that subnational governments should, as much as possible, self-insure against these occurrences. The chapter provides a summary of the most recent literature on this subject.

The chapter also illustrates the rationale for transfers on efficiency grounds. As mentioned above, there is a possibility of a crucial inefficiency of migration in decentralized systems, because when people they decide to migrate, they do not take into consideration the impact of their decisions on the rest of the society.

Further, transfers can reduce the inefficiencies generated by use of distortionary taxes at the local level, the inefficiencies of local tax competition and finally the efficiency costs of local tax administration.

In Chapter 15, Ehtisham Ahmad and Bob Searle survey the main issues that countries face when they implement a grants system, and provide an array of examples on how problems are solved or aggravated through proper or improper decisions. The chapter assesses the design and implementation of both special-purpose and equalization grants, and complements the illustration of the rationale for equalization grants provided by Boadway.

The multiplicity of special-purpose grants in many countries is a cause for concern. In many respects, earmarked transfers limit or override the subnational decision-making power in areas of local jurisdiction. Moreover, in many developing countries, central governments lack the tools to monitor earmarked transfers, and the plethora of such grants, including from international donors, are simply not implementable. Yet, given limitations of capacity and the need to maintain minimum basic standards, many countries continue to rely on special-purpose grants that might exceed by far amounts for untied transfers that could be distributed on an equalization basis (including in advanced countries, such as Canada).

The point of departure of the analysis of the overall grants system is the legal framework for grants. Increasingly, grants are defined by constitutions. However, excessive detail and specification to appease worries of subnational governments, which are particularly evident in societies with distinct population groups, might engender macroeconomic inflexibility and the (undesirable) need to change the constitution if there is a change in economic circumstances. The objectives of an equalization framework are important, and in some countries one might expect to see these in the constitution. An example is to ensure that subnational governments will have the capacity to provide a similar level of services at comparable levels of own-tax effort. The standards for equalization are important – full equalization may not be fiscally feasible, or desirable. Averages used by some developed countries might be too low in developing countries trying to improve minimum living standards.

Ahmad and Searle's chapter proceeds by surveying the main steps for the design and implementation of grants systems, namely the determination of the total pool of resources to distribute, and the main approaches for the allocation of equalization transfers: that is, fiscal capacity and expenditure needs. Decisions are also needed on whether or not special-purpose grants should be taken into consideration in the estimation of equalization transfers. Specific consideration is given to the use of minimum standards for the determination of expenditure needs.

The manner in which untied grants are provided can have an important effect on the subnational government's incentives to manage their finances efficiently. 'Gap-filling' transfers to meet subnational deficits are perverse in that they vitiate incentives for efficiency. Also, in determining equalization transfers, care should be taken to avoid factors that are under the control of the recipient governments, as this might encourage distortions of information or other forms of gamesmanship. Increasingly, countries resort to independent agencies for grants administration, in order to separate politics from administration, and which could enhance the transparency of the whole process.

A major issue in grants implementation relates to data requirements. This is a problem that is mostly overlooked in the literature. When countries start with grants programmes, availability of data operates as a constraint to the articulation of the grants system, but it might be possible to begin with relatively simple formulations building on data that are generally readily available at the subnational level, including demographic characteristics. In general, data collection and use are crucial ingredients for the success of grants mechanisms.

Governance and macroeconomic considerations

One of the main messages of this Handbook is that competition between government units at the same or at a different level explains fundamental characteristics of the working of decentralized systems, and is potentially a crucial factor for their efficiency. In fact, a parallel can be drawn between the private and the public sectors. This parallel can also be extended to institutions of financial control and management aimed at guaranteeing the achievement of the efficiency potential. Transparent and well-conceived accounting systems and statements of accounts by private firms are crucial for ensuring control of management by owners. Control and auditing bodies are equally essential. The same applies to the public sector in general, and especially to lower levels of administration.

When governments are not benevolent, they are not necessarily disposed to follow transparent financial management practices, which are essential ingredients for the success of decentralization. Good governance and transparent use of public funds, together with a need to maintain overall macroeconomic stability in order not to jeopardize all jurisdictions of a country as a result of profligate behaviour of some subnational governments, are discussed in Chapter 16, by Ehtisham Ahmad, Maria Albino-War and Raju Singh. This chapter focuses on the analysis of crucial institutions for fiscal management at the local level and devotes particular attention to subnational debt.

There is a need for standardized information for policy making and to evaluate the results of the policy actions *ex post*, and for institutions to ensure full accountability at each level of government. Unfortunately, administrative capacity is in short supply, and the rush to decentralize might have to be constrained by what is feasible in terms of reporting. The authors argue that local political constraints on policy making and policy makers are likely not binding in the absence of relevant and timely information. Given the limited administrative capacities in most subnational governments, especially in developing countries, the chapter argues that attempts to move prematurely to results-based budgeting (that would be required in theory), could be counterproductive.

In essence, institutions and good practices that have been applied at the central level have to be replicated at the subnational levels. It is particularly important to institute standardized minimum requirements using international standards, such as those established by the International Monetary Fund's *Manual of Government Finance Statistics* (IMF, 2001), to facilitate comparisons across jurisdiction, to monitor all operations of subnational government and to establish an 'early-warning' system to alert policy makers to potential macroeconomic problems.

At the same time, one has to take into consideration that subnational units are inherently financially and administratively weaker than the central government, although there may be exceptions with large metropolitan areas (for example, the district of Bogotá in Colombia is generally more advanced than the central government in many respects). In addition, common-pool problems can arise, as in the case of borrowing, since each local government does not fully internalize the cost of its decisions. These difficulties have led many developing countries, particularly though not exclusively in Latin America, to slide into macroeconomic crises. A menu of options to address various borrowing and macroeconomic situations is developed.

This chapter thus complements many of the theoretical assertions made in the various chapters of this volume.

Emerging issues
Finally, Part IV deals with important emerging issues. The sharing of natural

resources among levels of government has become a burning issue that risks tearing apart countries if not properly solved, particularly in natural resource-rich countries. This is addressed in the chapter by Giorgio Brosio. Similarly, environmental protection is in most countries at the heart of the aspirations of the general public and involves all levels of government. Silvana Dalmazzone's chapter provides useful insights into this expanding field for research. Corruption is clearly not a new issue, but its possible impact on decentralization is a crucial factor to be considered. The opposing views on this issue are strongly held, and are summarized by Anwar Shah. And as Richard Bird and Robert Ebel show, decentralization can consolidate or imperil national unity, according to the institutions that are created.

The political economy approach to federalism and decentralization is a pivotal feature of this Handbook. Despite this qualification, the approaches presented have mainly been from an economist's perspective and written by economists. To complete the picture, the editors considered that a view from a political science perspective would be a useful complement to other chapters in the volume. This view is provided by Brian Galligan.

The struggle over natural resources

The sharing of revenue from natural resources among levels of government is a crucial issue for decentralized systems in natural resource-rich countries, such as Bolivia, Iraq, Nigeria and Indonesia. If this issue is not properly addressed, it could feed rivalries between the constituent units and put a great strain on national unity.

Rents from natural resources can be very substantial. When assigned to local jurisdictions, per capita rent amount can reach relatively high levels, generating substantial disparities with non-producing regions. Decentralization expands the role of subnational governments and makes them more vocal in demanding a share of the revenues generated within their jurisdiction. These issues are examined by Giorgio Brosio (Chapter 17), who presents, first, the main instruments for extraction and sharing rent among different layers of government. These can be various taxes, as well as non-tax instruments, such as auctioning exploration and exploitation rights, production-sharing agreements, and the acquisition of equity in natural resource-extracting enterprises. There can also be shares in overall revenues, or gross natural resource revenues, between different levels of government.

The chapter notes the trend for an increasing access by subnational governments to natural resource revenues, and examines arguments against and in favour of sharing the rent with subnational governments. Sharing gross petroleum revenues, for example, could subject subnational governments to the fluctuations in international prices that may place excessive strains on basic spending during price downturns, and waste and unsustainable spending during periods of rising prices. It also could exacerbate horizontal inequalities at the lower level of administration. The chapter also presents innovations in the practice of intergovernmental relations, mechanisms and solutions that can soften the political and economic impact of the assignment of natural resource revenues to subnational governments. The fluctuations could be avoided by assigning tax bases that might be invariant to prices – for example, taxes related to the volume of production – which would be more closely linked to compensation for environmental damage caused by the extraction of natural resources. To some extent, horizontal imbalances engendered by assignments of natural resources to subnational jurisdictions could be addressed through the transfer systems described in Part III.

An example of decentralization and environmental concerns
The protection of the environment is increasingly attracting attention at all levels of government, in response to a corresponding increase in the aspirations of the general public. The assignment of responsibilities in this area has stimulated the growth of an important literature that is reviewed in Chapter 18, by Silvana Dalmazzone, which concentrates largely on issues related to decentralization and the control of pollution. The message of the fiscal federalism component of this literature is straightforward: those forms of environmental protection that generate benefits contained within the boundaries of local jurisdictions present a strong case for decentralized assignment, whereas control of polluting emissions that tend to spillover local boundaries – and all the more global environmental problems – requires central government intervention.

However, there are many exceptions to this rule. One of these exceptions, favouring the assignment to the central government, is the importance of scientific knowledge. The environment is an area where policies rely heavily on scientific and technical information. A problem of scale may act as a constraint on the extent of feasible decentralization: small local authorities may not have the capacity to produce or even to process the existing information.

A large body of literature suggests two other reasons against assigning environmental regulation at the local level. The first of these reasons refers to 'the potential trade distortions that may arise from locally differentiated environmental standards'. The second one is that devolution of these responsibilities to the local level 'could set in motion a competitive "race to the bottom" leading to inefficiently high levels of pollution'. The race to the bottom has attracted considerable attention, but it does not appear to be a phenomenon of significant empirical relevance. Pollution abatement costs are only one element among the many factors that impact on relocation of firms. Local governments have at their disposal other instruments to compensate firms for the imposition of these costs, as suggested in Salmon's chapter.

Drawing from the specific literature on environmental economics, Dalmazzone provides supplementary warnings against decentralization of environmental responsibilities. First, the chapter mentions the complexity of ecological systems. It implies that policy decisions concerning, for example, the regulation of a specific kind of pollution in a given jurisdiction generally indirectly affects more than one ecological component, although the impact is sometimes lagged and difficult to predict. Second, there is a temporal dimension. Ecological functions have different temporal cycles: for some the cycle is seasonal; for others, it may be of longer duration. If governments at different levels use different intertemporal discount rates, this should be taken into account. If, for example, higher-level governments use lower discount rates in making their decisions, then the decentralized solutions would lead to an allocation nearer to efficiency for environmental resources whose ecological functions have shorter temporal cycles, and vice versa. Again this is largely an empirical matter and further enquiry is needed.

Decentralization and corruption

Anwar Shah (Chapter 19) examines decentralization and corruption: a crucial factor in determining the relative merits of decentralized against centralized government. A growing number of studies have recently been devoted to this issue, but there are no clear results. A segment of the recent literature views decentralization as an effective antidote to corruption because it should render local public authorities more accountable to citizens. Another stream initiated by Madison (Madison et al. 1788) in the *Federalist Papers*, holds the opposite view: federalism and/or decentralization disperses power in the hands of a larger number of public authorities and increases opportunities for extracting illegal advantages from government activities.

Shah's chapter provides a balanced view of this literature. It presents the main theoretical approaches starting with a typical Becker-type model and continuing with a brief account of the most recent contributions of the new institutional economics. The chapter also surveys the growing number of applied studies, which do not yet provide convincing evidence on the links between decentralization and corruption. This is possibly due, among other factors, to the lack of appropriate data. Most of the information on corruption that can be used for cross-country comparisons is built on surveys of business people dealing with public administrations. This offers a partial view of corrupt practices – excluding those that refer to citizens as consumers of public services. Moreover, most calculated indexes of corruption refer to the number of corrupt practices recorded and not their economic incidence. As decentralization increases the potential loci of corruption, it is likely to increase the number of corrupt practices. But the incidence of corruption should be the main focus of analysis.

Shah's chapter provides useful and frank insights and also shows that the literature still has a long way to go to get definite results in this area.

Maintaining national unity

Federalization is an instrument of state creation. Decentralization is an instrument for maintaining states and to ease domestic conflicts in fragmented societies. This is an argument of Chapter 20, by Richard Bird and Robert Ebel. In fact, this tendency is seen increasingly across the world: Bosnia–Herzegovina, Spain, Ethiopia, South Africa and Iraq provide the leading examples. When the distinct components of a country, ethnic or otherwise, find it increasingly difficult to stay together, devolution to them of political autonomy becomes an obvious option. However, this is not entirely devoid of risk. In other words, decentralization could increase, rather than decrease, political instability. The design of decentralization is crucial, but very few generalizations emerge.

Interregional equalization comes at the top of the list. Divided countries stay together if each territorial component perceives that benefits outweigh costs. When income and wealth disparities are the main source of differences, or they combine with ethnic or other differences, regional redistribution is called for. It could, obviously, be complemented or substituted by interpersonal redistribution, but that would not always appease local elites. If brought too far, regional equalization becomes a factor of conflict, as in Germany, a solid federation with a well-developed welfare state.

Asymmetric decentralization is another possibility for addressing conflict situations. Bird and Ebel's analysis complements that of Congleton. In the latter's chapter, distinct regional preferences for policies do not have ethnic or cultural origins, but are mostly based on pure economic considerations.

A view from political science

Far from being obsolete, federalism is spreading across the world, albeit with evolving characteristics. It also provides an impetus and an instrument for solving challenges to governance coming from globalization. This is the main argument of Brian Galligan in Chapter 21, which concludes the volume from a constitutional and political science perspective. The chapter also singles out the distinct institutions that are essential to define federations and to ensure their survival.

Federations are strong decentralized systems, not because of the more extensive responsibilities assigned to subnational governments, but because of the high level of constitutional protection given to the jurisdictions that federate. When more protection is guaranteed, advantages from decentralization, such as competition, flow more easily. The three essential features of federations are: (i) a written constitution that is difficult to amend; (ii) a bicameral legislature; and (iii) judicial review. Federations are born out of agreements between constituents units submitted to popular referendum. A written text, the constitution, is a crucial pillar. It defines the spheres of autonomy of the federal government and of the federated jurisdictions. It also allocates responsibilities and revenues, or, in Breton's terminology, powers of government. Then, a crucial choice is faced by federations when the need for revision emerges: a lengthy participatory process, or a speedy process to ensure rapid adaptation of constitution mandates to the evolution of intergovernmental relations. Approval of constitutional amendments elaborated by the federal legislature by the constituent units of the federation, through a popular referendum or adoption by state legislatures, may be essential to maintain the vertical division of powers and the federal character. The process is clearly speeded up when the second chamber is selected according to the federal principle, as in Germany and South Africa, where the states (provinces) send their representatives to the second chamber.

The third institution, judicial review, is a channel for constitutional adjustment that does not require constitutional amendments. The problem here is that courts should never take decisions that deviate from the mainstream of political consensus. When conflicts among spheres of governments are brought to the Supreme Court, this implies that decisions should reflect the existing equilibrium of powers. But this has not usually been the case in a number of federations.

The interactions between political scientists focusing on institutions, and political economists examining how institutions interact and influence behaviour and economic outcomes, promises to be a fruitful one in further research in the area of intergovernmental fiscal relations.

References

Brennan, J. and J. Buchanan (1980), *The Power to Tax: Analytical Foundations of a Fiscal Constitution*, Cambridge University Press, Cambridge and New York.
Breton, A. (1965), 'A theory of government grants', *Canadian Journal of Economics and Political Science*, **31**, 175–87.
Breton, A. and A. Scott (1978), *The Economic Constitution of Federal States*, University of Toronto Press, Toronto.
International Monetary Fund (IMF) (2001), *Manual of Government Finance Statistics*, Washington, DC.
Madison, James, Alexander Hamilton and John Jay (1788), *The Federalist Papers*, republished in Penguin Classics, 1987.
Montesquieu, Charles de Secondat, Baron de (1914), *The Spirit of Laws*, G. Bell & Sons, London (public domain edition).
Musgrave, Richard (1959), *The Theory of Public Finance*, International Student Edition, McGraw-Hill, New York.
Musgrave, Richard (1961), 'Approaches to a fiscal theory of political federalism', reprinted in Musgrave (1986), *Public Finance in a Democratic Society*, Collected Papers, Vol. 2, Wheatsheaf Books, Brighton, UK.
Oates, Wallace (1972), *Fiscal Federalism*, Harcourt-Brace, New York.

Olson, Mancur (1969), 'The principle of "fiscal equivalence": the division of responsibilities among different levels of government', *American Economic Review*, **59**, 479–87.
Tiebout, Charles (1956), 'A pure theory of local expenditures', *Journal of Political Economy*, **64**, 416–24.
World Bank (2003), *The World Development Report 2003*, Washington, DC.

PART I

APPROACHES TO FISCAL FEDERALISM

1 The political economy of decentralization
Ben Lockwood[1]

Introduction

This chapter surveys recent contributions to the study of fiscal decentralization that adopt a political economy approach. By a political economy approach, I mean a systematic attempt to model the behavior of government – whether at the national or local level – taking into account institutions and processes, such as elections and legislatures, which determine the choice of fiscal policies in practice. This is in contrast to the 'standard' or traditional approach to the study of fiscal decentralization, which treats each level of government as a benevolent social planner, maximizing the welfare (for example, sum of utilities) of the residents of its jurisdiction, and is thus forced to make the ad hoc assumption of 'policy uniformity' in order to explain why decentralization can ever be efficient. The standard approach was stimulated by the pioneering work of Oates (1972) and since developed by a number of authors.[2]

What is the distinctive contribution of the political economy approach? In discussion of the costs and benefits of decentralization, it is usually argued that the costs of decentralization are due to various kinds of coordination failure: specifically, the failure to internalize tax and expenditure externalities of various kinds, or to exploit economies of scale (Oates 1999). The political economy approach has little to say about these coordination failures that is distinctive from the standard approach.

There is less of a consensus on the benefits of decentralization, but generally, the idea is that it is 'closer to the people'. There are two ways in which this can manifest itself. First, it is claimed to improve allocative efficiency, in the sense that the goods provided by governments in localities will be better matched to the preferences of the residents of those localities. This is sometimes known as the *preference-matching* argument. Second, decentralization is argued to increase the *accountability* of government. This term is used in rather a broad sense, and refers to the extent to which rent-seeking activities of office holders, such as taking bribes, favoring of particular interest groups, and insufficient innovation and effort, are held in check.[3] There is a growing body of empirical evidence (developed in other chapters of this Handbook) that does suggest fiscal decentralization impacts on government accountability and preference matching.

It is the thesis of this chapter that the standard approach has little to say

about either preference matching or accountability, but that a political economy approach can give an account of these two effects that is both rigorous
and plausible. So, the distinctive contribution of the political economy
approach is that it can rigorously explain two of the key benefits that are
widely believed to arise from increased fiscal decentralization, and give more
precise predictions about when such benefits might be achieved.

To understand the distinctive contribution of the political economy
perspective, consider first a simple version of the 'standard' model. Assume
two levels of government, central and regional, for simplicity. Both types of
government are assumed to be benevolent: that is, they maximize the sum (or
average) of utilities of the residents in their jurisdiction. The activity of
government is to provide local public goods, which may generate externalities
(positive or negative) for other regions.

With decentralization, regional governments fail to internalize these
spillovers. On the other hand, with centralization, as the government is benevolent, such spillovers are internalized. So, the standard model easily captures
the 'coordination failure' cost of decentralization. But, to capture the preference-matching benefit, it is forced to make the ad hoc assumption of policy
uniformity: central government is simply *assumed* to set a uniform level of
local public good provision in all regions. Moreover, as policy makers are
assumed to be benevolent, the 'problem' of non-accountability is not even
defined within the standard model.

The newer political economy approach can address both these shortcomings. First, models of legislative decision making with centralization developed by Lockwood (2002) and Besley and Coate (2003) explain why, even
when regional delegates are benevolent in the sense that they represent the
interests of the voters in the regions from which they are elected, levels of
regional public good provision decided upon by the legislature can be insensi-
tive to regional preferences; in other words, why there is reduced preference
matching with centralization.

Again, models of electoral control developed by Besley and Case (1995),
Besley and Smart (2003), Persson and Tabellini (2000) and others formally
endogenize the degree of accountability of policy makers to voters in an environment where: (i) policy makers may not represent the interests of the voters;
for example, they may be motivated by rent seeking; and (ii) initially, voters
do not know whether the incumbent policy maker is good or bad, but can make
inferences about the incumbent's type from the fiscal policy he/she chooses.
In this environment, Persson and Tabellini (2000) and Hindriks and Lockwood
(2005) have studied how the degree to which incumbents are accountable to
voters differs between centralization and decentralization. Belleflamme and
Hindriks (2003), Besley and Case (1995), Besley and Smart (2003) and
Bordignon et al. (2004), among others, have investigated how tax and yard-

stick competition between jurisdictions (with decentralization) might improve accountability. There is also a related emerging literature on decentralization and lobbying (for example, Bardhan and Mookherjee 2000): this literature explains how capture of government by special-interest groups may differ between centralization and decentralization.

Finally, this chapter also surveys recent work on the political economy of the choice between centralization and decentralization. This is a key part of the political economy perspective: after all, in practice, political institutions determine these choices, as well as the performance of government under a given allocation of fiscal powers.

The remainder of this chapter is organized as follows. The following section gives a brief account and critique of the standard model. The next section describes the type of political economy model (the legislative model) that has been used to look at the preference-matching argument, and then reviews the distinctive results of this recent literature. The penultimate section describes the type of political economy model (the electoral accountability model) that has been used to look at the accountability argument, and then again reviews results of this recent literature, including work on lobbying, which from a modeling point of view, is much more heterogeneous. The final section considers the political economy literature on the *choice* of the level of fiscal decentralization.

The standard model of the costs and benefits of decentralization

The economic environment
First, we shall set up a simple economic framework, which we shall use throughout this chapter. Consider a country comprising n administrative regions. In each region, government (regional or central) can provide a good that is purely public[4] within the region, but has spillovers for other regions. The public good can be produced from a second, private, good, and is financed out of taxes on the private good endowments of households. At this stage, let preferences for the public good vary only between regions, so that all households in a given region are identical. Finally, for convenience only, assume that there are only two regions with equal populations, which we normalize to unity.

Given the above assumptions, the utility of the household in region $i = 1, 2$ can be written $u_i = u(g_i, g_j, \theta_i, x_i)$, where g_i is the level of the regional public good in i, x_i is the level of consumption of the private good, and finally θ_i measures the willingness to pay for the local public good in region i (and depending on the functional form of u, may also measure the valuation of the spillover effect from the good in j). So, there are spillover effects if u_i depends on g_j. These can be positive or negative.

The household budget constraint for the household in region i is $x_i = X_i - \tau_i$, where X_i is the endowment of the private good, and τ_i the tax levied in region i. One unit of g_i can be produced from each unit of the private good (that is, the marginal cost of g_i is unity).

Finally, again for convenience, we assume that u_i is linear in x_i: that is, $u_i = u(g_i, g_j, \theta_i) + x_i$, so preferences are quasi-linear. In this case, it is well known that any Pareto-efficient allocation of public goods in the economy must maximize the sum of utilities, so the efficient levels of public good provision are uniquely defined by the familiar Samuelson rule.

Centralization and decentralization   Within this framework, we shall consider two possible allocations of tax and spending powers.

- *Fiscal centralization*   A single central government sets both local public good levels g_1, g_2 and taxes τ_1, τ_2 to maximize $u_1 + u_2$ subject to the budget constraint $g_1 + g_2 = \tau_1 + \tau_2$.
- *Fiscal decentralization*   A regional government in i sets the public good level g_i and tax τ_i in its own region to maximize u_i subject to the budget constraint $g_i = \tau_i$.

As remarked above, in the standard model, the objective of government is to maximize the sum of utilities of residents in its jurisdiction (welfaristic objectives). Then, with fiscal decentralization, in each region i the marginal benefit of the good to that region (that is, $u_1(g_i, g_j, \theta_i)$, where u_l denotes the derivative with respect to the lth element) is equated to the marginal cost of the good, unity. Clearly, regional government i ignores the spillover effect $u_2(g_j, g_i, \theta_j)$ of its public good provision on the other region, and this is a well-known source of inefficiency.[5]

Now consider central government. In this case, without any restrictions on the choice of g_1, g_2, central government will choose the efficient levels of g_1, g_2, because it internalizes spillover effects. Thus, in order to generate some disadvantage to centralization, the standard approach makes the *policy uniformity* assumption that public good provision (per capita) must be the same in both regions (that is, $g_1 = g_2 = g$). What does this imply about choice of g? Given that central government maximizes the sum of utilities in both regions, then government chooses g so that[6] the average of the marginal benefits of an increase in the public good in both regions is equal to the marginal cost of unity. Centralization has a cost: the level of public good provision cannot now be tailored to each region.

Then, we can immediately state some quite obvious, but important, conditions, under which centralization or decentralization can be more efficient. Recall that because we have assumed quasi-linear preferences, the efficiency criterion is the sum of utilities, or aggregate surplus, as it is sometimes known. So, one fiscal arrangement is more efficient than the other if it generates a higher sum of utilities.

Then, the *decentralization theorem* states:

1. If there are no spillovers ($u_2 = 0$) and regions are identical ($\theta_1 = \theta_2$), then centralization and decentralization are equally efficient.
2. If there are no spillovers ($u_2 = 0$) and regions are not identical ($\theta_1 \neq \theta_2$), then decentralization is more efficient than centralization.
3. If there are spillovers ($u_2 \neq 0$) and regions are identical ($\theta_1 = \theta_2$), then centralization is more efficient than decentralization.

The proof of this result follows directly from the above discussion. In particular, (2) is a more formal statement of Oates's original 'decentralization theorem':

> In the absence of cost savings from the centralized provision of a (local public) good and of inter-jurisdictional externalities, the level of welfare will be at least as high (and typically higher) if Pareto-efficient levels of consumption are provided in each jurisdiction than if any single uniform level of consumption is maintained across all jurisdictions. (Oates 1972, p. 54)

It is worth noting that these statements (1)–(3) are quite general. First, tax uniformity ($\tau_1 = \tau_2$) with centralization is not necessary to generate a cost of centralization: in the above analysis, we have not assumed it. Second, although we have assumed for simplicity that there is no preference heterogeneity within regions, this can easily be introduced without changing the main conclusions.[7] Third, in the above analysis, expenditure spillovers provided the reason why fiscal decentralization is not efficient. An equally important – if not more important – kind of spillover is that due to tax competition (Wilson 1999). The key difference here is that with tax competition there are spillovers between regions only with decentralization (that is, existence of spillovers is no longer technologically determined, but is endogenously determined by the allocation of fiscal powers). But in this case, an extension of (3) applies, replacing the word 'spillovers' by the phrase 'spillovers with decentralization'. Finally, the goods g_1, g_2 do not need to be purely public within the region: there may be some congestion, or the goods may be purely private.

A critique
We conclude this section by asking how good are the assumptions of benevolent government and policy uniformity. First, as a positive hypothesis about how government behaves, the hypothesis of benevolent government is very difficult to refute, as it is simply a statement that the outcome of the political

process must be consistent with maximization of some social welfare function. Economists' objections to it are really methodological: the 'benevolent government' model of the political process is a black-box one which ignores institutions.

But the policy uniformity assumption is testable. As it is stated and used in formal modeling (that is, that expenditures on a local public good are literally the same in different regions), it is clearly incorrect. For example, in many countries, there is considerable evidence that the level of spending per capita varies across regions in predictable ways. For example, Knight (2004) finds that in the US, funds for projects[8] earmarked in annual House of Representatives and Senate Appropriations Bills are unequally distributed by state, with small states that have higher per capita representation in the Senate and the House having significantly higher per capita expenditure.

But often, the policy uniformity assumption is justified by appeal to the idea that the central government has some information about local preferences, but not as much as local government. This is not obviously incorrect. But in many countries, central government has a large amount of information at its disposal.[9] Moreover, at a theoretical level, if central government were benevolent, and has unrestricted use of transfers, the incentives literature (for example, Mas-Colell et al. 1995) tells us that it could, given quasi-linear preferences, design incentive schemes to elicit this information from regions, and then implement the efficient outcome.

The most compelling criticism of policy uniformity is perhaps not that it is empirically refuted, but that it is probably not the most important reason why centralization leads to lower preference matching. The most important reason in practice is likely that with centralization, especially in a majoritarian system, legislators are primarily answerable to the voters in their constituency or region, and care less (if at all) about voters in other regions, even if they know their preferences. We now turn to a literature that formally models this idea.

The preference-matching argument

We begin by setting out the political economy model (or class of models), which has been used to study preference matching. In developing this model, we shall continue to assume the same economic environment as in the previous section (that is, the activity of government is to provide regional public goods, financed by a tax on the endowment of the private good). We shall therefore continue to use the same kind of notation as developed in the previous section.

Legislative models

In this class of models, decisions are made not by a benevolent social planner, but by political representatives. With decentralization, the order of events is as follows. All citizens[10] in a region elect a policy maker from the set of citizens[11] in a region. Then, the policy maker in i chooses fiscal policy (g_i, τ_i) to maximize his/her payoff, taking public good supply g_j in regions $j \neq i$ as given and subject to the regional budget constraint $g_i = \tau_i$. With centralization, it is assumed that the tax is uniform.[12] The order of events is then as follows. All citizens in a region elect a delegate (or legislator) to a national legislature. This legislature then chooses (g_i, τ_i), $i = 1, \ldots n$ and subject to the national budget constraint, $\sum_{i=1}^{n} g_i = \sum_{i=1}^{n} \tau_i = n\tau$, where τ is the uniform tax.

So, the key difference[13] between the legislative and the standard models is in the case of centralization: in the legislative model, decisions are no longer made by a benevolent social planner, but by a legislature whose representatives have conflicting interests over regional public good provision: specifically, this conflict is due to the fact that through uniform taxation, all regions pay for a public good in any particular region, but region i may get only a small benefit, or no benefit at all, from an increase in g_j.

A model of how the legislature behaves is obviously key to this approach. The first problem that arises is a technical one. The policy space (a vector of public good levels $g_1, g_2, \ldots, g_n$) is multidimensional, and so unrestricted voting over the alternatives will lead to an indeterminate outcome (that is, voting cycles). So, in order to proceed, some rules of agenda formation and voting must be imposed in order to generate a unique prediction about spending levels.

Probably the leading model[14] of legislative behavior[15] is that proposed in a seminal paper by Baron and Ferejohn (1989). In its simplest form, with closed-rule legislative bargaining, the model is the following. One of the n legislators (say i) is recognized as proposer with probability $1/n$. He/she can then make a proposal of a vector $\mathbf{g}^i = (g_i^1, g_i^2, \ldots, g_i^n)$ of public good levels, which is then put to a majority vote against the status quo $\mathbf{g}^0$. The status quo is generally some inefficient allocation: in what follows, we take it to be a situation with no expenditures (that is, $\mathbf{g}^0 = (0, 0, \ldots, 0)$). If $\mathbf{g}^i$ wins, it is implemented; if it loses, another of the n legislators, say j, is recognized as proposer. He/she can then make a proposal $\mathbf{g}^j$, and so on. The game continues until some proposal beats the status quo. All agents discount payoffs by δ between successive rounds of bargaining.

The basic argument

In the legislative model, it is easy to formalize the idea[16] that fiscal decentralization is more responsive to the preferences of citizens, without resorting to ad hoc policy uniformity assumptions. To make the argument as clearly as possible, we make the following simplifying assumptions. Assume three regions only, that the public good is a discrete 'project' (that is, $g_i \in \{0, 1\}$, and costs c_i in region i). Also assume that households are homogeneous within a region, with every household in region i gaining benefit θ_i from a project in its region, and there are no interregional spillovers from projects. In that case, the payoff to any citizen in region i under decentralization is $u_i^D = g_i(\theta_i - c_i)$, and under centralization it is:

$$u_i^c = g_i\theta_i - \frac{1}{3}\sum_{i=1}^{3} c_i g_i. \tag{1.1}$$

Note that the uniform taxation assumption generates the feature that there is *cost sharing*: each region pays one-third of the cost of any public project.

With decentralization, the outcome is simple. As all households are identical in any region, any policy maker will share their common preference for the public project, θ_i. So, a project in region i is supplied if its local benefit θ_i exceeds the cost c_i (that is, there is maximum preference matching).

To see what might happen with centralization in this framework, consider the behavior of the legislature assuming the Baron–Ferejohn legislative bargaining model. Moreover, to focus ideas, we assume that the project in region 3 is (i) the most costly ($c_1 < c_2 < c_3$), but (ii) at the same time generates the most economic surplus (that is, $\theta_3 - c_3 > \theta_2 - c_2 > \theta_1 - c_1$, and $\theta_3 > c_3$). So, a welfare-maximizing social planner would always choose $g_3 = 1$. But, because the project in region 3 is the most expensive, we shall assume that:

$$\frac{c_1 + c_2}{3} < \theta_i < \frac{c_i + c_3}{3}, \, i = 1, 2. \tag{1.2}$$

In combination with equation (1.1), equation (1.2) means that each of the legislators representing regions 1 and 2 would prefer the status quo of no projects to participating in a 'coalition' with the legislator from region 3 only (that is, funding projects in his/her region and region 3 only).

Now consider the outcome in this legislature first under the simplest form of closed-rule legislative bargaining, where there is only one round of bargaining. If i is chosen as agenda-setter, he/she cannot propose only his/her project for funding, as this will be opposed by the other two legislators (they pay the cost of i's project, and get no benefit, making them worse off than under the status quo). So, the agenda-setter will offer a project to one of the other two regions (we call this region the coalition partner). But which one? If $i = 1$ is the agenda-setter, he/she will choose 2 as his/her coalition partner, and vice versa. So, with probability 2/3, only projects in regions 1 and 2 are funded.

With probability 1/3, legislator 3 is chosen as coalition partner. What happens then? If he/she proposes a bundle of projects including his/her own, this will be rejected by both 1 and 2, as it is too expensive (by equation (1.2)). He/she does not wish to propose projects in just regions 1 and 2, because if that proposal is accepted, he/she will be worse off than with the status quo. So, legislator 3 cannot do better than propose the status quo of no projects, and this will be the outcome.[17]

So, the conclusion is that with centralization, only the cheaper projects will be funded in equilibrium, not the projects that generate the greatest economic surplus. This is ultimately because there is cost sharing through uniform taxation (the common-pool effect). So, an increase in c_i will affect the majority of legislators negatively, whereas an increase in θ_i will leave the majority of legislators indifferent. So, there is a *bias in the legislature to minimize cost of projects, not to maximize their net benefit.*

Lockwood (2002) provides a general analysis of this bias toward minimum cost projects. His framework has discrete[18] public goods, but allows for n regions and public good spillovers between regions. Under centralization, preferences over vectors of public goods, taking into account cost sharing via the government budget constraint, are of the form:

$$u_i = \theta_i g_i + \sum_{i \neq 1} s_{ij} g_j - \frac{1}{n} \sum_{j=1}^{n} c_j g_j, \ i = 1, \ldots, n, \qquad (1.3)$$

where s_{ij} is the spillover effect of a project in j on the citizens of i. So, public good spillovers can – at this stage – be completely general, other than being additively separable, and also costs can vary across regions.

Lockwood works with a slightly different model of the legislature from the Baron–Ferejohn one. This is (i) because the analysis of legislative bargaining equilibrium with an infinite number of rounds of bargaining in the general case is very difficult; and (ii) because even then, the closed rule does not allow for other legislators to amend the proposal 'on the floor' even though in practice, this is an important feature of procedure in legislatures. The following decision-making procedure in the legislature is assumed:

1. With probability $1/n$, one of the legislators, j, is recognized as the proposer, and proposes a list of projects to be funded, that is, a $g^j \in \{0, 1\}^n$:
2. with probability $1/(n-1)$, one of the remaining legislators other than j, say k, can offer an amendment g^k;
3. the proposal and the amendment are then brought to a vote, with the winner, say g', becoming the amended proposal; and
4. one of the remaining legislators other than j, k – say l – can offer an

amendment **g** to $\mathbf{g}^0$, and so on, with the final amended proposal voted on against the status quo of no projects.

Lockwood (2002) shows that under some assumptions, the outcome is *independent* of the order in which the legislators are chosen to propose and amend. In particular, this is the case if there exists[19] a Condorcet winner (CW) in the subset of policy alternatives that are preferred to the status quo (a restricted CW); in this case, the only possible equilibrium outcome is this restricted CW – say $\mathbf{g}^{CW}$. One of the main topics of Lockwood (2002) is a detailed investigation of how $\mathbf{g}^{CW}$ is inefficient, and in particular, how it results in lower preference matching than in the decentralized case.

There are two striking features of $\mathbf{g}^{CW}$ which are most easily stated when spillovers are uniform (that is, $s_{ji} = s$). Then, note that every region i imposes a *net spillover* $\sigma_{ji} = s - (c_i/n)$ on every other region j, which comprises the public good spillover, minus j's tax share of the cost of funding i's public good.

First, subject to conditions on the θ_i sufficient for the existence of $\mathbf{g}^{CW}$ being satisfied, the projects that are provided are *independent* of regional preferences $\theta_1, \ldots, \theta_n$, and depend only on the net spillovers. This captures formally the concept of centralization having lower preference matching. In fact, in equilibrium, the wrong public goods may be provided if the spillover is non-positive.[20] This generalizes what we found in the simple example above.

Second, the number of public goods funded is not always increasing in the spillover, s. The reason is that if s is negative, or positive and small, so that the net spillover is negative, then (under some weak conditions) a minimum winning coalition forms so that public goods are provided in a bare majority of regions $m = (n + 1)/2$ where project costs are lowest (as in the example above). If s is high, so that a majority of projects have positive net spillovers, then those projects are funded. But, if s is intermediate, a minority of projects have positive net spillovers, then under certain conditions, only those projects are funded – fewer than when s is small, or negative. Lockwood (2002) shows that this non-monotonicity in s implies that as a consequence, it is not generally true that the higher the spillover s, the greater the welfare gain from centralization. This is in contrast to what would occur in the standard model, where (given discrete projects, and preferences of the form (1.3)), there is a critical value of s above (below) which centralization (decentralization) is preferred.

Strategic delegation
So far, the analysis has assumed that all agents within a region are the same. In a recent paper, Besley and Coate (2003) argue that in a version of the

legislative model, if there is heterogeneity within regions, strategic choice[21] of delegates by voters can cause centralization to be inefficient, in the sense that aggregate surplus is not maximized. This can be thought of as a form of reduced 'preference matching' with centralization. But, the argument is logically distinct from the preference matching developed in the previous section.

Their intuitive argument is the following. Consider the case of just two regions, as Besley and Coate do. If region i chooses a delegate to the legislature who places a high value on the public good, this delegate will be more 'aggressive' in the legislature in demanding a higher g_i. This works to the benefit of citizens of i because part of the cost of higher g_i is borne by the other region. But, of course, if both regions delegate to 'aggressive' delegates, this will be self-defeating: the end result is that both g_1 and g_2 will be higher than their efficient levels.

The details are as follows. There are two regions, with utilities from the public good of the form:

$$u(g_i, g_j, \theta_i) = \theta_i[(1 - s) \ln g_i + g_i \ln g_j], 0 \le s < 0.5.$$

So, s parameterizes the size of the public good spillover between regions. Moreover, the preference parameter θ_i varies within a region, but has a symmetric distribution, with mean and median both equal to m_i. Finally, as in the previous section, utility is linear in the private good, and taxes are uniform. These assumptions ensure that the efficient level of provision of the public goods maximizes the sum of the utilities of the median voters in each region, which is

$$\sum_{i=1,2} u(g_i, g_j, m_i) - g_i.$$

Rather than model the agenda-setting and voting rules in the legislature explicitly, Besley and Coate assume that the outcome of bargaining between delegates in the legislature is that the policy chosen maximizes the sum of legislator utilities, that is,

$$\sum_{i=1,2} [u(g_i, g_j, r_i) - g_i],$$

where r_1 and r_2 are the preference parameters of the representatives elected from regions 1 and 2 in the legislature. They call this the 'cooperative legislature'. At the policy choice stage, then, the legislature will choose the $g_1^*(r_1, r_2)$, $g_1^*(r_1, r_2)$ that maximize this sum. It is easy to check that g_i^* is increasing in both r_1, r_2: indeed, $g_i = (1 - s) r_i + s r_j$.

Now, turn to consider the first stage where representatives are chosen through majority voting in each region. All citizens vote for their most preferred type of fellow citizen, rationally anticipating that if policy makers r_1, r_2 are elected, then (i) the outcome will be $g_1^*(r_1, r_2)$, $g_2^*(r_1, r_2)$; and (ii) the cost will be equally shared through the tax system. Then, there is a well-defined 'delegation game' between the median voters[22] in the two regions: in i, the median voter chooses r_i to maximize his/her utility given a choice r_j in the other region, and vice versa. Besley and Coate (2003) showed[23] that, with identical median voter preferences in both regions ($m_i = m_j$) each median voter will vote for a representative with a higher public good preference than his/her own, that is, $r_i > m_i$. As $r_i \neq m_i$, the outcome is not efficient. Moreover, this effect does not vanish as the spillover s becomes small.

What are the implications of strategic delegation for the choice between centralization and decentralization? As the spillover s goes to zero, the efficiency loss from strategic delegation remains. So, it is no longer true that if there are any spillovers and regions are identical, then decentralization produces a lower level of surplus than centralization (that is, statement (3) above no longer holds). Indeed, Besley and Coate (2003) show that with strategic delegation, there is some strictly positive level of s, $\tilde{s}$, such that below (above) this level, decentralization (centralization) is more efficient.

A drawback of Besley and Coate (2003) is that while simply *assuming* the rules of behavior of 'cooperative' legislature is a convenient analytical device for clearly identifying the strategic delegation effect, it is not clear that it can be justified with reference to any explicit game of agenda-setting and voting in the legislature. Lockwood (2005) investigates conditions under which the 'cooperative' legislature can be justified, in terms of the legislative bargaining model of Baron and Ferejohn (1989) described above. He shows that if the legislators can make side-payments to each other, then in the legislative bargaining model, delegates act as if they were maximizing the sum of their utilities. Moreover, if these side-payments are not made through the tax system, but are 'personal' transfers, then the strategic delegation argument applies exactly as in the Besley–Coate paper.

By contrast, if taxes are differentiated, and are used to make side-payments, all voters either pay or receive the side-payment. Thus, the median voter also takes into account the effect on the side-payment of delegating to some $r_i \neq m_i$. It can be shown that this exactly cancels the delegation incentive analysed by Besley and Coate, meaning that when side-payments occur through differentiated taxes, there is no strategic delegation in equilibrium and therefore, fiscal centralization is fully efficient.[24]

The accountability argument

As noted in the introduction, although this argument is frequently made, the concept of 'accountability' is difficult to pin down precisely. One problem is that if defined broadly, it is difficult to distinguish from preference matching. So, in order to focus the discussion, we shall focus on two possible aspects of accountability:

- The degree to which institutions allow the government (or officials within the government) to *divert rents*: that is, to transfer tax revenues away from productive expenditure on public goods, and to some other use that more directly benefits the government (such as campaign finance, or the outright use of these funds for personal consumption).
- The degree to which institutions allow special-interest groups to distort government decision making by *lobbying*.

Note here that accountability is defined negatively: the higher the rent diversion or lobbying activity, the lower is the accountability. The theoretical literature has considered the impact of decentralization on both these aspects of accountability. We consider each in turn.

We begin by setting out the political economy model, which has typically been used to study accountability issues. In developing this model, we shall continue to assume the same economic environment as above (that is, the activity of government is to provide regional public goods, financed by a tax on the endowment of the private good). We shall therefore continue to use the same kind of notation as developed above.

Electoral accountability models
In this class of models, decisions again are made not by a benevolent social planner, but by political representatives. There are two periods. With decentralization, the order of events in any region i is as follows. In period 1, an incumbent policy maker is in power, and chooses fiscal policy (g_i, τ_i), taking public good supply g_j in regions $j \neq i$ as given. At the end of period 1, there is an election: all citizens in i can vote for the policy maker or a challenger. In period 2, the winner then again chooses fiscal policy (g_i, τ_i). With centralization, the order of events is the same, except that (i) there is only one incumbent policy maker, who chooses (g_i, τ_i) $i = 1, \ldots, n$ or, if taxes are assumed uniform, (g_i, τ) $i = 1, \ldots, n$, and (ii) a national election with only one challenger.

This model has two key features. First, both the incumbent and the challenger can be 'good' or 'bad' from the point of view of the citizens. Specifically, it is usually assumed that the incumbent's and the challenger's types (good or bad) are random draws from some binary distribution (so that each is good with probability π). What 'good' or 'bad' is depends on the model at hand: generally, both incumbent and challenger can differ in competence in producing the public good (Rogoff 1990; Persson and Tabellini 2000), or benevolence, in that the bad type is interested in diverting rent (Besley and Case 1995; Besley and Smart 2003).

Second, citizens are initially uninformed about the type of both incumbent and challenger, whereas (usually) the incumbent and challenger know their own type. The result of this information asymmetry is that the bad type may imitate the good type in order to be re-elected (a pooling equilibrium), or act in his/her short-run best interests, thus revealing his/her type, and losing the election (a separating equilibrium).

So, the key difference between the electoral accountability model and the standard model is that with both centralization and decentralization, decisions are no longer made by a benevolent social planner, but by policy makers whose objectives may conflict with the electorate; thus, elections are used as a means of partial control of the incumbent. As stressed by Besley and Smart (2003), elections provide accountability in two senses. First, they allow voters to de-select bad incumbents (selection effects). Second, the selection effect provides an incentive for incumbents to change their behavior in order to increase the probability of re-election (incentive or discipline effects). A key question, therefore, is what effect (de)centralization will have on these two accountability mechanisms.[25]

Decentralization and rent diversion

In an important contribution, Seabright (1996) stressed two incentive effects of centralization, working in different directions. His setting is a two-period model of the type described above, except that all policy makers are the same: a pure moral hazard version of the model. The incumbent can vary the amount of rent he/she diverts from tax revenue to his/her own pocket. The voters observe the level of a public good provided by the incumbent in the first period, and the level of public good provided is equal to (exogenous) tax revenue, minus diverted rents, plus a productivity shock. As is standard in this kind of model (see, for example, the classic paper of Ferejohn 1986), the voters set a performance standard g', by voting the incumbent out of office if his/her production of the public good is lower than g'. This gives the incumbent an incentive to restrain rent diversion in the first period.

Now suppose that the economy is composed of n regions, and with decentralization, there is one policy maker in each region, and with centralization, a single policy maker. Suppose also initially that the productivity shocks are region-specific, rather than specific to the policy maker (that is, all policy makers are identical). Then, moving from decentralization to centralization, there are two ways in which the incentive for the policy maker to restrain rent diversion changes. First, and most obviously, with centralization, if the policy maker wins the election, he/she can expect more rent in the second period (in fact, in the second period, he/she will extract maximum rent in all regions, rather than one, so in the absence of any exogenous ego-rent from office (Persson and Tabellini 2000), his/her future rent rises by a factor of n). We call this the *rent scale* effect of centralization; this effect improves incentives for the incumbent (that is, lowers his/her incentive to divert first-period rent).

But there is a second, more subtle effect of centralization, loss of account-ability through the reduction in the probability that the voters in any one region are pivotal in determining the outcome of the election (we shall call this the *reduced pivot probability* effect of centralization). To illustrate, consider the case of three regions, and suppose that in any region, the incumbent policy-maker can choose high rent diversion, in which case he/she wins with proba-bility 0, or low rent diversion, in which case he/she wins with probability p. So with decentralization, the incumbent can raise his/her probability of winning by p by cutting rent diversion. With centralization, suppose the incumbent cuts his/her rent diversion in region i, assuming it is already low in the other two regions. Region i is only pivotal if the incumbent wins in one of the other regions and loses in the other, an event which occurs with probabil-ity $2p(1 - p)$. So, with centralization, the incumbent can raise his/her proba-bility of winning by only $q = p \times 2p(1 - p)$ by cutting rent diversion. Obviously, $q < p$, so the reduced pivot probability effect reduces the incentive to limit rents with centralization.

A weakness of Seabright's model is that the voters are not following a voting rule that can be easily justified: all policy makers are identical, and so whatever their performance in office, voters are *ex post* indifferent about voting them out of office or retaining them at the end of the first period. One way of resolving this indeterminacy is to suppose that the productivity 'shock' which maps tax revenue minus rent into public good provision, is an inherent competence characteristic of the incumbent. Then, voters are not indifferent about a performance cutoff *ex post*, because the higher g', the more likely it is that the incumbent who passes it is competent. Persson and Tabellini (2000, Chapter 9.1) present a model of this form, retaining Seabright's assumption that the first-period incumbent does not observe his/her competence level. An equilibrium of this model is thus described as (i) a level of first-period rent diversion by the incumbent, r', and (ii) a cutoff g' such that given r', his/her competence is judged to be at least as great as the challenger. Persson and Tabellini show how the rent scale effect and the pivot effect work in the deter-mination of r'.

A key limitation of both Seabright (1996) and Persson and Tabellini (2000) is that effectively they say nothing about how centralization impacts on the *selection* effects of elections. In Seabright, there are no selection effects, as all policy makers are identical. In Persson and Tabellini (2000), by construction, the probability that an incumbent of given competence loses the election (which we shall call the separation probability) is the same with centralization and decentralization. In both cases,[26] the incumbent loses office with probability 0.5.

So, for separation probabilities to be truly endogenous (and thus vary between centralization and decentralization), there must be asymmetric information: the incumbent must be better informed about his/her own competence (or some other characteristic) than the electorate. Hindriks and Lockwood (2005) study such a model. They find that (i) there is a tendency for separation probabilities to be lower with centralization, and (ii) conditional on a given separation probability, the amount of rent diverted is higher with centralization, and therefore voter welfare is lower.[27] The second effect is the analogue of the reduced pivot probability effect in the moral hazard case, and arises because with centralization the policy maker can win the election by selectively pooling only in a bare majority of regions where it is most profitable to do so, and then diverting maximum rents in all the others. Hindriks and Lockwood also find that with centralization, uniform taxation provides voters in one jurisdiction with partial information about fiscal policy in other regions: this constrains the ability of the incumbent to selectively pool. *Ex ante*, all voters would choose a uniform over a differentiated tax rate. This provides a novel explanation of why uniform taxes with centralization are so widely observed.

Decentralization and competition

Another way in which decentralization can alter the incentive and selection effects of elections is via competition among local or regional governments. Competition can be of two kinds, tax competition and yardstick competition, and we discuss each in turn.

Informally, it has long been recognized that if policy makers are rent seeking, competition for mobile tax bases can constrain their rent-seeking behavior (for example, Buchanan 1987) and thus improve vote welfare. The basic result is a second-best one; if governments are benevolent, tax competition creates a bias towards too little taxation, and undersupply of public goods, but if governments are rent seeking, they are biased in favor of overtaxation. Under some conditions, the first bias offsets the second, to the benefit of voters.

This point has been made more formally by Edwards and Keen (1996), where it is assumed that if the incumbent regional government maximizes some combination of voter welfare and the rents from office, and conditions are developed under which tax coordination is welfare improving for voters, this requires the 'weight' the government puts on rent diversion to be sufficiently low. In other words, if the 'weight' the government puts on rent diversion is high, stronger[28] tax competition raises voter welfare.

The limitation of this line of argument is that in their model, governments are simply assumed to be non-benevolent, but voters have no electoral control over them – there are no elections in the model. In a more recent paper, Besley and Smart (2003) take a major step forward[29] in developing a model of electoral accountability exactly as described above, where the incumbent policy maker can be benevolent or a rent maximizer. In this model, they show that an increase in the (exogenous) marginal cost of public funds – which can be interpreted as an intensification of tax competition – will decrease voter welfare if it leaves the equilibrium separation probability[30] unchanged, but may increase voter welfare if the change causes the bad incumbent to switch to a separating strategy – thus revealing his/her type – in equilibrium.

The second form of competition that is possible under fiscal decentralization is yardstick competition. This occurs when voters in any tax jurisdiction use the taxes (or expenditures) set by their own political representative relative to those in neighboring jurisdictions when deciding how to vote. (Of course, a necessary condition for yardstick competition is that voters can observe fiscal policy in neighboring jurisdictions.) To model this in a rigorous way, what is required is a version of the electoral accountability model as described above, with two (or more) jurisdictions and some positive correlation in the random cost of public good provision across jurisdictions. Theoretical models of yardstick competition along these lines have been developed by Besley and Case (1995), Belleflamme and Hindriks (2003), Besley and Smart (2003) and Bordignon et al. (2004).

In this type of model, voters can (under some conditions) improve their welfare by using yardstick competition (that is, by voting on the performance of their incumbent relative to the incumbent in the other region). The reason is quite intuitive: if the voters in region 1 observe that their incumbent has set a high tax, but that the incumbent in region 2 has set a low tax, this outcome is more likely to be generated by a 'bad' incumbent in region 1 than is the outcome where both set a high tax, because of the correlation in cost of public good provision across regions. Thus, in equilibrium, it is possible that voters vote for the challenger in the first case, and the incumbent in the second, even though in both cases, the tax in region 1 is high. Besley and Smart (2003) show that this has the consequence of making the pooling equilibrium more likely.[31] In turn, allowing yardstick competition may increase voter welfare, but does not necessarily do so, because pooling, while good for incentives, is bad for selection.

Finally, it is worth noting that while both tax competition and yardstick competition may, in some circumstances, provide arguments (under the general heading of increased accountability) as to why fiscal decentralization may be desirable, it is often difficult to distinguish in practice[32] between tax and yardstick competition. This is problematic because in a particular country that is initially highly fiscally centralized, preconditions for the two types of competition are rather different. Tax competition requires decentralization of (in particular), taxes on business. Yardstick competition requires, rather, transparency in government decision making and a mass media that are not subject to censorship.

Decentralization and lobbying
The economic theory of lobbying has been extensively developed and applied in recent years (see, for example, Grossman and Helpman 2001), and there are now several theoretical papers which explicitly consider the interaction between fiscal decentralization and lobbying (Bardhan and Mookherjee 2000; Bordignon et al. 2003; and Redoano 2003). One motivation of all these papers is to examine analytically a belief, going back to the US Federalist Papers in the eighteenth century, that local government is more susceptible to 'capture' by lobbies.

We can compare and contrast the contribution of these papers in a number of ways. First, it is important to understand first what the 'baseline' form of decision making is in the model, in the absence of lobbying: the distortion of policy making induced relative to lobbying is then measured by this benchmark. In both Bordignon et al. (2003) and Redoano (2003), the welfaristic assumption of the standard model is made: each level of government maximizes the sum of utilities of the residents in their jurisdiction (region or nation). In Bardhan and Mookherjee (2000), the 'baseline' form of decision making is Downsian competition between two political parties: each party sets policy so as to maximize the probability of winning, so both parties converge on policy that maximizes the median voter's payoff.[33]

A second difference is in the use to which payments by lobbies are put. In Bordignon et al. (2003) and Redoano (2003), lobbies' payments fund the personal consumption of policy makers. In Bardhan and Mookherjee (2000), lobbies fund campaign spending by the two parties: this spending in turn affects the voting behavior of 'uninformed' voters. The latter is an attractive assumption for several reasons: it is realistic, and it endogenizes the power of the lobby (see below).

A third difference is in the type of policy chosen by government. In Bardhan and Mookherjee, the policy space is rather general. In Bordignon et al., the policy is a level of provision of a good that positively affects the demand for a good produced by the firms who lobby,[34] or in a second variant of the model, also a decision about which firm(s) should have access to a given market. In Redoano, the policy is the level of provision of a regional public good.

Finally, in all these papers, the lobbying is to some extent endogenous. In Bardhan and Mookherjee, the number and size of lobbies is fixed (one per region with decentralization, one at the national level with centralization), but the size of the contribution the lobby wishes to make depends on the probability of the party winning the election, which in turn depends on the size of the contribution. In Bordignon et al., again, the number and size of lobbies is fixed (two firms) but with decentralization, firms can choose to lobby both, one or neither of the regional governments. In Redoano, a lobbying is organized by preference for the public good. A set of residents of a given preference type can potentially form a lobby: the free-rider problem is overcome by assuming that a lobby only forms if all residents of a given preference type agree to make a contribution.

All of these papers find that the traditional intuition that local government is more susceptible to 'capture' by lobbies is true only under certain conditions. In Bardhan and Mookherjee, in the baseline model without lobbies, centralization and decentralization are equivalent if regions are homogeneous, in particular, if (i) the income distribution in each region is the same, and (ii) the size of the lobby (the organized rich) is the same in each district. So, not surprisingly, Bardhan and Mookherjee find that there is less capture[35] with centralized decision making if citizens are better informed at the national level, and the rich are less organized at the national level. A more interesting result is that if both these factors are the same at the national and regional levels, and the shocks to informed voter preferences are uncorrelated (or, more generally, less than perfectly correlated) across regions, the outcome of the election is more certain at the national level, and so the rich are more willing to lobby the party most likely to win, raising capture at the national level. Other notable results are that there is less capture with centralized decision making if (i) there are more parties at the national level; and (ii) the electoral system is based on proportional representation, rather than majoritarian.

In Bordignon et al. (2003), in the baseline model without lobbies, centralization is the more efficient arrangement, as it internalizes a spillover effect of the publicly provided good between regions. With lobbying, this advantage of centralization may be neutralized or even reversed. In particular, without lobbying, centralization is efficient, so when lobbying is allowed, the publicly provided good is overprovided, whereas lobbying offsets the initially inefficient undersupply with decentralization. In other words, this is a second-best result: introducing a new source of inefficiency (lobbying) can help offset an initial inefficiency. In Redoano (2003), without lobbies, by contrast, decentralization is the most efficient arrangement, as there are no interregional public good spillovers, and there is inefficient policy uniformity (uniform public good provision) with centralization, but this needs to be the case without lobbying.

A political economy perspective on the allocation of fiscal powers

As emphasized in the Introduction, there are two aspects to the study of the allocation of fiscal powers from a political economy perspective. First, given an allocation of powers, how does the political process by which decisions are made (voting, behavior of the legislature and so on) determine the performance of government? We have dealt with this issue at length in the previous section. We now turn to the second question;[36] how does the political process by which decisions are made determine the choice of allocation of powers?

Broadly speaking, there are two ways in which a (re)allocation of fiscal powers between center and regions can be made: by voting in the national legislature, and by referendum. Both methods are used in practice. For example, in the UK, reallocation of powers is almost always implemented by ordinary legislation in the national parliament: for example, in the bill that devolved power to a Scottish parliament. However, there are exceptions, in the case of 'upward' allocation of power to the European Union (EU): the UK's 1975 entry into the EU was decided by referendum, and more recently, the UK government has promised a referendum on the new EU constitution.

An additional important issue is that whether a vote in legislature or a referendum is used, the use of either procedure is often quite different in federal and unitary states. In federal states, the allocation of powers is usually specified in the constitution and may require[37] a constitutional amendment. Constitutional amendments are used routinely in Switzerland, and less frequently in the US, Canada and Australia, to reallocate tax and spending powers (Wheare 1963).

In all major federal states, rules for constitutional amendment require that at least a majority of regions must approve the amendment, either by vote in the regional legislature, or by referendum (ibid.). For example, in the US, any amendment to the constitution must be approved by at least three-quarters of all state legislatures. Constitutional amendments in Australia and Switzerland require majority approval of the population as a whole, and also majorities in all the regions (that is, unanimity among the regions (ibid.)).

Assuming that decisions are always made by ordinary majority, for simplicity there are thus four logical possible decision rules, as indicated in Table 1.1. The table also covers situations where fiscal powers are reallocated 'above' the level of the nation state. The leading example, here, of course, is the European Union, where ratification of treaties – which often lead to centralization of powers at the EU level – can be done in any member country by either a national referendum or a vote in the legislature. For example, in the UK, the Maastricht Treaty was ratified by a vote in parliament, but in Denmark and France, it was ratified via referendum. The same choice between referendum or vote faces countries[38] now when ratifying the treaty establishing a constitution for Europe, which was signed on 29 October 2004.

Table 1.1 also allows us to locate the existing literature in a systematic way. First, an early contribution by Cremer and Palfrey (1996), and a more recent

Table 1.1 *The allocation of fiscal powers*

	Vote by referendum		Vote in legislature	
	Approval by region not needed (unitary state)	Approval by region needed (federal state)	Approval by region not needed (unitary state)	Approval by region needed (federal state)
Decision rule	Majority vote in national referendum	Two-stage procedure: 1. Majority vote in regional referendum to determine regional preference 2. Majority vote by regions to determine national preference	Majority vote in national legislature	Two-stage procedure: 1. Majority vote in regional legislature to determine regional preference 2. Majority vote by regions to determine national preference
Literature	Cremer and Palfrey (1996); Lockwood (2002, 2004); Lorz and Willman (2004); Redoano and Scharf (2004)	Cremer and Palfrey (1996), Lockwood (2004)	Lorz and Willman (2004); Redoano and Scharf (2004)	

one by Lockwood (2004) compare the performance of a national referendum and the two-stage procedure (federal referendum for convenience). Second, Lockwood (2002) considers the choice of decentralization via a national referendum only, but compares majority and unanimity rule. Third, Lorz and Willman (2004) and Redoano and Scharf (2004) compare choice of allocation of fiscal powers either via a national referendum (direct democracy) or via voting in a legislature (representative democracy).

National and federal referenda
In Cremer and Palfrey (1996), regional or central governments choose some value of a policy variable (a real number) via majority voting. In their model, the cost of centralization is that the policy variable must be set at the same level in all regions (Oates's policy uniformity): the benefit is that 'extreme' policies are less likely.[39] They obtain a remarkable result:[40] as the number of (equal-sized) regions become large, whenever the national referendum selects centralization, the federal referendum also selects centralization (but not necessarily vice versa), so federal referenda unambiguously lead to more centralization. They call this result 'the principle of aggregation'.

Lockwood (2004) addresses the same question in a model of discrete regional public goods, much closer to the legislative model of the previous section. There are no spillovers, so the benefit of centralization is in economies of scale. Policy uniformity is not assumed. The outcome with centralization is modeled in a legislative bargaining framework.[41] Finally, unlike[42] Cremer and Palfrey (1996), the model avoids imposing strong assumptions on the distribution of preferences for projects within and between regions.

With a fixed and finite number of regions, and no restrictions on the distribution of project benefits, either within or across regions, there is no particular reason to think that the federal referendum will be systematically more decentralizing than the national referendum or vice versa. The main (asymptotic) results of the paper concern what happens as the number of regions becomes large, under certain regularity conditions.[43] Under some symmetry assumptions on preferences, it is shown that the federal and national unitary referenda are asymptotically equivalent if the distribution of median project benefits across regions is uniform, irrespective of how preferences are distributed within regions. In the 'usual' case where the distribution of median project benefits across regions is positively single peaked (that is, has a quasi-concave density), then the federal referendum is asymptotically more likely to select centralization than the unitary referendum, confirming Cremer and Palfrey's result.[44]

Finally, Lockwood (2002) studies choice of decentralization in the legislative bargaining model described above. In that model, decentralization is efficient when the spillover is zero, but when the spillover is large and positive, the reverse is the case. Conditions are investigated under which unanimity or majority rule will select decentralization when the spillover is zero, and centralization when the spillover is large and positive.

Voting in the legislature versus referendum

This is a case that is of particular interest in the context of the European Union, where as already noted, ratification of EU treaties can be done via referendum or vote in the legislature. Redoano and Scharf (2004) were the first to study this choice. The main insight from their model is that (relative to a referendum), the delegation of the choice of centralization to the legislature can effectively act as a precommitment device by a procentralization region to induce the delegate from an anti-centralization jurisdiction to agree to centralization. Redoano and Scharf compare two ways of allocating fiscal powers, a referendum and a vote in the legislature. With a referendum, allocation of fiscal power is chosen through a referendum of the two-stage type (that is, the alternative chosen must be chosen by a majority of voters in both regions). With a vote in the legislature, delegates are first simultaneously elected from each of the two regions. Then, the delegates choose the allocation of fiscal power by majority vote. Finally, in either case, if centralization has been chosen, the legislature makes a decision on public good provision; if decentralization has been chosen, the two regions independently choose public good provision.

With only two regions, majority is unanimity, and so the status quo is relevant: the implicit assumption in Redoano and Scharf's paper is that the status quo is decentralization. So, with either a referendum (or a vote in the legislature), a move to centralization requires the agreement of the voters in both regions (or their delegates).

The willingness to pay for the public good of any voter can take on only two values, high or low. In region 1, a majority of the agents have a high willingness to pay, whereas in region 2, a majority of the agents have a low willingness to pay. The difference between a referendum and a vote in the legislature arises when preferences are additionally such that: (i) a high-preference voter in region 1 prefers centralization to decentralization, whereas a low-preference voter prefers the reverse, given that the two delegates to the legislature represent the majority of voters in their region, and (ii) a high-preference voter in region 1 even prefers centralization when his/her delegate is a low-preference type.

Then, with a referendum, as the majority of voters in region 2 prefer decentralization, they will prevail, and decentralization will be chosen. In this situation, the majority of agents in region 1 would like to make a side-payment to the majority in region 2 to persuade them to agree to centralization, but the referendum does not provide a mechanism for doing this. But, with a vote in the legislature, the majority in region 1 can make a 'strategic concession' to region 2 by choosing a low-preference delegate. If they do so, the delegate from region 2 will certainly vote for centralization, as the legislature will then contain two low-preference delegates. Anticipating this, the majority in region 1 will wish to delegate in this way, and so centralization will be chosen.

Lorz and Willman (2004) build on Redoano and Scharf. There, the focus is on which (of a continuum of) public goods should be provided centrally. Regions do not differ in preferences for the public goods, but legislators can make side-payments when bargaining over which goods to decentralize. So, voters strategically delegate to legislators who have a relatively low willingness to pay for the public good in order to win higher side-payments. This leads to too few goods (relative to the efficient benchmark) being provided centrally. As a referendum over which public goods to decentralize leads to the efficient outcome, voting in the legislature leads to less centralization than does a referendum.

Conclusions

This chapter has surveyed some recent contributions to the study of fiscal decentralization from a political economy viewpoint. The unifying theme of the survey is that the standard approach, based on the idea of benevolent governments and policy uniformity, cannot give a rigorous account of the preference-matching and accountability benefits of decentralization, but the political economy approach can do this. This matches with a growing empirical literature, which often demonstrates a link between fiscal decentralization and increased preference matching and accountability.

Notes

1. I would like to thank participants at the Seminar on Fiscal Federalism in August 2004 at the Centro di Studio di Federalismo and Yuji Tamura for helpful comments.
2. The policy uniformity assumption is widely used in papers on many topics in fiscal federalism as an easy way of generating some cost of centralization, including work by Alesina and Spolare (1997) on the size of nations, Bolton and Roland (1997) on the effects of threat of secession, and Alesina et al. (2001) on endogenous international unions. While these papers do not assume a benevolent social planner, they use the policy uniformity assumption as an easy way of generating some cost of fiscal centralization.
3. This argument goes back to Buchanan and Brennan's 'Leviathan' hypothesis (1977), in which they 'envision a monolithic government that systematically seeks to exploit its citizenry through the maximization of tax revenues that it extracts from the economy' (Oates 1985). They argue that decentralization checks the ambition of a Leviathan government.
4. This is the conventional assumption, but the results below go through if the good is a congestible public good, or even private.
5. An objection sometimes made to this argument is that the two regional governments can *bargain* with each other to improve on the non-cooperative outcome. So, to be non-trivial, the standard approach must assume that Coasian bargaining between regions to internalize externalities is impossible or prohibitively costly. This seems plausible in many cases (for example, sulfur dioxide pollution crossing state boundaries in the United States).
6. Formally, $1/2\sum_{l,k=1,2} u_1(g_l, g_k, \theta_l) + u_2(g_l, g_k, \theta_l) = 1$, $k \neq l$.

7. Suppose household preference θ_i is distributed within regions with mean $\bar{\theta}_i$ and median m_i. Then all the results go through unchanged, but $\bar{\theta}_i$ replaces θ_i, if preferences can be written $u_i(g_i, g_j, \theta_i) = \theta_i u_i(g_i, g_j, \theta_i)$.

8. These projects correspond very closely to the theoretical concept of a local public good, as they are items such as public buildings, transportation projects and so on.

9. For example, in the UK about 60 per cent of local government spending is financed by central government, primarily through the Revenue Support Grant. This grant is calculated according to a complex formula based on a large number of demographic, social and economic characteristics of local jurisdictions.

10. In what follows, we shall refer to the household equivalently as a citizen.

11. This implicitly assumes that all citizens are willing (or are compelled) to stand for election. If we assume some ego-rent from office, and no cost of candidacy, then all citizens will (weakly) be willing to stand. This assumption can be refined by introducing costs of candidacy (on which, see Besley and Coate 1997), in which case, not all citizens will wish to stand.

12. Uniform taxation is consistent with the 'stylized fact' that tax rates set by national legislatures are almost always uniform across regions (although actual taxes paid per head may of course, differ by region).

13. In this framework, we are assuming also that there is complete information and that legislators are benevolent (that is, they have neither the desire nor the opportunity to divert tax revenue away from spending on public goods and into spending on goods or services that will benefit them personally). So, this framework abstracts from any agency problem between voters and policy makers – see the penultimate section.

14. Another model, used by Lockwood (2002), is that of Ferejohn et al. (1987).

15. The legislative bargaining model with a closed rule has been widely applied to public finance issues, particularly in work by Persson and Tabellini (see, for example, Chapter 7 of Persson and Tabellini 2000). However, they do not address issues of fiscal decentralization in this framework.

16. This section is based on Lockwood (2005).

17. One might object that legislator 3's effective veto power over projects is due to the assumption that only one round of legislative bargaining is allowed. With an infinite number of rounds, and $\delta < 1$, what will happen is that legislator 3 will continue to propose the status quo, but this will be rejected by 1 and 2, and at some point 1 or 2 will become the agenda-setter. So, the equilibrium outcome is that the bundle $g_1 = g_2 = 1$, $g_3 = 0$ will be adopted, but possibly only after some delay.

18. Discreteness is not always unrealistic; many publicly funded infrastructure projects, such as airports, roads, universities and so on are discrete, although there is often a range of options on the scale of the project.

19. Lockwood (2002) presents some general conditions (Assumptions A0–A5) sufficient for the existence of a unique restricted CW. They are not too restrictive.

20. Consider the case of no spillovers, and $n = 3$. Take $\theta_1 = \theta_2 = 1$, $\theta_3 = 2$, $c_1 = 1.1$, $c_2 = 1.2$, $c_3 = 1.3$. Then, the two cheapest projects, 1 and 2, are funded in equilibrium, but it is clearly inefficient to do so, as $\theta_1 - c_1 = -0.1$, $\theta_2 < -0.2$. Conversely, project 3 is not funded in equilibrium, but it is efficient to fund it, as $\theta_3 - c_3 = 0.7$.

21. Although strategic delegation through elections is a well-understood effect (Persson and Tabellini 1992), so far it seems to have been mainly studied in the context of tax competition.

22. It is possible to show that the median voter in i, with willingness to pay m_i, is dictator in country I (that is, he/she effectively chooses the type of representative, r_i).

23. In fact, the delegation incentives of the median voter are quite subtle. Starting at a position of no strategic delegation ($m_i = r_i$), an increase in r_i will increase g_i, and also g_j, but by a lesser amount. The first effect makes the median voter in i better off (because he/she can get the other jurisdiction to pay for half the cost of the increase in g_i), and by the same argument, the second effect makes him/her worse off. Nevertheless, the first effect dominates as $s < 0.5$.

24. The reason for this is fairly obvious: the equilibrium side-payment equalizes the surplus that

each voter gets from a given g_1, g_2, thus giving each voter the incentives of the social planner.

25. It is important to note that (in the models considered in this literature) a good selection effect is usually associated with a bad incentive effect, and vice versa. For example, if a bad incumbent decides to pool rather than separate, he/she imitates the behavior of the good incumbent (a good incentive effect), but then retains office until the second period, when he/she diverts maximum rent (a bad selection effect).

26. In the equilibrium with both centralization and decentralization, an incumbent with a competence level higher (lower) than the expected competence of the challenger wins (loses) the election. As both competence levels are random draws from the same distribution, the probability that the initial incumbent has a competence level above the expected level of the challenger is simply 0.5.

27. It does not follow from this that voter welfare is always unconditionally lower with centralization, however, as voters may prefer a lower separation probability if they discount the future a lot, and this can outweigh the selective pooling effect.

28. A 'global' result along these lines is easy to prove: if the government (national or regional) puts a sufficiently high weight on rent diversion, fiscal decentralization will increase welfare.

29. A related paper is Gordon and Wilson (1999), which studies how results on the optimal tax structure change when a bureaucracy with its own objectives chooses government expenditure, but a legislature (effectively, a benevolent social planner) chooses taxes.

30. Recall that this is the probability in equilibrium that the rent-seeking incumbent loses the election.

31. Bordignon et al. (2004) have shown, however, that this result is rather specific to the parameter values that Besley and Smart consider: it is also possible to find cases where allowing yardstick competition makes the pooling equilibrium less likely.

32. See for example, the discussion on this issue in the survey paper by Brueckner (2003).

33. In fact, as there is probabilistic voting in the model (voters have random shocks to preferences), this means that each party chooses policy to maximize a form of social welfare function.

34. Bordignon et al. (2003) call this an infrastructure good, but this is an unusual way of modeling an infrastructure good, which is usually assumed to enhance the productivity of the firm.

35. In their model, capture is measured by the weight that the two parties place on the preferences of the informed rich in their objective functions (relative to the case without lobbying).

36. There are also a few empirical studies of the determinants of fiscal decentralization, notably Obholzer-Gee and Strumpf (2002) and Panizza (1999). These empirical studies do not, however, attempt to distinguish the effects of different political procedures for deciding on the allocation of powers (rather, they are concerned with whether more basic variables, such as preference heterogeneity, are significantly correlated with decentralization) and so we do not discuss them further here.

37. However, the degree to which reallocation of powers leads to constitutional amendment varies considerably across federal countries. In the US, there has been only one constitutional amendment for this purpose (in 1913, to allow a federal income tax), whereas in Switzerland there have been a large number of amendments over the last 100 years, enhancing the tax powers of central government (Wheare 1963, Chapter 6).

38. According to the official EU website (http://europa.eu.int/): 'This Treaty can only enter into force when it has been adopted by each of the signatory countries in accordance with its own constitutional procedures: this is called the ratification of the Treaty by the Member States. Depending on the countries' legal and historical traditions, the procedures laid down by the constitutions for this purpose are not identical: they comprise either or both of the following two types of mechanism: the 'parliamentary' method: the text is adopted following a vote on a text ratifying an international Treaty by the State's parliamentary Chamber(s); the 'referendum' method: a referendum is held, submitting the text of the Treaty directly to citizens, who vote for or against it'.

39. They assume that voters are incompletely informed about the preferences of other voters, both in their regions and in other regions. It turns out in this set-up that the benefit of central-

ization is policy moderation. That is, when the number of regions becomes large, the subjective probability for any particular voter that the policy variable will, in voting equilibrium, take on an extreme value (that is, far from that voter's most preferred value) is lower with centralization.

40. This follows from Figure 1 in their paper, where it is clear that if the proportion of voters preferring centralization is greater than 0.5, then the proportion of regions preferring centralization must also be greater than 0.5.

41. In the legislature bargaining equilibrium, every one of the n regions gets a public good with the (equal) probability $(n + 1)/2n$ that they are in the minimum winning coalition (which I call 'endogenous policy uniformity'). This is inefficient, as while all goods are assumed to be equally costly, some regions have a higher average willingness to pay than others, and so only some regions should get projects, and should get them with probability 1.

42. Due to the information structure in Cremer and Palfrey (1996), their model is tractable only if very specific assumptions on the distribution of preferences within regions and between regions are made, and indeed, they assume for the most part that both these distributions are normal.

43. These are: (i) regional median project benefits are random draws from a fixed distribution; (ii) conditional on the regional median, the distribution of tastes within any region is the same.

44. These findings relate to Cremer and Palfrey's 'principle of aggregation' as follows. The two cases analysed in their model were when preferences were normal. But the normal distribution is single peaked, in which case our result is that the federal referendum is more centralized, consistently with their principle of aggregation.

References

Alesina, A. and E. Spolare (1997), 'On the number and size of nations', *Quarterly Journal of Economics*, Vol. 112, pp. 1027–56.

Alesina, A., I. Angeloni and F. Etro (2001), 'The political economy of international unions', National Bureau of Economic Research Working Paper 8645.

Bardhan, P. and D. Mookherjee (2000), 'Capture and governance at local and national levels', *American Economic Review*, Vol. 90, No. 2, pp. 135–9.

Baron, D. and J. Ferejohn (1989), 'Bargaining in legislatures', *American Political Science Review*, Vol. 87, pp. 34–47.

Belleflamme, P. and J. Hindriks (2003), 'Yardstick competition and political agency problems', *Social Choice and Welfare*, Vol. 24, pp. 155–69.

Besley, T. and A. Case (1995), 'Incumbent behavior: vote-seeking, tax-setting, and yardstick competition', *American Economic Review*, Vol. 85, pp. 25–45.

Besley, T. and S. Coate (1997), 'An economic model of representative democracy', *Quarterly Journal of Economics*, Vol. 112, pp. 85–114.

Besley, T. and S. Coate (2003), 'Centralized versus decentralized provision of local public goods: a political economy approach', *Journal of Public Economics*, Vol. 87, pp. 2611–37.

Besley, T. and M. Smart (2003), 'Fiscal restraints and voter welfare' (unpublished; London School of Economics).

Bolton, P. and G. Roland (1997), 'The break-up of nations: a political economy analysis', *Quarterly Journal of Economics*, Vol. 112, pp. 1057–90.

Bordignon, M., F. Cerniglia and F. Revelli (2004), 'Yardstick competition in intergovernmental relationships: theory and empirical predictions', *Economics Letters*, Vol. 83, pp. 325–33.

Bordignon, M., L. Colombo and U. Galmarini (2003), 'Fiscal federalism and endogenous lobbies' formation', CESifo Working Paper No. 1017, Munich.

Brennan, G. and J.M. Buchanan (1977), 'Towards a tax constitution for Leviathan', *Journal of Public Economics*, Vol. 8, pp. 255–7.

Brueckner, J.K. (2003), 'Strategic interaction among governments: an overview of empirical studies', *International Regional Science Review*, Vol. 26, pp. 175–88.

Buchanan, J.M. (1987), 'The constitution of economic policy', *American Economic Review*, Vol. 77, pp. 243–50.

Cremer, J. and T. Palfrey (1996), 'In or out? Centralization by majority vote', *European Economic Review*, Vol. 40, pp. 43–60.

Edwards, J. and M. Keen (1996), 'Tax competition and Leviathan', *European Economic Review*, Vol. 40, pp. 113–35.

Ferejohn, J. (1986), 'Incumbent performance and electoral control', *Public Choice*, Vol. 50, pp. 5–26.

Ferejohn, J., M. Fiorina and R.D. McKelvey (1987), 'Sophisticated voting and agenda independence in the distributive politics setting', *American Journal of Political Science*, Vol. 31, pp. 169–94.

Gordon, R. and J.D. Wilson (1999), 'Tax structure and the behavior of government', National Bureau of Economic Research Working Paper 7244.

Grossman, G.M. and E. Helpman (2001), *Special Interest Politics*, Cambridge, MA: MIT Press).

Hindriks, J. and B. Lockwood (2005), 'Centralization and political accountability', CEPR Discussion Paper 5125, London: Centre for Economic Policy Research.

Knight, B. (2004), 'Legislative representation, bargaining power, and the distribution of federal funds: evidence from the US Senate', National Bureau of Economic Research Working Paper 10385.

Lockwood, B. (2002), 'Distributive politics and the costs of centralization', *Review of Economic Studies*, Vol. 69, No. 2, pp. 313–37.

Lockwood, B. (2004), 'Decentralization via federal and unitary referenda', *Journal of Public Economic Theory*, Vol. 6, pp. 79–108.

Lockwood, B. (2005), 'Centralized versus decentralized provision of local public goods: a legislative bargaining approach', University of Warwick Economics Working Paper.

Lorz, O. and G. Willman (2004), 'On the endogenous allocation of decision powers in federal structures' (unpublished; University of Gottingen).

Mas-Colell, A., M.D. Winston and J.R. Green (1995), *Microeconomic Theory*, Oxford and New York: Oxford University Press.

Oates, W. (1972), *Fiscal Federalism*, New York: Harcourt-Brace.

Oates, W. (1985), 'Searching for Leviathan: an empirical study', *American Economic Review*, Vol. 79, pp. 748–57.

Oates, W. (1999), 'An essay on fiscal federalism', *Journal of Economic Literature*, Vol. 37, pp. 1120–49.

Oberholzer-Gee, F. and K.S. Strumpf (2002), 'Endogenous policy decentralization: testing the central tenet of economic federalism', *Journal of Political Economy*, Vol. 110, pp. 1–36.

Panizza, U. (1999), 'On the determinants of fiscal centralization: theory and evidence', *Journal of Public Economics*, Vol. 74, pp. 97–140.

Persson, T. and G. Tabellini (1992), 'The politics of 1992: fiscal policy and European integration', *Review of Economic Studies*, Vol. 59, pp. 689–701.

Persson, T. and G. Tabellini (2000), *Political Economics: Explaining Economic Policy*, Cambridge, MA: MIT Press.

Redoano, M. (2003), 'Does centralization affect the number and size of lobbies?', Warwick Economic Research Paper No. 674.

Redoano, M. and K. Scharf (2004), 'The political economy of policy centralization: direct vs. representative democracy', *Journal of Public Economics*, Vol. 88, pp. 799–817.

Rogoff, K. (1990), 'Equilibrium political budget cycles', *American Economic Review*, Vol. 80, pp. 21–37.

Seabright, S. (1996), 'Accountability and decentralization in government: an incomplete contracts model', *European Economic Review*, Vol. 40, pp. 61–91.

Wheare, K.C. (1963), *Federal Government*, Oxford and New York: Oxford University Press.

Wilson, J.D. (1999), 'Theories of tax competition', *National Tax Journal*, Vol. 52, pp. 269–304.

2 Horizontal competition among governments
Pierre Salmon[1]

Introduction

Governments situated on the same level of a multilevel governmental system compete with one another as well as with those higher or lower in the hierarchy. Except for a few remarks towards the end, this chapter is concerned with horizontal competition only. The proposition that governments on the same tier compete among themselves – horizontal competition – is now widely accepted. This was not always the case. In many models or discussions of local government and finance, as well as of decentralization and federalism, competition had no place or, more often, played only an implicit role.

An obstacle to perceiving competition is that it can take many forms. The rivalry between Airbus and Boeing is intense. It would be difficult to deny its existence, which is ascertainable from the competitors' awareness of it and from their revealed behaviour. To visualize competition in an equilibrium situation in which decision makers are price takers, though, one must raise hypothetical questions such as what would happen if a supplier were to price its product above the market price. Another intellectual obstacle is the presence and necessity of coordination. It must be stressed that competition among governments as well as among business firms does not preclude coordination (Breton 1996). Two automobile firms may coordinate their actions on various dimensions, and even cooperate on some well-defined projects, without the overall competition between them ceasing to be intense. The same is true of governments. Yardstick competition, which will play an important role in the analysis below, raises a particular problem. Because it does not take place on markets in the usual sense, to become conscious of its existence one must look directly at the behaviour of the competitors and of the principals (the voters, most often) who induce them to compete.

Different variables may be the objects of horizontal competition. The most studied is taxation. The literature on tax competition is very large. Within that literature, many discussions concede that governments compete also with regard to the services they provide, or, even better from a logical point of view, in terms of the combinations of taxes and services they offer. Closely related to that, there is a lively discussion on the effects of competition on welfare benefits, and then on regulations associated with welfare, in the domain of labour in particular. Law, and law and economics scholars are mostly concerned with regulatory competition as applied to corporations, banks, insurance companies, financial markets, competition (anti-trust) and the environment – many economists being also involved, of course, in these subjects. These differences, however, are often, in a sense, superficial. Competition in terms of the same variable, say taxation, may be based on different processes, each of them being in turn quite general, that is, the basis of competition over different variables. In other words, there is a typology of processes or mechanisms that is largely independent of the typology of the variables considered. Thus tax competition can be based on the mobility of individuals, goods, factors or firms, but it can also happen without any kind of mobility, being founded instead, for instance, on the fact that the performance of policy makers is assessed comparatively – tax competition taking then the form of yardstick competition.[2] Conversely, mobility-based or yardstick competition may be relevant in different contexts (taxation, regulation and so on), in fact most of those mentioned above.

The typology of mechanisms must be further specified. Both mobility-based and yardstick competition can be assumed to operate in a world of perfect competition, in which governments are price, utility or yardstick takers. Alternatively, they can be modelled as a case of oligopolistic competition, in which governments interact strategically. And there are other possibilities – that is, other ways to conceive competition – that may sometimes be better able than the previous two to account for salient observations.

What are the motives that underlie the behaviour of governments? In the case of yardstick competition, although there are, as we shall see, at least two different possibilities, the answer remains fairly straightforward. In the case of mobility-based competition, it is less clear. In local public finance, it has often been assumed that jurisdictions maximize the profits or rents of developers, or of land- or home-owners. In more general settings, the often implicit assumption is that governments maximize tax bases, some net resource flow, some net gain, or something of the kind – discretionary spending power, for example. It seems natural for economists to think of intergovernmental competition as quite similar to the market competition they are familiar with. Still, governments do not always display the kind of behaviour that similarity would require. Thus, some allowance must be made for less standard assumptions about policy makers' objectives or about the setting in which they have to work.

The chapter is organized around underlying mechanisms and political assumptions rather than around the variables over which competition takes place. The larger part of the literature concerned, explicitly or not, with horizontal competition among governments assumes that it is based on mobility and, furthermore, as noted, that it is governed by mechanisms similar to those ascribed to competition on ordinary markets. The next section is devoted to this central strand. Because the literature is so large, the section will eschew the usual questions about spillovers and efficiency and focus instead on the degree of policy discretion that mobility leaves to governments. In the third section, we turn to non-standard assumptions, also based on mobility but leading to outcomes at odds with those usually considered as compelling. In the fourth section, we discuss the forms that competition among governments may take when based on information. Some of these forms – including the one defended by the neo-Austrian school – are related to what is sometimes called 'laboratory' federalism, which does not necessarily involve yardstick competition. In turn, the latter can be divided into different mechanisms. We focus on the one that gives a major role to comparisons across jurisdictions made by voters or by other potential sources of support to incumbents. In the real world, the various processes or mechanisms generally operate simultaneously. The fifth section explores the ways in which mobility-based and yardstick competition may interact.

Several forms of horizontal competition are not mentioned in the chapter. Junior governments compete to get grants from government(s) at a higher tier or from other sources. They use loopholes in their regulated environment to engage in mercantilist if not outright protectionist policies. They promote the adoption in a wider setting of their own regulations and standards. In the penultimate section, however, we discuss some aspects of horizontal competition not addressed before in the chapter but too central to be completely overlooked. These aspects are spillovers, empirical studies, normative assessments and institutional implications. The reason for this macedoine is not mainly one of convenience. Very little can be said from a normative or prescriptive perspective that does not rely on relatively precise empirical evaluations but, in the domain, empirical analysis encounters many obstacles, which suggests that normative positions are fragile.

Mobility-based competition: markets with some politics

Perfect competition-cum-mobility

Many contributions to the theoretical literature on local finance, decentralization and federalism are based on the assumptions of perfect competition among subcentral governments or jurisdictions and costless mobility of agents. The literature started with the assumption of jurisdictions as clubs. However, as was eventually realized, once the concept of territoriality, space or land is made central to the reasoning, as it should be, the theory of clubs may be misleading and intricate problems arise. One source of complication is that, in this setting, price affects quality, contrary to what is usually assumed about ordinary markets. I shall not summarize the problems or the solutions offered (see, for example, Epple and Nechyba 2004). I simply note that the two assumptions, in a less strict form, have escaped the world of scientific models and found their way to that of policy-oriented discussions. This provides a reason to adopt a more relaxed interpretation of perfect competition. Among the arguments exchanged in the media or among politicians on issues such as decentralization, federalism, European integration and globalization, some are based on the image of a world in which the two assumptions of perfect competition and zero mobility costs conspire to deprive governments, on the level concerned, of all capacity to act autonomously. Because the public debate often focuses on the question of autonomy or freedom to act rather than on the problems, central to the theory, raised by externalities, distortions and other departures from optimality, and also for convenience, as indicated, I shall also concentrate on the capacity to act.

In the field of taxation, the assumptions of perfect competition among governments and on all markets on the one hand, and of the mobility of agents, on the other, yield the proposition that, at equilibrium, taxes paid by mobile individuals, factors and firms will all be benefit taxes. The result seems arresting but it is not. It allows much diversity across jurisdictions with considerable policy discretion in each. Taxes are definitely not equalized across jurisdictions because individuals and firms have heterogeneous wants. So there will be much variation in the combinations of taxes and benefits that are offered (Tiebout 1956). In addition, taxes paid by mobile agents will not be fully dissipated through the cost incurred by the public sector to produce goods and services. There will be a surplus that the government and/or voters will be able to spend as they wish. In Epple and Zelenitz (1981), the surplus is the consequence of fixed interjurisdictional boundaries, the presence of heterogeneous amenities being also acknowledged.

This last reality is important. Space is heterogeneous, not only because of the artificial boundaries of jurisdictions. Differences in natural endowments are an obvious cause or manifestation of that fact. But, more importantly, at any point in time heterogeneity also follows from differences in the stocks of collective capital (including social capital) that inhabitants have built up in the course of time. As a consequence, some of the benefits provided to individuals and firms, and even to capital, are largely independent of the current output of the public sector. They are situational rents which do not have to accrue only to the owners of the land; they may be shared with the jurisdictions themselves, as represented by their governments. This creates, in most if not all jurisdictions, a tax base that can be tapped, among other possibilities, to finance the goods and services that mobile agents are not willing to pay for.

Let me introduce here an additional consideration – reflecting still more liberty with the usual specification of the competitive framework. In practice, competition among jurisdictions tends to be of the monopolistic competition variety. The specific character of the services provided by each jurisdiction and the heterogeneity of the preferences of the mobile agents cannot be fully dealt with by the Tiebout sorting process or taken into account by the tax system even when the latter tends towards benefit taxation. As a consequence, in a given jurisdiction some mobile agents will benefit from a consumer or producer surplus related to their presence or establishment in that jurisdiction. Even if there are no mobility costs, a tax increase will then not necessarily make them leave the jurisdiction.

The capacity to regulate may be treated more or less in the same way as the capacity to finance. The notion of benefits must be widened once more so as to include the utility (or disutility) provided to mobile agents by the laws and regulations in force in the various jurisdictions – also a part of the collective capital of these jurisdictions, albeit not to be interpreted now as fully exogenous and, in particular, as independent of what the current incumbents decide. Under perfect competition and no mobility costs, at equilibrium, mobile agents must find in any jurisdiction a level of utility at least equal to what they could obtain elsewhere. Utility here must be seen as a function of goods and bads of all kinds, including public output, taxes, situational rents, law and regulations, and so on. Focusing on an individual variable, like a tax, or a regulation of pollution, or the school system, though often unavoidable in practice, may be quite misleading because competition does not take place over single variables but over very complex and idiosyncratic packages. There is substantial fungibility in the components of these packages. Compensations are the rule. This is another factor of diversity across jurisdictions. For instance, the implementation of rules (concerning work conditions, lay-offs, the environment and so on) that impose a burden on mobile firms heavier than the one imposed in other jurisdictions may raise no problem if it is compensated, say, by a lower direct cost of labour or by less taxation. In spite of the high level of competition-cum-mobility, jurisdictions remain in this way capable of deciding important aspects of their social arrangements.

Does this capacity, in the same competitive environment, extend to income redistribution or some of its aspects (helping the poor, taxing the rich and so on)? The foregoing discussion provides part of the answer. First, as argued, most if not all jurisdictions keep some discretionary financing capacity – that is, a tax base they can use inter alia for redistribution. Second, a large part of what is usually considered as income redistribution is, for various reasons (insurance, peace seeking, altruism and so on), voluntary on the part of those who pay for it. In this sense, it is Pareto improving (Hochman and Rodgers 1969). In the context of competition among jurisdictions, income redistribution of this type can be simply included in the idiosyncratic packages already mentioned and submitted, as other components of these packages, to compensations of all kinds (see Breton 1996).

A problem, however, remains. Taken together the two reasons just offered suggest that resources may well be found to redistribute income, including by taxing the mobile rich. What seems more problematic, under the perfect competition-cum-mobility assumptions, is subsidizing the mobile agents and, in particular, helping the poor. The assumption of costless mobility, particularly plausible in the case of the poor or relatively large subsets thereof, implies, in the pure competition framework, that the demand curve for the assistance offered by a particular jurisdiction is infinitely elastic. Should we conclude, as is sometimes done in the literature on fiscal federalism, that no policy of assistance to the poor is sustainable at the subcentral level of government? Formulated as a proposition concerning the real world, such an inference would be quite unacceptable since helping the poor is exactly what lower-level governments in many countries do. What we should conclude instead is that with this difficulty we reach the limits of the compatibility between perfect competition-cum-mobility and autonomous decentralized policy making. To deal with the particular problem of subsidies to mobile agents – in any case to the poor – at least one of the two assumptions must be given up as we shall see in the next subsection.

The last important aspect of the perfect competition-cum mobility setting I want to mention is its implications for the well-known Leviathan view of government developed in particular in Brennan and Buchanan (1980) and, in somewhat different terms, in Weingast (1995).[3] The literature often assumes that the objective of governments, at all levels, is the welfare of the people. According to the Leviathan view, on the contrary, governments will use any discretionary power that they may be left with in a way which, as a rule, is unfavourable to the people. Under that perspective, one of the main advantages of federalism, if organized so as to produce the environment we referred to as perfect competition-cum-mobility, is to deprive government in general of its discretionary power. The foregoing discussion suggests that, even in an environment as favourable to that goal as the perfect competition-cum-mobility one, discretionary tax bases would not in general be eliminated. This is bad news for supporters of the extreme Leviathan view, good news for those who trust democratic mechanisms to align governments' and citizens' objectives, and in any case are particularly attached to government intervention in some domains. In between, where probably most economists stand, the result would generate mixed feelings – both disciplining effects and the capacity to act being legitimate concerns (see Edwards and Keen 1996).

Oligopolistic competition[4]
The analysis of horizontal relations among governments is increasingly formulated nowadays, as in other domains of economics, in terms of strategic interaction among a limited number of players – only two in many models. The analytical instrument used is non-cooperative game theory. I shall again

eschew the technicalities involved and speculate only about how the change in the assumed setting modifies the foregoing discussion. I continue to assume that mobility is costless.

If policy discretion could not be completely eliminated in the very constraining setting of perfect competition-cum-mobility, it will not either under oligopolistic competition; it will even, in general, be greater. The equivalence between the outcomes of Bertrand (price) competition under oligopoly and pure competition does not usually apply when the competitors are governments or jurisdictions because, again, of the different incidence of territorial constraints (being the only one to undercut price cannot entail taking all the market as is the case under Bertrand competition). These territorial effects are sometimes absent or negligible, as is the case with business firm registration or incorporation. Then, in principle something like Bertrand competition could apply, with the price (or the price/quality ratio) tending to what it would be under perfect competition. To some extent, the role played by Delaware in matters of incorporation provides an illustration. In general, however, even if there is no coordination or cooperation of any kind, a departure from equilibrium on the part of one government would entail a less dramatic response from outside the jurisdiction in the case of oligopoly than it would in the case of perfect competition.

It is unlikely, though, that interaction between a small number of governments will not lead them to cooperate or to coordinate their actions in some areas or on some points (which, as noted in the Introduction, does not imply that they will not compete actively, at the same time, in other respects or in general). Of course, the number of participants is an important determinant. We have seen that many models assume the number to be small (two participants, often). In the real world, it is also often the case that the number of jurisdictions on the same tier is small (three regions in the case of Belgium, ten provinces in the case of Canada). Then coordination costs are likely to be manageable. The situation is different when the numbers are larger (50 states in the case of the United States, 28 states in the case of India). What can be done in Belgium or Canada may thus be impossible in the United States or India and this certainly explains some of the differences in their federal arrangements or practices.

Inequality of size may also affect the possibility of cooperation. Two mechanisms, at least, may be at work. One, favourable to coordination and cooperation, is based on the willingness of the larger jurisdictions to finance by themselves a service that has the dimension of a collective good benefiting all. A large province or a large city (or a group of two or three of them) assumes all the cost of coordination and accepts that other provinces or cities shirk. The other mechanism, this time unfavourable to cooperation if not also to coordination, operates when a small jurisdiction (for instance a tax haven) draws a large profit, relative to its size, from not cooperating.

With a few exceptions (see Cardarelli et al. 2002), however, the literature has not devoted enough attention to the possibilities opened by repeat business. As is well known, with a sufficiently long time horizon and a sufficiently low rate of discount, the prospect of repeat business may make cooperation emerge where it would not if only the short run counted. What is, to my knowledge, even more underestimated is the potential of combinations of repeat business and issue linkage, as that latter phenomenon is known in political science. When numbers are relatively small or when a large jurisdiction assumes the costs of leadership, the reluctance of a government to cooperate in one domain (say, tax competition) can often be overcome by side-payments in other policy areas. In the relationship among the member countries of the European Union, deals of that kind are not only important but in fact institutionalized (Salmon 2002). They cannot but also be present in small-number or asymmetric federations like Canada and Belgium.

In some set-ups and on some issues, coordination can also be achieved by relatively large numbers. Assume, as argued in the preceding subsection, that, up to a certain amount, assistance to the poor can be financed by decentralized governments without problem, either because it can be included in the packages of benefits that at least some mobile agents (other than the poor) find valuable and are willing to pay, or because it can be one of the uses of the discretionary tax base discussed earlier. In many jurisdictions, the democratic pressure on policy makers makes them willing to implement a policy of assistance provided that this does not generate an excessive inflow of recipients. Clearly, if a large number of jurisdictions implement the policy, no excessive inflow in any of them may occur. Because the set-up here is that not of the prisoner's dilemma but of a game of coordination or assurance, a happy outcome is quite possible. Provided many other jurisdictions go on helping the poor, and so long as the said pressure from voters remains the same, the incentive for the policy makers of any jurisdiction is to pursue the assistance policy.

In spite of this particular case, one might be tempted to argue that the blend of coordination, or even cooperation, and competition will bend more towards competition when the level considered includes many jurisdictions, none of which is of a size much larger than the others. However, the example, cited in the Introduction, of intense competition between two aircraft manufacturers should dissuade us to attempt such generalization. The combination of tough small-number competition along most dimensions and coordination – and even cooperation – on some matters is as much a characteristic of federalism and decentralization as it is of the modern economy.

Mobility costs
In the real world, most agents, whether households, firms, or factors of production, cannot move without incurring significant costs, in terms of

money or sometimes only utility. Even within a single metropolitan area, house ownership and contractual obligations may make the costs significant whereas they may be very high when the jurisdictions concerned are regions or, in the European Union, member countries.

This fact is often considered as a decisive objection to models – like the Tiebout model or the Oates and Schwab model (1988) – that are dependent on the assumption of mobility. One might argue that the objection need not be taken too seriously as long as one respects two defining characteristics of the main approach, namely concentration on equilibrium and no explicit role for politics. Mobility costs are likely to be large only in the short and medium terms. In the long run, thanks to depreciation, obsolescence or the renewal of generations, real capital, whether tangible or intangible, moves much more easily across jurisdictional boundaries. In the said models, however, what counts is that adjustment takes place (that mobility costs eventually cease to count), *when* – that is, at what point in time – does not matter. In practice, the way to combine these models and the existence of costs of mobility is to divide agents or factors among those who are mobile and those who are not. In the European context, it is usual to assume that labour is not mobile across member countries.

In reality, costs of mobility vary continuously across agents and in time.[5] To take this into account, one must introduce in the analysis, in an explicit way, politics and something like dynamics and path dependency. Let us start from equilibrium, with a perfect correspondence between what is offered by a jurisdiction and what is demanded from it, and assume the occurrence of a shock, creating a difference between the two. Some inhabitants or firms will instantly leave the jurisdiction; others will be prevented from leaving quickly by the costs of mobility they would have to assume. The first consequence of their delaying their departure is that they will bear a utility loss. Thus it can no longer be argued that only land-owners are vulnerable to ill-effects of government policies. The second, related, consequence, then, is that losers, constrained by mobility costs to stay for some time, will have an incentive to turn to policy makers and press them to change policies. Their demands will not be fully satisfied, most likely, but some change of policy will take place if the political system is responsive – an additional reason why mobility-based competition is not exempt from politics. The third, also related, consequence, is path dependency. Even if ultimately a new equilibrium is reached, the situation in the jurisdiction will have been constantly different (including at that new equilibrium) from what would have obtained both with no mobility at all and with costless mobility. Soon after the shock, some agents will have left, others will have already induced some policy changes, not sufficient however to prevent other agents from leaving, and so on until a new equilibrium is reached (possibly). On the path to this new equilibrium, assuming that it exists, the two processes of 'exit' and 'voice' (Hirschman 1970) will interact in a highly idiosyncratic fashion, and this will also shape the final outcome.

Mobility-based competition: politics without markets
It seems natural to assume, as I have done so far, that the office-holders and the inhabitants of a jurisdiction assess in a positive way the resources available in that jurisdiction or flowing into it. This applies in particular to the abundance of land, the level of activity, the speed of economic development and the magnitude of the tax base. Conversely, it may seem strange that the politicians and voters in a jurisdiction prefer that it remains poor, that its economic development and the part of its territory used for human activities be as limited as possible, and that, as a consequence of the out-migration of many of its taxable agents, its tax base be made to shrink. Observation does confirm the manifestation, in some cases, of apparently perverse preferences such as these. To understand them, one must focus on politics, even at the cost of neglecting some market mechanisms. There has not been much research undertaken in that direction, at least in economics. I shall mention three instances, devoting more space to the first, which I happen to know more in depth.

In Mingat and Salmon (1988), the analysis is specific to circumstances particular to France in the 1960s and 1970s but its relevance is more general. Assume two political parties, Left and Right, that operate at the national and at the local levels, and assume that voters are loyal to one of the two parties depending on their relative income position (weighed up at the national level). To simplify, assume that the 'poor' vote is for the Left and the 'rich' for the Right at both the national and local levels.[6] All elected office-holders belong either to Right or to Left. Communes whose inhabitants are mostly poor tend to be governed by a Left mayor and communes inhabited mostly by the rich tend to be governed by a Right mayor. But this is only a statistical regularity, in particular (but not only) because the underlying relationship is submitted to exogenous shocks, for instance oscillations in public opinion at the national level. Thus incumbents are not certain to be re-elected even if the composition of their electorate does not change.

Now assume that mayors have at their disposal policy instruments that they can use to affect the inflows and outflows of poor and rich, and thus the rich/poor ratio among the voters of their jurisdictions. The hypothesis formulated in the model is that they will use these instruments to increase their probability of being re-elected. Thus mayors belonging to Right will want to increase this ratio and mayors belonging to Left will want to reduce it. If mayors can, for instance, foster or hinder the construction of rent-controlled and other types of 'social' dwellings, a relatively direct way to manipulate the ratio is, on the part of a Left municipality, to support such construction and, on the part of a Right one, to prevent it.[7] Less directly, if, in an inner city whose boundaries are fixed, the ratio is positively correlated with the price of dwellings and of land useable for the construction of dwellings (as was the case in France), and if these prices are increased by scarcity, indirect ways to increase the ratio are, for example, limiting the permissible height of new buildings, encouraging the construction of offices, or freezing as public parks a part of the city's territory. These policies are likely to be followed by mayors belonging to Right. Economic development in the whole metropolitan area puts pressure on the land available in the central city, makes its price rise, and, if the underlying mechanisms work as they did in France, increases the rich/poor ratio. This favours Right. A Left mayor of the central city may thus try to counter or slow down the economic development of the metropolitan area. He or she may, for instance, attempt to block the extension of the airport.

At any point in time the total number of poor and rich, and thus of voters voting for Left and Right, is fixed, both at the level of the country and at that of the metropolitan areas if we assume migrations to stop at the confines of the latter. Thus, with regard to the induced movements of population, competition takes place between incumbents of the same party. Less poor in the central city, which is good for its Right mayor, means more poor in the suburbs, which improves the electoral prospects of Left in those areas. There is a convergence of interest between the Right mayor of the central city and the Left suburban mayors taken as a group (including the Left challengers to Right incumbents, for that matter). There is a rivalry among these suburban mayors for a share of the windfall. Conversely, the re-election prospects of those mayors of suburban communes who belong to Right are worsened. Thus there is a conflict of interest and, potentially at least, some rivalry or competition between them and the mayor of the central city.

The foregoing suggests that once they get into power in a jurisdiction, parties will seek to strengthen their electoral support in that jurisdiction, but it leaves implicit the idea that, if incumbents are particularly successful or lucky, they will make that jurisdiction into an electoral stronghold for their party. The idea that competition between two parties could end up in providing them with 'safe districts' is developed by Caplan (2001) who, however, uses a mechanism different from that specified in Mingat and Salmon. Assume that there are two parties, the Democrats and the Republicans, each active at the two levels of jurisdiction. Voters are loyal to one of the two parties but have a different preferred policy along one single dimension. Office-holders in a subcentral jurisdiction adopt the policy favoured by the median voter in that jurisdiction. Suppose that, in the two cases by a very small margin, the Democrats come to power in one jurisdiction and the Republicans in another. They implement the policy preferred by the respective median voters, which is more or less the same – moderate. However, in the first jurisdiction the most extreme voters among those who support the Republicans are so unhappy to be governed by Democrats that they move to the second jurisdiction. Similarly, the most militant Democrat voters move from the second jurisdiction to the first so as to be governed by Democrats. As a consequence, the two median voter positions become more apart and incumbents adopt, in opposite directions, less moderate policies. This makes new subsets of Democrat and Republican voters unhappy in the jurisdictions governed by Republicans and Democrats respectively, and thus induces more migrations and so on. As a result, the policies followed in the two jurisdictions become very different and each party benefits from a safe district. Elections are not competitive any more, which justifies the author to consider the process as perverse.[8] There is no explicit intergovernmental competition in the model, but it would be easy to make it emerge by assuming a larger number of jurisdictions. Then, as in the previous story, there would be competition among incumbents of the same party, again for a share in a fixed total of sympathizers.

Whereas the essential decision makers are the incumbent office-holders in Mingat and Salmon (1988), and the mobile extremist voters in Caplan (2001), they are the immobile median voters in the third model, that of Brosio and Revelli (2003). In their framework, which is one of overlapping generations, there is no explicit government. The median voters are the sole policy makers. Their concern is that, when they retire in the next period, the median voters in power then will decide on a level of redistribution insufficient for providing them (the current median voters) with the pensions they will need. There is no way of binding the median voters of the next period. The only solution is to change them. This can be achieved by deciding now to have an inflow in the next period of low-income immigrants. During that next period, these immigrants will work and vote, and by their sole presence will change the income distributions. In each of the new income distributions, the median income, which is also by assumption the median voter's income, will be lower and more distant from the mean income than it would have been if there had been no low-income immigrants. In itself, this will tend to induce a collective decision, aligned to the preferences of the person who will now be the median voter, to redistribute more than would have been decided in the absence of migration. At the same time, however, the presence of the low-income immigrants will reduce the mean incomes, which by itself will have a negative effect on recipients of redistribution. Thus there is a trade-off. The median voters will favour immigration of low-skilled workers only if the negative effect of the entailed reduction of the mean income is less than the positive effect of the reduction of the median income. Calculations of this kind will yield different outcomes across jurisdictions. Only some of these jurisdictions will adopt the policy. There is no explicit interjurisdictional competition in the model because low-income workers are assumed to come from abroad, not from the other jurisdictions. Their supply is also implicitly assumed to be infinitely elastic. But if they were in limited supply, or if induced migrations took place only among the subcentral jurisdictions concerned, there would certainly be a competition among jurisdictions seeking inflows (and some of the others).

Information-based competition

In the previous sections, the existence of information flows across jurisdictional barriers was of course a necessary condition for mobility to take place. People who decide to move to another jurisdiction must know something about what is waiting for them there. We can refer to this kind of information as 'mobility-facilitating' or 'arbitrage-facilitating' information. Its imperfections are part of the transaction costs that constrain mobility. But information about what obtains in other jurisdictions is not reducible to this important but none the less auxiliary function. In this section, I shall consider three types of analysis that give information a larger role. I focus here on the third.

Laboratory federalism

The idea that social experimentation is a good way to introduce new policies and that decentralization is a good way to practise social experimentation is widely considered as making sense. In a decentralized system, each jurisdiction can experiment, and successful innovations can be adopted by other jurisdictions on the same level or by the central government (a possibility that I shall ignore). There have been many empirical studies – though seldom by economists – of policy experimentation and innovation diffusion at the subcentral level of government.[9] Among economists, two main views emerge, one that considers the phenomenon as very important and the other that doubts its significance. The nature of the assumptions about intergovernmental competition may explain the difference between the two.

The first view is a major feature of the neo-Austrian analysis of decentralization. It is related to the neo-Austrian perspective in general, which stresses ignorance and its mitigation. Given generalized ignorance, market competition is an evolutionary process whose main output is discovery. New methods of doing things, new modes of organization and so on are tried, and only some survive the selection process, which, in a capitalist economy, is based on competition among firms. In a sense, thus, this competition is instrumental. In the background of market competition among firms, there is a competition, perhaps more important for society (because it generates new knowledge) which is competition among more abstract items.

When the idea is transposed to the relations among jurisdictions, the duality remains. Interjurisdictional competition is a vector for competition among institutional features. The two, taken together, form a discovery procedure (Vihanto 1992; Vanberg and Kerber 1994; Gerken 1995). The underlying mechanism is based on the mobility of agents (households, firms, capital and so on).[10] A new institutional feature is tried in a jurisdiction. Eventually it proves its worth. Thanks to it, the jurisdiction is successful in the competition with other jurisdictions to attract or retain mobile resources. Because these processes take time, the traditional institutional features in the other jurisdictions are not dismantled right away. Eventually, however, to avoid losing ground as a consequence of resource mobility, all jurisdictions will have adopted the new institutional feature, which can be said thus to have won the institutional competition.

A theoretical formulation of the pessimistic view about laboratory federalism was developed first (as far as I know) by Rose-Ackerman (1980). It is elaborated with more modern analytical tools by Strumpf (2002). The main idea is a kind of transposition to the context of policy experimentation by decentralized jurisdictions of an argument often made against spending resources on basic research in a small country. This argument points to the advantage of free riding or, if one prefers that formulation, to the existence of positive externalities. If a discovery is made, even those who have assumed no cost to seek it can freely benefit from it.[11] In the decentralization context, the jurisdiction which experiments with a new policy incurs costs and runs risks, whereas its benefit if the experiment succeeds is only the increase in the welfare of the inhabitants of the jurisdiction. The usually larger benefits provided to the other jurisdictions, which will have simply to copy the innovation if successful, are not internalized. This creates at the subcentral level a disincentive to experiment.

In Rose-Ackerman, success of the innovation increases the probability of re-election of the incumbents and failure decreases it. In Strumpf, the political mechanism remains largely implicit but can be more or less the same; policy makers, in a set-up of strategic interaction, maximize a pay-off presumably related both to the welfare of inhabitants and to support by voters. In both papers, the decision is the outcome of a comparison between the benefit of the 'sure solution', which consists in doing nothing now and copying in the future the result of experimentation pursued elsewhere when it is successful, and the benefit and cost of the risky solution, which consists in experimenting.[12] Implicitly in Rose-Ackerman and explicitly, albeit briefly, in Strumpf, a potential alternative to the main reasoning assumes a process which Strumpf refers to as 'yardstick competition'. The process fully deserves to be referred to in this way, even though in the context of competition among governments or office-holders it is not the process usually discussed under that name. I consider both variants of yardstick competition, starting with the one considered in Strumpf.

Yardstick competition to be promoted
As noted by both Rose-Ackerman and Strumpf, a successful office-holder in

a subcentral jurisdiction may seek a reward in the form of an office higher up in the governmental system.[13] Examples supporting this point come to mind immediately. Thus it is not unusual for presidents of the United States, federal chancellors of Germany, or presidents of the EU Commission to have proved their worth earlier as state governors, minister-presidents of *Länder*, or prime ministers in member countries. The relative evaluation can be made by all or some of those who have the power to promote to the new office. In the brief discussion devoted to the mechanism by Strumpf, the voters of the higher tier evaluate and promote. Depending on the political system, evaluation and promotion could be done by parliament, representatives of the subcentral governments, political parties and so on. The criteria used for these assessments will vary accordingly, as will the exact incentives provided to the promotion seekers.

In the framework assumed by Rose-Ackerman and Strumpf, the decision to experiment entails costs, risks and possible benefits with net effects that can be positive or negative both in terms of the probability of being re-elected and in terms of promotion. Office-holders who decide not to experiment have an unchanged probability of being re-elected to the office they already hold if no innovation proves successful elsewhere. One may also suppose that they have an increased probability of being re-elected if an innovation does succeed elsewhere and they immediately copy it. In addition, they have a chance to do better than innovators in the yardstick competition for promotion. Altogether these assumptions tend to favour the decision not to experiment.[14]

Yardstick competition to be re-elected

In this second form of yardstick competition, the main role is assigned to the voters of the jurisdiction whose officials are appraised. They make the comparative assessments of performance. For the incumbents, comparative performance no longer has an impact on promotion but on the probability of being re-elected. Contrary to the assumptions made in the previous subsection, losing the comparative performance race does reduce that probability. There is no 'sure solution'; it is impossible not to participate in the race and take risks.[15]

The mechanism is exposed in some detail, in an informal way, in Salmon (1987).[16] A more formal treatment and a test are offered in Besley and Case (1995). The main problem encountered by voters, in a world in which there are many changes and much uncertainty, is assumed to be information asymmetry. Given circumstances that they do not know, or whose impact they cannot assess, the voters of one jurisdiction, say J, cannot say whether the performance of their government is good or bad. If disturbances are not wholly idiosyncratic to J but, to a sufficient degree, correlated across different jurisdictions, the observation of what obtains in some other jurisdictions may help voters in J to form an opinion on that performance. If the said jurisdictions are on the same level as J, yardstick competition is horizontal, if they are not, yardstick competition is vertical.[17]

I shall consider only horizontal competition. In some versions of the reasoning, voters have very different interests. If a voter of J, in a domain of interest to him/her, considers the services delivered by the government of J to be insufficient, compared to those in the same domain offered in some other jurisdictions that the said voter considers as comparable, this may decrease the probability that he/she will vote for the incumbent on the next occasion. Incumbents do not know exactly the domains that count most to that voter or others, or with what other jurisdictions he/she or others will compare what obtains in J. They know that exerting themselves as much and in as many areas as possible enhances the chance that their performance will be judged comparatively good by the voters of their own jurisdiction, and thus increases the probability that they will win the next election. If this is their main concern, it may produce in incumbents an incentive towards good performance, and moreover performance of a kind that tends to be aligned with the way voters themselves perceive their interests. In some cases, however, the mechanism may either not work or have perverse effects. It is impossible here to explain why, or to mention all the problems, issues and applications that the mechanism raises or suggests (see, for example, Salmon 2003; Bordignon et al. 2004, and the references therein). I shall make only four comments.

First, even though all voters have idiosyncratic interests, in some circumstances some variables are a concern common to many. Thus, rather than the very general formulation above, it is often both more convenient and productive for certain purposes to assume that yardstick competition takes place over one or a few salient variables (taxes, crime, inflation, unemployment, economic growth and so on).

Second, a probabilistic view of voting makes the mechanism much more plausible than it is under the median voter assumption. Making the median voter respond to information from outside the jurisdiction can be a tall order. Under the probabilistic view, candidates consider all voters as having a positive endogenous probability of voting for them. Thus the opinion of even relatively small groups might count, and consequently deserves some attention. If electoral competition is sufficiently tight, politicians will be attentive to interjurisdictional comparisons even if they know that only a minority of voters make them. This has some bearing on the foregoing discussion on decentralized policy innovations. Even if most voters consider only the costs and/or outputs of policies, under the probabilistic perspective it may be enough for motivating the decision to experiment in a single jurisdiction that a subset of its voters rewards incumbents for having introduced policies whose innovative character is proved by their diffusion to other jurisdictions.

Third, as stressed by Breton (1996), voting is only one of the ways for the population or segments thereof to award or withdraw support. This explains that yardstick competition can also be very powerful in a non-democratic context, as the fall of the Iron Curtain demonstrated. In such cases, however, the performance gap must be particularly pronounced and enduring. Even in democratic settings, incumbents may be attentive to public opinion independently of elections, or, in specialized domains, to the judgement of groups such as the military and artists which have no significant electoral power (and do not threaten to move out). It should also be noted that yardstick competition may generate conflicting assessments, depending on the party, group or category making the comparisons, and this may have a destabilizing effect (Heyndels and Ashworth 2003).

Fourth, two important distinctions structure the existing literature on yardstick competition. One concerns the nature of the accountability problem raised by information asymmetry. Many discussions of yardstick competition, following Besley and Case (1995), are mainly focused on the adverse selection problem met by voters. The central question is whether yardstick competition offers voters a way to re-elect politicians whose 'type' is 'good' rather than those whose type is 'bad'. In other contributions (for example, Salmon 1987), however, the problem is more one of moral hazard. Office-holders are more or less alike and the focus is on the impact of yardstick competition on their incentives. The moral hazard problem is perhaps more central than the selection problem to democratic governance and decentralization, but both are certainly important and worth studying.

The second distinction extends to yardstick competition the distinction which was made above, that is between perfect competition, allowing parametric assumptions, on the one hand, and small-number competition, requiring in principle a framework of strategic interaction, on the other. Contrary to what is supposed in a large part of the literature, the way information may reach the voters of a jurisdiction does not necessarily dictate the assumption that the office-holders of that jurisdiction are exclusively influenced by what happens in a small number of other jurisdictions, in general the neighbouring ones, which implies in principle recourse to a strategic interaction framework.[18] Voters can evaluate the performance of their government by comparing it to an index or a ranking calculated over or including a large number of jurisdictions. There is a growing supply of statistics, from both public and private sources, that enable voters to do exactly that. The counterpart to the price- or utility-taker assumption made in the case of mobility-based perfect competition will then be (in the index case at least) something like a yardstick- or benchmark-taker assumption.

Some remarks on how the two forms of competition might interact

The strength of mobility-based horizontal competition among governments is overestimated. Many people, academics as well as journalists and politicians, too easily accept the view that the actual or potential mobility of firms, factors and individuals will constrain governments to the point of depriving them of all real powers to design and implement policies. The tendency is particularly apparent in discussions of globalization and of integration in the EU context. In the third section, above, we saw some of the reasons why mobility is likely to leave considerable discretion to the governments and/or citizens of subcentral jurisdictions. A more direct way to arrive at that conclusion is simply to take the measure of what states, provinces, regions and cantons can achieve in fully integrated federations.[19] In fact, the most important limitations to the freedom to decide of subcentral governments should often be sought not in the constraints entailed by mobility-based competition but in those imposed by the centralized assignment of powers in the overall system and/or by the de facto extension of the activities of the central government (or of 'Brussels' in the EU context). I shall return to this in the next section.

By contrast, the acceptance of even a minimal influence of information-based or yardstick competition encounters serious intellectual obstacles, some of them ideological.[20] Consequently, the strength of that second form of horizontal competition is seriously underestimated. Yet, information of a comparative kind is increasingly made available by various organizations (a recent example being the publications of the CESifo Institute in Munich) or by the media and is used or referred to in public debates. In some of the member countries of the EU – and, on the occasion of municipal elections, in some cities – comparative notions like 'falling behind', 'winning the race' or 'catching up' play an increasing role. These facts may explain why somewhat more attention is given to the phenomenon in the economic literature.

How do the two main mechanisms that underlie horizontal competition interact? In general, they should be mutually reinforcing (Breton 1996). Yet, we know from Hirschman (1970) that *exit* may undermine *voice*. The potential of the latter can be weakened if the agents most likely to use it leave the jurisdiction. Some of the models discussed above illustrate this possibility. But the interaction between the mechanisms is typically more complex.

In some cases, it seems clear that only one of the two counts. I have already mentioned the case of incorporation in the United States. For large American firms the cost of incorporating in one state rather than in another is negligible (the situation is different in Europe). As a consequence, with regard to incorporation, mobility-based competition pre-empts yardstick competition. Sometimes, it is yardstick competition which seems relevant and mobility-based competition insignificant. Some categories of voters will compare the way their government addresses some environmental or ecological global issues (biodiversity, global warming and so on) with policies that deal with them in other jurisdictions. The outcome of such comparisons may be quite significant in electoral terms, whereas it is unlikely to induce significant mobility.

But let us examine that example more closely. Voters, even when particularly interested in environmental matters, are unlikely to respond to differences in environmental policies of that global type by moving from one jurisdiction to another. But the said policies typically have consequences outside the domain of the environment. For instance, they impose financial or regulatory burdens on industrial firms. Interjurisdictional differences in these burdens may have significant effects in terms of mobility-based competition. In this example, the complexity of the interaction between the two forms of competition stems from the fact that the agents concerned by them are not the same and are involved differently. This proposition is applicable more generally. Some categories of agents, often firms and capital, will respond to policy differences across jurisdictions largely by mobility, actual or potential, whereas other categories, typically labour and consumers, will react mainly by voting. The incentives given to office-holders by the two forms of competition may converge because voters take into account the consequences of mobility, actual or potential. But convergence may be incomplete, and, in some circumstances, the two forms of competition will provide completely contradictory incentives.

I have already discussed the degree to which mobility-based competition, by eroding the autonomy and capacity to act of subcentral governments, has a negative effect on the relevance of information-based competition. The two mechanisms interact in many other ways. I shall note one more. Mobility may increase diversity, that is spatial heterogeneity. The Tiebout mechanism leads to similar citizen preferences within, and different preferences across, jurisdictions. In the theory of international and interregional trade, under some plausible assumptions about transaction and transportation costs, more integration in the form of fewer obstacles to mobility will lead to increased specialization of production (as a consequence of a difference in factor endowments or, even in its absence, of economies of scale, internal or external). Should the diversity that may ensue not constitute an obstacle to the comparisons that play an essential role in yardstick competition? One should note, however, that interjurisdictional specialization of production does not extend to consumption, or to the production of many categories of non-exchangeable goods and services, both of which can remain quite homogeneous over the whole integrated area. Thus mobility-induced economic integration may not cause, via production specialization, much increase in the diversity, across jurisdictions, of citizen preferences, whereas the said diversity may tend to diminish as a consequence of informational integration. On the aggregate, interjurisdictional diversity with regard to consumption is probably diminishing with increasing integration (as travellers may verify for themselves). This should have a positive effect on the potential of yardstick competition.[21]

Spillovers, empirical studies, normative assessments and institutional implications

Several categories of questions about horizontal competition usually considered essential have been overlooked in the foregoing. One is policy spillovers; another is empirical analysis; a third is normative assessments; and a fourth is institutional or constitutional implications. Let me stress that, on several dimensions, all four are closely related. The controversies that they raise – especially in the domain of regulation – make that clear.

Interjurisdictional externalities of private activities and spillovers of subcentral governments' policies are probably, together with 'race to the bottom', the main concerns raised by horizontal competition. Their claimed existence and importance often serve as highly persuasive reasons to eliminate or reduce competition by way of centralization and harmonization of policy making. This tendency is particularly notable in the EU context but it is detectable in most countries, whether federal or not. The recommendations typically generate controversies that involve the four elements mentioned.

There is first the question, in a given domain or set-up, of what exactly should be considered as an externality or a spillover. Answering the question is not always straightforward from the moment competition among governments or jurisdictions is deemed legitimate in principle. The fact that one jurisdiction or its inhabitants succeed in something most often harms some people or governments in other jurisdictions. On markets it is generally agreed that externalities do not include damages caused only by competition (driving another firm to close down, in particular, is not considered as an externality in spite of all the social consequences involved). A similar limitation of the concept of policy externality must be found in the case of intergovernmental competition but, because the legitimacy of competition among governments is much less secured than that of market competition, its precise identification is more difficult. This explains why, even when the facts are well known, their interpretation as an externality remains often highly controversial (see the contributions in Esty and Geradin 2001).

There is then the difficulty of establishing facts. This applies to spillovers but even more clearly to the mechanisms that may lead to a 'race to the bottom' – or, for that matter, 'to the top'. Empirical studies on horizontal competition encounters many difficulties in general.[22] On the particular issue of the 'race to the bottom' effect, most of them yield answers that are ambiguous, do not converge or lack general significance – among other reasons, because, as stressed by Revesz (2001), the mechanisms held responsible for the said race are in fact different in important respects. A large part of the empirical or applied debate is about what might happen rather than about what has happened (see Sinn 2003). If we stick to the latter criterion, casual observation is often reassuring. Thus, in the European Union, over the last twenty years, although the rates of taxes on corporate income have declined – possibly eroded by mobility-based competition among governments – the revenues from these taxes have *increased* both as a share of GDP and of total tax revenue (Bond et al. 2000). According to a recent book (Thakur et al. 2003), the welfare state of Sweden is a 'bumblebee' which, so far, has 'kept flying'; and so have the welfare states of most other 'old Europe' EU countries.

Normative issues are already implicit in the problem of definition of spillovers just mentioned. A large part of the theoretical literature is more openly normative. On a less theoretical level, there is also a tendency, in particular in some of the ways the Leviathan thesis is presented, to be a bit ideological. Even in well-defined issue areas, general presuppositions on the role of the public sector and of markets often inspire the arguments exchanged about decentralization and horizontal competition. In the EU, in particular, there is a tension between the goal of completing the single market in all its dimensions, eliminating all impediments to trade and all sources of fragmentation of the market, as well as all possible distortions of competition among private producers (the 'level playing field' objective) on the one hand, and fostering competition among governments at all levels on the other hand – innovative governments necessarily contributing, by their actions, to the fragmentation of the market (Breton and Salmon 2002). In some comments, it seems clear that concerns for market competition dominate by and large the sympathy for intergovernmental competition that remains from the moment this competition is not confined to discipline Leviathan.

It can hardly be doubted that intergovernmental competition must be monitored and/or stabilized. The central government has clearly a major role to play for that purpose (Breton 1996). It can employ all of the many instruments, financial and regulatory, that it has in its possession. The mere fact, in some domains, that the central government can always intervene is often sufficient to compel junior governments to coordinate some aspects of their policies or to take into account – that is, to internalize – some of the benefits and costs that each of them exports outside its jurisdiction (Breton and Salmon 2002; Roe 2003). To trust the central government in its role of monitor or stabilizer of horizontal competition among subcentral governments, a serious problem, however, must be addressed because the central government is itself in (vertical) competition with the subcentral governments. Institutional solutions have been proposed to mitigate the problem (Breton 1996; Vaubel 1999). Another difficulty is that competition among subcentral jurisdictions may also take place within central government itself, in particular when members of parliament are induced by the electoral system to defend the interests of the districts in which they are elected (see Besley and Coate 2003).

Conclusion

Governmental systems, whether federations, unitary states, or a *sui generis* entity such as the European Union, always include many governments, which always compete with one another. Thus competition among governments is first of all a fact – a feature of existing arrangements whose importance varies in time and space but is never completely absent and is seldom negligible. But it is also a perspective. As such its adoption could easily lead to addressing under a different angle practically all the questions and topics discussed in the vast literature devoted to federalism and decentralization. Being limited to competition among governments situated on a same tier – horizontal competition – makes the task less daunting. Still, if only to avoid duplication with the others, this chapter has largely glossed over aspects of the subject that are often considered essential, in particular the more normative aspects (including considerations of efficiency). Conversely, much space – with the objective of convincing readers that they deserve more attention – has been devoted to forms of intergovernmental competition that have remained relatively unheeded.

The literature on forms of competition among governments that are based on mobility is particularly rich. Their treatment in this chapter has been unusual in two ways. One is a focus on the capacity of governments to compete. The other has been the attention devoted to analyses in which the prevalence of political considerations yields highly unconventional results. The work done so far on forms of competition among governments that are not based on the mobility of agents but on information flows, in particular yardstick competition, is still comparatively limited. Yardstick competition is slowly gaining some recognition but much remains to be done to elucidate the numerous questions that it raises. With regard to it, the ambition of the chapter has been limited to making a case for its relevance and to explaining some of the major processes it may involve.

Notes

1. I wish to thank participants in the Handbook of Fiscal Decentralization Seminar in Moncalieri for their comments, in particular Albert Breton for his written remarks and suggestions. The usual disclaimer applies.
2. Brueckner (2003) treats yardstick competition on taxation as an externality and does not include it in tax competition. For a particularly clear typology, see Kerber and Budzinski (2004).
3. See also Sinn (1992).
4. In the context, 'small-number competition' might be a better expression than 'oligopolistic competition'. I employ both.
5. Mobility costs, discussed in this subsection, should not be confused with the consumer surplus mentioned in the previous one. In both cases, an increase in tax will not make all mobile agents leave the jurisdiction. But the effect of the consumer surplus is valid in static terms, independently of time, whereas the effect of mobility costs normally diminishes over time.
6. The assumption mimicked reality fairly well over the period studied, 1953–83. It would not at present, mainly because many 'poor' vote for the extreme right.

7. According to *The Economist* (cited in Mingat and Salmon 1988), the former policy was followed by the Labour Party, in power at the time in London, with the objective of countering an exogenous trend of 'gentrification'.
8. In Mingat and Salmon, in spite of 'strongholds', competition never vanishes – that is, incumbents are never sure to be re-elected – because of exogenous shocks taking place at the central level.
9. See the references in Rose-Ackerman (1980), Breton (1996) and Strumpf (2002).
10. However there is nothing in the basic neo-Austrian perspective that prevents reliance also (or instead) on the mechanism of yardstick competition (see Kerber and Budzinski 2004).
11. Except if risky projects are 'structured so that it is difficult for others to copy the results' (Rose-Ackerman 1980, p. 594). Kamar (1998, p. 1954) shows that one reason for Delaware's pre-eminence in the market for corporate chartering is 'the indeterminate nature of its law, which makes it impractical to copy'.
12. The 'sure solution' may not be the surer one if, in the case of a decision not to experiment, the probability of being re-elected is low.
13. See also Bodenstein and Ursprung (2005).
14. This type of yardstick competition makes one think of the incentives generated in the market for managers as analysed by Fama (1980). In Fama, however, the risk of losing one's present position cannot be avoided. Everybody may be moved downwards as well as upwards. For a closer analogy with Fama's world, see Eichenberger (2003).
15. Whether this difference affects the main conclusions of the preceding analysis and not only its formulation remains to be verified. But there are other ways to modify the assumptions made by Rose-Ackerman and Strumpf and account for the fact that innovative policies in the context of yardstick competition typically yield electoral benefits. One way is suggested by Strumpf himself. I provide another below in the text.
16. In the literature on information, monitoring and incentives, yardstick competition is usually associated with Shleifer (1985) even though it was modelled earlier. In Salmon (1987), whose topic was decentralization in a governmental system, the analysis was inspired by the then recent literature on tournaments, in particular Lazear and Rosen (1981). Differences between tournaments and yardstick competition can be disregarded for our purpose.
17. On vertical yardstick competition, see Breton (1996) and Breton and Fraschini (2003).
18. However, the justification for assuming that comparisons are made with neighbouring jurisdictions may be not that information circulates more easily with them than with more distant ones, but that the correlation between exogenous shocks or disturbances is likely to be higher.
19. For the particularly interesting case of Switzerland, see Kirchgässner and Pommerehne (1996) and Feld (2000).
20. To my surprise, I have discovered that, in some subsets of the profession, a typical objection to yardstick competition in an electoral context is based on an interpretation of voters' 'rational ignorance' so extensive that it renders democracy pointless.
21. That potential may be affected negatively, however, if the increased specialization in production leads to random shocks being less correlated.
22. See Brueckner (2003).

References

Besley, Timothy and Anne Case (1995). 'Incumbent behavior: vote-seeking, tax-setting, and yardstick competition', *American Economic Review* **85**(1), 25–45.
Besley, Timothy and Stephen Coate (2003). 'Centralized versus decentralised provision of local public goods: a political economy approach', *Journal of Public Economics* **87**, 2611–37.
Bodenstein, Martin and Heinrich Ursprung (2005). 'Political yardstick competition, economic integration, and constitutional choice in a federation: a numerical analysis of a contest success function model', *Public Choice* **124**(3–4), 329–52.
Bond, Stephen, Lucy Chennells, Michael P. Devereux, Malcolm Gammie and Edward Troup (2000). *Corporate Tax Harmonisation in Europe: A Guide to the Debate*, London: Institute for Fiscal Studies.

Bordignon, Massimo, Floriana Cerniglia and Federico Revelli (2004). 'Yardstick competition in intergovernmental relationships: theory and empirical predictions', *Economics Letters* **83**, 325–33.
Brennan, Geoffrey and James M. Buchanan (1980). *The Power to Tax: Analytical Foundations of a Fiscal Constitution*, Cambridge: Cambridge University Press.
Breton, Albert (1996). *Competitive Governments: An Economic Theory of Politics and Public Finance*, Cambridge: Cambridge University Press.
Breton, Albert and Angela Fraschini (2003). 'Vertical competition in unitary states: the case of Italy', *Public Choice*, **114**(1–2), 57–77.
Breton, Albert and Pierre Salmon (2002). 'External effects of domestic regulations: comparing internal and international barriers to trade', *International Review of Law and Economics* **21**(2), 135–55.
Brosio, Giorgio and Federico Revelli (2003). 'The assignment of the income redistribution policy in the presence of migration', in Manfred J. Holler, Harmut Kliemt, Dieter Schmidtchen and Manfred E. Streit (eds), *European Governance*, Tübingen: Mohr Siebeck (*Jahrbuch für Neue Politische Ökonomie*, vol. 22), 148–66.
Brueckner, Jan K. (2003). 'Strategic interaction among governments: an overview of empirical studies', *International Regional Science Review* **26**, 175–88.
Caplan, Bryan (2001). 'When is two better than one? How federalism mitigates and intensifies imperfect political competition', *Journal of Public Economics* **80**(1), 99–119.
Cardarelli, Roberto, Emmanuelle Taugourdeau and Jean-Pierre Vidal (2002). 'A repeated interactions model of tax competition', *Journal of Public Economic Theory* **4**(1), 19–38.
Edwards, Jeremy and Michael Keen (1996). 'Tax competition and Leviathan', *European Economic Review* **40**, 113–34.
Eichenberger, Reiner (2003). 'Towards a European market for good politics: a politico-economic reform proposal', in Manfred J. Holler, Harmut Kliemt, Dieter Schmidtchen and Manfred E. Streit (eds), *European Governance*, Tübingen: Mohr Siebeck (*Jahrbuch für Neue Politische Ökonomie*, vol. 22), 221–37.
Epple, Dennis and Thomas Nechyba (2004). 'Fiscal decentralization', in J. Vernon Henderson and Jean-François Thisse (eds), *Handbook of Regional and Urban Economics, Vol. 4: Cities and Geography*, Amsterdam: Elsevier, North-Holland, 2423–80.
Epple, Dennis and Allan Zelenitz (1981). 'The implications of competition among jurisdictions: does Tiebout need politics?', *Journal of Political Economy* **89**(6), 1197–217.
Esty, Daniel C. and Damien Geradin (eds) (2001). *Regulatory Competition and Economic Integration: Comparative Perspectives*, Oxford: Oxford University Press.
Fama, Eugene F. (1980). 'Agency problems and the theory of the firm', *Journal of Political Economy* **88**(2), 288–307.
Feld, Lars P. (2000). 'Tax competition and income redistribution: an empirical analysis for Switzerland', *Public Choice* **105**(1–2), 125–64.
Gerken, Lüder (ed.) (1995). *Competition among Institutions*, London: Macmillan.
Heyndels, Bruno and John Ashworth (2003). 'Self-serving bias in tax perceptions: federalism as a source of political instability', *Kyklos* **56**(1), 47–68.
Hirschman, Albert O. (1970). *Exit, Voice, and Loyalty: Responses to Decline in Firms, Organizations, and States*, Cambridge, MA: Harvard University Press.
Hochman, Harold M. and James D. Rodgers (1969). 'Pareto optimal redistribution', *American Economic Review* **59**(4), 542–57.
Kamar, Ehud (1998). 'A regulatory competition theory of indeterminacy in corporate law', *Columbia Law Review* **98**(8), 1908–59.
Kerber, Wolfgang and Oliver Budzinski (2004). 'Competition of competition laws: mission impossible?', in Richard A. Epstein and Michael S. Greve (eds), *Competition Laws in Conflict: Antitrust Jurisdiction in the Global Economy*, Washington, DC: AEI Press, 31–65.
Kirchgässner, Gebhard and Werner W. Pommerehne (1996). 'Tax harmonization and tax competition in the European Union: lessons from Switzerland', *Journal of Public Economics* **60**(3), 351–71.
Lazear, Edward P. and Sherwin Rosen (1981). 'Rank order tournaments as optimal labor contracts', *Journal of Political Economy* **89**(5), 841–64.

Mingat, Alain and Pierre Salmon (1988). 'Alterable electorates in the context of residential mobility', *Public Choice* **59**(1), 67–82.

Oates, Wallace E. and Robert M. Schwab (1988). 'Economic competition among jurisdictions: efficiency enhancing or distortion inducing?', *Journal of Public Economics* **35**, 333–54.

Revesz, Richard L. (2001). 'Federalism and regulation: some generalizations', in Esty and Geradin (eds), 3–29.

Roe, Mark (2003). 'Delaware competition', *Harvard Law Review* **117**(2), 588–646.

Rose-Ackerman, Susan (1980). 'Risk-taking and reelection: does federalism promote innovation?', *Journal of Legal Studies* **9**(3), 593–616.

Salmon, Pierre (1987). 'Decentralisation as an incentive scheme', *Oxford Review of Economic Policy* **3**(2), 24–43.

Salmon, Pierre (2002). 'Decentralization and supranationality: the case of the European Union', in Ehtisham Ahmad and Vito Tanzi (eds), *Managing Fiscal Decentralization*, London: Routledge, 99–121.

Salmon, Pierre (2003). 'Assigning powers in the European Union in the light of yardstick competition among governments', in Manfred J. Holler, Harmut Kliemt, Dieter Schmidtchen and Manfred E. Streit (eds), *European Governance*, Tübingen: Mohr Siebeck (*Jahrbuch für Neue Politische Ökonomie*, vol. 22), 197–216.

Shleifer, Andrei (1985). 'A theory of yardstick competition', *Rand Journal of Economics* **16**, 319–27.

Sinn, Hans-Werner (2003). *The New Systems Competition*, Oxford: Blackwell (Yrjö Jahnsson Lectures).

Sinn, Stefan (1992). 'The taming of Leviathan: competition among governments', *Constitutional Political Economy* **3**(2), 177–96.

Strumpf, Koleman S. (2002). 'Does government decentralization increase political innovation?', *Journal of Public Economic Theory* **4**(2), 207–41.

Thakur, Subhash, Michael Keen, Balazs Horvath and Valerie Cerra (2003). *Sweden's Welfare State: Can the Bumblebee Keep Flying?*, Washington, DC: IMF.

Tiebout, Charles M. (1956). 'A pure theory of local expenditures', *Journal of Political Economy* **65**(5), 416–24.

Vanberg, Viktor and Wolfgang Kerber (1994). 'Institutional competition among jurisdictions: an evolutionary approach', *Constitutional Political Economy* **5**(2), 193–219.

Vaubel, Roland (1999). 'Enforcing competition among governments: theory and application to the Europan Union', *Constitutional Political Economy* **10**(4), 327–38.

Vihanto, Martti (1992). 'Competition between local governments as a discovery procedure', *Journal of Institutional and Theoretical Economics* **148**, 411–36.

Weingast, Barry R. (1995). 'The economic role of political institutions: market-preserving federalism and economic growth', *Journal of Law, Economics and Organization* **11**, 1–31.

3 Modelling vertical competition
Albert Breton[1]

Introduction

This chapter is aimed at modelling vertical competition, that is, at understanding a mechanism that helps determine equilibrium assignments of powers in federal states and in decentralized unitary states. A perusal of economic writings on decentralization and federalism – often labelled 'fiscal federalism' – makes it clear that, except for some applications of Charles Tiebout's (1956) mobility model and for the yardstick competition model introduced in the literature by Pierre Salmon (1987a and 1987b), approaches to the subject have been essentially normative – indeed normative in a nominalist tradition. This is particularly the case regarding the problem of the assignment of powers which, from the earliest times, has been one of the central problems of decentralized and federalist arrangements. The normative character of economic writings is apparent in the fact that, except for the models just noted, the literature proposes no automatic mechanisms based on maximizing (or other) behaviours capable of generating equilibrium outcomes. Instead, the literature is replete with what we may call principles or norms which, it is claimed, would lead to more efficiency in political systems and to greater welfare for citizens.

Among the principles that have been and continue to be bandied about, I note, to illustrate, the following: (a) powers should be assigned in such a way that the span of public goods – the number of persons to whom the benefits of a public good accrue or are made available in equal amount (see Breton and Scott 1978, Chapter 4 on the definition of spans) – should match as closely as possible the spatial boundaries of jurisdictions;[2] (b) powers should be assigned on the basis of subsidiarity – the principle which calls for assigning powers, to the extent possible, to governments that are closest to the people;[3] (c) powers should be assigned so as to encourage experimentation and innovation by more junior and consequently smaller governments, thus reducing the risks of larger cost failures when experiments are undertaken by more senior and consequently larger governments; (d) powers should be assigned in such a way as to preserve diversity; and (e) powers should be assigned so as to guarantee a maximum of individual political and economic liberty and, as a complement, to give minorities a maximum of protection. There are other such principles, but they have in common with the five I have listed that they are difficult to make operational, they are not easily reconciled with one another and, perhaps most damaging, they come with no hint of how they can be implemented and especially of who – persons, agency and/or force – will perform that task.

Kenneth Wheare, who was not an economist and who did not make use of the methods and language of economics, formulated a principle that, he thought, should govern the assignment of powers. What came to be known as 'classical' (or 'dual') federalism is the political arrangement that exists when the assignment of powers is governed by what Wheare (1963, p. 10) called 'the federal principle' by which he meant 'the method of dividing powers so that the general and regional governments are each, within a sphere, co-ordinate and independent'. It is because of the reference to 'general and regional governments' that the principle is sometimes labelled dual federalism. Although Wheare discussed it at length and examined its application in great detail, it is remarkable that the principle has played no role in the development of the economic analysis of federalism. Wallace Oates (1972, p. 17) even went as far as to write that '[t]he problem of federalism is, however, quite different [from Wheare's conception] for an economist'. In the next section I shall propose an interpretation of Wheare's federal principle which is consistent with a positive economic theory of federalism.

Before proceeding, note that the first principle in the above list has played a particularly nefarious role in blocking a genuine understanding of real-world federalism and decentralization. First introduced in the literature by Breton (1965), and rediscovered by Mancur Olson (1969), it was elevated by Oates (1972, pp. 35–45) to the rank of a 'theorem'. It is still very popular. There are many problems with the approach (theorem?), but two are particularly damning. The first is that those who continue to adopt the approach seem to be unaware that changes in assignments, or in the degree of decentralization, will impact on the costs of operating governmental systems – on what Breton and Anthony Scott (1978) called organizational costs, namely administration, coordination, mobility and signalling costs (see the third section, below): it is by minimizing these costs that the degree of decentralization is determined, not by choosing assignments without paying attention to these costs. The second problem raised by the approach is that it implies that external shocks or disturbances of necessity lead to changes in the degree of decentralization – in the assignment of powers. Casual observation reveals that this is not the sort of adjustment to shocks that usually takes place – variation in organizational activities is the favoured *modi operandi* following external disturbances.

In the next section, I address some definitional matters: what are the powers that are to be assigned; what element distinguishes federal, confederal and unitary states; how should we think of decentralization and of its virtues. In the subsequent section, I outline the Breton–Scott (1978) model of the assignment of powers. That is required as I aim to show that vertical competition is an essential component of this model. The fourth section looks at the *modi operandi* of vertical competition. The fifth section discusses some of the forces that mould that competition. The penultimate section is concerned with asymmetric assignments. The final section concludes the chapter.

Some definitions

Given that the notion of powers plays such a central role in the analysis of vertical competition, it is important that we be clear about what the concept means. A power is the authority granted to or acquired by a public or a private body to legislate, regulate and/or to have a general capacity to act in particular areas or domains. This definition is broad enough to encompass the privatization of powers that had been in the public arena as well as the socialization of previously private powers.[4]

Virtually all powers confer authority to act in more than one area. It is therefore impossible to say a priori how a particular power will be subdivided among the various bodies in which authority to act may be vested. For example, in Canada the power to define what is a crime and what constitutes criminal behaviour is assigned to the federal government, while the responsibility for the implementation of criminal law is granted to provincial governments as is the responsibility for the maintenance of courts – except the Supreme Court of Canada. This multidimensionality of powers is one reason why concurrency is so widespread and why, under one heading or another, explicit or implicit doctrines and/or rules of paramountcy are formulated and used. Furthermore, the many dimensions are not fixed for all time – their number and their meaning change with circumstances and the appearance of new problems. For example, the interpretation by the courts of Section 91(2) (related to 'Trade and Commerce') of the Constitution Act, 1867 – Canada's Constitution – was altered by as much as 180 degrees over a century, essentially through a re-definition of what constitutes 'national' and 'local' markets. One implication of the above is that constitutions and constitutional documents are always incomplete, just as contracts are always incomplete and for many of the same reasons. We shall discover as we proceed that these realities have important implications for the way vertical competition manifests itself.

I note by way of conclusion on the definition of powers that the Musgrave (1959)–Oates (1972) amalgamation of policy-making authority into redistribution, allocation and stabilization powers has been and remains a source of confusion because these are not powers that can be assigned, as constitutions are never and can never be formulated in terms of these three categories. Take redistribution as an example. Policies to redistribute income may be carried out under powers assigned to the centre to design and implement policies related to unemployment insurance, pensions or loan guarantees through commercial banks. Income can also be redistributed by policies derived from powers assigned to more junior governments, such as daycare centres, food banks, or low-cost housing achieved through zoning regulation.

A second matter that must be addressed relates to the difference between unitary, confederal and federal states.[5] It is easy when reading the literature on federalism to come to the conclusion that centralization or decentralization is the defining trait of the difference. However, once the fact is recognized that all democratic unitary states are decentralized, sometimes even more than some federal states, that trait must be jettisoned. I have argued (Breton 2000) that what distinguishes governmental systems is the ownership of powers. In unitary states, all powers are ultimately owned by the central government, in confederal states they are owned by associated members, and in federal states some powers are owned by the central and some by the peripheral governments.[6]

The economic theory of ownership (property rights) makes one thing clear: ownership is always circumscribed – it is always incomplete in that it always lacks certain characteristics. This fact plays a crucial role in shaping the character of vertical competition. Wheare, of course, was not concerned with competitive intergovernmental relations. Indeed, classical federalism which he invented, would seem to have been conceived to ensure the impossibility of any form of competition among governments. However, it is possible to read the first two chapters of *Federal Government*, which are concerned with a defence of the 'federal principle', as being in effect concerned with the ownership of powers and with the incompleteness of that ownership. In Chapter I, the principle itself is defined 'rigidly' to use Wheare's own word (1963, p. 15), but Chapter II can be read as an effort to salvage the principle in a world where it cannot be applied rigidly! It is rewarding to read Wheare with this in mind.

What are the virtues of decentralization? There are two ways to approach this question: that of welfare economics and that of public choice economics. If one chooses the first of these, then there are no intrinsic virtues to decentralization since a government that maximizes a social welfare function, while it may face informational constraints, will always strive to address all the problems that arise in the entirety of the country. This has been known since Jack Weldon's (1966) to-the-point criticism of Breton's (1965) 'theory' of government grants based on the spans of public goods. The recognition of the point is explicit in Robin Boadway and Frank Flatters's (1982, p. 6) analysis of equalization. Observed decentralization is taken to be an unfortunate accident of history. In Boadway and Flatters, that accident leads to inefficiencies. That is a logically consistent view. Those in the welfare economics tradition who attach virtues, such as 'closeness to the people', 'risk reduction in socio-political experimentation and innovation', or 'the promotion of liberty', to decentralization are logically inconsistent because a social-welfare-function-maximizing institution always strives to be close to the people, always tries to experiment and innovate at minimum risk, and always toils to promote liberty.

If, on the other hand, one opts for the second approach to the virtues of decentralization – the public choice economics approach – then these virtues are simply that an ideal decentralized institutional structure may possess the 'balance' needed to make effective 'checking' possible. The checks (and the balance) are a manifestation of competition.[7] The case for decentralization is that it produces competition and, by virtue of that competition, a degree of control over the office-holders who, the approach assumes, seek to maximize their own interest. If competition is strong enough, separate reference to subsidiarity, to experimentation and innovation, and to liberty is redundant. Decentralization by itself does not remove the informational constraints that public bodies such as the social planners of welfare economics are up against, but the competition that it begets does address the informational problems through the channels identified and analysed in particular by the Austrians (Friedrich Hayek, Ludwig von Mises and others).

I must address another definitional matter, one that is closely related to that pertaining to the virtues of decentralization. One encounters in the literature on decentralization a number of concepts – such as deconcentration, devolution, delegation – aimed at providing a classificatory matrix that would make it possible to pigeonhole all countries in such a way as to acknowledge all the differences between them in regard to the way they are decentralized. Reading that literature, I am often led to reflect that the scholars who engage in this sort of activity are lucky to have specialized in the study of political systems (of which there are few), as they would have been driven to insanity if they had chosen to specialize in the analysis of markets (of which there are millions)! Be that as it may, in what follows I shall assume that a governmental system is decentralized when checks and balances, and therefore vertical competition, are present. The fact that the governments of Liguria, Lombardy and Piedmont take the central government in Rome before the Constitutional Court – and vice versa – is evidence of checks and balances and of vertical competition in Italy. The fact that mayors elected by the citizens of *départements* sue prefects appointed to *départements* by the central government in Paris – and vice versa – is evidence of checks and balances and of vertical competition in France. The list could easily be extended.

If checks and balances and vertical competition are absent, decentralization, by this or by any other name, will not support an automatic mechanism operating to assign powers. The phenomenon is still, however, a legitimate and worthy object of study. But those who study it should be careful before identifying it as a 'principal–agent' problem. In agency theory, principals are assumed to hire agents. In many real-world decentralized systems, the agents (the junior governments) are often 'hired' by the citizens as are the principals (the senior governments). The task of analysing whether the constraints under which the agents operate are incentive-compatible does not consist in repeating the findings of agency theory. Moreover, one would think that the ultimate principals in that scheme of things – the citizens – must have some role to play in the principal–agent game!

The Breton–Scott assignment model
It is somewhat baffling, given the importance of the matter, that so little work has been done on the assignment problem beyond rather perfunctory discussions of the principles listed above that are taken to be relevant guides to the division of powers. It is even more baffling that among the work that has been done, only a small fraction is concerned with forces or mechanisms operating automatically to generate equilibrium outcomes. There are, I conjecture, two reasons for this. A first is the Musgrave–Oates definition of powers that I have discussed above; the second is the assumption that the Tiebout model of preference revelation – a model in which assignments are given as a matter of definition – provides the building-blocks needed to understand federalism.

The assignment problem or the problem of the division, among political bodies in a given society, of the authority to legislate, regulate and, generally, to act and govern is a problem that pertains to the organization of governmental systems. In 1978, Breton and Scott argued that there were four – and, by definition, only four – activities that had a role to play in resolving the assignment problem. They called them 'organizational activities'. Two of these are activities of governmental bodies and therefore associated with the supply of goods and services: they are administration, defined to include all the undertakings of legislatures as well as executives and their bureaucracies at all jurisdictional levels, and coordination which encompasses all that has to be done to ensure that what governments at all levels produce is synchronized and that interjurisdictional spillovers are internalized. The other two activities are engaged in by citizens and are therefore associated with the demand for goods and services: citizens signalling their preferences through the various means at their disposal – voting, lobbying, protesting and so on – is one of them; moving from jurisdiction to jurisdiction in search of a better bundle of goods and services is another.[8]

All these activities absorb resources. A basic assumption of the Breton–Scott model is that the volume of resources absorbed varies with the degree of decentralization of the governmental system.[9] For example, Breton and Scott (1978, Chapter 5) argued that when governmental systems become more decentralized, the amount of resources absorbed in coordination activities increases because more public sector business must be conducted and because the flows of interjurisdictional spillovers are likely to be more numerous and larger. At constant unit resource costs, this implies that as governmental systems become more decentralized, the total cost of the activities identified as coordination will increase. Having formulated hypotheses regarding each of the four activities, Breton and Scott were able to show that, as the degree of decentralization increases, the total cost of the four activities traces a U-shaped organizational cost curve.[10]

Breton and Scott argued that the minimum point on the U-shaped total cost curve was the point that had to be selected to obtain the ideal or optimal degree of decentralization. Who or what would do the selection? Their answer was that a 'constituent assembly' would. While the book was being printed, I gave a seminar on the book's findings to the Public Economics Workshop at the University of Toronto. John Dales, a friend and colleague, immediately pointed out that the Breton–Scott constituent assembly played a role not unlike that of the social welfare function of welfare economics in determining the equilibrium outcome. He was right. As we shall see in the fifth section, below, constituent assemblies – and what they produce, namely constitutions and constitutional amendments – have a role to play in the assignment of powers, but to be ascribed responsibility for the virtually incessant reassignments we observe in the real world, they would have to meet more often than they actually do.[11] A different building-block was needed.

Vertical competition
Salmon (1987a) argued that if the citizens of a jurisdiction appraise the performance of their government by comparing it to the performance of governments elsewhere but at the same jurisdictional level, they would induce their own government to do as well as or better than these governments. In Salmon (1987b), the horizontal intergovernmental competition implicit in the earlier paper was analysed more systematically along the lines of the theory of labour tournaments, initially proposed by Edward Lazear and Sherwin Rosen (1981).[12] One virtue of that mechanism – not shared by a mechanism based on fiscal mobility – is that it can provide a rationale for vertical competition whenever citizens use the performance of governments located at other jurisdictional tiers as benchmarks to evaluate what their own government is doing. That evaluation, as we shall discover, can serve as an element in a model in which vertical competition operates to shape the assignment of powers.

The initial formulation of what we may call the Salmon mechanism and all subsequent formulations assumed that citizens compared the performance of their own government to that of a benchmark government in terms of the 'levels and qualities of services, of levels of taxes or of more general economic and social indicators' (Salmon 1987b, p. 32). It is reasonable to take the view (see Breton 1996, p. 189), that governments situated at a given jurisdictional level provide goods and services that are close enough substitutes to goods and services provided by governments at other levels to guarantee sufficient homogeneity of supply to permit legitimate comparisons. Breton and Angela Fraschini (2003a) adopted a different approach.[13] They used Breton's (1996) model of compound governments which develops the view that competition in governmental systems compels all centres of power to forge Wicksellian connections (defined in the next two paragraphs) that are as tight as possible so as to be granted the (expected) consent (vote) of citizens.[14] In the light of this result, Breton and Fraschini argued that citizens will evaluate the relative performance of governments in terms of the tightness of Wicksellian connections – both for horizontal and for vertical competition. That is, they argued that if there are n centres of power indexed i and if w_i $(i = 1, \ldots, n)$ is a measure of the tightness of the Wicksellian connection generated by centre of power i, with w_i normalized to yield $0 \leq w_i \leq 1$, citizens will rank the centres of power that make up compound governments in terms of w_i.

What is a Wicksellian connection and why is it a defensible alternative to a formulation of the Salmon mechanism in terms of goods, services, taxes and other indicators on which the mechanism has hitherto been articulated? A Wicksellian connection is a link between the quantity of a particular good or service supplied by centres of power and the tax price that citizens pay for that good or service. Knut Wicksell ([1896] 1964), Erik Lindahl ([1919] 1964) and Leif Johansen (1965) showed that if decisions regarding public expenditures and their financing were taken simultaneously and under a rule of (quasi-)unanimity, a perfectly tight nexus between the two variables would emerge. Breton (1996) developed the point that competition between centres of power, if it was perfect and not subject to informational constraints, would also generate completely tight Wicksellian connections. In the real world, competition is never perfect and informational constraints are numerous; as a consequence, Wicksellian connections are less than perfectly tight. Still, as long as some competition exists and as long as institutions are in place to soften informational constraints, there will be Wicksellian connections.

The virtue of a Salmon mechanism expressed in terms of Wicksellian connections is that a given citizen can carry out comparisons of performance in terms of a common standardized variable, whether the benchmark government inhabits the same or a different jurisdictional level from that in which the citizen dwells. A variable that serves that purpose well is the size of the utility losses inflicted on citizens whenever the volume of the goods and services provided by centres of power differs from the volume desired at given tax prices. In other words, citizens experience the same kind of utility losses from decisions made by governments whatever the jurisdictional tier the governments inhabit. The goods and services supplied can differ between governments inhabiting different jurisdictional tiers, but the efforts to achieve tightness in Wicksellian connections need not. Indeed, the ability to compare performance horizontally is likely to reinforce the ability to execute vertical comparisons and vice versa.

How does vertical competition manifest itself? In a large number of ways, few of which have so far been explored. I focus on only one of these in this chapter, namely 'occupation' (defined immediately), therefore neglecting such important manifestations as yardstick competition *à la* Salmon. Assignments, like contracts, are always incomplete for two reasons. First, contracts are incomplete because their meaning, though possibly obvious to the signatories of the documents, will generally be ambiguous to third parties (judges, for example); similarly assignments of powers are incomplete because even if their meaning was absolutely transparent to those who negotiated and/or wrote the initial constitutional documents or initial assignment statutes, that meaning will be less clear to successors who are the de facto third parties of contract theory. Second, as with contracts, it is not possible to produce assignments – constitutional or statutory – that will take into account all possible future contingencies; for that reason also, assignments are incomplete. As a consequence of this incompleteness, there is always scope for governments at one jurisdictional tier to occupy the policy domain of governments located at a different tier.[15] Occupation can be a consequence of the way competitive politics is played. But it can also be the product of the way institutions are structured and function. For example, conditional intergovernmental grants are instruments of occupation,[16] as are mandates – whether funded or unfunded – in the United States and mandate-like injunctions from the American Environmental Protection Agency. Disallowance clauses, found in certain constitutions, that are used to ensure that a central government policy (say) will not be undercut by a policy of a more junior government are instruments of occupation. The 'directives' handed down by the European Commission in Brussels have a family resemblance to American unfunded mandates.

Let us now assume that governing politicians maximize expected consent. It follows that, given tax prices, these politicians will endeavour to supply goods and services (including redistribution and regulation) to their citizens in quantities and qualities that match as closely as possible what these citizens desire. As a consequence, governing politicians will only occupy the policy domain of governments located at other tiers when they expect the occupation to increase the consent their own citizens will grant them. Sometimes the occupation will not be successful; the reassignment will then be transitory. At other times, however, it will be successful and become permanent – a new static equilibrium will have been reached. In this second case the occupation will, in time, become entrenched in a constitutional document or in a convention to which all parties acquiesce. When that happens, vertical competition will have led to a new (static) permanent division of powers between jurisdictional tiers.

This mechanism is important. It generates reassignments of powers that reflect the comparative advantage of governments at different tiers to generate tight Wicksellian connections in the provision of particular bundles of goods and/or services. Vertical competition, driven by the modified Salmon mechanism, therefore generates assignments of powers that force governments to supply goods and services at the lowest tax prices possible. It exists and is activated by the desire of all centres of powers at all the jurisdictional tiers that constitute a governmental system to maximize expected consent.[17]

Some properties of equilibrium assignments

Vertical competition is an important (and to date the only known) automatic mechanism that contributes to the determination of equilibrium assignments of powers or of their division among governments located at different jurisdictional levels. Acceptance of this proposition requires, however, that we recognize that the working or operation of vertical competition – and therefore of the way it manifests itself – is conditioned by what are in effect institutional constraints.[18] In this section, I identify and examine four of these which I suggest are among the most important in shaping vertical competition and its outcomes.

The federal or unitary character of governmental systems

Salmon makes clear that attributing the outcome of vertical competition to a 'constitutional protection of powers' (2000, p. 240) alone – in the language used above, to the nature of the ownership of powers that derives from the federal or unitary character of governmental systems alone – misses much that is crucially important for understanding vertical competition. In other words, it is insufficient to reason from the facts concerning the ownership of powers alone; the institutional system inside of which vertical competition articulates itself is also important.

Salmon looks at some of the institutions that help mould vertical competition, and therefore the assignment of powers, in France. He begins by mentioning 'the representation of the lower level within the decision-making apparatus of the higher level' as with the German *Bundesrat* which brings the interests of the *Länder* in the decision-making process of the centre – an institution which is, in fact, a feature of a federal system and which may act to reduce vertical competition while protecting decentralization! But Salmon is right to point to this particular institution to introduce the very French *cumul des mandats*. That institution is best described in Salmon's (2000, p. 249) own words:

> Most decision makers who count at the national level are also important decision makers at the subnational levels, and vice versa. Thus mayors of large cities and

presidents of regional or general councils are typically also members of one or the other of the two houses of Parliament in Paris, whereas about half the members of Parliament also have important functions in local, *départemental*, or regional governments.

Because of this, there are many individuals who have a vested interest as well as the capacity to protect the decentralized character of the governmental system.[19]

In Italy all powers are owned by the central government. Prior to the constitutional revisions of October 2001, Article 117 of the constitution, which had been approved by a constituent assembly and had come in force on 1 January 1948, assigned 19 powers to regional governments. That these powers were owned by Rome is made evident by the fact that from 1948 to the early 1970s, Rome opposed the utilization of the 19 powers, and the regions did not use them. A reluctant transfer of powers in the 1970s was largely symbolic. It was only by the mid-1980s that the Constitutional Court, responding to the separatist pressures building up in the north, refused to uphold directives of the central government unless these were supported by laws passed by parliament. Thus the transfer of Article 117's powers to the regional governments effectively took place. Since then, the division of powers has been guaranteed by the Constitutional Court (see Breton and Fraschini 2003a).

That the powers are owned by Rome is also confirmed by the fact that the October 2001 modification to Title V of the constitution, which incorporates in a 'new' Article 117 a distinction between exclusive and concurrent powers, and which lists the exclusive powers of the central government, was effected by the government in Rome.

It is rewarding to contrast the workings of vertical competition in Canada, France and Italy given that Canada is a strict two-tier federation, France a unitary state in which the division of powers receives virtually no constitutional protection, and Italy a unitary state in which the division of powers is constitutionally protected but only if the Constitutional Court acts independently – which some critics argue it does not always do.[20] In Canada, there is vigorous competition between Ottawa and the provinces and therefore a continual reassignment of powers between them through the operation of that competition. There is, however, virtually no competition between the provincial and the municipal governments that affects the division of powers, so the division between these jurisdictional levels is the result of unilateral diktats originating at the provincial level.[21] In France, as argued by Salmon (2000, p. 249) the competition between the centre and the governments at the subnational levels is relatively weak, whereas competition among subnational governments is strong and plays a role in changing the assignment of powers. In Italy there is more competition between the central and regional govern-

ments than between the latter and the more junior governments, with consequences for the assignment of powers not too dissimilar from what takes place
in the Canadian federation. (As noted earlier, forms of vertical competition
can exist that will not affect the assignment of powers.)

Initial conditions and path dependence

Constituent assemblies or constitutional conventions sometimes produce
constitutions. These may ordain, among other things, a division of powers
among levels of government. It is generally recognized, except by unrecon-
structed contractarians, that the constitutions approved by assemblies and
conventions reflect compromises negotiated by decision makers (Galeotti
2000), accommodations to historical events, and adjustments to other idiosyncratic circumstances. Furthermore, before the ink on the approved documents
has had a chance to dry, constitutions begin to be interpreted by courts which
often give a meaning to the documents or parts thereof that may depart sharply
from that given them by the original signatories.

As a consequence, assignments ordained in initial constitutional documents
will be different, *ceteris paribus*,[22] from country to country simply because
initial conditions will differ among countries. We must also recognize that
systems that evolve over time, whether driven by a force such as vertical
competition or by another, will often exhibit a dependence on initial conditions – the evolution will be path dependent. The evolution may be 'lock[ed]
in by historical events' to use Brian Arthur's (1989) words, but it need not be
if the source of the path dependency atrophies with the passage of time (Young
1996). I should stress, in view of a welfare economics analysis of path dependence in some of the literature on the subject (for example, Liebowitz and
Margolis 1995 and Roe 1996), that I am not claiming that path dependence
leads to public sector failure or to inefficiencies, though it possibly could. The
burden of the foregoing is that vertical competition will organize and manifest
itself differently in different governmental systems – uniqueness and singular-
ity is the norm. Let me illustrate with three examples:

- *Example 1* The negotiations that led to the creation of the Canadian
  federation in 1867 were constrained by the necessity that the legal
  system of the Province of Quebec had to be the civil law, whereas the
  common law would be the legal system in the other provinces of the
  country. That in turn implied that, except for a few heads of legislative
  power – trade and commerce, banking, bills of exchange and promissory
  notes, interest, bankruptcy and insolvency, patents of invention and
  discovery, copyrights, and marriage and divorce – all remaining heads of
  power under property and civil rights had to be assigned to the provinces.
  This assignment, virtually unique in the world for the 'property and civil

rights' power, has had and continues to have a profound effect on the organization of vertical competition in the Canadian governmental system. For example, a number of laws concerned with property and civil rights that are designed and ratified by the central government often require, to be implemented, that they be 'completed' by provincial legislatures. The opportunity for federal and provincial governments to compete can hardly be richer.

* *Example 2*   In 1982, an Act of the British Imperial Parliament, known as the British North America Act, was 'patriated' to Canada; the country's constitution had come home. On the occasion of its patriation, a Charter of Rights and Freedoms was added to it. Brian Dickson was chief justice of the Supreme Court of Canada when the Charter provisions came into effect. In the words of Jameson Doig (2004, p. 1):

    Dickson's strategies in interpreting the *Charter* to protect minority rights, and his critical approach to *Charter* powers that could override these rights, shaped the Court's policies during his years as chief justice (1984–1990) and have significantly influenced Canadian jurisprudence in the past fourteen years as well.

    Dickson's early interpretation of some of the language in the Charter – language that could have been interpreted differently than he did – became the initial conditions that shaped the path taken by the Supreme Court's understanding of rights and freedoms in Canada.

* *Example 3*   Under the guidance and influence of James Madison, the Constitutional Convention that met in Philadelphia in 1787 decided to draft a new constitution and not simply to amend the Articles of Confederation as per the formal Terms of Reference drafted by the Continental Congress. Even if most of the framers were American nationalists looking towards a central government capable of nation-building and of effective governance, they were also wary of a government that would become large and powerful (see Rossiter 1966). For this reason the powers assigned to the centre were enumerated in the constitution, with those not in the enumeration reserved to the states. It is among the enumerated powers that one finds the famous Commerce Clause – sometimes referred to as the Dormant Commerce Clause to indicate that even when Congress does not act (even when Congress 'sleeps'), the states cannot undertake to regulate interstate commerce.[23] One of the most remarkable things about the clause is the number of definitions that have been given to the word 'commerce' over the years. Depending on the circumstances, the clause has been used by Congress to disallow state laws which were deemed to be protectionist of state activities – state laws seen as hindering the building of a national state

– and those that were viewed as interfering with the will of Congress to legislate in domains such as civil rights (the Civil Rights Act of 1964, for example – see Lens 2001). The Supreme Court also used the Commerce Clause to disallow federal laws and to support state laws. In these ways, the clause has shaped vertical competition and its outcome for over 200 years. Had the deliberations in Philadelphia not been so strongly influenced by the problems of the confederal arrangement of 1776, the initial conditions inscribed in the US constitution would in all likelihood have been very different, causing the path travelled by vertical competition to have been different.

Dynamic instability

In the literature on federalism and decentralization an element in what I call dynamic instability has been labelled 'race to the bottom'. The expression is due, I believe, to William Carey (1974, p. 666) who used it to characterize what he thought he was observing in what came to be known as the market for incorporation and reincorporation. It is generally agreed that the expression was inappropriate (see, for example, Wilson 1996; Oates 1999), but for one reason or another, it has continued to be widely used. The main problem with the race to the bottom expression is that it conveys the impression of adjustments that never set in motion countervailing forces or, to use Kelvin Lancaster's (1974, p. 287) term, 'restoring forces' that prevent collapse and can even bring whatever factor has been displaced back to its initial equilibrium or to some other equilibrium position far away from the bottom.

The variety of forms that dynamic instability has historically taken points to the probability that it is not likely that one theoretical model will fit all of the various forms. It is not clear how one should model the dynamic instability that could afflict vertical competition in governmental systems. I have elsewhere (Breton 2002, pp. 39–41) suggested a possible approach which I now think is lacking because I did not incorporate in it the organizational activities of the Breton–Scott model of assignment. Be that as it may, the point I wish to emphasize does not require that the phenomenon be modelled. It only demands that we acknowledge that dynamic instability is a possibility.

A number of scholars believe that races to the bottom are not de facto empirically important (see Oates and Schwab 1988; Wilson 1996; Oates 1998, 1999; and Scott 2000). I believe, to the contrary, that the presumption must be that the phenomenon is, if not ubiquitous, frequent. Indeed, tariff wars (Kindleberger 1986), competitive exchange devaluations (Nurkse 1944), and destructive tax competition (Rowell–Sirois Report 1940; Break 1967; Oates 1999) during the 1930s did take place. I think it significant, in addition, that in the post-Second World War era, we have not had serious tariff wars – some skirmishes but no wars – and no sustained competitive devaluations of currencies. This, I suggest, is not an accident. Indeed, a large literature attributes the relative stability of the post-war era in currency valuations and peace on the tariff front to the existence of international bodies such as the General Agreement on Tariffs and Trade (GATT) (now the World Trade Organization: WTO) and the International Monetary Fund (IMF). I concur with the conclusions of that literature. The absence of competitive devaluations and of tariff wars point to dynamic instabilities that are under control.

Just as the mechanism in place, through the WTO, to prevent tariff wars is different from the mechanism utilized by the IMF to frustrate competitive currency devaluations, we must presume that the mechanism that forces vertical competition to be dynamically stable varies across countries. Moreover, it is probable that the mechanisms are related to the operation of the Breton–Scott organizational activities and to their costs. If, for example, we focus only on coordination activities, we will see that coordination is not managed in the same way in Canada, in France, in India, in Italy and in the United States, all countries that have managed somehow to keep dynamic instability, actual or potential, under control.

Constitutional courts and revenue powers
In addition to the above three institutional constraints that help determine how vertical competition manifests itself, there are other constraints that are well known even if they are seldom if ever conceived in the role that I give them in this chapter. I mention two that are of undoubted importance as illustrations: first, the decision-making influence of constitutional courts; and, second, the division of revenue powers between jurisdictional tiers.

In decentralized governmental systems, governments often sue other governments of the same system in matters that pertain to the assignment of powers before courts that may or may not be called constitutional courts, but act in that capacity. The decisions and the jurisprudence that flow from these courts have a profound effect on the operation of vertical competition. That is not controversial. If we recognize that constitutional courts differ in respect of their composition, the length of the judges' tenure on the bench, the ideological bent of judges, and a host of other things, we should expect the slant given to vertical competition by constitutional courts to vary among countries.

There is considerable variation in the division of the authority to collect revenues: sometimes virtually all tax bases are assigned to the government at the central level; in other cases, the authority is more evenly distributed; and in still other cases, most tax bases are accessible to all governments whatever the level they inhabit. It is not necessary to insist that this constraint will have a crucially important influence on the way vertical competition will manifest itself.

Asymmetric assignments

Suppose that the power to legislate and regulate on matters related to, say, immigration has been assigned to the central government. If that power is relocated to one or more of the provinces, states or regions of the governmental system *but not to all of them*, the outcome is an asymmetric assignment of powers.[24] Asymmetry is not concurrency, nor is it a contractual undertaking whereby a province, state or region agrees to implement, for a fee, decisions made by the centre. Nor is it a sale or lease to some province, state or region of a service produced by a government at another level. Thus, the Canadian arrangement under which some provinces have their own police force while others hire, for a fee, the services of the federal police force, is not an asymmetric assignment.

What asymmetry of assignments requires is that the ownership of the authority to legislate, regulate and implement be reassigned. In Canada, the authority to design and implement immigration policies is federal, but that ownership has recently been relocated to the Province of Quebec (and not to the other provinces). That is, with respect to the immigration head of power, the assignment is asymmetric.

In the last section, I focused on some of the institutional constraints that shape vertical competition and the visage it reveals to those who observe it. I did not mention that another, more or less obvious, effect of the operation of the institutional constraints is asymmetry in intergovernmental relations and therefore in the responsibilities of governments located at different jurisdictional tiers. If, in addition, we acknowledge the existence of intergovernmental conditional grants, mandates, injunctions, directives and disallowances introduced and discussed in the fourth section, it should be clear that asymmetry in assignments is the general rule in decentralized governmental systems. One of the reasons why the asymmetry of assignments has not received more attention in the literature is that ascertaining its existence requires information that is often not readily available on the relationship that governments located at different levels entertain with one another. One must conclude that asymmetric assignments are an inevitable consequence of vertical competition.

Conclusion

The forgoing discussion has been concerned with the analysis of vertical competition as an automatic mechanism that operates to reassign powers in federal states and in decentralized unitary states. Care has been taken to provide concepts and building-blocks that are logically consistent with each other. An effort has been made in the discussion of the institutional context in which vertical competition unfolds to provide historical and factual material that makes it possible to 'observe', as it were, the workings of the mechanism in the real world.

Notes

1. I am grateful to Amaresh Bagchi, Anne Des Ormeaux, Silvana Dalmazzone, Stefanie Engel, Angela Fraschini, Pierre Salmon, Anthony Scott, the editors of the Handbook, and the participants in the Seminar on Fiscal Federalism for comments that have not only led to improvements, but that have also saved me from a few egregious mistakes. The usual disclaimer applies.
2. The literature seldom adds to the spatial dimension, captured by the idea of spans, the notion of economies of scale in supply which ensures that the powers under which such policies as foreign aid or a military navy could not be assigned to local governments, whatever their spans. One important exception is Tullock (1969).
3. For a history of the concept of 'subsidiarity' and the difficulties inherent in its application, see Breton et al. (1998).
4. In the remainder of the chapter, to economize on space and to avoid sentences that are uselessly contorted, I refer simply to 'governmental systems' defined to include, besides governmental bodies, quasi-public institutions, such as non-governmental organizations (NGOs), as well as private bodies that are competitors of public and quasi-public entities.
5. The European Union (EU) poses a special problem in this connection, because it is a governmental system that is not fully confederal, fully federal or fully unitary. Article 3b of the Treaty of Maastricht, which defines the principle of subsidiarity, contains the following subsentence: 'in areas which do not fall within [the Community's] competence', a statement which appears to be saying that those powers that had already been transferred to the Community in 1993 when the Treaty came into effect, are henceforth Community powers. That would imply that in respect of those powers, the EU is a federal governmental system. However, the most important powers are still vested in the Council of Ministers, which is a confederal institution, rather than in parliament. One could take the position that the EU is a governmental system in transition towards a federal or a confederal equilibrium or instead opine that it is really a new type of governmental system. However that may be, I shall have no more to say on the EU in this chapter.
6. If powers are owned by governments at three levels, one has a three-tier federation as is the case for some western states in the United States.
7. For a detailed analysis of that proposition, see Breton (1996, Chapter 3).
8. Mobility is unambiguously defined only when the governmental system is limited to two tiers – a national and a local one, as in Tiebout's (1956) preference revelation model. With three tiers, things are not as clear. If, for example, I want to live in Toronto, I *must* live in Ontario even if I would prefer to live in a different Canadian province. As the number of tiers increases, the mobility problem worsens. That is one of the reasons why the Tiebout model is a barrier to understanding decentralization and federalism.
9. If one draws a table listing all the *bona fide* (see above on the meaning of decentralization) jurisdictional levels vertically and all the powers horizontally, and if one inserts a one or a zero to indicate that a given power has or has not been assigned to a jurisdictional level, once all powers have been assigned in this way one obtains an 'assignment table' which provides a picture of the degree of decentralization. Note that the same power can be assigned to more than one jurisdictional level thus creating concurrency. If powers are weighted by some relevant variable, the table can be reduced to a coefficient (see Breton and Scott 1978, Chapter 3). To each coefficient, however, an infinite number of tables are attached. In other words, one can go from a table to a single coefficient, but not from the latter to the former.
10. Inman and Rubinfeld's (1997, pp. 96–101) discussion of organizational activities is carried out in a model of federalism different from that developed by Breton and Scott. Their definitions of organizational activities, inspired by Breton and Scott's work, are, however, different from those used in that work.
11. On the incidence of real-world reassignments of fiscal powers, see Winer (2000).
12. The comparison may be with governments within a country or it can be international. In the last case, informational constraints may be more difficult to overcome, but they are surely not insuperable (see Salmon 1991).
13. In terms of publication, Breton (2002) and Breton and Ursprung (2002) precede Breton and

Fraschini (2003a), but in terms of conceptualization (and drafting) the latter came before the former.

14. For a defence of that assumption, see Breton (1996, pp. 48–57). See also the literature on probabilistic voting in, for example, Calvert (1986).
15. Breton and Fraschini (2003a) used the word 'invade', while acknowledging that it was not a very satisfactory expression. In this chapter, I use the word 'occupy'. If we distinguish between active and passive occupation, we could think of the first as a product of invasions – or inroads, forays, intrusions, encroachments, infringements, trespasses, breaches and other more or less similar actions – and of the second as resulting from joint ventures, cooperative undertakings, exchanges of good services or a jumble of events that leave unclear how the occupation was achieved. The ways and means used by governments to access the policy domains of other governments is almost limitless.
16. It is, indeed, on that ground that conventional public economics declares them inferior to unconditional grants.
17. Vertical competition as I have described it, may also lead to the creation of new permanent or transitory tiers – temporary or permanent associations of a limited number of provinces, states or regions for the provision of a particular good or service.
18. That is also true incidentally of the working of electoral rules (Breton and Galeotti 1985) and of constitutions (Breton and Salmon 2003).
19. Even if the *cumul des mandats* were to disappear – there are signs that it might – there can be little doubt that it played a role in motivating the decentralization that was put in place in the early 1980s.
20. For a defence of the view that the Court is independent, see Breton and Fraschini (2003b).
21. I use the word 'virtually' because there are a few recent cases of occupation of provincial powers by some municipal governments (see Valiante 2002).
22. In other words, even if preferences, technologies, geography, population size and so on were similar.
23. The Commerce Clause reads: 'The Congress shall have the power to regulate commerce with foreign nations, and among the several states, and with the Indian tribes' (US Constitution, Article I, Section 8, Clause 3).
24. My concern is asymmetric assignments and not asymmetric federalism in the sense given that expression in Rao's (undated) very interesting paper.

References

Arthur, W. Brian (1989), 'Competing technologies, increasing returns, and lock-in by historical events', *Economic Journal*, **99**(394), 116–31.

Boadway, Robin and Frank Flatters (1982), *Equalization in a Federal State: An Economic Analysis*, Ottawa: Supply and Services Canada.

Break, George F. (1967), *Intergovernmental Fiscal Relations in the United States*, Washington, DC: Brookings Institution.

Breton, Albert (1965), 'A theory of government grants', *Canadian Journal of Economics and Political Science*, **31**(2), 175–87.

Breton, Albert (1996), *Competitive Governments. An Economic Theory of Politics and Public Finance*, Cambridge and New York: Cambridge University Press.

Breton, Albert (2000), 'Federalism and decentralization: ownership rights and the superiority of federalism', *Publius: The Journal of Federalism*, **30**(2), 1–16.

Breton, Albert (2002), 'An introduction to decentralization failure', in Ehtisham Ahmad and Vito Tanzi (eds), *Managing Fiscal Decentralization*, London and New York: Routledge, 31–45.

Breton, Albert, Alberto Cassone and Angela Fraschini (1998), 'Decentralization and subsidiarity: toward a theoretical reconciliation', *University of Pennsylvania Journal of International Economic Law*, **19**(1), 21–51.

Breton, Albert and Angela Fraschini (2003a), 'Vertical competition in unitary states: the case of Italy', *Public Choice*, **114**(1–2), 57–77.

Breton, Albert and Angela Fraschini (2003b), 'The independence of the Italian Constitutional Court', *Constitutional Political Economy*, **14**(4), 319–33.

Breton, Albert and Gianluigi Galeotti (1985), 'Is proportional representation always the best rule?', *Public Finance*, **40**(1), 1–16.

Breton, Albert and Pierre Salmon (2003), 'Constitutional rules and competitive politics: their effects on secessionism', in Albert Breton, Gianluigi Galeotti, Pierre Salmon and Ronald Wintrobe (eds), *Rational Foundations of Democratic Politics*, Cambridge and New York: Cambridge University Press, 222–46.

Breton, Albert and Anthony Scott (1978), *The Economic Constitution of Federal States*, Toronto: University of Toronto Press.

Breton, Albert and Heinrich Ursprung (2002), 'Globalization, competitive governments, and constitutional choice in Europe', in Henryk Kierzkowski (ed.), *Europe and Globalization*, Basingstoke: Palgrave Macmillan, 274–301.

Calvert, Randall L. (1986), *Models of Imperfect Information in Politics*, Chur, Switzerland: Harwood Academic.

Carey, William L. (1974), 'Federalism and corporate law: reflections upon Delaware', *Yale Law Journal*, **83**(4), 663–705.

Doig, Jameson W. (2004), 'New constitutions and vulnerable groups: Brian Dickson's strategies in interpreting the 1982 Charter', Typescript.

Galeotti, Gianluigi (2000), 'Founding fathers versus rotten kids: a positive approach to constitutional politics', in Gianluigi Galeotti, Pierre Salmon and Ronald Wintrobe (eds), *Competition and Structure. The Political Economy of Collective Decisions: Essays in Honor of Albert Breton*, Cambridge and New York: Cambridge University Press, 104–25.

Inman, Robert P. and Daniel L. Rubinfeld (1997), 'The political economy of federalism', in Dennis C. Mueller (ed.), *Perspectives on Public Choice: A Handbook*, Cambridge and New York: Cambridge University Press, 73–105.

Johansen, Leif (1965), *Public Economics*, Amsterdam: North-Holland.

Kindleberger, Charles P. (1986), *The World in Depression, 1929–1939*, revised and enlarged edition, Berkeley, CA: University of California Press.

Lancaster, Kelvin J. (1974), *Introduction to Modern Microeconomics*, 2nd edition, Chicago: Rand-McNally.

Lazear, Edward P. and Sherwin Rosen (1981), 'Rank-order tournaments as optimum labor contracts', *Journal of Political Economy*, **89**(5), 841–64.

Lens, Vicki (2001), 'The Supreme Court, federalism, and social policy: the new judicial activism', *Social Service Review*, **75**(2), 318–36.

Liebowitz, Stanley J. and Stephen E. Margolis (1995), 'Path dependence, lock-in, and history', *Journal of Law, Economics, and Organization*, **11**(1), 205–26.

Lindahl, Erik ([1919] 1964), 'Just taxation – a positive solution', in Richard A. Musgrave and Alan T. Peacock (eds), *Classics in the Theory of Public Finance*, London: Macmillan, 168–76.

Musgrave, Richard A. (1959), *The Theory of Public Finance. A Study in Public Economy*, New York: McGraw-Hill.

Nurkse, Ragnar (with William A. Brown) (1944), *International Currency Experience*, New York: League of Nations.

Oates, Wallace E. (1972), *Fiscal Federalism*, New York: Harcourt Brace Jovanovich.

Oates, Wallace E. (1998), 'Environmental policy in the European Community: harmonization or national standards', *Empirica*, 25, 1–13.

Oates, Wallace E. (1999), 'An essay on fiscal federalism', *Journal of Economic Literature*, **37**(3), 1120–49.

Oates, Wallace E. and Robert M. Schwab (1988), 'Economic competition among jurisdictions: efficiency-enhancing or distortion inducing', *Journal of Public Economics*, **35**(3), 333–54.

Olson, Mancur, Jr. (1969), 'The principle of fiscal equivalence', *American Economic Review*, **59**(2), 479–47.

Rao, M. Govinda (undated), 'Asymmetric federalism in India', Typescript.

Roe, Mark J. (1996), 'Chaos and evolution in law and economics', *Harvard Law Review*, **109**, 641–68.

Rossiter, Clinton (1966), *1787, The Grand Convention*, New York: Norton.

Rowell–Sirois Report (1940), Royal Commission on Dominion–Provincial Relations, Ottawa: Queen's Printer, 1954.

Salmon, Pierre (1987a), 'The logic of pressure groups and the structure of the public sector', in Albert Breton, Gianluigi Galeotti, Pierre Salmon and Ronald Wintrobe (eds), *Villa Colombella Papers on Federalism, European Journal of Political Economy*, **3**(1–2), 55–86.

Salmon, Pierre (1987b), 'Decentralization as an incentive scheme', *Oxford Review of Economic Policy*, **3**(2), 24–43.

Salmon, Pierre (1991), 'Checks and balances and international openness', in Albert Breton, Gianluigi Galeotti, Pierre Salmon and Ronald Wintrobe (eds), *The Competitive State. Villa Colombella Papers on Competitive Politics*, Dordrecht: Kluwer Academic, 169–84.

Salmon, Pierre (2000), 'Vertical competition in a unitary state', in Gianluigi Galeotti, Pierre Salmon and Ronald Wintrobe (eds), *Competition and Structure. The Political Economy of Collective Decisions: Essays in Honor of Albert Breton*, Cambridge and New York: Cambridge University Press, 239–56.

Scott, Anthony D. (2000), 'Assigning powers over the Canadian environment', in Gianluigi Galeotti, Pierre Salmon and Ronald Wintrobe (eds), *Competition and Structure. The Political Economy of Collective Decisions: Essays in Honor of Albert Breton*, Cambridge and New York: Cambridge University Press, 174–219.

Tiebout, Charles M. (1956), 'A pure theory of local expenditure', *Journal of Political Economy*, **64**(5), 416–24.

Tullock, Gordon (1969), 'Federalism: problems of scale', *Public Choice*, **6**, 19–29.

Valiante, Marcia (2002), 'Turf war: municipal powers, the regulation of pesticides and the *Hudson* Decision', *Journal of Environmental Law and Practice*, **11**(3), 325–57.

Weldon, Jack C. (1966), 'Public goods (and federalism)', *Canadian Journal of Economics and Political Science*, **32**(2), 230–38.

Wheare, Kenneth C. (1963), *Federal Government*, 4th edition, London: Oxford University Press.

Wicksell, Knut ([1896] 1964), 'A new principle of just taxation', in Richard A. Musgrave and Alan T. Peacock (eds), *Classics in the Theory of Public Finance*, London: Macmillan, 72–118.

Wilson, John Douglas (1996), 'Capital mobility and environmental standards: is there a theoretical basis for a race to the bottom?', in Jagdish Bhagwati and Robert E. Hudec (eds), *Fair Trade and Harmonization. Prerequisites for Free Trade?*, Vol. I, Economic Analysis, Cambridge, MA: MIT Press, 393–427.

Winer, Stanley L. (2000), 'On the reassignment of fiscal powers in a federal state', in Gianluigi Galeotti, Pierre Salmon and Ronald Wintrobe (eds), *Competition and Structure. The Political Economy of Collective Decisions: Essays in Honor of Albert Breton*, Cambridge and New York: Cambridge University Press, 150–73.

Young, H. Peyton (1996), 'The economics of convention', *Journal of Economic Perspectives*, **10**(2), 105–22.

4 Spatial interactions among governments
Federico Revelli[1]

Introduction
The theoretical local public finance literature has studied extensively the reasons why local governments might not set their fiscal policies in isolation, but rather tend to interact with neighboring jurisdictions (see chapters in this Handbook). Similar arguments hold for interactions among states within federal countries as well as for fiscal interdependence among nation states at the international level. This chapter aims at illustrating how those theoretical models of intergovernmental fiscal interaction can be implemented empirically. In particular, it reviews the recent empirical literature on intergovernmental fiscal interaction and focuses on the specification and estimation of fiscal interaction models that give rise to a spatial pattern in local government expenditures and revenues. The chapter first groups the existing empirical studies into three broad categories, depending on the assumed channel of interaction (preferences, constraints and expectations), and shows how different theoretical hypotheses of strategic interaction among governments – such as expenditure spillover, tax competition for mobile resources, and yardstick competition – can be implemented empirically in order to ascertain the sign and magnitude of spatial interdependence. Careful analysis of the recent empirical literature shows that estimation of a reduced-form interjurisdictional reaction function might not by itself allow us to discriminate among competing theoretical hypotheses. Consequently, a number of approaches for identifying the theoretical model generating the observed spatial auto-correlation in fiscal variables are outlined, which are based either on auxiliary predictions that can be directly derived from the theory, or on the existence of institutional arrangements or reforms that generate a sort of 'natural experiment'. Finally, the chapter provides some methodological guidelines for the spatial econometric analysis (modeling, testing and estimation) of strategic interaction models based on local government data, and offers some concluding remarks and suggestions for future empirical work.

Spatial model specification
Similarly to the social interactions approach (Manski 1993, 2000), governments can be thought of as interacting with one another along three main channels: preferences, constraints and expectations.

First, according to the preferences interaction hypothesis, an action chosen by a (local welfare-maximizing) government affects directly the preferences of another government, in the sense that the public services provided by a jurisdiction enter the welfare function of another jurisdiction (Brueckner 2003). Empirically, one observes either positive or negative correlation among public expenditures as a result of the spillover, depending on the patterns of complementarity/substitutability among local public services.

Second, according to the constraints interaction hypothesis, the fiscal policy of a jurisdiction influences the size of a 'resource' that locates in nearby localities and consequently affects the budget constraint of other governments (ibid.). As a result, a jurisdiction's policy affects indirectly the fiscal policies of neighboring jurisdictions, leading to interdependence in local fiscal choices.

Finally, in the presence of expectations interaction, an action chosen by a government affects the information set and, as a result, the expectations of an imperfectly informed electorate in another jurisdiction. In the presence of an informational spillover from nearby jurisdictions, voters evaluate the performance of their own government relative to other governments. Comparative performance evaluation on the part of voters consequently generates a yardstick competition among governments and a correlation in their fiscal policies (Besley and Case 1995). The rest of this section is devoted to examining in detail the empirical implications of the three forms of interaction sketched above.

Direct preference interaction
In the presence of a direct preference interaction, the benefits of local public services provided in a jurisdiction tend to spill over into neighboring localities. While examples of spillover generating public expenditures abound – including spending on roads, public transport, education, training and environmental protection – the empirical literature that investigates the size and direction of such spillovers is rather thin.

Case et al. (1993) estimate an expenditure determination equation using a panel dataset of the US states' budgets, where the presence of spillover effects is due to the fact that expenditures by one state – such as expenditures on roads – benefit residents in neighboring states.[2] Murdoch et al. (1993) estimate a model where recreation expenditures by local governments in California affect the well-being of non-residents as well. Finally, Revelli (2003) estimates the impact on neighboring jurisdictions' expenditures of English districts' spending on environmental and cultural services.

In expenditure spillover models, the welfare of jurisdiction i depends – apart from private consumption of residents c_i and a vector of own characteristics $X_i = [x_{i1}, x_{i2}, \ldots]$ – both on own spending on local public services (g_i) and on spending in a nearby jurisdiction $n(g_n)$:

$$u_i = u[c_i\,(y_i,\,g_i,\,l_i),\,g_i,\,g_n,\,X_i], \tag{4.1}$$

where private consumption c_i depends, via the budget constraint, on income (y_i), on the level of public spending (g_i) and on the amount of it that is funded by grants from central government (l_i).

Depending on the type of spillover, g_n can either raise or diminish the marginal utility of own spending ($\partial u_i/\partial g_i$), therefore leading either to positive correlation – in the case of complementary public goods provided by jurisdictions i and n – or to negative correlation – in the case of substitute public goods – among neighbors' expenditures.[3] In fact, maximization of local welfare (4.1) yields that the optimal level of expenditure in jurisdiction i ends up depending on jurisdiction n's expenditure:

$$g_i = g(g_n,\,y_i,\,l_i,\,X_i). \tag{4.2}$$

In a linear specification, (4.2) can be expressed as:

$$g_i = \theta_0 + \theta_1 g_n + \theta_2 y_i + \theta_3 l_i + X_i\,\kappa + \zeta_i, \tag{4.3}$$

where ζ_i is a random term, κ is a vector of parameters, θ_2 and θ_3 capture the response of local spending to income and grant respectively, θ_0 is a constant, and the size and significance of parameter θ_1 expresses whether the choices of jurisdictions i and n are actually interdependent.

A potential problem with equation (4.3) arises because, since public spending and local tax effort are related via the budget constraint, a relationship between neighbors' spending levels might in reality be caused by some form of interaction along the revenue side of the budget – such as tax or yardstick competition – and not by a benefit spillover (Revelli 2002b). As a result, in order to discriminate between the expenditure spillover hypothesis and alternative fiscal interaction hypotheses, it is necessary to explore carefully the empirical implications of tax competition and yardstick theories.

Indirect constraints interaction
Models of tax competition – usually competition for mobile capital – represent the classical example of indirect constraints interaction (Wilson 1999). Tax competition theory yields two main empirical predictions. First, the optimal tax rate (in more general terms, the entire policy vector affecting a mobile tax base) in a jurisdiction depends on the tax rates set in nearby jurisdictions (Brett and Pinkse 2000; Brueckner and Saavedra 2001; Buettner 2001; Fredriksson et al. 2004). Second, the resource (the tax base) that locates in a jurisdiction is affected by the tax rate (in more general terms, by the entire fiscal policy) in

that jurisdiction, as well as by neighboring jurisdictions' tax rates (Brett and Pinkse 2000; Buettner 2003).

A strand of the literature looks in particular at international tax competition and estimates policy reaction functions among countries at an international level (Goodspeed 2000; Devereux et al. 2002a, 2002b), while another strand looks at environmental and regulatory competition, that is competition among authorities in setting environmental regulation, standards and growth control measures (Brueckner 1998; Fredriksson, and Millimet 2002a; Levinson 2003).

Moreover, Tiebout-like models (Tiebout 1956) that look at fiscal competition and residential decisions of mobile voters/taxpayers belong to this group (Dowding et al. 1994; Feld 1997; Feld and Kirchgässner 2001).

Finally, welfare competition models – reviewed by Brueckner (2000) – belong to this category, if one sees the number of welfare recipients as the mobile 'resource'. In the presence of mobile welfare recipients, every jurisdiction realizes that, by increasing welfare benefits, it tends to attract poor people from other jurisdictions – the 'welfare magnet' hypothesis. Consequently, the optimal welfare policy of a jurisdiction tends to be affected by neighbors' policies, in the sense that a reduction in neighbors' benefits is accompanied by a reduction in own benefits – the 'race to the bottom' hypothesis (Smith 1991; Shroder 1995; Figlio et al. 1999; Saavedra 2000; Wheaton 2000; Baicker 2005).[4]

Following Brueckner (2003), the main idea underlying all of the above models can be formalized and implemented empirically in the following simple way.

The basic assumption is that, apart from a vector of exogenous characteristics of jurisdiction i (denoted by $Y_i = (y_{i1}, y_{i2}, \ldots .))$,[5] the policy enacted in jurisdiction $i(t_i)$ as well as that in a nearby jurisdiction $n(t_n)$ affect the tax base (or, more generally, the 'resource') that locates in jurisdiction $i(b_i)$:

$$b_i = b(t_i, t_n, Y_i). \tag{4.4}$$

In general, $\partial b_i/\partial t_i < 0$ and $\partial b_i/\partial t_n > 0$, because a tax increase in jurisdiction i (a tax cut in jurisdiction n) makes i less attractive for the mobile resource, by reducing its net return. In tax competition models, b_i ought to be interpreted as the stock of capital that locates in jurisdiction i and is employed, along with an immobile factor of production (labor), in the production of a private good with constant returns to scale.

Jurisdiction i's welfare (u_i) depends on local residents' private consumption (c_i), as well as on the public goods that the local government provides (g_i), and it is assumed that both of them depend on the size of the resource b_i that locates in jurisdiction i:[6]

$$u_i = u[c_i(b_i), g_i(b_i), X_i] \tag{4.5}$$

where $X_i = [x_{i1}, x_{i2}, \ldots]$ in the equation is a vector of characteristics of the jurisdiction, such as demographic and ethnic composition of the resident population.

Maximization of local welfare (4.5) subject to (4.4) yields that the optimal tax policy in jurisdiction i depends on the exogenous characteristics of the jurisdiction (X_i, Y_i), as well as on jurisdiction n's tax policy:

$$t_i = t(t_n, X_i, Y_i). \tag{4.6}$$

Consequently, one can test a tax competition model by estimating the reduced-form reaction function, which is usually expressed in linear (or log-linear) form as:

$$t_i = \rho_0 = \rho_1 t_n = X_i\beta + Y_i\delta + \varepsilon_i, \tag{4.7}$$

where ρ_0 is the constant term, ρ_1 is a scalar parameter, β and δ are parameter vectors, and ε_i is a random term. The tax competition model prediction is that $\rho_1 \neq 0$.[7]

However, the tax competition model also implies – equation (4.4) – that the own tax rate should have a negative impact on the tax base, while neighbors' tax rates should have a positive impact on it. Consequently, as shown later, full testing for indirect constraints interaction requires modeling explicitly, along with the policy reaction function, the constraint/resource equation, and ascertaining whether local fiscal policies actually affect the location of the resource.

Expectations interaction
Interaction in expectations within a political agency framework gives rise to the phenomenon of yardstick competition (Salmon 1987), by which imperfectly informed voters in a local jurisdiction use other governments' performance as a yardstick to evaluate their own government, and politicians try not to get too far out of line with the policies enacted in nearby jurisdictions.

Yardstick competition models yield two main empirical predictions. First, tax rates tend to be correlated among neighboring jurisdictions, because local authorities mimic each other's behavior, as the evidence in the work of Ladd (1992) for US counties, Case et al. (1993) for US states, Heyndels and Vuchelen (1998) for Belgian municipalities, Bivand and Szymanski (1997, 2000) and Revelli (2001) for UK local governments, Schaltegger and Kuttel (2002) for Swiss Cantons, and Solé-Ollé (2003) for Spanish municipalities tends to suggest.

Second, the electoral results in a jurisdiction depend both on own tax rates and on neighboring jurisdictions' tax rates. In this regard, Besley and Case (1995) present a political agency model where voters and politicians are sensitive to events outside their boundaries and test their yardstick competition hypothesis on US states' income taxes from 1960 to 1988. They find that own tax changes have a negative effect and geographic neighbors' tax changes have a positive and significant effect on a governor's chances of re-election. Revelli (2002a) obtains similar results for UK local election results and local property tax rates in the 1980s.

In the standard yardstick competition model, it is assumed that the cost of public services in a local jurisdiction i (g_i) equals a non-stochastic component (f_i) that is not under the control of politicians, plus a cost shock, again not controlled by politicians (s_i). It is usually assumed that voters know the former, but not the latter, while politicians observe the realizations of both:

$$g_i = f_i + s_i. \tag{4.8}$$

Moreover, some politicians (the 'bad' ones) do not charge the actual cost of public services, g_i, but rather $t_i > g_i$, because they misappropriate (own rents) or waste (w_i) the tax in excess of the cost:

$$t_i = g_i + w_i. \tag{4.9}$$

Assuming a maximum of two terms in office for an incumbent government (due, for example, to term limits), the bad politicians' lifetime utility (vl_i) depends on the rents they can appropriate in the first period (w_i) and in the second period (w_{i+1}), if they manage to get re-elected (an event that occurs with probability p_i):

$$vl_i = v(w_i) + p_i v(w_{i+1}). \tag{4.10}$$

However, politicians are aware that their chances of being re-elected and remaining in power in the second term (p_i) depend – apart from a vector of politicians' characteristics $Z_i = [z_{i1}, z_{i2}, \ldots]$ – on their relative fiscal performance while in power in the first period:

$$p_i = p(t_i, t_n, Z_i). \tag{4.11}$$

In particular, the higher the own tax t_i, the higher the probability that voters will think that the governing politicians are accumulating rents, and the lower their probability of re-election ($\partial p_i / \partial t_i < 0$). However, in a decentralized system of government, voters look to other jurisdictions' t's in order to get another perspective on the cost of providing public services, thus solving the asymmetry of local information. Such behavior is rational, as long as neighboring jurisdictions are subject to correlated cost shocks ($Cov(s_i, s_n) > 0$). Observing a high t_n can convince voters that their own jurisdiction has been hit by a bad cost shock (s_i in (4.8)). Consequently, a government that sets a high t_i might get away with it and manage to be re-elected. This implies that a higher t_n in equation (4.11) will raise, *ceteris paribus*, the incumbent's chances of re-election ($\partial p_i/\partial t_i > 0$). However, if the information from the neighborhood jurisdictions suggests that there has not been any bad cost shock (low t_n), a high t_i will likely lead to electoral defeat for the incumbent in jurisdiction i.

Maximizing (4.10) subject to the electoral constraint (4.11) yields that the optimal tax for the politician in jurisdiction i, depending on jurisdiction n's tax:

$$t_i = t(t_n, f_i, Z_i).\tag{4.12}$$

In a linear specification, the tax reaction function can be expressed as:

$$t_i = \phi_0 + \phi_1 t_n + \phi_2 f_i + Z_i \nu + \eta_i,\tag{4.13}$$

where ν is a vector of parameters to be estimated along with ϕ_0, ϕ_1, ϕ_2 and η_i is a random term reflecting unobserved shocks to local fiscal policy. Yardstick competition can consequently be tested by estimating equation (4.13), where in general it is expected that $\phi_1 > 0$.[8]

Actually, equation (4.13) is no different from the reaction function that would be derived from a tax competition model. Consequently, as shown later, identification of yardstick competition requires taking explicitly into account the electoral constraints that face incumbent governments.

Empirical implementation

Up to now, the analysis has considered the policy of one jurisdiction (n) and its potential impact on the policy of another jurisdiction (i). Clearly, though, in most applied settings each local jurisdiction will interact with a (possibly large) number of other jurisdictions. Moreover, in most instances the influence of jurisdictions' policies will be reciprocal. This is chiefly a result of the multidirectional nature of dependence among spatial units, that makes the empirical analysis of spatial economic data – termed 'spatial econometrics' – different from the clear unidirectional dependence in time that is typical of standard time-series econometrics (Anselin 1988).

In fact, empirical work on spatial data requires making the information on other jurisdictions' variables tractable. Including in the policy determination equation of a jurisdiction the policies of all other jurisdictions separately – such as $t_i = f(t_n \mid n = 1, 2, \ldots, N)$ – or even only the subset of relevant jurisdictions, such as $t_i = f(t_n \mid n \in \tilde{N} \subset N)$, is in general not possible, due to lack of degrees of freedom.

The typical approach consists in summarizing in a unique variable the entire information that is contained in the other jurisdictions' policies, by means of a spatial weights matrix.

Spatial weights matrix construction
The main role of the spatial weights matrix consists in translating the information on the location of the jurisdictions – that is, the information that is contained in a map – into a suitable form for analytical treatment. The spatial weights matrix, denoted by W, is of dimension equal to the number of observations $(N \times N)$. The basic criterion driving its construction is that the element corresponding to row r and column c (w_{rc}) is set to be different from zero if observations – spatial sites – r and c are considered to be neighbors according to the chosen definition of neighborhood, and zero otherwise, with $w = 0$ if $r = c$.

While the original matrix is symmetric, it is usually standardized such that the elements of a row sum to one. This is obtained by dividing each element in the matrix by its row sum. Thus, the product of the $(N \times N)$ matrix and the $(N \times 1)$ vector of the relevant policy variable (t) yields, for each jurisdiction i, a spatially weighted average of neighboring jurisdictions' variables:

$$
Wt = \begin{pmatrix} \sum_{j=1}^{N} w_{1j}t_j \\ \\ \sum_{j=1}^{N} w_{2j}t_j \\ \\ \cdots \\ \\ \sum_{i=1}^{N} w_{Nj}t_j \end{pmatrix}
\tag{4.14}
$$

Whether or not the neighborhood matrix should be row-standardized clearly depends on the underlying economic model, and in some instances the use of a standardized matrix might not be economically meaningful. The fact that the spatial weights sum to one for each local jurisdiction means that the total effect of all neighbors is the same, regardless of the number of neighbors. This implies that, the fewer the neighbors, the stronger their individual influence on the central unit will be.

As for the criterion driving the construction of the matrix, the simplest one is a basic binary weights system, according to which two local jurisdictions are neighbors if they share a border. In that case, w_{rc} is equal to one if they do, and is equal to zero otherwise. Other common weighting criteria are based on inverse distance between (the central points of) two spatial units, or negative exponential of distance (as in the empirical analysis of expenditure spillovers in Murdoch et al. (1993). Alternatively, the weight can take into account the relative length of the shared border and the relative area of the spatial units (Anselin 1988).

The above purely spatial criteria can be relaxed in two ways. First, while admitting the importance of proximity, one could argue that not all neighbors should be given equal weight, and use a spatial matrix whose elements are weighted by relevant neighbors' characteristics, such as population size or income level (Brueckner 1998; Heyndels and Vuchelen 1998; Brueckner and Saavedra 2001; Fredriksson and Millimet 2002a, 2002b). Particularly in spillover models, local jurisdictions might attribute a stronger weight to jurisdictions with relatively larger population (*pop*), while allowing for distance (*dis*):

$$w_{rc} = \frac{pop_c}{\sum_{j=1}^{N} pop_j} \cdot \frac{1}{dis_{rc}}. \tag{4.15}$$

On the other hand, a reasonable weighting criterion in welfare competition models might be based on the gross migration flow between jurisdictions r and c, relative to migration flows between jurisdiction r and the rest of the country (Shroder 1995):

$$w_{rc} = \frac{migration_{rc}}{\sum_{j=1}^{N} migration_{rj}}. \tag{4.16}$$

In other frameworks, it may be sensible to build neighborhood matrices whose weights are based on similarity in demographic or economic characteristics between jurisdictions, regardless of distance. In fact, local jurisdictions may regard as neighbors other jurisdictions that are similar to them from an economic or demographic point of view, regardless of geographic proximity, particularly in models of yardstick competition (as in Case et al. 1993).

Since the elements of W cannot be estimated, it is clear that the choice of the neighborhood criterion is to some extent arbitrary. For most spatial processes of interest in applied local public economics, the use of a geographical criterion seems reasonable, because close-by jurisdictions are more likely to affect each other than far away ones, particularly as far as constraints and preferences interaction is concerned.

In general, the definition of the weighting criterion should be driven by the theoretical model.[9] In particular, a model-driven approach helps prevent the analysis from being affected by the so-called 'modifiable a real unit problem', that is the sensitivity of the results to the way the spatial units are organized (Anselin 1988). Second, the definition of the spatial matrix should be inspired by parsimony. Unless the theoretical model predicts differently, a parsimonious specification of the weights matrix – such as a binary one – is usually to be preferred to more structured (and often more arbitrary) ones, in that the use of 'neutral' weights prevents us from introducing spurious correlation among the variables or even to cause circularity, that is to impose on the data the spatial structure that the analysis wishes to discover (ibid.).

Testing

A sensible way of constructing and specifying a spatial public finance model starts from testing, that is from looking at whether the local government data suggest that a non-spatial model is inappropriate, and that some form of spatial dependence should be allowed for in the empirical implementation.

Actually, the first reason why a non-spatial model may be inappropriate for studying local government fiscal decisions is that the error term in the policy determination equation – such as, for instance, ε_i in equation (4.7) – might be spatially auto-correlated. In fact, any influence which is omitted from the model and is spatially auto-correlated – such as, for instance, regional shocks to income or tax base – will lead to a spatial pattern in the dependent variable.

This form of spatial dependence is referred to as 'spatial error dependence', and requires modeling a spatial process in the error term explicitly, such as a first-order spatial auto-regressive process (Anselin 1988).

Alternatively, if any of the substantive interaction processes outlined above occur, the policy determination equation must take into account that local jurisdictions' policies are determined simultaneously – as in equations (4.3), (4.7) and (4.13), above. Following Anselin, we refer to this kind of interaction as 'substantive spatial dependence' or 'spatial lag dependence', because the equation includes a 'spatial lag' of the dependent variable – such as t_n in equation (4.7) – among the explanatory variables.

The consequences on the model parameter estimates from omitting the two forms of dependence are different. If substantive spatial dependence is present, but the spatial lag term is omitted from the model, the estimates for the regression coefficients will be biased and inconsistent. On the other hand, when spatial error dependence is present, but ignored, the ordinary least squares (OLS) estimates are no longer efficient, but they remain unbiased, with the inefficiency arising from the non-diagonal structure of the disturbance matrix (ibid.). Consequently, it is important to investigate whether the policy of a local jurisdiction is actually correlated with the policies of other jurisdictions, and whether spatial lag or spatial error dependence are the more likely sources of correlation.

In this respect, a number of tests for spatial auto-correlation have been suggested in the spatial econometrics literature. Those tests are derived from the null hypothesis that space does not matter, or that the assignment of values to particular locations is not relevant. Under the alternative hypothesis of spatial auto-correlation, either large (small) values of the variable of interest tend to be surrounded by large (small) values – positive auto-correlation – or large (small) values tend to be surrounded by small (large) values – negative auto-correlation. Whereas positive spatial auto-correlation implies a spatial clustering of similar values, negative spatial auto-correlation implies a checkerboard pattern of values. Tests for spatial auto-correlation are based on the magnitude of an indicator that combines the value observed at each location with the values at neighboring locations, and basically represent measures of the similarity between association in value (correlation) and association in space (contiguity).

The most commonly used measure for spatial auto-correlation is Moran's I statistic (Cliff and Ord 1981). Moran's I statistic for N observations on a variable t is expressed as:

$$I(t) = \frac{N}{S_0} \frac{\sum\limits_{i,j=1}^{N} w_{ij}(t_i - \bar{t})(t_j - \bar{t})}{\sum\limits_{i=1}^{N} (t_i - \bar{t})^2},$$
(4.17)

where t_i is the level of the fiscal variable observed at location i, $\bar{t}$ is the average of the variable across all jurisdictions, w_{ij} is the element corresponding to row i and column j in the spatial weights matrix, and S_0 is the sum of the elements of the weights matrix: $S_0 = \sum_i \sum_j w_{ij}$.[10]

Inference for the I statistic is carried out by computing its mean and variance, under the hypothesis that the t's are drawn from a normal distribution (ibid.).

Furthermore, one can test for spatial correlation, after conditioning on the non-stochastic determinants of t. A widely applied diagnostic for the residuals of an OLS regression of t on a set of exogenous variables is the following application of Moran's I statistic:

$$I(e) = \frac{N}{S_0} \frac{e'We}{e'e},$$
(4.18)

where *e* are the OLS regression residuals of, say, equation (4.7), where parameter ρ_1 has been set to zero. For normal error terms, the $I(e)$ statistic is asymptotically normal (ibid.).

However, Monte Carlo simulation experiments have revealed that Moran's *I* for OLS regression residuals suffers from two major drawbacks (Anselin and Rey 1991). First, the test is very sensitive to the presence of other forms of specification error, such as non-normality and heteroscedasticity. Second, Moran's $I(e)$ is not able to discriminate properly between the two forms of spatial auto-correlation cited above – spatial error dependence and spatial lag dependence – in the sense that it tends to reject the null in the presence of either, leaving the crucial question open of whether the observed spatial pattern should be attributed to a behavioral interaction process or to spatially correlated shocks.

An alternative to Moran's $I(e)$ is the use of tests based on the Lagrange Multiplier (LM) principle, which again require only the OLS regression residuals from a non-spatial model. In particular, Anselin et al. (1996) have proposed two robust tests based on the LM principle that can give a clearer indication of what is the most likely source of spatial dependence (spatial error or spatial lag dependence).

While the above tests can be performed by simple OLS estimation of a non-spatial equation, proper estimation of the spatial models needs to be performed in order to learn more about the process that is responsible for the observed spatial auto-correlation.

Estimation
Upon detection of spatial auto-correlation through testing, the empirical model should be implemented with the spatial structure suggested by the test results: spatial lag or spatial error dependence.

Spatial lag dependence   Spatial lag dependence occurs when the dependent variable corresponding to each spatial unit depends upon a weighted average of that dependent variable for neighboring units. The model to be estimated can be expressed as in equation (4.19) below – or as the matrix form and multiple neighbors analogue of (4.7):

$$t = \rho_1 Wt + H\tau + \varepsilon, \qquad (4.19)$$

where: $H = [1, X, Y]$, $\tau' = [\rho_0, \beta', \delta']$, and ε is a $(N \times 1)$ vector of i.i.d. error terms with variance σ_ε^2. OLS yields biased estimates of the parameters in (4.19) because own and neighbors' spending levels are determined simultaneously and the spatial lag of the dependent variable (Wt) is correlated with the error term:

$$E[(Wt)\varepsilon'] = W(I - \rho_1 W)^{-1} \sigma_\varepsilon^2 \neq 0. \tag{4.20}$$

Basically, two approaches exist for estimating consistently a spatial reaction function such as (4.19) above.

The first approach – which owes its increasing popularity to its intuitive rationale and computational simplicity – is based on an IV (instrumental variables)/2SLS (two-stage least squares) principle, and consists in finding variables that are correlated with neighbors' endogenous variable (Wt), while not being correlated with ε.

In their estimation of a state tax reaction function, Besley and Case (1995) use a 2SLS procedure, where neighbors' taxes (Wt) are instrumented with neighbors' demographic and economic exogenous variables (WH). Similarly, in testing the 'race to the bottom' hypothesis in welfare spending, Figlio et al. (1999) use a subset of the matrix of neighbors' covariates (unemployment rate, ratio of females to employed males, and wages) as instruments for neighboring states' benefit level. Finally, in their analysis of intercounty spillovers, Kelejian and Robinson (1993) suggest building an instrument matrix that contains own and neighbors' exogenous variables. Consequently, in a first stage Wt is regressed on the instrument matrix: $[H, WH, W^2H, \ldots]$. The predicted value from such regression is then used as a regressor in the reaction function (4.19).

The second approach is based on an ML (maximum likelihood) principle and is more demanding in terms of computational effort involved (Anselin 1988). It basically consists in inverting the spatial reaction function (4.19) and in exploiting the properties of the error term ε:

$$t = (I - \rho_1 W)^{-1} H\tau + (I - \rho_1 W)^{-1} \varepsilon. \tag{4.21}$$

For independently distributed and normal error terms with variance σ_ε^2, the log-likelihood for model (4.19) is:

$$L = c + \ln(J_p) - \frac{N}{2} \ln(\sigma_\varepsilon^2) - \frac{1}{2\sigma_\varepsilon^2} (W_\rho t - H\tau)'(W_\rho t - H\tau) \tag{4.22}$$

where c is a constant, $W_\rho = I - \rho_1 W$, and $J_\rho = |\det(W_\rho)|$ is the Jacobian of the transformation between ε and t (ibid.).

Spatial error dependence   The spatial error dependence model is obtained by setting $\rho_1 = 0$ in (4.19) and modeling a spatial process in ε:

$$t = H\tau + \varepsilon \tag{4.23}$$

$$\varepsilon = \varphi W \varepsilon + \mu, \tag{4.24}$$

where φ is the crucial auto-regressive spatial parameter to be estimated, with $|\varphi| < 1$ to ensure spatial stationarity (Cliff and Ord 1981), and μ is i.i.d. over space.

ML estimation of the spatial error dependence model (4.23)–(4.24) is based upon the properties of μ. The log-likelihood for a sample of N observations, if the error term μ is normally distributed with variance σ_μ^2, is:

$$L = c + \ln(J_\varphi) - \frac{N}{2}\ln(\sigma_\mu^2) - \frac{1}{2\sigma_\mu^2}(t - H\tau)\,'W_\varphi'\,W_\varphi\,(t - H\tau), \tag{4.25}$$

where $W_\varphi = I - \varphi W$, and $J_\varphi = |det(W_\varphi)|$ is the Jacobian of the transformation between μ and t (Anselin 1988).

Alternatively, the error term can be assumed to have a spatial moving average process (SMA), with spatial coefficient γ:

$$\varepsilon = \gamma W \psi + \psi, \tag{4.26}$$

where $|\gamma| < 1$ and ψ is i.i.d. over space.

Spatial lag and error dependence An empirical analysis of intergovernmental fiscal interactions would ideally control for spatial lag and error dependence, thereby allowing both for the possibility of a genuine interaction process – due, say, to yardstick or tax competition phenomena – and for the existence of common non-behavioral shocks to local policies – such as correlated shocks to the costs of providing local public services. A spatial auto-regressive process in the dependent variable with auto-regressive error terms can be expressed as:

$$t = \rho_1 W t + H\tau + \varepsilon \tag{4.27}$$

$$\varepsilon = \varphi W \varepsilon + \mu. \tag{4.28}$$

Kelejian and Prucha (1998) suggest a GMM (generalized method of moments) estimator for the parameters of model (4.27)–(4.28).[11] Basically, the Kelejian and Prucha procedure involves three steps. First, one needs to build an instrument matrix $[H, WH, W^2H, \ldots]$ that contains spatial lags of the exogenous variables, and that is used as an instrument for Wt in order to obtain an estimate of ρ_1 from equation (4.27). In a second step, the residuals $\hat{\varepsilon}$ are used to obtain a non-linear least squares estimate of the spatial auto-correlation parameter $\hat{\varphi}$. Finally, in the third step $\hat{\varphi}$ is used to 'spatially filter' the variables, that is to invert equation (4.28) and substitute it in (4.27), and then to estimate – with a feasible 2SLS estimator – the resulting model:

$$(t - \hat{\varphi}Wt) = (Z - \hat{\varphi}WZ)\,\beta + \mu, \tag{4.29}$$

where: $Z = (Wt, H)$, $\beta' = (\rho_1, \tau')$, and the predicted values of a regression of $(Z - \hat{\varphi}WZ)$ on $[H, WH, W^2H, \ldots]$ are used as instruments. Once obtained, the 2SLS estimates of $\beta' = (\rho_1, \tau')$ from the third step, the procedure starts again with the first step and continues until convergence is achieved.

Alternatively, ML methods can be employed in the estimation of models (4.27)–(4.28) (Case et al. 1993). However, due to the fact that the two spatial processes in (4.27) and (4.28) tend to 'mimic' each other (Case 1991) identification is difficult, especially if it is thought that the two processes are driven by the same spatial matrix. In particular, it can be shown that two different estimates of ρ_1 can be obtained from models (4.27)–(4.28) (Anselin 1988).

Anselin and Florax (1995) suggest using instead a SARMA (spatial auto-regressive moving average) specification in order to identify the two forms of spatial dependence in the dependent variable and in the errors, that is a model with a first-order spatial auto-regressive process in the dependent variable, and a first-order SMA process in the error term – equation (4.26).

Finally, in order to discriminate among the two forms of spatial dependence, it can be useful to notice that the spatial error model can be rewritten in the 'common factor' form as:

$$t = \varphi Wt + H\tau + WH\tilde{\tau} + \mu, \tag{30}$$

where: $\tilde{\tau} = -\varphi\tau$. One can consequently estimate (4.30) and test the non-linear restriction. Moreover, a test on the significance of the $\tilde{\tau}$ coefficients is a test of the spatial lag dependence model ($\tilde{\tau} = 0$) against the spatial error dependence specification.

Identification issues

Earlier it was shown that alternative theoretical models – expenditure spillover, tax competition, yardstick competition – can give rise to similar forms of spatial dependence in local fiscal variables. Consequently, even employing the estimation techniques outlined in the previous section, it can be difficult to attribute the observed pattern of spatial auto-correlation to a precise and unique theoretical explanation.

This section outlines three empirical strategies aimed at identifying the underlying economic model that is responsible for the observed spatial pattern in local government data.

Fully exploiting the theory

In some instances, the theory provides additional empirical predictions that can help discriminate among alternative theoretical hypotheses. In particular, both tax and yardstick competition theories yield auxiliary equations that can be implemented empirically.

First, as far as tax competition is concerned, a fundamental empirical prediction of the theory – besides the tax reaction function (4.7) – is that the tax base actually reacts to local tax rate differentials by moving across jurisdictions (Brett, and Pinkse 2000; Buettner 2003).

In particular, tax competition models imply – from equation (4.4) – that the own tax rate should have a negative impact on the tax base that locates in a jurisdiction ($h_1 < 0$ in equation (4.31)), while neighbors' tax rates should have a positive impact on it ($h_2 > 0$):

$$b_i = h_0 + h_1 t_i + h_2 t_n + Y_i \lambda + o_i. \tag{4.31}$$

Consequently, instead of estimating the reduced-form reaction function (4.7), testing for tax competition can be performed by estimating equation (4.31), as in Buettner (2003), which estimates a variant of equation (4.31) on a panel dataset of German jurisdictions, and adopts an IV approach to control for potential endogeneity of the tax variables on the right-hand side of the equation.

Moreover, a thorough test of tax competition can be based on estimation of the structural model represented by equations (4.31) and (4.32), below, where the tax rate in jurisdiction i is affected – via maximization of the welfare function (4.5) – by the size of the tax base:

$$t_i = k_0 + k_1 b_i + X_i \alpha + \eta_i. \tag{4.32}$$

From an inspection of the structural models (4.31)–(4.32), it turns out that the parameters of a reduced-form tax competition reaction function are non-linear combinations of the structural equations' parameters:

$$t_i = \rho_0 + \rho_1 t_n + X_i \beta + Y_i \delta + \varepsilon_i, \tag{4.33}$$

where:

$$\rho_0 = \frac{k_0 + k_1 h_0}{1 - k_1 h_1}; \rho_1 = \frac{k_1 h_2}{1 - k_1 h_1}; \beta = \frac{\alpha}{1 - k_1 h_1}; \delta = \frac{k_1 \lambda}{1 - k_1 h_1}; \text{ and } \varepsilon_i = \eta_i + k_1 o_i.$$

A structural model approach is pursued in Brett and Pinkse (2000), who estimate the two-equation model (4.31)–(4.32) on a panel dataset of Canadian municipalities, and use instruments for the endogenous variables on the right-hand side (t_i and t_n in (4.31), and b_i in (4.32)).

As far as yardstick competition is concerned, a specific prediction of the theory refers to the determinants of incumbents' popularity (Besley and Case 1995; Revelli 2002a). According to yardstick competition, voters hold the government responsible for its fiscal performance relative to neighboring jurisdictions. Consequently, the popularity of the incumbent party in jurisdiction $i - p_i$ in equation (4.11) – should be negatively correlated with the own tax t_i ($\pi_i \leq 0$ in equation (4.34), below) and positively correlated with the tax in jurisdictions that experience similar cost shocks t_n ($\pi_2 > 0$ in equation (4.34)):

$$p_i = p(t_i, t_n, Z_i) = \pi_0 + \pi_1 t_i + \pi_2 t_n + Z_i \iota + u_i, \qquad (4.34)$$

where u_i is a random shock affecting the popularity of the incumbent, and ι is a vector of parameters to be estimated along with π_0, π_1 and π_2.

Estimation of equation (4.34), however, poses some econometric problems. In fact, the policy variables on the right-hand side of a popularity equation – t_i and t_n – cannot be assumed strictly exogenous (Paldam 1997). The shock to the incumbent's popularity (u_i) may be correlated with the local tax, if incumbents try to counterbalance those shocks by varying their policies and adapting them to their perceived popularity (Revelli 2002a).[12]

As a result, the proper way of estimating equation (4.34) is to adopt an IV approach, which consists first in regressing t_i and t_n on a set of exogenous variables, and then in using the predicted values of t_i and t_n as instruments. Clearly, then, the best way to estimate a yardstick competition model is to estimate the tax determination equation (4.13) and the popularity equation jointly in a system of simultaneous equations (as in Besley and Case 1995).

Finally, it could be argued that voters are concerned about the relative change in taxes, rather than their levels, in the sense that a government that increases taxes during its term of office is more likely to be punished at the polls if the other governments are not doing so. In that case, the popularity equation should be expressed as:

$$p_i = p(t_i, t_n, Z_i) = \pi_0 + \pi_1 \Delta t_i + \pi_2 \Delta t_n + Z_i \iota + u_i \qquad (4.35)$$

where again own and neighbors' tax changes require instrumentation to solve the endogeneity problem.

The appealing aspect of estimating a popularity equation is that an impact of neighbors' taxes on an incumbent's chances of re-election can hardly be reconciled with theories other than yardstick competition. In particular, it has been argued (Besley and Case 1995; Bordignon et al. 2003) that the empirical implications of yardstick competition theory depend on the information set of voters, in the sense that if voters understand the determinants of tax changes, they should penalize incumbent governments only for 'unanticipated' tax changes. In particular, if voters know the non-stochastic determinants of the costs of public services in own and neighboring jurisdictions (such as the basic costs of public services, as well as, in a more general framework, the quality and variety of public services that are provided), only the tax change that is 'unexplained' should have a negative impact on the popularity of the incumbent in equation (4.35). As a result, testing whether anticipated versus unanticipated tax changes have a heterogeneous impact on the popularity of incumbents represents a potentially powerful test of the voter information hypothesis upon which yardstick competition theory is based.[13]

Natural experiments
In some instances, identification of the theoretical model generating the observed spatial pattern in the data is eased if external information can be used that affects the intergovernmental interaction pattern in an exogenous way. In other words, sometimes the researcher might exploit the fact that the framework, rules or institutions within which local authorities operate vary exogenously, either across local jurisdictions and/or over time, providing identification conditions in a sort of natural experiment.

As far as the exploitation of exogenous intergovernmental differences is concerned, the first examples in the literature are represented by Case (1993) and Besley and Case (1995). They rely on the different electoral prospects of US state governors due to the existence of term limits, and find that governors who cannot run for re-election because of a binding term limit – an exogenous constraint on some state governors – are less sensitive to neighbors' tax changes than are governors who are eligible for re-election.

A similar term limit effect is found for Italian municipality mayors by Bordignon et al. (2003), in the sense that mayors who cannot run for re-election appear to be less sensitive to neighbors' fiscal policies. Furthermore, Bordignon et al. exploit a further form of exogenous crosssectional heterogeneity among incumbent governments. Controlling for the size of majorities supporting the mayors in power, they find that mayors who are supported by large majorities, and for which the electoral threat is consequently less severe, tend to be less sensitive to neighboring jurisdictions' policies. A similar result emerges in Spanish local government (Solé-Ollé 2003).

Evidence of heterogeneous behavior of politicians depending on their exogenous status reinforces the hypothesis that yardstick competition – and not other forces, such as the sheer presence of correlated shocks – is driving local government taxing decisions and spatial interaction patterns.

On the other hand, in her test of strategic interaction among US states, Case (1993) exploits the fact that, after the US reform of 1986, which reduces federal marginal tax rates (TRA86), increases in state taxes are costlier to taxpayers who deduct state taxes. She finds that after TRA86, governors become more sensitive to neighbors' behavior and align their tax changes more closely with those observed in neighboring states.

Along a similar line of reasoning, in an analysis of UK local government, Bivand and Szymanski (1997, 2000) find that, while there is substantial spatial dependence in the costs of domestic garbage collection in the UK districts, due to contracts based on performance comparison and local yardstick competition, spatial interactions are substantially reduced after the nationwide introduction of compulsive competitive tendering (CCT), which imposes standard contracting rules and reduces the scope for local authorities to pursue idiosyncratic policies. Clearly, if spatial interaction were due to factors other than yardstick competition, the introduction of CCT would not affect it substantially.

Finally, Revelli (2006) analyses the impact of national systems of evaluation of local government performance on local patterns of spatial interaction. In an analysis of local provision of social services, Revelli finds that spatial interaction is substantially reduced after the introduction, in 2001, of a national performance assessment system that has the main objective of improving public information on social service provision performance. It is then possible to conclude that the interaction observed before 2001 was most likely due to yardstick competition arising from a local information spillover, instead of being the result of other possible sources of interdependence (such as welfare competition or sheer correlated shocks).

Horizontal and vertical interactions
It could be argued that, within a multi-tiered structure of government, the policies enacted by upper levels of government might have a potentially important impact on the policies of lower-tier governments – such as, say, changes in federal tax rates on state and local tax rates and expenditures. However, it seems that the fiscal federalism literature, and particularly the tax competition one, has mainly focused on horizontal interactions, while mostly disregarding vertical fiscal interactions. As Keen (1998) puts it: 'A key ingredient of any coherent theory of fiscal federalism must be a clear understanding of the interaction between federal and state governments, an interaction that has commonly been neglected in the traditional literature' (p. 457).

The above point has only recently been seriously considered within the empirical strategic interaction literature. In particular, recent papers by Esteller-Moré and Solé-Ollé (2001), Goodspeed (2002), Hayashi and Boadway (2001) and Devereux et al. (2004) estimate more general models that allow both for various forms of vertical fiscal externalities and for horizontal fiscal interaction.

Esteller-Moré and Solé-Ollé (2001, 2002) estimate an income tax rate setting equation for US states (Canadian provinces) that allows both for vertical tax interaction with the federal government and for horizontal tax interactions among neighboring states (provinces). Hayashi and Boadway (2001) analyse corporate income tax setting by federal and provincial governments in Canada, and estimate separate tax setting equations with vertical and horizontal effects for the federal government, the two major provinces, and an aggregate of the other provinces. Goodspeed (2002) focuses on local–national tax externalities in a number of OECD countries, and controls for horizontal tax competition by introducing a proxy for tax base mobility (a poverty index) in a country-based local income tax equation. Finally, Devereux et al. (2004) analyse interstate and federal–state competition in excise taxes on cigarettes and gasoline in the United States.

While considering both forms of interaction can somewhat complicate the analysis, it might be true that allowing for vertical fiscal interactions can help identify horizontal fiscal interactions. In an analysis of local government property taxation by the two tiers of local government in non-metropolitan areas of England, Revelli (2001) argues that controlling for correlation in tax rates between lower-tier (district) authorities and upper-tier (county) authorities can help conclude whether a spatial pattern in property tax rates among lower-tier authorities ought to be attributed to spatially auto-correlated shocks or to genuine interaction. The idea is that, if spatial correlation in local tax rates between governments of the same level is simply attributable to the presence of spatially correlated shocks and has no substantive relevance, then one will also expect the tax rates of the lower tier of government to be correlated with the tax rates of the upper tier, because they share the same tax base and are likely to be hit by the same shock. On the other hand, if tax mimicking is driving the spatial dependence in local tax rates, one should expect to find no vertical correlation in tax rates between districts and counties.

In a further study of English local government expenditures on environmental services, Revelli (2003) finds that, when vertical expenditure externalities among upper- and lower-tier authorities are explicitly taken into account (because of complementarity/substitutability between public expenditures of the two levels of government), the estimated magnitude of between-districts interaction is substantially reduced, and concludes that the observed positive spatial auto-correlation among district expenditures can be attributed to a large extent to common reaction to county expenditures, rather than to actual strategic interaction.

Clearly, thorough consideration of vertical fiscal externalities in an empirical model of horizontal strategic interactions is a rather challenging task, mostly because it requires making specific assumptions – and properly testing for them – about the nature of the relationship between upper- and lower-tier governments, and exploring the impact of such vertical interaction process of horizontal spatial patterns. However, investigating in depth the role of central government in affecting the spatial patterns in subnational government taxes and expenditures seems to represent an important topic for future research.

Concluding remarks

The past decade has witnessed a surge of empirical research on strategic interaction among local governments. This chapter has reviewed such literature, by first grouping the existing studies into broad categories, depending on the assumed channel of interaction (preferences, constraints and expectations), and then highlighting the main issues that emerge in the specification of the empirical model and pointing towards the most frequent problems that one encounters in empirical implementation.

The analysis of the existing empirical literature shows that model specification and estimation are crucial steps for correctly identifying the underlying source of spatial interaction. In particular, it turns out that alternative theoretical models give similar empirical predictions in terms of spatial reaction functions. Consequently, any attempt to uncover spatial interaction phenomena should take into account that estimation of a reduced-form interjurisdictional policy reaction function might not by itself allow discriminating among competing theoretical hypotheses of spatial interaction, such as tax competition, expenditure spillovers and yardstick competition.

As a result, further theoretical effort seems to be required to get neater predictions on the sign – and possibly on the shape – of the fiscal reaction function, as well as to give guidance as far as more realistic yet complicated interaction patterns are concerned, such as the possibility of multidimensional policy reaction functions. The latter approach could be particularly suited to analyse empirically the competition for businesses and tax bases in an economically integrated world, where a number of heterogeneous policy instruments are involved.

Moreover, it turns out that using the appropriate estimation techniques – which can be based either on an IV/2SLS principle, or on ML techniques – is essential to avoid mistaking the sheer presence of correlated shocks (a fairly common phenomenon when dealing with local government data) for actual strategic interaction. Actually, it seems that proper modeling of a spatial structure in the error term is crucial for discriminating between 'exogenous' correlated effects that have no behavioral significance, and 'endogenous' effects that reflect a process of strategic interaction. This modeling effort seems particularly important in yardstick competition research, where the presence of common or correlated shocks is a necessary condition for relative performance evaluation to be meaningful.

It seems that a promising way to improve our understanding of strategic interaction phenomena in future empirical research is represented by fully exploiting the theory, in particular by estimating – along with the traditional fiscal reaction function – 'auxiliary' equations that can be directly derived from the theory, such as popularity equations in yardstick competition models and tax base determination equation in tax competition and welfare competition models.

While estimation of such auxiliary equations is admittedly costly in terms of data requirements, and can pose formidable theoretical as well as empirical problems when spatial considerations are taken into account, it promises to represent a substantial step forward in our understanding of strategic interaction phenomena. In fact, estimation of structural political economy models seems to constitute a very powerful instrument in order to discriminate between competing theoretical explanations of local strategic interaction that have indeed very different normative and policy implications.

Finally, the main insight of the chapter for the estimation of spatial reaction functions in empirical local public finance consists in exploiting the presence of exogenous factors that can affect subnational governments in different ways and consequently yield heterogeneous spatial interaction responses. Those factors can be represented either by the presence of particular institutional arrangements (such as the presence of a multi-tiered structure of government that generates vertical fiscal externalities, or the existence of asymmetric federal structures) or by the role of exogenous policy shocks (such as the introduction of central government caps on local government expenditures, or the presence of exogenous sources of cross-sectional heterogeneity, such as different electoral rules or term limits) as identification conditions in a sort of 'natural experiment'.

Clearly, a lot remains to be learned about strategic interaction among subnational governments in multi-tiered fiscal structures. In particular, the employment of spatial econometric techniques to the analysis of fiscal interactions at the international level promises to be a most fruitful research topic in this area, due to the increasing importance of tax and yardstick competition phenomena that seem to go well beyond the traditional national boundaries.

Notes

1. I would like to thank participants in the 'Handbook on Fiscal Federalism' seminar held in Moncalieri-Turin (August 2004), and particularly the editors Ehtisham Ahmad and Giorgio Brosio for very helpful comments. All remaining errors and omissions are my responsibility.
2. However, they also envisage other possible rationales for interaction among the states – see the expectations interaction discussion in the next section.

3. Formally, whether $\partial g_i / \partial g_n$ is positive or negative depends on the second partial derivatives of the local welfare function (Case et al. 1993).
4. A particular 'resource flow' is considered in Kelejian and Robinson (1993), who find that police expenditures in US counties are significantly and positively influenced by neighboring county police expenditures, based on the idea that, since counties inflict a negative externality on their neighbors by spending more on police services due to crossovers between the borders, the need for police services in a given county tends to increase as such services in neighboring counties increase.
5. Y_i can include climate, availability of natural resources, infrastructure and overall business climate, depending on the model.
6. In tax competition models, a higher level of b_i raises private consumption c_i by raising the marginal productivity of labor (wages). As for public spending, a higher level of b_i increases tax revenues for a given tax rate.
7. Brueckner and Saavedra (2001) show that the slope of the reaction function may be positive or negative.
8. However, Bordignon et al. (2004) argue that in some instances correlation could be negative, as long as a bad government's chances of re-election are so low that, in the presence of low taxes in the neighborhood, it prefers to accumulate the maximum rent in the first period, at the expense of losing the elections.
9. Actually, the property of being a model-driven approach instead of a data-driven orientation is what makes spatial econometrics different from spatial statistics (Anselin 1988).
10. For a row-standardized spatial weights matrix, the term (N/S_0) disappears.
11. The Kelejian and Prucha (1998) procedure is employed in a local public finance context by Buettner (2003).
12. For instance, an incumbent seeking re-election in a time of low popularity can try and gain consensus by cutting the local tax. On the other hand, if an incumbent is confident of re-election (either because a certain target of popularity is surpassed, or because he/she expects not to be opposed by any serious contender), he/she can pursue his/her surplus goal, raise the local tax and expect to remain in office.
13. Furthermore, yardstick competition should then generate spatial auto-correlation in tax rates (or tax rate changes) only as far as the unpredicted component of the tax is concerned, thus making it possible to discriminate empirically tax from yardstick competition phenomena (Bordignon et al. 2003).

References

Anselin, L. (1988), *Spatial Econometrics: Methods and Models,* Dordrecht: Kluwer Academic.
Anselin, L., K. Bera, R. Florax and M. Yoon (1996), 'Simple diagnostic tests for spatial dependence', *Regional Science and Urban Economics*, Vol. 26, pp. 77–104.
Anselin, L. and R. Florax (1995), 'Small sample properties of tests for spatial dependence in regression models: some further results', in Anselin and Florax (eds), *New Directions in Spatial Econometrics,* Heidelberg: Springer, pp. 21–74.
Anselin, L. and S. Rey (1991), 'Properties of tests for spatial dependence in linear regression models', *Geographical Analysis*, Vol. 23, pp. 112–31.
Baicker, K. (2005), 'The spillover effects of state spending', *Journal of Public Economics*, Vol. 89, pp. 529–44.
Besley, T. and A. Case (1995), 'Incumbent behavior: vote seeking, tax setting, and yardstick competition', *American Economic Review*, Vol. 85, pp. 25–45.
Bivand, R. and S. Szymanski (1997), 'Spatial dependence through local yardstick competition: theory and testing', *Economics Letters*, Vol. 55, pp. 257–65.
Bivand, R. and S. Szymanski (2000), 'Modeling the spatial impact of the introduction of compulsive competitive tendering', *Regional Science and Urban Economics*, Vol. 30, pp. 203–19.
Bordignon, M., F. Cerniglia and F. Revelli (2003), 'In search of yardstick competition: a spatial analysis of Italian municipality property tax setting', *Journal of Urban Economics*, Vol. 54, pp. 199–217.

Bordignon, M., F. Cerniglia and F. Revelli (2004), 'Yardstick competition in intergovernmental relationships: theory and empirical predictions', *Economics Letters*, Vol. 83, pp. 325–33.

Brett, C. and J. Pinkse (2000), 'The determinants of municipal tax rates in British Columbia', *Canadian Journal of Economics*, Vol. 33, pp. 695–714.

Brueckner, J. (1998), 'Testing for strategic interaction among local governments: the case of growth controls', *Journal of Urban Economics*, Vol. 44, pp. 438–67.

Brueckner, J. (2000), 'Welfare reform and the race to the bottom: theory and evidence', *Southern Economic Journal*, Vol. 66, pp. 505–25.

Brueckner, J. (2003), 'Strategic interaction among governments: an overview of empirical studies', *International Regional Science Review*, Vol. 26, pp. 175–88.

Brueckner, J. and L. Saavedra (2001), 'Do local governments engage in strategic property tax competition?', *National Tax Journal*, Vol. 54, pp. 203–29.

Buettner, T. (2001), 'Local business taxation and competition for capital: the choice of the tax rate', *Regional Science and Urban Economics*, Vol. 31, pp. 215–45.

Brueckner, J. (2003), 'Tax base effects and fiscal externalities of local capital taxation: evidence from a panel of German jurisdictions', *Journal of Urban Economics*, Vol. 54, pp. 110–28.

Case, A. (1991), 'Spatial patterns in household demand', *Econometrica*, Vol. 59, pp. 953–65.

Case, A. (1993), 'Interstate tax competition after TRA86', *Journal of Policy Analysis and Management*, Vol. 12, pp. 136–48.

Case, A., J. Hines and H. Rosen (1993), 'Budget spillovers and fiscal policy interdependence', *Journal of Public Economics*, Vol. 52, pp. 285–307.

Cliff, A. and J. Ord (1981), *Spatial Processes: Models and Applications*, London: Pion.

Devereux, M., R. Griffith and A. Klemm (2002a), 'Corporate income tax reforms and international tax competition', *Economic Policy: A European Forum*, Vol. 17, pp. 450–95.

Devereux, M., B. Lockwood and M. Redoano (2002b), 'Do countries compete over corporate tax rates?', CEPR Discussion Paper No. 3400, London.

Devereux, M., B. Lockwood and M. Redoano (2004), 'Horizontal and vertical indirect tax competition: theory and some evidence from the USA', Warwick Economic Research Papers No. 704.

Dowding, K., P. John and S. Biggs (1994), 'Tiebout: a survey of the empirical literature', *Urban Studies*, Vol. 31, pp. 767–97.

Esteller-Moré, A. and A. Solé-Ollé (2001), 'Vertical income tax externalities and fiscal interdependence: evidence from the US', *Regional Science and Urban Economics*, Vol. 31, pp. 247–72.

Esteller-Moré, A. and A. Solé-Ollé (2002), 'Tax setting in a federal system: the case of personal income taxation in Canada', *International Tax and Public Finance*, Vol. 9, pp. 235–57.

Feld, L. (1997), 'Exit, voice and income taxes: the loyalty of voters', *European Journal of Political Economy*, Vol. 13, pp. 455–78.

Feld, L. and G. Kirchgassner (2001), 'Income tax competition at the state and local level in Switzerland', *Regional Science and Urban Economics*, Vol. 31, pp. 181–213.

Figlio, D., V. Kolpin and W. Reid (1999), 'Do states play welfare games?', *Journal of Urban Economics*, Vol. 46, pp. 437–54.

Fredriksson, P. and D. Millimet (2002a), 'Strategic interaction and the determination of environmental policy across US states', *Journal of Urban Economics*, Vol. 51, pp. 101–22.

Fredriksson, P. and D. Millimet (2002b), 'Is there a "California effect" in US environmental policy making?', *Regional Science and Urban Economics*, Vol. 32, pp. 737–64.

Fredriksson, P., D. Millimet and J. List (2004), 'Chasing the smokestack: strategic policymaking with multiple instruments', *Regional Science and Urban Economics*, Vol. 34, pp. 387–410.

Goodspeed, T. (2000), 'Tax structure in a federation', *Journal of Public Economics*, Vol. 75 493–506.

Goodspeed, T. (2002), 'Tax competition and tax structure in open federal economies: evidence from OECD countries with implications for the European Union', *European Economic Review*, Vol. 46, pp. 357–74.

Hayashi, M. and R. Boadway (2001), 'An empirical analysis of intergovernmental tax interaction: the case of business income taxes in Canada', *Canadian Journal of Economics*, Vol. 34, pp. 481–503.

Heyndels, B. and J. Vuchelen (1998), 'Tax mimicking among Belgian municipalities', *National Tax Journal*, Vol. 51, pp. 89–101.

Keen, M. (1998), 'Vertical fiscal externalities in the theory of fiscal federalism', *IMF Staff Papers*, Vol. 45, pp. 454–85.

Kelejian, H. and I. Prucha (1998), 'A generalised spatial two stage least squares procedure for estimating a spatial autoregressive model with autoregressive disturbances', *Journal of Real Estate Finance and Economics*, Vol. 17, pp. 99–121.

Kelejian, H. and D. Robinson (1993), 'A suggested method of estimation for spatial interdependent models with auto-correlated errors, and an application to a county expenditure model', *Papers in Regional Science*, Vol. 72, pp. 297–312.

Ladd, H. (1992), 'Mimicking of local tax burdens among neighboring counties', *Public Finance Quarterly*, Vol. 20, pp. 450–67.

Levinson, A. (2003), 'Environmental regulatory competition: a status report and some new evidence', *National Tax Journal*, Vol. 56, pp. 91–106.

Manski, C. (1993), 'Identification of endogenous social effects: the reflection problem', *Review of Economic Studies*, Vol. 60, pp. 531–42.

Manski, C. (2000), 'Economic analysis of social interactions,' NBER Working Paper No. 7580, Cambridge, A: National Bureau of Economic Research.

Murdoch, J., M. Rahmatian and M. Thayer (1993), A spatially autoregressive median voter model of recreation expenditures', *Public Finance Quarterly*, Vol. 21, pp. 334–50.

Paldam, M. (1997), 'Political business cycles', in D. Mueller (ed.), *Perspectives on Public Choice: A Handbook*, Cambridge, New York: Cambridge University Press, pp. 342–70.

Revelli, F. (2001), 'Spatial patterns in local taxation: tax mimicking or error mimicking?', *Applied Economics*, Vol. 33, pp. 1101–7.

Revelli, F. (2002a), 'Local taxes, national politics, and spatial interactions in English district election results', *European Journal of Political Economy*, Vol. 18, pp. 281–99.

Revelli, F. (2002b), 'Testing the tax mimicking versus expenditure spillover hypotheses using English data', *Applied Economics*, Vol. 34, pp. 1723–31.

Revelli, F. (2003), 'Reaction or interaction? Spatial process identification in multi-tiered government structures', *Journal of Urban Economics*, Vol. 53, pp. 29–53.

Revelli, F. (2006), 'Performance rating and yardstick competition in social service provision', *Journal of Public Economics*, Vol. 90, pp. 459–75.

Saavedra, L. (2000), 'A model of welfare competition with evidence from AFDC', *Journal of Urban Economics*, Vol. 47, pp. 248–79.

Salmon, P. (1987), 'Decentralization as an incentive scheme', *Oxford Review of Economic Policy*, Vol. 3, pp. 24–43.

Schaltegger, C. and D. Kuttel (2002), 'Exit, voice, and mimicking behavior: evidence from Swiss cantons', *Public Choice*, Vol. 113, pp. 1–23.

Shroder, M. (1995), 'Games the states don't play: welfare benefits and the theory of fiscal federalism', *Review of Economics and Statistics*, Vol. 77, pp. 183–91.

Smith, P. (1991), 'An empirical investigation of interstate AFDC benefit competition', *Public Choice*, Vol. 68, pp. 217–33.

Solé-Ollé, A. (2003), 'Electoral accountability and tax mimicking: the effects of electoral margins, coalition government, and ideology', *European Journal of Political Economy*, Vol. 19, pp. 685–713.

Tiebout, C. (1956), 'A pure theory of local expenditures', *Journal of Political Economy*, Vol. 64, pp. 416–24.

Wheaton, W. (2000), 'Decentralized welfare: will there be underprovision?', *Journal of Urban Economics*, Vol. 48, pp. 536–55.

Wilson, J. (1999), 'Theories of tax competition', *National Tax Journal*, Vol. 53, pp. 269–304.

5 Asymmetric federalism and the political economy of decentralization

Roger D. Congleton

Introduction

A broad range of theoretical and empirical work on federalism is based on the implicit assumption that subnational governments within federal systems are more or less equally sized and equally influential. This idea seems to be based on the intuition that the production and distribution of public services by local governments have properties similar to those of competitive firms. At a competitive Tiebout equilibrium, each government at a given level of governance in a federal system tends to be that which provides services to its residents at least cost. Consequently, all jurisdictions that produce the same mix of government services are approximately the same efficient size, and a federal system will be composed of more or less homogeneous local governments. Only efficiently-sized communities survive in a fiscally competitive environment, because least-cost producers of government services always attract residents and tax base away from less optimally-sized jurisdictions.

The Tiebout model is a useful characterization of many locational decisions in which production economies and competition may be presumed to play a significant part in the decisions reached. However, the assumption of uniform jurisdictional size and power is a less useful foundation for county, city and state levels of analysis. Here we observe significant differences in physical size, population, income and political representation for state and local governments. In the United States, California is physically the third-largest state with 11 per cent of the citizens, whereas Wyoming, the sixth-largest state includes less than 1 per cent of the US population. Requejo (1996) notes that New South Wales includes 35 per cent of the population of Australia, whereas Tasmania includes less than 3 per cent. North Rhine Westfalia includes some 21 per cent of the population of Germany, whereas Bremen includes less than 1 per cent of the population. Uttar Pradesh includes 16 per cent of the population of India, whereas Sikkim includes less than a twentieth of 1 per cent. That population and population densities vary so widely implies that demands for local services also tend to vary widely among these regional governments and, moreover, implies that political power within their respective democratic central governments is also likely to vary widely by state, *Land* and province.

That regional interests and bargaining power vary is important for fiscal federalism, because national constitutions do not fully specify the degree of decentralization within a nation at any single point in time or through time. Rather, the degree of decentralization is determined by a series of political bargains within and between national and regional legislatures in which both the details of policy and the powers to make policies are negotiated and rene-gotiated through time. Consequently, any differences in the bargaining power and interests among participating governments is likely to affect the distribution of fiscal and regulatory authority adopted.[1]

Of course, it is possible that unequal populations and resources have no effect on the political bargains that determine decentralization. Each state, province, autonomous region, *Land* and city might have essentially identical regulatory, tax and expenditure authority. The distribution of political power within a federal system could be bound by a political generality rule, as implicitly assumed in most analyses of fiscal federalism. However, in practice unequal bargaining power has often led to agreements that generate different degrees of authority to different state and local governments.

For example, in Spain, Navarra and the Basque communities have formal tax and expenditure powers beyond those of the other 'autonomous communi-ties'. Galicia and Catalonia have special authority over education, language and culture. In Canada, Quebec has special powers to encourage the use of the French language and protect the French-Canadian culture. In the United Kingdom, the Scottish parliament has significantly more policy-making authority than the Welsh parliament. In the United States, Indian reservations have their own specific taxing and regulatory authority that differ from those of ordinary state governments. California, the most populous state, has unique powers of environmental regulation.[2] In China, Hong Kong has been granted unique legal and political institutions: 'one country, two systems'. Indeed, large cities in many countries often have powers of taxation and regulation that smaller cities lack or rarely use. New York City and Washington, DC have their own income and sales taxes.

Asymmetries are also common among the members of large international organizations. In the European Union (EU), some members retain more auton-omy than others inasmuch as they have opted out of or delayed membership in the menu of treaties that define the responsibilities of affiliated countries. The responsibilities of members of the United Nations with respect to military armaments, human rights and environmental regulations are similarly defined through a series of treaties with quite different signatories. Different nations formally retain different degrees of autonomy both within and without these very decentralized confederations.

Overall, the more carefully one examines the distribution of fiscal and regulatory authority within nation states and international organizations, the more asymmetries one finds. Congleton et al. (2003) refer to such voluntary systems of centralization and decentralization as 'menu federalism'.

Although constitutional documents often specify federal structures of governance that constrain the permissible range of political bargains that may be reached, it is ordinary legislation that ultimately determines which levels of government control which policies, taxes and legislation, at least at the margin. This also tends to be true of unitary governments that lack some of the formal institutional features of a federal government (a provincial or regional council, or senate). Fiscal responsibilities within unitary states are often distributed among many layers of more or less independent governments in which the power to make fiscal decisions at provincial and local levels is the result of negotiations within legislatures and between particular levels of governance. As a consequence, many federal and unitary states have highly decentralized fiscal and regulatory systems, while others are highly centralized. The German *Länder* have little power of taxation, while the substantial income tax of Sweden is a local matter, rather than a national one.

This chapter attempts to explain in economic and political terms the emergence of decentralized governance in general, and of asymmetric federalism in particular, and their implications for government finance, service levels and intergovernmental competition.

The following section provides an illustrating example of the consequences of unequal policy-making authority at one level of governance. In general, communities with greater authority to make their own policies have a competitive advantage over their fellow communities that lack such powers. The subsequent two sections analyse why communities, none the less, often have somewhat unequal authority to make public policies. The analysis shows that the federal structures are a natural consequence of fiscal bargaining, and that asymmetries emerge, because of differences in the perceived political risk and economic advantages associated with delegating policy-making authority to central governments. The penultimate section explores other political implications of asymmetric fiscal federalism. For example, the average degree of asymmetry that emerges in under- and overcentralized states tends to differ, because different marginal states control the degree of centralization that is adopted. The asymmetries that emerge are also affected by the institutional setting in which negotiations take place. Asymmetries tend to be smaller in democracies with a very mobile population than in authoritarian regimes with a relatively less mobile population. The final section summarizes the results and suggests further extensions.

The approach is contractarian in spirit in that decentralization is analysed as a consequence of voluntary agreements between communities and central governments. This is not to deny that methods other than negotiation have generated multilevel governance, but for the most part asymmetric decentralization within modern states reflects agreements rather than wars of conquest or threats of secession. Moreover, the existence of mutual gains provides a survivorship rationale for the continuation and success of more or less decentralized states once established. The standard tools of public choice, public finance and constitutional political economy are used to analyse the agreements that might be reached between central and provincial governments. Historical examples are used to illustrate the relevance of the analysis.

Mobility and the long-run economic consequences of asymmetric fiscal federalism

Asymmetric federalism exists whenever governments at the same level of geographic responsibility – towns, counties, cities or states – have different regulatory and fiscal powers. Such differences in policy authorities create a 'supply-side' source of variation in government services, regulations and taxes in addition to the standard demand-side variation in local demand stressed in models of local fiscal competition, as developed elsewhere in this volume. Asymmetries in the supply side of the fiscal contest can have substantial effects on the distribution of services, persons and income within a nation state or international community.

For example, consider the case in which only a single city is granted authority to use eminent domain to produce 'rights of way' for light rail transport services. Suppose that the favored city sells or rents the rights of way to private railroad companies. This provides the city with a unique source of revenue and also a unique economic advantage. Both effects allow the more autonomous government to provide a more attractive fiscal and economic environment for its residents than is possible for otherwise similar governments.

Light rail has the effect of reducing transport costs to city apartments, shops and factories that operate in an otherwise competitive market. Individuals prefer to work for firms that are close to the rail lines, and consumers prefer to live and shop at stores near the rail lines – other things being equal – because the net of transport real wages are higher and net of transport prices are lower along the rail lines. This increases net benefits and profits for consumers and firms located near the rail lines. Moreover, rental revenue from the right of ways allows the favored city to reduce other tax rates within the city.

Given these economic advantages, persons and firms from within the favored city *and throughout the country of interest* will attempt to relocate near to the rail lines of the favored city. In principle, the favored city continues expanding its rail network and attracting tax base up to the point where the marginal increase in revenue and tax base generated by an extra kilometer of new right of way equals the marginal cost of the right of way less any loss in tax base generated by investor fears concerning the use of eminent domain – or until no private firm is willing to expand its rail network because traffic densities are too low to recover its costs. The latter, of course, expands outward from the city center as immigration of capital and labor occurs.

Although there is a limit to the urban growth encouraged by this city's unique power of eminent domain, the favored city becomes an important commercial and cultural center well before this limit is reached. Its internal market and population expands; specialization increases; and wages and profits increase as productivity rise. Other cities that have to rely entirely upon private provision of rail services falter, because holdout problems make assembling long rights of way very difficult – indeed intractable – for private firms acting alone. The more autonomous city grows and prospers – while other similar cities that would have copied the strategy of the favored city are legally unable to do so.

Other local fiscal and regulatory 'privileges' can have similar effects, in so far as the additional authority allows favored governments to provide a more attractive fiscal package than is legally possible for other similar governments.

If favored governments take advantage of their additional authority, residents and tax base will be attracted to their communities, and those communities will prosper relative to others. In this manner, asymmetric distributions of fiscal and regulatory power may amplify pre-existing asymmetries in population, wealth and political power. The expectation of these greater regional inequalities, in turn, tends to produce additional political demands for provincial, urban and local autonomy – but also creates demands that such asymmetries be limited.

The next two sections analyse political gains to trade associated with reallocating fiscal and regulatory authority within under- and overcentralized states. These political gains to trade imply that asymmetries in the legally permitted scope of local policy formation will be commonplace. The fourth section discusses some political and economic limits to the process of reallocating political authority among levels of government.

Emergence of asymmetric federalism within an 'undercentralized' state

Historically, most national governments emerged by assembling and merging local and provincial governments. In some cases, the amalgamation of regional governments was the result of military force, as might be said of modern states of Great Britain, Japan, Italy and Germany. In others, national governments have been formed by a series of treaties among regional governments, many of which were catalysed by military threats, as might be said of the Netherlands, the United States and Switzerland. In either case, the resulting nation states tend to be composed of many levels of governance, and gains to political exchange between local, state and national governments often exist. Such gains to trade tend to exist both at the time the nation state is assembled and through time as political circumstances change.

Many of these intranational political gains from trade affect the extent of decentralization – the extent to which state, county and local governments have independent policy-making authority on particular fiscal policies and regulations. This section of the chapter analyses the advantages of transferring authority from local to central authorities in an initially undercentralized state.

Mutual advantages from further coordination of policies at a particular level of government may arise for a variety of economic reasons, as noted in the other chapters: sharing the fixed costs of new or expanded public services, increased opportunities for social risk pooling, the internalization of regional and international externalities, advantages associated with expanded markets, and, in some cases, reduced tax competition among regional governments.

The advantage of centralizing policy-making authority, however, is largely *reduced decision costs*, rather than the economic advantages associated with greater coordination, because centralization is not the only method of solving coordination problems or of realizing economies of scale. Multilateral agreements among governments, however, are often difficult to negotiate, because they require unanimous agreement among the contracting parties. In agreeing to centralize some policy decisions, member governments (states) normally sacrifice complete political control (veto) for partial control. That is to say, centralization of policy-making authority often replaces unanimity with a somewhat less inclusive decision rule. As a consequence, the costs of coordinating policy choices fall, but a new risk is created. The service levels and cost allocations of the central authority may make one or all participants worse off – even if constrained to policy areas in which mutual advantages from centralizing policy-making authority exist (Buchanan and Tullock 1962).

Thus, both the advantages and the disadvantages of centralization, *per se*, are largely political in nature, although the benefits from increased policy coordination and from the realization of economies of scale are largely economic – as noted by several of the other chapters in this volume.

To centralize or not? Political and economic considerations
Consider the case in which local governments may individually choose whether to participate or not in a new centralized program that will henceforth determine a particular public policy for all member states using some form of majority rule.[3]

The net benefit of joining a centralized authority is partly determined by anticipated cost savings from the greater scale or scope of production as well as reduced negotiation costs and also by expectations about the manner in which potential savings are to be distributed among member states. Local governments agree to the centralized control of a service if their governments expect to realize net advantages from that control. For the purposes of this chapter, it is assumed that local political incentives are correlated with local net benefits, as tends to be the case in competitive democratic governments.

Let P_{ij} be the probability that local government j is a member of the decisive coalition on issue i, and let $1 - P_{ij}$ be the probability that it is in the minority coalition. The anticipated benefit if government j is a member of the majority (on service i) is B^M_{ji}, which rationality implies cannot be smaller than that associated with minority status, B^N_{ji}. Member states in the majority coalition bear cost C^M_{ji} for public service i which cannot be larger than j would have paid as a member of the minority coalition, C^N_{ji}. If state j does not join the confederation, or if the confederation chooses not to provide service i centrally, state j produces government service i independently and realizes a net benefit of N_{ji} from its own independent production.[4]

State j favors service i being provided by the central government iff:

$$P_{ji}(B^M_{ji} - C^M_{ji}) + (1 - P_{ji})(B^N_{ji} - C^N_{ji}) > N_{ji} \text{ and } N_{ji} \geq 0. \qquad (5.1)$$

Equation (5.1) makes it clear that both economic and political factors enter into decisions to provide services centrally. If both $B^M_{ji} - C^M_{ji}$ and $B^N_{ji} - C^N_{ji}$ exceed N_{ji}, then economic considerations are sufficient to justify centralizing provision of service i – given the existing political and technological constraints. In cases in which the net advantage for the advantaged (majority) groups exceeds that of independent production, $B^M_{ji} - C^M_{ji} > N_{ij}$, but those associated with the disadvantaged (minority) group are below those of independent production, $B^N_{ji} - C^N_{ji} < N_{ij}$, it is clear that political considerations largely determine whether state j favors centralized or independent provision of service i. In this latter case, both the size of the fiscal differential across majority and minority groups and the probability of being in the minority (non-decisive) coalition influence the demand for centralized services.

Once the range of services to be centrally provided is determined, the expected net benefit of participation can be computed by adding up the expected net benefits across all services. Within service areas bound by a generality rule, membership is essentially an all-or-nothing choice and all members will receive more or less the same array of services. State j transfers policy-making authority in these areas to the central government if:

$$\sum_i [P_{ji}(B^M_{ji} - C^M_{ji}) + (1 - P_{ji})(B^N_{ji} - C^N_{ji})] > \sum_i N_{ji}. \qquad (5.2)$$

The last member to join the centralized authority, the marginal member, is essentially indifferent between confederal and independent production.

Non-members believe that the net advantage of the entire political and economic package is less than zero. Their net benefits from additional coordination and economies of scale are too small to offset the political risks of centralization.

The importance of political institutions for voluntary centralization
If confederal members are attempting to realize economies of scale in the production of government services or internalize regulatory externalities, it is clear that the number of participants matters. The more members, the greater are the economies of scale and the more fully are regulatory externalities taken into account. Consequently, both members and non-members have an interest in adopting institutions that reduce the perceived political risk of centralization, at least at the margin. Reduced risks induce more governments to participate and increase the *economic* advantages of membership.

Equations (5.1) and (5.2) imply that two general categories of institutions can reduce the downside risk of minority status: (i) adopting voting rules with a more demanding qualified majority and (ii) reducing the central confederal government's ability to discriminate among potential members. Such institutions increase the range of services that member states can agree to provide jointly, because they increase the expected net benefits of non-member states.

It bears noting that favorable collective choice rules can allow essentially all the potential gains from centralization to be realized. For example, a collective choice method that gives every member state the same probability of being in the majority as in the minority, as with a lottery or explicit rotation in government, generates a unanimous agreement to allow confederal production of all services in which the *average* net benefits of centralized joint production, adjusted for risk, are greater than those of decentralized production. Political risks are not eliminated by such institutions, but are substantially reduced for marginal members of the confederation.[5] (There always remains the possibility, neglected in the present analysis, that the 'natural' majority will evade the constitutional constraints.)

The risk associated with being outside the decisive coalition can also be reduced by adopting constitutional or procedural rules that limit the extent to which the central authority can discriminate among member states. For example, a policy constraint may be adopted that requires uniform treatment of all member states, as with the generality rule examined by Buchanan and Congleton (1998). A generality rule limits prospects for targeting the benefits and costs of centrally provided services, because it requires equal treatment of all members. In the limit, a generality rule makes service levels and costs identical among regions (or persons). If the disadvantage of minority status disappears, equation (5.1) implies that all services for which centralization yields positive net benefits will be centralized.[6]

Menu federalism: an alternative political risk-reducing institution
Another institutional method of reducing political risk and expanding service membership and service areas is menu federalism. Under menu federalism, member states choose which services they will have produced centrally in much the same way that consumers select services from large firms in the marketplace. The voluntary nature of each 'subscription' allows non-uniform service levels to be provided while reducing the political risk associated with discriminatory central governments, and also allows central authorities to be constrained to provide uniform services in order to avoid such discrimination.

The range of services provided for members remains limited to those accepted by all member states under both symmetric and asymmetric forms of federalism. However, the 'all or nothing' choice of symmetric federalism is replaced by a series of 'marginal' choices by member states. The least-advantaged member of a symmetric system accepts more centralized services than really desired, while the most advantaged member states accept less centralization than is ideal for them. The menu approach allows each government to choose which services to centralize. This reduces membership costs for marginal and near-marginal members of the confederation, while providing opportunities for additional centralization for members otherwise constrained by the concerns of marginal members.

Ignoring non-partitionable global public goods, which make up a very small portion of government services, asymmetric federalism allows both membership and the range of centralized services to expand relative to that of uniform centralization in much the same way that ordinary consumers benefit from scale economies and coordination by purchasing goods from large firms and joining private clubs. Local governments 'purchase' centrally produced services whenever the cost is lower or the quality of service better than is possible under independent production.[7]

In cases in which a menu-like approach to centralization cannot be used on a day-to-day basis because of transaction costs, or hold-out problems, opportunities to create new asymmetric federal or confederal arrangements are limited to 'constitutional moments'. Such moments often arise when the terms of membership are varied or new service areas are to be centralized.

In either case, both formal and informal asymmetries are likely to emerge under menu federalism as the confederal charter evolves in a piecemeal fashion to address the concerns of current and potential members, as has been the case for the European Union and the United Nations.

The unequal economic consequences of centralization
In all of these cases, as noted above, the economic consequences of unequal policy-making authority tend to be unequal, because some states benefit more than others from centralization and others choose not to participate in some of

the agreements to centralize policy-making authority. Non-members retain more policy autonomy than member states, although at the cost of reduced scale, coordination and network economies.

If the centralized policy-making authority is well designed so that all of its policies make all member communities better off, then some members are still likely to do better than others under centralization. The communities that benefit most from increased scale and coordination are the smallest members, other things being equal. The smallest members will, thus, tend to prosper as their net of tax service and regulatory pattern improves relative to the status quo and to other members whose net gains are more modest. Communities that do not participate in the centralization are somewhat worse off, because they face stiffer competition for residents and capital.

On the other hand, if the centralized policy-making organization is not well designed, some members will find themselves worse off than they would have been under decentralization. Non-members in this case may find that their circumstances improve relative to members, as residents and capital flow from losing member states to winning member states and to non-member states.

Emergence of asymmetric fiscal federalism from an overly centralized state

Now consider the opposite case, in which control of some government services is initially over- rather than undercentralized. A common situation both historically and in modern times is that in which local and state governments petition their central government for specific local privileges or new authority in a policy area of mutual interest. For example, local authorities may seek special authority to regulate, produce, tax or distribute services that are currently exclusively within the jurisdiction of the central government. When the central government expects to profit from allowing such local authority, it will draft a charter or promulgate a law that delegates new policy-making authority to the community seeking it. When some, but not all, regions or communities secure additional policy-making authority, the result is asymmetric federalism.

Mutual gains from decentralization: the underprovision of public services by Leviathan

Brennan and Buchanan (1977, 1980) demonstrate that a revenue-maximizing central government tends to overtax its subjects and discuss several institutional methods for curtailing Leviathan's power to tax. The complementary analysis of government expenditures suggests that a net revenue-maximizing state tends to underprovide government services. For example, Olson (1993, 2000) and Olson and McGuire (1996) note that a net revenue-maximizing government produces services only to the extent that the expected net tax revenue is increased by providing those services. All provinces may receive local services from the central government, but central government services are likely to be provided at levels that differ from the local ideal.

This point can be easily demonstrated by considering the underlying mathematics of the tax and public service provision by a net revenue-maximizing central government. The tax revenue of such a government may be characterized as the sum of the revenues from each of its territories:

$$T = \Sigma_j \, t_j \, N_j Y_j(t_j, \, G_i).$$ (5.3)

The taxable income of each territory is its population, N_j, times its average income, Y_j, which increases with government service level, G_i, and falls with the national tax rate, t_j. G_i is assumed for purposes of illustration to be a national public good such as transport infrastructure, law and order, environmental quality, or national defense. The cost of providing public service i is:

$$C = c(G_i).$$ (5.4)

The public service output and tax rates that maximize net tax receipts can be characterized by differentiating the difference between equations (5.1) and (5.2) with respect to t_j and G_i:

$$\Sigma_{tj} \, N_j Y_{jti} + N_j Y_j(t_j, \, G_i) = 0$$ (5.5)

and

$$\Sigma_{tj} \, N_j Y_{jG_i} - C_{G_i} = 0.$$ (5.6)

Note that the government service is underprovided for the nation as a whole as long as $t_j < 1$ and $C_{G_i} > 0$, since maximizing national income requires $\Sigma N_j Y_{jG_i} - C_{G_i} = 0$.

A net revenue-maximizing government underprovides both national and local public goods, because local services are provided only to the point at which the marginal increase in tax revenue equals the marginal cost of public services. Public services that increase taxable income are provided by the central government, but are underprovided, because the central government receives only part of the increase in taxable base generated by the public service. (Marginal and average tax rates are necessarily less than 100 per cent in order to provide a return for the private initiative that actually generates the taxable base.) Public services that are valued by local residents but do not increase taxable income are not provided at all!

The political market for local autonomy

The underprovision of governmental services noted by Olson implies the existence of unrealized gains to trade between a net revenue-maximizing central government and local communities. That is to say, at least some local communities will have an interest in negotiating with the central administration for the right to provide extra services.[8]

Each community's interest in greater autonomy varies with the endowments (wealth) of its citizenry and with the intensity of their desire for the underprovided services. Each community's ability to pay for local autonomy, whether in dollars or political favors, varies with its ability to organize negotiations with the sovereign and locally finance payments to the central authority and additional production. Together these imply that there is a maximum sacrifice that each community is willing to make to obtain local authority in every policy area. That is to say, each community has a reservation price for obtaining the power to provide (and fund) its ideal service level and these reservation prices vary among communities. The *effective demand for decentralization* can be characterized by ordering community reservation prices for service autonomy from high to low. Figure 5.1 depicts such a demand schedule for local autonomy.

As the monopoly provider of autonomy in the service areas of interest, the central government can manipulate the political and economic 'price' of autonomy to maximize the net advantage realized by the crown. Grants of autonomy are, after all, simply another source of revenue and/or other valued services for Leviathan. The central government's marginal cost for allowing local autonomy consists largely of increased administrative and security costs associated with ruling more autonomous and therefore more independent regions. Except in cases with unusual security or administrative costs, the cost of granting additional local autonomy appears to be more or less the same across communities.[9]

For purposes of illustration, Figure 5.1 assumes that the central government does not engage in price discrimination among communities or across service areas and that those seeking autonomy use the same methods of settlement with the sovereign.[10] These assumptions allow the marginal cost curve faced by those seeking limited local autonomy to be characterized as a horizontal line. The marginal cost confronting regional, urban and local governments is assumed to be the monopoly price of autonomy, although the specific price is not of special interest for the present analysis. The focus of the present analysis is the degree to which autonomy is 'purchased' by localities at a positive price. The more fiscal and regulatory areas in which local authority is obtained, the greater is the average degree of fiscal and regulatory decentralization.

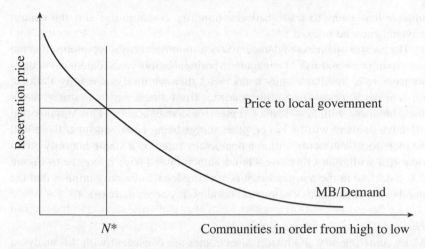

Figure 5.1   The political market for local authority within a particular policy area

Note that asymmetric federalism is the normal result of a political market for local autonomy. Only communities to the left of the intersection of the autonomy demand and marginal cost curve obtain local autonomy in the policy area(s) of interest. Communities to the right of N^* accept the centrally provided fiscal package. As in ordinary markets, only communities willing to pay the price receive the product sold.

The comparative statics of the demand for local autonomy under Leviathan are similar to those of ordinary monopoly markets. As the willingness to pay for autonomy increases and as the 'price' faced by autonomy-seeking communities declines, the extent of autonomy 'purchased' from the central government tends to increase. Conversely, autonomy may be relinquished by towns whose benefits from autonomy decline or costs increase as noted in the previous section.

Decentralization within overly centralized democracies

Incentives within overly centralized democracies ruled by stable majority coalitions are in many ways similar to the autocratic case. A stable majority is interested in providing services and transfers to its membership. In so far as local service levels and transfers are set to advance majority interests, tax rates tend to gravitate toward levels that maximize revenues, although elected governments normally advance broader interests than an autocrat does and normally confront binding constitutional constraints. This provides the majority with an encompassing interest in income-generating public services, but not necessarily for other public services favored by the minority. The latter implies that gains to trade between minority communities and the central government tend to exist.

The greater openness of democratic communities, however, implies that the underlying cost and risk of engaging in political activity to secure local authority tends to be smaller within democracies than within dictatorships. Political movements favoring greater independence from central authorities may, therefore, organize with less fear of repressive consequences. This implies that effective demand will be larger, other things being equal, and that there will be more local autonomy within a democracy ruled by a stable majority coalition than within an otherwise similar autocracy.[11] (With reference to Figure 5.1, a decline in the marginal cost of seeking local autonomy implies that the number of autonomous communities and policy areas increases.)

Historical examples of decentralization
Many contemporary and historical examples are consistent with this analysis. For example, during the early Middle Ages, towns began to prosper as overland trade routes were perfected and expanded. The population of towns and cities increased and land within towns became more intensely used. As community wealth and the value of town services increased, relatively autonomous cities emerged along the major trading routes throughout Europe. Such communities often negotiated a special charter from the ruling barony or bishopry in order to secure local autonomy, or, in some cases, simply acted to secure greater service independence (Pirenne [1925] 1970: 190):

> The charter granted to St. Omer in 1127 may be considered as a point of departure of the political programs of the burgers of Flanders. It recognized the city as a distinct legal territory, provided with a special law common to all inhabitants, with special aldermanic courts and full communal autonomy. Other charters in the course of the Twelfth century ratified similar grants to all the principal cities of the county. Their status was thereafter secured and sanctioned by written warrants.

These medieval charters are relevant for modern Europe, because many of its contemporary urban centers were launched by such medieval charters of privilege.

Of course, there are many other more recent cases around the world in which a few local communities seek or simply claim a degree of local fiscal autonomy that others do not demand. For example, the major Belgian language communities recently negotiated for and received substantial increases in regional autonomy. Similarly, devolutions were negotiated by the Welsh, Scottish and Northern Irish communities within the United Kingdom and by the autonomous communities of Spain.

Such negotiations are not always successful, but they are commonplace. For example, close to this author's home, the communities of Northern

Virginia, the wealthiest region of Virginia, recently sought special authority to create a local sales tax to fund high construction and mass transit. Local governments received permission from the State of Virginia to impose such taxes – but subject to a local referendum – which sales tax proponents lost.

The communities that secure additional local control over public services are those that are willing to 'pay' the most at the margin for additional local services. Others find the political and economic costs of additional local control to be greater than the anticipated benefits; they may be too small, too weak, or too poor to benefit from increased local autonomy or to pay the price required for it. In this manner, the most demanding communities and regions create through their discretionary actions a more decentralized structure of governance, although often an asymmetric one.

Political limits to decentralization and centralization

Contrasting the degree of decentralization under the two scenarios
The degree of centralization that emerges from a gradual shift of policy-making authority from local to central confederal governments differs from that of a gradual shift of policy-making authority from central to local governments, because *the price of autonomy differs in the two cases*. In the over-centralization case first examined, the central government charged local governments the monopoly price for the right of autonomous production. In the undercentralized case, autonomy is freely available, and centralization is voluntarily adopted to the extent that centralization yields local net benefits given that price. Indeed, local governments might have to pay a price to transfer their autonomy to a pre-existing central authority. These differences in the price of local authority imply that gradually centralizing states tend to be more decentralized in equilibrium than gradually decentralizing states.

Differences in the general pattern of local authority are less clear. In the overcentralized case, asymmetric federalism results when relatively more prosperous high-demand jurisdictions lobby for greater authority to provide additional services. In the case of the undercentralized state, it is possible that relatively large prosperous states with relatively high service demands will also be the ones that choose autonomy over centralized provision. They have less to gain from economies of scale and coordination, because they already operate at a relatively large scale. On the other hand, as larger states their political risks for membership tend to be smaller than those of smaller states, because they are more likely to be members of the majority coalition.

Another possible pattern of local autonomy involves the order of membership. The analysis suggests that non-members generally prefer more autonomy than those that initially formed the confederation. And, it is non-members, of course, that form the pool of potential new members. The analysis above suggests that completely new services, political assurances or opportunities for lesser degrees of centralized control have to be offered to attract new members. In the last case, the order of membership will tend to generate asymmetries, with the latest members retaining more local autonomy or being relatively more influential within the central authority.

Political limits to asymmetric fiscal federalization in democracies:
a centralization trap
The political bargains that can be struck within democracies differ from those within autocracies, because majority rule tends to be more constrained by distributional effects than one-man rule. Indeed, majority approval for narrow increases in local authority are relatively easy to secure only in cases in which the new authority can be exercised without imposing externalities on other communities. In such cases, allowing some or all minority communities a bit more local authority is a Pareto-superior move, and those uninterested in greater authority for themselves will not attempt to block it for others and may easily be induced to vote in favor of it. However, states or provinces that are uninterested in increased authority for themselves will attempt *to block it* for others if the local authority sought tends to reduce prosperity in regions that do not obtain (or desire) the same degree of authority. Moreover, in cases in which local areas already possess powers that impose externalities on the majority, the majority will eliminate those powers, unless those powers are constitutionally protected.

In so far as a majority of regions or communities are harmed by additional fiscal or economic competition, their representatives will vote against granting other communities additional powers and will repeal such powers if they already exist.

Democratic politics, thus, tends to generate relatively more homogeneous (uniformity) distributions of fiscal and regulatory powers among their subnational governments than stable autocracies, although a more decentralized one as noted above. Asymmetries will still exist within democracies, but their asymmetries favor the majority, tend to have relatively few fiscal externalities, or are constitutionally protected. Such asymmetries are predicted whether or not decentralization increases overall political and economic efficiency.

Internal organization and asymmetric fiscal federalism
Asymmetric federalism may take a variety of institutional forms. Specific asymmetries may be created by a nation's constitution by assigning different areas of competency to various regions of the country. Alternatively, the constitution may allow the possibility of alternative *internal arrangements* that allow the formation of many levels and combinations of fiscal authority. For example, a national constitution may simply allow states to organize them-

selves into various subnational organizations of states, cities or counties. An international treaty organization may allow a subset of member states to pursue their own interests within the terms of the treaty.

This possibility allows a range of federal structures that is more complex than normally analysed by economists and more so than can be fully analysed here. However, it is clear that that many internal organizational structures tend to produce asymmetric forms of fiscal federalism. Figure 5.2 illustrates one such internal structure.

If we interpret the interregional government as another level of centralized control, it is clear that local government 1 retains more autonomy than local governments 2 and 3, because it is not bound by the decisions of the regional government, if the regional government is not granted exclusive areas of competency. Alternatively, if the regional government is granted powers that no member state possesses by itself, local government 1 has less authority than local governments 2 and 3. In either case, the result is an asymmetric distribution of policy-making authority.

Such internal 'governmental clubs' are commonplace. Metropolitan governments often form regional transportation authorities to coordinate regional transport services. Regional environmental councils are often formed via accord or treaty to coordinate the development environmental rules by the state and national governments affected by a regional environmental problem.

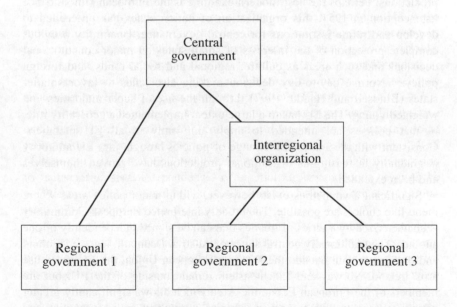

Figure 5.2   Internal asymmetry

Non-members are not be bound by council decisions, but retain complete local autonomy in the policy areas that others delegate to the central authority.[12]

Empirical implications and some evidence from existing confederations
The analysis has generated several predictions about symmetric and asymmetric confederations. First, more-encompassing regional and international organizations will specify collective decision-making processes and other institutional arrangements that protect the interests of smaller states *vis-à-vis* larger members as a means of increasing the scope for mutually advantageous centralization. Second, the number of areas in which competencies are shifted to the central government will tend to increase as such institutions are adopted to reduce political risks associated with centralization. Third, asymmetries emerge whenever a menu approach to confederalism is adopted and as new members or policy areas are added through time to an existing confederation. Fourth, the degree of decentralization is affected by the historical starting point, whether the service areas of interest are initially over- or undercentralized. Fifth, asymmetries tend to be smaller within democratic states than within dictatorships. Sixth, asymmetries that emerge within democracies tend to have few fiscal externalities and/or tend to favor members of long-standing majorities.

Several central authorities and federal systems around the world that have formed gradually and voluntarily through time seem to accord well with these predictions. Perhaps the best modern example is the European Union. Since its inception in 1951, this organization of nation states has proceeded to develop and refine institutions for central governance. Unanimity provides complete protection of the interests of small states on major constitutional decisions and such areas as culture, regional and social funds, and foreign policy.[13] Normal day-to-day decision making also tends to favor smaller states (Bindseil and Hantke 1997) through the use of super-majorities and weighted voting. The EU has to a large extent implemented a generality rule, in that policies are intended to apply uniformly to all EU members. Consistent with the analysis, the range of policies brought into EU authority is gradually increasing as institutional protections have proven themselves and been extended.

Significant asymmetries exist, however, within major policy areas where menu-like choices are possible. The broadly interpreted European Community is characterized by a series of treaties that can be signed independently of one another. The traditionally neutral states of Austria, Denmark, Iceland, Finland and Sweden remain outside the Western European Union, the EU's defense arm. Ireland, Norway and Liechtenstein remain outside of the EU, but are members of the European Economic Area which allows significantly greater national autonomy with respect to fisheries, agriculture, indirect taxation and tariffs than full membership does.

Exceptions to the core treaties of the EU have been granted at constitutional moments: at times when new services have been brought under EU authority or as new members have been added. Confederal asymmetries largely take the form of exemptions that provide additional local autonomy over specific policy areas. The United Kingdom has obtained 'opt-outs' from the Social Charter of the Maastricht Treaty. The United Kingdom, Denmark and Sweden retain more autonomy over macroeconomic policy than other member states by opting out of the European currency union. Some recent members have received permission to maintain stricter environmental standards in some areas (subject to EU review). Consistent with the analysis, the original members (Germany, Italy, France, Belgium, the Netherlands and Luxembourg) have given up relatively more autonomy to the EU than have subsequent members.

Conclusion and summary
This chapter has analysed the politics of decentralization. The analysis demonstrates that the degree of centralization is affected by both political and economic considerations. Moreover, no single uniform level of centralization emerges, but rather the degree of centralization differs according to the original circumstances of the polities involved and the distribution of demands for regional autonomy. Decentralization is not an exogenous feature of a polity, as often assumed, but rather an endogenous result of ongoing negotiations over the assignment of central and local authority. The latter implies that the degree of local autonomy is likely to vary by region, because the demand for local authority tends to vary according to local needs, income and organization.

The processes of centralization and decentralization analysed were broadly contractarian and Coasian (Coase 1960) in spirit. However, in contrast to the unique result of the classic Coase discussion of agreements to internalize externalities, there are many possible agreements that can be negotiated between levels of government and among governments at a particular level of governance. As in any Edgeworth box, initial 'endowments' affect which parts of the constitutional contract curve may be reached via a series of voluntary agreements. Thus, different historical starting points allow communities to reach different regions of the Pareto constitutional frontier via voluntary exchange.

Although the analysis has mainly been concerned with explaining some fundamental institutional features of federal and confederal systems of governance, the conclusions parallel and extend those of the conventional welfare-economic analysis of fiscal federalism, which largely neglects institutional and political aspects of federal states. The analysis suggests that intragovernmental negotiations often produce efficiency-increasing political institutions, because improved political institutions often produce economic benefits for both central and local governments. For example, the rule of law and the generality principle allow economies of scale and scope to be more fully realized by increasing membership in so far as such legal constraints reduce the cost of being a member of a politically disadvantaged group (Congleton 1997). Super-majority requirements, regional vetoes, weighted voting, bicameralism and explicit power-sharing arrangements similarly reduce the probability that a region or member state will find itself powerless in the central government. Menu systems of fiscal federalism can also promote efficiency by facilitating centralization in policy areas and for groups of communities in which centralization is efficient, without imposing it in areas where it is not. Such institutions encourage the formation and continuation of centralized fiscal systems, and also allow government services to be provided more efficiently.

Competition among local governments within an asymmetric federal system, however, differs from that in symmetric systems, because there are supply- as well as demand-side variations in services in asymmetric systems. Clearly, only communities that have the power to set tax and service levels can compete on such taxes and services. Consequently, asymmetries in fiscal and regulatory authority often generate asymmetries in population and wealth as favored cities or regions adjust their fiscal packages to attract new capital and labor, while other cities and regions that lack the power to make their own policies fall behind. The consequences of regional favoritism can be reduced by reducing the price of local autonomy, as with a menu-based system in which communities are free to join or opt out of centralized control.

Overall, the analysis suggests that asymmetric federalism is likely to emerge in a wide variety of circumstances and is likely to be efficiency enhancing in so far as local governments promote local interests. The latter are fortunate indeed, because asymmetric solutions are likely to become increasingly widespread around the world as regional organizations and globalization induce disparate countries and regions to pursue new mutual advantages from cooperation, while minimizing the political risks associated with centralized control.

Notes

1. Yet, surprisingly very little work has been done on asymmetric federalism. Tiebout (1956) and Oates (1972) pioneered the economic analysis of fiscal federalism and intergovernmental relationships. Inman and Rubinfeld (1997) provide a nice survey of issues in subsequent literature. Molander (2004) provides a more international review of fiscal federalism in unitary states. Qian and Weingast (1997) elaborate the role that federalism can play in solving various commitment and information problems. None of these papers or books includes any reference or comments on asymmetric forms of federalism. Requejo (1996) analyses some general features of existing asymmetries within modern states. Congleton et al. (2003) analyse the political foundations of asymmetric distribution of authority within nation states and international organizations.
2. Service differences across communities may also emerge in a completely unified state where

policy-making authority is completely centralized, in so far as communities may have unequal influence over the decisions of the central government because of differences in population, political heterogeneity, history, or size. For example, equal representation by population often implies unequal representation by regions or economic interests, and vice versa. Unequal *influence* within the central government implies that central government policies will often favor some regions or communities over others.

Analysis of variation voting power has a long and distinguished history in the public choice literature (see, for example, Mueller 1989). However, this form of asymmetry is not the same as that analysed here in which regional governments acquire different degrees of local policy-making authority.

3. There are several reasons for focusing on 'confederal' decisions. First, an exercise in creating a new central authority more naturally focuses attention on centralized decision-making procedures and constraints. The emergence of new governmental policy-making bodies is a fairly common outcome of negotiations between a central government and local jurisdictions. Even very narrow agreements to centralize policy-making authority within a particular area often devote considerable resources to institutional design. For example, international environmental treaties generally devote more text to specifying institutional arrangements for collective decision making than to specifying environmental problems and remedies (Congleton 1995). Second, the analysis of voluntary transfers of authority to the central government focuses attention on the decisions of potential confederal partners or service subscribers. The process of intergovernmental bargaining is too easily neglected if one focuses exclusively on the central government's interests, in which case all fiscal structures might be assumed to reflect the interests of the national government alone.

4. It is assumed that the favored group consists of members of the ruling majority coalition. However, in some cases, minority protections may assure small states relatively preferential treatment, as for example when a minority is given effective veto power over policy. In such cases, the political risk is simply that the majority will evade the constitutional constraints. Olson and Zeckhauser (1966) note that cost sharing in NATO favored smaller nations who were able to free ride to some extent on the contributions of the United States. Vaubel (1994) argues that unanimity grants member states equal power and thereby an equal claim on the gains from cooperation. In this manner, Vaubel argues that unanimity rules favor the smaller states of the European Union.

5. Weak forms of confederation often specify unanimous agreement for the highest levels of policies. For example, under a standard international treaty, a joint political body is often created which specifies that the decision rule post-signing remains some form of unanimous agreement. Within a 'stronger' form of federal or confederal system the central government will use a less inhibiting form of political decision making such as majority rule. In the limit, a unanimity rule can increase the probability of being in the decisive coalition to unity, but as noted by Buchanan and Tullock (1962), collective decision-making costs may be rather large, which as noted above is a reason for replacing multilateral agreements with a standing central authority.

6. Buchanan and Congleton (1998) note that a generality restriction both increases majoritarian stability and reduces the burden of majoritarian cycles. Deadweight cost increases with the square of the marginal tax rate (Browning 1987), consequently, the deadweight burden of concentrating the tax burden on the minority is greater than it would have been under more uniform methods of taxation. That is to say, the average cost of programs increases under discriminatory majority rule with an 'evenly rotating majority' relative to that under a generality rule.

7. Here, it bears noting that most of the services that are produced by governments are not pure public goods available globally, as is often assumed in public finance models, but rather services for which laws rather than factories are the principal method of production. Laws, taxes and most government services are inherently excludable because law enforcement and other services are provided by *individual governments*. Of course, as in the 'right of way' illustration, many of these services will attract emigrants from other communities. But, whether new immigrants are entitled to the same services as current residents is, itself, a matter of law.

8. Opportunities for mutually advantageous tax reductions may also exist if the community has a comparative advantage in providing services for Leviathan.
9. In addition to adopting Mancur Olson's (1993) model of the provision of public services within an autocracy (under a stationary bandit), this section also adopts Olson's benign neglect of security issues. Security issues are neglected as a method of simplifying the prose and reducing modeling complexity. In the context of the present analysis, security concerns are interpreted as additional costs or benefits associated with decentralization. Grants of regional autonomy may increase or reduce security costs according to the particular circumstances. Autonomy makes it easier for opponents to organize and resist control by the central government; on the other hand it also reduces incentives to do so.
10. Differences in local organizational costs have historically played a role in securing local autonomy as well. For example, the existence of political, regional or ethnic organizations clearly reduces the difficulty of organizing to 'demand' local autonomy from a central government. A common language, religion or ethnicity reduces organization costs, as does the existence of standing organizations such as churches, guilds or local governments. Differences in organizational costs will, naturally, affect a group's reservation price for autonomy.
11. Evidence of the effect of democracy on the degree of centralization can be taken from the histories of many countries that have cycled between democratic and autocratic regimes. Spanish history provides several good illustrations. The Basque country and Catalonia are two of the wealthiest regions of Spain. Both regions have enjoyed limited autonomy for much of the past five hundred years that other regions of Spain have rarely obtained, and have been by far the most active seekers of regional autonomy during modern Spanish history. In the past two hundred years there have been several cases where Spanish central governments have shifted briefly between democratic (republican) and authoritarian regimes. Consistent with the above analysis, each time a republican form of governance took hold, local autonomy increased in these two regions. Each time the autocratic authority regained control, regional autonomy was reduced, but not eliminated. (See, for example, Hennessy 1989, or Brassloff 1989.) Similar examples could be taken from recent developments in South America, Africa and Asia.
12. Casella and Frey (1992) and Frey and Eichenberger (1996) analyse the welfare implications of overlapping jurisdictions which, as noted, tends to imply asymmetric forms of federalism. Their emphasis is on how competition between or within states can be usefully promoted. We do not emphasize the competitive implications of federalism but rather the political and economic advantages of decentralized control. As indicated by these and other more traditional analyses of federalism, competition among communities also tends to improve the economic performance of local governments, and therefore provides another normative defense of federalism.
13. Consistent with this, Bendar et al. (1996) note that the areas in which public support is greater for the EU are those which rely upon unanimity for decision making. The move to majoritarianism embodied in successive integrative steps lessened public support for the EU.

References

Bendar, J., Ferejohn, J. and Garrett, G. (1996), 'The politics of European federalism', *International Review of Law and Economics* **16**: 279–94.

Bindseil, U. and Hantke, C. (1997), 'The power distribution in decision making among EU member states', *European Journal of Political Economy* **13**: 171–85.

Brassloff, A. (1989), 'Spain: the state of autonomies', in M. Forsyth (ed.), *Federalism and Nationalism*, London: Palgrave Macmillan.

Brennan, G. and Buchanan, J.M. (1977), 'Towards a tax constitution for Leviathan', *Journal of Public Economics* **8**: 255–73.

Brennan, G. and Buchanan, J.M. (1980), *The Power to Tax. Analytical Foundations of a Fiscal Constitution*. Cambridge: Cambridge University Press.

Browning, E.K. (1987), 'On the marginal welfare cost of taxation', *American Economic Review* **77**: 11–23.

Buchanan, J.M. and Congleton, R.D. (1998), *Politics by Principle Not Interest*. Cambridge: Cambridge University Press.

Buchanan, J.M. and Tullock, G. (1962), *The Calculus of Consent*. Ann Arbor, MI: University of Michigan Press.

Casella, A. and Frey, B. (1992), 'Federalism and clubs. Towards an economic theory of overlapping political jurisdictions', *European Economic Review* 36: 639–46.

Coase, R.E. (1960), 'The problem of social cost', *Journal of Law and Economics* 3: 1–44.

Congleton, R.D. (1994), 'Constitutional federalism and decentralization: a second best solution', *Economia delle Scelte Pubbliche* 12: 15–29.

Congleton, R.D. (1995), 'Towards a transactions cost theory of environmental treaties: substantive and symbolic environmental agreements', *Economia Delle Scelte Pubbliche* 13: 119–39.

Congleton, R.D. (1997), 'Political efficiency and equal protection of the law', *Kyklos* 50: 485–505.

Congleton, R.D., Bacarria, J. and Kyriacou A. (2003), 'A theory of menu federalism, decentralization by political agreement', *Constitutional Political Economy* 14: 167–90.

Elazar, D.J. (ed.) (1991), *Federal Systems of the World: A Handbook of Federal, Confederal, and Autonomy Arrangements*. Harlow: Longman Group Limited.

Frey, Bruno and Eichenberger, Reiner (1996), 'FOJC. Competitive governments for Europe', *International Journal of Law and Economics* 16: 315–27.

Hennessy, C.A.M. (1989), 'The renaissance of federal ideas in contemporary Spain', in M. Forsyth (ed.), *Federalism and Nationalism*, London: Palgrave Macmillan.

Inman, R.P. and Rubinfeld, D.L. (1997), 'Rethinking federalism', *Journal of Economic Perspectives* 11: 43–64.

Molander, P. (2004), *Fiscal Federalism in Unitary States*. Dordrecht, NL: Kluwer Academic.

Moraw, P. (1994), 'Cities and citizenry as factors of state formation in the Roman–German Empire of the Late Middle Ages', in Tilly and Blockmans (eds), pp. 631–62.

Mueller, D.C. (1989), *Public Choice II*. Cambridge: Cambridge University Press.

Oates, W.E. (1972), *Fiscal Federalism*. New York: Harcourt, Brace, Jovanovich.

Olson, M. (1993), 'Dictatorship, democracy, and development', *American Political Science Review* 87: 567–76.

Olson, M. (2000), *Power and Prosperity: Outgrowing Communist and Capitalist Dictatorships*. New York: Basic Books.

Olson, M. and McGuire, M.C. (1996), 'The economics of autocracy and majority rule: the invisible hand and the use of force', *Journal of Economic Literature* 34: 72–96.

Olson, M. and Zeckhauser, R. (1966), 'An economic theory of alliances', *Review of Economics and Statistics* 48: 266–79.

Pirenne, H. ([1925] 1970), *Medieval Cities: Their Origins and the Revival of Trade* (Translated by F.D. Halsey). Princeton, NJ: Princeton University Press.

Qian, Y. and Weingast, B. (1997), 'Federalism as a commitment to preserving market incentives', *Journal of Economic Perspectives* 11: 83–92.

Ra'anan, U., Mesner, M., Armes, K. and Martin, K. (eds) (1991), *State and Nation in Multiethnic Societies: The Breakup of Multinational States*. Manchester and New York: Manchester University Press.

Requejo, F. (1996), 'Diferencias Nacionales y Federalismo Asimétrico', *Clares de Razón Practica* 59: 24–37.

Tiebout, C. (1956), 'A pure theory of local expenditures', *Journal of Political Economy* 64: 416–24.

Tilly, C. and Blockmans, W.P. (eds) (1989), *Cities and the Rise of States in Europe, A.D. 1000 to 1800*. Boulder, CO: Westview Press.

Vaubel, Roland (1994), 'The public choice analysis of European integration: a survey', *European Journal of Political Economy* 10: 227–49.

6 Functional, overlapping and competing jurisdictions (FOCJ): a complement and alternative to today's federalism

Reiner Eichenberger and Bruno S. Frey

I. Introduction

Traditional types of federalism and decentralization exhibit many important advantages over centralization, but they also face some serious problems. In this contribution we develop a new concept of functional federalism which exploits the advantages of decentralization, but which at the same time avoids the inherent problems. Our concept, called *FOCJ* as the acronym of functional, overlapping and competing jurisdictions, is well suited to improve politics in industrial as well as developing countries. This new kind of competitive federalism we put forward may seem radical in various respects, but we shall show that the concept has been successful in the past as well as the present. Thus, we believe that it constitutes an idea worthy of serious consideration. The remainder of this chapter is organized as follows. In the next section we discuss the advantages and problems of traditional federalism. The third section specifies the concept of FOCJ, and discusses its main beneficial effects. The fourth section puts it into theoretical perspective. The fifth section shows that some aspects of FOCJ have existed throughout European history and continue to do so today. Furthermore, the relationship to US special districts and in particular to functional communities in Switzerland is emphasized. While the sixth section discusses how FOCJ can be institutionalized in Europe, the seventh section focuses on the relevance of FOCJ for developing countries. The last section concludes.

II. Advantages and problems of federalism

The economic theory of federalism yields one clear and overriding result: a federal (that is, decentralized) state is superior to a centralized one in the sense that it fulfils the demands of the citizens more effectively. A federal constitution that endows the federal subunits (provinces, *Länder*, states or cantons as well as municipalities, cities or communities) with sufficient decision making rights and taxing power has three major advantages over a unitary state:

1. *More flexible politics* In all societies, citizens differ widely in their

demand for services provided by the state. These differences in demand are not only the result of heterogeneous tastes due to differences in tradition, culture, language and so on, but also of unequal economic conditions. The latter are caused by, for example, leads or lags in the general business cycle and, of course, special structural conditions such as differences in infrastructure, unemployment, the concentration of particular industries and so on. These differences in the demand for public services must be met by differentiated supply policies if citizens' preferences are to be fulfilled. Federal subunits are best able to meet this challenge. While the politicians in charge are better endowed with information about the local requirements, they have the incentives to provide these services according to the preferences of the citizens because they are directly accountable for local policy and their re-election depends on the satisfaction of the voters they represent.[1] In contrast, centralized states tend to produce unitary policies which are less capable of responding to differences in local demands.

2. *More efficient provision of public services* The efficiency of the public sector is extremely important due to the very large size of today's public sector in terms of government expenditure as a share of national income, public servants as a share of the total workforce, the dependence of a substantial portion of the population on income redistributed by government (for example, in the form of subsidies, social security and old-age pensions) and, of course, the many resources that go into tax collection. In federally organized states, efficiency is enhanced by at least three mechanisms. First, individuals and firms which are not satisfied with the balance between the supply and cost of public services may move to jurisdictions where this balance is more favourable. Such exit and entry thus establish competition among the various local suppliers of public services, giving them a strong incentive to be efficient. The exit/entry mechanism does not depend on the full mobility of individuals or firms (there are, of course, costs of moving); it suffices if *some* such mobility is induced (in analogy to the marginal traders leading to equilibrium prices on normal goods markets). Indeed, spatial competition between jurisdictions in a federal system mimics competition among firms for the supply of private goods and services (Tiebout 1956). Second, decentralization enhances efficiency by decreasing the cost of information for the citizens. As the voters can compare politics and policy outcomes in their own jurisdictions with those variables in other jurisdictions, it becomes easier for them to assess the performance of their governments and politicians. Such comparisons lead to 'yardstick competition' among local governments (see Salmon 1987, and Ch. 2 in this volume; Besley and Case 1995) which enforces the incentives of the governments to cater for the preferences of

the citizens. Third, there is not only horizontal competition among govern-ments of the same level, but also vertical competition among governments of different levels which fortifies the governments' incentives to provide their services efficiently (Breton 1996, and Ch. 3 in this volume).

3. *More innovation*   In a federal system, innovations in the supply of public goods or taxation can be implemented first in those local units where the conditions are ideal for success. Moreover, a particular local unit finds it less risky to undertake innovations in the supply of public goods or taxa-tion because the effects are limited and can be better observed and controlled. If the innovation is unsuccessful, not much is lost. However, if it proves to be successful, it will be quickly adopted by other jurisdictions and eventually the entire nation. For this Hayekian process to take place, the innovators must reap at least some of the benefits. This is much more the case when the innovation starts from a clearly defined local jurisdic-tion where the success (or failure) can be clearly attributed to the respec-tive politicians and governments.

In spite of these heavyweight advantages, federalism is not an ideal system. However, there is *no* ideal system. Following the well-established 'compara-tive analysis of institutions', it is fruitless to judge any existing system or a new proposal by comparing it with a theoretical optimum. Rather, a compari-son must be made with actual systems existing in reality. In the case of feder-alism, it is appropriate to compare it with a centralized state. From this point of view, it has often been argued that a federal constitution is faced with four major problems:

1. *Spillover effects*   Spatial positive and negative externalities produce systematic distortions in the allocation of publicly supplied goods and services. 'Fiscal equivalence' (Olson 1969; Oates 1972) is not secured: some benefits of local public supply go to citizens of other jurisdictions who have not paid the corresponding tax cost (which induces under-supply); some costs are carried by citizens outside a particular jurisdiction (which induces oversupply). This cause for the distorted allocation of public services cannot be neglected. In reality, it can often be observed that such spillovers are substantial and part of the fiscal crises of cities can be attributed to this factor. As an example, the cultural institutions (for example, the opera house) whose costs are carried by the local taxpayers but whose benefits are enjoyed by many people living and paying taxes outside the city. Acknowledging that such positive and negative spillovers may be serious under many circumstances, we hereby propose a solution: the size of the jurisdiction should correspond to the 'geography of the problems'.

2. *Smallness* In traditional federalism, jurisdictions are often too small to exploit economies of scale. Think, for example, of nuclear power plants or universities, which normally require heavy capital investments for a local jurisdiction (city, communities) to run efficiently. In our proposal for a new federalism, we are trying to confront the problem directly. We envisage flexible (functional) jurisdictions which are able to adjust to the lowest cost size.

3. *Need for coordination* It is often claimed that federalism makes cooperation difficult or impossible. However, this is only part of the real problem. In federal states, cooperation among the various national subunits emerges endogenously because it is obviously advantageous for all actors concerned. Moreover, it should be noted that coordination problems also exist within unitary states, in particular among the various national ministries whose competencies and interests overlap. Thus, a unitary state is neither a necessary nor sufficient condition for effective cooperation.

4. *Redistribution of income* This argument says that when a local unit tries to tax the rich in order to support the poor, the rich will leave and the poor will enter. The redistribution policy therefore cannot be maintained in a federalist state, but is only feasible in a unitary state. This argument has some truth in it. However, empirical evidence shows that federalist structures admit a substantial amount of income redistribution (see, for example, Gold 1991; Ashworth et al. 2002). One example is Switzerland where the (partly very small) 26 cantons together with about 3000 communities levy more than 80 per cent of total income and capital taxes. Although each canton is free to set its own tax schedule, all cantons rely on progressive taxes and engage heavily in income redistribution (see Kirchgässner and Pommerehne 1996; Feld 2000). Moreover, quite a large amount of redistribution exists between rich and poor cantons. Nevertheless, the problem of redistribution in a decentralized governmental system has to be taken seriously. In our proposal for a new kind of federalism, we argue that this is one of the functions for which the national state is sometimes an appropriate jurisdiction.

III. FOCJ: beyond traditional federalism

The federal units proposed here are named FOCJ due to their four essential characteristics: they are

- *functional (F)*, that is, the new political units extend over areas defined by the tasks to be fulfilled;
- *overlapping (O)*, that is, in line with the many different tasks (functions), there are corresponding governmental units extending over different geographical areas;

- *competing (C)*, that is, individuals and/or communities may choose to which governmental unit they want to belong, and they have political rights to express their preferences directly via initiatives and referenda; and
- *jurisdictions (J)*, that is, the units established are governmental, they have enforcement power and can, in particular, levy taxes.

These *functional, overlapping, and competing jurisdictions* form a federal system of governments that is not dictated from above, but emerges from below as a response to citizens' preferences. For this to become reality, a fifth freedom has to be enacted, which in some ways is the political counterpart to the four well-known economic freedoms as established by the European Union. It simply has to permit the formation and continued existence of FOCJ. Such a fifth freedom requires a *constitutional decision* (see, for example, Frey 1983; Mueller 1996) which ensures that the emergence of FOCJ is not blocked by existing jurisdictions such as direct competitors or higher-level governments. In the European Union, this would mean that every citizen and community would have the right to directly appeal to the European Court if barriers to the competition between governments are established. A European Union directive must be enacted to give the lowest political units (communities) a measure of independence so that they can engage in forming FOCJ. The citizens must be given the right to establish FOCJ by popular referenda, and political entrepreneurs must be supported and controlled by the institution of popular initiatives. The FOCJ themselves must have the right to levy taxes to finance the public services they provide.

The concept of FOCJ is based on theoretical propositions advanced in the economic theory of federalism. It nevertheless leads to a governmental system that is completely different from the one suggested in that literature. While the economic theory of federalism (see Oates 1991, or the various contributions on federalism in the Fall 1997 issue of the *Journal of Economic Perspectives*) analyses the behaviour of *given* political units at the different levels of government, FOCJ *emerge* in response to the 'geography of problems'.[2]

FOCJ with their four main elements are now compared with existing federal institutions and theoretical concepts, pointing out both similarities and differences and the beneficial effects of FOCJ.

The main characteristics

Functions   A particular public service which only benefits a certain geographical area should be financed by the people living in this area, that is, there should be no spillovers. Under this rule, the different political units can cater for differences in the populations' preferences or, more precisely, to its demands. To minimize cost, these units have to exploit economies of scale in production. As these may strongly differ between functions (for example, between schools, police, hospitals, power plants and defence) there is an additional reason for single-function (or linked-function) governmental units of different sizes. While this idea is central to 'fiscal equivalence' as proposed by Olson (1969) and Oates (1972), the endogeneity of the size of governmental units constitutes an essential part of FOCJ. Moreover, fiscal equivalence theory has been little concerned with decision making within functional units. The supply process is either left unspecified or it is assumed that the mobility of persons (and of firms, a fact rarely mentioned) automatically induces these units to cater for individual preferences. This criticism also applies to a closely related concept of fiscal federalism, namely 'voting with one's feet' (Tiebout 1956). This preference-revealing mechanism makes comparatively efficient suppliers grow in size, and the others shrink. According to this model of federalism, the political jurisdictions are exogenously given, are multipurpose, and do not overlap, while the political supply process is left unspecified. In contrast, we emphasize the need to explicitly study the political supply process. In line with Epple and Zelenitz (1981), exit and entry is considered insufficient to eliminate rent extraction by governments. Individuals must have the possibility of 'raising voice' in the form of voting. Buchanan's 'clubs' (see Buchanan 1965; Sandler and Tschirhart 1980) are similar to FOCJ because their size is determined endogenously by club members' benefits and costs.

Overlap   FOCJ may overlap in two respects: (i) two or more FOCJ catering for the same function may geographically intersect (for example, a multitude of school FOCJ may exist in the same geographical area); (ii) FOCJ catering for different functions may overlap. The two types of overlap may coexist; however, a constitutional decision can be taken to restrict FOCJ of specific functions to the second type because this alleviates free-riding problems (see also Vanberg 2000). An individual or a political community normally belongs to various FOCJ at the same time. FOCJ need not be physically contiguous, and they need not have a monopoly over a certain area of land. In this respect the concept of FOCJ is similar to Buchanan-type clubs which may intersect, but it differs completely from archaic nationalism with its fighting over pieces of land. It also breaks with the notion of federalist theory that units at the same level may not overlap.

Competition   In FOCJ, two mechanisms guarantee that empowered politicians conform closely to their members' preferences: while the possibility for individuals and communities to exit mimics market competition (Hirschman 1970), their right to *vote* establishes political competition (see Mueller 2003). It should be noted that migration is only one means of exit. Often, membership in a particular FOCUS (we define a FOCUS to be the singular of FOCJ) can be discontinued without changing one's location. Exit is not restricted to individuals or firms; as said before, political communities as a whole, or parts of them may also exercise this option. Moreover, exit may be total or only partial. In the latter case, an individual or community only participates in a restricted set of FOCUS activities. This enlarged set of exit options makes 'voting with one's feet' a real constraint for politicians.

'Secession', that is, exit of jurisdictions such as states or regions, has been recognized in the literature as an effective mechanism for restricting the power of central states (for example, Zarkovic Bookman 1992; Drèze 1993; Backhaus and Doering 2004). Secession has been suggested as an important ingredient for a future European constitution (Buchanan 1991; European Constitutional Group 1993). The right to secede stands in stark contrast to the prevailing concepts of nation states and federations where this is strictly forbidden and often prevented by force, as is illustrated, for example, by the American Civil War, 1861–65, by the Swiss *Sonderbundskrieg* 1847, or more recently by the wars in Katanga (1960–63), Biafra (1967–70), Bangladesh (1970–71), and in the past decade in the former Yugoslavia.

For FOCJ to establish competition between governments, exit should be as unrestrained as possible. In contrast, entry need not necessarily be free. As for individuals in Buchanan-type clubs, jurisdictions may be asked to pay a price if they want to join a particular FOCUS and benefit from its public goods. The existing members of the particular FOCUS have to democratically decide on the entry prices. 'Free' mobility in the sense of a disregard for the cost imposed on others is overcome by internalizing the external cost of movement. In addition, FOCJ do not have to restrict entry by administrative and legal means such as zoning laws. Explicit, openly declared entry fees substitute for implicit restrictions resulting in high land prices and housing rents. The commonly raised concern that pricing could be exploitative and mobility strongly curtailed is unwarranted as FOCJ are subject to competitive pressure. Moreover, the possibility of imposing an explicit entry fee gives incentives to FOCJ governments to cater for the preferences not only of actual, but also of prospective members.

However, the exit option does not suffice to induce governments to act efficiently. Thus, competition needs to be enhanced by political institutions. The citizens should directly elect the persons managing the FOCJ, and should be given the right to initiate popular referenda on specific issues. These democratic institutions are known to raise efficiency in the sense of fulfilling individual preferences (for elections, see Downs 1957 and Mueller 2003; for referenda, see Frey 1994; Frey and Stutzer 2001; Feld and Kirchgässner 2001; and Feld and Matsusaka 2003).

Jurisdiction   A FOCUS is a democratic governmental unit with authority over its citizens, including the power to tax. According to the two types of overlap, two forms of membership can be distinguished. First, the lowest political unit (normally the community) is a member, and all corresponding citizens automatically become citizens of the FOCJ to which their community belongs. In that case, an individual can only exit via mobility. Second, individuals may freely choose whether they want to belong to a particular FOCUS, but while they are its citizen, they are subject to its authority. Such FOCJ may be non-voluntary in the sense that one must belong to a FOCUS providing for a certain function, for example, to a school FOCUS, and must pay the corresponding taxes (an analogy here is health insurance which in many countries is obligatory but where individuals are allowed to choose an insurance company). The citizens of such a school FOCUS may then decide that everyone must pay taxes in order to finance a particular school, irrespective of whether one has children. With respect to FOCJ providing functions with significant redistributive effects, a minimal amount of regulation by the central government may be in order so that, for example, citizens without children do not join 'school FOCJ' which in effect do not offer any schooling but have correspondingly low (or zero) taxes. In this respect, Buchanan-type clubs differ from FOCJ, because they are always voluntary while membership in a FOCUS can be obligatory.

FOCJ as jurisdictions provide particular services but do not necessarily produce them themselves if contracting out to a public or private enterprise is advantageous. It is noteworthy that present-day outsourcing by communities does not automatically lead to FOCJ. The former is restricted to production, while FOCJ typically concentrate on provision and are democratically controlled. FOCJ also differ from existing functional and overlapping institutions such as the various kinds of specific administration unions (or *Zweckverbände* as they are aptly called in German-speaking countries). These institutions normally do not have the legal status of governments but are purely administrative units. The same applies to the many types of corporations which usually have no power to tax but have to rely on charges.

Beneficial effects of FOCJ
Due to its four essential characteristics, FOCJ compare favourably to traditional forms of federalism. One aspect concerns the governments' incentives and ability to satisfy heterogeneous preferences of individuals. As a consequence of the concentration on one functional area, the citizens of a particular FOCUS have better information on its activity, and are in a better position to compare its performance with that of other governments. As many benefits and costs extend over a quite limited geographic area, we envisage FOCJ to be often small which is also helpful for voters' evaluations. The exit option opened by the existence of overlapping jurisdictions is not only an important

means to make one's preferences known to governmental suppliers but it also strengthens the citizens' incentives to be informed about politics (see Eichenberger and Serna 1996).

On the other hand, FOCJ are able to provide public services at low cost because they are formed in order to minimize interjurisdictional spillovers and to exploit economies of scale. When the benefits of a specific activity indivisibly extend over large areas, and there are decreasing costs, the corresponding optimal FOCUS may cover many communities, several nations, or even Europe as a whole. An example may be defence against outward aggression where the appropriate FOCUS may most likely extend over the whole of Europe (even beyond the European Union). That such adjustment to efficient size is indeed undertaken in reality is shown by the Swiss experience. Communities decided by referendum whether they wanted to join the new Canton of Jura established in 1978, and in 1993 communities in the Laufental opted to belong to the Canton of Basel-Land instead of Berne. Communities also frequently change districts (the federal level below cantons) by referendum vote, which suggest that voters perceive the new size of jurisdictions and the new bundle of services to be more efficient. The same holds for American special districts.

The specialization in one or a few functions further contributes to cost efficiency due to the advantages of specialization. As FOCJ levy their own taxes to finance their activity, it pays to be economical. In contrast, in APJ (all-purpose jurisdictions) financed from outside lacking such fiscal equivalence, politicians have an incentive to lobby for ever-increasing funds, thereby pushing up government expenditures. The incentive to economize in a FOCUS induces its managers to contract out whenever production cost can thereby be reduced. While FOCJ are more market oriented than APJ, they reduce the size of the public sector. However, they differ from today's one-shot privatization, which usually does not impact on the government's basic incentives and thus is often reversed by re-regulation and de-privatization. In contrast, in a system of FOCJ privatization emerges endogenously and is sustainable, as the politicians' incentives are fundamentally changed.

The threat of dissatisfied citizens or communities exiting the FOCUS, and the benefit of new citizens and communities joining, gives an incentive to take individual preferences into account and to provide public services efficiently. Quite another advantage of FOCJ is that they open up the politicians' cartel (*classe politique*) to functionally competent outsiders. While in APJ people with broad and non-specialized knowledge tend to become politicians, in FOCJ those with a well-grounded knowledge in a particular functional area (for example, education or refuse collection) are successful.

FOCJ not only make it possible for the citizens to change from one supplier to another, but they also increase the mobility of politicians. In transborder

FOCJ, politicians will be allowed to supply their services in several countries. This is in stark contrast to current regulations, which prevent politicians from doing so. In FOCJ, it is also more likely than in traditional territorial units that foreigners and institutional providers are allowed to enter the political market (on the favourable effects of open markets for politics, see Eichenberger and Frey 2002; Eichenberger 2003). While many people reject the idea of allowing policy consulting firms and foreigners to run directly for office in general-purpose units, they are quite favourable to the idea when it is applied to the politics of FOCJ. Examples are FOCJ that concentrate on the supply of fresh water and sewage systems, which could be governed by international firms specializing in water resource management.

The right to form FOCJ helps to address issues raised by fundamentalist sentiments. Political movements focused on a single issue (for example, ethnicity, religion, environment and so on) are not forced to take over governments *in toto* but can concentrate on those functions they are really interested in. An ethnic group need not dissociate itself from the state they live in as a whole but may establish FOCJ which cater for their particular preferences. South Tyroleans, for example, unhappy with the language domination imposed by the Italian state, need not leave Italy in order to have their demands for cultural autonomy fulfilled, but may establish corresponding FOCJ. Such partial exit (for example, only with respect to ethnic issues) does not lead to trade barriers often following the establishment of newly formed all-purpose political jurisdictions. FOCJ thus meet the criterion of market preserving federalism (see Qian and Weingast 1997).

A federal web composed of FOCJ undoubtedly affects the role of nation states. They will certainly lose functions they presently do not fulfil according to the population's preferences, or which they produce at higher cost than FOCJ designed to exploit cost advantages. On the other hand, the scheme does not purport to do away with nations but allows for multinational as well as small-scale alternatives where they are desired by the citizens. Nation states subsist in so far as they provide functions efficiently according to the voters' preferences.

IV.   FOCJ in perspective

Our proposal is purely process oriented. It is neither necessary nor possible to determine at the European and at the national levels all the functions which should be provided by FOCJ and how these entities should be organized. The internal organization of a particular FOCUS lies solely in the competence of the communities and individuals who decide to establish such a jurisdiction. Nevertheless, it is possible to specify the conditions for FOCJ to emerge and to fulfil their tasks effectively. Thus, our approach follows the logic of constitutional economics, which aims to design beneficial decision processes without closely defining the outcomes (Buchanan and Tullock 1962; Mueller 1996).

One condition is crucial for FOCJ to work properly: economic and political competition must be guaranteed. Thus, economic markets in FOCJ have to be open; in particular, the four freedoms referring to the free movement of goods, services, and capital, and the free mobility of individuals have to be secured. At the same time, the political markets of FOCJ have to be competitive, that is, human rights and fundamental democratic rights have to be guaranteed. This includes the right for citizens to make use of the instruments of direct democracy.

Not only traditional governments, but also the governing bodies of FOCJ, pursue their own interests and tend to undermine competition and to build cartels or even monopolies. Therefore, the rules have to be monitored by a 'competition supervisory board'. This body also has to fix rules for determining the ceiling on entry and exit fees. If they are too high, mobility is hampered. However, such prices for mobility prove effective in preventing individuals from exploiting the redistributive policies in FOCJ. Regulative measures may also be necessary to enable FOCJ to supply public services effectively (see also Vanberg 2000), as has been discussed above for the case of school FOCJ. In such cases, it may be advantageous to declare membership in a FOCUS to be obligatory, and to fix minimum service levels. The competition supervisory board must be given the competencies to step in if such regulations are violated. This board has to be empowered in a constitutional decision at the national (or, even better, international) level. However, it would be a mistake to delegate the monitoring of competition among FOCJ to the national bureaucracies which are interested in restricting FOCJ. Rather, an independent agency seems appropriate. A possible solution could be a constitutional court (in the European Union, the European Court of Justice). Even though such institutions tend to favour national at the expense of regional and local interests, their decisions tend to be less biased than those of national political institutions.

In light of the stiff resistance functional jurisdictions will meet, they can emerge successfully only if two conditions are met:

1. To establish and to operate FOCJ must be a constitutionally guaranteed right – the 'fifth freedom', as we would like to call it. The newly founded political units must be allowed to operate as jurisdictions with (restricted) enforcement rights. The power to tax in order to finance a clearly specified service is the key to efficiency. However, this right of FOCJ will be disputed by other political units with which FOCJ will compete for the same tax base.

    Principally, the communities (as the lowest-level political units) as well as individuals should be allowed to form FOCJ. However, depending upon the function to be fulfilled, membership may be restricted to the former. It is, for example, highly possible that individuals form a FOCUS which provides a special type of schooling; for other services, especially for those with stronger public good appeal, for example, waste water treatment or local police, communities or parts of them are the 'natural' agent. It is important to note that the decision to which of these two classes a function belongs can be left to the local level itself. This decision should not be transferred to the European level.

2. Existing political units may not hinder the formation of FOCJ. Most importantly, the higher-level political units have to appropriately reduce the taxes of those citizens who become members of a FOCUS or of various FOCJ providing governmental services. The competition supervisory board has to force the existing units to openly declare the cost, that is, the tax prices of the various services they provide. These 'tax price lists' can then serve to fairly rebalance the tax rate of the citizens who receive services from newly emerging FOCJ instead of from traditional political units. The existing governments' tendency to underrate the cost in order to minimize tax reductions to FOCJ members can be broken simply by demanding that the tax prices for a specific service serve not only to compensate exiting citizens, but also to tax former and newly entering service recipients. This rule makes the market for politics contestable. The potential existence of FOCJ is enough to compel all levels of government to give an account of the real cost of their services. However, it need not be said that existing political units will use all possible measures to impede the new competitors. Thus, the competition supervisory board does not have an easy job. Again, the constitutional court seems to be the appropriate institution to undertake this task. It could rely on the competencies of the audit office (or the court of accounts or *Rechnungshof*) to control the calculations of the tax prices. This latter institution has the necessary knowledge which has so far been wasted, as audit offices are typically only allowed to formulate non-binding recommendations which are most often ignored by the political decision makers.

V. FOCJ in the future and in the past

Future opportunities

There is a wide range of functional issues to which FOCJ could profitably be applied. A practical example is the policing of Lake Constance (which borders on two German *Länder*, two Swiss cantons and one Austrian *Land*) which involves the regulation of traffic, environmental protection, the suppression of criminal activities and the prevention of accidents. Formally, the various local police departments are not allowed to directly collaborate with one another, not even to exchange information. Rather, they must advise the police ministries of the *Länder* and cantons, which then have to notify the respective central governments which then interact with one another. Obviously, such a formal procedure is in most cases vastly inefficient and unnecessarily time consuming. In actual fact, the problems are dealt with by direct contact among the local police commissioners and officers. However, this is outside the law and depends, to a substantial extent, on purely personal relationships (which may be good or bad). A FOCUS committed to policing the lake would allow a pragmatic, problem-oriented approach within the law – and would, moreover, be in the best 'spirit' of Europe.

FOCJ are not restricted to such small-scale functional issues but are relevant for all levels of government and major issues. An example would be Alsace which, while remaining a part of France in other respects, might partially exit by joining, say, the German social security or school system (with German as the main language), or might join a university FOCUS involving the Swiss University of Basle and the German universities of Freiburg and Karlsruhe. Actually, the first steps for establishing such a university FOCUS are under way. But these efforts contrast with the idea of regions as set out in the Maastricht Treaty (or elsewhere), not least because one of the participants (the University of Basle) is not part of the European Union. Another example refers to Corsica which according to Drèze's (1993) suggestion should form an independent region of Europe because of its dissatisfaction with France. However, most likely the Corsicans are only *partially* dissatisfied with France. This suggests that one or several FOCJ provide a better solution in this case; they may, for example, especially focus on ethnic or language boundaries or on Corsica's economic problems as an island. This would make it possible for the Corsicans to exit France only partially instead of totally. Quite generally, tourism and transport issues, in particular railroads, are important areas for FOCJ. It should be noted that, despite the membership of various countries in the (then) European Community, railroad policy was not coordinated to exploit possible economies of scale; a FOCUS may constitute an appropriate organization to overcome such shortcomings.

Contemporary and historical forerunners

The original European Community started out as a FOCUS designed to establish free trade in Europe, and was from the very beginning in competition with other trade areas, in particular North America, Japan and the European Free Trade Association (EFTA). Due to its economic success, it has attracted almost all European countries. But entry has not been free, the nations determined to enter had to pay a price. They have (with partial exceptions) to accept the *acquis communautaire* as well as to pay their share to the Union's outlays which to a large extent serve redistributive purposes. In several respects there exist FOCJ-like units within Europe with respect to law enforcement, education, environment, transport, culture or sports, though they have been prevented from becoming autonomous jurisdictions with taxing power.

Most of these functional units are not contiguous with the area of the European Union. Some are smaller (for example, those organized along ethnic or language functions), and some are larger. Several East European countries and Switzerland, which are not EU members, are certainly fully involved in, for example, European culture, education or crime. FOCJ of the nature understood in this chapter may therefore build upon already existing structures, and are in the best of European traditions.

There are two countries in which functional, overlapping and competing jurisdictions exist, that is, the United States and Switzerland (though they do not in all cases meet the full requirements of FOCJ specified above).

United States   Single-purpose governments in the form of 'special districts' play a significant role in the American federalist system (ACIR 1982, 1987; Foster 1996; Nuun and Schoedel 1997). Their number has increased considerably, between 1967 and 1972 by 30.4 per cent, and between 1972 and 1984 by 19.7 per cent, in both cases more quickly than other types of jurisdiction (Zax 1988). There are both autonomous and democratically organized as well as dependent special districts (for example, for fire prevention or recreation and parks). Empirical research suggests that the former type is significantly more efficient (Mehay 1984). In contrast to all-purpose jurisdictions, functionally specialized units are able to exploit economies of scale. While, in school districts, increasing size leads to lower cost of production, in all-purpose communities there is no size effect as they fulfil many functions with decreasing economies of scale, and their citizens lose control over politicians (Zax 1989).

Our theoretical hypothesis of the opposition of existing jurisdictions to the formation of special districts is well borne out. In order not to threaten the monopoly power of existing municipality statutes, 18 states prohibit new municipalities within a specified distance from existing municipalities (ACIR 1982; Zax 1988); in various states there is a minimum population size required, and various other administrative restrictions have been introduced (see, for example, Nelson 1990). Empirical studies reveal that these barriers imposed by local agency formation commissions (LAFCOs) tend to reduce the relative efficiency of the local administration (Di Lorenzo 1981; Deno and Mehay 1985), and tend to push the local government expenditures upwards in those municipalities which have introduced LAFCOs (Martin and Wagner 1978).

Switzerland   Many Swiss cantons have a structure of overlapping and competing functional jurisdictions which share many features of FOCJ. In the canton of Zurich (with a population of 1.2 million), there are 171 geographical communities which in themselves are composed of three to six independently managed, direct democratically organized communities devoted to specific functions and levying their own taxes on personal income: in addition to general-purpose communities, there are communities that exclusively provide for elementary schools and others specializing in junior high schools, and there are the communities of three different churches. All these governmental units have widely differing rates of income taxes. Moreover, there are a vast number of 'civil communities' (*Zivilgemeinden*) providing water, electricity, TV antennas and so on, which are 'direct-democratic' but finance themselves by user charges. These communities often overlap with neighbouring political communities. In addition there are 174 functional units (*Zweckverbände*), whose members are not individual citizens but communities. These *Zweckverbände* are responsible, for example, for waste water and purification plants, cemeteries, hospitals and regional planning. The Zurich canton is not the only Swiss canton with various types of functional communities. A similar structure exists, for example, in the Glarus or Thurgau cantons (for the latter, see Casella and Frey 1992). Various efforts have been made to suppress this diversity of functional communities, usually initiated by the cantonal bureaucracy and politicians. However, most of these attempts were thwarted because the population is largely satisfied with the public supply provided. The example of Switzerland – which is generally considered to be a well-organized and -administered country – demonstrates that a multiplicity of functional jurisdictions under democratic control is not a theorist's wishful thinking but has worked well in reality.

Decentralized, overlapping political units have also been an important feature of European history. The competition between jurisdictions in the Holy Roman Empire of German Nations, especially in today's Italy and Germany, was intensive. Many of these jurisdictions were small. Many scholars attribute the rise of Europe to this diversity and competition of governmental units which fostered technical, economic and artistic innovation (see, for example, Hayek 1960; Jones 1981; Weede 1993; and Baumol and Baumol 1994, who also give a lively account of how the musical genius of Wolfgang Amadeus Mozart benefited from this system of government). While the Chinese were more advanced in very many respects, their superiority ended with the establishment of a centralized Chinese Empire (Rosenberg and Birdzell 1986; Pak 1995). The unification of Italy and Germany in the nineteenth century, which has often been praised as a major advance, partially ended this stimulating competition between governments and led to deadly struggles between nation states.[3] Some smaller states escaped unification; Liechtenstein, Luxembourg,

Monaco, San Marino and Switzerland stayed politically independent, and at the same time grew rich.

The above-mentioned governmental units were not FOCJ in the sense outlined in this contribution but they shared the characteristic of competing among themselves for labour and capital (including artistic capital). However, history also reveals examples of jurisdictions close to FOCJ, most importantly in multicultural and plural societies (Coakley 2003; Kyriacou 2004). For instance, the problems connected with Poland's strong ethnic and religious diversity (Catholics, Protestants and Jews) were at least partly overcome by jurisdictions organized according to these features, and not on geographical lines (see, for example, Rhode 1960; Haumann 1991). The highly successful Hanse prospered from the twelfth to the sixteenth century, and comprised among others Lübeck, Bremen, Köln (today Germany), Stettin and Danzig (today Poland), Kaliningrad (today Russia), Riga, Reval and Dorpat (today Baltic republics) and Groningen and Deventer (today the Netherlands); furthermore, London (England), Bruges and Antwerp (today Belgium) and Novgorod (today Russia) were *Handelskontore* or associated members. It was clearly a functional governmental unit providing for trade rules and facilities and was not geographically contiguous.

VI. FOCJ and Europe

In its present form, EU enlargement solves some old problems, but also creates many new ones. With progressing enlargement, the economic and institutional disparities grow among the member countries, as well as between the existing members and the new neighbouring countries at the shifting outer borders. The envisaged integration of Turkey, for instance, would make Georgia, Armenia, Iran, Iraq and Syria neighbours of the EU.

For several reasons, it will prove impossible to fully integrate all the present neighbouring countries and, *a fortiori*, the new neighbours, without changing the whole concept and institutions of the EU:

1. *Decreasing potential for full integration* The increasing economic and institutional gap at the outer border makes it unlikely that border countries can, in due time, meet the formal requirements regulating the entry into the EU,[4] which stipulate that acceding states must have a stable democracy and a functioning market economy, follow the rule of law, observe appropriate standards of human rights and protect minorities, and most importantly must agree to the obligations of EU membership which include adherence to the aims of political and economic union. This means that they have to fully accept the *acquis communautaire*. This legal corpus of the EU has now reached a considerable size, involving more than 16,000 pages of text.

2. *Overcharged redistribution system* It is most unlikely that the EU
    member states will be willing to grant ever poorer applicant countries the
    free movement of labour, and integrate them into the EU income redistri-
    bution mechanisms, the most important being the common agricultural
    policy and the structural funds. For a long time to come, the income
    differences between the existing member states and the countries apply-
    ing for entry will be too large (see Carius et al. 2000).
3. *The growing democracy deficit* Enlargement does not even begin to
    tackle the basic problem of the EU, the democracy deficit. On the
    contrary, it has even worsened. In a growing EU without fundamental
    institutional reforms, the negotiation processes among the member coun-
    tries become more complex and the responsibilities more blurred. Thus,
    the citizens' influence on politics diminishes and the discretionary leeway
    of the EU decision making bodies grows. The large increase in the
    number of member countries, with even more divergent preferences
    among the population, necessitates new decision making mechanisms in
    the Council of Ministers and the Commission. Without such structural
    changes, there is a risk of deadlock, or at least a standstill, because the citi-
    zens' resistance to widening and deepening the EU will increase.

How will the European Union respond to these challenges? A likely
scenario is already partly visible. The negotiations will most probably extend
over a long period, in any case much longer than desired by the applicants. The
formal entry conditions will be maintained, but long adjustment periods will
have to be granted. Most importantly, the free movement of labour will more
than likely be blocked by the current members, while the countries applying
for membership will ask for exemptions from the free movement of goods,
services and capital. The challenges will therefore be solved only at the legal
level, while the underlying economic problems of integration will remain
unsolved.

As the income discrepancies at the borders increase, migration will pose a
growing problem. The huge economic discrepancies and disequilibrium
creates opportunities for rent seeking and interventionism, which result in
protectionism, stagnation and corruption.

At the same time, the political structure of the EU will not be fundamentally changed, but only the weights of the respective countries in the decision
making procedures will be somewhat adjusted, and the requirements of
unanimity and qualified majorities will be somewhat softened. At the end, the
discussion on the democracy deficit tends to be undermined by the strong
focus on enlargement. On the whole, this scenario suggests that the EU will
continue to 'muddle through' instead of squarely facing the problems of
enlarged membership.

The concept of FOCJ suggests a totally different approach. Countries which want to be integrated more closely with the EU should have the option of forming FOCJ with some or all EU member states. Thus, they would get the possibility of *partial* entry rather than the all-or-nothing decision to accept the whole *acquis communautaire* in one go. These FOCJ should not be imposed from above, but should emerge as the result of the voluntary negotiations between the new partners. To the extent that the partially integrated countries develop (partly as a result of the existence of these flexible partnerships), an increasing number of such FOCJ with different members and functions will arise so that an ever closer integration can take place. With FOCJ, variable geometry is a desirable feature of integration rather than a shortcoming. It goes far beyond the proposal for a multispeed integration of some 'chosen' countries into a 'core Europe' (as recently proposed by the former German foreign minister Joschka Fischer), or the special cases of the treaties of Schengen and of the Economic and Monetary Union (EMU), which not all EU member countries need to join.

Flexible widening and deepening
FOCJ allow for differentiated, tailor-made integration. Thus, they are in stark contrast with the *acquis communautaire*, which stands for equalized integration. With FOCJ, countries and regions can establish cooperation in those matters in which it is really important that they cooperate, and they are not forced into cooperation with respect to those matters where they would rather act alone. However, for three reasons FOCJ do not lead to less integration than the *acquis communautaire*. First, FOCJ decrease the price of integration for the citizens and thus increase the demand for integration, as they make integration more efficient and enhance citizens' democratic influence. Second, thanks to FOCJ, integration of partner countries is no longer a question of 'all or nothing'. The countries which are not able to quickly incorporate the *acquis communautaire* can be integrated better with FOCJ than without. Third, a FOCUS may aim at stronger integration with respect to its specific function than the *acquis*.

Of course, differentiated integration is not a totally new concept. Today's standard procedure of integration of new member countries also entails some differentiation, as the countries are granted different adaptation periods. These, however, are only looked at as temporary exceptions and unwelcome deviations from the current *acquis*. They neither allow for stronger integration with respect to certain functions, nor do they give the new entrants the right to search for different degrees of integration with a special selection of today's members. Partial integration has also been institutionalized in the European Economic Area (EEA) with Norway, Iceland and Liechtenstein, or with Switzerland via bilateral treaties. However, the concept of FOCJ goes far beyond a partial integration via treaties. It provides for a common government composed of all the members. The extended rights of political co-determination strengthen identification and provide the basis for solidarity among the members.

Multilevel integration

Transborder FOCJ can emerge at all levels of government. With respect to European integration, three kinds of FOCJ may be identified:

1. *FOCJ formed by all the EU member and some non-member states*   The EU and its neighbours have a common interest in fighting transnational mafia-type activities. Today, this problem is approached in a purely technocratic way via EUROPOL and INTERPOL, often with very limited success. A police FOCUS comprising the affected nations would bring about a more efficient anti-mafia policy because governance and taxation would be matched. The FOCUS would make it possible to deploy police resources in the areas where they could most effectively be used. In contrast, the EU does not have any joint police forces, not even for special purposes. Such a police FOCUS would thus go beyond the integration now existing in the EU.

2. *FOCJ formed by some EU member and non-member states*   An example is the reciprocal acceptance of technical norms for goods and services. With present arrangements, trade between the EU member and non-member states is severely hindered, as the norms differ and the countries do not accept each other's norms – that is, the 'Cassis de Dijon' principle is only valid within the EU. However, it is impossible to apply this important principle to non-EU members, as there are always some member countries in which some influential special- interest groups stand to lose from freer trade, and thus object to liberalizing trade. Under the regime suggested here, those members of the EU could partially integrate their economies with selected neighbouring countries by establishing a joint FOCUS for the reciprocal acceptance of norms. Such a FOCUS would most probably not only represent a treaty stipulating the reciprocal acceptance of norms, but it would also have an institutional structure, which guarantees that the norms of the EU partner countries satisfy some reasonable standards and that the norms are followed by the producers. Thus, such a FOCUS would be an institution which comes close to a special government for the setting, controlling and reciprocal acceptance of norms. This allows all the FOCUS members to exploit their international comparative advantage, and thus to experience a welfare gain, even if full integration according to the *acquis communautaire* is impossible.

3. *FOCJ formed by communities and regions of some EU member and non-member states* This is a new form of cross-border cooperation. A pertinent example refers to local environmental degradation, say water pollution. One or several communities of, for example, Finland, Estonia and Russia, may form an environmental FOCUS. The government of the FOCUS would be elected by the citizens of all the communities involved. The FOCUS would be responsible for water quality in the area, would set the standards best meeting the preferences of all the citizens and would impose the taxes necessary to reach these goals. The Russian communities can therewith adopt an environmental standard higher than that generally obtained in the rest of their nation. Such an institutional arrangement is also advantageous for the respective Finnish and Estonian communities because of the negative spillovers connected with Russian emissions.

Obviously, FOCJ not only facilitate the integration of new countries, but they also make it possible for the current members to flexibly deepen integration. Therefore, the general rules of full integration into the EU can be relaxed to some extent, as the countries that want to integrate more closely have an effective institutional tool for doing so (which differs sharply from existing instruments such as the regions as envisaged in the INTERREG programmes, see, for example, European Commission 2001; Jensen and Richardson 2001).

Meeting the challenges
By making use of the concept of FOCJ, the three main challenges faced when enlarging the EU can be successfully addressed.

1. *Outer-border problems* The use of FOCJ allows a differentiated expansion of the EU instead of an abrupt rupture when it comes to non-EU countries. This can be achieved in two ways: first, a country which is not yet able to accept the *acquis*, would nevertheless be able to enter the EU partially, that is, with respect to only some functions. Thus, integration of potential member countries is accelerated and facilitated. Such partial enlargement will have much farther-reaching geographical implications than the all-or-nothing approach. Second, the institutional development of partially integrated countries will be accelerated. EU transborder FOCJ are ideal vehicles for the transfer of democratic culture to neighbouring countries, as their citizens come in contact with, and become accustomed to, well-functioning democratic institutions.
2. *Income redistribution* FOCJ reduce the number of problems connected with redistribution by two means. First, the demand for receiving subsidies by current members of the EU will be reduced because with FOCJ it is feasible to cooperate mainly with respect to those functions which yield

particularly high benefits of cooperation. The applicant countries are not forced to compromise on functions from which they do not profit much, or even lose, when accepting the *acquis communautaire*. Therefore they need less compensation.

Second, it is likely that the full entry of some or all neighbouring countries will be blocked by those members which would lose from a new targeting of redistributive flows. With FOCJ, instead, particular neighbouring countries and the EU could establish a redistribution FOCUS acceptable to all existing EU members.

3. *EU decision making structure and democracy deficit*   The existing EU members which do not agree with the partial admission of one or several neighbouring countries can opt out instead of having to use their veto power. Thus, the current decision-making mechanisms in the EU need not be changed. However, FOCJ can help to overcome the democracy deficit of the EU because they are based on effective democratic principles.

VII.   FOCJ and developing countries

The concept of FOCJ is not only suited for industrial countries. It can also be fruitfully applied to developing countries whose problems are mainly due to inadequate institutions.

Too much and too little government

Economic growth in many developing countries is hampered by excessive government. The state tends to interfere in, and minutely regulate, almost all activities. The government sector, which is often very large, employs a high proportion of the population outside agriculture. The administration tends to be more bureaucratic than in industrial countries. Rent-seeking distortions are rampant and waste is pervasive. This combination of interventionism and bureaucracy stifles investment and innovation in the private sector, making over-government a reality.

At the same time, however, many governments do not adequately fulfil the functions necessary for rapid economic growth. Most importantly, property rights are only insufficiently secured. Investors are faced with a high degree of uncertainty and are, therefore, reluctant to commit themselves to long-term investments. Instead of concentrating on productive endeavours, investors devote their resources to finding substitutes for the deficient property rights.

But governments in developing countries are also inadequate in a second, quite different sense. They are far from meeting the wishes of the citizens; many are either strongly paternalistic or even dictatorial. While the preferences of the city dwellers – in particular of the capital – are at least taken into account in so far as to avoid an uprising, the preferences of the peasantry are almost totally disregarded. While some Third World countries are officially federal, central governments regularly neglect local problems and demands. Often, it even actively destroys well-working production and distribution arrangements, in particular in self-governing units.

Thus, developing countries are faced with a paradoxical situation: at the same time there is 'over-government' (that is, interventionism), and 'under-government' (that is, too little consideration for fragmented local problems). The concept of FOCJ can overcome this unproductive situation as it allows for a large number of jurisdictions that are based on grassroots local democracy to check government and prevent it from evolving into an oppressive and inter-vening bureaucracy. Of course, the concept of FOCJ deviates strongly from existing development plans. It is worth observing that a large part of the economic literature on development does not address the government struc-ture. The failures of government are duly noted but no remedies are proposed. To just hope that the future will bring 'better politicians' is unfounded opti-mism. Government will only improve if the underlying institutional conditions are changed. This is exactly what FOCJ do. These jurisdictions are formed according to the geography of problems, that is, by the citizens seeking to cope with issues with which they are confronted.

The local power to impose taxes as an essential ingredient to FOCJ will also prove decisive for developing countries. Whenever the central govern-ment allocates funds (as it is the rule in today's 'federal' developing countries) the lower-level units become dependent on it and have biased incentives so that most of the advantages of decentralization are lost. Under these circum-stances, decentralization is not necessarily beneficial. In a system with impor-tant central allocations, the lower-level units are liable to become fiscally irresponsible. They tend to borrow too much on the (normally correct) assumption that they will be bailed out by the central government if they run into trouble. In contrast, if FOCJ have the power to levy their own taxes, the population would have to carry the cost of bad politics, therefore, governments have an incentive to observe the budget constraint and to behave fiscally responsibly.

Benefits of FOCJ for developing countries
FOCJ produce major advantages over the existing form of government in developing countries:

1. They break the central government's effort to monopolize politics which would otherwise stifle economic development and oppress the citizens. FOCJ shift the power to initiatives from below. Effective local govern-ments become viable because they have authority over particular govern-ment functions, and may raise taxes to finance the respective expenditures.

2. FOCJ make it possible to combine various forms of political rules. They blend not only federalism with democracy, that is exit and voice, but also modern and traditional styles of governing such as meetings by village elders. Time-proven local ways of public decision making are not eliminated, but are used and fostered in those areas in which they prove to be effective.
3. FOCJ solve the 'fundamental organizational dilemma' between an open polity and decentralized development at the local level: 'one of the necessary (though far from sufficient) conditions of a development state is a large degree of insulation that the development-minded decision makers can have against the ravages of short-run pork barrel politics and their ability to use the discipline of the market . . . against the inevitable follies of group predation' (Bardhan 1993, p. 46). Indeed, FOCJ provide such insulation by the establishment of new, growth-oriented development units which are, however, disciplined by economic and political competition.
4. FOCJ deal with another 'fundamental dilemma of government' (Montignola et al. 1995, pp. 54–5). The state has to be strong enough to enforce legal rules, especially property rights which are prerequisites for economic development. At the same time, government institutions have to be 'weak' in the sense of not exploiting the citizens by, for example, expropriation or excessive taxation. FOCJ are able to convey credible limits against such exploitation because each FOCUS is self-financed and may go bankrupt if its members choose the exit option. In a system of FOCJ, individuals and firms do not face a monopolistic and therefore oppressive state but may resort to substitutes.
5. There is an emphasis on local public production and efficient polycentric organization. This aspect has been much neglected in the literature.
6. The fiscal decentralization induced by FOCJ reduces the volatility in macroeconomic variables (for instance, in budget deficits and income growth).
7. The concept of FOCJ overcomes the fruitless contradiction of 'government versus market' which was typical of many of the writings on developing countries. FOCJ mark a radical departure from much of the earlier literature on developing countries that emphasized the need for a strong, well-organized central state and bureaucracy to steer and support economic growth. They depart from the more recent exclusive emphasis on private property and free market as the key to successful development. In both cases local governments needed for economic growth are neglected.

Arguments against FOCJ in developing countries
Some people consider the claim that FOCJ are also advantageous to developing countries to be too optimistic and naively neglect the specific conditions reigning there. The following three related assertions are discussed below:

1. *FOCJ will not work in developing countries which are neither federalis-tic nor democratic*   The pre-colonial political system in most developing countries was characterized by various forms of self-government, though they, of course, did not meet the criteria of democracy with which we are familiar. Vestiges remain even today, but this traditional way of govern-ing was on the whole destroyed by the authoritarian colonial rule. Post-colonial governments wanted to centralize as much power as possible in their hands, and consequently destroyed traditional local rule.

2. *FOCJ are unsuitable for developing countries*   This 'culturalist posi-tion' maintains that individuals in developing regions are basically different from Westerners and, therefore, need a different form of government, arguably a more authoritarian one. A popular version of this belief is that people in developing countries lack the discipline and initia-tive to form FOCJ. However, the economic approach to human behaviour suggests the opposite causation. The lack of observed discipline and initiative is the consequence, and not the cause, of unfavourable institu-tional settings.

    Three types of empirical observations strongly support the economic view: (i) Empirical evidence shows that to the extent self-government could be preserved, it often functions well and is even able to solve diffi-cult common property resource problems (Wade 1988; Ostrom 1990; Ostrom et al. 1993). (ii) When individuals in developing countries shed the stifling restrictions imposed upon them by government bureaucracies, they become active and venturesome. While this applies to all developing countries, it has been particularly impressively demonstrated for Peru by de Soto (1989), who shows that people who are passive within the confines of the highly regulated and inimical official sector become enter-prising and energetic once they act in the unofficial or shadow economy. (iii) Even experiences with an extreme form of democracy, popular refer-enda, are positive provided they are devoted to substantive issues and not simply plebiscites to support the authoritarian or dictatorial rulers (Rourke et al. 1992). If citizens in developing countries are taken seriously, they participate in political affairs (for Africa, for example, Chazon 1994; for Mexico, see Oberreuter and Weiland 1994).

3. *FOCJ worsen inequality*   Many people believe that central governments promote inequality while federal systems make the rich richer and the poor poorer. Central governments are at best formally committed to an 'equal' provision of public services but in actual fact, there are huge differences in the services provided across the country – Ostrom et al. (1993, p. 211) even speak of a 'myth of equality'. Typically the popula-tion in the capital is grossly favoured, in particular by highly subsidized food, while the much poorer inhabitants in the rural areas are taxed. FOCJ

redress such imbalances because they are based on decentralized decision making and subsequently allow regional and local development of the natural and human resources to be made available.

VIII.   Conclusions

Our concept of functional, overlapping and competing jurisdictions provides a radical alternative to today's policy in industrial and developing countries. However, the idea of FOCJ is not driven by any particular ideology (except for the normative position that politics should function according to the citizens' preferences), and it does not suggest perfect, simple or ready-made solutions. Nor does it require an all-or-nothing decision. It may sometimes appear surprising and perhaps even shocking, but it may be introduced on a step-by-step basis. The beneficial features of the concept already become evident even when it is only applied with regard to some functions and a few members. This does not mean that FOCJ emerge all by themselves. Even if political competition works well to the advantage of citizens, established politicians who see their power reduced will make an effort to block or at least undermine the concept. It is, therefore, necessary to openly and seriously discuss the proposal in order to make the advantages generally known and accepted by the population. In democratic societies the citizens then have the means to make FOCJ become a reality by rewriting the constitutions such that FOCJ may emerge.

Notes

1. It could be argued that locally elected politicians in central states also face incentives to cater for the local preferences. However, in many countries, the members of the national parliament are only partly, or not at all, elected in local districts. In the Federal Republic of Germany, for instance, a substantial share of the members of the Bundestag are not elected by winning in a particular precinct but because they are placed on a list which is controlled by the party they belong to. Moreover, in national parliaments, a local delegate's accountability is low as he/she is only one of several hundred parliamentarians.
2. The concept of FOCJ is extensively discussed in Frey and Eichenberger (1999). Similar ideas have already been found in Montesquieu (1749). Burnheim (1985) and Wehner (1992) mention similar elements. In the economics literature, a related concept has been pioneered by Tullock (1994), who calls it 'sociological federalism'. Casella and Frey (1992) discuss the concept and refer to relevant literature. A Centre for Economic Policy Research Publication (CEPR 1993) briefly mentions the possibility of establishing overlapping jurisdictions in Europe (pp. 54–5) but does not elaborate on the concept or refer to previous research (except for Drèze 1993 on secession).
3. According to Sperber (1994, p. 24), in the first half of the nineteenth century, average income was higher in strongly decentralized Germany than in strongly centralized France, which may at least partly be attributed to the difference in the degree of centralization.
4. See Cameron (1998); Dehousse (1998); Laurent and Maresceau (1998); Wagener and Heiko (1998).

References

Advisory Commission on Intergovernmental Relations (ACIR) (1982), *State and Local Roles in the Federal System*, Report A-88, Washington, DC: US Government Printing Office.

Advisory Commission on Intergovernmental Relations (ACIR) (1987), *The Organization of Local Public Economies*, Report A-109, Washington, DC: US Government Printing Office.

Ashworth, John, Bruno Heyndels and Carine Smolders (2002), 'Redistribution as a local public good: an empirical test for Flemish municipalities', *Kyklos* **55**: 27–56.

Backhaus, Jürgen G. and Detmar Doering (2004), *The Political Economy of Secession – A Source Book*, Zürich: Neue Zürcher Zeitung Publishing.

Bardhan, Pranab (1993), 'Symposium on democracy and development', *Journal of Economic Perspectives* **7**: 45–9.

Baumol, William J. and Hilda Baumol (1994), 'On the economics of musical composition in Mozart's Vienna', *Journal of Cultural Economics* **18**: 171–98.

Besley, Timothy and Anne Case (1995), 'Incumbent behaviour: vote-seeking, tax-setting, and yardstick competition', *American Economic Review* **85**: 25–45.

Breton, Albert (1996), *Competitive Governments. An Economic Theory of Politics and Public Finance*, Cambridge and New York: Cambridge University Press.

Buchanan, James M. (1965), 'An economic theory of clubs', *Economica* **32**: 1–14.

Buchanan, James M. (1991), 'An American perspective on Europe's constitutional opportunity', *Cato Journal* **10**: 619–29.

Buchanan, James and Gordon Tullock (1962), *The Calculus of Consent*, Ann Arbor, MI: University of Michigan Press.

Burnheim, John (1985), *Is Democracy Possible? The Alternative to Electoral Politics*, Cambridge: Polity Press.

Cameron, Fraser (1998), *Preparing for Enlargement: Policy and Institutional Reform in the EU*, Brussels: European Commission Directorate General IA.

Carius, Alexander, Ingmar von Hohmeyer and Stefani Bär (2000), 'The Eastern enlargement of the European Union and environmental policy: challenges, expectations, speed and flexibility', in Katharia Holzinger and Peter Knoepfel (eds), *Environmental Policy in a European Union of Variable Geometry? The Challenge of the Next Enlargement*, Basel: Helbing & Lichtenhahn: 141–80.

Casella, Alessandra and Bruno S. Frey (1992), 'Federalism and clubs: towards an economic theory of overlapping political jurisdictions', *European Economic Review* **36**: 639–46.

Centre for Economic Policy Research (CEPR) (1993). *Making Sense of Subsidiarity: How Much Centralization for Europe?*, London: CEPR.

Chazon, Naomi (1994), 'Between liberalism and statism: African political cultures and democracy', in Larry Diamond (ed.), *Political Culture and Democracy in Developing Countries*, Boulder, CO: Lynne Rienner, 59–97.

Coakley, John (ed.) (2003), *The Territorial Management of Ethnic Conflict*, 2nd edition, London: Frank Cass.

de Soto, Hernando (1989), *The Other Path: The Invisible Revolution in the Third World*, New York: Harper & Row.

Dehousse, Renaud (ed.) (1998), *An Ever Larger Union? The Eastern Enlargement in Perspective*, Baden-Baden: Nomos.

Deno, Kevin T. and Stephen L. Mehay (1985), 'Institutional constraints on local jurisdiction formation', *Public Finance Quarterly* **13**: 450–63.

DiLorenzo, Thomas J. (1981), 'Special districts and local public services', *Public Finance Quarterly* **9**: 353–67.

Downs, Anthony (1957), *An Economic Theory of Democracy*, New York: Harper & Row.

Drèze, Jacques (1993), 'Regions of Europe: a feasible status, to be discussed', *Economic Policy* **17**: 266–307.

Eichenberger, Reiner (2003), 'Towards a European market for good politics: a politico-economic reform proposal', *Jahrbuch für Neue Politische Ökonomie* **22**: 221–37.

Eichenberger, Reiner and Bruno S. Frey (2002), 'Democratic governance for a globalized world', *Kyklos* **55**: 265–87.

Eichenberger, Reiner and Angel Serna (1996), 'Random errors, dirty information, and politics', *Public Choice* **86**: 137–56.

Epple, Dennis and Allan Zelenitz (1981), 'The implications of competition among jurisdictions: does Tiebout need politics?', *Journal of Political Economy* **89**: 1197–217.

European Commission (2001), *A Guide to Bringing INTERREG and Tacis Funding Together*, Luxemburg: Office of Official Publications of the European Communities.
European Constitutional Group (1993), *A Proposal for a European Constitution*, London.
Feld, Lars P. (2000), *Steuerwettbewerb und seine Auswirkungen auf Allokation und Distribution: Eine Überblick und eine empirische Analyse für die Schweiz*, Tübingen: Mohr.
Feld, Lars P. and Gebhard Kirchgässner (2001), 'The political economy of direct legislation: direct democracy and local decision making', *Economic Policy* **16** (33): 331–67.
Feld, Lars P. and John G. Matsusaka (2003), 'Budget referendums and government spending: evidence from Swiss cantons', *Journal of Public Economics* **87**: 2703–24.
Foster, Kathryn A. (1996), 'Specialization in government: the uneven use of special districts in US metropolitan areas', *Urban Affairs Review* **31**: 283–313.
Frey, Bruno S. (1983), *Democratic Economic Policy*, Oxford: Blackwell.
Frey, Bruno S. (1994), 'Direct democracy: politico-economic lessons from Swiss experience', *American Economic Review* **84**: 338–42.
Frey, Bruno S. and Reiner Eichenberger (1999), *The New Democratic Federalism for Europe: Functional, Overlapping and Competing Jurisdictions*, Cheltenham, UK and Northampton, MA, USA: Edward Elgar.
Frey, Bruno S. and Alois Stutzer (2001), *Happiness and Economics: How the Economy and Institutions Affect Human Well-Being*, Princeton, NJ: Princeton University Press.
Gold, Steven D. (1991), 'Interstate competition and state personal income-tax policy in the 1980s', in Daphne A. Kenyon and John Kincaid (eds), *Competition among States and Local Governments*, Washington, DC: Urban Institute Press, 205–17.
Haumann, Heiko (1991), *Geschichte der Ostjuden*, Munich: Deutscher Taschenbuch-Verlag.
Hayek, Friedrich August von (1960), *The Constitution of Liberty*, Chicago: Chicago University Press.
Hirschman, Albert O. (1970), *Exit, Voice and Loyalty*, Cambridge, MA: Harvard University Press.
Jensen, Ole B. and Tim Richardson (2001), 'Nested visions: new rationalities of space in European spatial planning', *Regional Studies* **35**: 703–17.
Jones, Eric L. (1981), *The European Miracle*, Cambridge: Cambridge University Press.
Kirchgässner, Gebhard and Werner W. Pommerehne (1996), 'Tax harmonization and tax competition in the European community: lessons from Switzerland', *Journal of Public Economics* **60**: 351–71.
Kyriacou, Andreas P. (2004), 'Functional, overlapping, competing jurisdictions and ethnic conflict management', Manuscript, University of Girona.
Laurent, Pierre-Henry and Marc Maresceau (eds) (1998), *The State of the European Union: Deepening and Widening*, Boulder, CO and London: Lynne Rienner.
Martin, Dolores and Richard Wagner (1978), 'The institutional framework for municipal incorporation', *Journal of Law and Economics* **21**: 409–25.
Mehay, Stephen L. (1984), 'The effect of governmental structure on special district expenditures', *Public Choice* **44**: 339–48.
Montesquieu, Charles Louis (1749), *De l'esprit des lois*, Paris: Garnier.
Montignola, Gabriella, Tingyi Quian and Barry R. Weingast (1995), 'Federalism, Chinese style: the political basis for economic success in China', *World Politics* **48**: 50–81.
Mueller, Dennis C. (1996), *Constitutional Democracy*, Oxford and New York: Oxford University Press.
Mueller, Dennis C. (2003), *Public Choice III*, Cambridge: Cambridge University Press.
Nelson, Michael A. (1990), 'Decentralization of the subnational public sector: an empirical analysis of the determinants of local government structure in metropolitan areas in the U.S.', *Southern Economic Journal* **57**: 443–457.
Nuun, Samuel and Carl Schoedel (1997), 'Special districts, city governments, and infrastructure. Spending in 105 US metropolitan areas', *Journal of Urban Affairs* **19**: 59–72.
Oates, Wallace E. (1972), *Fiscal Federalism*, New York: Harcourt Brace Jovanovich.
Oates, Wallace E. (1991), *Studies in Fiscal Federalism*, Aldershot: Edward Elgar.
Oberreuter, Heinrich and Heribert Weiland (eds) (1994), *Demokratie und Partizipation in Entwicklungsländern*, Paderborn: Schönig.

Olson, Mancur (1969), 'The principle of "fiscal equivalence": the division of responsibilities among different levels of government', *American Economic Review* **59**: 479–87.

Ostrom, Elinor (1990), *Governing the Commons: The Evolution of Institutions for Collective Action*, Cambridge: Cambridge University Press.

Ostrom, Elinor, Larry Schroeder and Susan Wynne (1993), *Institutional Incentives and Sustainable Development*, Boulder, CO: Westview Press.

Pak, Hung Mo (1995), 'Effective competition, institutional choice and economic development of Imperial China', *Kyklos* **48**: 87–103.

Qian, Yingyi and Barry R. Weingast (1997), 'Federalism as a commitment to preserving market incentives', *Journal of Economic Perspectives* **11**: 83–92.

Rhode, Gotthold (1960), 'Staaten-Union und Adelsstaat: Zur Entwicklung von Staatsdenken und Staatsgestaltung in Osteuropa, vor allem in Polen/Litauen, im 16. Jahrhundert', *Zeitschrift für Ostforschung* **9**: 185–215.

Rosenberg, Nathan and L.E. Birdzell (1986), *How the West Grew Rich. The Economic Transformation of the Industrial World*, London: I.B. Tauris.

Rourke, John T., Richard P. Hines and Cyrus E. Zirakzadeh (1992), *Direct Democracy and Institutional Politics. Deciding International Issues Through Referendums*, Boulder, CO: Lynne Rienner.

Salmon, Pierre (1987), 'Decentralization as an incentive scheme', *Oxford Review of Economic Policy* **3**: 24–43.

Sandler, Todd and John T. Tschirhart (1980), 'The economic theory of clubs: an evaluative survey', *Journal of Economic Literature* **18**: 1488–521.

Sperber, Jonathan (1994), *The European Revolutions 1848–51*, Cambridge: Cambridge University Press.

Tiebout, Charles M. (1956), 'A pure theory of local expenditure', *Journal of Political Economy* **64**: 416–24.

Tullock, Gordon (1994), *The New Federalist*, Vancouver: Fraser Institute.

Vanberg, Viktor J. (2000), 'Functional federalism: communal or individual rights?', *Kyklos* **53** (Fasc. 3): 363–86.

Wade, Robert (1988), *Village Republics: Economic Conditions for Collective Action in South India*, Cambridge: Cambridge University Press.

Wagener, Hans-Jürgen and Fritz Heiko (eds) (1998), *Aspekte der EU-Osterweiterung*, Bonn: Dietz.

Weede, Erich (1993), 'The impact of interstate conflict on revolutionary change and individual freedom', *Kyklos* **46**: 473–95.

Wehner, Burkhard (1992), *Nationalstaat, Solidarstaat und Effizienzstaat. Neue Staatsgrenzen für neue Staatstypen*, Darmstadt: Wissenschaftliche Buchgesellschaft.

Zarkovic Bookman, Milica (1992), *The Economics of Secession*, New York: St. Martin's Press.

Zax, Jeffrey S. (1988), 'The effects of jurisdiction types and numbers on local public finance', in Harvey S. Rosen (ed.), *Fiscal Federalism: Quantitative Studies*, Chicago: University of Chicago Press, 79–106.

Zax, Jeffrey S. (1989), 'Is there a Leviathan in your neighborhood?', *American Economic Review* **79**: 560–67.

7 Contract federalism
Paul Bernd Spahn

Introduction
A fundamental reform of existing federal arrangements is especially difficult. Although one could agree that federal constitutions are neither optimal nor forward looking, reflecting past developments and disregarding future challenges, a complete redesign of these arrangements is illusive given that they constitute the very foundation on which the state and intergovernmental relations are built. The constitutional core is almost 'cast in stone', and radical reforms are possible only after catastrophes such as wars. Even then there is need for extensive political compromise. Contracts between governments at different levels are increasingly being used to address weaknesses in the existing intergovernmental structures. This represents a consensual attempt to replace otherwise hierarchical relationships, and also reflects increasing autonomous decision-making capabilities at the subnational level.

This chapter explores some of the consequences of contracts on future intergovernmental relations to render public service delivery more effective and responsive to modern challenges.

Individualistic versus corporatist views of the state
Alliances and other forms of cooperation across public entities are as old as humanity. They were typically created among states sharing common interests such as religious worship and defense of the region. A famous example is the Delian League (fifth and fourth century BC), a confederation of Greek city states under the leadership of Athens for the purpose of protecting the region against intruders from Persia. Another is the Latin League, a cooperation of cities in Latium that was formed against enemies such as the Etruscans, Volscians and the Aequians. However, such confederations typically broke down once the external pressures had disappeared. In these alliances each public entity struggled to preserve its independence although this often meant internal rivalries and contending quests for leadership.

The Romans were particularly apt in using a differentiated network of treaties (*foedera*) or bilateral agreements to establish lasting political and economic relations among its provinces. These treaties were often established 'among equals' (*foedus aequum*) ensuring political independence but placing Rome de facto in a leading position. Another characteristic of these treaties was the asymmetric nature of such contractual relations: provinces could exist basically on equal terms with Rome; others would join as juniors only loosely; and again others had to endure the *Pax Romana* by imposition. Over time, however, many of these alliances eliminated the sense of independence, which would eventually lead to the absorption of cities and people into the Roman sphere of influence, the *Imperium*. The Romans were probably the first to form a multicultural nation through the notion of the *civis Romanus*.

At the same time, the status of citizens was highly differentiated and discriminatory. This was a source of continuous tension and inner strife that solicited legitimacy of the state. It was found, among other things, in the intriguing analogy between the state and living organisms. A famous example is that of *The Belly and the Limbs* in which Senator Menenius Agrippa, in 494 BC, is reported to have appeased rebellious plebeians by bringing them back into the City to work out a compromise. This suggests a corporatist view of the state, and it continues to permeate state doctrines throughout history. It was further developed by philosophers such as Thomas de Aquino and Johannes Althusius,[1] and put to work by politicians such as António de Oliveira Salazar, Juan Domingo Perón and Getúlio Vargas in the twentieth century.

Corporatist thinking is at odds with individualistic views of the state in the tradition of French and German rationalists (René Descartes and Gottfried Leibniz) and British and Irish empiricists (John Locke, David Hume and George Berkeley) who view the state in terms of contractual arrangements among free subjects. These ideas found their culmination in Jean Jacques Rousseau's celebrated *Social Contract*. They were highly influential in shaping the Constitution of the United States and its offshoots in the rest of the world – from federal Latin American countries to Switzerland. And they are fundamentally different from 'cooperative' federal arrangements as exist, for example, in Austria or Germany where the corporatist view of the state still predominates.

In the following I shall attempt to work out the basic differences between corporatist and contractual federal arrangements. I argue that the latter are much more flexible and hence adaptive to a changing social and economic environment than the former. But cooperative federal provisions are not necessarily doomed to fail either.

Federal design and economic principles
The American constitution is more disposed to the fostering of contractual arrangements than the corporatist elements that predominate in the German constitution. In a nutshell the difference between the American model of federalism on the one hand and the German on the other can be described as follows:

- The American constitution aims at neatly delineating public responsibilities between national and state governments. Administration follows this demarcation of responsibilities, and so does financing. Every level of government and every public agency exists on its own, defines its policies, implements and administers them and exploits its own tax bases and other sources of financing. There is a market for government debentures where every agency carries its proper default risk. One can therefore speak of a clear separation of powers, which secures both transparency and political accountability. Unlike other models of federalism with a similar separation of powers, but little interaction among government and a strict segmentation of responsibilities, the current American practice of federalism is characterized by lively interagency competition based on contractual arrangements, such as the mutual recognition of standards at the horizontal level, and vertical competition among the federal and state governments.
- The German constitutions, including the actual *Grundgesetz*, follow the American model to some extent (for instance, for defense or education), but the vertical sharing of powers is mainly allocated according to functions (for example, policies and administration), *not* responsibilities (or areas, such as education or health). Over the years policies had more and more shifted onto the central government, while administration remained at the state level. The Reich of 1871 depended on existing state administrations (including for taxation) rather than its own, except for the army and diplomacy.
- Over the years the German federal government has progressively taken up a leading role in setting national policy standards, while states were limited to an implementing function even in areas of exclusive state responsibilities, such as education.[2]

The corporatist interpretation of federalism in Germany and more so in Austria, has had a number of typical outcomes. There are intergovernmental cooperative arrangements and bodies; there are 'joint tasks' and cofinancing among levels of government; there is uniformity of tax legislation even for the few genuine state taxes remaining; there is a trend toward financing all government functions – federal, state and local – from a common tax pool; there is a substantial redistribution of financial resources among governments, both vertically and horizontally for interstate equalization; there is a mutual bailout guarantee among governments for their public debts. In the same way as it is sensible for the body to make use of its resources in an equitable and balanced fashion without neglecting any one of its organs or limbs, so it is reasonable for the corporatist state to perceive its components as constituent parts of a consistent whole.

All federations in the world possess their own characteristics, but they will contain both corporatist and contractual elements to varying degrees. It is therefore useful to examine the potential impact of these elements on economic and social developments. But before doing so, there is a need to characterize more precisely what corporatist and contractual approaches mean to intergovernmental coordination and cooperation.

Corporatist and contractual approaches to intergovernmental coordination and cooperation

As mentioned, the corporatist interpretation of federalism views intergovernmental arrangements under the principle of 'to every one his own' (*suum cuique*) or concurrency of responsibilities. Thus, every government entity is to exercise its specialized function. For example, within education, the center establishes policy directives in view of coherent national objectives; and others implement and administer these policies. The political and economic benefits lie in rules-based coordination; the costs of such arrangements lie in a loss of transparency and accountability. Moreover they produce economic inefficiencies due to blurred assessments of cost, especially where there is no accrual accounting. Not surprisingly, the current discussion on constitutional reform in Germany turns around issues such as 'disentanglement' (*Entflechtung*) and 'budget equivalence' (*Konnexität*), where the former addresses issues of political accountability and the latter aims at connecting decision making and financing of public services to enhance efficiency. In fact, if the federal government legislates on social aid, for instance, and hence on transfers to households, these transfers represent unfunded mandates that have to be paid from municipal budgets – as in Germany. Budget equivalence is violated and there is neither accountability nor efficiency.[3]

For a corporatist constitution, disentanglement poses a serious dilemma. It appears to call for rearrangements similar to those adopted in the United States, where there is an assignment of policy, administration and financing of a function for a specific level of government. This is impossible without surrendering the basic values of the corporatist state, so it is a non-starter for reforming the German constitution. But why should one aim at disentangling functions in the public sector given that the private sector of a modern economy thrives on a widening network of business contracts, outsourcing of functions, associations of enterprises, cofinancing arrangements and complex financial holdings?

Fortunately, disentanglement of functions is *not* required to establish accountability and transparency within government. All that is needed is to bring intergovernmental relations closer to those governing business relations within the private sector. This is easier said than done because procedural arrangements differ significantly between the public and the private sectors.

However, those differences can and must be overcome if coordination is to become more flexible and responsive. The following may serve to guide the debate:

- The network complexity of a modern private economy ensues from a host of contractual arrangements among organizations, firms and individuals, where service flows are directed by economic and financial incentives. An ideal contract is focused on specific services, realizes a *quid pro quo*, assigns clear responsibilities, allocates and hedges risks, contains effective sanctions in the case of non-compliance, and is limited in time and hence flexible. Changing existing arrangements within the limits set by contracts typically offers rewards, which fosters commitment, entrepreneurship and innovation.
- By contrast, interaction *within* the public sector rests basically on legal and bureaucratic structures and processes. These processes are often rigid, ill-defined or inappropriate to specific needs, and they often assign circular responsibilities that can be shifted on indefinitely. Moreover these processes typically fail the *quid pro quo* test, and they do not offer rewards for institutional or procedural developments.

If the public sector were to make use of private sector mechanisms, transparency and efficiency could be enhanced significantly. This is particularly true for intergovernmental relations within federal structures. Moreover, contractual arrangements among government entities could serve to work out responsibilities in a clear fashion, which would foster political accountability. This would require an independent 'third party or legal framework' or system that would be capable of adjudicating disputes and enforcing penalties pursuant on the breach of contract. This involves independent and unbiased courts with appropriate jurisdiction to operate at all levels of government. To the extent that bureaucratic structures could perhaps break down in view of the challenge imposed by a contract, some disentanglement of bureaucracy would follow automatically.

This is not to say that intergovernmental relations should all be 'de-bureaucratized' in favor of a contractual approach to federalism. Bureaucratic rules if well defined have advantages. These only call for identifying those federal arrangements that could be developed more flexibly on the basis of contracts rather than bureaucratic rules.

Approaches to contractual arrangements among governments

Contractual arrangements to achieve coordination among governments do not necessarily have to be based on a market-like *quid pro quo*. Intergovernmental redistribution of resources, for instance equalization grants, might be based on concepts such as equity, fairness, social justice, cohesion or political stability, and *not* on market equivalence. None the less such grants could still be based on contracts by which recipient governments accept certain obligations in exchange for grant entitlements. It could go as far as earmarking the grant to specific uses, but it could also embrace qualitative commitments attached to the grant, such as pursuing non-discriminatory actions or implementing a certain type of social policy. In each case some bureaucratic control mechanism is needed to monitor the fulfillment of the contract. However, a complete contract should also include clauses on a possible breach of the contract and on ensuing sanctions. This goes beyond the pure administrative approach that disregards mutual obligations, the essence of contractual arrangements.

Contractual arrangements could be developed to address interjurisdictional spillovers or externalities. If it is possible to assess the monetary equivalent of external costs and benefits of policies among layers of government, or among government of any one level, then there is a case for coordinating interagency decisions through intergovernmental resource flows based on contracts. This would both lead to greater efficiency and foster political accountability.

Contracts could be tailored to meet particular circumstances and contract federalism is therefore closely related to the concept of 'laboratory federalism' which stresses the innovative power of decentralized intergovernmental relations.[4] Proponents of laboratory federalism have argued that – with imperfect information – learning by doing and testing different options may enhance the quality of public policy. And experimentation is in fact a particularly attractive feature of federal systems.[5]

It is common for the corporatist state to bedevil contractual grants as 'unbalanced', 'inequitable' and 'socially unfair'. Indeed transfers on a contractual basis tend to deviate from the usual pattern of equalization grants that are typically based on some formula. What is more, contractual grants motivated by externalities or spillovers tend to produce asymmetries that are at variance with a corporatist vision of the state. Asymmetry is suspected to be unconstitutional in corporatist societies although it is difficult to imagine evolution without asymmetries. In order to resolve this apparent conflict, is important at this juncture to thoroughly distinguish between equalizing grants that serve to generate equity or fairness among regions, and contractual grants that aim at compensating external effects between and among governments or public agencies. They must coexist. If all grants are viewed as equalizing only, there is no scope for compensating interjurisdictional externalities, and important instruments for promoting efficiency within the public sector are excluded.

Vertical spillovers
Vertical spillovers or externalities occur where two or more layers of government encounter costs, or draw benefits from, a policy or action. An example

is state education that will be advantageous to both the nation *and* the region. Another example is the protection of external frontiers by regional police. Vertical spillovers also form the rationale for the co-called 'joint tasks' of the German constitution, which identify areas of conjoint decision making and cofinancing between the federal government and the states. The German joint tasks are confined to the following areas: extension and construction of institutions of higher education, including university clinics; improvement of regional economic structures; improvement of the agrarian structure; and coast preservation.

From an efficiency point of view, cooperation and cofinancing between layers of government is essential to enhance social welfare. It results from the fact that each level of government, from its own perspective, would supply only insufficient amounts of the public service because it will disregard spillover effects that accrue to other entities of the public sector. Contractual arrangements including cofinancing provisions are needed to achieve an optimal outcome for the federation as a whole. Moreover, contracts could also be used to coordinate local policies and to resolve conflicts that may materialize among lower tiers of government. For example, if one state or public agency has achieved a comparably high level of public service delivery already, the marginal return on investment in this region, and hence national spillovers, will be small relative to others. By offering cofinancing in accordance with national spillovers, the federal government would not only have a say in setting priorities for subnational investments, but also play an indirect role in optimizing subnational budgets. Of course there are other forms of contractual arrangements that could be used to coordinate government actions. For instance, the central government could also facilitate cooperation among local governments as a 'broker' rather than through cofinancing or grants.

Breton (1965) emphasizes the role of a higher level of government in achieving a Pareto-efficient allocation of resources in such instances. He mentioned the possibility of treaties, organizations and committees, but considered them only imperfect substitutes for interventions by higher levels of government. This is in contrast to Buchanan (1965) who explicitly assumes that individuals facing certain externalities or having similar preferences for certain collective goods will form clubs. Benefit taxation could then be used to finance the provision of collective good to the members of a club. Buchanan apparently emphasizes Coasian bargaining,[6] while Breton does not. This might be explained by the fact that Breton considered agreements between jurisdictions while Buchanan was originally concerned with agreements between individuals forming jurisdictions to supply particular public goods.[7]

Although there is a strong case for policy coordination and cofinancing in the presence of vertical spillovers, the joint tasks are under heavy attack in Germany. They represent *the* prime target for 'disentanglement' and constitutional reform. Again, this flows from the corporatist perspective embedded in the German constitution. Cofinancing is *not* based on contracts, but on a uniformity objective and on the principle of non-discrimination. Each and every state can claim federal funding at identical terms, not on the basis of marginal contributions to national welfare. This has encouraged the states forming a cartel to reap certain benefits from the federal government, which they share evenly among themselves. Under these conditions they give up both efficiency and sovereignty, altogether, by agreeing to a rationing device whose rules are set exclusively by the federal government. So again: efficiency through contractual arrangements would result in regional asymmetries, not uniformity, which is at odds with the spirit of the corporatist state.

Moreover, by forming a cartel against the federal government, the group of states enters into a bilateral monopoly with the federation producing uncertain outcomes that can only be resolved politically, not through market-oriented pricing.[8] Again the key to resolving such conflicts between layers of government lies in asymmetries through flexible contractual provisions among governments or public agencies, *not* uniformity.

An example where a reasonable degree of flexibility in intergovernmental dealings was attained is represented by the European Union (EU). Although heavily influenced by the German federal constitution, and still twisted toward uniformity through the concept of the *acquis communautaire*, the EU has achieved greater flexibility in relation with its member states than Germany. This is because:

1. It respects fiscal equivalence, or the policy makers' pay principle.
2. Core national policy objectives are protected against intrusion by European policy makers. The principle of subsidiarity is firmly entrenched, and reciprocity with home-based quality control (see below) has won over the older paradigm of 'single policies' for integration.
3. There is no significant interstate equalization scheme, let alone one inspired by the 'uniformity of living conditions' as in Germany. On the contrary, the grants system is geared toward efficiency through contractual cofinancing arrangements with highly asymmetric outcomes.
4. Finally, the corporatist spirit of the *acquis* has been supplanted by a so-called *géométrie variable* or multispeed approach with contractual opting-in and opting-out provisions that add flexibility. The latter had been resisted for decades by politicians (and is still being resisted today by some) although it has proven to be of major importance in fostering political and economic integration.

The EU is said to represent an entity *sui generis*, not a federation, although this might be contested. It has all the institutions of a federation including a

Second Chamber in the form of the European Council (modeled after the German *Bundesrat*). And it has powerful exclusive policy competencies such as on competition and interstate commerce. It is noteworthy that the EU has developed through negotiations, treaties and intergovernmental contracts that allow for multiple speed and asymmetries while still pursuing a common goal: the integration of markets. There is no corporatist vision of the EU, and much could be drawn from this example in dealing with vertical interjurisdictional spillovers in federal countries all over the world.

Horizontal spillovers
Horizontal spillovers or externalities occur where two or more jurisdictions at the same level of government encounter costs, or draw benefits from, some policy or action. An example is university education or specialist hospital services whereby citizens of one state may benefit from services provided by another one. Such spillovers may also occur among public agencies and even within one single public entity. Citizens from a number of jurisdictions living in the catchment areas of hospitals and universities could benefit from these services. Again, every state government, from its own perspective, would supply insufficient amounts of the public service because it will disregard spillover effects accruing to citizens of neighboring states. For university education, for instance, it would make sense to provide this service to the citizens of overlapping areas by one of the States concerned, for instance, but not by both. Efficiency is enhanced by contractual agreements between the two states according to which one will supply the service receiving compensation from the other in the form of a grant. Similar contractual arrangements can be found in Switzerland, for example. In France the government makes use of mission-led and performance-driven *contrats de plan* with the regional authorities. And Canada has traditionally been using contracts with its provinces, for instance on value-added tax administration and collection with the Maritime Provinces, or with Quebec. This grant or compensation should ideally correspond to the value of the public service consumed by the citizens of the grantor state. Moreover, regional homogeneity in service delivery, that is, every state and region providing the same level of service, is highly inefficient. For the bulk of public services, agglomeration benefits point toward focusing such services onto concentrated areas rather than dispersing them according to a uniformity of living condition rule.

In addition to existing externalities, states and municipalities might face a continuum of new problems that might call for collective action. Three possibilities have to be considered, according to Olson – the collective benefits might reach beyond the boundaries of a providing jurisdiction; they might be of the same size; or they might be smaller. Again, of these possibilities, the case where collective goods/bads or their utilities/disutilities reach beyond a jurisdiction's border will pose efficiency problems.[9] These possibilities call for interagency bargaining and perhaps the setting up of joint institutions with contractual arrangements as they are common in the private sector. Most likely, contract federalism requires *more* interagency cooperation rather than less through disentanglement. But of course, cooperation must be based on transparent rules according to a *quid pro quo* in order to achieve greater efficiency and to preserve political accountability.

Frey (1997) goes as far as breaking down the public sector into so-called functional, overlapping and competing jurisdictions (FOCJ) that not only have the power to tax, but are also run and ruled by their constituents.[10] The division is by responsibility, not by territory. And of course a host of contractual arrangements would be required to coordinate the different jurisdictions among themselves and with actors of the private sector. This is the other extreme to disentanglement, but it would foster efficiency while preserving accountability of each one of the competing jurisdictions. As in the Tiebout model, individuals would constrain government behavior through their option to leave or join jurisdictions at their discretion, whereby any individual can be a member of several jurisdictions and face several governments at the same time.[11] While it is improbable that FOCJ could function in the real world for several reasons (for example, the high cost of voting required, control costs, time and resources spent by individuals in deciding which FOCJ to join and so on), the concept is useful in guiding proposals to tackle the problem of interjurisdictional spillovers with contractual arrangements.

Fortunately a multitude of functional jurisdictions is not necessary to enhance competition within the public sector. A powerful institution for coordinating policies at the horizontal level represents the concept of reciprocity. Reciprocity means *implicit* contractual or institutional arrangements by which one jurisdiction accepts the standards set by the legislature or agencies of another public entity under the proviso that this other entity will reciprocate. By abandoning the quest for uniformity and common policies, the EU has now adopted the mutual recognition of standards with home-based quality control, a powerful interstate coordination mechanism that has immediately broken the deadlock of 'Eurosclerosis', which had prevailed during the 1970s. Its power lies in the fact that it fosters cooperation while maintaining diversity.

But even reciprocity and its coordinating power can be corrupted by corporatist thinking. Education in Germany is again a tarnished example. By forming a cartel among the states with the aim of achieving uniformity even in the realm of exclusive state competencies, each state government has not only given up its respective sovereignty, but the states have conjointly abandoned the innovative power that lies in asymmetry and diversity, the crucial elements of laboratory federal arrangements.

Contract federalism in its various shades does not require a fundamental revision of the constitution, however. While the basic constitution remains untouched, new institutions can be set up and operate on the basis of single-purpose contracts among states, eventually only for a limited period of time. The political reality in Germany renders contract federalism, that is, bargaining among states (or municipalities) attractive in a second-best world.[12]

Contract federalism and public service delivery

Contractual forms of federalism can significantly improve the quality of service delivery in the public sector.[13] There is one simple reason for this – contractual forms of governance affect the relationship between the parties involved, that is, they create supplier–user relationships. Interagency financial flows triggered by public service delivery would correspond, more or less, to *quid pro quo* transactions, and any partner dissatisfied with the quality of the service could exit as under market conditions. Of course citizens can be considered 'customers' of public services even under present conditions, but so far this relationship is problematical in two instances:

- by and large consumers' potential to organize themselves is weak, *and*
- consumers now typically face monopolies for providing public services, that is, there is no choice or exit option.

While contract federalism does not necessarily alter the relationship between a public administration and the citizen/consumer, the perception is different from the viewpoint of states or municipalities. If one assumes that bargaining would indeed take place and that certain jurisdictions might specialize in the production of specific public goods, the 'producer' possesses a 'make-or-buy' option.[14] If it decides not to buy the public good, that is, the contract goes to another jurisdiction or a private business, the quantity of goods and the level of quality expected within the agreements' lifetime are inevitably at stake. It is important to recognize that while, at a first glance, contractual governance replaces one multilevel principal–agent relationship (voter–politician–public service) with another (voter–politician–service provider), this will effectively terminate supply-side monopolies.[15]

Contracts enrich options and choice and one can be optimistic about their economic virtues – even though it may be restricted to politicians because consumer-led FOCJ do not appear to be a realistic option:[16]

- Politicians who face such choices are likely to use contracting because this could improve the quality of service delivery or reduce costs.[17] This would be popular with consumers/voters, and politicians who ignore these options will become vulnerable to critique by party peers and consumers alike.

- Theory predicts that consumer welfare will rise as more options become available.

Contractual federalism and Germany's fiscal constitution

What does contract federalism mean for the future of corporatist federations such as Germany?

There are numerous spillover problems within the German federal structure. While the relevance – in some cases even the existence – of these spillovers is debated, the phenomenon clearly points to a more general problem: the size of jurisdictions and the structure of the German federation. Certain states are extremely small compared with others; there are major differences in the number of inhabitants and tax potentials. Nine out of 16 states are currently receiving supplementary grants for compensating costs endured in political management, that is, they are considered incapable of financing governance, the administration of their own states.[18] Using Breton's or Olson's phraseology, respectively, there are indications that Germany does not possess an economically optimal constitution and that budget equivalence is not reached within all jurisdictions (see Olson 1969). However one must accept that the actual set-up of states is a direct consequence of historic developments, that is, it is path dependent. It must therefore be considered an exogenous trait of Germany's fiscal federal relations even though economists might be able to identify superior structures.[19] If one accepts the political reality, there is need for techniques to help jurisdictions in coping with regional spillovers affecting horizontal and vertical relationships among jurisdictions.

Despite difficulties to implement contractual arrangement in practice, negotiations and contractual agreements between states resulting from such bargaining should be used to internalize spillovers that are now compensated by grants. This is especially true for the city states that constitute agglomeration centers within their respective regions. At present, their fiscal burden is carried by *all* other states. Compared to bilateral or multilateral negotiations, this may lead to an oversupply of local public goods by the city, because the individuals whose preferences determine demand do not bear all resulting costs. This problem would not exist in bilateral or multilateral negotiations involving only those states that benefit directly from the provision of public services. If an agglomeration center plans a new infrastructure project, for instance, it must decide on its scale and scope.[20] It will use cost–benefit analysis to decide whether the project should be undertaken. Generally there are two possible outcomes:[21]

- The center or the center's voter/citizens are willing to undertake the project alone – that is, the combined utility of the center is larger than the project's costs.

- The center is not willing to undertake the project alone – that is, the costs of the project are higher than the combined willingness to pay.

In the first case it is rational to complete the project even though the surrounding state may free ride on its benefits. This is the classic Olson case where one 'individual' has preferences that are strong enough to produce a public good on its own (Olson 1971). Still the center might try to bargain with the periphery but chances of success are slim as long as preference-revealing mechanisms cannot be used.

The second case is the more interesting one as the center could negotiate with relevant regions or states, which, again, may have two rational outcomes:

- The combined willingness to pay for the project is smaller than its costs and therefore the project is not executed.
- The center and the states agree to realize the project conjointly because a distribution of costs is found leaving all participants better off than without the project. A club of two or more states is formed in line with Buchanan's original concept, which results in a Pareto improvement.

The example could easily be transferred to a situation in which there are several smaller states of public agencies, all of which have preferences for statehood and are facing a situation of scarce resources, for example, because special grants for costs endured in political management have indeed been abolished. These states will have every incentive to bargain on a number of issues and institutions that they might be able to use and finance in concert.[22]

These are strong reasons for abolishing the supplementary grants for costs incurred in political management and the weighing by inhabitants, respectively. Stronger budgetary pressures would then encourage less expensive and problem-oriented solutions.[23] It should be clear that this point depends on the question of how the future transfer schedule for horizontal equalization will be conceived. If states cannot retain at least as much of their bargaining rents as they would save by trying to socialize their problems, bargaining will either break down, or not start at all.

Conclusions
Coordinating intergovernmental relations within a federation through laws and bureaucratic processes has significant drawbacks, which lie in the loss of accountability and efficiency. This is particular obvious for so-called cooperative or corporatist models of federalism. In Germany these deficiencies have been identified and there is a quest to 'disentangle' processes that are deemed to blur political responsibilities.

It is argued in this chapter that this approach is unnecessary and doomed to fail. In a modern economy there is a trend toward creating more interaction, not less. The key to restoring accountability and promoting economic efficiency in the public sector lies in intergovernmental contracts that clearly specify responsibilities for delivering services and use transfers to compensate interjurisdictional spillovers that accrue both vertically and horizontally. These transactions are necessarily asymmetric and have to be thoroughly distinguished from grants whose rationale is interagency equalization rather than compensation of externalities.

Conventional budget procedures have to be opened up by focusing democratic control on outcomes, rather than a rigid allocation of funds and budgetary processes, and to be replaced by more open contractual forms of interjurisdictional cooperation. This would certainly improve the quality of public service delivery and could lead to a greater variety of such services if laboratory conditions are created on a larger scale.[24] Open forms of contractual relations would also be reflected in interregional resource flows as counterparts to the costing of public service provisions via greater interjurisdictional cooperation.

It is hoped that the benefits of interjurisdictional contracts and the need to redesign intergovernmental resource flows are recognized by German politicians, and that the pending revision of the fiscal constitution will promote them. Disentanglement might be an outcome where existing arrangements fail to meet the market test, but eventually one must expect *more* intergovernmental relations within contract federalism rather than less.

The irony of the German system could be that its basic philosophies and actual fiscal arrangements could be interpreted to foster such developments, as cooperative federalism is in fact the nucleus and archetype of more open forms of contractual federalism. The so-called 'joint task' represents a prominent example. However, the need for consensus and a partisan-driven misinterpretation of regional solidarity may ultimately prevent this modernization of German federalism from coming to fruition.

Notes

1. Althusius (1563–1638) is not only considered to be the first writer on federalism, but is also thought to have supported a corporatist view of federalism. In Chapter I of his *Politica* he writes: 'Politics is the art of associating [*consociandi*] men for the purpose of establishing, cultivating, and conserving social life among them. Whence it is called "symbiotics". The subject matter of politics is therefore association [*consociatio*], in which the symbiotes pledge themselves each to the other, by explicit or tacit agreement, to mutual communication of whatever is useful and necessary for the harmonious exercise of social life.'
2. However, in education the corporatist spirit also permeated through horizontal coordination among states with a tendency toward forming interstate cartels.
3. The term 'fiscal equivalence' typically means equivalence between public services rendered and fiscal burden onto a taxpayer. Here it is interpreted in the sense of a linkage between public responsibilities and compensatory payments among entities or agencies *within* government.
4. Compare Oates (1999, pp. 1131–4) for a survey on the literature concerned with laboratory federalism.

5. The argument in favor of laboratory federalism is derived from Friedrich von Hayek's critique of centralized economies. He argued that the ability to process information of a central planning commission is weak compared to the market system's facility to process that same information. Thus the ability of a nation to process information may increase as more than one level of government (or different governments on the same horizontal level) can test different options. Historians have argued, for instance, that the European economies and nations of the Renaissance period constituted nothing else but laboratories, and that competition among those states spurred innovations and propelled them into leading positions in the world. See North (1981, Chapter 11).
6. More recent thinking on the Coase theorem and its information requirements has shown that it will deviate from the Pareto optimum if not all participants are fully informed *ex ante*. This is likely to be the case when states bargain with each other. However, one may still be skeptical whether a higher jurisdiction is better suited to overcome this information asymmetry.
7. Nevertheless there is a certain realism to the idea of one club per public good; as Olson (1969) reports, there are 1400 governments in the New York metropolitan area alone – counting school, sewerage, pollution control districts, and the like, as governments.
8. At the extreme such a situation may lead to blockages of national decision making as is the case, at present, for much of the German federal legislation that has to pass the Second Chamber of the federal parliament, the *Bundesrat*.
9. As an example of relevance for Germany, consider infrastructure projects such as major airports. As the discussion on a new Berlin/ Brandenburg airport or the discussion about an expansion of the Rhine-Main airport in Frankfurt demonstrate, the scope of a regional project often goes far beyond the borders of a single state.
10. See also Eichenberger and Frey, Ch. 6 in this volume.
11. See Frey (1997). As an example for FOCJ, Frey refers to Swiss municipalities that are generally ruled by their citizens in direct democracy.
12. The usage of 'second best' in this context may be questionable theoretically, but highlights the fact that contract federalism is a superior solution under given political and institutional constraints.
13. Second-generation reforms like improvements in the provision of services in the public sector are receiving more attention lately as it becomes clear that policy reforms alone will not generate desirable and durable effects. See Tanzi (2000, pp. 22–3).
14. Two additional points might be in order here. First, jurisdictions with traditionally large public sectors might specialize in providing services to others with the aim of using their capital and labor more efficiently. Secondly, jurisdictions facing a 'make-or-buy' option are basically redefining the borders of their 'firm'. Here, as in many other cases, theory that was originally designed for a private business environment, for example Coase (1937) and Williamson (1985) on transaction costs, contracts and principal–agent relationships may yield powerful insights for the public sector.
15. Of course the supply-side monopoly would eventually be replaced by a bilateral monopoly, which has its own drawbacks. However, it would still represent an improvement of the situation compared to present arrangements.
16. It should be noted in passing that new technologies such as the internet enhance the possibilities of participatory governance such as participatory budgeting (a model initiated by the city of Porto Alegre in Brazil) or e-government which allows quality controls through consumer feedbacks.
17. Again, Lindahl tax prices could render consumers accountable for the consequences of the politician's actions more directly.
18. One should not overlook that a state not only consists of government. In addition to its executive, it has legislative and judicative branches with corresponding bureaucracies to render them effective. In the case of some German states, one must add the public broadcasting systems, state central banks (subdivisions of the Deutsche Bundesbank), school systems and so on, which were established almost regardless of efficiency considerations.
19. See Oates (1999, pp. 1130–31) for similar thoughts concerning the US states. One might be skeptical about such computing as the result it produces will probably lose its validity

quite quickly in a changing environment, that is, the rise and decline of certain sectors alters the buoyancy of regional tax bases.

20. Even now – without bargaining – it is hard to imagine Hamburg, for example, building a new museum or theatre without considering how many potential users of such an enterprise might be living outside Hamburg's geographical region.

21. See Homburg (1994, pp. 319–21) for a similar argument.

22. There are already some examples of German states making use of joint institutions, for example, Baden-Württemberg and Rhineland-Palatine merged their public broadcasting systems, which is a considerable success in so far as the two separate systems (running against states' borders) had existed since the Allies had created them in the late 1940s. Equally, regional central banks were not automatically tolerated for the new Eastern states, which was an incentive to create supraregional institutions.

   There are notable examples for contacts among states on a number of issues, although only at an informational base. For instance, Bremen and Lower Saxony have set up a body that coordinates regional planning in the Northwest of Lower Saxony. However, incentives to reach bilateral solutions are non-existent as it is always possible for Bremen or any other city/small states to socialize the costs and let all fellow states carry their share of the burden.

23. There is one qualification to this conclusion: the Constitutional Court's judgment on the handling of budgetary distress of certain states that allows them to socialize their debts too.

24. Laboratory federalism now begins to bear fruit, chiefly at the municipal level in Germany.

References

Breton, Albert (1965), 'A theory of government grants', in *Canadian Journal of Economics and Political Science*, Vol. 31, pp. 175–87.

Buchanan, James M. (1965), 'An economic theory of clubs', *Economica*, Vol. XXXII, pp. 1–14.

Coase, Ronald H. (1937), 'The nature of the firm', *Economica*, Vol. 4, pp. 386–405; reprinted in R.H. Coase (1988), *The Firm, the Market, and the Law*, Chicago: University of Chicago Press.

Frey, Bruno S. (1997), *Ein neuer Föderalismus für Europa: Die Idee der FOCJ*, Beiträge zur Ordnungstheorie und Ordnungspolitik 151, Tübingen: Mohr Siebeck.

Homburg, Stefan (1994), 'Anreizwirkungen des deutschen Finanzausgleich', *Finanzarchiv N.F.* **51**, pp. 312 ff.

North, Douglass C. (1981), *Structure and Change in Economic History*, New York: Norton.

Oates, Wallace E. (1999), 'An essay on fiscal federalism', *Journal of Economic Literature*, Vol. 37, pp. 1120–49.

Olson, Mancur (1969), 'The principle of "fiscal equivalence": the division of responsibilities among different levels of government', *American Economic Review Proceedings*, Vol. 49, pp. 479–87.

Olson, Mancur (1971), *The Logic of Collective Action: Public Goods and the Theory of Groups*, Cambridge, MA: Harvard University Press.

Tanzi, Vito (2000), 'The role of the state and the quality of the public sector', IMF Working Paper 00/36, Washington, DC.

Williamson, Oliver E. (1985), *The Economic Institutions of Capitalism*, New York: Free Press.

PART II

DECENTRALIZATION AND DEVELOPMENT

8 Decentralization and development
Pranab Bardhan

Introduction
The centralized state, on account of its many well-recognized failures, has lost a great deal of legitimacy everywhere, and decentralization of governance is widely believed to promise a range of benefits. It is often suggested as a way of reducing the role of the state in general, by fragmenting central authority and introducing more intergovernmental competition and checks and balances. It is viewed as a way to make government more responsive and efficient. Technological changes have also made it somewhat easier than before to provide public services (like electricity and water supply) relatively efficiently in smaller market areas, and the lower levels of government have now a greater ability to handle certain tasks. In a world of rampant ethnic conflicts and separatist movements, decentralization is also regarded as a way of diffusing social and political tensions and ensuring local cultural and political autonomy.

These potential benefits of decentralization have attracted a very diverse range of supporters. For example, free-market economists tend to emphasize the benefits of reducing the power of the overextended or predatory state. In some international organizations pushing structural adjustment and transitional reform, decentralization had sometimes been used almost as a synonym for privatization; similarly, in the literature on mechanism design an informationally decentralized system of individual decisions coordinated by a price mechanism is pitted against a system of central commands and plans. Even those who are still convinced of the pervasiveness of market failures are increasingly turning for their resolution to the government at the local level, where the transaction costs are relatively low and the information problems that can contribute to central government failures are less acute. They are joined by a diverse array of social thinkers: post-modernists, multicultural advocates, grassroots environmental activists and supporters of the cause of indigenous peoples and technologies. In the absence of a better unifying name, I would describe this last group as 'anarcho-communitarians'. They are usually both anti-market and anti-centralized state, and they energetically support assignment of control to local self-governing communities.

As is usually the case when a subject draws advocates from sharply different viewpoints, different people mean different things by decentralization. But in this chapter, we shall focus on a particular kind of decentralization in developing (and transition) economies, the devolution of political decision making power to local-level small-scale entities. In countries with a long history of centralized control (as in the old empire states of Russia, China or India) public administrators often mean by decentralization the dispersion of some responsibilities to regional branch offices at the local level of implementation on a particular project. For the purpose of discussion in this chapter we shall distinguish decentralization in the sense of devolution of political decision making power from such mere administrative delegation of functions of the central government to their local branches. We should also separate the political and administrative aspects of decentralization from those of fiscal decentralization, and in the latter, the more numerous cases of decentralization of public expenditure from those involving decentralization of both tax and expenditure assignments. We shall include cases where local community organizations get formally involved in the implementation of some centrally directed or funded projects. Not all these aspects of decentralization operate simultaneously in any particular case and it is quite possible that a given economy may be decentralized in some respects, and not in others.

It should also be clear that the effects of a policy of deliberate decentralization – which is our concern here – can be qualitatively different from those following from an anarchic erosion of central control (either due to the collapse of the state, as has happened in some countries in Africa, or lack of administrative or fiscal capacity on the part of the central authority leading to abandonment of social protection functions, as has happened in some transition economies). The latter case is also increasingly common in both developed and developing countries where facing a fiscal crisis the central government devolves responsibilities for social sector spending to local governments in the form of 'unfunded mandates'. This also caters sometimes to a strategic conservative agenda of 'starving the beast' of social welfare programs. Another strategic use of decentralization, serving the political power of the central government, is to disperse some authority with a view to 'divide and rule' when there are diverse clamoring regional interests that threaten central control. In Uganda, Pakistan and elsewhere, military rulers have used decentralization as an instrument of consolidation and legitimization of power.[1] In South Africa under apartheid, decentralization was used as an instrument of central control and racial division. On the more positive side, decentralization has emerged out of the recent transition from authoritarianism to democracy, as in countries like Brazil or Indonesia. These different historical–political contexts of the evolution of decentralization in a country clearly affect the nature of its functioning and impact.

The territorial domain of subnational governments, of course, varies enormously from country to country. A typical province in India or China is larger (in size of population) than most countries in the world, and so federalism in the sense of devolution of power to the provincial state governments may still keep power over people pretty centralized. Unfortunately, data below the provincial government level are often very scarce, and most quantitative studies of decentralization (for example, those based on share of the central government in total expenditure or revenues) do not pertain to the issues at the local community level (even apart from the fact that the share of expenditure or revenues is not a good index of decision-making authority). Even at the latter level the units are diverse (ranging from megacities to small villages) and the boundaries are often determined by accidents of history and geography, not by concerns of decentralization of administration. In this chapter we shall in general confine the analytical focus of decentralization to the governing authority at the local community level (say, village, municipality or county levels of administration).

Our discussion begins with a description of why decentralization poses some different issues in the institutional context of developing (and transition) countries, and thus why it may sometimes be hazardous to draw lessons for them from, say, the experiences of US states and city governments. We try to give the flavor of some new theoretical models that extend the discussion to political agency problems that may resonate more in the context of developing and transition economies. We then refer to some of the ongoing empirical work in evaluating the impact of decentralization on delivery of public services and local business development.

Decentralization has undoubted merits and strengths. However, the idea of decentralization may need some protection against its own enthusiasts, both from free-market advocates who see it as an opportunity to cripple the state and from those anarcho-communitarians who ignore the 'community failures' that may be as serious as the market or government failures that economists commonly analyse.

Departures from the fiscal federalism literature

There is a large literature on decentralization, often referred to as 'fiscal federalism', mostly relating to the case of the United States.[2] The principles discussed in this literature have been fruitfully applied to the national–provincial relations in developing countries like Argentina, Brazil, Colombia, South Africa, India or China, but in this chapter we shall go beyond this and stress the special issues that arise in decentralization in developing (and transition) economies primarily because the institutional context (and therefore the structure of incentives and organization) are in some respects qualitatively different from that in the classical US case (or the recent case of the European Union).

Much of the fiscal federalism literature focuses on the economic efficiency of intergovernmental competition, which often starts with a market metaphor that is rationalized by the well-worn Tiebout (1956) model. In this approach, different local governments offer different public tax-expenditure bundles and mobile individuals are supposed to allocate themselves according to their preferences. The assumptions required for the Tiebout model are, however, much too stringent, particularly for poor countries.[3] The crucial assumption of population mobility (fully informed citizens 'voting with their feet' in response to differential public performance) that enables governments in the Tiebout framework to overcome the well-known problem of inducing citizens to reveal their preferences for public goods largely fails in poor countries. In any case many of the public goods in question are community and site specific and it is often possible to exclude non-residents. Rural communities of poor countries, in particular, are often face to face, and social norms sharply distinguish 'outsiders' from 'insiders', especially with respect to entitlement to community services.

Second, the information and accounting systems and mechanisms of monitoring public bureaucrats are much weaker in low-income countries. In the standard literature on decentralization and fiscal federalism, the focus is on allocation of funds and it is implicitly assumed that allocated funds automatically reach their intended beneficiaries. This assumption needs to be drastically qualified in developing countries, where attention must be paid to special incentives and devices to check bureaucratic corruption – and thus the differential efficacy of such mechanisms under centralization and decentralization.

Third, even in the relatively few democratic developing countries the institutions of local democracy and mechanisms of political accountability are often weak. Thus, any discussion of delivery of public services has to grapple with issues of capture of governments at different tiers by elite groups more seriously than is the custom in the traditional decentralization literature.

Fourth, the traditional literature on decentralization, even though not impervious to issues of distribution, is usually preoccupied with those of efficiency in public provision. When a major goal of decentralization in developing countries is to effectively reach out to the poor (or to diffuse unrest among disadvantaged minority groups), often in remote backward areas, targeting success in poverty alleviation programs is a more important performance criterion than the efficiency of interregional resource allocation. In the traditional discussion of decentralization and federalism, the focus is on checks and balances, on how to restrain the central government's power, whereas in many situations in developing countries the poor and the minorities, oppressed by the local power groups, may be looking to the central state for protection and relief. Stepan (1999) has made a useful distinction between 'coming-together federalism' like the United States, where previously sovereign polities gave up part of their sovereignty for efficiency gains from resource pooling and a common market, and 'holding-together federalism' like the multinational democracies of India, Belgium and Spain, where the emphasis is on redistributive or compensating transfers to keep the contending polities together. In heterogeneous societies, such redistributive pressures sometimes lead fiscal decentralization to allow for state and local borrowing that may be large enough to cause problems of macroeconomic stabilization, as has happened in South Africa, Brazil and Argentina.[4] Not all state-mandated redistribution, however, is inflationary or unproductive rent creation, as is usually presumed in the traditional literature. Some redistribution to disadvantagd groups or regions (say in the form of decentralized delivery of health, education or infrastructural services) need not be at the expense of efficiency, and may even improve the potential for productive investment, innovation and human resource development on the part of communities long bypassed by the elite or the mainstream.

Fifth, the fiscal federalism literature typically assumes that lower levels of government both collect taxes and spend funds, so localities can be classified as low-tax/low-service or high-tax/high-service. This connection between local revenues and spending is rather tenuous. In most countries, much of the more elastic (and progressive) sources of tax revenue lie with the central government, and there is a built-in tendency toward vertical fiscal imbalance. Income is often geographically concentrated, both because of agglomeration economies and initial endowments of natural resources and infrastructural facilities. Thus, certain local areas will find it much easier to raise significant tax revenue than others.[5] In addition, there are limits to interregional tax competition. In many low-income countries, the decentralization issues discussed there are primarily about providing centrally collected tax revenue to lower levels of government, rather than seeking to empower lower levels of government to collect taxes. The focus is on public expenditure assignments, unaccompanied by any significant financial devolution.

Sixth, the decentralization literature typically assumes that different levels of government all have similar levels of technical and administrative capacity. This assumption is questionable for all countries. On account of agglomeration economies in attracting qualified people, in most countries central bureaucracies attract better talent. But the problem is especially severe in many developing countries, where the quality of staff in local bureaucracies – including basic tasks like accounting and record-keeping – is very low. Even their more professional and technical people suffer from the disadvantages of isolation, poor training and low interaction with other professionals. As Bird (1995) puts it, information asymmetry thus works both ways: the central government may not know *what* to do, the local government may not know *how* to do it.[6] Of course, this problem is of differential importance in different services. Providing for street cleaning or garbage collection may not require sophisticated expertise, but power production and transmission, bulk supply of clean water and public sanitation do. Decentralization to the local level will often work better in the former kind of services than the latter. It should also be recognized that there is learning by doing in local administration which improves the performance of local democracies over time.

In our subsequent discussion we shall consider the issues of decentralization in developing countries, bearing in mind these points of difference with the traditional literature.

Adapting the theory of decentralization for developing countries
The conventional wisdom in the fiscal federalism literature, as in Oates (1972), is that decentralization is to be preferred when tastes are heterogeneous and there are no spillovers across jurisdictions. With spillovers and no heterogeneity a central government providing a common level of public goods and services for all localities is more efficient; with spillovers decentralization leads to underprovision of local public goods, as local decision makers do not take into account benefits going to other districts. The issue of spillovers is relevant to investment in highway transport and communication, public research and extension, controlling pollution and epidemics, and so on. It is less relevant when the public goods are more local, as in local roads or minor irrigation, village health clinics and sanitation, identification of beneficiaries of public transfer programs, and so on.

Centralization can also exploit economies of scale better in the construction of overhead facilities, but these economies of scale are less important in local management and maintenance. In a canal irrigation system, for example the one in South Korea described by Wade (1997), construction was in the hands of the central authority, but maintenance was devolved to local communities. Similarly, in primary education while the local government may run the day-to-day functioning of schools, the upper-tier government can have the economies of scale in designing curricula and prescribing and enforcing minimum quality standards. In the public delivery of electricity, economies of scale in generation and transmission may be the responsibility of centralized power plants and grids, while the distribution may be decentralized to local governments.

The traditional theory of fiscal federalism is now being extended to a political economy setting, with the introduction of transaction costs in the political markets, or political agency problems between the ruler and the ruled, between the politicians/bureaucrats and the electorate, and for reasons mentioned above these transaction and agency costs may be much more serious in the context of developing countries. It is usually argued that the local government has an information advantage over the upper-tier governments. But it may be asked why a central government cannot procure for itself the same information advantage of proximity through local agents. In some countries the central government uses such representatives at the local level (like the *préfets* in France and Italy or the *intendentes* in Chile) for this purpose. It may even be argued that the central government can have economies of scope in the collection of information. But the main reason why in practice the local government still retains the informational advantage has to do with political accountability. In democratic countries the local politicians may have more incentive to use local information than national or provincial politicians, since the former are answerable to the local electorate while the latter have wider constituencies (where the local issues may get diluted).

Focusing on accountability, rather than information *per se*, leads to thinking about how the public can monitor and affect elected officials at different levels of government. Seabright (1996) discusses the problem of political accountability theoretically in terms of allocation of control rights in the context of incomplete contracts, where breaches of contract are observable – though not verifiable in administrative or judicial review – and are subject to periodic electoral review. His model has both central and local elected officials. In his framework, centralization allows benefits from policy coordination, which is especially important if there are spillovers across jurisdictions. However, centralization has costs in terms of diminished accountability, in the sense of reduced probability that the welfare of a given locality can determine the re-election of the government. Elections are, of course, extremely blunt instruments of political accountability, and other institutional devices and unelected community organizations (such as non-governmental organizations) may be deployed to strengthen local accountability.

The mechanism of accountability may also be strengthened by 'yardstick competition', where jurisdictions are compared to each other.[7] The effort or competence of public officials is not directly observable by citizens, and if poor results occur, public officials can always plead that they did the best that was possible under the circumstances. However, if the shocks that create a wedge between effort and outcomes are correlated across jurisdictions, then yardstick competition can act as an indicator of relative effort on the part of agents. As Seabright (1996) points out, this argument of yardstick competition under decentralization, which may help voters to know whether they should seek to replace their governments, is to be distinguished from his own argument that decentralization may increase their ability to do so.

The combination of decentralization and yardstick competition allows the possibility of experimentation in the way a given public service is provided, and then demonstration and learning from other jurisdictions. In China in the early years of its market reforms, decentralization with jurisdictional competition allowed some coastal areas to experiment with institutional reform, the success of which showed the way for the rest of the country. Economic historians have pointed to the fragmentation and decentralization in early modern Europe – sometimes called 'parcellized sovereignty' – as a source of strength, in enabling experimentation and competition, leading to technological and institutional innovations that helped Europe to ultimately overtake the more centralized empire states of Asia.

Tommasi and Weinschelbaum (1999) pose the political agency problem in terms of the number of principals (relative to agents) in comparing centralization and decentralization. Citizens are viewed as principals and their elected representatives as agents. The local government has better means (in the form of information) to be responsive, also better (electoral) incentives. In the case of centralization the number of principals is very large while the number of agents is few, whereas in the case of decentralization there is one agent per locality. The larger the number of principals, the more serious is the problem of lack of coordination in contracting with agents. Decentralization is preferable to centralization when the problem of interjurisdictional externality is less important than the coordination effect.[8]

Besley and Coate (2003) focus on the importance of political aggregation mechanisms in the trade-off between centralized and decentralized provision of local public goods. Under decentralization, public goods are selected by locally elected representatives, while under a centralized system, policy choices are determined by a legislature consisting of elected representatives from each district (so that conflicts of interest between citizens of different jurisdictions play out in the legislature). They then reconsider the traditional questions of the fiscal federalism literature in terms of alternative models of legislative behavior (one in which the decisions are taken by a minimum winning coalition of representatives and the other where legislators reach a bargaining solution). They show that the familiar presumption that larger spillovers across jurisdictions help the case for centralization is not so clear under such political economy considerations.

Political accountability in poor countries is particularly affected by the likelihood of corruption or capture by interest groups. While local governments may have better local information and accountability pressure, they may be more vulnerable to capture by local elites, who will then receive a disproportionate share of spending on public goods.[9] (This is in contrast to the Seabright (1996) model where political accountability is always greater at the local level.) On the other hand, the central bureaucrat who is in charge of the delivery of, say, an infrastructural service like electricity, telecommunication or canal irrigation may be corrupt in a way that leads to cost-padding, targeting failures and generally an inefficiently low and inequitable service delivery. The problem for the central government which employs the bureaucrat is that it has very little information on the local needs, delivery costs and the amount actually delivered. Many programs in developing countries have thus a large gap between a commitment of resources at the central level and delivery of services at the local level. For a particularly egregious example, see Reinikka and Svensson (2004), who study the leakage in the flow of educational funds from the central government to schools in Uganda in the 1991–95 period. They found that only 13 per cent of the total grant transferred from the central government for non-wage expenditures in schools (on items like textbooks, instructional materials and other costs) actually reached the schools. The majority of schools actually received no money at all from the central transfers for non-wage expenditures. On unannounced visits to a nationally representative sample of government primary schools in India, Kremer et al. (forthcoming) found that 25 per cent of teachers were absent and only about half were teaching. The absence rates were higher in poorer areas.[10]

Bardhan and Mookherjee (2000a) develop a simple analytical framework that formalizes the trade-off between these conflicting aspects of centralized and decentralized delivery systems. Decentralization, by shifting control rights from the central bureaucrat (who otherwise acts like an unregulated monopolist) to a local government, typically tends to expand service deliveries as authority goes to those more responsive to user needs. But with capture of the local government (in the sense of elites receiving a larger weight in the local government's maximand of a weighted sum of welfare), there is a tendency for the service to be overprovided to local elites at the expense of the non-elite. The extent of such inefficient and inequitable cross-subsidization will depend on the extent of local capture and on the degree of fiscal autonomy of the local government. On the latter question three different financing mechanisms for local governments are considered: local taxes, user fees and central grants. With local tax financing there is the risk that the captured local government may resort to a regressive financing pattern whereby the non-elite bear the tax burden of providing services to the elite. Restrictions on the ability of local governments to levy taxes may then be desirable, even at the cost of reducing flexibility of service provision to local need.

User charges may be a useful compromise between the need for matching provision to local needs and avoiding an unduly heavy burden on the local poor. Since no user is compelled to use the service, this imposes a limit on the extent of cross-subsidization foisted on the poor. So with user-fee financing, decentralization unambiguously welfare-dominates centralization as well as local tax-financed decentralization, irrespective of the extent of local capture. Central grant financing, on the other hand, may encourage local governments to claim higher local need or cost, leading to a restriction of the level of service delivery; the welfare implications are ambiguous, depending on a range of relevant political and financing parameters.

User charges cannot, however, be used to finance anti-poverty programs (like targeted public distribution of food, education or health services), which by their very nature are targeted at groups that do not have the ability to pay for the service (or pay bribes to the central bureaucrats). In such cases, as is shown in Bardhan and Mookherjee (2005), the extent of capture of local governments relative to that of the central government is a critical determinant of the welfare impact of decentralization. If local governments are equally or less vulnerable to capture than the central government, decentralization is then likely to improve both efficiency and equity. But the opposite may be the case when capture at the local level is much greater than at the central level.

Even though the extent of relative capture of governments at different levels is crucial in understanding the likely impact of decentralization initiatives, there has been very little work on the subject, either theoretical[11] or empirical. The extent of capture of local governments by local elites depends on levels of social and economic inequality within communities, traditions of political participation and voter awareness, fairness and regularity of elections, transparency in local decision-making processes and government accounts, media attention, and so on. These vary widely across communities and countries, as documented in numerous case studies.[12] Of course, central governments are also subject to capture, and it may be more than at the local level on account of the larger importance of campaign funds in national elections and better information about candidates and issues in local elections based on informal sources. On the other hand, particularly in large heterogeneous societies, the elites are usually more divided at the national level, with more competing and heterogeneous groups neutralizing one another. At the local level in situations of high inequality, collusion may be easier to organize and enforce in small proximate groups (involving officials, politicians, contractors and interest groups); risks of being caught and reported are easier to manage, and the multiplex interlocking social and economic relationships among the local influential people may act as formidable barriers to entry into these cozy rental havens. At the central level in democratic countries more institutional mechanisms for checks and balances are usually in place: these include various constitutional forms of separation of powers and adjudicatory systems in some countries, more regular auditing of public accounts, more vigilance by national media, and so on, much of which are often absent or highly ineffective at the local level.

Even in undemocratic but largely egalitarian societies the problem of local capture may be less acute. It is generally overlooked in the widely noted success story of decentralized rural–industrial development of China in the 1980s and 1990s that the decollectivization of agriculture since 1978 represented one of the world's most egalitarian distributions of land cultivation rights (with the size of land cultivated by a household assigned almost always strictly in terms of its demographic size), and this may have substantially mitigated the problem of capture of local governments and other institutions by the oligarchic owners of immobile factors of production (like land), which afflicts other rural economies (for example, India).

When the potential for capture of local governments is serious, decentralization programs have to focus a great deal of attention on strengthening local accountability mechanisms. In fact, in policy debates when we consider the costs and benefits of redistributive policies (such as land reforms, public health campaigns or literacy movements), we often ignore their substantial positive spillover effects in terms of enlarging the stake of large numbers of the poor in the system and strengthening the institutions of local democracy. Comparing across the various states in India, it is clear that local democracy and institutions of decentralization are more effective in the states (like Kerala and West Bengal) where land reforms and mass movements for raising political awareness have been more active. The 1996 National Election Survey data in India suggest[13] that in West Bengal 51 per cent of the respondent voters expressed a high level of trust in their local government, whereas in the adjoining state of Bihar (where both land reforms and local democracy institutions have been very weak) the corresponding figure is 30 per cent. Near-universal literacy in Kerala has helped sustain widespread newspaper readership which has encouraged a vigilant press on issues like corruption in local governments.

In both Kerala and West Bengal it has also been observed that theft and corruption at the local level are more effectively resisted if regular local elections to select representatives in the local bodies are supplemented by an institutionalized system of periodic public hearings on items of major public expenditure.[14] But even that is inadequate if the complaints made in public are not acted upon by the ruling party. There is evidence that sometimes the opposition parties or minority factions stop attending the village council meetings or the public hearings, as they perceive that they cannot do much about the ruling party's spending of public funds that takes the form of widespread distribution of patronage (like 'jobs for the boys' or what Italians call *lottizzazione*) which sometimes consolidate its electoral advantage. It is important to install public accounts committees at the local legislative level with their leading members taken from the opposition party (as is the case at the central parliamentary committees in India or Britain). In general the auditing process at the local level is extremely deficient, not always by design, but by the sheer dearth in the villages of technical capacity for accounting, record-keeping and auditing.

In the preceding paragraphs we have discussed the elite capture problem in local governments and how publicly provided goods and services may be diverted. But sometimes an equally serious problem is that of 'elite secession'. In many areas the rich no longer use some of the public services (they send their children to private schools, they use private medical facilities, and so on) and are therefore less active than before in politically supporting (or lobbying for) these services, and do not care much if the public delivery mechanisms fall into disarray. This is a general political economy problem that afflicts many targeted anti-poverty programs: a transition from a universal to a narrowly targeted program often erodes its necessary political support base in the rich and middle classes. Gelbach and Pritchett (2000) have given examples of this from food subsidy programs in Sri Lanka and Colombia, and Moene and Wallerstein (2001) from the welfare state programs in industrially advanced countries.

In sum, in considering the theory of decentralization in developing countries, it is important to move beyond the traditional trade-off of how centralization is better for dealing with spillovers and scale economies and decentralization is better for dealing with heterogeneity. It is necessary to delve into political economy issues of institutional process and accountability at both the local and central levels.

Empirical evaluation of decentralized delivery of public services
In this section we shall briefly indicate some of the attempts that have been made to empirically evaluate the impact of decentralization on the delivery of social services in developing countries. Even though decentralization experiments are going on in many of these countries, hard quantitative evidence on their impact is rather scarce. In any such empirical work, one has to be particularly wary of important econometric problems that arise in this context. One issue is that some of the data involved in evaluating local community participation and project performance may be subjective. For instance, some investigators start with the prior belief that participation is good, which creates a 'halo effect' in their observations. A second problem is one of simultaneity: better beneficiary participation may cause improved project performance, but improved project performance often also encourages higher participation.[15] Finally, there is the commonly encountered endogeneity problem. In claiming that decentralization brought about certain outcomes, it is worth considering that decentralization may have resulted from ongoing political and economic changes that also affected these same outcomes. Besides these econometric issues, there is the general problem, as we have indicated in the preceding section, that the impact of decentralization depends both on the context where it is implemented (particularly the political tradition that is germane to the functioning of local accountability mechanisms) and on the way it is designed (particularly as the design itself may be endogenous with respect to the underlying political economy). General presumptions that transcend institutional details are difficult to sustain, and the impact studies have to be very much context and design specific.[16] Let us report here a few scattered impact studies that are available in the literature, and arrange them in terms of the nature of empirical methodology followed.

In two successful cases of decentralization in Latin America there is some evidence available on the 'before–after' comparison of service delivery outcomes. One is the widely noted case of participatory budgeting in municipal government in the city of Porto Alegre in Brazil, and the other is the less well-known but quite dramatic success of the post-1994 decentralization initiative in Bolivia. In Porto Alegre, where assembly meetings of local citizens and neighborhood associations in different regions discuss investment priorities, review accounts and elect representatives to a citywide council (COP) that allocates available resources across wards, impressive results have followed: between 1989 and 1996 access to basic sanitation (water and sewage) as well as enrolment in elementary or secondary schools nearly doubled, while increasing revenue collection by 48 per cent; see Santos (1998). Although it is difficult from this study to isolate the impact of participatory budgeting reforms from those of other ongoing changes, it seems likely that there has been a substantial impact on the pattern of resource allocation across localities, particularly to poor ones, and in the lessening of the misappropriation of resources compared to the past and to other areas in Brazil. But it is worth noting that successful participatory budgeting practices in Brazil have been so far largely confined to better-off areas and those with a tradition of active civil society.

In Bolivia in 1994 the number of municipalities as well as the share of national tax revenue allocated to municipalities doubled, along with devolution to the municipalities of administrative authority, investment responsibility and title to local infrastructural facilities. This has been associated with a massive shift of public resources in favor of the smaller and poorer municipalities and from large-scale production to social sectors. Faguet (2001) finds that public investment in education, water and sanitation rose significantly in three-quarters of all municipalities, and investments responded to measures of local need (for example, the expansion in public education spending was larger on average in municipalities with a lower literacy rate or with fewer private schools). However, Faguet's analysis is in terms of levels of public spending rather than outcome variables such as school enrolments or school performance or access to water and sanitation services. In the studies of Porto Allegre or Bolivia there is not much information available on the allocation of resources within a community across households in different socioeconomic classes. This means that issues like cost-effectiveness of programs, targeting performance or the extent of capture of local governments cannot be addressed.[17] Without household-level data on access to public services these crucial aspects of the impact of decentralization cannot be properly assessed.

In a longitudinal sample of 89 West Bengal villages over 1978–98, Bardhan and Mookherjee (2004) examine the performance of local governments with respect to pro-poor targeting of credit, public distribution of agricultural inputs, and employment programs. They find that intra-village allocations were targeted quite well in favor of the poor, with only mild adverse effects of land inequality in the village and low caste status and illiteracy among the poor. In contrast, inter-village allocations exhibited a substantially stronger and significant anti-poor bias. The results suggest that the accountability problems stem in this case more from political discretion at the upper tiers of government in inter-village allocations,[18] rather than intra-village elite capture. One should, of course, bear in mind that West Bengal is one of the few states in India where village land reforms have been relatively successful.

There is hardly any household-level analysis in the literature of the comparative effects of centralized versus decentralized delivery. One detailed study of targeting performance of a decentralized program using household-level information in a developing country is that of Galasso and Ravallion (2005), who investigated a decentralized food-for-education program in Bangladesh. In this central government program, in which two million children participated in 1995–96, the identification of beneficiary households within a selected community was made typically by a local school management committee (consisting of parents, teachers, education specialists and school donors). Galasso and Ravallion use data from a 1995–96 Household Expenditure Survey to assess the targeting performance of the program. They find that the program was mildly pro-poor (that is, taking all villages, a somewhat larger fraction of the poor received benefits from the program than the non-poor). But they also find some evidence of local capture. For example, within the set of participating villages, targeting performance was worse in communities with larger land inequality or in remote locations. But the targeting improved as the program expanded, suggesting that the program shifted the balance of power in favor of the poor. It is also clearly the case that the level of targeting *within* communities was superior to that achieved *across* communities by central allocation, thus offering little support for the view that the central government is more accountable to the poor than local communities. This is in some contrast to the experience of the widely acclaimed anti-poverty transfer program[19] of *Progresa* (now expanded into the *Oportunidades* program) in Mexico. The program follows a two-stage targeting process. Coady (2001) finds that most of *Progresa*'s targeting effectiveness is achieved at the first stage when poor localities are selected, rather than in the second stage when households are selected within localities, not on the basis of identification of beneficiaries by local communities as in the food-for-education program in Bangladesh, but on the basis of information collected from a census undertaken for this purpose.

Alderman (1998) examines, on the basis of a household survey conducted in 1996, a targeted social assistance program (*Ndihme Ekonomika*) in Albania that was decentralized in 1995. He finds that there have been modest gains in targeting efficiency and cost-effectiveness following decentralization, that local authorities use some additional information in allocating program benefits among households, and that the central allocation of social assistance funds to local authorities is ad hoc and not strongly correlated with the level of poverty in the local communities. He does not find evidence that the decentralization initiative caused the benefits of the program to be captured by the well-off members of the community.

There is some quantitative evidence on the impact of mandated representations of historically disadvantaged groups like women in leadership positions in local governance in India. Since 1998, one-third of all positions of chief of the village councils in India have been reserved for women: only women may be candidates for the position of chief in a reserved village council and the latter is selected randomly. Taking advantage of this random assignment (thus avoiding an econometric problem in usual cross-section studies on this question that communities which are more likely to take women's needs into account may also be more willing to let them be in leadership positions), Chattopadhyay and Duflo (2004) have measured the impact of this political reservation policy on outcomes of decentralization with data collected from a survey of investments in local public goods made by 265 village councils in West Bengal and Rajasthan. They find that the women leaders of village councils invest more in infrastructure that is directly relevant to the needs of rural women (for example, drinking water supply), and that village women are more likely to participate in the policy-making process if the leader of their village council is a woman. (In other studies they have similar findings for location of public goods – such as wells – in their residential parts of the village when the leadership is reserved for disadvantaged castes.) Besley et al. (2004) on the basis of their household and village survey in south India find that special group reservation of the leadership position in the village council improves the chance that a household in a disadvantaged social group (either 'scheduled caste' or 'scheduled tribe') would have access to some facilities (such as private electricity or water connection) from a government scheme.

In a statistical analysis on the basis of village surveys and satellite and topographic data, Somanathan et al. (2005) show that in the central Himalayas forests managed by village councils are conserved no worse, and possibly better, than those under state management, and at a cost that is an order of magnitude less per unit area. Foster and Rosenzweig (2001) use a panel dataset of villages across India to examine the consequences of democratization and fiscal decentralization. They find that an increase in the demographic weight of the landless households in a village under democratic decentralization has a positive effect on allocation of public resources to road construction (which, according to them, primarily benefits the landless workers) and a negative effect on that to irrigation facilities (which are to primarily benefit the landed). It is not clear, however, how much of a leeway elected local village councils have in matters of allocation to projects like road construction (which are often centrally sponsored and quite bureaucratically controlled from above, and at most the local government gets involved only in the decision where to locate the road and to identify the beneficiary workers). In general it is as yet misleading to generalize the specific outcomes of decentralization from an all-India dataset, since in most parts of India there is hardly any *de facto* (as opposed to *de jure*) decentralization. In only about four out of the twenty-plus major states has there been any significant decentralization to speak of.[20]

There are also some case studies on the effects of decentralization in different parts of the world which provide some descriptive and suggestive correlations, but not enough to clinch any hypothesis. Azfar and Meagher (2002) survey households and government officials at municipal and provincial levels in the Philippines with respect to the stated public investment priorities in a given locality. Stated priorities of officials at the municipal level turned out to weakly match those of local residents, while those of officials at the provincial level did not, suggesting that decentralization may improve the quality of information used in public investment decisions. There is also some evidence in the survey of more perceived corruption at the central level than at the local level. A similar survey for Uganda is reported by Azfar, Livingston and Meagher in their chapter in Bardhan and Mookherjee (forthcoming) with qualitatively similar results. They also find in Uganda a greater reliance on community leaders for news concerning local corruption and local elections than for national news, which they interpret as evidence of greater potential for local capture.

In the 1990s, Nicaragua started a program of transferring key management tasks in public schools from central authorities to local councils involving parents. An evaluation of this program by King and Ozler (1998) on the basis of school and household surveys and student achievement tests suggests that de facto autonomy has not yet been given to many of the councils, but where it has been there is a significant positive effect on student performance.

The *World Development Report* 1994 on infrastructure cited several cases of quality improvement and cost savings in infrastructure projects after local communities were given part of the responsibility in management. A review of World Bank data for 42 developing countries found that where road maintenance was decentralized, backlogs were lower and the condition of roads better. Data for a group of developing countries revealed that per capita costs of water in World Bank-funded water projects were four times higher in centralized than in fully decentralized systems. A study of 121 completed rural water supply projects, financed by various agencies, showed that projects with high participation in project selection and design were much more likely to have the water supply maintained in good condition than would be the case with more centralized decision making.

Wade's (1997) contrasting account of the operations of irrigation bureaucracy in South Korea and in South India brings out the importance of local accountability in delivery of infrastructural services. There are also many examples that there is no one-to-one relationship between the strength of democracy at the national political level and that of institutions of accountability at the local level. Local accountability in rural health clinics may be stronger in authoritarian Cuba than in much of democratic India.

Taken as a group, these studies suggest generally positive effects of decentralization, but it is hard to draw conclusive lessons. Many of the studies are largely descriptive, not analytical, and often suggest correlations rather than causal processes. Most of them are not based on household survey data, making the comparative impact of centralized versus decentralized programs on different socioeconomic groups of households difficult to assess. (It should also be noted that household surveys that incorporate valuation of public goods sich as roads, irrigation or sanitation to a particular household are more challenging than the usual ones based on valuation of private goods.)

Decentralization and local business development

Most of the cases of decentralization in developing countries examined in the theoretical and empirical literature relate to delivery of social services. But in recent years there has been an extension of the traditional literature on federalism to the case of the role of local government in promoting local business development, particularly in the context of transition economies, especially China, and this has potential implications for developing countries where so far public delivery issues have been more prominent. In Qian and Weingast (1997) and Qian and Roland (1998), for example, decentralization of information and authority and interjurisdictional competition have been considered as commitment devices on the part of the central or provincial government to provide market incentives, both the 'positive' incentive rewarding economic success at the local level and the 'negative' incentive in terms of punishing economic failure. The local government-run township and village enterprises (TVEs), which served as the engine of growth in China in the 1980s and 1990s, have been cited as a major example of the outcome of a successful 'market-preserving federalism'. In terms of 'positive' market incentives the TVEs had full control over their assets and they were largely left alone (as a residual claimant) to 'get rich gloriously', and the limited knowledge of the upper-tier governments about the 'extra-budget' and 'off-budget' accounts of local governments acted as check on upper-tier interventionism. In contrast, as we can see from an econometric study of the fiscal relations between local and regional governments in Russia by Zhuravskaya (2001) on the basis of a panel dataset for 35 large cities, local governments could retain only about 10 per cent of their revenues at the margin, thus providing only weak incentives to foster local business development and thus to increase their tax base. In terms of the 'negative' incentive, by denying bailout to many failing TVEs, Chinese upper-tier governments enforced a dynamic commitment. Having no access to state banks and facing mobility of capital across jurisdictions raised the opportunity costs of local governments for rescuing inefficient firms, thus leading to the endogenous emergence of a hard budget constraint.

Without denying the importance of these market incentives, it is possible to argue, however, that the case of market-preserving federalism is institutionally underspecified in these studies. Depending on the political–institutional complex in different countries, the same market incentives may have different efficacy. As Rodden and Rose-Ackerman (1997) have pointed out in a critique of market-preserving federalism, whether political leaders of a local government respond to highly mobile investors or instead pay more attention to the demands of strong distributive coalitions dominated by owners of less mobile factors depends on the institutional milieu. Owners of capital vary widely in the specificity of their assets and institutional incentives facing political leaders may vary even for the same jurisdictional competitive pressure. Even in a democracy, not to speak of authoritarian systems, electoral competition does not necessarily punish local leaders who fail to respond to exit threats of mobile asset owners and are instead more responsive to coalition-building and the 'voice' of well-organized lobbies. We have pointed out earlier the problem of local capture by the oligarchic owners of immobile factors of production, such as land in rural India, and how in the Chinese case the lack of such strong rural lobbies (owing largely to the egalitarian land distribution) may have made a difference in the local governments' vigorous pursuit of rural industrialization.[21] In Russia, many have pointed out that over much of the 1990s, local governments have shown features of being captured by erstwhile rentholders and old firms which sometimes blocked the rise of new firms that could compete away their rents.[22] Of course, even in China by some accounts, for example that by Shirk (1993), local officials have often used their financial authority under decentralization to build political machines, collecting rents in exchange for selective benefits and patronage distribution, and federalism may not always have been that market preserving. Poncet (2004) provides some evidence that internal trade barriers may have even increased in the 1990s.

It seems that jurisdictional competition is not enough to explain the emergence of endogenous hard budget constraints for local governments without a lot more specification of the local political process. Even ignoring the lobbies of land oligarchies, in some countries (democratic or otherwise) if a local business fails, threatening the livelihood of thousands of poor people, it is difficult for the local government (or if that is bankrupt, upper-tier governments) to ignore the political pressure that will be generated in favor of bailing them out. Wildasin (1997) has rightly pointed out that federal grants to local governments may be less 'soft' in the small jurisdictions as opposed to the large (which are 'too big to fail'), but even small jurisdictions may have key politicians representing (or lobbying for) them and in any case it is cheaper to come to their rescue.

Conclusion

It is quite plausible to argue that in the matter of service deliveries as well as in local business development, control rights in governance structures should be assigned to people who have the requisite information and incentives, and at the same time will bear responsibility for the (political and economic) consequences of their decisions. In many situations this calls for more devolution of power to local authorities and communities. But at the same time it is important to bear in mind that structures of local accountability are not in place in many developing countries, and local governments are often at the mercy of local power elites, who may frustrate the goal of achieving public delivery to the general populace of social services, infrastructural facilities and conditions conducive to local business development. (In other cases the elite may secede from the system of public services and the political support base of the latter may collapse.) This means that decentralization to be really effective has to be accompanied by serious attempts to change the existing structures of power within communities and to improve the opportunities for participation and voice, and engaging the hitherto disadvantaged or disenfranchised in the political process. This is an important indirect effect of redistributive reforms (such as land reform or mass education campaigns) which is usually ignored in the study of the impact of these reforms. Participation or enfranchisement, of course, has its own feedback effects in terms of energizing awareness and involvement on the part of a hitherto silent or apathetic majority and building local capacity.

After all, the logic behind decentralization is not just about weakening the central authority, or about preferring local elites to central authority, but it is fundamentally about making governance at the local level more responsive to the felt needs of the large majority of the population. To facilitate this the state, far from retreating into the minimalist role of classical liberalism, may sometimes have to play an activist role in enabling (if only as a 'catalyst') mobilization of people in local participatory development, in neutralizing the power of local oligarchs, in providing supra-local support in the form of pump-priming local finance, supplying technical and professional services toward building local capacity, acting as a watchdog for service quality standards, evaluation and auditing, investing in larger infrastructure and providing some coordination in the face of externalities across localities.

The literature on decentralization in the context of development is still in its infancy. On the theoretical side, perhaps the key challenge is to find better ways to model the complex organizational and incentive problems that are involved, in a situation with pervasive problems of monitoring and enforcement. On the empirical side, there is a great deal of scope for rigorous work in evaluating the impact of ongoing decentralization initiatives, using detailed household and community surveys, comparing it with the experience with centralization or some other counterfactual. Separating decentralization from its political and economic causes and contexts, so that decentralization is not just a proxy for an ill-defined broad package of social and economic reforms or the outcome of the characteristics and the institutional details of a more broad-based and progressive community, is a delicate and challenging problem. Thus it may be too early to pass judgment on its effectiveness, but most scholars agree that decentralization has opened up a new political space and opportunities for public policy in many countries.

Notes
1. See, for example, the chapters by Azfar, Livingston and Meagher for Uganda and Cheema, Khwaja and Qadir for Pakistan in Bardhan and Mookherjee (forthcoming).
2. Many of the issues have been well surveyed in the *Journal of Economic Perspectives* 'Symposium on Fiscal Federalism' in Fall 1997.
3. There are doubts about just how the Tiebout mechanism operates even in relatively mobile societies like that of the United States. For instance, very few poor people move from state to state in search of higher welfare benefits – see Hanson and Hartman (1994).
4. This chapter will not have much to say on the impact of decentralization on macroeconomic stabilization. For a game-theoretic model of how decentralization or local democratization may increase the level of central redistribution to prevent spirals of regional revolt and how the macroeconomic consequences depend on the initial levels of cultural division and decentralization, see Treisman (1999).
5. Some localities, strapped for finance, may raise it through local regulations and the resulting bribes as a form of indirect revenue source. Henderson and Kuncoro (2004) utilize a dataset collected from 1808 firms to focus on this kind of corruption at the local (*kabupaten*) level in the recent decentralization in Indonesia. Cai and Treisman (2004) give examples from Russia, China and the US to show that local governments may sometimes compete to attract capital by offering businesses corrupt collusive deals.
6. Occasionally, however, the local people come up with ingenious low-cost solutions, whereas centralized systems use unnecessarily expensive services of specialized technicians. For some of the basic needs for poor people, local youths with some minimum training as primary health workers or primary school teachers can be adequate. In other, more technical, projects there is a lot of scope for improving access to engineering, project design and administrative skills. Organizations like AGETIP in Africa or the Brazil-based IBAM have in recent years been helpful in developing local technical capacity.
7. See, for example, Besley and Case (1995).
8. The idea of fewer principals in smaller jurisdictions having more political control clearly resembles the relationship between group size and free riding in the voluntary provision of a public good first discussed by Olson (1965). As is well known, this relationship can be ambiguous.
9. In the *Federalist Papers* (no. 10) James Madison comments on the notion that local govern-

ments are more prone to capture by elites and special interests: 'The smaller the society, the fewer probably will be the distinct parties and interests composing it; the fewer the distinct parties and interests, the more frequently will a majority be found of the same party; and the smaller the number of individuals composing a majority, and the smaller the compass within which they are placed, the more easily will they concert and execute their plans of oppression. Extend the sphere and you take in a greater variety of parties and interests; you make it less probable that a majority of the whole will have a common motive to invade the rights of other citizens; or if such a common motive exists, it will be more difficult for all who feel it to discover their own strength and to act in unison with each other.'

10. Jimenez and Sawada (1999) evaluate the case of El Salvador, where teacher and student absenteeism dropped substantially after the government introduced the EDUCO program which gave responsibility to local community organizations known as ACEs.

11. For a theoretical analysis of the problem, see Bardhan and Mookherjee (2000b). We argue that the overall comparison of capture at central and local levels in a democracy would depend on the interplay of a large number of underlying institutional factors, such as relative degrees of voter awareness and cohesiveness of special-interest groups, the extent of heterogeneity across districts, and the nature of the national electoral system, and so the issue is ultimately context and system specific.

12. See, for example, Crook and Manor (1998) and Conning and Kevane (2002).

13. See Mitra and Singh (1999).

14. Besley et al. (forthcoming) show on the basis of their household and village survey of local governments in four South Indian states that members of socially and economically disadvantaged groups are both more likely to attend village meetings and be chosen as beneficiaries in villages which have these meetings.

15. For an attempt to take this latter set of econometric problems into account in an evaluation of 121 rural water projects, see Isham et al. (1995).

16. For a discussion of the dimensions of context and design with respect to decentralization, see the introductory chapter in Bardhan and Mookherjee (forthcoming).

17. The other problem in empirical studies is that the index of decentralization used in these studies or in 'before–after' comparisons does not fully capture the multidimensional nature of decentralization, involving various aspects of devolution of power.

18. The need-based formulae-bound interregional allocations in Bolivia and Indonesia seem to have produced better results. See the chapters by Faguet, and by Hoffman and Kaiser in Bardhan and Mookherjee (forthcoming).

19. Programs like *Progresa* are also distinctive as demand-side interventions. In the accountability literature it is presumed that the main problem is on the supply side of delivery of public services. In many cases there are also demand-side problems, such as parents pulling their children out of school or not taking them to the public health clinics, even when these facilities are available.

20. For a comparative assessment of the progress (or lack of it) of decentralization across the states in India, see Chaudhuri's chapter in Bardhan and Mookherjee (forthcoming).

21. Even in India, in areas where land distribution is relatively egalitarian and local democracy is more solidaristic, as in Kerala, there are now some instances of municipal governments taking a leading role, in collaboration with bankers and social groups, in local business development. For some examples, see Das (2000).

22. The explanation of China's relative success attributed to political centralization in Blanchard and Shleifer (2000) does not seem very plausible. A strong central political authority can punish local governments (reducing the risk of their capture and the scope of their rent seeking), but one needs a plausible story of a benevolent non-rentier central authority to go with it.

References

Alderman, H. (1998), 'Social assistance in Albania: decentralization and targeted transfers', Living Standards Measurement Study (LSMS) Working Paper no. 134, World Bank, Washington DC.

Azfar, O., S. Kähkönen and P. Meagher (2002), 'Conditions for effective decentralized governance: a synthesis of research findings', IRIS Center Working Paper, University of Maryland.

Bardhan, P. and D. Mookherjee (2000a), 'Corruption and decentralization of infrastructure delivery in developing countries', University of California, Berkeley, forthcoming in *Economic Journal*.

Bardhan, P. and D. Mookherjee (2000b), 'Relative capture of government at local and national levels', *American Economic Review*, **90**(2), 135–39.

Bardhan, P. and D. Mookherjee (2004), 'Pro-poor targeting and accountability of local governments in West Bengal', forthcoming in *Journal of Development Economics*.

Bardhan, P. and D. Mookherjee (2005), 'Decentralizing anti-poverty program delivery in developing countries', *Journal of Public Economics*, **89**(4), 675–704 .

Bardhan, P. and D. Mookherjee (forthcoming), *Decentralization to Local Governments in Developing Countries: A Comparative Perspective*, MIT Press, Cambridge, MA.

Besley, T. and A. Case (1995), 'Incumbent behavior: vote-seeking, tax-setting and yardstick competition', *American Economic Review*, **85**(1), 25–45.

Besley, T. and S. Coate (2003), 'Centralized versus decentralized provision of local public goods: a political economy analysis', *Journal of Public Economics*, **87**(12), 2611–37.

Besley, T., R. Pande, L. Rahman and V. Rao (2004), 'The politics of public goods provision: evidence from Indian local government', *Journal of the European Economic Association*, **2**(2/3), 416–26.

Besley, T., R. Pande and V. Rao (forthcoming), 'Participatory democracy in action: survey evidence from South India', *Journal of the European Economic Association*.

Bird, R. (1995), 'Decentralizing infrastructure: for good or for ill?', in Estache (ed.).

Blanchard, O. and A. Shleifer (2000), 'Federalism with and without political centralization: China versus Russia', NBER Working Paper no. 7616, National Bureau of Economic Research, Cambridge, MA.

Cai, H. and D. Treisman (2004), 'State corroding federalism', *Journal of Public Economics*, **88**(3/4), 819–43.

Chattopadhyay, R. and E. Duflo (2004), 'Women as policy makers: evidence from a randomized policy experiment in India', *Econometrica* **72**(5), 1409–43.

Coady, D. (2001), 'An evaluation of the distributional power of *Progresa*'s cash transfers in Mexico', International Food Policy Research Institute Working Paper, Washington, DC.

Conning, J. and M. Kevane (2002), 'Community based targeting mechanisms for social safety nets: a critical review', *World Development*, **30**(3), 375–94.

Crook, R. and J. Manor (1998), *Democracy and Decentralization in South Asia and West Africa*, Cambridge University Press, Cambridge.

Das, M.K. (2000), 'Kerala's decentralized planning', *Economic and Political Weekly*, **35**, 4300–4303.

Estache, A. (ed.) (1995), *Decentralizing Infrastructure: Advantages and Limitations*, World Bank Discussion Papers 290, Washington, DC.

Faguet, J.-P. (2001), 'Does decentralization increase government responsiveness to local needs? Decentralization and public investment in Bolivia', Centre for Economic Performance Working Paper, London School of Economics.

Foster, A.D. and M.R. Rosenzweig (2001), 'Democratization, decentralization and the distribution of local public goods in a poor rural economy', unpublished, University of Pennsylvania, Philadelphia.

Galasso, E. and M. Ravallion (2005), 'Decentralized targeting of an anti-poverty program', *Journal of Public Economics*, **89**(4), 705–27.

Gelbach, J. and L. Pritchett (2000), 'Indicator targeting in a political economy: Leakier can be better', *Journal of Policy Reform*, **4**(1), 113–45.

Hanson, R.L. and J.T. Hartman (1994), 'Do welfare magnets attract?', Institute for Research on Poverty, University of Wisconsin, Madison.

Henderson, J.V. and A. Kuncoro (2004), 'Corruption in Indonesia', NBER Working Paper no. 10674, National Bureau of Economic Research, Cambridge, MA.

Isham, J., D. Narayan and L. Pritchett (1995), 'Does participation improve performance? Establishing causality with subjective data', *World Bank Economic Review*, **9**(2), 175–200.

Jimenez, E. and Y. Sawanda (1999), 'Do community-managed schools work? An evaluation of El Salvador's EDUCO Program', *World Bank Economic Review*, **13**(3), 415–42.

King, E. and B. Ozler (1998), 'What's decentralization got to do with learning? The case of Nicaragua's school autonomy reform', Development Research Group Working Paper, World Bank, Washington, DC.

Kremer, M., N. Chaudhuri, F.H. Rogers, K. Muralidharan and J. Hammer (forthcoming), 'Teacher absence in India: a snapshot', *Journal of European Economic Association*.

Mitra, S.K. and V.B. Singh (1999), *Democracy and Social Change in India: A Cross-Sectional Analysis of the National Electorate*, Sage, New Delhi.

Moene, K. and M. Wallerstein (2001), 'Inequality, social insurance and redistribution', *American Political Science Review*, **95**(4), 859–74.

Oates, W. (1972), *Fiscal Federalism*, Harcourt Brace Jovanovich, New York.

Olson, M. (1965), *The Logic of Collective Action*, Harvard University Press, Cambridge, MA.

Poncet, S. (2004), 'A fragmented China', Tinbergen Institute Working Paper 103/2, Erasmus University Rotterdam.

Qian, Y. and G. Roland (1998), 'Federalism and the soft budget constraint', *American Economic Review*, **88**(5), 1143–62.

Qian, Y. and B.R. Weingast (1997), 'Federalism as a commitment to preserving market incentives', *Journal of Economic Perspectives*, **11**(4), 83–92.

Reinikka, R. and J. Svensson (2004), 'Local capture: evidence from a central government transfer program in Uganda', *Quarterly Journal of Economics*, **119**(2), 679–705.

Rodden, J. and S. Rose-Ackerman (1997), 'Does federalism preserve markets?', *Virginia Law Review*, **83**(7), 1521–72.

Santos, B.D.S. 91998), 'Participatory budgeting in Porto Alegre: toward a redistributive democracy', *Politics and Society*, **26**(4), 461–510.

Seabright, P. (1996), 'Accountability and decentralization in government: an incomplete contracts model', *European Economic Review*, **40**(1), 61–89.

Shirk, S. (1993), *The Political Logic of Economic Reform in China*, University of California Press, Berkeley.

Somanathan, E., R. Prabhakar and B. Singh Mehta (2005), 'Does decentralization work? Forest conservation in the Himalayas', unpublished, Indian Statistical Institute, New Delhi.

Stepan, A. (1999), 'Federalism and democracy', *Journal of Democracy*, **10**(4), 19–33.

Tiebout, C.M. (1956), 'A pure theory of local expenditures', *Journal of Political Economy*, **64**(5), 416–24.

Tommasi, M. and F. Weinschelbaum (1999), 'A principal–agent building block for the study of decentralization and integration', University of San Andres, Argentina.

Treisman. D. (1999), 'Political decentralization and economic reform: a game-theoretic analysis', *American Journal of Political Science*, **43**(2), 488–517.

Wade, R. (1997), 'How infrastructure agencies motivate staff: canal irrigation in India and the Republic of Korea', in A. Mody (ed.), *Infrastructure Strategies in East Asia*, EDI, World Bank, Washington, DC.

Wildasin, D.E. (1997), 'Externalities and bailouts: hard and soft budget constraints in intergovernmental fiscal relations', World Bank Policy Research Paper 1843, Washington, DC.

Zhuravskaya, E.V. (2000), 'Incentives to provide local public goods: fiscal federalism, Russian style', *Journal of Public Economics*, **76**(3), 337–68.

9 Fiscal federalism in planned economies
Govinda Rao

Introduction

This chapter deals with the challenges of fiscal federalism in planned economies. The discussion on fiscal federalism in the mainstream literature refers to decentralization and not federalism *per se*. The benefits attributed to and costs associated with fiscal federalism refer to decentralization.[1] However, fiscal federalism is supposed to deal with all multilevel fiscal systems irrespective of whether the system is federal or unitary. As stated by Oates (1977, p. 4),

> [T]he term federalism for the economist is not to be understood in a narrow constitutional sense. In economic terms, all governmental systems are more or less federal; even in a formally unitary system, for example, there is typically a considerable extent of *de facto* fiscal discretion at decentralized levels.

Thus, the analysis in this chapter refers to multilevel fiscal systems in all planned economies irrespective of whether they are formally unitary or federal.

This discussion relates to planned economies. Of course, centralized planning is negation of federalism. In centrally planned economies, the decisions on prices, outputs and allocation of resources are taken by the central planner and here, neither the market nor the subnational governments have any role in resource allocation. The subnational governments simply implement the functions assigned to them as agents of the central government. However, most of the centrally planned economies have made, and are making, a transition from command to market, and in some countries such as India, planned development strategy has historically coexisted with market determined resource allocation. In economies that have followed a central planning strategy for a long time, even as they make a transition to the market, the vestiges of planning continue to impact resource allocations and institutions of market are yet to be developed fully. They impact through controls over prices, outputs, inputs, impediments to free movement of factors and products and, above all, lumpiness of past investments persist, altering both intersectoral and interregional resource allocations in ways different from the market or their endowments. In other developing countries, the market institutions are yet to be developed. In the context, the norms of intergovernmental finance developed in the context of developed market economies need to be modified.

The objective of this chapter is to identify the salient features of developing and transition economies impacting on intergovernmental fiscal arrangements and to suggest modifications in the policies and institutions. The next section brings out the specific characteristics of planned developing economies impacting on interregional resource allocation. The third section speculates on the impact of planning on interregional resource flows in developing countries and identifies the areas requiring particular attention reforming fiscal decentralization policies and institutions in these economies. The final section summarizes the major conclusions.

Planning and federalism

The classical concept of federalism refers not only to an 'indestructible union of indestructible states' (Chanda 1965, p. 40) but is also 'the method of dividing powers so that the general and regional governments are each, within a sphere, co-ordinate and independent' (Wheare 1964, p. 10). Examples of such countries are rare and Wheare, writing in the 1940s, could find only four federations. In most developing and transitional countries the subnational governments are neither co-ordinate nor independent and, moreover, they are not indestructible either.

A major reason for the existence of relatively centralized fiscal systems in developing and transitional countries is the adoption of planned development strategy. The apparent success of the Soviet economy in achieving rapid progress by adopting centralized planning led many developing countries in the 1950s and 1960s to adopt a planned strategy for investment allocation with heavy reliance on the public sector. While the Soviet Union and similar socialist countries adopted a centralized planning strategy, many other developing countries such as India and Pakistan adopted a planned development strategy in a mixed economy framework with coexisting private and public sectors.

The nature and operation of the public sector in these socialist and other planned economies differed vastly from developed market economies and the subnational governments in the former countries were, to a greater or lesser degree, deconcentrated units of the central government. This was true even in countries that were formally called 'federations' such as the USSR and Czechoslovakia (Bird et al. 1995). In the case of federal countries that adopted planning in a mixed economy framework with the public sector assigned the 'commanding heights' role, there was a sharp increase in centralization as planning developed deeper roots.

Economic reforms providing a greater role for the market in resource allocation in developing and transitional economies in recent years have had an important bearing on multilevel finance in two important ways. The first relates to privatization in which many economies have moved from a command economy to liberalized markets. Another key aspect is the decentralization of the government itself. These two factors have had far-reaching implications for the functioning of the multilevel fiscal system in these countries.

With transition, subnational governments secured important roles in redistribution (providing social safety nets), stabilization and allocation of resources. At the same time, the problem of mobilizing revenues has assumed a critical dimension as efficiency considerations required the governments to assign major tax bases to the central governments. Besides, declining fortunes of public enterprises with greater competition and privatization deprived subnational governments of their traditional revenue source.

The transition from centralized planning to market-determined resource allocation has important implications for the fiscal role of the subnational governments. It is, therefore, important to understand the salient characteristics of these countries having a bearing on the assignment system, vertical and horizontal intergovernmental competition and interregional resource flows. Many of the instruments of planning create implicit interregional resource transfers, which are often invisible and difficult to take into account in the explicit transfer systems. In this section, some important characteristics of the planned economies with implications for assignment of taxes and expenditures on the one hand, and creating invisible transfers on the other are highlighted.

The rapid progress achieved in the initial years after the Bolshevik revolution led many developing countries to adopt Soviet-style economic planning. These included the countries of the Soviet bloc and other, similar socialist countries including China and Vietnam. With all investments centrally directed, the subnational units in these countries were merely deconcentrated implementing agencies of the center. The absence of property rights rendered the role of taxing properties, incomes and wealth largely irrelevant in these fiscal systems. With public enterprises taking a pivotal role to generate resources for investment, the location of these enterprises determined the pattern of regional development. Furthermore, often, the difference between government administration and public enterprises in the provision of public services becomes blurred in these economies, as many enterprises are directed to provide public services like schools and hospitals. In general, there is a soft budget constraint, particularly at subnational levels. The closed nature of these economies takes away the role of competition altogether. In these economies, the advantages arising from the 'largeness' and 'smallness' of nations attributed to federations by Alexis de Toqueville ([1838] 1945) over a century ago do not simply accrue. In these economies, there is no meaningful role for the subnational governments. As stated by Chelliah (1991, p. 7), 'Comprehensive central planning, involving as it does, centralized decision making in relation to production activities and disposal of resources in the "national interest" is the negation of the principle of true federalism'.

The perverse incentives and institutional weaknesses in socialist economies made them inherently unsustainable. 'Economic federalism', in which the decentralized structure of government internalizes all economic externalities, fails in such economies because of a lack of competition, impediments to mobility, and price and quantity controls.[2] There has been a dramatic reform not only in Central and Eastern Europe, but also in large Asian countries with strong socialist persuasion such as China and Vietnam. The most notable features of reform in these countries are privatization and restoration of the role of markets, opening up of the economies and decentralization (Bird et al. 1995). The three features are complementary and reinforce one another to make a transition from command to market economy.

Although considerable progress has been made in each of these areas, many transition economies function in a relatively centralized institutional environment, and planning in some form or other coexists with market-based resource allocation. In some cases, the continued use of administered prices as an instrument of resource allocation, is accompanied by the prevalence of soft budget constraints, contingent liabilities and associated fiscal risk, physical restrictions and impediments to internal trade, restrictions on the mobility of labor and capital and finally, the historically given spread of physical infrastructure and stock of capital invested in state enterprises.

The transition from command to market has impacted decentralization in a variety of ways. The attempts to control fiscal pressures at the center have led to pushing the deficits down. While some countries, notably Vietnam, accomplished just under a six percentage point reduction in the expenditure–GDP ratio over the 1990–94 period to reduce the inflation rate from a three-digit number to a single-digit level, the general approach has been to reduce transfers to local governments while keeping the functional assignment unchanged. This has led to either declining standards in public service provision, as in Russia, or in countries with a tradition of soft budget constraints, an accumulation of arrears and contingent liabilities as in China (World Bank 2002) and Hungary (Bird et al. 1995). In many cases, the central government continues to play the dominant role in resource allocation, and this is true of countries like Russia that have adopted formally federal constitutions. Thus, in many transition economies, subnational governments are yet to acquire a meaningful role in the provision of public services. In particular, no transition country has assigned any broad-based revenue sources to subnational governments. Local governments tend to have limited autonomy in expenditure decisions in the initial stages of the transition.

The second category of economies are those which have adopted development planning as a strategy to accelerate growth in a mixed economy framework. India and Pakistan fall into this category. In the 1950s and 1960s, low levels of saving and investment, the existence of poor infrastructure and the absence of an industrial base combined with export pessimism motivated these countries to channel available savings to priority areas of investment. In the Indian context, this involved assigning 'commanding heights' to the public sector, and the private investments had to be channeled into priority areas through a system of industrial licensing. Elimination of domestic competition was combined with a high degree of protection, through a combination of physical restrictions on imports and very high tariffs to eliminate external competition altogether. As this could lead to large monopolies and highly skewed distribution of incomes and wealth, various legislations to control restrictive trade practices on the one hand, and confiscatory levels of taxation on the other, were introduced.

Thus, fiscal policy in planned economies with private sector participation was designed to (i) finance investment by raising the level of domestic saving, especially public saving; (ii) transfer household savings to public investment; (iii) reduce inequalities in income and wealth; and (iv) aid in social engineering of the volume and direction of economic activity (Bagchi and Nayak 1994). The way in which fiscal policies were calibrated in these large economies had a significant impact on the operation of multilevel fiscal systems. In particular, while the size and diversity of such economies required a significant fiscal decentralization, the adoption of planned development strategy called for a high degree of centralization in both fiscal and financial systems.

Although economic liberalization in these economies has brought in significant changes in the policy environment, the legacies of the past policies and structure of institutions continue to have an impact on the operation of the multilevel fiscal system. In both India and Pakistan, there has been a tendency to decentralize operations – but for different reasons. As Bardhan (Ch. 8 in this volume) points out, in Pakistan the decentralization is the result of a top-down decision planned by a military government. In India, the development of the *panchayat* system has been a result of political pressures.

Development planning and fiscal federalism

As mentioned earlier, despite the progress achieved in fiscal decentralization, privatization and freeing of product and factor markets, the autarchic fiscal system and the institutions set up to implement the systems continue to impact on the functioning of multilevel fiscal operations in these economies in a variety of ways.

Impact of planning on budgeting systems
The development planning strategy has affected the way in which investment

budgets are determined in developing and transitional economies. In India, for example, the process has resulted in the segmentation of both central and state budgets into 'plan' and 'non-plan'. While in principle, the expenditure on new schemes is supposed to be classified as plan, that incurred for the maintenance of the completed schemes is considered non-plan. Thus, spending classified as plan does not necessarily represent investment expenditures. This segmented budgeting practice has prevented a comprehensive and consistent approach to the provision of public services. The emphasis on having larger plans at the state level has resulted in three important outcomes. First, the states have made larger allocations to plans without paying attention to the maintenance of assets such as roads, bridges and irrigation works, which are in their domain. Second, competing claims for scarce resources and eagerness to take up a large number of schemes have led to spreading the resources thinly with significant cost and time over-runs. Finally, the need to increase the plan size has led to raising resources by the state governments with little regard to their distortionary implications (Rao 2002).

The most important aspect of the planning process in countries such as India is that segmentation of the budget into plan and non-plan categories has led to the separation of the transfer system for plan and non-plan purposes. Both the streams are general-purpose transfers intended to offset fiscal disabilities, but are distributed on the basis of different, and often conflicting, criteria. The separate mechanisms employed to determine plan and non-plan transfers have led to the states adopting strategies with adverse incentives to fiscal management, besides inequity and inefficiency in the delivery of public services.[3]

In many of the transitional economies such as Vietnam, Laos and China, the investment budget is also determined differently from the recurring budget. The investment budget is determined by a combination of bottom-up and top-down processes with the central governments eventually including only a small fraction of the projects demanded by the local governments. The process distorts prioritization, causes underfunding and time and cost over-runs. In these countries too, segmented treatment of investment and recurrent expenditures has prevented a comprehensive view and strategy of their budgets.

In transitional and developing economies, rationalizing the budgeting systems is an important component of reform agenda. As the economies decentralize their fiscal systems further, it is important to have comparable and uniform systems, proper processes of determining budgets, and internal and external control mechanisms. Many transitional countries still do not have an adequate or consistent accounting framework involving uniform budget codes and nomenclature. In many of these countries, the accounting system does not enable decentralized expenditure management, the treasury control is not effective and external control through independent audit does not exist. The reporting systems from line ministries and local governments are not standardized, besides being weak. Countries such as Vietnam, Cambodia and Laos follow the erstwhile French system of budget classification, while countries such as India, Pakistan and Bangladesh follow the Anglo-Saxon tradition. In these countries, considerable effort is needed to change over to the Government Finance Statistics (GFS) classification system.

In most socialist countries, the budget was traditionally considered to be a secret document. Reforms in the systems of budgeting and reporting are extremely important as these economies decentralize their fiscal systems further.

Commanding state enterprises: implications on fiscal federalism
An important feature of the planned economies is the lead role played by state enterprises in economic activities. In these economies, resource mobilization is done thorough capturing state enterprise profits. Thus, the volume and pattern of resource mobilization is determined by the way in which public sector prices are administratively determined. With economic liberalization and opening up of the economy, the revenue importance of state enterprises declines. Besides, as taxes replace public enterprise profit transfers, there are implications for relative prices and allocative efficiency and for the assignment of revenue sources to central and subnational governments.

In many planned fiscal systems, subnational governments derive significant revenues from the state enterprises owned by them and, as the economy is liberalized, subnational taxes have to be developed. However, assignment of taxes in most of the planned economies to local governments is meager. Nevertheless, in India, state governments collect almost 37 per cent of their total revenues from their own sources. In many of these economies, property markets are not well developed, property owners are a powerful elite and obviously property taxes do not contribute much to the revenue of local governments. Thus, in many transitional economies, inability to substitute declining revenues from locally state enterprises with local taxes can reduce the fiscal autonomy of local governments.

The impact of declining state enterprise revenues on fiscal decentralization is generally seen in both reducing enterprise revenues and reducing transfers to subnational governments. In most transitional economies, the subnational governments' declining revenues because of the substitution of taxes for profit transfers, and because of inability to face greater competition in a liberalized open environment, increases their fiscal dependence. One probable result of overall declining revenues, particularly for the center, is to push the deficits down by transferring expenditure responsibilities to subnational governments. In Hungary, the responsibility for welfare expenditure and the social safety net was transferred to local governments in 1993. In Russia the central government transferred social expenditures amounting to 6 per cent of GDP to local governments and in the next year also transferred the responsibility for important national investments to subnational governments (Bird et al. 1995).

The consequence of pushing down the functions in planned economies such as India, has been to reduce the standards of public services or to raise revenues from revenue handles assigned to them without any regard to the economic effects of such levies. The state and local governments in India, for example, are known to raise revenues from residence-based and distortionary taxes, which has created impediments to internal trade and violated the principle of the common market (Rao 2002). This can also lead to a build-up of expenditure arrears in payments, as seen in Bulgaria, Romania, Russia and Ukraine, or undesirable borrowing, as was the case of Budapest in the early 1990s[4] and Russian *oblasts* (Bird, et al. 1995, p. 25).

Public enterprise revenues of subnational governments can be an important source of distortion and inequity. In the case of commodities that are relatively inelastic with respect to prices, sales outside the jurisdictions result in the collection of monopoly profits from the non-residents, and this is akin to inter-jurisdictional tax exportation. Apart from the strategy followed by the jurisdictions in determining administered prices, they may set low prices in the case of commodities that are price elastic to attract trade diversion, or high prices in the case of commodities that are relatively price inelastic to earn monopoly rents from non-residents.

An important outcome of public enterprise activity in many planned economies is the off-budget financing of public services. In such cases, state enterprises directly provide many public services, such as running of schools, hospitals, housing, and construction and maintenance of roads and bridges. Although with privatization these activities had to be transferred to subnational governments, in many countries, enterprises continue to finance public service provision to a considerable extent. The use of extra-budgetary sources to finance public services is particularly significant at local levels. In China, for example, it was estimated that the off-budget financing of expenditures in 1996 was over 20 per cent of GDP. This included quasi-fiscal expenditures of enterprises for the provision of public services at less than full compensation, estimated at 1 per cent of GDP (Wong 1999; World Bank, 2002). In Russia, local tax offices permitted illegal tax breaks to firms setting up their own kindergartens and providing other social services. Similarly, in Bulgaria, the state enterprises played an important role in health, education, infrastructure and culture (Martinez-Vazquez 1995). This obscured the roles of central and subnational governments, created overlapping authorities, and posed difficulties in establishing accountability and incentives in the provision of public services.

Another important implication of the public enterprises is the way they have been used to soften the budget constraints at subnational levels. In many countries the local bond market is yet to be developed, and borrowing from the financial system involves considerable liabilities. In India, acute fiscal difficulties by the state governments have led them to use the state enterprises as conduits to undertake additional borrowing on their behalf and soften the budget constraint (Rao 2001). Thus, an outcome of the predominant public sector has been to add significant contingent liabilities and fiscal risk to subnational governments in planned economies.

Developing subnational tax systems

An important feature of the planned development strategy, seen in both developing and transitional economies, is the determination of prices according to the government fiat rather than the market principles. This is a part of the public sector dominated import-substituting strategy. The consequence of this has been that the allocation of resources, both between different industries and between regions in these economies, is markedly different if the prices were market determined. Thus, administered prices have important implications for both efficiency and equity in a multilevel fiscal system.

The most important local tax that needs to be developed to strengthen fiscal decentralization is the local property tax. However, in order to develop the property tax as a significant contributor to local revenues, it is important to establish clear property rights and develop legal and regulatory systems.[5] In many socialist countries, such as Vietnam and China, assignment of property rights and development of a legal system are still in their infancy. In India, property rights have been assigned and legal institutions exist. But often, the records are not properly maintained and vestiges of the planned regime – the Rent Control Act and the Urban Land Ceiling Act – continue to plague rationalization of the property tax system. Also, the property-owning class as a pressure group in a local government can be a formidable hindrance to the development of a modern property tax system.

Substituting the administered prices with taxes is a major reform agenda in many planned economies. This changes the revenue assignment system for, in many transitional economies, the subnational governments do not have tax powers and enterprise income has to be substituted by transfers. Some countries, such as Romania, still assign local enterprise taxes to subnational governments and in some others local governments stake 'source entitlement' claims. Nevertheless, by and large, the substitution of administered prices with taxes has been to centralize tax collections. On the one hand, moves to decentralize functions have resulted in greater expenditure responsibilities and on the other, substitution of enterprise income with taxes leads to centralization of tax powers.

Meaningful fiscal decentralization requires significant subnational taxing powers. Linking tax and expenditure decisions at the margin is critical to ensuring expenditure efficiency and accountability. In most transitional economies, local governments did not have significant tax powers – though this is changing especially in eastern Europe. Even when they are given some tax powers, the subnational governments have shown a general reluctance to raise revenues from the sources assigned to them. In countries such as India, decentralization in tax powers is only up to the state level (Rao et al. 2004). Even so, the states levy a host of inefficient taxes including a cascading sales tax and tax on the inter-state sales. Below the state level, even in urban areas, the property tax is not well developed and this has led the local governments to levy inefficient taxes such as the tax on the entry of goods (*octroi*) into local areas.

There is much to be done in assigning appropriate tax bases and developing tax administration in these economies. Despite the claim that administration at the local level provides incentive for revenue collections by increasing tax compliance, the experiences of a number of socialist countries, such as Russia and Laos, have shown that tax compliance will actually decline when the tax collection is decentralized – and in China the creation of a central tax administration has led to a significant improvement in overall revenue collection. Therefore, it is important to pay attention to the design of decentralization in these economies as they make a transition to the market.

Substituting physical controls with market-based instruments
An important feature characterizing transitional economies is the prevalence of price and quantity controls. With market-based liberalization and the opening up of these economies, price (including interest rate) and quantity controls will have to give way to monetary and fiscal policy instruments. Disbanding command and control systems associated with Soviet-style planning and replacing them with fiscal and regulatory instruments calls for changes in the responsibilities of multilevel administrations as well.

A number of other controls and regulations introduced at various levels also hinder the development of a common market. The impediments have been erected to serve the needs of planning or rationing to meet scarcity situations. These have imposed several hindrances to the movement of factors and products across the country. In India, for example, the restrictions placed on the movement of foodgrains continue to pervade under the Essential Commodities Act. In many socialist countries such as China and Vietnam, migration from one region to another and often from rural to urban areas is prohibited, resulting in a large number of illegal migrants in the fringes of major cities without proper access to basic services. In many countries the easiest way to collect revenues is by erecting barriers on highways and arterial roads and collecting (often illegal) taxes. In addition, in countries like India, the poor information base has led to the establishment of checkpoints at several places to facilitate tax collection. Thus, there are checkpoints for administering sales taxes, state excises on alcoholic products, taxes on motor vehicles, to check the exploitation of forest products, besides regular police checkpoints. These have been set up not only on state borders but also inside the states. In addition, there are taxes on the entry of goods into local area (*octroi*) for which separate checkpoints are set up by the municipalities.

Despite a reduced emphasis on the plan and change in scarcity conditions over the years, a number of fiscal and regulatory impediments have continued in most developing and transitional economies. Besides physical controls, there are also fiscal impediments with unintended allocative consequences. The removal of obstacles to ensure free movement of factors and products throughout the country is necessary to improve competitiveness, and this will be an important challenge in the transitional economies of Asia. An important advantage of federalism is the access to a large common market, but this is not realized in most planned economies.

Balanced regional development, interregional inequity and invisible transfers
In planned economies, there are two explicit ways by which regional allocation of resources is generally brought about. First, the central government's own investment in different regions or regional policy pursued by it determines the level of economic activity and the private sector resource flows. Central investment in infrastructure in different regions determines the flow of private investments. In most planned economies, the objective of 'balanced regional development' pursued by the governments distorts the investment pattern by central investments. Often, despite the claims about balanced regional developments, the investment decisions are taken on political considerations – on the basis of bargaining powers and political influence of different regions.[6] Thus, the claims made on behalf of balanced regional development are often more rhetoric than reality. Even as large investments were made in steel plants in states with large deposits of manganese and coal as in Bihar, Madhya Pradesh, Orissa and West Bengal, the forward linkages from these large investments were nullified by a 'freight equalization policy' – a policy of subsidizing freight charges to equalize the prices of steel across the country. Although the policy has since been abandoned, the investment decisions undertaken when the policy existed cannot be unmade and it will be a long time before a more rational resource allocation is made.

The second explicit method of impacting on regional resource allocation is through intergovernmental transfers. In some socialist planned economies, the expenditure assignment is delegated or deconcentrated and the transfers are given mainly to carry out these functions. However, in large countries, fiscal decentralization is a reality and the determination of the volume and design of the transfer system are important reform issues. In most countries, the transfer system is negotiated. There is no objective mechanism to determine the volume of transfers nor are there distribution formulae. In many countries, transfers were initially determined in the process of determining budgets. These included Hungary, Poland and even Vietnam. In the last case, actually, norms are built into the determination of expenditures (World Bank 2000). In Russia until 1994, the *ex post* subventions were negotiated between deficit regions and the Ministry of Finance with serious incentive problems. Institution of a rule-based transfer system is an important challenge in these countries.

In India, the constitution itself provides a mechanism for determining the transfer system. The Finance Commission appointed by the President of India every five years is supposed to determine the total tax devolution and grants as well as their distribution among various states. The functioning of the Finance Commission, however, has left much to be desired. The Commission, in effect follows the 'gap-filling' approach, with serious disincentives for fiscal management. In addition, with the emergence of the Planning Commission as an institution determining the resource allocation of the public sector, a parallel transfer system evolved to plan expenditure requirements. Both planning and finance commissions give unconditional transfers, and the Planning Commission, in addition, channels central government loans to state governments. In addition to these agencies, individual ministries allocate specific-purpose transfers.

The most important issue in both developing planned economies, and transitional economies with a strong plan legacy, is that considerable improvements need to be made in the transfer systems. Negotiated transfer systems and those with significant disincentives to fiscal management should be replaced by formulae-based systems to offset fiscal disabilities. Further, the institutional mechanism to devolve the transfer system needs to be evolved to make the system objective and transparent.

In addition to regional policies and intergovernmental transfers, there are various sources of implicit interregional transfers that alter resource allocation across regions. One source of such transfers is various price and quantity controls. Administered determination of prices and quantities affects the profitability of different industries and, depending on the resource endowments, different regions. Another important source of implicit transfer is the collection of revenues from origin-based taxes and consequent interregional tax exportation. Origin-based tax systems, and cascading taxes, can cause significant interregional resource transfers. In economies characterized by oligopolistic markets and with mark-up pricing, the producing subnational units collect significant revenues from the consumers in consuming units. In the Indian case, the implicit transfers estimated from subsidized lending to states significantly eroded the progressively of explicit transfers in India during the 1985–95 period (Rao 1997).

Distortions and inequity

Planned economies, through their various policy instruments to control the resource allocation, introduce several sources of distortion and inequity. Thus, fiscal federalism in these countries ceases to be an efficient institutional arrangement. The distortions are introduced by the way the budgets are determined and prices administered, impediments to internal trade and movement of labor and capital, the closed nature of the economy and the commanding height of the role assigned to the public sector. Most planned economies are making a transition to more market-oriented decentralized systems. However, until the transition is complete, the multilevel fiscal arrangements will have to take these distortions and inequity into account in formulating their federal fiscal policies.

Impediments to internal trade and allocative distortions

An important characteristic of planned economies is the impediments on the mobility of factors of production on the one hand and finished products on the other. The restrictions could be imposed by fiscal instruments, or there may simply be physical restrictions to serve the objectives of regional distribution. Fiscal impediments arise when taxes are levied on the sale of goods from one province or region to another (export taxes) and taxes are levied on the entry of goods into a region (import taxes). The levy of interstate sales tax on the export of goods from one state to another and the taxes on the entry of goods into a local area by the local bodies are examples. Given the poor information systems in these countries, the administration of such taxes requires erecting physical barriers and collecting taxes at the point of exit or entry into a province or a region. This not only results in dividing the country into several tariff zones but also involves very high compliance cost and delays in transportation. Furthermore, as the tax is not account based but purely collected at the point of entry or exit, it leaves a lot of discretion to the tax officials, resulting in large-scale corruption.

Physical restrictions on the movement of goods were introduced as a rationing device to meet scarcity conditions in respect of essential goods. Although in countries like India scarcity conditions no longer exist, restrictions on the physical movement of essential foods, particularly food items, have continued. These create additional implicit taxes and subsidies. In addition, in many socialist economies like China and Vietnam, formal restrictions on the mobility of people from one region to another impede free mobility of labor. Although this causes large-scale illegal migration of labor from rural and urban areas, the result is inadequate provision and pressure on urban infrastructure, substitution of capital for labor and various other types of distortions.

Concluding remarks

This chapter has examined the special features of planned economies affecting intergovernmental fiscal arrangements and indicated the areas where mainstream literature on fiscal federalism needs modification.

The chapter has identified a number of areas where the planned development strategy can impact on fiscal federalism. Of course, central planning is the negation of federalism. However, virtually all economies have made a transition from command economy to market-based resource allocation, but vestiges of planning continue to impact on resource allocation. Similarly, some countries have adopted a planned development strategy within a mixed economy framework. The chapter has analysed the impact of planning on assignment systems, overlapping in the assignments and the implications for intergovernmental transfers arising from the planned development strategy.

There are a variety of ways in which a planned development strategy affects the efficiency and equity in multilevel fiscal systems and fiscal federalism can become an optimal institutional arrangement in these countries only when significant reforms are undertaken. These include reforms in planning and budgeting practices, reforms to substitute public enterprise profits with taxes at subnational levels, developing market-based instruments to substitute physical controls, evolving the transfer system to take into account invisible transfers and reforms in the fiscal system to reduce distortions.

On the policy side, the scope of reforms in fiscal federalism in developing countries is much more complex and broader than merely looking at the issues in assignment and transfer systems. The reforms in fiscal federalism are inextricably intertwined with privatization, planning and budgeting, reforms in administered price mechanisms, various regulations relating to the movement of factors and products, and also the issues discussed in fiscal federalism proper. Any attempt to look at the issues in isolation will render the reforms less potent and ineffective.

Notes

1. Breton (2000) distinguishes federalism from decentralization in terms of the ownership of inextinguishable constitutional powers of the levels of government.
2. The concept of 'economic federalism' propounded by Inman and Rubinfeld is close to Oates's 'fiscal federalism' in his seminal work (Oates 1972). See, Inman and Rubinfeld (1997, pp. 45–8) for a discussion on economic federalism.
3. For a detailed analysis of the adverse incentives and efficiency and equity implications of the transfer system, see Rao and Singh (2005).
4. The passage of municipal bankruptcy legislation in Hungary has subsequently been a major structural reform (see Ahmad, Albino-War and Singh, Ch. 16 in this volume).

5.   For a detailed discussion of evolving property tax systems in transitional countries, see Malme and Youngman (2001).
6.   In India, for example, despite a lot of emphasis given to regional equity, as on March 2002, four high-income states with 29.5 per cent of the population and generating state domestic product of 34 per cent accounted for 22.1 per cent of investments and 31.6 per cent of employment in central enterprises. In contrast, five low-income states with a population of 44.7 per cent and generating income of 28.4 per cent of the country accounted for only 26 per cent of investments and 42.1 per cent of employment (Rao and Singh 2005).

References

Bagchi, Amaresh and Pulin Nayak (1994), 'A survey of public finance and planning process', in Amaresh Bagchi and Nicholas Stern (eds), *Tax Policy and Planning in Developing Countries*, New Delhi: Oxford University Press, pp. 21–87.

Bird, Richard M., Robert D. Ebel and Christine I. Wallich (eds) (1995), *Decentralization of the Socialist State*, Washington, DC: World Bank.

Breton, Albert (2000), 'Federalism and decentralization: ownership rights and the superiority of federalism', *Publius: The Journal of Federalism*, Vol. 30. No. 2 (Spring), pp. 1–16.

Chanda, Asok (1965), *Federalism in India*, London: George Allen & Unwin.

Chelliah, R.J. (1991), *Towards a Decentralised Polity: Outline of a Proposal*, L.K. Jha Memorial Lecture, Fiscal Research Foundation, New Delhi.

Inman, Robert and David Rubinfeld (1997), 'Rethinking federalism', *Journal of Economic Perspectives*, Vol. 11, No. 4, pp. 3–33.

Malme J.H. and Joan M. Youngman (eds) (2001), *The Development of Property Taxation in Economies in Transition*, Washington, DC: World Bank.

Martinez-Vazquez, Jorge (1995), 'Intergovernmental fiscal relations in Bulgaria', in Bird et al. (eds), pp. 183–222.

Newberry, David (1987), 'Taxation and development', in David Newberry and Nicholas Stern (eds), *The Theory of Taxation for Developing Countries*, Oxford: Oxford University Press.

Oates, W.E. (1972), *Fiscal Federalism*, New York: Harcourt, Brace & Jovanovich.

Oates, W.E. (1977), 'An economist's perspective of fiscal federalism', in Oates (ed.), *Political Economy of Fiscal Federalism*, Massachusetts: Lexington Books, pp. 3–20.

Oates, Wallace E. (1999), 'An essay on fiscal federalism', *Journal of Economic Literature*, Vol. 37, No. 37, pp. 1120–49.

Rao, Govinda (1997), 'Invisible transfers in Indian federation', *Public Finance/Finances Publiques*, Vol. 52, No. 3, pp. 299–316.

Rao, Govinda M. (2001), 'State finances in India', *Economic and Political Weekly*, Vol. XXXVII, No. 31, pp. 3261–671.

Rao, Govinda M. (2002), 'Dynamics of Indian federalism', Paper Presented at the Conference on Indian Economic Reforms, Center for Economic Development and Policy Reform, Stanford University, Stanford, CA.

Rao, M. Govinda and Nirvikar Singh (2005), *Political Economy of Indian Federalism*, New Delhi: Oxford University Press.

Rao, M. Govinda, H.K. Amar Nath and B.P. Vani (2004), 'Fiscal decentralization in Karnataka', in Geeta Sethi (ed.), *Fiscal Decentralization to Rural Governments in India*, Oxford: Oxford University Press.

Tocqueville, Alexis de ([1838] 1945), *Democracy in America*, New York: Vintage Books Random House; quoted in Oates (1999).

Wheare, Kenneth C. (1964), *Federal Government*, 4th edition, London: Oxford University Press.

Wong, Christine (1999), 'Converting fees into taxes: reform of extra-budgetary funds and inter-governmental fiscal relations in China, 1999 and beyond', Paper presented at the Association of Asian Studies Meetings, Boston, MA.

Wong, Christine (2000), 'Central–local relations revisited: the 1994 tax sharing reform and public expenditure management in China', Paper presented at the International Conference on 'Central–Periphery Relations in China: Integration, Disintegration or Reshaping of an Empire?', Chinese University of Hong Kong, 24–25 March.

World Bank (2000), *China: Managing Public Expenditures for Better Results*, Report No. 20342 – CHA.

World Bank (2002), *China: National Development and Sub-National Finance*, World Bank Report No. 22951 – CHA.

10 Decentralization and service delivery

Junaid Ahmad, Shantayanan Devarajan, Stuti Khemani and Shekhar Shah

Introduction

This chapter provides a framework that explains both why decentralization can generate substantial improvements in service delivery, and why it often falls short of this promise. Services seem to work when there are strong relationships of accountability between the actors in the service delivery chain – between providers, clients and policy makers. Decentralization can both strengthen and weaken these relationships of accountability.

The next section describes the motivation for recent decentralization efforts worldwide and their impact on service delivery. It develops the framework for thinking about why decentralization can lead to substantial service delivery improvements but can also fall short of that potential. The third section examines how different types of accountability mechanisms between central and local government (fiscal transfers, regulation, borrowing rules and so on) affect the incentives facing service providers, and how these translate to service delivery outcomes.

The fourth section examines the effect of decentralization on political incentives at all levels – central and local. It asks how a system where politicians at the central level were not facing the right incentives to provide good services will change in the wake of decentralization. For instance, if there were information asymmetries, are these reduced or exacerbated by decentralization? How are social polarization and elite capture affected? And how do electoral rules and political institutions affect the outcome?

In the penultimate section, we explore some open questions in the link between decentralization and service delivery, most of which have to do with the transition from a centralized to a decentralized system. The final section concludes.

Background

In the last 25 years, over 75 countries have attempted to transfer responsibilities of the state to lower tiers of government. Significantly, most of these lower-tier governments have been elected, so that the decentralization is not just administrative or fiscal, but also political. The motivation for the decentralization has varied. In Eastern Europe and the former Soviet Union, it was part of the political and economic transformation; in Latin America, it was to reinforce the transition to democracy; in South Africa, Sri Lanka and Indonesia, it was a response to ethnic or regional conflict; and in Chile, Uganda and Côte d'Ivoire, it was to improve the delivery of basic services (Shah and Thompson 2004). Even when it is not explicit, improving service delivery is an implicit motivation behind most of these decentralization efforts.

The reasons are twofold. First, these basic services, such as health, education, water and sanitation, all of which are the responsibility of the state, are systematically failing – and especially failing poor people (World Bank 2003b). That governments are falling short of their responsibility to ensure adequate health, education, water and sanitation to their people can be seen at various levels. At the macroeconomic level, the main instrument with which governments exercise this responsibility – overall public spending – seems to have only a weak relationship with outcomes. Public spending on health has no significant association with reductions in child or infant mortality; and public spending on education has an extremely weak relationship with primary school completion rates (Filmer and Pritchett 1999a, 1999b; Filmer et al. 2000).

The microeconomic evidence indicates why government spending does not translate to better outcomes. For one thing, the money does not often reach the frontline service provider. In Uganda, the share of non-salary spending on primary education that actually reached primary schools was 13 per cent (Reinikka and Svensson 2001). For another, the quality of these services is often extremely poor. In Bangladesh, the absenteeism rate for doctors in primary health centers was 74 per cent (Chaudhury and Hammer 2005).

The second reason is that these services are consumed and provided locally, and centralized decision making might not correspond to local preferences. Norway's health system was run by locally appointed health commissions until the 1930s; schools in Nepal were managed by communities until the 1960s. Yet today the central government in these two countries (as well as most others) assumes responsibility for the delivery of these services. Many governments and their electorates associate the problems of service delivery with the centralization of these services.

For instance, the fact that only a fraction of the money that is due service providers actually reaches them may be due to the power of the central government *vis-à-vis* local government, through whom the money gets transferred. Similarly, centralization means that the allocation of resources among these local services may not reflect local preferences. Faguet (2004) shows that decentralization in Bolivia led to a better match between local preferences and budgetary allocations.[1] Faguet's study points to another problem of centralization: some regions might get completely neglected. Prior to decentralization in

Bolivia, an overwhelmingly disproportionate amount of public resources were concentrated in the capital city and its surroundings. Finally, central government provision could also lead to greater corruption and misuse of funds, as the service recipients in a local district cannot monitor the bureaucrat or politician in the capital city (Bardhan and Mookherjee 2000).

However, despite these problems associated with central delivery of services, the experience with decentralization itself has been quite mixed (World Bank 2003b; Burki et al. 1999). While success or failure is difficult (and premature) to judge, some common problems associated with decentralization's impact on service delivery have begun to emerge.

The most frequently cited problem is the lack of capacity at subnational levels of government to exercise responsibility for public services. In Uganda and Tanzania, the lower tiers of government lacked the ability to manage public finances and maintain proper accounting procedures. Since these were a requirement for transferring money to the lower tiers, they actually received less money than before decentralization. In Uganda, spending on primary health care fell from 33 to 16 per cent during decentralization (Akin et al. 2001). In Ethiopia, where decentralization goes down to the third tier or *woreda* level, some *woredas* lack sufficient people who can read and write to operate the district governments.

A second problem is that decentralization has led to misaligned responsibilities, possibly because the process is incomplete, possibly for political reasons. Although Pakistan has devolved responsibility for education to the districts, school teachers remain employees of the provincial government.[2] The district *nazim* or elected executive has little authority over the hiring, firing, evaluation or placement of teachers.

Third, while decentralization was in some cases intended to strengthen the political power of lower tiers of government *vis-à-vis* the center, it has also increased the possibility of political capture within these lower tiers. In 1979, Indonesia established 'village governments' with locally chosen village heads accountable to village councils that would determine budget priorities. A study of 48 rural villages showed that, since village heads chose the members of the council, accountability to the villagers was weak; only 3 per cent of the village proposals were included in the district budgets. Those villagers who participated in government organizations were more likely to speak out at village council meetings, crowding out the voice of others in the village (World Bank 2001).[3]

Fourth, a host of other problems, not associated with service delivery, have nevertheless helped to undermine service delivery in decentralizing economies. For instance, the 'soft budget constraint' facing subnational governments has led to overborrowing (Rodden et al. 2003) and, in the case of Argentina, a major macroeconomic crisis at the end of 2001.[4] The social impact of the Argentinian crisis has clearly been a deterioration in service quality: poverty rates jumped 40 per cent, 12 per cent of the people with formal health insurance discontinued their policies, medical supplies were in short supply throughout the public hospital network and in 2002 a third of the provinces experienced school closings of 20–80 days out of a 180-day school year (World Bank 2003b).

Why does decentralization sometimes substantially improve services and why does it often fall short of this promise? To explain this, we provide a framework based on the *2004 World Development Report* (World Bank 2003b). The essence of the framework is that the delivery of services requires strong relationships of accountability between the actors in the service delivery chain (Figure 10.1). In contrast to the delivery of goods or services in a private, competitive market, where the service provider is directly accountable to the client or consumer of the service, the delivery of public services involves at least two relationships of accountability. First, clients as citizens have to hold policymakers or politicians accountable for allocating resources towards these services. Second, policymakers in turn need to hold the service providers accountable for delivering the service. We refer to this as the 'long route of accountability', as opposed to the 'short route' which is the direct accountability of providers to clients.

Weaknesses in service-delivery outcomes can be attributed to a breakdown in one or both of the links along the long route of accountability. For instance, the fact that public spending on health and education mainly benefits the non-poor reflects the inability of citizens, especially poor citizens, to hold politicians accountable for resource allocation decisions. In some cases, this is because there is no electoral democracy in the country. In others, there may be a functioning electoral system, but due to information asymmetries or social polarization, the outcomes may still be biased against the poor (Keefer and

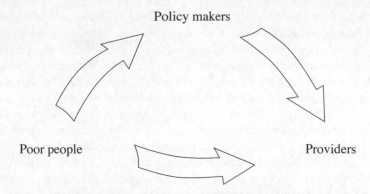

Policy makers

Poor people

Providers

Figure 10.1   The framework of accountability relationships

Khemani 2005). Even if poor citizens can hold politicians accountable, the politician in turn may not be able to hold the provider accountable. The minister of education in the capital city will not be able to monitor school teachers in rural primary schools. Unless there is a mechanism by which clients can monitor and discipline the providers (that is, the short route of accountability is working), the result is that teachers are absent, and primary education suffers.

These problems with the long route of accountability are what lead some to advocate decentralization as a means of strengthening accountability and thereby improving service delivery. Devolving responsibility for public services to lower tiers of government means that the politician who is responsible is now a locally elected one (Figure 10.2). The hope is that this would make him more accountable to the citizens, as they can monitor him more closely and attribute changes in service quality to him more easily. That is, decentralization will strengthen the citizen–local politician relationship of accountability, and thereby the other relationships of accountability for service delivery.[5]

However, as shown in Figure 10.2, decentralization introduces one more relationship of accountability, namely between the central and local policy makers. In fact, much of the literature on decentralization focuses on this relationship – the rules and practices governing fiscal transfers, regulation and expenditures between central and local policy makers. As our earlier discussion pointed out, changes in these rules and practices affect service delivery

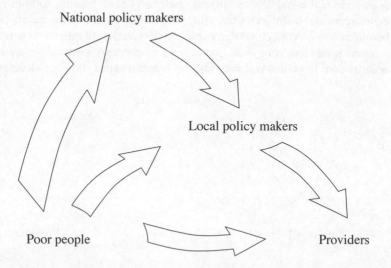

National policy makers

Local policy makers

Poor people

Providers

Figure 10.2   The framework of accountability relationships under decentralization

only through their effect on the accountability relationship between local policy makers and providers. For instance, as mentioned earlier in the case of education in Pakistan, even when devolution leads to fiscal transfers from the central to the local policy makers, if the local policy maker cannot hold the provider accountable (since he/she is an employee of the central government), the greater accountability of local politicians to their electorate may not result in better service delivery.

The accountability between central and local policy makers and providers

Decentralization introduces a new relationship of accountability, that between central and local policy maker (Figure 10.2), even as it seeks to make local politicians more accountable to their local clients. In addressing the difficulties with the 'long route of accountability', decentralization introduces its own complications. This section examines how the accountability between central and local policy makers – its fiscal, financing, regulatory and administrative dimensions – can have an important bearing on the incentives facing service providers and therefore on service delivery outcomes. Sound design and implementation of these aspects of decentralization is the starting point for improving local service delivery.

Fiscal issues

Four components define the fiscal dimensions of decentralization: (i) allocation of expenditure responsibilities by central and local tiers of government; (ii) assignment of taxes by government tiers; (iii) the design of an intergovernmental grant system; and (iv) the budgeting and monitoring of fiscal flows between different government tiers. Local governments will be less accountable for delivering good services if they can manipulate these components to shift fiscal liabilities to the center – what is often referred to as a 'soft budget constraint' (Litvack et al. 1998).

The assignment of expenditure and financing responsibility between different tiers of government can have a direct impact on service delivery. For example, in some countries in Latin America, the decentralization of water and sanitation services to small local governments has led to a loss of economies of scale in service delivery (see Foster 2002). On the other hand, recognizing that the spillover benefits of health and education outcomes and their impact on equity are national in scope have convinced many governments in Latin America and Africa to keep the financing of these sectors at a central level (Litvack et al. 1998). In the United States, the assignment of certain business taxes to local levels has led to inefficient tax competition – a race to the bottom – with consequences for the tax base of municipalities and their ability to finance service delivery (Inman 1992).

In principle, the factors that should come into play in deciding the optimal assignment of expenditure and tax responsibilities include economies of scale, spillover benefits, cost of administering taxes, tax efficiency and equity. In practice, political realities and historical legacies often determine the choices and, not surprisingly, give rise to mismatches. Political expediency led the Indonesian parliament to hastily pass laws in 1999 to implement a 'big-bang' decentralization, but left the expenditure law unclear on assignments. The laws have had to be subsequently revised (World Bank 2003a).

In addition, the assignment of responsibilities can affect service delivery by altering the accountability of lower- to higher-level governments. For instance, there is often a concurrence in expenditure and financing responsibilities. This issue is well exemplified by the way health and education services are funded and delivered in South Africa. Currently, each of these expenditures is constitutionally considered to be the concurrent responsibility of central and provincial governments. But the concept of concurrence – who is responsible for what aspect of the joint responsibility – has not been defined properly. While policy, delivery standards, and health and education financing are decided nationally, implementation is decentralized to provinces. Not surprisingly, this structure has created incentives for budget gaming. After spending their grants, many provinces leave the central government to worry about any funding gaps, arguing that central mandates need to be financed directly from the center. A system of properly defined concurrent responsibilities might have the center fund national standards, leaving the provinces with own resources to manage and if necessary pay for service delivery above the national minimum standards. Alternatively, responsibilities could be fully centralized with provinces contracted for service delivery through effective monitoring and enforcement mechanisms.

Second, the accountability of lower-level governments to local clients is enhanced if subnational governments have access to own-taxes with the right to adjust tax rates.[6] Indeed, the service delivery incentives facing subnational governments may improve if, at the margin, they have to raise their own revenues through tax increases rather than relying on central transfers or bailouts that soften the budget constraint. This potential impact of own-taxes suggests that proposals for national tax reforms should include tax instruments that can be devolved, or, at the very least, introduce a system of surcharges on national taxes.[7] In the United States, the adherence to sales tax as an important source of revenue for states is a reflection of the country's federal origins and a historical commitment to ensure the independence of states in economic management (McLure 1999). South Africa has considered allowing provinces a surtax on national income tax to enable them greater autonomy in decision making. India has considered a dual center-state VAT (with the power given to states to set rates) in order to strengthen intergovernmental fiscal relations and to enlarge the tax base (Government of India 2004).

Third, the design and implementation of intergovernmental fiscal transfers can influence the accountability of subnational governments for service delivery. Own-tax sources will rarely meet the funding requirements of subnational governments, nor does the theory of fiscal decentralization suggest that each tier of government should be self-sufficient. Fiscal transfers typically have a conditional and an unconditional portion. The former leads to a more hierarchical system of accountability – the center holding the subnational accountable for proper use of central transfers. The latter falls in the category of discretionary resources, for which subnational governments are directly accountable to their constituencies. Also critical is the predictability of fiscal transfers, essential in allowing subnational governments to plan local service delivery more effectively. Predictability is enhanced through the use of formula-based allocation systems driven by simple measures of equity and efficiency (Bird 2003).

In general, the use of unconditional, formula and block transfers enhances both the predictability and 'own-revenue' properties of such fiscal flows. However, transfers are also subject to political manipulation by central governments. There is an emerging consensus in the literature that resource distribution across subnational governments cannot be explained by efficiency and equity considerations alone, that political variables representing the incentives of central political agents are additional and significant determinants. Thus, politically disadvantaged subnational governments generate weak political incentives for central resource transfer towards them, and risk having poor capacity for service delivery. Recent evidence from India shows that even when transfers are supposed to be formula driven they can be influenced by political concerns and constitutional rules delegating decision making to independent agencies can make a difference in curbing political influence (Khemani 2006a). Several countries, such as India and South Africa, have adopted independent commissions to oversee and protect fiscal transfers from the center to the subnational from political vagaries. But, the performance of these commissions has been mixed. In the case of India, many states have not implemented state-level finance commissions. In South Africa, the Financial and Fiscal Commission, while playing an important role in the initial years of the new democracy, has progressively lost its influence as the country made its transition from conflict years. These examples suggest that the politics that influence the distribution of resources between different tiers of government will inevitably determine the design and effectiveness of independent commissions aimed at insulating intergovernmental finances from political capture.

Overdependence on central transfers can also undermine the accountability of subnational governments to the local electorate, and facilitate shifting of blame for breakdowns in service delivery to upper tiers of government

(Rodden 2002; Khemani 2006b). The extent to which the design of intergovernmental transfers affects local accountability depends upon the nature of political relations between national and subnational governments – if institutions of political competition promote accountability to the local electorate, there will be stronger incentives for quality service delivery (Khemani 2007).

Finally, fiscal interdependence between different tiers of government means that budgeting and evaluation of transfers are also important elements in ensuring efficient service delivery and getting value for money. In their budgeting process, a number of countries have implemented a medium-term expenditure framework (MTEF) that allows subnational entities to participate in a multiyear budgeting system (for example, South Africa). Even if the fiscal transfer system does not have a predictable, formula-driven division of total revenues between different tiers of government, the multiyear nature of the MTEF can provide some certainty, usually over a three-year span. To complement its MTEF process, South Africa has introduced a comprehensive Treasury Bill that focuses on financial management within the intergovernmental system, including the regular publication of comprehensive financial information for each tier of government to assist in the monitoring of public resources (see Momoniat 2001). This facilitates public monitoring by nongovernmental civil society groups that can make budget information comprehensible to citizens (Singh and Shah 2003). Some countries, such as Brazil, have gone one step further by involving communities in the budget process through a participatory approach such as in city municipalities in Porto Alegre and Belo Horizonte (Andrews and Shah 2003).

Financing
Access to capital markets by subnational governments is important for several reasons. First, long-term financing is necessary given the lumpiness of public expenditures for infrastructure services and the inefficiency of relying on pay-as-you-go schemes. Without access to long-term finance, investment in infrastructure may be suboptimal. Second, infrastructure investments benefit future generations, so equity requires that future generations should also bear the cost of financing. Financial markets offer this intertemporal linkage. Third, financial markets play an important role in signaling the performance of regional and local governments. The accountability created for subnational governments on the fiscal side by providing an own-revenue base can be further strengthened by providing access to capital markets on the debt side (although premature or uncoordinated subnational borrowing might also reduce accountability – see Ahmad, Albino-War and Singh, this volume). In fact, the implicit threat that poor policy management and service delivery may force local policy makers to raise own-taxes, or pay higher borrowing costs, are important incentives in ensuring that service delivery is managed efficiently.

How subnational governments access financial markets will determine the extent to which such markets will influence the overall health of the subnational government and its ability to ensure good service delivery. Generally, access can be achieved through the central government (where the central government borrows on behalf of subnational tiers), through a public financial intermediary (for example, a municipal bank or fund), or by raising funds directly (for example, commercial bank borrowing or bond operation by subnational governments). While borrowing through the central government certainly guarantees access by subnational governments to long-term finance, international experience suggests that the allocation of credit through this route may get embroiled in politics. Capital then does not necessarily flow to the most productive use but follows political incentives, with the result that government borrowing is inefficient, the subsequent investments are unproductive, and services suffer. Intermediation by a public financial intermediary (PFI), may also suffer from these drawbacks, with the additional disadvantage that the debt of the PFIs is generally an implicit – hence unplanned – obligation of the central government. In Argentina, for example, public banks provided loans to finance the deficits of subnational governments, contributing to macroeconomic imbalances as well as stifling the incentives for changing inefficient service delivery mechanisms (Ahmad 1996).

Direct access to capital markets offers the potential for a more market-based relationship to develop and for a greater chance of enforcing a hard budget constraint. But, moral hazard – the presumption by capital markets that borrowing by subnational governments will be backed by the central government – can be a concern for decentralized borrowing directly from the market. Resolving this problem is critical for ensuring that financial markets provide the appropriate signals to subnational governments in their investment decisions.

There are several regulatory mechanisms for reducing the moral hazard problem of decentralized borrowing. Measurement of the assets and liabilities of each tier of government on a regular basis and disclosure of this information is a necessary step. But, it is not sufficient. Explicit measures and mechanisms to manage public sector bankruptcy are essential to ensuring that both subnational governments and their creditors can be held accountable for their actions without assuming that upper-tier governments will play the role of banker of last resort. In New Zealand, the court system – given its independence and capacity – intervenes in cases of public sector bankruptcy. In the United States, the political process allows the formation of control boards. In both cases, local policy makers have to bear the consequences of poor financial decisions, that is, face a hard budget constraint.

An important component of the bankruptcy process is to define a mechanism for ensuring the continuity of a minimum level of service delivery. In principle this can be done by the courts or the control boards with the legal authority to ring fence local resources to maintain local services. This process ensures that the potential spillover effects of a city or local government going bankrupt are internalized and local policy makers are accountable for their decisions. In addition, it ensures that services such as water and sanitation and solid waste management, which have important health externalities – and can therefore lead to moral hazard – continue to function.

Other measures include legislating end-of-year balanced budget requirements, eliminating the access by local governments to indirect sources of funding such as using municipal corporation borrowing on behalf of local governments (Brazil in the early 1990s) or delaying contribution to pension funds (USA) to finance budgets, or at the very least ensuring that such liabilities are measured and officially reported.

Administrative responsibilities and building capacity

Alongside fiscal and financial resources and autonomy, a key issue facing subnational governments is the access to staff and human resources. Decentralized service delivery is difficult when subnational governments lack skills and institutional capacity. More often than not, administrative decentralization claims far less attention than political and fiscal factors, with decentralization proceeding without explicit staffing strategies or public administration reform. Administrative devolution is inevitably drawn out, often falling behind political and fiscal decentralization. Political and fiscal devolution may have proceeded apace, but administrative changes may only approximate deconcentration (local service providers continue to be full employees of upper-tier government) or delegation (local government has only limited ability to hire and fire providers).

Misalignment between the structure of the government bureaucracy and the assignment of service responsibilities to different tiers confuses incentives, weakens accountability for service delivery, and creates conflicts of interest instead of checks and balances. In many parts of the world – for example, India, Bangladesh, Malawi and Tanzania – administrative staff of subnational governments are either directly appointed by an upper-tier government or belong to a national service and are on the payroll of the central government. In these cases, local staff continue to respond to the incentives provided by upper-tier governments. In Pakistan, the decentralization to local tiers has been incomplete with local staff still part of a provincial administrative cadre. Their incentive has been to claw back powers from the local level to the provincial one.

The twin tasks of administrative devolution and building local capacity are closely linked, making the task of bringing about this alignment even more daunting. This leads to questions of sequencing between different aspects of decentralization and whether to wait to build local capacity before providing local governments the autonomy to respond to local needs, or to let local autonomy precede the creation of such capacity. There are no one-size-fits-all answers to these difficult questions, but there are some principles dealing with the role of the central government that are worth heeding in implementing decentralization.

The central government has a key role in building local capacity and has two approaches available to it. It can provide training in traditional, top-down ways. Or it can create an enabling environment, using its finance and regulatory powers to help subnational governments define their needs (making the process demand driven), to deploy training from multiple sources (local, national, overseas, public, private sector), to learn by doing as decentralization proceeds, and to establish learning networks among jurisdictions. This second approach is more consistent with devolution and more likely to produce capacity tailored to the many cross-sector responsibilities of subnational governments. It also avoids the pitfalls of a supply-driven approach. These sequencing issues are also addressed further in the penultimate section.

Accountability of local governments to local citizens
Proponents of decentralization expect that by narrowing the jurisdiction served by a government, and the scope of public activities for which it is responsible, citizens will find it easier to hold the local government accountable. Decentralization will improve outcomes to the extent that physical proximity increases voter information, participation and monitoring of performance, and to the extent that narrowing the scope of responsibilities of each tier of government decision makers reduces their ability to shirk on some responsibilities by performing better on others. But in order to fully analyse the question of whether locally elected governments have better incentives for service delivery we must begin with the question of why *any* level of democratic government in developing countries, where politicians presumably depend upon support from the majority of poor people, fail to provide the basic social services from which poor people benefit. Then we can attempt to understand why the incentives of locally elected governments might be different.

It is a common observation across countries, rich and poor alike, that substantial public expenditures are systematically misallocated, for example to wage bills for bulky state administrations, to farm subsidies that impose distortionary costs on the economy and fail to benefit the poor, and to large infrastructure projects that allow political rent extraction without creating sustainable assets, all at the expense of quality public services. These misallocations have a disproportionate impact on the poor, who are known to benefit from increased access to public services. Even resources allocated to broad public services, such as basic education and health, might be ineffective in actually delivering those services, if, for example, the posts of teachers and doctors are used to extend the patronage of government jobs, rather than to be held accountable for actual service delivery.

Misallocation has persisted despite a sea change in the way in which governments are selected and remain in office. From 1990 to 2000, the number of countries governed by officials elected in competitive elections rose from 60 to 100.[8] Democratization might be expected to benefit most the 'median' or average voter, who in most developing countries is 'poor'. Yet, public policy in emerging democracies does not seem to have benefited poor voters. Why do policy makers who depend upon political support from the poor not effectively deliver basic services to the poor?

In recent political economy analysis (Keefer and Khemani 2005), it is argued that imperfections in political markets explain this puzzle. Political market failures in this analysis are reduced to three broad features of electoral competition: (i) lack of information among voters about politician performance; (ii) social and ideological fragmentation among voters that leads to identity based voting and lower weight placed on the quality of public services; and (iii) lack of credibility of political promises to citizens. Informed voting is costly, and voters may have difficulty in coordinating information to reward (or punish) particular politicians or political parties for specific actions that improve (or worsen) the quality of public services. Similarly, socially and/or ideologically fragmented societies are less able to provide the incentives to their political agents to improve broad public services, because voting is more likely to occur along the dimension of narrowly defined identities. Even if voters are informed and coordinated in focusing on specific policies, if political competitors cannot make credible promises prior to elections, incumbents are more secure from challenge and have fewer incentives to be responsive to citizens. If politicians are credible only to a few voters, with whom they can maintain clientelist relations, public resources are allocated to targeted benefits for these 'clients', instead of to broad public services.

A strong conclusion of the analysis here is that the most adverse effects of political market imperfections are felt in the area of broad public services, such as health and education. It is especially difficult for voters to assess the quality and efficiency of service provision in these areas and to evaluate the responsibility of specific political actors for service breakdowns or poor outcomes. By the same token, political competitors find it especially difficult to make credible promises about service provision. Voters cannot easily collect information that would verify that politicians have fulfilled their promises.

Moreover, even if they could, politicians in many countries can only make credible promises to narrow groups of voters. For these voters, it may be politically more efficient to promise narrowly targeted goods – such as a farm subsidy, a contract for an infrastructure project (especially if it does not need to get built or if the contractor can get away with using poor quality materials), or a government job as a teacher or a doctor (especially if they are not held accountable to show up to work in schools and clinics). The large mass of unorganized voters would suffer from the resultant poor quality of services – bankrupt state utilities that bear the subsidy burden, dilapidated roads and undrinkable water, and empty schools and clinics where children do not learn and the sick remain untreated – but would find it difficult to coordinate action to improve political incentives. Social fragmentation in the electorate exacerbates these problems of voter coordination in determining reward and punishment based upon political actions towards the quality of public services.

To the extent that in developing countries, poor voters are more likely to vote in uninformed ways, being susceptible to campaign slogans, or polarized along non-economic, ideological dimensions such as religion or ethnic identity, and political promises are particularly lacking in credibility or prone to clientelism, it is precisely the broad public services that are likely to suffer.

Within this framework of analysis, decentralization to locally elected governments will improve political incentives and service delivery outcomes if voters are better informed and likely to use information about local public goods in their voting decisions for electing local governments, if there is greater social homogeneity and coordination of preferences for local public goods, and if political promises are more credible at local levels. If political markets function better at more centralized levels of government, then decentralization might not need to be political, but rather designed to help central politicians with agency problems, such as gathering information, monitoring performance, and enforcing norms for locally produced and consumed services. That is, understanding the nature of political market imperfections can help to optimally design the institutions of decentralization, or analyse the impact of available and operational institutions.

In the following three subsections we consider each political market imperfection in turn, and discuss whether these are likely to be more prevalent for centrally elected rather than locally elected governments. The general answer is, of course, that 'it depends', and the objective of the analysis is to begin to list on what this depends.

Information, participation, and monitoring
Voters may be better informed about the quality and availability of local public goods because of greater physical proximity, or more focused on using this information in voting decisions because of the narrower range of responsibilities for which to hold their representatives responsible. There are two ideas here, one that information is easier to come by at local levels, and that participation and monitoring by voters is less costly. The other is that if voters

care about multiple issues, a subset of which is decentralized to local levels, then they will be better able to hold each tier of government accountable for their respective responsibilities. For example, if voters care deeply about both education and national defense, national government decision makers can more easily remain in office by doing well on the latter and underperforming on the former. Decentralizing responsibility for education to a lower-level government allows voters to hold one set of officials strictly accountable for education and the upper tier strictly accountable for defense.

However, because of historically high degrees of centralization of resources, both public and private, there might not be regular or straightforward channels of information transmission at local levels. For example, information with regard to local policies may be of poorer quality if national newspapers, covering only national issues, are the main source of information for voters. Voters might be more apathetic to participation in local elections, perhaps because of poor media coverage and because they perceive that the bulk of the power and capacity to get things done resides with higher tiers of government. If local expenditures are financed entirely out of grants from higher tiers of government and not out of local tax bases (as is the case in most developing countries), local voters may have little or no information regarding the resource envelope available to their local government and what those resources are intended to provide.

There is very little data on political participation by households in developing countries so there is very little evidence on relative participation by citizens in local and national politics. Khemani (2001) finds evidence that Indian voters use more information in evaluating governments in state elections than they do in national elections. But, of course, states in India are large enough to be countries in their own right, so it is not clear how much this evidence tells us about real decentralization to local governments. Chhibber et al. (2003) surveyed voters in India and asked which tier of government they held responsible for the public goods they cared most about – medical facilities, drinking water, roads, education. The state governments were indicated as the most responsible agent by the majority of respondents, although locally elected village governments were also indicated as having significant responsibility for these public goods. This evidence suggests that the mere creation of locally elected governments does not ensure that citizens will hold local representatives responsible for public services.

Azfar et al. (2000) find that citizens in the Philippines and Uganda, both countries with recent decentralization reforms, rely on community leaders and local social networks for news about local corruption and local elections, and more on the formal media (TV, radio, newspapers) for news about national elections. However, there are no data about relative quality and range of information from these different sources.

Evidence from Nigeria suggests that local governments' overdependence on central transfers appears to have created uncertainty and lack of information about resources actually available to local governments, which facilitates local evasion of responsibility under the guise of fiscal powerlessness. What local governments do receive as transfers is therefore sometimes treated as the personal fief of local politicians (Khemani 2004a).

Social polarization and elite capture

In socially polarized and/or ethnically fragmented societies, voters tend to vote for those candidates with whom they most closely identify. Political competition between parties thus also concentrates on identity issues, and candidates are nominated from constituencies largely on the basis of demographic calculations of ethnicity and religion. Like uninformed voters, polarized voters are therefore also less able to hold politicians accountable for their overall performance in office in making services work. Public good provision would suffer most under these conditions, since politicians in polarized societies rarely internalize the society-wide costs and benefits of their policy decisions.

Decentralization might help by devolving decision making authority to more homogeneous groups. However, social homogeneity may decline rather than increase at more local levels. Social polarization between any two local groups may be more intense due to age-old differences across settled communities and weaker at the national level, perhaps through national campaigns of nation-building. Local politics may therefore be more likely to revolve around identity issues and hence not be geared towards providing strong incentives for political agents to deliver public goods.

If some groups of voters, perhaps the local elite, are more likely to mobilize themselves to influence public policies at more local levels, then decentralization might increase the risk of 'capture' of public resources for the benefit of the non-poor (Bardhan and Mookherjee 2000). For this express reason, the architects of the Constitution of India, a country with entrenched social and economic inequalities within communities, were reluctant to provide for formal institutions of local government (Mathew and Nayak 1996). There is substantial anthropological and anecdotal evidence from India that disadvantaged groups are systematically excluded from using public goods within their own villages by social processes of discrimination. Micro-level case studies and survey evidence from India show that within-village inequality in education access and achievement is significant, with the privileged castes in the village enjoying near-universal adult literacy for several decades while literacy rates are still close to zero among disadvantaged castes in the same village (Drèze and Sen 1996).

Comparing across states in India it appears that local democracy and institutions of decentralization are more effective in states where land reforms and social movements have consciously promoted social egalitarianism (Bardhan 2002).

Credibility of political promises

Political agents at appropriately decentralized levels may have greater credibility to voters at large because of their proximity, or reputation developed through community interactions over an extended period of time. However, these same features may allow clientelist promises to be easier to make and fulfill at more local levels due to closer social relations between the elected representatives and their clients, at the expense of broad public goods.

Keefer (2002) shows that clientelism can be viewed as the natural outcome of political competition when the credibility of political competitors is limited. In these cases, political promises are credible only to 'clients'. This has clear implications for public policy: the larger the number of clients, the greater the focus of government spending on items targeted to specific individuals (clients) and, ultimately, the less spent on public goods. Compared to a situation where no politicians are credible, clientelism generates less rent seeking or corruption – but only because instead of keeping resources for themselves, patrons are obligated to transfer the fruits of office to clients.

In an empirical application of his model, Keefer (2002) shows that as democracies age the impetus for clientelist policies first increases – as politicians are likely to increase their credibility first on a targeted basis by increasing the number of their clients – and then declines as broader reputations finally develop. Consistent with this argument, he finds that corruption and public investment spending (which is more targetable to particular constituencies) are both higher in younger than in older, well-established democracies. According to this argument, recently instituted decentralized political competition might take some time to move from clientelistic policies to broad public services, as local political agents develop reputations for providing services to a larger group of the population.

Greater social fragmentation among the electorate might make it more difficult for political agents to make promises about public service provision to large segments of voters, cutting across social divisions. Voters might only believe promises made by candidates belonging to their own ethnic or religious group; those promises are, therefore, necessarily narrow, and targeted to members of the respective ethnic groups. A combination of relatively young democratic processes and social heterogeneity at disaggregated levels might therefore create conditions for local politics to be particularly clientelistic. There is some evidence for this, once again from India, from the experience of decentralization to village-level governments. India has simultaneously instituted decentralization with political reservations for disadvantaged groups – women, and scheduled castes and tribes – in order to combat the problem of elite capture. Besley et al. (2004) find that if the leadership of a locally elected village government in India is reserved for a scheduled caste or tribe member (SC/ST), then SC/ST households residing in the group of villages represented by that government are more likely to receive targeted welfare transfers.

Foster and Rosenzweig (2001) find evidence that is consistent with greater capture and clientelism at local levels. They focus on three categories of public goods which together account for 73 per cent of the activities of village governments in their sample in India – roads, irrigation and schools. They find that villages with democratically elected governments are more likely to provide more of all three public goods, but the largest effect is for irrigation, as calculated at the sample average, which is the service most likely to benefit the rural elite. However, in villages with a very high proportion of landless (much above the sample average) public investment shifts from irrigation to road construction (rather than education, which is unaffected by the proportion of landless), which suggests that capture by elites can be ameliorated when the numerical strength of the poor increases, but in a manner that might not be the most efficient for extending benefits to the poor. Roads built by village governments primarily benefit the poor, but largely by raising their (short-term) wages, as local road construction and improvement initiatives in India serve as employment programs for the landless poor. Education, which one expects to have the most profound effect on poverty over the medium and long terms, seems least affected by decentralization.

In a similar vein, in a study of villages in the states of West Bengal and Rajasthan, Chattopadhyay and Duflo (2003) find that villages with women leaders, elected as a consequence of mandated political reservations for women in village governing bodies, are more likely to invest in public goods that are revealed preferred by women during interviews – water, fuel and roads (as it provides employment) and less likely to invest in education. Their findings do not necessarily reflect the success of decentralization, *per se*, but rather of political reservations at any level of government in environments where there are substantial social pressures operating against the political participation of particular groups.

Taken together, the work on political reservations and village decentralization in India suggests that traditionally disadvantaged groups that receive new democratic privileges tend to exert pressure to shift public resources *out* of education and *into* other targeted public goods that provide immediate benefit specifically to their group. While this suggests that political decentralization coupled with political reservations indeed succeeds in giving greater voice to these disadvantaged groups, it is also indicative of problems in the public provision of education services. Mandated reservations might worsen overall public service performance by strengthening clientelist relations and reducing incentives of political competitors to invest in broad policy reputations across the electorate.[9]

Political parties and electoral rules

A problem with large, centralized governments is that resources might be distributed across regions and groups with the purpose of winning only 50 per cent of votes, or the required votes from only 50 per cent of electoral districts (depending on the nature of electoral laws). Many regions with voters that are not the pivotal or 'swing' voters can get systematically and pointedly neglected. Bolivia provides the most dramatic example of this. In 1994, Bolivia created 198 new municipalities where previously none existed, and increased the share of national tax revenues going to municipalities from 10 to 20 per cent. Before decentralization, about 93 per cent of national resources were spent in the nine state or department capitals, while after decentralization this became 38 per cent, with a massive shift in resources flowing to the poorest and smallest municipalities (Faguet 2001), although there are questions about the effectiveness of the use of these resources (Bardhan; and Ahmad et al., this volume).

Diaz-Cayeros et al. (2001) find evidence for clientelist spending by the Partido Revolucionario Institucional (PRI) in Mexico to maintain its hegemonic control – non-supporting localities were denied public funds and public employment. They argue that decentralization reduced clientelism as opposition parties in states and municipalities began to publicly clamor for more transparent and egalitarian distribution of national resources.

In general, Seabright (1996) shows theoretically that decentralization can promote accountability by increasing the probability that welfare of a given locality can determine the re-election of government. But decentralization could promote more clientelist spending because there is less electoral gain to be had from providing broad public goods to a larger group of voters. Electoral rules like proportional representation and district magnitude might be more significant determinants of the extent to which governments provide broad public services than institutions of decentralization (Persson and Tabellini 2000).

There is so far very little research into the nature of political institutions at local levels. How do political party systems interact with local electoral politics? One can think of several competing hypotheses. On the one hand, lower barriers to entry in local elections might intensify political competition, break party hegemony, and encourage challengers that are committed to reform. On the other hand, if political parties are the real decision making bodies rather than individual politicians, it might be that the objective of local government leaders is something other than re-election at local levels (which is necessary for accountability to the local electorate). It might be that what political agents care about is rising through the party hierarchy or receiving benefits from party bosses. If this is the objective of locally elected governments, then their political incentives would be no different from the incentives of higher tiers of government. Policies at all levels of government would be determined by the nature of competition between rival political parties. We do not assert or argue this, but merely point out that decentralization needs to be viewed in the context of broader political institutions that have large implications for service delivery.

Emerging issues and policy implications
Until now, this chapter has discussed the implications of decentralization for service delivery as if decentralization were an outcome. But in reality, decentralization is a process, one that proceeds in fits and starts, occasionally with reversals. Furthermore, the way in which decentralization is carried out – the sequencing, the choice among different forms of decentralization, and how the politics is managed – can be just as important to service delivery as the decision to decentralize itself. This section explores issues associated with the process of decentralization. As there is much less known about the implications of these process issues for service delivery, the discussion is speculative, and suggestive of fertile ground for further research.

Sequencing political, fiscal and administrative decentralization
Ideally, subnational governments should first be given clarity about their functions and associated expenditure responsibilities and, based on these, the proper assignment and design of tax instruments and transfer systems should be made. The rule that finance follows function appropriately defines this sequencing. In addition, to ensure service delivery and the exercise of devolved powers in general, administrative decentralization should be implemented along with expenditure and fiscal arrangements. So function, finance, and functionaries all need to be sequenced properly.

Once the expenditure, fiscal and administrative bases are cemented, the rules about market access to finance should be clarified and subnational borrowing permitted. Setting the expenditure and fiscal framework first before decentralizing borrowing powers is an important rule in the sequencing of decentralization. The expenditure and fiscal base provides the 'collateral' to access capital markets: that is, the fiscal base determines access to finance. In most cases, lack of access to financial market is not a failure of capital markets but rather simply a failure to provide subnational governments the appropriate fiscal resources that can be pledged in the capital markets as collateral. In addition, ensuring a proper fiscal base provides a safeguard against creating moral hazard: a policy that enables local governments to borrow in the market in the absence of fiscal resources will inevitably signal to capital markets that upper-tier governments are responsible for the financial liabilities of lower-tier governments. Similarly, the policy of setting up public financial institutions to overcome the lack of access to capital markets is a step in the wrong direction when the required intervention is on the fiscal side. Under these conditions, capital markets are unlikely to play their role of disciplining local government expenditures and management of services. And local service delivery can suffer.

In reality, only on rare occasions do policy makers have carte blanche – the opportunity to sequence decentralization properly. In South Africa in 1994, the end of the apartheid era allowed the Mandela government to introduce a new constitution and completely restructure the country's intergovernmental system from scratch. Most countries however do not have such an opportunity to start anew; instead, decentralization proceeds as and when there is a political opening. Not surprisingly, decentralization has often led to mismatches with, for example, devolution of expenditure responsibilities outstripping fiscal devolution (for example, Eastern Europe), expenditure and (some) fiscal decentralization without administrative authority (Pakistan or Bolivia), design of fiscal transfers in the absence of taxing authority and lack of clarity in expenditure (South African provinces), and political decentralization – elections at the local level – without the fiscal authority (India and Bangladesh).

These types of mismatches may result in poor service delivery outcomes, though it is not clear whether the outcomes would necessarily be better without decentralization. More importantly, the mismatches may well provide the political impetus for change. For example, the proliferation of centrally sponsored development schemes in India with overlapping and contradictory objectives is now beginning to create a constituency for their consolidation and simplification. India may well see the shift from uncoordinated vertical schemes to consolidated, conditional grants that are tied to reforms and to a system eventually of unconditional block grants. Each shift can create the political opportunity for the next shift.

In general, the policy reality that the design and implementation of decentralization is not always systematic suggests that decentralization is not a one-off policy change; it is an ongoing process where the end point of accountable and efficient local governments may well take many decades to achieve. In this dynamic and uncertain process, ironically, it is the center that may be best positioned to manage the risks of improper sequencing and their impact. In addition, in such a dynamic process where decentralization processes across countries have different entry points with different mismatches, it is difficult to objectively measure decentralization and its impact. This may account for the dearth of empirical studies on the outcomes of decentralization and it calls into question cross-country econometric comparisons that draw conclusions based on common definitions and measurement of decentralization (Davoodi and Zou 1998). Much more needs to be done to assess the dynamics of decentralization to understand better the costs of inappropriate sequencing, the mismatches that really matter, how the mismatches may or may not provide further impetus to the decentralization process, and most importantly, whether and to what extent services succeed or fail during this dynamic process.

Different forms of decentralization: functional versus jurisdictional

Various studies have suggested that efficient service delivery requires policy making, service provision and regulation to be kept separate (World Bank 2003). The problem arises when the roles become blurred with policy makers taking on the role of providers and regulators or when providers are expected to fulfill regulatory functions. In these situations there are no checks and balances and accountability in service delivery diminishes. If separating the functions of policy making, service provision and regulation within each sector is the key to better service delivery, why have we focused the discussion on the linkage between decentralization of responsibilities to lower tiers of government and service delivery? Would it not have been more logical to discuss how to create separation of functions? For example, it may not matter whether a water utility is owned by a central, state or local government, but whether the water utility has operational independence and autonomy regardless of the tier of government with which it is associated. In other words, the issue for service delivery may not be jurisdictional decentralization – separation of powers between tiers of government – but functional decentralization – separation of powers between government and service provider.

There are several reasons why functional decentralization by itself does not allow us to address the problem of service delivery. To begin with, we face a political reality that service responsibilities have been devolved to lower-tier governments in many countries. In this context, 'getting the rules right' about decentralization is essential to improving service delivery. In addition, services that require the implementation of user charges or allocation of subsidies – both being political acts – cannot be isolated from the politics of local governments. Inevitably, local governments will be drawn into the process, that is, functional decentralization cannot in reality be kept separate from the politics of subnational governments. In Cochabamba in Bolivia water supply was privatized and the formal private provider was given exclusive rights and allowed to implement user charges in an area dominated by local independent providers. Given the local politics of water this led to riots in the streets and the cancellation of the contract (Nickson and Vargas 2002).

More importantly, jurisdictional decentralization may well be the political path for catalysing functional decentralization. At one level, by devolving powers to subnational governments an upper-tier government can play an independent role in supporting incentives for lower tiers to reform their service delivery. In South Africa, for example, the central government has implemented a conditional grant aimed at providing incentives for reform of urban services for large cities *after* having devolved powers to city governments (Ahmad 1996). In the United States, given that municipalities have devolved authority over service delivery, state governments can credibly play the role of an independent regulator. In contrast, in Indian states, the fragmentation of responsibilities between states and municipalities has created a situation whereby policy makers at the state level have very little incentive to devolve powers to providers or local governments. Their incentive is to centralize, thus preserving their power base.

In addition, during the process of devolution – the transition period between centralized to decentralized systems – upper-tier governments have the chance to enforce functional decentralization at the subnational level. For example, in Pakistan the federal government has offered fiscal incentives to the provinces to restructure their education services. During an early stage of decentralization when subnational governments may not have the requisite capacity and there are political incentives to show success in service delivery, such fiscal incentives can provide the incentives for subnational governments to restructure their services in ways that separate policy making, provision and regulatory functions.

Decentralization to community-based organizations

Decentralization of management authority down to the level of service providers and communities through the creation of community-based organizations with representation of service providers and users, such as education, health and water committees, is being explored as a promising approach to improving services. The hope is that it will institutionalize the participation of beneficiaries in the management of services and thereby improve performance. There are at least two problems with this decentralization strategy. The one that has received the most attention in the literature is that of 'capture' of these organizations by a local elite who would use them for their own benefit. If local communities have entrenched inequalities, such decentralization might facilitate elite domination of public services and systematic exclusion of disadvantaged groups. Baland and Platteau (1999) explore the role of inequality in the local management of resources. Mansuri and Rao (2003) provide a review of the empirical evidence on the functioning of community-based and -managed projects, distinguishing between the role of elites as benevolent facilitators versus pernicious captors of resources. These studies indicate that while local community organizations would have informational advantages to identify the poor, there is typically a strong role for centralized governments to devolve project funding in a way that creates the right incentives for local agents to properly target benefits to the poor.

The second set of problems derives directly from political incentives of governments. One is in implementation – if truly egalitarian community-based organizations were successfully created and invested with the authority of managing service providers, rewarding them for good performance and punishing them for service breakdowns, politicians would have to give up their claim on public employment as a form of political patronage. If politicians do not give up this claim then local communities would have a hard time making service providers like teachers and doctors respond to their pressures – these providers may simply ask to be transferred out of the demanding communities, and refuse to take certain postings, because they know their jobs are politically protected. Poor people might indeed be well aware that providers are not doing their job, but feel powerless to change anything because teachers and doctors are elite members of the community, or people with political connections. Drèze and Gazdar (1996) recount how village schools in the state of Uttar Pradesh in India were non-functional for as long as ten years due to teacher absenteeism and shirking, or used as a cattle-shed by the village head-man, without any collective protest being organized.

In a multi-tier structure of government, the institution of decentralization to community-based organizations might create opportunities for higher-tier governments to use these groups to bypass democratically elected governments in middle and lower tiers, and target benefits to individuals or groups that are critical to win political power (not necessarily the poorest or the most deserving). That is, it is difficult to get away from the impact of overall political incentives facing elected representatives at any tier of government.

Managing the politics of decentralization
Even if decentralization is aimed at improving service delivery, it will be resisted by those who have benefited from the previously centralized system. For instance, politicians and bureaucrats at upper tiers of government may have been earning rents from the system that gave them control over the allocation of resources. These groups will resist decentralization if it threatens their access to such rents. This creates at least two dilemmas facing decentralizing societies.

First, during the early phases of decentralization, as lower-tier governments adapt to their new responsibilities, the results in terms of service delivery may be disappointing. How can we distinguish between weak outcomes because of the transition and weak outcomes because of a fundamental flaw in the design of decentralization? In addition, decentralization opponents can use any early disappointing outcomes to build political momentum to slow down or even reverse decentralization. If the problem is one of transition, then how can these political forces be balanced by those who favor decentralization, even if they have little to show for it at the start? One obvious approach to managing the politics of decentralization is to try to show early results on service delivery.

This leads to a second dilemma. In order to show early results, it may be necessary to intervene and provide resources and technical assistance to lower-tier governments in ways that are different, and perhaps even inimical, to the long-run, sustainable success of decentralized service delivery. For instance, in Pakistan decentralization to districts is based on resources being transferred by the newly constituted provincial finance commissions. Yet these commissions are only beginning to develop the award mechanisms for transferring resources in ways that will yield results. There are other ways of transferring resources that are likely to generate better outcomes in the short run, but these would involve circumventing the commissions' formulae and the philosophy of Pakistan's decentralization. This is a classic dilemma in development, between short-term results and long-term institution-building, and it is reflected particularly sharply in the process of decentralization. There is clearly no simple answer to this dilemma, except to re-emphasize the principle of 'strategic incrementalism' – reforms that are not likely to fully address service delivery difficulties but can alleviate acute problems while creating the conditions for deeper and more favorable change. This can be contrasted with, for lack of a better term, 'incremental incrementalism' that merely solves one set of immediate problems but creates others, as might happen when donors continue to fund central, vertically organized development schemes to deal with the immediate service deficits but that crowd out local initiative or accountability.

Another insight emerging from the framework of accountability presented in this chapter is that if the evolving institutions of decentralization address political market imperfections, even if accidentally and not purposefully designed to do so, then they have enormous potential to *eventually* change the incentives of elected representatives to improve service delivery. In this view the progress in decentralization in any particular local context could be analysed in terms of its impact on information and participation of citizens, and the credibility of political agents when making promises about improving broad public services, even if actual gains in service delivery are not immediately forthcoming. For example, even with incomplete decentralization of service delivery resources and responsibilities, if the creation of locally elected governments is instrumental in mobilizing poor citizens to participate in political processes and increase monitoring of government performance, then this might improve the incentives of higher tiers of government that retain control over service delivery.

Concluding remarks

Dissatisfied with centralized approaches to delivering local public services, a large number of countries are decentralizing responsibility for these services to lower-level, elected governments. The results have been mixed. This chapter has provided a framework for evaluating the benefits and costs, in terms of service delivery, of different approaches to decentralization. We highlighted the fact that service delivery depends on the relationships of accountability of different actors in the delivery chain.

Decentralization introduces a new relationship of accountability – between national and local policy makers – while also altering existing relationships, such as that between citizens and elected politicians. Only by examining how these relationships change can we understand why decentralization can, and sometimes cannot, lead to better service delivery. In particular, the various instruments of decentralization – fiscal, administrative, regulatory, market and financial – can affect the incentives facing service providers, even though they relate only to local policy makers. Likewise, and perhaps more significantly, the incentives facing local and national politicians can have a profound effect on the provision of local services. Finally, the process of implementing decentralization can be as important as the design of the system in influencing service delivery outcomes.

Two of the more significant shifts in the twenty-first century have been the increased attention to the delivery of public services on the one hand, and greater decentralization of responsibility for these services on the other. This chapter has attempted to identify the linkages between these two phenomena, emphasizing that the relationship is complex and far from being fully understood. Yet countries are taking decisions that affect the welfare of millions of people, many of them poor. The challenge to researchers is to provide the knowledge base so that these decisions will improve the welfare of these poor people.

Notes

1. But see contrary views on the conclusions that might be drawn from Faguet's study, for example, by Bardhan (Ch. 8 in this volume), who argues that the evidence on the distribution of local services must be drawn from household survey data, and Ahmad, Albino-War and Singh (Ch. 16 in this volume) who point to the continuing weaknesses in local governance in Bolivia that make any generalizations problematic (eds).
2. Similar problems are associated with the overlapping assignments in education and health care in Bolivia (eds, see also Ahmad, Albino-War and Singh, this volume).
3. Note that in Indonesia, operations were largely deconcentrated at the subnational level until the reforms in 2000. The evidence on the effects of decentralization since then has been mixed.
4. See also Ahmad, Albino-War and Singh (this volume).
5. This section mainly addresses the implications for service delivery of this specific model of decentralization – to locally elected governments. However, in subsequent sections, we take up the issue of other types of decentralization that might be preferable for improving service delivery.
6. Even with decentralized tax instruments, administrative costs and efficiency criteria suggest that tax administration and setting of tax bases (as opposed to tax rates) can remain a central

function. In many countries, a national but independent tax administration is an option that is being considered as part of the fiscal decentralization process.

7. This raises several policy issues. For example, if promoting accountability of each tier of government is an important policy objective, the general conclusion that the value-added tax (VAT) is preferable to a sales tax may need to be reassessed, since it is difficult to administer the VAT at the subnational level (but a central administration with the local setting of rates might be feasible). Or, to take another example, one would need to reassess whether in a federal system, a combination of central VAT and a provincial sales tax is not 'superior' to a central VAT and revenue sharing. In the case of a system of surcharges, national tax reform may also need to consider the coordination of national and subnational tax rates.

8. According to the number of countries reported in the Database of Political Institutions (Beck et al. 2001) as having competitive elections for executive and legislative office, *EIEC* and *LIEC* equal to seven.

9. The shift away from education may be just a short-term effect of decentralization reforms. The immediate concern of new women political leaders, for example, may be to provide those essential public goods that disproportionately benefit women and have been historically underprovided. Demand for public resources in education may increase with time, as women are better situated to take advantage of improved opportunities. A full analysis of the dynamic impact of political decentralization in India, as the institutions stabilize over time, remains to be undertaken.

References

Ahmad, Junaid (1996), 'The structure of urban governance in South African cities', *International Taxation and Public Finance*, **3**(2): 193–213.

Akin, John, Paul Hutchinson and Koleman Strumpf (2001), 'Decentralization and government provision of public goods: the public health sector in Uganda', Abt Associates: MEASURE Evaluation Project Working Paper No. 01-35, Bethesda, MD.

Andrews, Matthew and Anwar Shah (2003), 'Towards citizen-oriented local-level budgets in developing countries', in Anwar Shah (eds), *Ensuring Accountability When There Is No Bottom Line*, Washington, DC: World Bank.

Azfar, Omar, Satu Kahkonen and P. Meagher (2000), 'Conditions for effective decentralized governance: a synthesis of research findings', Working Paper, IRIS Center, University of Maryland, College Park, MD.

Baland, Jean Marie and Jean-Philippe Platteau (1999), 'The ambiguous impact of inequality on local resource management', *World Development*, **27**(5): 773–88

Bardhan, Pranab (2002), 'Decentralization of governance and development', *Journal of Economic Perspectives*, **16**(4): 185–205.

Bardhan, Pranab and Dilip Mookherjee (2000), 'Capture and governance at local and national levels', *American Economic Review*, **90**(2): 135–9.

Beck, Thorsten, George Clarke, Alberto Groff, Philip Keefer and Patrick Walsh (2001), 'New tools in comparative political economy: the database of political institutions', *World Bank Economic Review*, **15**(1): 165–76.

Besley, Timothy, Rohini Pande, Lupin Rahman and Vijayendra Rao (2004), 'The politics of public good provision: evidence from Indian local governments', *Journal of the European Economic Association*, April–May; 416–26.

Bird, Richard M. (2003), 'Subnational revenues: realities and prospects', reading for course on Intergovernmental Fiscal Relations and Local Financial Management, World Bank Institute, World Bank, Washington, DC, http://www1.worldbank.org/wbiep/decentralization/Topic07_Printer.htm.

Burki, Shahid Javed, Guillermo Perry and William Dillinger (1999), *Beyond the Center: Decentralizing the State*, Washington, DC: World Bank.

Chattopadhyay, R. and E. Duflo (2003), 'Women as policy makers: evidence from an India-wide randomized policy experiment', MIT Department of Economics Working Paper, Massachusetts Institute of Technology, Cambridge, MA.

Chaudhury, Nazmul and Jeffrey S. Hammer (2005), 'Ghost doctors: absenteeism in Bangladeshi health facilities', *The World Bank Economic Review*, **18**(3): 423–41.

Chhibber, Pradeep, Sandeep Shastri and Richard Sisson (2003), 'The state, voluntary associations, and the provision of public goods in India', Mimeo, Department of Political Science, University of California at Berkeley, http://www.polisci.berkeley.edu/Faculty/bio/permanent/Chhibber,P/publicGoods.pdf.

Davoodi, Hamid and Heng-fu Zou (1998), 'Fiscal decentralization and economic growth: a cross-country study', *Journal of Urban Economics*, **43**(2): 244–57.

Diaz-Cayeros, Alberto, Beatriz Magaloni and Barry Weingast (2001), 'Democratization and the economy in Mexico: equilibrium (PRI) hegemony and its demise', Mimeo, Stanford University, Stanford, CA.

Drèze, Jean and Haris Gazdar (1996), 'Uttar Pradesh: the burden of inertia', in J. Drèze and A. Sen (eds), pp. 33–128.

Drèze, Jean and Amartya Sen (eds) (1996), *Indian Development: Selected Regional Perspectives*, Oxford and New Delhi: Oxford University Press.

Faguet, J. (2004), 'Does decentralization increase responsiveness to local needs? Evidence from Bolivia', *Journal of Public Economics*, **88**(34): 867–94.

Filmer, Deon, Jeffrey S. Hammer and Lant H. Pritchett (2000), 'Weak links in the chain: a diagnosis of health policy in poor countries', *World Bank Research Observer*, **17**(1): 47–66.

Filmer, Deon and Lant H. Pritchett (1999a), 'The impact of public spending on health: does money matter?', *Social Science and Medicine*, **49**(10): 309–23.

Filmer, Deon and Lant H. Pritchett (1999b), 'The effect of household wealth on educational aAttainment: evidence from 35 countries', *Population and Development Review*, **25**(1): 85–120.

Foster, Vivien (2002), 'Ten years of water service reform in Latin America: towards an Anglo–French model', in P. Seidenstat, D. Haarmeyer and S. Hakim (eds), *Reinventing Water and Waste Water Systems: Global Lessons for Improving Management*, New York: John Wiley and Sons.

Foster, A. and M. Rosenzweig (2001), 'Democratization, decentralization and the distribution of local public goods in a poor rural economy', Working Paper, Brown University, http://adfdell.pstc.brown.edu/papers/democ.pdf.

Government of India (2004), *Report of the Task Force on Implementation of the Fiscal Responsibility and Budget Management Act, 2003*, Ministry of Finance, Government of India, July.

Inman, R.P. (1992), 'Can Philadelphia escape its fiscal crisis with another tax increase?', *Business Review of the Federal Reserve Bank of Philadelphia*, September–October: 5–20.

Keefer, Philip (2002), 'Clientelism, credibility and democracy', Mimeo, Development Research Group, Washington, DC: World Bank.

Keefer, Philip and Stuti Khemani (2005), 'Democracy, public expenditures, and the poor', *World Bank Research Observer*, **20**(1), Spring: 1–27.

Khemani, Stuti (2001), 'Decentralization and accountability: are voters more vigilant in local than in national elections?', World Bank Policy Research Working Paper No. 2557, Washington, DC: World Bank.

Khemani, Stuti (2006a), 'Does delegation of fiscal policy to an independent agency make a difference? Evidence from intergovernmental transfers in India', *Journal of Development Economics*, forthcoming.

Khemani, Stuti (2006b), 'Local government accountability for service delivery in Nigeria', *Journal of African Economics*, **15**(2), 285–312.

Khemani, Stuti (2007), 'Party politics and fiscal discipline in a federation: evidence from the states of India', *Comparative Political Studies*, **40**(6), forthcoming.

Litvack, Jennie, Junaid Ahmad and Richard Bird (1998), *Rethinking Decentralization in Developing Countries*, Washington, DC: World Bank.

Mansuri, G. and V. Rao (2003), 'Community based (and driven) development: a critical review', *World Bank Research Observer*, **19**(1): 1–33.

Mathew, P. and P. Nayak (1996), 'Panchayats at work', *Economic and Political Weekly*, 6 July, p. 1765.

McLure, Charles E., Jr. (1999), 'The tax assignment problem: conceptual and administrative considerations in achieving subnational fiscal autonomy', Presented to Seminar on

Intergovernmental Fiscal Relations and Local Financial Management organized by the National Economic and Social Development Board of the Royal Thai Government and the World Bank, Chiang Mai, Thailand, 24 February–5 March, http://www1.worldbank.org/wbiep/decentralization/Topic06_Printer.htm.

Momoniat, Ismail (2001), *Fiscal Decentralisation in South Africa: A Practitioner's Perspective*, Pretoria: South African National Treasury.

Nickson, Andrew and Claudia Vargas (2002), 'The limitations of water regulation: the failure of the Cochabamba concession in Bolivia', *Bulletin of Latin American Research*, 21(1): 99–120.

Persson, Torsten and Guido Tabellini (2000), *Political Economics: Explaining Public Policy*, Cambridge, MA: MIT Press.

Reinikka, Ritva and Jakob Svensson (2001), 'Explaining leakage in public funds', World Bank Policy Research Working Paper No. 2709, Washington, DC.

Rodden, J. (2002), 'The dilemma of fiscal federalism: intergovernmental grants and fiscal performance around the world', *American Journal of Political Science*, 46(3): 670–87.

Rodden, Jonathan, Gunnar Eskeland and Jennie Litvack (eds) (2003), *Decentralization and Hard Budget Constraints*, Cambridge, MA: MIT Press.

Seabright, Paul (1996), 'Accountability and decentralization in government: an incomplete contracts model', *European Economic Review*, 40(1): 61–89.

Shah, Anwar and Theresa Thompson (2004), 'Implementing decentralized local governance: a treacherous road with potholes, detours and road closures', Policy Research Working Paper WPS 3353, Washington, DC: World Bank.

Singh, Janmejay and Parmesh Shah (2003), 'Making services work for poor people: the role of participatory public expenditure management', Background note for the *World Development Report 2004*, Washington, DC: World Bank.

World Bank (2001), *Indonesia Poverty Report*, Washington, DC: World Bank.

World Bank (2003a), *Decentralizing Indonesia: A Regional Public Expenditure Review: Overview Report, Report No. 26191-IND, East Asia*, Washington, DC: World Bank.

World Bank (2003b), *World Development Report 2004: Making Services Work for Poor People*, Oxford: Oxford University Press, and Washington, DC: World Bank.

PART III

IMPLEMENTING MULTILEVEL FISCAL SYSTEMS

11 The assignment of functions to decentralized government: from theory to practice

Bernard Dafflon

Introduction

Over the past ten years, the assignment of public responsibilities and functions to the different levels of government has emerged as a key question not only in federal, but also in many unitary countries, including some that have a long tradition of centralist government.[1] The resurgence of the federal idea and the need for decentralization basically has many different causes. Political development in post-communist countries and in the Balkans, recent discussions in the European Union, and new trends in Latin America, Asia and Africa show that this tendency is worldwide. The debate on fiscal federalism and decentralization demonstrates clearly that there is no 'one' correct economic model. Empirical evidence also suggests that there is a great variety of expenditure assignments among different countries reflecting varying social preferences. Facts and ideas depart from the canon of fiscal federalism. Hence the subject of this chapter originates in the discrepancies which have been experienced in many European countries between the economic literature concerned with the optimal size and responsibilities of decentralized governments and practices in the (re)assignment of functions to regional and local authorities as a result of political and institutional processes.

It is not surprising that academic arguments have not informed the political debate when one considers that the traditional economic theory in this field is prescriptive. It assigns allocative expenditure activities to lower government layers on the principle of territorial benefit, whereas distributional and stabilization (macroeconomic) functions require central responsibility. It treats allocative efficiency as being concerned only with resource use and with the *outcome of policies* rather than with the *procedures* that generate these outcomes. There is no particular interest in political federalism as such: the utility of federal arrangements and principles exists only as long as they are useful in attaining economic rationality.

But for political and constitutional scientists, multilevel government is not simply a form of organization for economic efficiency; it represents the acme of political and social relationships. It is a conception of power-sharing and democracy (Elazar 1977: 25; Blindenbacher and Koller 2003: 9ff.). Thus, attempts to apply the concepts of welfare economics to constitutional federalism provide little insight into the broader question of why the constitutional arrangements exist at all. Federal constitutions are not only economic: thus, 'a country's social preference, rather than economic theory, should be the major guide to defining the appropriate level of expenditure decentralization' (Ahmad et al. 1997: 27). Each method of sharing functions and financial powers inevitably reflects different histories and values. Decentralization requires us to rethink the role and responsibilities of the various government layers in relation to the traditional policy objectives of allocation, redistribution and stabilization.

The purpose of this chapter is to explore and identify some of the discrepancies that exist between theory and practice. The approach is conceived in the belief that decentralized public finance arrangements cannot plausibly be divorced from the nature of intergovernmental relations in general, especially in a sensitive topic such as the functioning of regional (local) authorities, in which the issues are loaded with value judgements. To understand the nature of the problem, normative theoretical arguments should be confronted with the criteria referred to in a particular federal system. For example, there always exists a layer of government (central, regional, local) which already performs specific (exclusive or shared) functions written in the constitution or to the law. This is indeed a trivial consideration; is it unimportant? The canons of fiscal federalism assume that the map of subcentral authorities can be totally re-drawn for the purpose of an optimal allocation of each separate function on the basis of its territorial benefit. But in practice, one has to deal with political jurisdictions – not just 'economic clubs' – invested with real political power and already performing some services. The problem is the reassignment at the margin of evolving functions and resources to existing political units.

To bridge the gap between theory and practice, the arguments are developed in three sections. The next section reviews the most relevant factors that are used in the traditional theory of fiscal federalism in describing the optimal government organization and, for this topic, the optimal size of local authorities. The following section enumerates a catalogue of criteria for the assignment of functions which has been discussed in Switzerland, first at federal/cantonal levels, then at cantonal/local levels. The main point is not about Switzerland; it is that the discussion in this country – as probably any other national debate on decentralization in the European tradition – focuses on rather different criteria from those noted in orthodox economics. The conclusion is that there is no general answer to the assignment of functions to a particular level of government since the solution depends upon the relevant value judgements of the individual voters in specific national circumstances as well as to the resource use required to provide given services. The outcome, described in the subsequent section, is a set of proposals on how better processes for assigning functions might be developed. The conclusion is that the political economy of fiscal federalism and decentralization should concentrate on procedure rather than on outcomes.

Political decentralization

If the effective pattern of decentralized functions reflects the particular character of the society inclusive of the protection of its minorities, cultural and social values, and political institutions in the country concerned, rather than being derived simply from economic theory (Watts 2001: 34), then political decentralization matters first. The distinguishing feature of a constitutional federation is the formal reservation of power to decentralized authorities.[2] Thus political tiers of government (political decentralization) and optimal public service precincts (fiscal decentralization) may not coincide. What is the relevance of this situation for the economic debate? As this introduction suggests, it is not possible to give a general answer to this question without considering the characteristics of institutional federalism. There are four preliminary issues.

First, it is not possible to transfer the discussion from theory to practice without referring to the particular political (constitutional) organization of federalism or decentralization in the country under examination. Decentralization is a top-down process; federalism is bottom up: yet top-down decentralization or bottom-up centralization may require different medication for the same diagnosis.

Second, constitutional boundaries at local and intermediate levels are not set according to the concepts of optimal government size as formalized in standard economic models. They have multidimensional causes, political, historical, socio-cultural, ethnic or geographic factors (King 1984: 79). Proposals to correct them in one (economic only) dimension might face stiff opposition irrespective of the merits that such proposals may have.[3] In those circumstances, the question is not that of creating the optimal-size authority for given local public goods. The problem is one of deciding which tier of existing political authority should be given responsibility for a new service or whether some existing services should be transferred to a level of government different from the one which actually produces them. If the existing political authorities are entrusted with many services, then the advantage of having fewer levels of government, each concerned with a number of public goods, would mean that most services are provided by authorities of non-optimal size from an economic point of view. In other words, the problem is that of minimizing observed inefficiencies in the geographical provision of local public goods, given the existing political map; it is not one of searching for a hypothetical allocative optimum that implies rearranging the size of local authorities. Of course, the solution of rearranging intermediate or local units is not excluded from the outset: what we underline here is that it cannot be imposed top down for one policy argument only, which is the efficient production of public services.

A third issue is the actual size of local governments, which may differ considerably from one place to another. In Europe, the average population size at the local level varies from more than 100,000 residents in the UK to less than 2000 in France; in 13 European countries, it is less than 10,000 inhabitants. In Switzerland, the average is 2500 inhabitants, with important differences from one canton to another; half of the communes number less than 900 inhabitants. This distribution of the population in local political units of government influences directly the possibility of implementing any system of 'optimal' size service precincts, as idealized by economic models, since this means merging smaller local governments and, perhaps, splitting up larger ones. Moreover, many communes are more populous than some small cantons, which raises a new issue (again, not exclusively Swiss): how do we cope with the situation where the 'optimal' economic size of a particular function might correspond at the same time with the local level in some places (a large city) and with the intermediate level in others (a small canton)? In this context, it is important to distinguish between the decision to produce, the physical production of the local public service and access to the service. Several solutions are possible which influence the reassignment process. Small local authorities may very well coordinate their decision and join in contracting out in order to benefit from economies of scale, but retain independent access to a service, for example, by tailoring what they need for their own population. Or, local authorities might form special service precincts of various sizes, for each of the many functions they have to perform. This procedure would leave out of the debate both the 'economies of scale' argument (see below) and the amalgamation issue.

Finally, solutions are not unique and require political choice. When local governments are too small to provide a function, what are the alternatives: cooperation, coordination, amalgamation or reassignment at the next higher level? The textbook answer is: 'when too small, pass over to the next level'. But coordinated decision making at the local level is an alternative solution that can replace the reassignment of functions at the next level of government. The important difference is that, with coordination, local governments must agree on, but also retain command over, the definition of a policy's objectives and means, whereas with the attribution of the same function to the next (intermediate) level of government, this command is abandoned altogether. The outcome may be different, from 'cooperative federalism' to 'creeping centralization'.

The economic theory of decentralization

The economic theory of decentralization has two facets. One concerns the general casting of the three 'branches' – allocation, redistribution and stabilization – between the government layers. The other focuses on the assignment of responsibilities between decentralized jurisdictions within the allocation branch. The argument that decentralization of spending responsibilities and revenue sources will promote efficiency and welfare has a long history in economics literature. We start with what we call the 'T.O.M.' model of fiscal federalism, after the first modern authors (Tiebout 1956 and 1961; Oates 1968 and 1972; Musgrave 1961) who built the existing theoretical parts into a coherent framework. The canonical view was that decentralization has definite advantages in the allocation branch, but can entail significant costs in terms of redistributive policy and macroeconomic management. The theory is based on four key assumptions: the existence of pure local public goods, the coincidence between the circles of taxpayers and beneficiaries, mobility and no spillovers. The main analytical task of fiscal federalism was to define the appropriate assignment of allocative responsibilities to decentralized government levels and matching revenue sources. Initially, stabilization and redistribution branches were considered to be essentially 'central' responsibilities (Oates 1999: 1121).

Centripetal federalism

There are sound orthodox economic arguments for assigning functional finance and redistributive policies at the centre: this is the case when decentralized jurisdictions are 'open' economies, when they indulge in strategic behaviours and take short-sighted fiscal decisions, or simply because of the mobility of individuals and businesses. We describe this situation as 'centripetal' federalism. However, the actual (de)centralized public finance may be somewhat removed from the textbook theory. Although the general trend is towards centralization in the stabilization and redistributive branches, there is still some room for manoeuvre at the local and regional levels.

Macroeconomic policies In theory, three arguments are generally proposed for central responsibility in stabilization (Rossi and Dafflon 2002: 20–25). Also 'stabilization' is the only macroeconomic policy that is considered; regional growth is another 'discipline' on its own. But this is too restrictive: let us consider what happens when both are taken together.

- *The 'openness' of local economies* Stabilization policy via the local budget is not possible because the multiplier effects of local additional expenditures for stabilization purposes would largely flow over the local border: both regions and local governments are in the position of a 'small' open economy (Balassone and Franco 1999). For example, there is little if any chance that additional public investment, however important but only local, would alone boost a depressed economy. And local entrepreneurial capacity can be insufficient to respond to invitations to tender – which in any case have to be open, nationally or internationally, according to their amount. The other argument is that revenues generated through those additional activities (wages, raw material, equipment and so on) will neither necessarily fall into local hands – entrepreneurs, traders or resident workers – nor be spent within the local borders.

* *Free riding*   Why then should a local government borrow to finance additional investment when its benefit is likely to spill over? It could as well wait and adopt a free-rider position, letting other jurisdictions implement macroeconomic policies and waiting for the benefits. Now, local politicians are not stupid; they will rapidly learn and implement strategic behaviours. This is a typical non-cooperative situation which requires an external hand to resolve this prisoner's dilemma. The theory asserts that the 'external' hand must be 'central'.

* *Deficit financing*   The last (and controversial) argument is whether and how the central government should control local deficits and borrowing. This is because regional and communal accountability involves the access to own revenue sources together with the right of the decentralized jurisdictions to borrow. Uncontrolled access to capital markets and mismanagement of the budgets by regional and local governments could jeopardize the efforts, if any, to stabilize the economy. For this reason, so the textbook argument runs, central government ought to have some monitoring or control power. However, one must distinguish whether the assignment of responsibilities and revenues to the intermediate and local tiers is in balance and regular, or volatile and subject to strong cyclical variation. In the first case, control can be restricted to the golden rule, that borrowing is allowed only for infrastructures, and amortization corresponds to the time-path of capital investment. In the second case, borrowing may be needed not only for investment, but also to compensate for cyclical variation in the budget (higher social assistance expenditures, with less revenue, in a downward cyclical turn, for example). The double argument for central regulation is: (i) to avoid bailout situations (Dafflon 1996: 239) and (ii) that primary reliance on market discipline does not function properly in the capital market (Ter-Minassian and Craig 1997: 162).

Now, there are at least two domains where the centralization of macroeconomic policies is contradicted: first, the capacity of the centre to gear stabilization policies by itself might be challenged; second, opinions about regional growth might diverge between governments, politicians and, indeed, economists. In stabilization, the fundamental questions are not only whether the centre has the legal, institutional and managerial capacity to react rapidly to economic downturns and upturns, but also whether its own budget volume is sufficient to act alone. There is no point asserting that stabilization belongs to the centre if, in practice, decentralization is such that the centre commands only a miserable fraction of total public expenditures and taxes. The Swiss experience may serve to illustrate the argument with reference to the economic classification of public expenditures. At the federal level, about 82 per cent of the total budget is spent on categories (personnel, interest payment, grants-in-aid, revenue sharing written in the constitution) that are very difficult, if not impossible, to modify in the short term for macroeconomic purposes. Outlays for goods, external services, equipment and investments barely reach 11 per cent of the total federal budget (and less than 4 per cent of the total public budget). This is by no means sufficient for any kind of functional finance. At the cantonal level, the picture is not much better: here, too, expenditure categories that are rigid in the short term are personnel, debt interest, revenue sharing and grants-in-aid in the current and capital accounts, in total 79 per cent of cantonal public expenditures. Only one-fifth of the total cantonal public expenditures (constituting the categories 'consumption' and 'own investment', with 12 and 8 per cent respectively) can be swiftly adapted to stabilization policy objectives – with the additional restriction on single investments discussed below. Not surprisingly, one finds that the communes spend much more on consumption (21 per cent) and investment (12 per cent) than the other government tiers: these categories amount to roughly 33 per cent of their total expenditures. This suggests that, in quantitative terms, local governments would be the most suitable tier to implement macroeconomic policy. However, as we said above, local governments are small open economies, with no interest in stabilization for reasons of spillover effects or because they have other investment objectives. The actual distribution of expenditure responsibilities between the three layers of government in Switzerland, and the very nature of these outlays, do not mean that any macroeconomic policy through fiscal instruments is impossible, at least from a conceptual point of view. Yet, because of the difficulty of acting on personnel expenditures and transfers in the short term, one must recognize that any macroeconomic policy cannot be driven by and at the centre only. It requires some form of consensus and vertical cooperation between the three government tiers. This is not an easy matter because the (26) cantons and (around 2880) communes can conduct their own fiscal management, in line with objectives not necessarily compatible with those of the federal government.

As regards growth, there is no reason to believe that any particular canton will abandon or modify its investment planning for macroeconomic reasons. Particular cantonal objectives concerning regional growth, fiscal competition for attracting new activities and the creation of jobs, or the political pressure of local interests, are powerful arguments that are foreign to any 'general' and diffuse interest of a central stabilization policy geared through fiscal instruments. In particular, more and more investment projects require important financial resources and long-term planning: when individual projects are ready to be voted on, it is doubtful whether any government would accept postponing a local investment for macroeconomic reasons. And inversely, it is almost impossible to accelerate a project for macroeconomic reasons, not taking the time to present a detailed investment programme and trying to rush it through the parliamentary process with no respect for democratic procedures. A canton or a commune may be very reluctant to abandon or postpone an investment for the sake of a centrally coordinated macroeconomic policy.[4] This also explains why the fiscal and budgetary policy plays only a limited role in fine-tuning surpluses or deficits for stabilization (Ayrton 2002), compared to monetary policies.

Redistribution   In redistribution, economists argue that the centre is more efficient than regional and local governments in ensuring income redistribution from the rich to the poor and in establishing minimum standards of public services across the regions (Ahmad et al. 1997: 29; Oates 2003: 40). The ability of decentralized jurisdictions to support redistribution from high- to low-income groups is limited by the very nature and extent of the local tax bases, and the mobility of the poor, the rich and business activities across local boundaries. Sharp redistribution by a given jurisdiction in isolation will attract the poor from neighbouring places and, at the same time, drive away mobile individual or corporate taxpayers in higher tax brackets to more clement skies. The consequence is a shrinking tax base and a self-defeating redistributive policy – a consequence that is worsened through tax competition.

In the theoretical approach, the crucial argument is mobility. If mobility is low either because exit opportunities do not exist or are too costly, or because the social and psychological attachment to one's region is high, then moderate redistributive policies at a local level are possible. But even in the quasi-absence of mobility, there could be good arguments for centralized social (redistributive) policies: it may simply be that the electorate favours federal welfare programmes – such as social security – for reasons of equal access, actuarial efficiency and costs, social national cohesion or possible disparities (risk selection), that would result if such insurances were left to the initiative and finance of decentralized units.

Yet, at the other end of the spectrum, local governments are not avoiding the issue. Specific responsibilities, such as social protection, education or health, are examples. A frequent argument is that local governments are better able to identify beneficiary groups and to mobilize support for them in a targeted way through social and redistributive policies. Also, segmented social and redistributive local aids generally have time-restrictive and selected criteria of eligibility, so they do not attract residents from outside. The costs of such policies are supported out of the general local budget, however with due attention to progressive direct taxation, if any, in order to avoid inducing the out-migration of the rich. Education also represents a classic of conflicting goals and different levels of assignment (Ahmad et al. 1997: 40–42). Many societies find it desirable to decentralize control of state-supported schools, while at the same time taking steps to ensure minimal quality standards. Reasons for decentralization are: reducing distance between decision-makers and beneficiaries, higher quality of teaching, direct involvement of the parents, quality-enhancing local monitoring, and protection of minorities. Minimum national standards are necessary to reduce inequality in educational services, to ensure that teachers are properly qualified, and to promote national social cohesion or economic development. Financial support is justified for cost differentials across jurisdictions, due to unavoidable spatial or demographic factors.

The choice between taxation or user charges to finance specific local public services is yet another example with redistributive connotations. Pricing for services such as kindergarten and nurseries, or levying cost-covering user fees on public utilities, such as water, sanitation and refuse collection, certainly improve budget responsibility and efficiency in pricing the individual benefit of certain local public goods. But this also has clear distributive implications for the poor, can reduce access and might necessitate accompanying individual social aid.

Allocation and the optimal size of local government
Generally speaking, economic models of the optimal size of subcentral authorities mostly ignore the constitutional organization of multilevel government. Orthodox theory initially retains the assumptions of a given and geographically fixed population and costless decision making. It considers the existence of an impure public good which may be consumed collectively in groups of different sizes. Exclusion of non-residents is possible at low or zero cost. In this framework, the problem becomes that of determining the optimal-size group to consume the good collectively. Size is measured in terms of population (the number of consumers). However, increasing the number of beneficiaries of a particular local public service is supposed to be obtained by extending the boundaries of the service precinct and having fewer political authorities in consequence rather than by depopulating some jurisdictions and moving the citizens from those areas to others. In doing so, private costs (in time and money) of access to a service, moving from domicile to the place of provision of the public service (school, hospital, recreational and cultural facilities) is ignored, as if distance does not exist.

The traditional economic approach is to assume that a function is initially performed by individual households at their own expense. It is then supposed that there could be both individual gains and losses if private provision is replaced by subcentral authority provision. The basic idea is that there should be coincidence among the three circles of those who decide about (the order of) local public goods, those who capture the benefits, and those who pay. Coincidence corresponds to local accountability which requires that the revenue consequences of locally determined/defined expenditures, the benefits of which are assumed to accrue only for local residents, should be passed on to the local payers through either taxation or user charges. Any divergence among these three circles calls for a modification of the size of the groups in order to restore coincidence and thus to achieve 'efficiency'. The present value of the future gains and losses will depend on the size of the groups into which the nation is divided and the optimal size is the one yielding the highest net gains. All these models have in common the broad proposition that the optimal degree of (de)centralization is the result of the/an interplay between centripetal and centrifugal forces (from the locus of the production) that lead to gains and losses. There is no simple *a priori* strategy to solve this problem of balance and determine whether a given jurisdiction ought to be increased or decreased in size. The fundamental differences between the models result from differing assumptions about the relevant gains and losses, the list of criteria to be taken into account and the weights which should be attached to each of them (King 1984: 51). There is no one-for-all solution.

The first difficulty is to address the criteria which influence the optimal size of provision of any local public good. Following Oates (1972: 38–53) or King (1996: 55–76), the simplest model includes the first five technical and microeconomic arguments given in Table 11.1.

Two points deserve attention. (i) The list of criteria can be expanded beyond the first five traditional arguments: what is essential is that additional arguments must be discussed and decided on their own merit before any attempt to apply the decision matrix represented by Table 11.3, below. One should avoid adding new ad hoc arguments in the course of discussing the (de)centralization of a public service, either for strategic reasons or because it propels the foreseen result in the 'adequate' direction – whatever this term covers. (ii) Second, the choice does not result in the two theoretical extremes mentioned in Table 11.1: local (decentralization) or central (centralization). Intermediate institutional forms could be adequate for the provision of quasi-decentralized public services and deserve careful consideration (Perritaz 2003: 61ff.). One example is the so-called 'special purpose district' (*Gemeindeverband* in the Swiss and German literature on local public finance) in which a number of local jurisdictions cooperate with each other in order to avoid the transfer of responsibility to the next government layer. Frey and Eichenberger (1999) have developed the concept of 'functional, overlapping and competing

Table 11.1   (De)centralization criteria

Criteria	Decentralization	Centralization
1. Individual preferences for local public goods and services	Heterogeneous	Homogeneous
2. Economies of scale	No	Yes
3. Spillovers or geographical externalities	No	Yes
4. Congestion costs	Yes	No
5. Information and decision costs	Increase with the number of participants	Remain low when the number of participants increases
6. Fiscal competition:		
seen as positive	Yes	No
seen as harmful	No	Yes
7. Additional (non-economic?) criteria	?	?
. . .		

jurisdictions', in which ad hoc service precincts would compete for local 'clients' in the delivery of local public services, with the argument that competition would make them 'efficient'. There is room for disagreement about the right pattern and size of jurisdiction at the intermediate level of government. Yet, economists have a key role to play in describing and evaluating each economic criterion in the list above, while other experts in political science, sociology or history, assume the same role if other non-economic criteria are added. And assigning weights to each of those criteria in the final addition is largely the role of politics.

One should not believe that the economic criteria for (de)centralization are unambiguous or that they can be selected in a straightforward manner for one column or the other of Table 11.1. Checks and balances are embedded in the very nature of each of them; nothing is simple and there is no mechanical determinism.

Preferences   First, if political decision making is decentralized among subnational units, and assuming heterogeneous preferences for public goods, each local government can tailor its tax and service package to the preferences of like-minded individual residents and thus minimize coercion. The logic suggests that the more heterogeneous the federal population, the higher is the necessity for decentralization. With varying tastes and incomes of all citizens in a group, collective provision – as opposed to private provision – may result in a loss of welfare: the distance between the deciders and the beneficiaries of the service increases. In orthodox economic models, welfare losses arise either from the fact that the individual consumers cannot choose their own consumption levels and lose control over the quality and quantity of the public service provided as the size of the group increases or because they have different views on the type of service to be provided. In contrast to the standardization inherent in centralization, decentralization enhances diversity in the decision outcome and consequently results in a supply of services that is better adapted to the various preferences of groups within the national population. The determination of the optimal size therefore involves a trade-off between the increased cost savings from joint consumption in larger groups versus the greater welfare from more responsive levels of consumption in smaller groups.

Information and decision costs   The problem of consumers' preferences becomes somewhat more intricate if the model extends from one to many local services. The optimal organization of federalism would consist of as many sets of local authorities as the number of public services to be provided. Each consumer would belong to as many 'clubs' as the number of public services he/she selects. Even if it were possible to create separate authorities to serve each group that jointly consumes a particular local public good, there are strong reasons for not doing so because of the individual cost of participating in too many decision-making processes. Information and participation costs have to be taken into account: there can be some major gains in reducing the levels and number of governments which would have the responsibility of providing many subcentral services.

Another argument is that the provision of local public services in ad hoc precincts leaves open the door to interjurisdictional contracts or arrangements passed between the executives, leaving local parliaments or citizens' assemblies outside of the discussion: they are confronted by a 'take-it-or-leave-it' situation which is qualified as a *democratic deficit*. However, the standard theory does not propose any key to solve this particular problem. It does not stipulate which tier of government must provide which combination of public services, nor does it articulate whether a basket of multiple services must be provided by a higher government level or by several local governments in association or merged in one larger jurisdiction.

Fiscal competition   A third argument in favour of decentralization is that local authorities provide multiple combinations of taxes, goods and services from which to choose. Tiebout (1956) suggested that it might be useful to view the provision of local public goods in a system of numerous jurisdictions as being analogous to a competitive market for private goods. Competition among jurisdictions would allow for a variety of taxes and public goods menus. Individuals would reveal their preference for one combination by moving into the jurisdiction that provides them with the maximal net benefit. Such a process, it is argued, would lead to more efficient outcomes.

The limits of the Tiebout model have been much debated. One line of economic research purports to demonstrate that the Tiebout model provides a narrow view of the world. But for lack of a fully satisfactory normative model, it still considers that the appropriate question is whether and under what assumptions the Tiebout model provides a good approximation of the local public economy. Then, the discussion is expanded either by relaxing some of the original assumptions or by adding realistic complications (Rubinfeld 1987: 571–2). More recent contributions suggest that this theory is not so useful for policy purposes: it ignores the political processes of decision (Breton 1998: 230; Feld 1999: 41). But politics cannot be eliminated from local government models without making extremely strong assumptions about individual tastes and opportunities. In a Tiebout situation, individuals who do not agree with the objective function determined by the majority leave the group. This is the 'exit' solution, which is conservative: not only does the majority's objective function remain unchanged when the opposing minority moves out, but the pressure for subsequent changes is considerably lessened. Yet the fundamental question remains: how have the initial tax and local public goods combinations been selected? There is also the 'voice' solution, which implies an incursion into models of local politics. The political economic analysis of local government systems must deal with two different issues. The first is the procedure by which choices are made (who makes the choice). Second, it must specify the information available to the (political) actors and isolate the things that matter to them. In practice, one can see that local functions have been attributed to local political authorities – with boundaries that result from historical and social factors rather than from the economic criteria mentioned previously.

The third problem of the Tiebout model is the 'mobility dilemma'. As developed by Breton (1998: 191–2), this dilemma is present in any democracy with two or more government layers. Imagine a resident in commune A of region (intermediate layer) X who is fully satisfied with the local public goods and tax mix, but not at all with the region's mix; he/she would prefer regions Y's mix, but in this region, he/she does not find the right local mix. Thus the resident is confronted with a really delicate choice of localization: he/she is forced to weight the communal versus the regional fiscal baskets to find an acceptable compromise. Things can be even more complicated with the addition of the central budget. If the resident is satisfied with the local and the regional budgets and tax policies, but not with those of the centre, should he/she (i) leave the country, (ii) accept the given situation, or (iii) act in politics if 'voice' is possible?

Economies of scale   If in the provision of local public services there are economies of scale that extend beyond the jurisdictional limits, it makes sense to have larger service precincts, for production purposes at least. Collective public provision may enable individuals to obtain any particular level of certain local goods and services at a lower unit cost because of production and managerial economies of scale, at least over some range of the production function. Lower prices bring in consumer surpluses. Any situation where the political boundaries are tighter than the scale of production which minimizes unit costs, calls for a larger size of the group up to the point where economies of scale are exhausted.

There are, however, restrictions to this conclusion. Tullock (1969: 21) and more recently King and Ma (2000: 258–62) have shown that the presence of economies of scale is not an appropriate criterion for determining the optimal size of the local authority. It is important to dissociate economies of scale in the production of local public services from economies of scale that arise from joint consumption. Economies of scale in production are relevant if a governmental unit itself must produce the particular service. But this is not necessarily so, particularly when decentralized governments can contract out. If it can purchase the service from a specialized producer, then the economies of scale cease to have relevance for the decision about the size of the governmental unit. In a competitive market, public tenders should enable local authorities of whatever size to obtain the full benefits of any economies of scale in production that may exist; if so, the optimal size of local authorities will depend entirely on other arguments.

Spillovers   A potential difficulty with subcentral provision is that subcentral authorities may ignore any external benefits (spillovers) to non-residents and so underprovide their services. Three traditional solutions are proposed to internalize spillovers: (i) compensatory subsidies, (ii) enlargement of the service area to obtain the coincidence of deciders, beneficiaries and payers, and (iii) restriction to entry. In solutions (i) and (ii), the basic idea is that the presence of spillovers implies potential gains from trade in eliminating outside free-rider behaviour. And cooperative federalism, in the form of negotiation between local government units, would solve the problem.

The first solution is rather straightforward and economic theory offers a toolbox of grant designs for almost all circumstances. The adequate general rule is that compensatory subsidies should be paid at the estimated value of the geographical externalities by the jurisdictions where beneficiaries live to the jurisdiction that provides the service. The stumbling block is not the difficulty of estimating spillovers – which is real but solvable – but far more the political will of the beneficiary jurisdictions to recognize in the first place that they are beneficiaries. This is not often the case under the 'no recognition equals no payment' rule.

Second, in the absence of an agreement between the group of beneficiaries and the authority that determines the local public good, an increase in the size of the jurisdiction which produces the service should itself allow the realization of at least some of the potential gains from trade through geographically internalizing most of the benefits. However, a fundamental difficulty arises in this context. If there is no agreement between jurisdictions for financial compensation, in the previous and simplest solution, would decentralized government units really agree on increasing the size of the jurisdiction that provides the service, either by creating an independent special purpose district or in merging? In the absence of an agreement, who decides: the authority at the next higher level of government? And what is the result of the decision: mandatory subsidies between existing political jurisdictions, or changing the size of the producer jurisdiction by merging of the beneficiary jurisdictions, or the creation of a special service district? In fact, higher-rank governments seldom intervene in this field and the free-rider behaviour of neighbouring local authorities remains one of the most crucial problems of urban agglomerations.

Third, restriction to entry is the least desirable solution – and a non-optimal one. On the other hand, non-residents who move to the production place in order to benefit from non-exclusive services might create congestion costs. For economic optimality, access should be restricted to residents only; but the practical question of how the access is to be restricted is not answered.

From theory to policy

According to theory, balancing gains and losses enables us to design the optimal set of local government organization for each function. The enumeration in the previous section includes individual preferences, economies of scale in production and joint consumption, benefit spillovers and congestion costs, information and participation costs, and competition among jurisdictions. But in practice, economists who present these arguments are often confronted with opponents who, although they admit the existence of these factors, qualify them as unimportant or not central to the debate. Unimportant, because possible arrangements allow to realize gains or to avoid losses without modifying the actual size of local government. Economies of scale in production, spillovers or congestion costs are good examples: the economic theory of federalism offers solutions that do not imply changing the size of political jurisdictions. The disadvantages of those solutions belong to another category of arguments: top-down orders, creeping centralizing coordination, democratic deficit and the like. How do we ensure a balance? Economic arguments are not central to the debate, because the debate is about the distribution of power – power to decide, power to spend and power to tax – between existing *political* tiers of government, not about arranging the 'optimal' size of local authorities in order to obtain efficient economic solutions. Constitutional economics suggests that the existing political jurisdictions perform as multifunction service precincts. This proposal rediscovers the fact that an optimal economic organization of government would consist of as many sets of authorities as the number of public services – one geographic division into service precincts per each decentralized public service: a pattern that would be too costly in terms of information, organization and collective decision making. Some simplifications are proposed, the most common being to promote multifunction entities and to assign them to existing political authorities. If this is so, it must be accepted that politico-institutional factors – such as local autonomy and participative democracy – as well as economic factors will have to be taken into account. Thus one cannot expect that 'efficiency' which serves to measure the performance of local authorities, to assign public functions and responsibilities or to design new boundaries of decentralized governments, will be 'economic' efficiency only.

The debate over the reassignment of functions among the three tiers of government, which started in the early 1970s in many European countries, was first linked with the question of the reorganization and the amalgamation of local jurisdiction (Derycke and Gilbert 1988: 104; Conseil de l'Europe 1995: 16). The discussion regained vitality at the turn of the century with the Maastricht Treaty and the criteria of subsidiarity set out in the European Charter of Local Self-Government (Council of Europe 1998). The rationale and the initial diagnosis are similar throughout the continent:

1. Successive political decisions about the provision of many public services, their production and finance, have produced a jungle. Responsibilities between government layers are too often intermingled, uncontrollable or divergent: their assignment reflects political feasibility at the time of their introduction without reference to general policy guidelines. There is no follow-up and no periodical performance assessment. These functions must be disentangled on the basis of budget responsibility (deciders = payers) and with regard to the benefit principle (beneficiaries = payers).
2. Both decisions about the provision of local (cantonal) public services and the procedures of choice themselves lack coordination and coherence. There is a need for a procedure that can improve the efficiency with which policy decisions are taken.

Starting from this diagnosis, many criteria have been used in practice for the reassignment of functions among government tiers and for coordination when political jurisdictions and 'optimum' service precincts (however this 'optimum' is defined) do not coincide.

A criteria catalogue

One of the first criteria catalogues was proposed by Wittmann (1973) and was thereafter used in Austria (Esterbauer and Thöni 1981: 79–93) and Switzerland (Buschor et al. 1984; Aebischer 1987). More recently, a very similar approach has been developed for decentralization in the context of the Balkan area and the transition economies in Eastern Europe (Conway et al. 2005). Following Wittmann, the arguments can be classified in three categories: (a) *general policy criteria*: subsidiarity, coherence with other horizontal and vertical policies, equal access to comparable categories of public goods and services; (b) *financial and technical criteria*: financial capacity and budget responsibility, functional and managerial abilities, flexibility; and (c) *efficiency criteria*: economies of scale, geographical externalities – a category which groups the arguments of Table 11.1 above.

General policy criteria   The assumptions for this category of criteria are:

1. By placing government closer to people, decentralization fosters greater responsiveness of policy makers to the tastes of individual jurisdictions.
2. In each decentralized jurisdiction, the 'distance' between citizens (demand) and politicians (supply) on one side, and between citizens and the bureaucracy (management and production) on the other, remains as short as possible. Thus signalling and control are effective, resulting in a better congruence between public preferences and public policies. Political clientelism and bureaucratic rent-seeking behaviours should be minimized or, even better, eradicated.
3. Minorities can also find local governments which offer a tax and service mix that satisfies their preferences without undue coercion. This is analogous to the equal-access argument below.

However, although the argument is that responsiveness and accountability are better served through decentralization, it must not be forgotten that the smaller the local authority, the easier it is for (unrepresentative?) pressure groups to influence and control the outcome of local public policies for their own profit. This, in turn, calls for a decision procedure which identifies and eliminates conflicts of interest and for some control of local activities at the next government level. The red line is not easy to draw. Local minorities joining in vote exchanges to obtain certain specific local public services remain in the realm of democracy. Land zoning in very small local jurisdictions could be the other (bad) example. When many persons in the executive or in the legislative municipal assembly are landowners and could gain private profit in arranging zones, control by the next government level of the proceedings and choices is necessary. But this situation, although repeated in many small local authorities, does not itself justify reassignment of this function at the higher level of government simply because in larger jurisdictions the same risk does not occur.

Coherence   The formal (constitutional) reservation of powers to decentralized authorities places the conflict of policy aims in the centre of the picture and raises the question of whether there are legitimate national interests in subnational policy choices. If so, the federal (regional) government may wish to assert its will to achieve an objective of greater value than the promotion of regional (local) choice. The fundamental issues are whether and how decentralized authorities participate in the definition of higher-level policy ends and means, or whether they act as mere deconcentrated agencies in a principal–agent relation. Local priority-setting processes may be limited by higher governments through imposition of mandated spending, predefined minimum levels of service, or fiscal limitations. The answer is political and depends on the nature of a particular policy. Economic growth is a familiar example because attempts to distribute growth between the regions might be realized only to the detriment of national growth. Tax competition between jurisdictions might have harmful results: should tax harmonization and coordination be horizontally negotiated or imposed top-down? The question of coherence is ultimately that of which government level (unit) has the last word.

Equal access   Decentralization might result in individuals receiving a different level of services for the same fiscal burden, raising the question of individual 'equal access' to the provision of comparable local public services. This does not mean standardization of the level and quality of the supplied services. Standardization is a concept that implies encroachment upon the freedom of local decision making, as opposed to a minimum level of service provision, which gives local authorities the freedom to decide whether to have more or better. Moreover, equal standards could be allocatively inefficient owing to differences in taste, income, and to geographic or demographic factors. Second, equal access may be a good substitute for mobility between local areas. Distance of access to the service and congestion costs play an important role in qualifying this concept. Hence, on the one hand, residents are not pushed into migration if they can accept minimum levels of provision for some local goods and services. On the other hand, 'equal access' is the inverse medicine to Tiebout's 'voting with one's feet' argument: the concept brings local public services to people and not people to services. 'Comparable' provision, however, will encompass only part of the function, the objective being that differences in local public services are no definite hindrance to mobility (for example, interjurisdictional migration would call for a minimum coordination in the school calendar and

the curricula – but this does not require centralization of compulsory education).

Financial criteria 'Budget responsibility' is a criterion that should not be
confused with 'financial capacity' which is a constraint. The question is one
of balance between the assigned functions to each level of government and to
government units at the same level, and their capacity to finance the budget
out of their own-revenue sources. The coincidence between responsibilities
and own revenues reinforces budget responsibility: expenditure decisions are
taken in the knowledge that local taxation is the consequence. But coincidence
is never guaranteed in the long run if the time-paths of expenditure growth and
tax elasticity to GNP differ. Orthodox economic models offer a variety of
means to correct fiscal imbalance: subsidies, tax or revenue sharing, equalization grants and so forth. But the crux of the matter is financial (fiscal) autonomy, and to a lesser extent fiscal flexibility. There are three arguments. First,
fiscal responsibility is needed at decentralized levels of government to link
taxing and spending decisions and avoid overspending. Second, fiscal responsibility increases accountability and the understanding of the electorate, with
the subsequent improvement of decision making in a democratic context.
Third, decentralized fiscal (budget) responsibility plays an important role in
the distribution and in the control of power, which characterize federalism.
Evidence has it that with intergovernmental grants or revenue-sharing formu-
las, the grantor – the higher tier of government – eventually makes the
payment dependent on some conditions on how the money should be spent on
different services and the type or quality of service to be provided. Rejection
of this dependence is strong: the usual claim is that the whole exercise will end
up only in an undesirable redistribution of costs without a real redistribution
of responsibility for provision or production. Thus, any acceptable reassignment of functions is subject to conditions such that the new situation must not
create (further) fiscal imbalance or, if imbalance is inevitable, that it must be
compensated through unconditional grants or constitutionally linked revenue
sharing from the higher level of government. The reverse argument does not
hold: a situation of insufficient local financial resources only – distinct from
general fiscal imbalance – cannot serve as a pretext to transfer local functions
to the next higher government layer. Financial imbalance of this sort must be
solved through a new allocation of revenue sources, revenue sharing or equalizing block grants.

Flexibility   In the debate about the (re)assignment of functions between
government levels, flexibility is associated with three issues: diversity in
public policies, innovation and risk, and the adaptability of the legal framework. First, decentralized structures promote diversity in public policies

because the delivery of local services is tailored to the needs and the tastes of local residents. The argument, articulated from the viewpoint of the offer, is analogous to the criterion of local preference, as expressed from the demand side. Second, decentralized government can serve as a laboratory for introducing new public policies and instruments, with the simultaneous advantages of testing several solutions to an identical problem while limiting the cost of failure, if any, to a single isolated programme. Diversity in innovation then benefits the other decentralized governments with the diffusion of the most successful policies and solutions. Another advantage is that the residents of one jurisdiction can evaluate the performance of service delivery in terms of information about similar policies in other jurisdictions. Such awareness can promote the spread of successful policies among local governments. Third, flexibility is also interpreted as the capacity to rapidly adapt the legal framework to evolving circumstances. Legal procedures are often less intricate and less time-consuming at the local level than at higher government levels.

<u>Managerial abilities</u>   These are discussed below.

Efficiency criteria   The two efficiency criteria which are listed, economies of scale and geographical externalities, correspond to those traditionally discussed in theory (see Table 11.1).

Subsidiarity
In its original formulation, the principle of subsidiarity introduces a presumption of competence in favour of the lower government layers. The theorem proposes two arguments: (i) local authorities *are* in a better position to supply public services to residents, in terms of preferences, efficiency and budget accountability; and (ii) reassignment of any local responsibility at the next higher government layer is acceptable only if the local level is no longer capable of providing a public service. Capacity is normally defined in productive and managerial terms – it is not 'financial' capacity, which would call for block grants or the reorganization of revenue sources.

In 1985, the Council of Europe promulgated the European Charter of Local Self-Government with a first reference to subsidiarity very close to the original concept (art. 4 par. 3): 'Public responsibilities shall generally be exercised, in preference, by those authorities which are closest to the citizen. Allocation of responsibility to another authority should weigh up the extent and nature of the task and requirements of efficiency and economy'. According to the explanatory report, article 4 paragraph 3 implies that 'unless the size or nature of a task is such that it requires to be treated within a larger territorial area or there are overriding considerations of efficiency or economy, it should generally be entrusted to the most local level of government' (Council of Europe

1998: 13). One remarkable feature in the definition and explanation is that the very nature of the local task is balanced against efficiency and economy arguments that should be 'overriding': one understands here that the 'very nature' of local responsibilities does not only pertain to economic arguments since the latter are opposed – 'weighted' against it. In addition, the extension is articulated in terms of territory and not in terms of population mobility or relocation/ migration – that is: special larger service precincts or the amalgamation of communes are possible solutions at the 'local' level before a task is transferred to the next government layer. This interpretation of the subsidarity principle is a constant in the Council of Europe's definition of local self-government (for example: Recommendation R 95 19, 12 October 1995 and annex II of the Ancona declaration, 16 October 1999).

Today the dominant concept of subsidiarity debated for the assignment of functions in the European Union (EU) between the member states and the European Commission departs from the original one: it reformulates (i) and ignores (ii) in the definition above. Within nations, reference to the 'modified' principle is more and more frequent as a guideline for state–local intergovernmental relations. But this is not an EU exclusivity; it is also used in transition economies.[5] Yet, if subsidiarity is often linked with decentralization, the two concepts are not synonyms. Decentralization can be organized without calling upon the subsidiarity principle; inversely, subsidiarity can inspire the process of decentralization (Fraschini 2001). A closer look reveals that the subsidiarity principle is more appropriate to fiscal federalism and 'bottom-up' (de)centralization than to 'top-down' decentralization. Figure 11.1 is an attempt to visualize this distinction.

In any more or less decentralized system, the effective assignment of tasks between the government layers is the result of opposite forces. Centralization criteria are rather technical and belong to the production function: economies of scale, spillovers, congestion costs (those already mentioned in Table 11.1), whereas decentralization forces relate rather to social objectives and participative democracy: a better respect for individual preferences in the demand for public services, less political leeway and better control of bureaucracy, better congruence between supply and demand. In the left-hand box of Figure 11.1, the criterion of interpersonal equity is the exception, being a 'non-technical' criterion which also calls for some degree of centralization. Democracy is the reason for this exception: majority votes might result in minorities' demands and rights being neglected, thus requiring that the centre steps in, for example in the form of minimum requirements concerning the quantity or quality of certain local public services. Minorities can have religious, linguistic or cultural identities, but they can also represent population categories, such as children or the working poor. The right-hand box of the figure introduces equalization in the principle of subsidiarity as a criterion *for* decentralization.

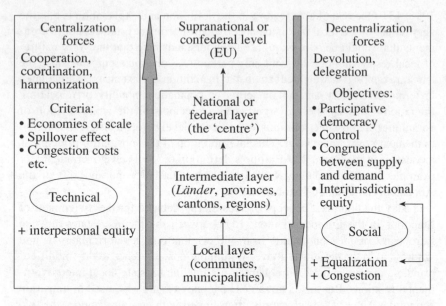

Figure 11.1   The subsidiarity principle

This position deserves an explanation. The argument here is that economic disparities among jurisdictions, differences in relative needs or costs – if they are out of the control of local authorities for geographic or demographic reasons – require equalizing transfers of some sort (horizontal and/or vertical). Or, to put it the other way round (hence the arrows in both directions): any equalization scheme, if it exists and partly compensates for fiscal disparities, reinforces decentralization. This is because 'poor', 'high-need' or 'high-cost' decentralized jurisdictions thus receive a guarantee that the fiscal consequences of devolution will be (partly) compensated. How much fiscal equalization is needed in order to establish some degree of equity between jurisdictions, to balance expenditure requirements and revenues so that devolution is feasible, and finally to ensure the survival of subsidiarity, is certainly at the core of fiscal federalism.

The right-hand box also introduces the concepts of devolution and delegation which should not be confused (Conway at al. 2005: 13–14; Bird 2001: 2). 'Devolution' refers to those cases in which there is 'full transfer of authority and responsibility to the lower levels of government' – that is, decentralized governments would be entirely responsible for the supply, the quality and the characteristics of production of the allocated tasks, and for their finance. Devolution is here synonymous with 'decentralization' in academic discussion – that is, 'the transfer of authority for certain functions from the national to local governments'. The term 'delegation' usually refers to 'those cases when the national government relies on local governments to perform all or part of its functions without actually ceding authority and responsibility for that function'. Of course, devolution and delegation could follow much of the same path and refer to similar criteria. But there is a difference. Devolution is the true assignment of total responsibility – for supply, production and finance – and, in this respect, must be considered the 'top-down' version of subsidiarity. Delegation contains a 'principal–agent' relation, in which the centre – the principal – commands (and should also pay for) the service; local governments are the executive agents.

Functional and managerial abilities
The assignment of functions to decentralized governments is not only a general objective for better public policies, but also poses new challenges in the management of public expenditures, service delivery and taxes. Local governments are in a better position to supply the right services because they are more familiar with the demands of their residents: but this information advantage is not *ipso facto* a guarantee of efficiency in the production of the functions that are to be decentralized. To satisfy the demand, governmental authorities cannot be simply 'local'; they also have to be 'managerial'. This qualification relates to the use of human resources and the capacity of local government to find persons with technical knowledge and the managerial abilities in the decentralized functions. Certainly it is conceivable to contract out professional competence for particular services. But it is not possible to maintain a meaningful local autonomy when expertise fails in many functions. When almost complete out-sourcing becomes the rule at the local level, residents will probably force the transfer of the responsibility to the next higher level in order to regain democratic command at another level.[6] The absence of managerial and organizational abilities at the local level leads to centralization, with local government losing both informal influence and constitutional power in the design of policies. Centralization can be straightforward, when a function is simply reassigned to the next level. Or it can take a more subtle form: in order that local governments do not neglect or abandon certain tasks, centralization is 'creeping in' in the form of cantonal minimum service levels and through regulations in organization and delivery procedures, up to the point where local governments act as mere implementation agencies.

In the last decade, several studies have tackled the question of governmental managerial capacities in the delivery of public services considered from the viewpoint of political economy rather than from a new public management perspective. Although addressed initially to 'the' government in general – which we take here to be the 'central' government (Grindle 1996) – Wallis and Dollery (2002) have reinterpreted the issue with regard to the intermediate and local levels. Table 11.2 summarizes some recent criteria.

Table 11.2   Organizational capacity of decentralized government

Grindle (1996)	Polidano (2000)	Weist (2003)

• political capacity
• institutional capacity
• administrative
  capacity
• technical capacity
	• policy capacity
	• implementation
	  authority
	• operational efficiency
		• organization
		• planning
		• personnel
		• infrastructure
		• resources
		• regulation

Wallis and Dollery (2002)
+ social capital

- 'Political capacity' is the ability of each elected member of the local government to understand the residents' preferences and demand, to apprehend the policy issues, and to behave appropriately in political assembly. It is also the ability to distinguish between private, pressure group and general local interests. 'Policy capacity' belongs to the same category: identify the demand and clarify the issues in order to define the objectives, fix the supply of local public services and find the appropriate means and tools.
- 'Institutional capacity' is about understanding the laws and statutes with respect to local government. It includes the comprehension of the vertical and horizontal, formal or informal relations between government layers and between governments at the same layer.
- 'Administrative capacity' refers to the efficient management of the local bureau in general: management of personnel; command over the budget process and the accounting procedure, cost calculation and controlling; knowledge of laws and rules – if not directly, at least in the capacity of hiring the right collaborators and expertise, and the ability to delegate and control. 'Implementation authority' also implies a local administration that can do what it has to do in general, without referring to a particular service.
- 'Technical capacity' or 'operational efficiency' relates to the production function of any particular local public service, whether it be produced directly or in outsourcing (Polidano 2000).

Weist (2003) refers to the same managerial qualities as requisites for decentralization, but organizes them somewhat differently. 'Organization' comprises the general institutional links that make it possible to run local government and produce local services: it contains at the same time political, institutional and administrative capacities. 'Planning' is the time horizon for the organization. 'Personnel' refers to internal employees and outsourcing human resources. 'Infrastructure' corresponds to the capacity of local government to decide about/on their own investments for the supply of local services and not merely to manage current affairs. With regard to 'resources', local entities should be entitled to adequate financial resources of their own, which they may dispose of freely within the framework of their powers and commensurate with local responsibilities. 'Regulation' addresses the supervision of local authorities.

For Wallis and Dollery (2002), 'social capital' is an additional ingredient of success in decentralized public expenditure management. The criteria in the list above are internal: in-built, acquired with experience; but they are by no means sufficient. The performance of local authorities also depends on reliable outside networks: citizen or professional groups, civil organizations, business associations, neighbouring jurisdictions, and regional or central authorities. In addition to formal or informal contact networks, the social capital of decentralized jurisdictions encompasses the quality of the relation, reciprocity, trust, the respect of decision, the absence of corruption and the like. Without these ingredients, participative democracy is not possible – and decentralization of responsibilities is an empty shell. With those social components, information and transaction costs are considerably lowered and local functions easier to perform.

Although they are important criteria for decentralization, functional and managerial abilities are not easy to define and measure (Weist and Kerr 2002). The advantages of decentralization, principally in terms of a better congruence between supply and demand for local public services, local preferences, control and responsibility, are realized only to the extent that local authorities and administrations have the matching abilities and knowledge to organize the jurisdiction, perform the functions and supply the local services. In some transition economies and developing countries, the national government refuses to transfer responsibilities and resources to lower government layers because it claims that those jurisdictions have no or insufficient organizational and managerial capacity – but at the same time, little effort is made to clarify and measure what the minimum requirement would be. In the spirit of the subsidiarity principle, responsibilities should not be taken away from local jurisdictions simply because of a lack of managerial capacities. First, local government should take part in the definition and measurement of the required capacities. Second, training programmes should be made available before any conclusion is drawn that weakness in local managerial capacities is a good reason for centralization.

Box 11.1 provides an example in the case of primary education.

BOX 11.1   POSITIVE FEDERALISM: THE CASE OF PRIMARY EDUCATION

Primary education is an interesting exercise of decentralization and a good example for explaining the positive assignment of responsibilities to government tiers following a multicriteria analysis where the criteria are not only economic but also social and political. Though it is generally assigned at the local level, one can question the nature and extent of discretionary local authority to perform and manage this responsibility. Considering that the production function of a primary school contains five factors (teachers' qualifications, teachers' salaries and social conditions, education programmes, organization of the school, equipment and buildings), there are good reasons to consider these factors from different perspectives in the (de)centralization process.

- Teachers' qualifications might require some degree of centralization, at least at the intermediate level of government, for two reasons. One is to guarantee the quality of the professional formation of teachers at an acceptable cost; the other is to respond to professional mobility through a curriculum of coherent and comparable content and requirements. Local government units are not in a position to respond individually to these requirements.
- When teachers' salaries and social working conditions are totally decentralized, there is a concern with the nature and extent of possible competition among local governments that may lead to inefficiencies. Past experience in Swiss cantons shows that local governments add a premium to attract a large number of candidates and select the best ones. Communes with low financial capacity are unable to compete for the better ones and are priced out of the market, which ultimately results in a dual education system. In a non-cooperative situation, this competition would also be to the detriment of the richer communes in the long term for they would be induced to push up the premium in order to attract the best teachers. On one hand, this is a typical prisoner's dilemma situation that requires higher-level coordination and standards. On the other hand, the nature and extent of standards set by the next government level is a frequent and often contentious issue. This is particularly the

case when local governments perform under delegation: they have to pay the teachers' salaries but without authority and responsibility thereupon. The more so when the higher government opts for the easy way in collective bargaining with teachers' unions, knowing that it does not have to foot the bill.

* Education programmes are another critical issue, concerning at the same time efficiency considerations, cultural values and diversity. First, with a high degree of mobility of economic agents within a country, there is an argument that school programmes should be very similar so that children can easily integrate into another class when their parents move from one place to another. Second, countries that place a high value on national cohesion and identity may be less inclined to decentralize these functions than other countries that place a higher value on local choice or control. But, on the other hand, cultural and social diversity, and the rights of (religious, ethnic or language) minorities justify that the programmes should be tailored to the needs and values of regional and local populations. There is no economic model for solving this bipolarity. One way to find a balance could be that central and local governments negotiate that part of the programme that should be common, but leaving sufficient time and room for local specificities.

* Should the organization of the school be decentralized or delegated? First, what does this term comprise: school hours and timetable, school week, holiday periods, beginning of the school year, school transport, school meals? Once a comprehensive definition is accepted, the immediate commonsense answer would be that the authority managing and organizing the service delivery should be local, possibly regional, to accommodate local (regional) preferences. But total decentralization creates problems in relation to the working hours of the parents, professional mobility, holiday periods in various economic sectors, bottlenecks in the use of leisure facilities and the like. Again, there is no definitive answer to these issues and economic theory does not help much. There are good efficiency arguments that the organization of school transport

and school meals should be local to respond to the variety of local conditions (climate, distance, dispersed population and so on). But there are also good efficiency reasons for more centralization in the school calendar. One example may illustrate the need for standards set at a higher government level. In Switzerland, the school year used to start in the autumn in some cantons and at Easter in others. This created huge problems when families moved from one system to another, and also for the beginning of the school year in further education (professional school and universities, for example). The cantons' positions were irreconcilable and it was necessary to write in the federal constitution that 'the school year shall begin between mid-August and mid-September' (art. 62 Cst.).

•   In the transition from a centralized to a decentralized form of government, a number of issues arise about the nature and the extent of local ownership and control over the assets associated with the functions and responsibilities assigned to local governments. The textbook argument is that school equipment and buildings should be decentralized at the local level for reasons of efficiency in use and responsibility in maintenance. If ownership of the assets does not follow automatically with the assignment of function, it can become an obstacle to the full exercise of their service authority (Conway et al. 2005: 19). There is also the financial question that the local governments should have sufficient resources for school investments, major repairs and maintenance.

All in all, the example of primary education shows that there is no clear line between centralization and decentralization, or between devolution and delegation. It also shows that economic-only arguments do not provide any clue to policy analysts and academics regarding the question of how much decentralization of which services is needed or efficient. Issues and problems, pros and cons must be made explicit and explained. Also a space for dialogue, evaluation and problem solving must be constructed. A multicriteria matrix such as the one proposed in this chapter contributes to a better understanding of the political economy of decentralization.

Conclusion and proposal

Conclusion

The outcome of this analysis offers no normative framework that would guide decisions about the assignment of functions at decentralized levels of government. We have only a list of pros and cons, distributed along economic criteria, augmented with general criteria, subsidiarity and managerial capacities as outlined above. The list is certainly not exhaustive. In addition, we have drawn attention to a number of unsettled questions which concern both the ends and means of policy making. The recognition that policy criteria might be conflicting, and that decentralized governments retain discretionary powers, leads to the conclusion that the problem of (re)assigning functions between government levels and between government units at the same level are not in the nature of things capable of ultimate, once-and-for-all general prescriptions. Orthodox theory gives many useful indications on the nature of federalism and on the complexity of (economic) ends and means, but no ready-made solution. The fundamentals have not changed: in fiscal federalism, efficiency is not economic efficiency. Equity is not only redistributive: it encompasses equal access, the right of diversity, consideration for the minority, solidarity and equalization. The political economy of the assignment of responsibilities in federal and decentralized nations is concerned with the general relationships between government units and government levels. In doing so, it forces those concerned with economic phenomena to carefully consider questions of political behaviour.

The problem of efficiency in policy making is therefore one of multifunctional coordination among different levels and units of government. If normative propositions about the nature of the federal–regional–local relations are to be avoided, political economists must be well satisfied if they are able to improve the efficiency with which policy decisions are arrived at by clarifying the nature of the relevant issues, whatever attitude is taken with regard to the ends themselves. In other words, it is not easy to make propositions of any significance in federal public finance arrangements that do not have any implication for the authority relationship which exists at any particular time between federal, intermediate and local governments. Yet, it is possible to avoid normative value judgements about this relationship and present a plausible alternative by suggesting a procedure which shows the implication of policy proposals for the welfare of the federal society and draws attention to the relation between the proposals discussed and the political and constitutional/institutional characteristics of the federation.

To summarize, the conclusion is that there is no 'best' framework within which the assignment of functions at central/intermediate/local levels of government can be evaluated; thus there is no 'best' policy to be proposed.

This approach suggests that it will be more useful to engage all knowledge derived from economic analysis not to make policy prescriptions, but to improve the policy ground rules and procedures, leaving the value judgements to those chosen by the community to make them. Bearing this in mind, the political economist's contribution should be that of developing a comprehensive model of negotiation in which the various objectives of federalism could be considered while the analysis remains ethically neutral.

Any attempt to do this must begin from the existing economic and constitutional environment. This is not to suggest that this environment cannot or should not be changed. On the contrary, in any federal system, it is likely that there will be continuous tension between the tiers of government and the constituent jurisdictions themselves over the years and that different balances between them will develop at different times. Conflicts arising from the economic and (other) political arguments cannot simply be overruled, as has been done in the economic literature on federal finance, by assuming a centralist form of federal government (Wiseman 1989). It follows from the argument developed so far that a general model of policy making, for the assignment of functions to different tiers of government, does not require the political economist to be able to specify what the objectives of the federation should be. Such a model, to be relevant, should rather optimize the possibility (and the procedure) that the best 'policy compromise' will be achieved. In short, it is a model of procedure and choices, not of outcomes.

Proposal

The assignment of responsibilities to (de)centralized levels of government can be organized along several criteria, not all of which are of an economic nature. No doubt those criteria have opposing forces, centrifugal or centripetal, and no doubt, local, regional and central government may have divergent opinions regarding which argument should be listed and how important each of them is. The role of the economist is neither to make choices, nor to prescribe weights, but to specify the characteristics of the system if the policy-making process is to work efficiently. Particular care should be given to the points of agreement and of conflict about policy ends and means, and to trace the convergences and divergences between the economics and the politics of federalism.

The most satisfying instrument for the purpose of assisting policy makers in deciding the appropriate level of (de)centralization could be formalized in a 'decentralization matrix'. With this method, the various criteria used for the assignment of responsibilities are listed explicitly and systematically in the rows. They are confronted with the various institutional arrangements, in the columns, acceptable for decentralization in the national context under examination. Table 11.3 exemplifies a possible decentralization matrix. The main

Table 11.3   (De)centralization matrix

Assignment criteria	Institutional government level				
	Local	. . .	Regional	. . .	Central

1. Macroeconomic policies
  • Openness
  • Free riding
  • Deficit financing					

2. Redistribution
  • Mobility
  • Guaranteed access
  • Targeted eligibility
  • Minimum service level					

3. Allocation
  • Preferences
  • Economies of scale
  • Spillovers
  • Congestion
  • Decision costs					

4. Managerial capacities
  • Political
  • Institutional
  • Administrative
  • Technical
  • Social capital					

5. Socio-political arguments
  • Preferences
  • Subsidiarity
  • Participative democracy
  • Information
  • Control
  • Accountability and
    transparency
  • Solidarity					

6. Other criteria (not
  discussed in the text)
  • Poverty alleviation
  • Fiscal competition
  • . . .					

purpose of the method is to create a policy environment in which the different views on ends or on technical questions of government units can be brought together.

The rows contain explicitly the assignment criteria that would be considered for the assignment of a particular function. Criteria should not only be enumerated, but a proper definition should be given for each, to which all the parties can adhere. Information on how each criteria would be measured, evaluated or appreciated is also necessary. This participative method is founded on two rules:

1. The list of criteria should be established first so that everyone knows in advance the rules of the game. Of course, the list given in Table 11.3 is tentative; it does not give the whole array of possible criteria. What is important is that additional criteria should be given – or non-relevant criteria abandoned – prior to the factual debate on (de)centralizing a particular function. If additional criteria are necessary *en cours de route*, then the analysis should restart in an iterative process for reasons of coherence and coordination between all the criteria.
2. Each criterion should be debated and defined first to remove any ambiguity that could exist over the vocabulary that will be used in the factual discussion on the function to be (de)centralized.

The columns indicate the government layers that exist in the particular nation under analysis. Table 11.3 offers a simplified version with three layers: local, regional and the central. The columns between local and regional level and between regional and central level are added simply to remember that other regional or ad hoc institutional arrangements are possible. Many forms of cooperative federalism exist or can be invented between local and regional levels: special service district, ad hoc jurisdiction, single-purpose or multi-purpose association of communes, urban agglomeration, and amalgamation of communes.

The general idea of the method is to fill the cells of the matrix when considering for each criteria how appropriate it is in the context of a specific level of government written in the columns. The role of economists would be to help with the criteria that concern fiscal federalism, while leaving to other experts the non-economic criteria, and to help fill the cells of the matrix – the pros and cons. They should also contribute to analysing the coherence or the opposition between criteria for specific functions and the level of decentralization. Political evaluation and weighting would be needed at this stage. The process would be iterative; the purpose being that of reducing the set of possible alternatives for individual policies after each round of negotiation has been completed, until no further gains from trade can be realized.

What is needed in essence is a decision framework; not a set of policy prescriptions, but a series of linked decision processes from which policy decisions would emerge. The decisions themselves would depend on the weights attached by policy makers to particular ends and means. There can be no technically determined 'right' answer to the question of reassigning public functions between government levels, as for other questions in fiscal federalism. But there can be more or less technically efficient procedures for reaching the 'best' policy compromise.

Notes

1. The last (at the time of writing this chapter) European example is the amendment of the French constitution recognizing that France is a decentralized republic, giving explicit fiscal power to local territories. See Law 2003-276, 28 March 2003 and art. 72.2 Cst.
2. There could be two or more government layers: our reference in this chapter is to a system with three levels of *political* government, the centre, the intermediate layer (provinces, *Länder*, cantons, regions) and a local or lower level (communes, municipalities, towns, villages).
3. The history of the amalgamation of communes in Europe (Dafflon 1998) and the 20 June 2004 vote on the 'défusion de communes' in Québec are good examples. The compulsory reorganization of local entities in Europe has been limited both in time (beween 1960 and 1980) and in space (to northern, especially German and Anglo-Saxon countries).
4. In addition, in most cantons and at the federal level, the tax rates are written in the law so that any change is submitted to popular vote. At the local level, the citizens' assembly decides about/on the annual tax rate coefficient needed to balance the current budget – which includes interest payments and the amortization of the debt. Thus a rapid change in taxation for stabilization purposes is virtually/nearly impossible.
5. The standard definition in transition economies is: 'In general, the assignment of responsibility for the function of producing public goods follows the principle of subsidiarity, that is, that the best results occur when these functions are assigned to the lowest level of government capable of performing them' (Conway et al. 2005: 15).
6. The possible alternative would be the amalgamation of small communes with a neighbouring larger one in order to restore local autonomy in the choice and performance of local public services, rather than passing the function over to the next government layer. The evidence in Switzerland is that around one-third of the amalgamation of communes originates in the persistent difficulty of finding managerial capacities to run the commune both at the political and bureaucratic levels. See Dafflon (1998: 139).

References

Aebischer, R. (1987), *Aufgabenverteilung zwischen Kanton und Gemeinden*, Universitätsverlag Freiburg, Wirtschaftswissenschaftliche Beiträge No. 34.
Ahmad, E., Hewitt, D. and Ruggiero, E. (1997), 'Assigning expenditure responsibilities', in Ter-Minassian (ed.), pp. 25–48.
Ayrton, R. (2002), *L'impossible politique budgétaire: l'Etat fédéral face aux turbulences économiques*, Presses polytechniques et universitaires romandes, Collection Le Savoir Suisse, vol. 3, Lausanne.
Balassone, F. and Franco, D. (1999), *Il federalìsmo fiscale e il Patto di stabilità*, in Banca d'Italia (ed.), *I controlli delle gestioní pubbliche*, Roma, Banca d'Italia, pp. 225–57.
Bird, R. (2001), 'Rationales and forms of decentralization', in Bird and Stauffer (eds), pp. 1–13.
Bird, R. and Stauffer, T. (eds) (2001), *Intergovernmental Fiscal Relations in Fragmented Societies*, Helbing & Lichtenhahn, Basel, Institute of Federalism, Fribourg, Études et colloques 33.
Blindenbacher, R. and Koller, A. (eds) (2003), *Federalism in a Changing World – Learning from Each Other*, McGill-Queen's University Press, Montreal and Kingston.

Breton, A. (1998), *Competitive Governments: An Economic Theory of Politics and Public Finance*, Cambridge University Press, Cambridge, first paperback edition.

Buschor, E., König, F., Rey, A. and Rondi, E. (1984), *Neue Finanzpolitik der Kantone*, Studie der Fachgruppe für kantonale Finanzfragen, Verlag Paul Haupt, Bern, Staat und Politik, No. 29.

Conseil de l'Europe (1995), *La taille des communes, l'efficacité et la participation des citoyens*, Communes et régions d'Europe, no. 56, Conseil de l'Europe, Strasbourg.

Conway, F.J., B. Desilets, P. Epstein, J.H. Pigey, G. Frelick and F. Rosensweig (2005), *Intergovernmental Fiscal Relations in Central and Eastern Europe: A Sourcebook and Reference Guide*, The International Bank for Reconstruction and Development/The World Bank, Washington, DC.

Council of Europe (1998), *European Charter of Local Self-Government and Explanatory Report*, CoE Publishing, Strasbourg, reprinted version October 1998.

Dafflon, B. (1996), 'The requirement of a balanced local budget: theory and evidence from the Swiss experience', in Pola et al. (eds) pp. 228–50.

Dafflon, B. (1998), 'Suisse: les fusions de communes dans le canton de Fribourg, analyse socio-économique', *Annuaire des collectivités locales*, Éditions du GRALE et du FNRS, Paris, pp. 125–66.

Derycke, P.-H. and Gilbert, G. (1988), *Économie publique locale*, Association de Science Régionale de Langue Française, Bibliothèque de science régionale, Economica, Paris.

Elazad, D.J. (1977), 'The ends of federalism: note toward a theory of federal political arrangements', in M. Frenkel (ed.), *Partnership in Federalism*, Peter Lang, Bern, pp. 25–6.

Esterbauer, F. and Thöni, E. (1981), *Föderalismus und Regionalismus in Theorie und Praxis*, Schriftenreihe des Instituts für angewandte Sozial- und Wirtschaftsforschung, Signum Verlag, Vienna.

Feld, L. (1999), *Steuerwettbewerb und seine Auswirkungen auf Allokation und Distribution: eine empirische Analyse für die Schweiz*, Doctoral dissertation no. 2222, University of St. Gall, Difo-Druck OHG, Bamberg (Germany).

Fraschini, A. (2001), 'Subsidiarity', *Rivista di diritto finanziario e scienza delle finanze*, **60**(1), I, 55–61.

Frey, B. and Eichenberger, R. (1999), *The New Democratic Federalism in Europe: Functional, Overlapping, and Competing Jurisdictions*, Studies in Federalism and State–Local Finance, Edward Elgar, Cheltenham, UK and Northampton, MA, USA.

Grindle, M. (1996), *Challenging the State: Crisis and Innovation in Latin America and Africa*, Cambridge University Press, Cambridge.

King, D. (1984), *Fiscal Tiers: The Economics of Multi-level Government*, Allen & Unwin, London.

King, D. (1996), 'A model of optimum local authority size', in Pola et al., pp. 55–76.

King, D. and Ma, Y. (2000), 'Local authority size in theory and practice', *Environment and Planning C: Government and Policy*, **18**, 255–70.

Musgrave, R. (1961), 'Approaches to a fiscal theory of political federalism', in NBER *Public Finance: Needs, Sources and Utilization*, Princeton University Press, Princeton, NJ, pp. 97–133.

Oates, W. (1968), 'The theory of public finance in a federal system', *Canadian Journal of Economics*, **1**, pp. 37–54.

Oates, W. (1972), *Fiscal Federalism*, Harcourt Brace Jovanovich, New York.

Oates, W. (1999), 'An essay on fiscal federalism', *Journal of Economic Literature*, **37**, 1120–49.

Oates, W. (2003), 'Assignment of responsibilities and fiscal federalism', in Blindenbacher and Koller (eds), pp. 39–50.

Perritaz, S. (2003), *Intercommunalité, agglomération et fusion de communes: l'optimal et le possible dans les zones urbaines suisses*, BENEFRI Centre d'Études en Économie du Secteur Public, Université de Fribourg, Doctoral thesis.

Pola, G., France, G. and Levaggi, R. (eds) (1996), *Developments in Local Government Finance: Theory and Policy*, Edward Elgar, Cheltenham, UK and Northampton, MA, USA.

Polidano, C. (2000), 'Measuring public sector capacity', *World Development*, **28**(5), 805–22.

Rossi, S. and Dafflon, B. (2002), 'The theory of subnational balanced budget and debt control', in B. Dafflon (ed.), *Local Public Finance in Europe: Balancing the Budget and Controlling Debt*, Edward Elgar, Cheltenham, UK and Northampton, MA, USA, pp. 15–44.

Rubinfeld, D.L. (1987), 'The economics of the local public sector', in A.J. Auerbach and M. Feldstein (eds), *Handbook of Public Economics*, vol. 2, North-Holland, Amsterdam, pp. 571–645.

Ter-Minassian, T. (ed.) (1997), *Fiscal Federalism in Theory and Practice*, International Monetary Fund, Washington, DC.

Ter-Minassian, T. and Craig, J. (1997), 'Control of subnational government borrowing', in T. Ter-Minassian (ed.), pp. 156–72.

Tiebout, C.M. (1956), 'A pure theory of local expenditures', *Journal of Political Economy*, **64**, 416–24.

Tiebout, C.M. (1961), 'An economic theory of decentralization', in NBER, *Public Finance, Needs, Sources and Utilization*, Princeton University Press, Princeton, NJ, pp. 79–96.

Tullock, G. (1969), 'Federalism: problems of scale', *Public Choice*, **4**, 19–29.

Wallis, J. and Dollery, B. (2002), 'Local government capacity and social capital', *Australian Journal of Public Administration*, **61**(3), 76–85.

Watts, R. (2001), 'The dynamics of decentralization', in Bird and Stauffer (eds), pp. 15–34.

Weist, D. (2003), 'Public services: assigning, designing and delivering expenditures', Presentation at the World Bank Conference 'Intergovernmental Fiscal Reforms in the EU Member and Applicant Countries', Ankara, 6–8 October.

Weist, D. and Kerr, G. (2002), *Budget Execution, Monitoring and Capacity Building*, Decentralization Briefing Notes, World Bank Institute, Washington, DC.

Wiseman, J. (1989), 'The political economy of federalism: a critical appraisal', in *Cost, Choice and Political Economy*, Edward Elgar, Aldershot, UK and Brookfield, USA, pp. 71–111.

Wittmann, W. (1973), 'Kriterien für die Aufgabenverteilung zwischen öffentlichen Körperschaften', in H. Haller and G. Hauser (eds), *Sozialwissenschaften im Dienste der Wirtschaftspolitik*, Mohr Verlag, Tübingen, pp. 157–78.

12 Normative versus positive theories of revenue assignments in federations

Maria Flavia Ambrosanio and Massimo Bordignon

Introduction

This chapter is organized around a number of questions. First, how are local governments financed around the world, and in particular what is the role of local taxation in this financing? Second, what has economic theory to say about this allocation, both on normative and positive grounds? In particular, can it explain what we observe? Third, which are the practical important issues that one should consider in designing a local tax system? For example, given the presence of increasing administrative costs for decentralization, how could one use the existing national taxes to create room for local tax autonomy? And how should tax enforcement powers be allocated across levels of government? A simple list of open problems may be of great help in understanding the issues involved in designing a local tax system. The bibilography at the end of the chapter offers a guide to the more specialized literature.

Even in this more limited framework, there are several issues that we can just touch on in the chapter. First, there is, or there should be, an obvious link between a local tax system and the expenditure which this tax system is supposed to finance. Both the level and the characteristics of the local expenditure should enter as variables in the equation concerning the determination of the optimal local tax system (see, for example, Gordon 1983). We recognize this problem, but do not investigate it to a great extent. Second, local taxation is only one of the instruments that could be used to finance local expenditure. Alternatively, tariffs, debt and grants from higher levels of government could also have been (and are in fact) largely used. Clearly, the presence and the features of these alternative financing instruments will affect the choices of local governments in terms of their tax instruments and should therefore also be considered in the analysis of an optimal local tax system. We briefly discuss some of these links, but do not attempt to offer a comprehensive analysis of the relationship between the different tools of financing, given the other chapters in this volume devoted to these. Finally, our discussion of local tax theory here aims to offer only a general framework for the analysis.

The data

What do the data show? What do local governments do around the world and how are their finances organized? Do general patterns concerning local taxes emerge?

Table 12.1 shows the degree of fiscal decentralization in some selected Organization for Economic Cooperation and Development (OECD) countries, based on subnational spending and revenues as a percentage of general governments' spending and revenues. This index varies significantly across countries; and the *form* of the state (for example, whether federal or unitary) constitutes at best only a very weak indicator of the actual degree of decentralization of a

Table 12.1   Subnational government spending and revenues

	Share in general government spending*		Share in general government revenues		Tax revenues as % of total revenues	
	1985	2001	1985	2001	1985	2001
Federal countries						
Austria	28.4	28.5	24.6	21.4	23.8	18.9
Belgium	31.8	34.0	11.4	11.3	4.8	28.6
Canada	54.5	56.5	50.4	49.9	45.4	44.1
Germany	37.6	36.1	31.9	32.4	30.8	29.2
USA	32.6	40.0	37.6	40.4	32.7	31.7
Unitary countries						
Denmark	53.7	57.8	32.3	34.6	28.4	33.8
Finland	30.6	35.5	24.8	24.7	22.4	22.4
France	16.1	18.6	11.6	13.1	8.7	9.3
Greece	4.0	5.0	3.7	3.7	1.3	1.0
Ireland	30.2	29.5	32.3	34.6	2.3	1.9
Italy	25.6	29.7	10.7	17.6	2.3	12.2
Luxembourg	14.2	12.8	8.0	7.4	6.6	5.6
Netherlands	32.6	34.2	11.4	11.1	2.4	3.5
Norway	34.6	38.8	22.5	20.3	17.7	16.3
Portugal	10.3	12.8	7.6	8.3	3.5	6.5
Spain	25.0	32.2	17.0	20.3	11.2	16.5
Sweden	36.7	43.4	34.3	32.0	30.4	30.8
UK	22.2	25.9	10.5	7.6	10.2	4.1

Note: *Excluding the transfers paid to other levels of government.

Source: OECD, Jourmaud and Kongsrud (2003).

country. Indeed, there are some unitary countries (most notably, the European Nordic countries) where subnational governments are responsible for a larger share of public spending and financing than in most federal countries. Some patterns emerge from the table, which are confirmed in more sophisticated econometric studies (for example, Cerniglia 2003). Richer and larger countries are usually more decentralized than smaller and poorer ones (this correlation should not be mistaken for a causal relationship, which could very well go in the opposite direction); and in almost all countries, subnational governments' share in total public expenditure exceeds the same share in total revenues, suggesting that grants from higher levels of government are an important part of local financing.

Table 12.1 tells us something about what local governments do in selected countries. But how do they finance their expenditure? Table 12.2 offers some information on the composition of local revenues among taxes, non-taxes and grants for selected countries. Local taxation plays an important role in most countries. But again, what is mostly impressive is the variance across countries, with the ratio of own-tax revenues on total local revenues ranging from more than 70 per cent in Iceland to just 5 per cent in the Netherlands.

Table 12.2 offers some further general insights. First, there is some substitution effect between local tax revenue and local tariffs; countries that rely more on taxes to finance local governments generally use fewer tariffs, and vice versa. Second, grants from higher levels of government also play an important role in all countries. Third, we can detect some tendency towards decentralization on the financing side in the last 20 years. Between 1985 and 2003, most countries increased the role of taxation in the financing of local governments, reducing the share of grants in local budgets. However, there are also some counterexamples to this general tendency, the UK and Ireland, among the unitary countries and Switzerland and Mexico, among the federal ones.

These contrasting tendencies can be partly explained in terms of the difference in the composition of local tax revenues (Tables 12.3 and 12.4). In large federal countries, local governments are largely financed by property taxes, which cover most of local tax revenues. This is particularly true for the countries belonging to the Anglo-Saxon tradition (Australia, Canada, the USA). On the contrary, federal countries in continental Europe rely heavily on income and profit taxes (Belgium, Germany, Switzerland); others, such as Spain and Austria, present a more balanced structure, involving property and consumption tax as well. Among unitary countries, the UK is exceptional in the sense of employing exclusively property taxation (or 'rates') to finance local government; on the contrary, Nordic European countries are exceptional in the sense of relying exclusively on income taxation (based on income from labour, whereas income from capital is subject to the corporate income tax rate under

Table 12.2 Revenues received by local government (as a percentage of total revenues)

	Tax revenues		Non-tax revenues		Grants	
	1985	2000	1985	2000	1985	2000
Federal countries						
Australia	42.5	40.3	37.0	45.4	20.5	14.3
Austria	53.8	52.4	32.1	27.4	14.2	20.1
Belgium	32.0	37.2	6.7	9.2	61.3	53.6
Canada	36.5	40.6	15.6	19.9	47.9	39.5
Germany	36.9	39.5	36.0	25.3	27.0	35.2
Mexico	35.2	19.4	57.2	29.2	7.6	51.4
Switzerland	50.9	48.2	32.4	34.5	16.7	17.3
USA	39.3	37.8	22.1	23.6	38.5	38.6
Unitary countries						
Denmark	44.0	52.9	10.0	7.8	46.0	39.3
Finland	46.2	55.1	19.6	22.6	34.2	22.3
France	46.7	45.1	18.9	19.3	34.4	35.5
Iceland	72.0	74.0	20.0	17.3	8.0	8.8
Ireland	5.4	4.9	20.0	18.7	74.6	76.4
Italy	6.3	37.2	11.7	13.5	82.0	49.3
Luxembourg	45.0	33.4	12.5	29.4	42.5	37.2
Netherlands	5.6	9.7	14.0	20.2	80.4	70.1
Norway	45.7	38.5	15.8	20.1	38.4	41.4
Spain	56.3	66.5	19.4	11.0	24.2	22.6
Sweden	57.7	74.9	20.5	5.7	21.8	19.4
UK	30.8	14.3	21.1	15.6	48.1	70.1

Source: OECD, Revenue Statistics, 2003.

a dual income tax system). The other countries use more widespread sources for local taxation. Italy and France also make heavy use of local business taxes, usually taxes which rely on a somewhat broader definition of tax base than just profits (that is, labour costs, imputed rents for industrial buildings and so on). As these different sources of taxation present a different elasticity with respect to national income, this is likely to affect the evolution of the decentralization index.

However, the figures discussed so far are only very rough indicators of the actual taxing power of subnational governments, as they mix together different

Table 12.3   *Tax revenues of the main local taxes, 2001, federal countries (as % of total tax revenues of local government)*

	Income and profits	Payroll	Property	General consumption taxes	Specific goods and services	Taxes on use etc.	Other taxes
Australia	–	–	100.0	–	–	–	–
Austria	37.7	19.1	10.0	22.7	3.8	1.7	5.0
Belgium	85.8	–	–	1.4	7.9	4.6	0.3
Canada	–	–	91.6	0.2	–	1.6	6.5
Germany	77.1	–	16.6	5.2	0.5	0.4	0.2
Mexico	–	0.1	88.5	–	1.9	0.9	8.6
Switzerland	83.1	–	16.6	–	0.2	0.1	–
USA	6.2	–	71.5	12.4	5.1	4.8	–

Source: OECD, Revenue Statistics, 2003.

Table 12.4   *Tax revenues of the main local taxes, 2001, unitary countries (as % of total tax revenues of local government)*

	Income and profits Individuals	Income and profits Corporate	Property	General consumption taxes	Specific goods and services	Taxes on use etc.	Other taxes*
Denmark	91.1	2.2	6.6	–	–	–	–
Finland	78.6	16.9	4.3	–	–	–	0.2
France	–	–	49.1	–	7.6	3.4	39.8
Greece	–	–	56.2	2.8	23.1	17.9	–
Hungary	0.8	–	22.2	71.1	1.0	4.5	0.4
Iceland	80.4	–	12.4	7.2	–	–	–
Ireland	–	–	–	100.0	–	–	–
Italy	8.8	–	18.0	–	8.7	10.6	53.9
Japan	47.5	27.4	31.1	7.0	8.1	5.4	1.0
Luxembourg	–	92.6	5.8	–	1.0	0.2	0.3
Netherlands	–	–	57.5	–	–	42.5	–
Norway	90.6	–	7.5	–	–	1.8	–
Portugal	22.4	7.9	44.3	17.3	12.3	3.3	0.3
Spain	25.3	21.9	37.4	11.7	9.9	13.7	1.9
Sweden	100.0	–	–	–	–	–	–
UK	–	–	99.9	–	–	–	0.1

Note: *Includes tax on net wealth (Norway), estate taxes (Finland and Portugal) and some residual taxes, mainly on business (France, Italy).

Source: OECD, Revenue Statistics, 2003.

Table 12.5   *Subnational government taxing powers in selected OECD countries,*[1] *1995*

	Sub-national government taxes related to:		Discretion to set taxes[2]	Summary indicator of taxing power[3]
	Total taxes	GDP		
Sweden	32.6	15.5	100.0	15.5
Denmark	31.3	15.5	95.1	14.7
Switzerland	35.8	11.9	92.4	11.0
Finland	21.8	9.8	89.0	8.7
Belgium	27.9	12.4	57.9	7.2
Iceland	20.4	6.4	100.0	6.4
Japan	24.2	6.8	90.3	6.1
Spain	13.3	4.4	66.6	2.9
New Zealand	5.3	2.0	98.0	2.0
Germany	29.0	11.1	12.8	1.4
Poland	7.5	3.0	46.0	1.4
UK	3.9	1.4	100.0	1.4
Netherlands	2.7	1.1	100.0	1.1
Austria	20.9	8.7	9.5	0.8
Portugal	5.6	1.8	31.5	0.6
Czech Republic	12.9	5.2	10.0	0.5
Hungary	2.6	1.1	30.0	0.3
Norway	19.7	7.9	3.3	0.3
Mexico	3.3	0.6	11.2	0.1

Notes:
1. The countries are ranked in descending order according to the value of the summary indicator of taxing powers.
2. The figures show the percentage of their total taxes for which subnational governments hold full discretion over the tax rate, the tax base, or both the tax rate and the tax base. A value of 100 designates full discretion.
3. The summary indicator is the product of the ratio of subnational governments taxes to GDP and the degree in the discretion to set taxes. Thus it measures subnational government taxes with full discretion as a percentage of GDP.

Source: OECD, Jourmaud and Kongsrud (2003).

tax instruments, from tax shares to own taxes. Not much is known about the effective taxing powers of local governments in the different countries, and empirical studies on fiscal federalism have often suffered from lack of proper data. Table 12.5 shows the results of a single study that has attempted to cast some light on this issue in a number of OECD countries (Jourmaud and Kongsrud 2003). In this study, taxing power is measured as the product of local discretion (in setting up tax rates and tax base by local governments) and local tax revenue on GDP. Clearly, the Northern European countries, plus a number of federal countries such as Belgium and Switzerland, show a higher level of decentralization. However, other countries, including federal ones such as Germany and Austria, present low levels of decentralization. Indeed, once discretion in setting tax rates is taken into account, Germany appears as centralized on the taxing side as the UK, in spite of the fact that in the latter local tax revenue on GDP is about one-tenth of that in the former.

Fiscal federalism and tax assignments: what does theory say?
Tax assignment concerns the optimal determination of the vertical structure of taxation. It tries to answer questions such as which level of government ought to choose the taxes to be imposed at any level, which level should define tax bases, which one the tax rates and, finally, which one should enforce and administer the various tax tools. There is no generally accepted framework to address this problem. Indeed, there are two extreme positions in this debate, which make reference to the traditional normative approach (Musgrave 1959; Oates 1972) on the one side, and to the public choice approach (Brennan and Buchanan 1980) on the other. According to the former approach, optimal tax assignment is strictly related to the normative optimal assignment of expenditure functions to levels of governments. According to Musgrave's famous distinction, there are three branches of government: resource allocation, income redistribution and macroeconomic stabilization. Because of spillover effects,[1] the responsibility for income redistribution and macroeconomic stabilization should be assigned to central government, whereas resource allocation may be performed by all levels of government. It follows that individual progressive income taxes and corporate income taxes should be assigned to central government, as the best instruments for both income redistribution and macroeconomic stabilization. With regard to the allocation branch, on efficiency grounds, central and local governments should mainly use benefit taxes. The conventional approach also provides some guidelines for the setting of subnational taxes. First, local governments should levy taxes on relative immobile bases or assets, in order to prevent tax competition and revenue losses; second, they should levy taxes on bases evenly distributed among jurisdictions, in order to prevent the generation of horizontal fiscal imbalances; and third, they should levy taxes whose yield is relatively stable in real terms, to ensure expenditure planning.

This approach has been criticized in many respects. It rests on the assumption that governments are benevolent, social welfare-maximizing unities; it does not take into account the exercise of political power and bargaining in designing tax assignment; it is a purely normative theory and provides a very poor explanation of the tax and expenditure assignments between central and local governments as we observe in the real world. Indeed, local governments are in many countries concerned with income redistribution, for instance in education and health-care sectors; and local governments in fact make little use of benefit taxation.

In contrast with this, the Brennan–Buchanan approach hinges upon a different view of government, and therefore leads to an opposite view of the optimal tax assignment. In this approach, governments are not benevolent, and even in strong democracies, effective control by citizens on politicians is weak. Thus, politicians behave as Leviathans, and taxes are used to maximize total revenue from the private sector as this allows politicians and bureaucrats to maximize their spending power. This involves choosing broad tax bases with the aim of minimizing tax evasion and tax erosion, and imposing higher rates on less elastic bases. Accordingly, within this framework, Brennan and Buchanan stress the positive effects of tax competition among local governments, as one of the forces restraining tax design and budget size; subnational taxes should then be imposed on mobile factors so as to trigger competition which limits the rapaciousness of Leviathan. Tax competition provides efficiency gains just as competition between private economic agents does, by reducing the monopoly powers of governmental units. As in the Tiebout model, where people 'vote with their feet', competition imposes a limitation on the ability of governments to expropriate citizens.

Many criticisms can be addressed to the Leviathan model as well. In the real world, governments are less monopolist than in the Brennan–Buchanan model. Competition among subnational governments may introduce serious allocative distortions as, for example, in the case of predatory tax competition, beggar-my-neighbour policies, which can then lead to an erosion of the tax base. Further, there is little evidence on the fact that the size of public sector 'should be smaller, *ceteris paribus*, the greater the extent to which taxes and expenditures are decentralized' (Brennan and Buchanan 1980, p. 15). In fact, empirical results concerning the Leviathan hypothesis are mixed at best (Edwards and Keen 1996).

In spite of all their differences, both approaches share the common feature of being fundamentally static and normative in nature. In the Oates–Musgrave tradition, tax assignment solves a benevolent social planner's problem; in the Brennan–Buchanan tradition, tax assignment solves – at the constitutional level – the opposite problem of limiting the predatory appetite of the Leviathan. As a result, none of them is really interested in explaining tax assignments in the real world. More interesting insights on these grounds come from the more *positive*-oriented approach of Hettich and Winer (2000) and more generally, by the modern literature on political economy (Persson and Tabellini 2000). In this literature, there is an attempt to endogenize the fiscal choices of governments, both on the revenue and the expenditure side, as the result of the incentives that the different features of the political system impose on politicians. For instance, Hettich and Winer (2000) develop a model of tax choices, where governments attempt to minimize the political costs of raising a given amount of revenue, in terms of votes lost at election time; parties propose fiscal programmes that maximize their probability of winning the next election. This model (a probabilistic spatial voting approach) does not provide normative principles, but tries to explain some features we observe in the tax system, such as complicated tax structures, multiple rates, bases and special exemptions, on the assumption that different people have different political responses to taxation.

In an interesting extension of this analysis to our problem here, the tax assignment (or rather tax reassignment) problem, Winer (2000) uses the Breton (1996) framework to argue that the distribution of tax powers inside a federation has very little to do with either the formal constitution of a country or the normative tax assignment view. Rather, as constitutions are incomplete contracts whose interpretation may change over time, the observed tax assignment in a federation is the result of a struggle between different levels of government to raise their respective share of taxing powers. In this struggle, exogenous shocks such as major international crises (for example, the two world wars) or technological advances (for example, in tax enforcement), by changing the relative bargaining powers of the different levels of governments, also change the effective distribution of taxing power.[2]

This approach is promising as it suggests looking at fiscal federalism as a mechanism to reallocate the effective use of governing instruments, including tax sources, among the various political jurisdictions in the face of unforeseen events. However, in this approach, it is unclear how one could judge on normative grounds the observed distribution of tax powers across jurisdictions. Furthermore, as already mentioned, there are many different models of political economy that can be applied to tax choices, and the results vary greatly according to the model considered (in particular, if politicians can or cannot commit to their electoral promises, so that electoral competition hinges on before or after the elections) and to the specific question addressed. It is then fair to say that no clear indication concerning the optimal tax assignment to different levels of government emerges from this literature (Profeta 2005).

Designing local taxation: a conceptual framework

In this section we present a unified framework that attempts to assess the usefulness of the insights of the different theories in terms of the design of an 'optimal' local taxation system. A useful starting point for such an analysis is a remark recently made by Wildasin (2004) for local debt, but which also applies to local taxation. Wildasin notes that as both local and central governments issue debt, but since at the same time central government also transfers resources to local governments, it would make no formal difference if all local debts were transferred to the central government, and in exchange the latter increased grants to local governments by exactly the same amount. The stance of both the private and the public sector as a whole would remain unchanged. By the same token, it would make no difference if a euro of local taxes were exchanged with a euro of extra transfers, transferring all tax revenue to the central government. Then, if it does make a difference on economic grounds, it can only be because there are some imperfections in the functioning of the markets or in the functioning of the political system, so that a euro of local tax revenue is not the same thing as a euro of national tax (plus transfers). In what follows, we discuss what can make a difference under situations of increasing complexity and realism. As we shall argue, a reasonable, although not uncontroversial, tax assignment model emerges from this exercise.

Identical regions with immobile agents
Consider first the simplest case where there are no differences whatsoever across jurisdictions; regions are identical in terms of population, resources, preferences and income of the resident individuals. Suppose further that there is no mobility, with all agents – firms, factors and individuals – being completely immobile across regions. In this highly abstract world, one may then ask whether there is any role at all for taxation at the local level. Indeed, in such a world, one may actually wonder if there is any role for local governments, as all decisions could be taken by the central government without any risk of inducing discrimination across different individuals.

The most recent literature suggests that there may indeed be still one rationale. If politicians are not perfectly benevolent, or are not uniformly competent, creating several jurisdictions, rather than having a single decision maker, may help citizens in learning about the quality of their governments, allowing them to compare the policy outcomes in their jurisdiction with respect to those in other similar jurisdictions. Citizens are 'rationally ignorant'; they do not have the same incentives to invest in learning the details of policy making as politicians do, and this puts them in a situation of informational asymmetry. This asymmetric situation may then be eased by having several jurisdictions rather than one, because, unless 'bad' local politicians are able to perfectly collude against citizens, their different choices offer potentially useful information to citizens,[3] which may then allow the latter to discriminate between bad and good politicians and to keep their behaviour in check.

This basic insight, which is presently under scrutiny by a growing literature under the general label of 'yardstick competition' (see Lockwood, Ch. 1, and

Salmon, Ch. 2, in this volume), is interesting because it suggests that there may be efficiency gains from decentralization, even in the absence of either heterogeneity of preferences (Oates), or mobility of agents (Tiebout). It is also interesting because it has some important implications for local taxation. First, it suggests that indeed, even in the very abstract setting we are considering here, there may be a role for taxation as a main source of finance for local governments. It is true that, in principle, one could think that yardstick competition might also be triggered by many other factors rather than local taxation. In practice, however, it is clear that local taxes are the most natural candidate for yardstick competition, for instance, because it is easier to compare tax rates instead of complicated expenditure structures,[4] or because if everything were financed with money coming from outside the jurisdiction, citizens living in that jurisdiction would have very little incentive to check how that money was spent.

Second, this approach also offers some novel insights about the desirable characteristics of local taxes. If one of the basic roles of local taxation is that of increasing the responsibility and accountability of local politicians, then local taxes should be chosen so as to maximize the ability of citizens to control the behaviour of local politicians. Hence, issues such as *visibility*, *transparency* and *accountability* of the local tax system become paramount. For instance, one should certainly prefer own taxes over tax surcharges and tax shares as a potential source for local taxation, as the allocation of responsibility across levels of government would then be clearer. Also, while one would certainly want to give autonomy to the local politicians in the setting up of the tax rates, it might be more questionable if we should also want to give the same autonomy on the tax base, as that would then make interregional comparison more difficult. Admittedly, it is unlikely that a satisfactory theory of tax assignments could be built just on the basis of yardstick competition theory; some suggestions are pertinent, however, as discussed below.

Identical regions with mobility
Next, suppose that we add to the picture the possibility that agents or factors can move freely across jurisdictions, as happens in real-world federations, while maintaining the hypothesis of identical jurisdictions, so as to rule out equity considerations and other efficiency aspects of local taxation. Factor, firm or household interregional mobility lies at the heart of most of the literature on fiscal federalism, which has at length investigated the effects of mobility on the equilibrium allocations. Results depend very much on who can move (firms, factors, households or just some of those?), at what cost (same or differentiated costs for the different agents?), and what exactly can be moved (only the place of residence or the actual employment of a factor?).[5]

Provided that governments are benevolent enough, the basic message of this literature is that mobility usually introduces inefficiency in the spatial allocation of private agents and therefore induces suboptimal equilibria. Only if regions have a complete set of fiscal instruments, can tax firms and households depending on their location, and moreover have access to a non-distorting tax (such as a tax on land rents) to cover costs above marginal crowding costs, will efficient allocations be reached. But this also requires either perfect competitive markets or perfectly mobile households. Otherwise, in the presence of migration costs, if these costs are differentiated across households, or if mobility is only limited to some firms or some factors (that is, capital), mobility again induces inefficient allocations (Wellich 2000).

This conclusion may be reversed if politicians are not benevolent, or if there are some other political failures. Tax competition, for instance, may be beneficial if politicians are Leviathans, because it reduces equilibrium tax rates. It might also be beneficial if politicians are benevolent but unable to commit, as it can then help to solve a time-inconsistency problem (for example, Persson and Tabellini 2000). Hence, the normative status of mobility depends very much on the view one has about local politics on the one hand, and on the plausibility of (efficient) Tiebout-type of equilibrium outcomes, on the other.

On the whole, our view is that interjurisdictional mobility should be better thought of *as a constraint* to be imposed on the source of taxation which can be given to local governments (Cremer et al. 1996). For instance, basic incidence theory suggests that a local tax on a factor that is perfectly mobile across jurisdictions is ultimately paid by the less mobile ones (Gordon 1986). It would then make very little sense to assign such a tax to a local government. And even if one could imagine complicated centrally made transfer mechanisms which would allow local governments to internalize the spillover effects from local taxation (for example, Wellich 2000), it is clearly much better to avoid these problems *ex ante* by an appropriate tax assignment, rather than trying to correct them *ex post* with informational costly transfer systems.[6]

Hence, this suggests that taxes on highly mobile assets, such as for instance (source-based) taxes on corporations or capital income, should not be given to local governments. On the other hand, it is a matter of degree. It is hard to think of tax bases that are totally immobile across jurisdictions (leaving aside taxes on land rents); and some amount of mobility in the local tax base might not be too harmful. It might induce inefficient choices from the benevolent politicians, but it might also restrain the choices of less benevolent ones and solve some other incentive problem as well. For instance, taxes on consumption offer some advantages as a form of local taxation (see below). True, they might also induce some inefficient cross-border shopping effects. But, for reasonable differences in the local tax rates, these effects are likely to be very limited (Kanbur and Keen 1993; Besley and Case 1995), especially if the size of the local jurisdictions is large enough. Similarly, local surcharges on personal income tax, although possibly in conflict with benefit taxation and the redistributing role of taxation, may have several advantages, for example, the merit of being highly visible to taxpayers, thus increasing the accountability of local politicians. The general lesson is that once the mobility of some tax base goes below a given threshold, this tax base has some chance of being considered, on efficiency grounds, as a source for local taxation. Some limited amount of tax competition should not forbid the use of that tax base for local financing.

Much more difficult to address is the opposite case of *tax exporting*. That is, the case where, due to the mobility of the tax base, or through the effects of taxation on the market mechanism, taxes levied in some jurisdictions are carried over to the residents of other jurisdictions. Tax exporting is deleterious for local tax autonomy, whatever model of government one has in mind. Benevolent governments interested in the well-being of residents, as well as Leviathan governments only interested in accumulating rents, would act in the same (inefficient) way in this context. Tax exporting immediately rules out some assets from the ambit of local taxation. For instance, excises on local productive services (that is, gas and petrol extraction and refinement) that are used as inputs nationwide, are an obvious example of tax instruments that should not be given to local administrations. On the other hand, once tax incidence is taken into consideration, many other tax instruments become suspect. As we saw above, some countries use local tax on business as a source of local revenue. However, if these taxes can be partly translated into prices, and the relevant goods are sold elsewhere in the country, it is clear that this source of taxation allows for tax exporting, and its use as a local tax should therefore be limited. One problem with this type of argument is that we do not really know much about tax incidence outside the simplest perfect competitive models, and the available empirical evidence is poor. It is therefore largely a matter of judgement and specific analysis to decide which tax allows or does not allow for tax exporting.

Very similar considerations apply to the case of another famous source of tax exporting, although not necessarily linked with mobility, that is, vertical tax externalities across levels of governments (Keen 1998). If several layers of government share, partially or totally, the same tax base, none would have an incentive to take into account the effects of own-tax choices on the tax base of the other level of government. This would imply higher taxes than optimal as each level of government tries to 'export' to the other level the burden of taxation, with the effect of overtaxing the same citizens. Consequently, it would be better to choose tax bases across levels of government so as to minimize this occurrence. But this is easier said than done, as basic economic equivalences suggest that many formally different taxes in reality share the same base.[7]

Indeed, in a more fundamental sense, all taxes overlap, as ultimately they all make reference to the same taxable asset, the national wealth produced in a country in a given period. Hence, there is little that can be done about this problem, except to try to understand how serious the problem is in practice. Empirical evidence is unfortunately absent. On theoretical grounds, an obvious and definite solution to the problem of tax externalities would be to concentrate all tax powers on a single level of government, a solution that has indeed been advocated in the literature.[8] But clearly this would have many negative side-effects, for instance in terms of the accountability of the different governments. Alternatively, one can think of some compensating transfer mechanism across levels of government that would force them to internalize the vertical externalities.

Difference in preferences
Our basic conclusion is that there is a role for tax autonomy at the local level even in the simplest case of identical regions. This role is weakened, but not eliminated, by the presence of mobility of the tax bases. Mobility reduces the set of tax instruments which can safely be offered to local governments and raises many other efficiency aspects which need to be considered, but does not change the nature of this basic insight. However, if we allow for differences in local preferences across regions (still maintaining the assumption of identical resources), the argument for local autonomy in the setting of the choice of the tax rates and tax bases can only be strengthened on efficiency grounds. It is hard to devise mechanisms that would allow local governments to reflect differences in local preferences, if these local governments did not have tax instruments to use to this effect. Local taxation may be used to finance different levels of expenditure as well as a mechanism to share the burden of taxation differently across the local population. True, other tools, such as tax expenditures and tariffs may also play this role. But whenever local expenditure presents characteristics of indivisibility and introduces distributive effects across the population (that is, in the overall majority of cases), the recourse to taxation appears unavoidable.

At the same time, this is also the type of setting where specific suggestions are difficult to make, without considering the specific characteristics of the allocation of competences across governments. As suggested by the traditional approach, benefit taxation is the main tool that should be used to solve allocative problems and to take into account the heterogeneity of preferences at the local level. On the other hand, this largely depends on what these local governments are asked to do. Benefit taxation, besides being very limited in practical terms, makes sense only if local governments play an allocative role. If this is not the case, as for most countries, then other local tax instruments need to be considered. For instance, if local governments also play a relevant role in the provision of important services such as education, health and social security, it would make little sense to deny a role to these governments in personal income tax, as this is traditionally the main tool used to finance these services. Hence, the answer to the question of which taxes to allocate at local level can only be case specific; it requires first a preliminary recognition of the attribution of functions. Of course, this only moves the fundamental question one step up the ladder; why is it that some competences are given to local governments in one country and to some others in a different country?

Differences in endowments

Finally, suppose that we now also relax the assumption of identical endowments across regions, so that by now local jurisdictions are also allowed to differ in terms of resource allocations. Differences in endowments also interact with the other efficiency aspects of taxation (for example, Wellich 2000) which we have already discussed, but it mainly introduces a new aspect in the discussion. It becomes crucial to consider the problem of *the distribution of the tax base* of the different tax instruments across the national community. If local governments are supposed to perform similar functions across the country,[9] but have very different resources to finance these functions, there is clearly a problem. This is largely to do with the issue of *horizontal equity*; individuals who are perceived to be identical at the national level (say, households with the same income and the same composition) might receive a very different basket of local services just because they happen to live in a region or local community with a very different endowment of resources. And unless we can count on perfect household mobility to take this problem into account automatically, so that people who live in poorer regions do so out of an autonomous choice,[10] this inequality can be perceived as unacceptable in many countries.[11]

Of course, one may think that intergovernmental transfers should take care of the problem. Indeed, as we saw above, there is basically no country where grants from higher levels of government do not play an important role in the financing of local governments. Still, there are very substantial reasons for believing that the role of the transfer system in this context can only be limited. First, fiscal equalization across local governments would require not equality of resources at a given tax rate for the local tax system (which can easily be obtained with a block grant at some reference tax rate), but rather equalization in the *local tax effort* for any tax rate one local government should decide to use. In other words, irrespective of own resources, each local government should raise the same amount of revenue with respect to some standardized basis (say, per capita) by raising its own tax rate at any equal level. Transfer mechanisms with this property can be designed, but suffer many inconveniences, above all that the overall amount of transfers to local governments cannot be defined *ex ante* but only *ex post*, as a result of the autonomous choices of local governments. Second, transfer mechanisms raise a number of incentive issues that have been addressed by a large literature (see Boadway, Ch. 14 in this volume). We cannot discuss this literature here, but it suffices to say that once these incentive problems are taken into account, transfer systems are a second-best instrument, inducing several welfare losses. Hence, it is certainly desirable to try to solve problems in the interregional distribution of resources by an appropriate choice of local taxation *ex ante*, rather than *ex post* through transfer mechanisms.

In our view, differences in endowment should be thought of as introducing yet another constraint in the choice of an optimal local tax system, akin to the mobility issue. *Ceteris paribus*, one should avoid choosing tax tools with a very unequal distribution at the territorial level, as this distribution can only be imperfectly corrected *ex post* through the grant system. For instance, in many countries, territorial differences in per capita income (or value added) are larger than differences in per capita consumption. This is because the richer parts of the country, either through the national government budget or through the donations of individual citizens (for example, transfers from emigrants in the richer regions), usually transfer resources to the poorer parts of the country, and this helps to maintain per capita consumption at a more equal level in spite of the difference in per capita income.[12] Hence, *ceteris paribus*, consumption taxes should be preferred as a source of local taxation.

This argument also allows us to touch briefly upon another important practical issue. In the world of normative fiscal federalism theory, functions are allocated on a one-function–one-level-of-government basis, depending on the characteristics of that function (see above). That is, each government should be responsible for a given function with no overlapping of competences across levels of government. In reality, as we observed above, this is not the case in most countries. Either as a result of an explicit normative decision taken at the constitutional level, or as a result of the political process, many functions are in reality jointly performed by different levels of government. This overlapping, variously explained in the literature as a consequence of a 'conflict' across levels of governments (Breton 1996) or as the attempt of benevolent national governments to limit excessive variance in the supply at the local level of basic services (education, health and so on), has probably some justifications even on purely efficiency grounds. Spillover effects across different functions are probably unavoidable, so that any rigid attribution of competencies across levels of government is bound to be overcome in reality. There are services that, although decided at the central level, are better executed at the local level for purely administrative and organizational reasons; and finally, there may be various political distortions that suggest that overlapping among levels of government could be in many cases a second-best solution to an incentive problem.[13] This means that it might be better to think of many public functions as a *continuum*, with different levels of government that act, sometimes overlapping, on some parts of this continuum. In such a world, it is obvious that the source of financing for local governments also needs to 'overlap', presenting a continuum from own taxation to grants from the central level, as the different levels of government attempt to influence the choices of the other level in its own part of the continuum. Hence, the role of local taxation should be assessed in the context of this continuum of functions and resources (Smart 1998).

Dynamic issues

So far we have discussed only static economies. But the real world is dynamic and one should also consider how the case for local taxation changes when we introduce dynamic issues. Many different features could of course be considered in this enlarged framework, and it would take us too far to discuss them here.[14] But there is at least one aspect that has received considerable attention in the recent literature, which is worth mentioning for its practical importance, and also because it hinges directly on the issue of local taxation. This is the problem of how to enforce a *hard budget constraint* at the local level. The traditional normative approach usually takes for granted that a local budget can be enforced at no cost; given its resources, a local government will always keep its (intertemporal) budget in equilibrium, by setting up expenditure accordingly. In reality, this does not always happen. Worse, it is sometimes the case that it is the central government that solves the financial problems of local governments by bailing out local debts or by increasing transfers *ex post*. In some countries, this problem has proved to be so pervasive as to threaten the financial stability of the country as a whole. Brazil and Argentina are the most obvious examples, but there are increasing worries that the soft budget constraint disease may spread over to many other developed countries, such as the rich European countries, as a result of the decentralization process currently taking place (Rodden et al. 2003; Bordignon 2005).

It is important to understand that the soft budget constraint problem is really a *dynamic issue*, a time-inconsistency problem. The central government sets up a given level of transfers *ex ante*; but *ex post*, after some choices have been made or threatened by the local government, the central government gives in, and takes care of local governments' financial problems. The crucial feature, however – the identifying element of a soft budget constraint problem – is that this behaviour on the part of the central government is *expected* by the local government (or we would not have a soft budget problem to start with). The latter misbehaves *ex ante* exactly because it knows that with some positive probability it is going to get financial help *ex post* by the centre. Why this happens – why central government cannot commit *ex ante* and why it may change its views after some decisions have been taken at local level – has been scrutinized by a large literature (Kornai et al. 2003; Bordignon 2005). More interestingly for our purpose, is what can be done to avoid the problem? A crucial suggestion from the literature is that *local taxation may play an important role in curbing expectations of soft budget constraints.* The threat by the central government not to intervene *ex post* to solve local governments' problems may simply not be credible *ex ante*, if the local government has no sufficient resources of its own to take care of unpredictable events. And as local expenditure tends to be fixed in the short run, these extra resources can only come from local taxation. Interestingly, there is some robust empirical evidence (Rodden 2002, 2005; Bordignon and Turati 2005), based on both interregional and intercountry comparison, which suggests that local governments which are mostly financed by own resources tend to be less prone to soft budget constraint problems. Hence, in the complex equation determining the optimal tax assignment issue, one should take into account that local taxation is also instrumental in coping with this kind of dynamic problem.

Which type of tax autonomy (methods of tax assignment)?
The previous section suggests that there may be a role for tax autonomy at the local level even in the simplest case of identical regions and immobile citizens, and that this role is further enhanced by the consideration of differences in local preferences and of dynamic issues and commitment problems. A related theme is how this autonomy can be implemented in practice. The literature suggests *three fundamental methods* of tax assignment: own taxes (independent legislation and administration); tax surcharges; and tax sharing. Each method is characterized by a different degree of fiscal autonomy or taxing power. We shall briefly discuss the merits and demerits of these alternative methods.

The maximum degree of subnational fiscal autonomy occurs under independent legislation and administration, where subnational governments enact their own tax laws independently of higher levels of government; each jurisdiction chooses which taxes to levy and the definition of the tax base, sets up the tax rates, and is responsible for tax administration and enforcement. Own revenues, in the sense of own taxing power and marginal source of revenues, enable subnational governments to have control over the level of taxation and expenditure. This has many advantages. First, subnational governments can predict their revenues with an acceptable degree of certainty and in consequence can plan their expenditure flows; second, they are able to increase or reduce their revenues and are clearly responsible for the consequences of their actions; third, under independent legislation, the level of local public services is strongly connected to the level of local revenues. In this respect, independent legislation is also consistent with the definition of 'assignment' as 'the authority to design and implement policy' – Breton (1996) – as it provides subnational governments with a real taxing power and political accountability for their fiscal policies, an increasingly important element as discussed above. Rational tax assignment may thus help to increase accountability.

Independent legislation, however, has potential disadvantages, especially if different jurisdictions design tax structures that are radically different: duplication of administration, higher compliance costs and tax exporting, which may produce inequities and inefficiencies. Another potential demerit of independent legislation is predatory tax competition,

> [E]specially in the case when sub-national governments are free to set tax bases rather than tax rates, and may erode the tax base . . . competition among the US states and Canadian provinces to attract business and households . . . has resulted in the erosion of some tax bases and to an increased complexity of tax system, hence raising transaction costs. (OECD 2003, p. 153)

The second method of tax assignment consists of *surcharges*, where central and subnational governments levy the same tax. The latter impose surcharges on the tax base defined by the central government. In this case, the taxing power of subnational jurisdictions is lower than under independent legislation and lies in the choice of tax rates, sometimes within limits decided by central government, on their share of the total tax base. This method of tax assignment retains some of the benefits of the independent legislation method, such as transparency, administrative ease and simplicity, without giving rise to the problems discussed above. On the other hand, it may give rise to horizontal fiscal disparities, as revenues arise where economic activity occurs and incomes are generated. As discussed above, if a comparable amount of local public services must be offered by the different jurisdictions and hence financed, it may then require a grant system to reach fiscal equalization. Furthermore, it may enhance the vertical externalities problem we referred to above, given 'the interdependence of taxing decisions when different levels of government tax the same base. . . . What is certain is that such spillovers make it highly unlikely that the right level of taxation and expenditure will be found in any jurisdiction' (Bird 1999, p. 32). Problems also arise with regard to the attribution of the tax base to (the use of formulae to divide the tax base among) subnational jurisdictions, as it is often difficult to decide where a given income is generated. For instance, in the case of corporate income taxes, revenue is often attributed to the different jurisdictions according to some appropriation formula. These formulae, in turn, are usually not waterproof with respect to the strategic behaviour of jurisdictions.

Finally, tax sharing may assume two different forms. Subnational governments are entitled to a fraction of particular tax revenues arising in their jurisdiction or to a given percentage of nationwide tax receipts. This third method of tax assignment has some of the same merits as tax surcharges, but subnational governments have very limited fiscal autonomy, as they do not directly control the level of their own revenues. Furthermore, although there are methods to ease this problem,[15] tax sharing makes the revenues of one level of government dependent on the choices taken by another level of government; say, decisions by the centre about the tax bases or the tax rates of national taxes immediately impact on the receipts of lower-level governments. Hence, tax sharing is often more precisely considered a particular form of grant or subvention than a method of tax assignment.[16] Under wholly tax-sharing rules, local jurisdictions' fiscal autonomy is restricted to spending autonomy – decisions on how to spend a given amount of revenues – and subnational governments have no marginal source of own revenues.

As we argued in the Introduction, tax assignment methods should not be considered in isolation from the other sources of funding for local governments. Indeed, Table 12.2 demonstrates that grants and transfers represent an important source of revenue for subnational governments in most developed countries, with the ratio of intergovernmental grants over total subnational revenues varying considerably from country to country in a range from 15–20 per cent to 70–80 per cent.[17] Grant and transfer systems play several important roles. They may offset both *horizontal* fiscal and *vertical* fiscal imbalances. They may help to internalize spillover effects, and they allow the centre to influence the pattern of local expenditure. However, they may also interact with the fiscal autonomy of the local governments and the exercise of their tax autonomy. Interregional distributive mechanisms, aimed at reducing fiscal capacity disparities, for instance, may have negative effects on the tax efforts of both rich and poor communities (for example, Bordignon et al. 2001).

Which taxes are best suited for different levels of government?
Finally, the allocation of taxing power to subnational governments raises the question of which are the best taxes to be attributed at local level, on efficiency and distributional grounds. Earlier we hinted at several arguments that may induce a preference for one source of taxation over another.

The traditional theory of fiscal federalism (Musgrave 1983) suggests some guidelines in the field of subnational taxation. Subnational governments should impose *benefit taxes*, in the form of charges or quasi-charges to the beneficiaries as payment for public services, on the assumption that local jurisdictions are mainly concerned with resources allocation functions. 'Benefit taxation by sub-national governments does not distort the allocation of resources; indeed it contributes to an economic allocation of resources' (McLure 1999b, p. 14), so that an extensive use of user fees and charges, under which people pay for what they get, can help to promote efficiency. But there are two relevant obstacles for the implementation of benefit taxation. First, public goods and services provided by local governments often produce *generalized benefits*, which cannot be closely related to taxes on beneficiaries. Second, in practice subnational governments are often assigned redistributive functions and the latter, by definition, cannot be financed by benefit taxes. Furthermore, user fees and charges might not provide sufficient resources to finance local public expenditure, especially in those countries where decentralization of functions proceeds rapidly.

In most OECD countries, subnational governments rely on income and profit taxes as well as on consumption and property taxes. Which of these are best suited for subnational governments? The answer is not straightforward. We start by listing some desirable features for subnational taxation. Subnational taxes should not distort resource allocation, should not produce tax-exporting and predatory tax competition, should not produce vertical and horizontal fiscal imbalance, and should be easily administered and enforced. Indeed, there may not be any tax satisfying all these requirements.

Property taxes (on land and housing) are often considered one of the best sources of revenue for local jurisdictions and an appropriate instrument to provide subnational governments with a real taxing power. No relevant problems arise from differences in rates and administrative practices across jurisdictions, the tax base being immobile; there are relatively few problems of tax fraud and avoidance; and tax revenue is relatively stable and predictable. Tax-exporting problems may, however, occur '[to] the extent [that] its incidence is on land and capital that are owned by non residents' (McLure 1999b, p. 13). One demerit of property tax – at local as well as at national level – concerns the difficulty in determining the tax base, because of the difficulty in assessing land and housing value, with much room for discretion. Furthermore, because of limited liquidity problems, the elasticity of property tax revenue to nominal income increase appears to be low everywhere (OECD 2003).

As far as *income taxes* are concerned, personal income taxes are generally levied by central governments for redistribution and macroeconomic stabilization, but subnational governments often have access to revenues from these taxes, generally applying a surtax on the national income tax base, according to a residence principle (revenues are assigned to the residence jurisdictions). The attribution of personal income tax to subnational jurisdictions can also be justified on a benefit basis, if one thinks that local public services are used especially by resident households (education for children, social services, health care); in this sense, subnational personal income taxes are related to generalized benefits of public services and should be imposed at a flat rate. Furthermore, income taxes are often highly visible for taxpayers and hence may promote accountability. Two problems, however, should be stressed.

First, generally the income tax base is not evenly distributed across jurisdictions and poorer jurisdictions might not be able to raise sufficient revenues for financing a minimum standard of public services. This makes the case for supplementary equalization schemes in conjunction with the tax.

Second, in the presence of different local tax rates, if individuals (and incomes) are relatively mobile across jurisdictions, distortions may occur. For example, individuals may be stimulated to change their formal place of residence or move altogether to avoid the communities with higher tax rates. Note further that it is very unlikely that this induced tax mobility would satisfy a Tiebout type of efficient allocation, as many assumptions behind the Tiebout efficient equilibrium are not satisfied in practice. Thus, local personal income tax may have undesirable spillover effects.

Finally, when more than one level of government levies the personal income tax, some inefficiency may occur, as each government has no incentive to internalize the choice made by the other government (a vertical tax competition issue). For example, in the case of the Scandinavian countries, where personal income taxes are important sources of subnational revenue, the OECD (2003) provides evidence that this may have induced tax rates to rise at inefficiently high levels, with negative effects on labour supply decisions.

Profit taxes (corporate income tax or enterprises income tax) are not considered a good source of revenue for subnational governments. First, if production is relatively mobile, local profit taxes, applied at different rates, are likely to distort the location of economic activity, so distorting resource allocation. They might be levied at the local level only if investment is specific to the locality such that a firm cannot easily relocate (Feld and Schneider 2001) but this is an unusual case. Second, subnational profit taxes present the same problems that arise in an international setting, administrative difficulties, the possibility of tax exporting, and difficulty in the determination of the geographic source of corporate income. In fact, in the case of enterprises operating in more than one jurisdiction, it is necessary to divide the base of the enterprise income tax among the subnational jurisdictions where income is earned, often arbitrarily. In addition, corporate income tax revenue is subject to cyclical fluctuations and is not a stable source of revenue.

As far as *consumption taxes* are concerned, excises are well suited for subnational governments. They are easily administered at local level and minimize distortionary effects, if applied according to the destination principle (attribution of the revenue to the jurisdiction where consumption occurs). But if levied at different rates in different jurisdictions, abuses may occur, as it may be relatively easy to buy and pay the tax in a low tax rate jurisdiction and transport the products to a high-rate jurisdiction. The relevance of the problem is of course empirical, as it depends on the costs involved in this 'cross-border' shopping behaviour. Excises are also suitable for the implementation of the benefit principle when they are benefit related, such as excises on tobacco products and alcoholic beverages that could be used to finance health care, or taxes on motor vehicles and motor fuel, used to finance the construction and maintenance of roads.[18] But, as for user fees and charges, excises might not provide sufficient resources to finance local public expenditure:

> Indeed, although it is true that in countries such as the United States and Canada a significant proportion of state revenue comes from excises, it does not seem particularly desirable to tie state finances in any substantial way to such inelastic levies when the pressure on those finances for the most part come from very elastic expenditure demands for health and education. (Bird 1999, p. 13)

General consumption and sales taxes might be a good source of revenue for local governments. The value-added tax (VAT) is one of the most important sources of revenue in all developed countries (only the United States does not make use of VAT) and many countries use a share of VAT revenue as a financing tool for local governments (see above). However, in the vast majority of countries, VAT is applied only by the central government, which has the power to set up tax bases and rates. The role of local governments is limited in sharing some of the proceedings of VAT. This fits well with conventional wisdom, which maintains that VAT is not a suitable instrument for lower-level jurisdictions in a federal system (Keen 2000). In fact, most authors think that VAT is a bad own tax for subnational governments, for many reasons: the effects on trade between different jurisdictions, problems of tax fraud if applied according to the destination principle, problems of tax exporting and transfer pricing if applied according to the origin principle, high administrative and compliance costs, problems of compliance asymmetry (the obligations on taxpayers should be the same wherever in the federation they sell) and so on.

However, there is an increasing literature that challenges this conventional wisdom, arguing that, by suitably reorganizing the VAT system, this may in fact provide an excellent autonomous source for local taxation. Bird and Gendron (1998), for instance, suggest that central and local levels of government could maintain independent VAT, by simply harmonizing bases and to some extent rates. VAT could become a joint central–local tax, administered by either level of government on a jointly determined base, but with each government choosing its own tax rate (this is known as the dual VAT system). In the same vein, other, more sophisticated, proposals have recently been advanced for decentralizing the VAT system, mainly the VIVAT system (viable integrated VAT, advanced by Keen and Smith) and the CVAT (compensating VAT, proposed by Ricardo Varsano and developed by McLure in 2000). The VIVAT mechanism, originally proposed by Keen and Smith (1998) for eliminating enforcement and tax rate setting problems within the European Union, could well be extended to finance local jurisdictions. Under the VIVAT system, a distinction is made between sales to registered traders and sales to households and unregistered traders. VIVAT would apply to all sales to registered traders at a uniform union (or national) wide rate; national (or local) different VAT rates would instead apply to sales to households and unregistered traders.

The CVAT system was originally proposed for developing countries, such as Brazil and India, where there is a significant federal tax presence. Under the CVAT system, sales to local purchasers (registered traders, households and unregistered traders) would be subject to the local VAT, but sales to purchasers in other jurisdictions would be zero rated for central VAT and subject instead to a compensating VAT. Credit would be allowed for VAT paid on purchases by registered traders, for the local VAT on intrastate purchases and for the CVAT on interstate purchases.

Merits and demerits of the three alternative schemes are illustrated in Table 12.6, with respect to the more relevant issues. Tax rate setting autonomy is fully preserved only under the dual VAT system; under the VIVAT scheme, the tax rate applied to intermediate transactions is uniform and set by the central government, but VAT rates applied to sales at the retail stage are under the control of local jurisdictions; also under CVAT interjurisdictional exports are taxed at a rate that is out of jurisdiction control. As far as compliance cost symmetry is concerned, this is guaranteed only by VIVAT, since uniform procedures are applied to transactions within and between local jurisdictions, through the application of the same tax rate to all sales to registered traders whether or not they cross internal borders of local jurisdictions. So traders do not need to distinguish between their customers according to where they are located, and this is 'important precisely in order to get away from geography-based distinctions that are increasingly meaningless' (Keen and Smith 2000, p. 747). On the other hand, VIVAT presents the disadvantage that it would require a distinction to be made between sales to registered traders and sales to final consumers, since they would be taxed differently. This imposes additional compliance costs on business and additional administrative costs on tax authorities, which should account separately for these two categories of sale.

On the contrary, dual VAT appears to be superior to either CVAT or VIVAT in terms of administrative costs and simplicity, since it does not impose additional costs with respect to interjurisdictional trade (see Table 12.6).

Another relevant issue concerns collection incentives and clearing. Both CVAT and VIVAT would require that tax levied on exports from one jurisdiction be credited/refunded against tax due in another. There is therefore the need to introduce a *clearing* system, ensuring that revenue collected on exports from one jurisdiction is available to finance credit/refunds claimed in another. These incentive problems might be resolved by internalizing the

Table 12.6   Merits and demerits of dual VAT, CVAT and VIVAT

	Dual VAT	CVAT	VIVAT
Rate autonomy	Yes	Some	Some
Central rate setting	No	Some	Some
Collection incentive	Some	?	?
Compliance symmetry	No	No	Yes
Identify destination state	No	No	Yes
Administrative cost	Low	Higher	Highest?
Distinguish types of purchasers	No	Yes	Yes
Credit tracking	No	No	Yes
Excess credit	Few	Some	Yes
Needed administrative capacity	High	Low	High
Central agency	Yes	Yes	No

Source: Bird and Gendron (2000), p. 756.

transfers within a single administration that collects the tax and pays for the rebate.[19] In conclusion, both systems would require the presence of an overarching administration to guarantee appropriate clearing and do not distort collection incentives.

Finally, a reference should also be made to Bird (1999) who proposes to replace the various unsatisfactory state and local taxes imposed on business by a local low-rate value-added tax levied on the basis of income (production, origin) rather than consumption (destination). According to Bird, such a tax (BVT, business value tax) would be less distorting than subnational profits and capital taxes, more neutral (on the investment as well as on consumption) and more stable than the usual corporation income tax. Any problems that might occur with the BVT, such as for example tax competition or tax exporting, may be eased by appropriately setting floor and ceiling for the local tax rates. And indeed, Bird mentions the examples of some countries, such as Germany and Italy, which have introduced forms of BVT (respectively, *local trade tax*, *Gewerbesteuer*, and *regional business tax*, IRAP[20]) in their tax systems, in order to provide subnational governments with own additional revenues to finance local public expenditure.

Who should enforce local taxation?
The final point concerns the issue of administration of local taxation. Who should be in charge of administering and enforcing (local) taxation, the central or the local level? As usual, the literature does not provide clear-cut responses to this question (Ebel and Taliercio 2004); nevertheless, we shall briefly

survey the major merits and demerits of the centralized and decentralized models of tax administration.

As far as *efficiency* is concerned, the primary objective of the tax administration is to collect revenues at the lowest possible cost. On these grounds, most of the literature suggests assigning the function of tax administration to the central government, because of the existence of economies of scale[21] and scope, through which tax collection costs are minimized.[22] Furthermore, a centralized tax administration may provide some other advantages (Mikesell 2003):

- A centralized tax administration may reduce taxpayers, compliance costs, since it provides a single structure for dealing with all taxpayers throughout the country, and all taxpayers will be subject to exactly the same administrative rules and procedures; it also eliminates the possibility that the taxpayer will be confused about what tax organization is responsible for answering questions, receiving filings and enforcement.
- A centralized tax administration can help to reduce incentives to corruption, because of the larger possibility of rotation of personnel and the ability to pay higher salaries.[23]
- A central tax administration may afford more qualified personnel, allow personnel to specialize to a degree which is not feasible with smaller administrative units, and have budgets that permit the use of more sophisticated information technology.
- Finally, a national tax administration can be better equipped, legally and in terms of resources, to deal with national and global business entities and with taxable activities that cross regional or local jurisdiction boundaries within the nation.

What are the arguments instead in favour of decentralized tax administration and enforcement? They are several. Decentralizing tax collection and enforcement functions may help to enhance local government autonomy. Since the level of enforcement activity affects the level of taxes collected, a subnational government that had control over enforcement activities would be able to increase own revenues at the margin (Ebel and Taliercio 2004). Furthermore, a decentralized administration may help to enhance tax transparency and the accountability of subnational government officials to their constituencies. When tax administration of local taxes is decentralized, taxpayers know which government is levying what taxes and can hold the appropriate government accountable. In contrast, transparency can be lost when a central authority administers the tax levied by a lower level of government (Martinez-Vazquez and Timofeev 2005).

But perhaps the most relevant issue concerns the design of the organizational structure of tax administration and the incentives that it provides to tax officials. The question is whether a national administration would have the same incentives to collect local taxes than a local one. As Mikesell puts it: 'When higher governments . . . administer [local] taxes, there is the danger that administrators will give collection and enforcement of lower tier taxes less attention and lower priority than taxes levied by the higher tier' (2003, p. 9). In other words, local governments may have more forceful incentives to collect their own taxes than national officials.[24] On the other hand, if, for the reasons already stressed, local administration is likely to be less competent than central administration, the choice between national and local enforcement of local taxation is in reality a choice between indifference and incompetence (Dillinger 1991).

Of course, how these contrasting incentives can be reconciled in practice depends very much on the tax under consideration, and in particular on the type and the complexity of the tax structure. For instance, individual income taxes, corporate income taxes, value-added taxes and social security contributions are perhaps better administered at the central level, because of information externalities, cost structures, and the high skill levels required. On the other hand, property taxes or user charges may be more efficiently administered at the local level.

Finally, in assessing the case for local tax administration and enforcement, one should also consider the more general financing system of the local governments, as this may affect their incentives for tax enforcement. This is a point which we have raised several times in this chapter, but which is worth repeating again. In the presence of interjurisdictional redistribution mechanisms, for instance, local jurisdictions may have fewer incentives to collect taxes, as part of these revenues would be attributed to other jurisdictions or may reduce the grants received from the centre.[25] In general, one should expect that the incentives to collect local taxes will be the higher, the higher the degree of fiscal autonomy of the local government.

Summing up, there is no clear-cut recipe for the assignment of tax administration powers. This requires a fine balance among many conflicting criteria, and the recognition of several forms of constraints and political economy issues, in particular the alignment of the incentives of tax authorities with those of the government. These criteria and constraints may balance differently in different countries or regions, and with respect to different taxes (Martinez-Vazquez and Timofeev 2005).

Concluding remarks

Let us briefly summarize some of the main themes raised in this survey. On theoretical grounds, we have argued that there would be a role for local taxation even in a highly abstract world of identical regions and immobile and identical citizens, and that this role could only be enhanced by the presence of differences in local preferences and by the consideration of dynamic issues and commitment problems. Mobility, at least above a certain threshold, and inequality in resource endowments across territories, should instead be considered more correctly as constraints to be taken into account in the choice of the tax resources which should be offered at the local level. The recent literature, concerned with issues of accountability of local governments, certainly stresses more than in the past the role that transparency, visibility and autonomy should play in the setting up of local taxation and local tax enforcement.

We have also attempted to offer a review of the main tools which could be used to build up a local tax system, discussing the *form* that local taxation could take (own taxes, surcharges and tax shares), the *source* of tax bases which could be used for local financing (wealth, income, consumption, value added) and the issue of the *optimal tax assignment* of responsibility for tax administration and enforcement of local taxation. This part does not provide, nor should it be expected to, ready-to-make recipes for establishing local taxation; it is mainly a list of the several trade-offs that are unavoidably linked with all options. Furthermore, this part is burdened by the almost complete lack of convincing empirical evidence, both in terms of case studies and in terms of cross-country analysis. We have arguments and counterarguments, but very little empirical basis for establishing which is the right one. Nevertheless, some general themes emerge from this part of the survey. First, the most recent literature has finally come at to recognize that benefit taxation, although still an important component of local tax instruments, can have only a limited role in local taxation. Given what local governments actually do, and the administrative difficulty of setting up benefit taxation, other tax sources should also be considered.

In particular, there is a renewed interest in the literature for attempts to decentralize the VAT system, allowing tax rate autonomy at the local level for at least some component of the tax base, and for attempts to establish a local value-added business tax, raised at the production level on a larger base than profits only. Second, the debate on tax enforcement has finally left the traditional opposition (increasing returns to scale for central administration versus enhancing of local autonomy for the local one) to focus on the analysis of incentives that the different systems may provide to local governments and tax officials in collecting and enforcing local taxation. Here, again, the role of other funding mechanisms (grant system) in affecting these incentives should be emphasized.

Notes

1. To be sure, the Coase theorem tells us that under well-defined property rights assignment, bargaining across rational agents should lead to a complete internalization of any externality. However, the Coase theorem relies upon lack of transaction costs, symmetric information and enforceable agreements. All these assumptions are highly questionable in the present context.

2. Winer illustrates his point with reference to the very different evolution of taxing powers in two similar federations during the last century, Canada and Australia.
3. This of course implies that there is some spatial correlation among local economies, which seems, however, reasonable in the light of the fact that we are talking about local governments inside a single country.
4. And indeed most empirical investigations on yardstick competition focused on local taxation, with results broadly supporting the theory (Besley and Case 1995).
5. For households it may be complicated to move their place of residence without carrying their labour endowment with them. But this is not true for big corporations, for example.
6. Furthermore, yardstick and tax competition may conflict; local taxes on a wholly mobile tax base are less informative for the citizens than a tax on a less mobile factor.
7. The classical example is that of a tax levied on consumption, attributed to a local government, and a tax on labour income, given instead to the national government. But by the budget constraint of the individual taxpayer, the two tax bases are in reality very close, in particular for all those consumers who live on their labour income.
8. This was, for example, the conclusions in the paper by Boadway and Keen (1996).
9. This does not need to be the case. Indeed, there are several examples in the real world of 'different speed federalism'; that is, a situation where the tasks of regions or of lower-level governments are differentiated across the country. The *ex ante* distribution of resources may play a role in this differentiated assignment of functions; see, for example, the Spanish case in the 1990s (Garcia-Mila and McGuire 2005). Typically, weaker and poorer regions are more 'protected' by the centre, receiving more grants and more administrative support. In exchange, they have less autonomy.
10. Meaning that there are elements in the structure of individual preferences which more than compensate individuals for living in the poorer regions. Note that the sort of mobility needed would require, for example, full employment and no productive ability loss for moving elsewhere. In other words, we would be back to a Tiebout framework, where perfect mobility solves not only an efficiency problem but also an equity problem, in the sense that in equilibrium no individual is worse off for living in one region rather than in another.
11. Still, it is not clear what the notion of horizontal equity really means in a federal context. If one interprets it as meaning that no difference across identical individuals due to location choices is acceptable on ethical grounds, it is difficult to resist the impression that the only allocation compatible with perfect horizontal equity is one of perfect centralization, with no role left to local governments. The literature on fiscal federalism has always had serious problems coming to terms with the issue of horizontal equity in a territorial context; see Buchanan (1950) for an earlier attempt and Bordignon and Peragine (2005) for a more recent one.
12. In Italy, for instance, the per capita difference in income between the north and the south of the country is close to 100 per cent (almost 200 per cent for per capita value added); it is only around 30 per cent in terms of per capita consumption.
13. See, for instance, Persson and Tabellini (2000) on separation of powers and Bordignon et al. (2003) on lobbying.
14. With myopic governments, for instance, a crucial issue is whether the many efficiency results in the literature of fiscal federalism would still hold in an intertemporal setting, for instance with overlapping generations.
15. For instance, tax sharing may be computed in terms of a percentage of the *tax base* of the national tax rather than in terms of a percentage of the *tax revenue* of the same tax. This isolates local governments' resources from discretionary decisions taken at the central level about tax rates and tax allowances.
16. Again, it is a matter of degree. The key issue here is how discretional grants and tax sharing are on political grounds. Tax sharing of national taxes whose percentages are established at the constitutional level (as is the case, for instance, with VAT revenues in Germany) 'insures' the local government against the risk of adverse decisions taken at the central level more than grants which can be decided discretionally at the national level. In this case, grants and tax sharing do not coincide, although it is still true that tax sharing does not offer tax autonomy at the local level.

17. And it would have been even larger if we had considered developing countries; see, for instance, Kraemer 1997.
18. For a detailed analysis of vehicle-related taxes at the subnational level, see Bird (2000).
19. Under CVAT, the central authorities would collect the CVAT on interjurisdictional sales and credit it against central output tax liabilities; if central tax exceeds CVAT paid on inputs, the central authorities would provide refunds. Under VIVAT, incentive problems might be internalized by entrusting the administration of the intermediate rate to central authorities, all tax charged to registered traders would be paid to, and registered traders would claim all their credits and refunds from, the central authority.
20. The IRAP was challenged in the Constitutional Court in Italy and the European Court of Justice, and the government undertook to replace it (eds).
21. The available evidence from government budgetary information clearly indicates that the budget cost of collecting individual income, business income and sales taxes is generally in excess of 1 per cent of the revenues from these taxes, and can sometimes be substantially higher (Alm 1999, p. 17).
22. The question is whether the potential greater cost efficiency of a centralized approach to tax administration actually holds in reality. Unfortunately, there has been little empirical research on cost efficiency and economies of scale in tax administration, and there are practically no studies that have directly compared the centralized and decentralized approaches (Ebel and Taliercio 2005, p. 7).
23. But duplicate enforcement may provide a check against omissions when central and subnational administrations exchange information, and may make corruption more difficult because two sets of enforcement officials must be paid off.
24. Fees, that is, allowing the national government to retain a portion of the lower-tier tax it administers, may ease the problem, but are unlikely to solve it. See Martinez-Vazquez and Timofeev 2005, for a discussion.
25. Bordignon et al. (2001) model it in terms of an asymmetric information problem. If tax enforcement is attributed at the local level and at the same time there is an equalization mechanism in place, local jurisdictions may have an incentive to hide their true fiscal capacity, by reducing the effort level in collecting taxes.

Bibliography

Alm, J. (1999), 'Tax compliance and administration', in W.B. Hildreth and J.A. Richardson (eds), *Handbook on Taxation*, New York: Dekker, pp. 741–68.
Asian Development Bank (1999), *Fiscal Transition in Kazakhstan*, Manila: ADB.
Atkinson, P. and Van den Noord, P. (2001), 'Managing public expenditures: some emerging policy issues and a framework for analysis', OECD Economic Department Working Paper no. 485, Paris.
Bailey, S.J. (1999), *Local Government Economics: Principles and Practices*, Basingstoke: Macmillan.
Baker, P.J. and Gould, A.C. (2001), *Democracy and Taxation*, Notre Dame, IN: University of Notre Dame, Paris.
Besley, T. and Case, A. (1995), 'Incumbent behavior: vote seeking, tax setting and yardstick competition', *American Economic Review*, 85(1), 25–45.
Besley, T. and Coate, S. (2003), 'Centralized versus decentralized provision of local public goods: a political economy approach', *Journal of Public Economics*, 87, 2611–37.
Bird, R.M. (1999), 'Rethinking sub-national taxes: a new look at tax assignment', International Monetary Fund, WP/99/165, Washington, DC.
Bird, R. (2000), 'Subnational revenues: realities and prospects', in S.J. Burki and G. Perry (eds), *Decentralization and Accountability of the Public Sector*, Annual World Bank Conference on Development in Latin America and Caribbean, 1999, Washington, DC: World Bank, pp. 319–39.
Bird, R.M. and Gendron, P. (1998), 'Dual VATs and cross-border trade: two problems, one solution?', *International Tax and Public Finance*, 5, 429–42.
Bird, R.M. and Gendron, P. (2000), 'CVAT, VIVAT, and dual VAT: vertical "sharing" and inter-state trade', *International Tax and Public Finance*, 7, 753–61.

Boadway, R. and Keen, M. (1996), 'Efficiency and the optimal direction for federal state transfers', *International Tax and Public Finance*, **3**, 137–55.

Bordignon, M. (2005), 'Fiscal decentralization: how to harden the budget constraint', paper presented at the EU Commission Workshop 'Fiscal Surveillance in EMU: new issues and challenges', Brussels.

Bordignon, M., Colombo, L. and Galmarini, U. (2003), 'Fiscal federalism and endogenous lobbies' formation', Quaderni dell'Istituto di Economia e Finanza, no. 52, Catholic University of Milan.

Bordignon, M., Manasse, P. and Tabellini, G. (2001), 'Optimal regional redistribution under asymmetric information', *American Economic Review*, **91**(3), 709–23.

Bordignon, M. and Peragine, V. (2005), 'Horizontal equity in a regional context', mimeo, Catholic University of Milan.

Bordignon, M. and Turati, G. (2005) 'Bailing out expectations and health expenditure in Italy: an empirical approach', manuscript, Catholic University of Milan.

Brennan, G. and Buchanan, J. (1980), *The Power to Tax: Analytical Foundations of a Fiscal Constitution*, Cambridge: Cambridge University Press.

Breton, A. (1996), *Competitive Governments: An Economic Theory of Politics and Public Finance*, Cambridge, New York: Cambridge University Press.

Buchanan, J.M. (1950), 'Federalism and fiscal-equity', *American Economic Review*, **40**, 583–99.

Cerniglia, F. (2003), 'Decentralization in the public sector: quantitative aspects in federal and unitary countries', *Journal of Policy Modeling*, **25**(8), 749–76.

Cremer, H. Fourgeaud, Leite-Mointeiro, V.M., Marchand, M. and Pestieau, P. (1996), 'Mobility and redistribution: a survey', *Public Finance/Finances Publiques*, **51**, 325–52.

Dahlby, B. and Wilson, L.S. (1994), 'Fiscal capacity, tax effort, and optimal equalization grants', *Canadian Journal of Economics*, **27**(3), 657–72.

Dillinger, W. (1991), *Urban Property Tax Reform*, Washington, DC: World Bank.

Ebel, R.D. and Taliercio, R. (2004), 'Subnational tax policy design and administration in transition and developing economies', paper presented at the International Symposium on Fiscal Decentralization in Asia revisited, 5–6 November, Hitotsubashi University, Kunitachi, Tokyo.

Ebel, R.D. and Yilmaz, S. (2002), 'On the measurement and impact of fiscal decentralization', World Bank, Policy Research Working Paper 2809, Washington, DC.

Edwards, J.S.S. and Keen, M. (1996), 'Tax competition and Leviathan', *European Economic Review*, **40**, 113–34.

Esteller-Morè, A. (1999), 'The politics of tax administration: evidence from Spain', Working Paper, Institut d'Economia de Barcelona (IEB).

Feld, L.P. and Schneider, F. (2001), 'State and local taxation', in R. Liesenfeld, J.F. Richard, N.J. Smelser and P.B. Baltes (eds) (2001), *International Encyclopedia of the Social and Behavioral Sciences*, Oxford: Elsevier, p. Bd 12.

Garcia-Mila, T. and T.J. McGuire (2005), 'Fiscal decentralization in Spain: an asymmetric transition to democracy', in R.M. Bird and R. Ebel (eds), *Subsidiarity and Solidarity: The Role of Intergovernmental Relations in Maintaining an Effective State*, Cheltenham, UK and Northampton, MA, USA: Edward Elgar.

Gordon, R.H. (1983), 'An optimal taxation approach to fiscal federalism', *The Quarterly Journal of Economics*, **98**, 567–86.

Gordon, R.H. (1986), 'Taxation of investment and savings in a world economy', *American Economic Review*, **76**, 1086–102.

Hettich, W. and Winer, S.L. (1984), 'A positive model of tax structure', *Journal of Public Economics*, **24**, 67–87.

Hettich, W. and Winer, S.L. (1997), 'The political economy of taxation', in D.C. Mueller (ed.), *Perspectives on Public Choice: A Handbook*, Cambridge: Cambridge University Press, pp. 481–505.

Hettich, W. and Winer, S.L. (2000), *Democratic Choice and Taxation: A Theoretical and Empirical Analysis*, Cambridge: Cambridge University Press.

Heyndels, B. and Vuchelen, J. (1998), 'Tax mimicking among Belgian municipalities', *National Tax Journal*, **51**(1), 89–101.

Hines, J.R. Jr (2000), 'What is benefit taxation?', *Journal of Public Economics*, **75**, 483–92.

Jourmaud, I. and Kongsrud, P.M. (2003), 'Fiscal relations across government levels', OECD Economic Department Working Paper no. 375, Paris.

Kanbur, R. and Keen, M. (1993), 'Jeux sans frontières: tax competition and tax coordination when countries differ in size?', *American Economic Review*, **83**(4), 877–92.

Keen, M. (1998), 'Vertical tax externalities in the theory of fiscal federalism', IMF Staff Papers, **45**(3), 454–85.

Keen, M. (2000), 'VIVAT, CVAT, and all that: new forms of value-added tax for federal systems', International Monetary Fund, WP/00/83, Washington, DC.

Keen, M. (2002), 'Some international issues in commodity taxation', IMF Working Paper WP/02/124, Washington, DC.

Keen, M. and Kotsogiannis, C. (2002), 'Does federalism lead to excessively high taxes?', *American Economic Review*, **92**(1), 363–70.

Keen, M. and Smith, S. (1998), 'The future of the value added tax in the European Union', *Economic Policy*, **23**, 375–471.

Keen, M. and Smith, S. (2000), 'Viva VIVAT!', *International Tax and Public Finance*, **7**, 741–51.

Kornai, J., Maskin, E. and Roland, G. (2003), 'Understanding the soft budget constraint', *Journal of Economic Literature*, **41**(4), 1095–136.

Kraemer, M. (1997), 'Intergovernmental transfers and political representation: empirical evidence from Argentina, Brazil and Mexico', Inter-American Development Bank, Working Paper 345.

Lockwood, B. (2000), 'The assignment of powers in federal and unitary states', Warwick Economics Research Paper Series 580, Department of Economics, University of Warwick.

Lockwood, B. (2004), 'Decentralization via federal and unitary referanda', *Journal of Public Economic Theory*, **6**, 79–108.

Ma, J. (1997), *Intergovernmental Fiscal Transfers: A Comparison of Nine Countries (Cases of the United States, Canada, the United Kingdom, Australia, Germany, Japan, Korea, India, and Indonesia)*, Washington, DC: World Bank, Economic Development Institute.

Martinez-Vazquez, J. and Timofeev, A. (2005), 'Choosing between centralized and decentralized models of tax administration', Andrew Young School of Policy Studies, Working Paper 05-02, Georgia State University.

McLure, C.E. Jr (1999a), 'Tax assignment', in *Fiscal Transition in Kazakhstan*, Manila: Asian Development Bank, Chapter 8, pp. 273–316.

McLure, C.E. Jr (1999b), *The Tax Assignment Problem: Conceptual and Administrative Considerations in Achieving Subnational Fiscal Autonomy*, Washington, DC: World Bank.

McLure, C.E. Jr (2000), 'Implementing subnational value added taxes on internal trade: the compensating VAT (CVAT)', *International Tax and Public Finance*, **7**, 723–40.

McLure, C.E. Jr (2001), 'The tax assignment problem: ruminations on how theory and practice depend on history', *National Tax Journal*, **54**(2), 339–63.

Mikesell, J. (2003), 'International experiences with administration of local taxes: a review of practices and issues', paper prepared for the World Bank Thematic Group on Taxation and Tax Policy, Washington, DC: World Bank.

Musgrave, R.A. (1959), *The Theory of Public Finance: a Study in Public Economy*, New York: McGraw-Hill.

Musgrave, R.A. (1983), 'Who should tax, where, and what?', in C.E. McLure, Jr (ed.), *Tax Assignment in Federal Countries*, Canberra: Centre for Research on Federal Financial Relations, Australian National University, in association with the International Seminar in Public Economics; distributed by ANU Press. pp. 2–19.

Norregard, J. (1997), 'Tax assignment', in T. Ter-Minassian (ed.), *Fiscal Federalism in Theory and Practice*, Washington, DC: International Monetary Fund, pp. 42–79.

Oates, W.E. (1972), *Fiscal Federalism*, New York: Harcourt Brace Jovanovich.

Oates, W.E. (1999), 'An essay on fiscal federalism', *Journal of Economic Literature*, **37**, 1120–49.

OECD (1994), *State Budget Support to Local Governments*, OCDE/GD(94)116, Paris.

OECD (1997), *Managing across Levels of Government. Part one: Overview*, Paris: OECD.

OECD (1999), *Fiscal Decentralization: Benchmarking the Policies of Fiscal Design*, Paris: OECD.

OECD (2001), *Fiscal Design Across Levels of Government: Year 2000 Surveys*, Directorate for Financial, Fiscal and Enterprise Affairs, Paris: OECD.

OECD (2002), *Fiscal Decentralization in EU Applicant States and Selected EU Member States*, Centre for Tax Policy and Administration, Paris: OECD.

OECD (2003), 'Fiscal relations across levels of government', *Economic Outlook*, **74**, 143–60.

OECD (2004), *Tax Administration in OECD Countries: Comparative Information Series (2004)*, Forum on Tax Administration, Paris: OECD.

Persson, T. and Tabellini, G. (2000), *Political Economics: Explaining Economic Policy*, Cambridge, MA: MIT Press.

Profeta, P. (2005), 'The political economy of taxation and tax reforms', in L. Bernardi, M.W.S. Chandler and L. Gandullia (eds), *Tax Systems and Tax Reforms in New EU Members*, London: Routledge, pp. 55–75.

Rodden, J.A. (2002) 'The dilemma of fiscal federalism: grants and fiscal performance around the world', *American Journal of Political Science*, **46**, 670–87.

Rodden, J.A. (2005), *Hamilton's Paradox: The Promise and Peril of Fiscal Federalism*, Cambridge, New York: Cambridge University Press.

Rodden, J.A., Eskeland, G.S. and Litvack, J. (eds) (2003), *Fiscal Decentralization and the Challenge of Hard Budget Constraint*, Cambridge, MA: MIT Press.

Salmon, P. (2003), 'The assignment of powers in an open-ended European Union', CESifo Working Paper no. 993, Munich.

Smart, M. (1998), 'Taxation and deadweight loss in a system of intergovernmental transfers', *Candian Journal of Economics*, **31**(1), 189–206.

Thießen, U. (2003), 'Fiscal decentralization and economic growth in high-income OECD countries', *Fiscal Studies*, **24**(3), 237–74.

Varsaro, R. (2000), 'Substantial taxation and the treatment of interstate trade in Brazil: problems and a proposed solution', in S.J. Burki and G. Perry, *Decentralization and Accountability of Public Sector*, Washington, DC: World Bank.

Wellich, D. (2000), *The Theory of Public Finance in a Federal State*, Cambridge, New York, Cambridge University Press.

Wildasin, D.E. (2004), 'Competitive fiscal structures', paper presented at the International Institute of Public Finance conference on 'Fiscal and regulatory competition', Milan, 23–26 August.

Winer, S.L. (2000), 'On the reassignment of fiscal powers in a federal state', in G. Galeotti, P. Salmon and R. Wintrobe (eds), *Competition and Structure: The Political Economy of Collective Decisions*, New York: Cambridge University Press, pp. 150–73.

13 Tax competition in a federal setting
John D. Wilson

Introduction

Early models of tax competition, developed by Wilson (1986) and Zodrow and Mieszkowski (1986), were based on Oates's (1972, p. 143) insight that, 'In an attempt to keep taxes low to attract business investment, local officials may hold spending below those levels for which marginal benefits equal marginal cost'. The basic source of the inefficiency in these models has been called a 'horizontal tax externality': a rise in one region's tax rate causes mobile capital to relocate to other regions, benefiting them because their tax bases contain this capital. This view of tax competition is not without controversy. In particular, there is now a literature on welfare-improving tax competition, much of it based on the notion that this competition leads governments to behave more efficiently than they would in its absence. See Wilson (1999) for a recent review of the various approaches to modeling tax competition.

One relatively recent development has been the construction of tax competition models that contain an important role for a central government. This role introduces a new externality, known as a 'vertical tax externality'. If the central government and lower-level governments share the same tax base, then an increase in the taxation of this base by one level of government may lower the size of this base for the other level of government. In other words, higher tax rates now create negative externalities, which tend to lead to excessive taxation. We can therefore no longer say that local taxes and expenditures are too low.[1]

Whereas vertical tax externalities tend to increase local taxes and expenditures, their impact on central government behavior depends on the central government's objectives. In this chapter, I consider two views. First, the central government is a welfare maximizer, where welfare encompasses the well-being of all regions. Second, central government behavior is described by a political process that prevents it from operating efficiently. This chapter will begin with the first approach. Even here, however, the central government is likely to be constrained in its ability to eliminate inefficiencies at the local level. I identify three potential problems: limitations on the available forms of policy intervention, informational asymmetries, and the inability of the central government to commit to policies prior to the actions taken by lower-level governments. Throughout the chapter, I focus mainly on efficiency issues, though income distribution problems are briefly discussed.

As a vehicle for analysing tax competition in a federal system, I use a model based on the models recently developed by Janeba and Wilson (2003) and Wilson and Janeba (2005). The next section describes the horizontal and vertical externalities in this model, and the third section investigates the use of intergovernmental transfers to achieve an efficient equilibrium. The fourth section describes the inefficiencies that arise when such transfers are not possible, and the following two sections examine how these inefficiencies can be mitigated by appropriately allocating public spending responsibilities between the two levels of government. The second of these two sections also replaces the assumption of a welfare-maximizing central government with an inefficient political process for designing expenditure programs at the central level. The final section contains some conclusions and extensions. Throughout the chapter, the analysis is limited to competition for mobile capital. Other types of competition, such as for individual firms or shoppers, are not considered here, though some of the same insights apply to these cases.

Horizontal and vertical externalities in an illustrative model

Consider a country that is initially divided into identical regions, meaning that their size, production technologies and residential population are all alike. Assume also that decision making within a region can be modeled as though it is controlled by a single representative resident. This resident possesses endowments of labor and capital, which are supplied to competitive firms. Capital is treated as mobile across regions, which means that it is allocated across regions until the after-tax return on capital, r, is everywhere equal. In contrast, labor is treated as immobile. Following the standard Zodrow–Mieszkowski (1986) model, assume that these firms produce output that is purchased by the representative resident as a final consumption good, or by the region's government and transformed into public goods that benefit the resident. Examples of such public goods might include schools and police protection. Unlike Zodrow–Mieszkowski, however, there may exist many such public goods, which are imperfect substitutes from the resident's viewpoint. Another departure from Zodrow–Mieszkowski is that capital is not only mobile across regions within the country, but also between the country and the rest of the world. Thus, the after-tax return, r, is determined on international markets. Alternatively, the country described here may be reinterpreted as an economic union consisting of many, but not all, countries, such as the European Union (EU).

Now a critical assumption in this model is that each region's public good expenditures are financed by a tax on the capital employed within its borders. By modeling such a tax, I conveniently capture the fact that modern tax systems do tax mobile factors at source to some degree.[2] By assuming that both the regional governments and the central government employ such a tax,

I may also model the shared tax base that gives rise to vertical externalities, as described above. For the central government, the tax base is all capital within the country's borders, summed across all regions.

I shall assume that the central government also supplies public goods. Thus, the representative resident in a region may be thought of as obtaining utility from the private good, a set of regionally-provided public goods, and a set of centrally-provided public goods.

The problem confronting a region's government is to choose the unit tax rate on capital, t_i for region i, to maximize the representative resident's utility, subject to a budget constraint requiring that tax revenue equals public good expenditures. Tax revenue is expressed, $t_i K(r + T + t_i)$, where T is the central government's tax rate and $K(r + T + t_i)$ is a capital demand schedule, describing the relation between the capital employed by firms in the region and the before-tax return on capital, $r + T + t_i$. As this before-tax return rises, K falls.

For now, let us treat foreign governments as passive, in the sense that they tax capital at exogenously given rates. We may then look at the tax competition game played within the 'home country'. Again following Zodrow–Mieszkowski, assume that the regional governments use taxes as their strategy variables in a simultaneous-move Nash game; that is, each region chooses the tax rate that is optimal from its viewpoint, given the tax rates chosen by the other regions and the central government. A critical issue will be whether the central government's tax rate is chosen at the same time as the regions' rates. If this is the case, the central government is simply another player in this simultaneous-move game. Alternatively, the central government may be assumed to choose its tax rate prior to the regional decisions. Using common terminology, the central government is then a Stackelberg leader, giving it a strategic advantage over regional governments because it can influence their policy choices through its own choices. For now, I assume that the central government can anticipate exactly how regional governments respond to its choices.[3]

With taxes serving as the strategy variables, public good levels adjust to satisfy the government budget constraints. Alternatively, we could treat the public good levels themselves as strategy variables, with taxes adjusting to satisfy these constraints. See Wildasin (1988) for a discussion of how the choice of the strategy variables affects the equilibrium for the system of regions.

Regardless of whether the central government is a Stackelberg leader, regions treat the central government's tax as fixed when making their decisions. Their choices are then characterized by the horizontal and vertical externalities described above. When one region increases its tax rate, firms in the region reduce their demands for capital. To restore equilibrium in the capital market, the after-tax return, r, must fall enough to induce other regions to demand more capital, though this fall in r will be tiny if the region is tiny.[4] Thus, capital will be reallocated away from this region and into both other regions of the home country and also the rest of the world. This means that a rise in one region's tax rate has two important effects: it increases the capital used by other regions, but it reduces the country's total capital. In symbols, a rise in t_i raises the sum of $K(r + T + t_j)$ over all j not equal to i, but it lowers the sum of $K(r + T + t_j)$ over all j, including j equal to i. The first effect is the horizontal externality: a rise in region i's tax increases the availability of capital to other regions. If there were no other sources of inefficiency, this 'positive externality' would cause region i to set its tax rate too low from the viewpoint of the entire country. By equating the marginal benefit of public good provision to the marginal cost, measured from its viewpoint, it would be ignoring the benefits other regions receive from the greater availability of capital.

On the other hand, the fall in the sum of all $K(r + T + t_j)$, denoted $\Sigma_j K_j$ for short, is the vertical externality, because this sum represents the tax base for the central government. With a lower tax base, the central government must lower its provision of public goods to lower-level governments, thereby harming other regions. In the absence of other sources of inefficiency, this 'negative externality' would cause regions to set their tax rates too high. With the two externalities possessing opposite signs, we cannot say whether public good provision is too high or too low.[5]

There is yet a third potential source of inefficiency in this model. As already noted, a rise in one region's tax rate reduces the after-tax return, r, required to clear the world capital market. If the country as a whole is a net importer of capital, the lower r represents a lower price that must be paid to foreigners for imports of capital. All regions benefit from this lower price of imports, implying a positive externality. As with the horizontal externality, this consideration tends to produce inefficiently low tax rates. On the other hand, the sign of the externality would be reversed in the case of a capital-exporting country. I refer to this third source of inefficiency as the 'terms-of-trade effect'.

To conclude, these three considerations fail to all work in the same direction, so public goods may be under- or oversupplied at the regional level. The question then is what the central government can do about the resulting inefficiency.

Central government intervention
Consider now a central government whose objective is to maximize welfare, summed across all regions (that is, the sum of the utilities of the representative residents). I start by investigating the circumstances under which the central government is able to intervene in a way that eliminates the inefficiencies described above. Then I consider more restricted forms of intervention.

Assume first that the central government has access to intergovernmental transfers. In particular, it is able to transfer revenue between its treasury and the treasuries of the regional governments (that is, 'lump-sum transfers'). The crucial implication of this assumption is that the central government can undo any inefficiencies in the division of capital tax revenue across the two levels of government. Consequently, it need only set its tax rate T so that the combined rate, $T + t$, is set at the welfare-maximizing level for the country as a whole (where t is the common tax rate set by all regions in a symmetric equilibrium), while using revenue transfers to ensure that the allocation of revenue between the two levels of government supports the efficient division of public expenditures between these levels. Although t itself may be influenced in various ways by the vertical and horizontal externalities, what matters for the country as a whole is the combined tax rate, $T + t$, not t itself. Essentially, the use of intergovernmental transfers links the budget constraints of the two levels of government, so that only the combined tax rate matters.

Note also that it does not matter whether the central government plays a Stackelberg or Nash game with the regions. In both cases, it may choose T to ensure that $T + t$ is optimally set. Thus there is no tax competition problem.

These conclusions contrast with Wildasin's (1989) analysis of a 'corrective subsidy' for eliminating the inefficiencies from tax competition. This subsidy is levied by the central government on a region's revenue from capital taxation, tK, and its purpose is to eliminate the horizontal externality. But in Wildasin's model, the central government does not provide public goods or tax capital itself. With $T = 0$, the value of t alone matters, and the central government must be a Stackelberg leader to optimally influence this value. Moreover, it must supplement its corrective subsidy, imposed at some flat rate, s, on tK, with a lump-sum tax on regional governments that raises the revenue needed to finance s. In the current model, only the lump-sum transfer is needed, not the subsidy, since only $t + T$ matters. Interestingly, Boadway and Keen (1996) demonstrate that optimality may require that the transfer go from regions to the central government, not in the opposite direction. Although they use a somewhat different model, similar considerations appear to apply here.

Central government intervention obviously becomes more complicated when regions differ in important ways, such as differences in their production technologies or consumer preferences for public goods. In this case, income distribution considerations become important. Welfare maximization for the country as a whole requires that t_i be identical across all regions, since otherwise the allocation of capital would be distorted. The central government cannot generally satisfy this requirement, using only its uniform tax on capital and intergovernmental transfers. Rather, additional policies are needed, such as Wildasin's corrective subsidy, or a corrective tax if the vertical externalities are sufficiently important. But this subsidy/tax must generally differ across regions to induce them to choose the same tax rate. Note, finally, that the central government must be a Stackelberg leader to implement such policies.

Clearly, a policy of tailoring subsidies to the individual characteristics of regions imposes large information requirements on the central government. Recognizing these requirements, Bucovetsky et al. (1998) and Dhillon et al. (1999) have analysed forms of central government intervention where the central government is not able to observe important differences between regions and therefore must confront them all with the same subsidy schedules.[6] In this case, the optimal form of central government intervention will generally allow regional tax rates to differ. Although the central government could essentially mandate that all regions set the same tax rate, it would then lose its ability to redistribute income across these regions in desirable ways, given its lack of information about how they differ. Essentially, some regions obtain 'information rents', reflecting the central government's informational disadvantage.

We now return to the case of identical regions. The use of intergovernmental transfers to achieve an efficient equilibrium has been emphasized by Hoyt (2001), using a model with commodity taxation rather than capital taxation. An added complication here is that governments face multiple tax bases, one for each taxed commodity. If the central government has access to the same tax bases available to regional governments, then efficiency can be obtained. Once again, only the combined tax rate matters (one for each commodity), given that intergovernmental transfers are possible. If the central and regional governments use different tax bases, however, then the central government may not be able to offset inefficiencies in the regional tax systems.

A nice example of these principles, provided by Hoyt, is the federal subsidies provided to housing by the US federal government, combined with high rates of taxation on housing by local governments. He observes, 'While high rates at one level and subsidization at another level may seem perverse, they may reflect the optimal response by state and federal governments to local tax rates on housing far above what would be optimal' (p. 510).

No intergovernmental transfers

If intergovernmental transfers are not available, then the regional and central tax rates matter separately, rather than the combined tax rate, since the budget constraints of the two governments are no longer linked. Regional taxes, along with regional public good levels, may be too high or too low, depending on the relative strength of the vertical and horizontal externalities.

To understand the considerations involved here, let us consider the extreme case where not only are regions within the country small, but the country itself is small relative to the rest of the world. In this case, there are no horizontal externalities. When one region raises its tax rate, capital is reallocated from the region to the rest of the world, not to other regions. Thus, these other regions fail to benefit from one region's increase in its tax rate. On the other hand, there is certainly a vertical externality, because regions and the central government continue to share the same tax base, which declines when any one of them increases its tax rate. To see the problem, start with a Nash equilibrium for the tax competition game played among regions, and suppose that all regions simultaneously reduce their tax rates. Then capital will flow into the country, because the cost of capital has declined. (There are no terms-of-trade effects, because r is fixed under the small-country assumption.) As a result, centrally provided public good supplies will rise, benefiting all regions. This benefit represents the vertical externality. When only a single region lowers its tax rate, it fails to account for the externality, because the benefit of increased tax revenue at the central level is spread among all regions. For a tiny region, no single region benefits much from this externality, but it is still important when summed over many tiny regions.[7]

To conclude, small countries are characterized by only vertical externalities, implying that regions overtax capital and provide inefficiently high levels of public goods. At the other extreme, consider a country that is closed to cross-border capital movements, as would be the case if the home country under consideration actually represented the entire world economy. In this case, there exists only a horizontal externality, since the tax base for the entire country is fixed. The standard result that tax competition leads to the under-provision of public goods then applies.

Thus, the size of a country matters for whether horizontal or vertical externalities dominate. Keen and Kotsogiannis (2002) reach similar conclusions, but for a model of a closed economy where the supply of capital is given by an upward-sloping supply curve for savings. If the supply of savings is sufficiently elastic, then the vertical externality dominates, whereas the horizontal externality dominates if the savings supply is independent of the net interest rate. These results correspond to the current small- and large-country assumptions.[8]

Keen and Kotsogiannis also extend the analysis by adding the possibility that regions tax the returns on their fixed factor at 100 per cent (interpreted as economic rent in their model). In this case, the horizontal tax externality dominates. This result may be understood by considering the case of many small regions, each facing an infinitely elastic supply of mobile capital. In this case, a single region would not choose to tax capital, because doing so would actually cause its revenue to decline, through the negative impact of the tax on economic rent. Since the supply curve is finite for the nation as a whole, however, regions could raise additional revenue while creating only second-order deadweight losses, if they all simultaneously taxed capital by a small amount.

We now turn to central government behavior. If both the central and regional governments choose their tax rates simultaneously, then a welfare-maximizing central government will clearly choose the T that is efficient from the viewpoint of the entire nation, given the (inefficient) taxes chosen by regions. But if the central government enjoys a first-mover advantage, then its choice of T can be used to influence regional tax choices. The marginal impact of T or regional taxes has been found to be theoretically ambiguous, turning this issue into an empirical matter. Hayashi and Boadway (2001) find the relation to be negative for business taxes in Canada: lower federal taxes lead to higher provincial taxes. This study suggests that if regional taxes are too low, then the central government should undertax business income, causing regions to respond by raising their taxes.

Optimal federalism: strategic considerations

The relative sizes of the vertical and horizontal externalities should also depend on the relative sizes of the different levels of government, measured by their share of total expenditures on public goods. For an economy with many public goods, the vertical externality will not be important if the central government provides only a small number of these goods. This idea has been exploited by Wilson and Janeba (2005), who consider the possibility that a country might manipulate the division of public goods between the two levels of government in a way that gives it a strategic advantage in tax competition with foreign rivals.

To illustrate this idea, consider a world economy consisting of a home country and a foreign country, each divided into several identical regions, as before. Assume that both central governments and the regional governments all play a Nash game in tax rates, and let the combined tax rates of each country (denoted $T + t$ above) be strategic complements: that is, an increase in one country's combined tax rate leads to a rise in the other country's combined tax rate. In other words, reaction curves slope up, as illustrated in Figure 13.1.[9] Now suppose that before this game is played, each country can choose which public goods are supplied at the central level, and which are supplied locally. To isolate strategic issues, Janeba and Wilson assume that all public goods enter consumer utility functions in a symmetrical way, and that public good provision is characterized by constant returns to scale. Thus, there is no reason for a particular public good to be supplied centrally or locally, other than for the strategic considerations analysed here. Moreover, these considerations dictate only the fraction of public goods supplied at each level of government, not which particular goods are supplied.[10]

The basic insight from this model is that the central government will desire to increase the share of public goods provided centrally to the point where the vertical externality dominates the horizontal externality. Doing so will raise

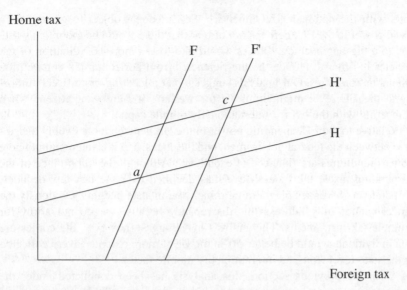

Figure 13.1 Home and foreign reaction curves

the country's combined tax rate, which graphically means that its reaction curve will shift up, as shown by the shift in the curve from H to H′ in Figure 13.1, where curve H is defined for the case where the two externalities offset each other (or where the central government controls all public good provision, implying no externalities). As a result, the equilibrium moves up the foreign's reaction curve, F, raising foreign's tax rate (ignore curve F′ for now). The higher foreign tax rate benefits home, since it tends to encourage a reallocation of capital from foreign to home. Of course, foreign has the same incentive to raise its reaction curve. When both choose their optimal levels of centralization, curves H′ and F′ represent the home and foreign reaction curves, and the equilibrium shifts from point *a* to point *c*. Wilson and Janeba (2005) show that both countries are better off in this new equilibrium, since public goods are underprovided at point *a*, from the viewpoint of the world economy.

The stylized model described here may hold some lessons in the context of capital mobility within and across the US and the EU. Both areas have central and regional governments, and at the same time there is a fair amount of investment across the Atlantic. In general, debates over fiscal federalism in the EU and the US typically ignore aspects of international capital mobility. Thus, our analysis provides new arguments for these debates.

For example, in the EU most of the existing spending and taxing power rests with the national governments.[11] Some people object to giving more fiscal power to the EU, perhaps out of fear that there would be too much waste due to a big bureaucracy. Others would like to see more coordination of tax policies in order to reduce the inefficiencies from horizontal tax competition among nation states. Our analysis suggests that allocating more fiscal authority to the EU level might improve the welfare of European citizens when competing with the US for internationally mobile capital.

Relative to the EU, spending power in the US is much more evenly distributed between the federal government and the states. Yet it is interesting to note how expenditures are financed at each level. Although the importance of the corporation tax at the federal level has declined over the last few decades, corporate tax revenues play a more minor role in state budgets. Obviously the model cannot fully address this discrepancy because we do not allow for multiple tax instruments. The analysis may suggest, however, the conjecture that individuals would be better off in the US if more revenues were collected at the state level from the internationally mobile factor.

As in the previous section, this analysis has been conducted under the assumption that intergovernmental transfers are not available. In the current context, one possible justification for this assumption is that such transfers might be misused, due to imperfections in the political processes, whereas the design of the federal system involves constitutional arrangements that are perhaps less easy to manipulate in undesirable ways. Moreover, this design is less easily changed, so that a government is better able to use it as a commitment device for gaining a strategic advantage over foreign rivals in competition for internationally mobile capital. Once inefficiencies in political processes are recognized, however, we must ask whether these inefficiencies provide a reason for decentralizing public good provision. This issue is investigated next.

Optimal federalism: inefficient central governments

The analysis so far has treated central government behavior as efficient, focusing instead on the central government's role in correcting inefficiencies caused by tax competition at the regional level. In practice, however, the political processes that determine central government policies are characterized by separate inefficiencies. This section shows how the trade-off between inefficiencies and the central and regional level lead to a theory of optimal fiscal federalism. The analysis is based on Janeba and Wilson (2003).

Once again, the issue is how to allocate spending responsibilities and taxing powers between the central and lower-level governments. One of the more prominent approaches, originally put forward by Oates (1972), views central provision of public goods as characterized by inefficient uniformity across regions, whereas cross-border spillovers of public good benefits create inefficiencies under decentralized provision. Oates's decentralization theorem states that decentralization is preferable in the absence of spillovers. In a related approach, Besley and Coate (2005) also view public goods as being inefficiently allocated across localities under centralization. But by giving careful attention to the exact form of legislative bargaining and strategic delegation under centralization, their approach yields inefficiencies involving the unequal distribution of public good expenditures. In a complementary paper, Lockwood (2002) also compares the benefits from centralization relative to decentralization. He shows that legislative outcomes under centralization are not sufficiently sensitive to the within-region benefits of the public projects that are being allocated across regions. The results in both papers suggest that spillovers must be sufficiently small for decentralization to be more efficient than centralization.

Following Besley and Coate, let us view centralization as generating inefficient interregional differences in the provision of public goods. In particular, these differences result from the control of the central government's legislature by a 'minimum winning coalition' (MWC), consisting of representatives from $(N + 1)/2$ of the N regions in the country.[12] In contrast, regions are characterized by inefficiencies from tax competition, as modeled above. I again impose the simplifying assumption that regions are identical, but I also fix the supply of capital in the country (that is, no international mobility), so that there are no vertical externalities. With only horizontal externalities, regions tend to undersupply public goods, and this inefficiency must be traded off against the inefficiencies created by the decision making of the MWC at the central level.

Public goods and taxes are modeled as in the previous section; that is, there are many public goods,[13] they are all financed by taxing capital, there are no scale economies, and public goods affect consumer utility in a symmetric manner. Thus, the issue again is what fraction of public goods should be provided centrally, rather than locally. I now assume that the central government moves first, anticipating the subsequent behavior of regional governments. The central government is assigned a set of particular public goods to provide, the question being how many of these public goods should belong to this set. I assume that the central government may vary the levels of its public good supplies across regions, as in Besley and Coate, but that a uniform tax on the nation's capital is employed (denoted T above). After this provision is determined, regional governments then provide their own public goods. In addition, they may supplement any deficiencies in the supplies of centrally-provided public goods.

The resulting equilibrium is easily understood. The regional taxes generate horizontal externalities, resulting in the underprovision of public goods. By contrast, the central government has the advantage of taxing capital at a uniform rate across regions, which does not distort the allocation of capital.

But the MWC favors providing its public goods only to the members of the MWC, or 'insider regions'. Since part of the cost of this public good provision is financed by taxing the 'outsider regions', the MWC has an incentive to raise the levels of public goods supplied to insider regions beyond their efficient levels. Thus, there are two types of inefficiencies at the central level: public goods are inefficiently distributed across regions, and those regions that do receive these public goods are oversupplied with them from an efficiency viewpoint.

The question then is what fraction of public goods should be centrally provided, if the objective is to maximize total welfare, summed across regions.[14] While the exact answer will depend on a detailed description of consumer preferences and production technologies, some general observations may be provided. First, Janeba and Wilson (2003) demonstrate that it is always desirable to decentralize some public goods; that is, it is never optimal for all public goods to be centrally provided. The explanation involves a well-known property of distortionary taxes: the deadweight losses from small taxes are only second-order, not first-order. Intuitively, when the set of public goods provided by regional governments is small, the tax rates needed to finance them are small as well, and hence the efficiency losses from tax competition are small as well. As a result, a small amount of decentralization dominates complete centralization, under which all public goods would be overprovided to the MWC. In contrast, a small amount of decentralization might not be beneficial if there were cross-border spillovers of public good benefits.

The argument is more involved than this intuition suggests, since the asymmetric treatment of regions inside and outside the MWC gives rise to interregional capital flows and general equilibrium changes in the after-tax return on capital. But these additional considerations do not normally alter the main insight. Decentralizing a fraction of public goods means that insider regions must raise their tax rates, causing capital to flow to outsider regions. Since outsider regions have the higher tax rates, given the lack of help from the central government in public good provision, capital is therefore flowing from low- to high-tax regions, which represents an efficiency gain.

In contrast to the desirability of some decentralization, it is possible that no central provision is optimal. In particular, a low substitution elasticity between labor and capital in production implies that taxes have little impact on the allocation of investment, making the tax competition problem relatively unimportant. But with a sufficiently high substitution elasticity, the welfare-maximizing federal structure involves both centralized and decentralized public good provision.

Janeba and Wilson (2003) also consider cases where public goods are characterized by region-specific fixed costs, which differ across these goods. It is then optimal for the central government to provide those public goods with relatively high fixed costs. The basic idea is that tax rates must be increased by relatively large amounts to provide such goods, creating relatively large horizontal externalities.

This last result may explain the strong financial support that the federal government in Germany is constitutionally obliged to give (Article 91a and b Grundgesetz) for the construction and renovation of universities as well as general research institutions (see Bundesministerium für Bildung und Forschung). Under this arrangement, the costs are split in half between German *Länder* and the federal government. The financing concerns only investment expenses (including university medical clinics and procurement of equipment above a minimum threshold level) but not operating expenses (like wages or rents). Since the former can be considered fixed costs, the German federal government helps out where the *Länder* alone would not be able to support such institutions.

Concluding remarks

As described above, much of the literature on tax competition in a federal system has focused on the trade-off between horizontal and vertical externalities. More recently, Wilson and Janeba (2005) have argued that the federal system can be designed in a way that influences the relative strengths of these externalities. Interestingly, this design (which involves specifying the division of public good provision between the different levels of government) works not so much by reducing the size of horizontal and vertical externalities, but rather by offsetting one against another until their net effect is optimal (but non-zero, given their use as a strategic device in this model). The analysis therefore departs quite dramatically from the first-best analysis of externalities, which says that they should be targeted directly with the appropriate subsidies or taxes. Instead, it points to the value of analysing different externalities together, rather than in isolation, and designing a federal system that optimally controls their net impact.

Whereas the tax policies of lower-level governments are characterized by horizontal and vertical externalities, policies at the central level are subject to different types of inefficiencies, depending on the political process. I have characterized optimal fiscal federalism as involving a trade-off between these different sets of policies. Future work in this area should examine more closely the political processes that characterize decision making at the central level. In Besley and Coate (2005) and Janeba and Wilson (2003), centrally provided provided public goods are unequally allocated across regions in an inefficient way. In contrast, Oates (1972) emphasizes inefficient uniformity in their provision. Both approaches have validity, perhaps depending on the nature of different public goods, but more research is needed to produce models that combine elements of both approaches. The paper by Lockwood (2002), mentioned above, represents a useful step in this direction.

Even if a central government were concerned about the welfare of all regions, it would still be at an informational disadvantage when trying to regulate the behavior of lower-level governments. I have mentioned papers by Bucovetsky et al. (1998) and Dhillon et al. (1999), which explicitly incorporate informational asymmetries into tax competition models, but more work needs to be done in this area, particularly on how these asymmetries arise and persist.

In contrast to central government behavior, regional governments have been assumed throughout this chapter to act in the best interest of their representative citizen. But for the same reason that central government is inefficient, one might expect that further decentralization of regional decisions to even lower levels of government would be beneficial. It would be interesting to examine under what conditions the typical three-tier government structure, consisting of federal, regional and local governments, emerges as an optimal response to the trade-off between the benefits and costs of decentralization.

Finally, future research should more thoroughly examine the implications of different federal structures for the distribution of income. In the model considered in the previous section, centralization helps regions inside the minimum winning coalition at the expense of outsiders. Thus, the analysis suggests that centralization has the potential to worsen the distribution of income. In contrast, a theme of the local public economics literature is that distributional policies should be centralized, given the limitations that factor mobility places on the ability of lower-level governments to redistribute income. While these limitations are certainly important, the type of model considered above highlights the potential for bad politics at the central level to lead to capricious changes in the distribution of income.

Notes

1. Wilson's (1999) survey contains some discussion of vertical externalities, but Keen (1998) devotes an entire survey to this issue. This chapter builds on Keen's informative survey, emphasizing some more recent contributions.
2. Wilson (1999) reviews several papers that extend the standard tax competition model to include multiple tax instruments. See, in particular, Bucovetsky and Wilson (1991).
3. Yet another possibility, not considered here, is that the central government chooses its tax rate after the choices made by the regional governments. A richer model might build on this order of moves by modeling the lobbying efforts undertaken by regional governments to influence the central government's choices.
4. I assume that the supply of capital is fixed for the entire world economy, though it is mobile between the country considered here ('home') and the rest of the world.
5. Throughout this chapter, the expenditures financed by public goods are assumed not to affect tax bases. Dropping this assumption would create the possibility that higher regional taxes actually increase total tax revenue at the central level, due to complementarities between the central government's tax base and public expenditures at the regional level. Dahlby (1996) emphasizes the variety of forms that vertical externalities may take. In the

current set-up, one possibility would be that regional governments use their tax revenue to finance public inputs, which enhance the productivity of capital, thereby potentially more than offsetting the disincentive effects of the taxes used to finance these inputs.

6. Both of these papers assume that regions have access only to a tax on mobile capital for financing public goods, as assumed here. In contrast, Raff and Wilson (1997) assume that labor is mobile, rather than capital, and they examine the optimal form of intervention by a central government when the purpose of this intervention is to improve the distribution of income.

7. Another example of this type of large-numbers externality would be automobile congestion, where adding one car to a road slows down other cars by only a tiny amount, but the externality is still important because a large number of cars are being slowed down.

8. In an interesting follow-up paper, Keen and Kotsogiannis (2004) demonstrate that intensified tax competition, represented by a rise in the number of regions, must lead to lower welfare, regardless of which type of externality dominates.

9. This case is often assumed, but reaction curves may also slope down in tax competition models.

10. Wilson and Janeba (2005) assume a continuum of public goods, which is a convenient approximation because it allows them to treat this fraction as a continuous variable.

11. The EU budget is about 1 per cent of member countries' GDP, whereas national government spending at all levels is often in the range of 40–50 per cent of national GDP.

12. This concept has been used by Buchanan and Tullock (1962), Riker (1962) and Baron and Ferejohn (1989). Qualitatively similar insights would be obtained by instead assuming that more than a simple majority is required to pass a fiscal package. A higher threshold level, or supermajority requirement, would increase the attractiveness of centralization in the current model.

13. More accurately, Janeba and Wilson (2003) again assume a continuum of public goods, as a convenient approximation.

14. This objective would coincide with the maximization of each region's expected welfare, if the regions were randomly selected for inclusion in the MWC, and this decision was made after the design of the federal system.

References

Baron, D. and J. Ferejohn (1989), 'Bargaining in legislatures', *American Political Science Review* **83**, 1181–206.

Besley, T. and S. Coate (2005), Centralized versus decentralized provision of local public goods: a political economy analysis', *Journal of Public Economics* **87**, 2611–37.

Boadway, R. and M. Keen (1996), 'Efficiency and the optimal direction of federal–state transfers', *International Tax and Public Finance* **3**, 137–55.

Buchanan, J. and G. Tullock (1962), *The Calculus of Consent*, Ann Arbor, MI: University of Michigan Press.

Bucovetsky, S., M. Marchand and P. Pestieau (1998), 'Tax competition and revelation of preferences for public expenditure', *Journal of Urban Economics* **44**, 367–90.

Bucovetsky, S. and J.D. Wilson (1991), 'Tax competition with two tax instruments', *Regional Science and Urban Economics* **21**, 333–50.

Bundesministerium für Bildung und Forschung, http://www.bmbf.de.

Dahlby, B. (1996), 'Fiscal externalities and the design of government grants', *International Tax and Public Finance* **3**, 397–412.

Dhillon, A., C. Perroni and K.A. Scharf (1999), 'Implementing tax coordination', *Journal of Public Economics* **72**, 243–68.

Hayashi, M. and R. Boadway (2001), 'An empirical analysis of intergovernmental tax interaction: the case of business income taxes in Canada', *Canadian Journal of Economics* **34**, 481–503.

Hoyt, W.H. (2001), 'Tax policy coordination, vertical externalities, and optimal taxation in a system of hierarchical governments', *Journal of Urban Economics* **3**, 491–516.

Janeba, E. and J.D. Wilson (2003), 'Optimal fiscal federalism in the presence of tax competition', unpublished manuscript, Michigan State University.

Keen, M. (1998), 'Vertical tax externalities in the theory of fiscal federalism', *International Monetary Fund Staff Papers* **45**, 454–84.

Keen, M. and C. Kotsogiannis (2002), 'Does federalism lead to excessively high taxes?', *American Economic Review* **92**, 363–70.

Keen, M. and C. Kotsogiannis (2004), 'Tax competition in federations and the welfare consequences of decentralization', *Journal of Urban Economics* **56**, 397–407.

Lockwood, B. (2002), 'Distributive politics and the costs of centralisation', *Review of Economic Studies* **69**, 313–38.

Oates, W. (1972), *Fiscal Federalism*, New York: Harcourt Brace Jovanovich.

Raff, H. and J.D. Wilson (1997), 'Income redistribution with well-informed local governments', *International Tax and Public Finance* **4**, 407–28.

Riker, W. (1962), *The Theory of Political Coalitions*, New Haven, CT: Yale University Press.

Wildasin, D.E. (1988), 'Nash equilibria in models of fiscal competition', *Journal of Public Economics* **35**, 393–421.

Wildasin, D.E. (1989), 'Interjurisdictional capital mobility: fiscal externality and a corrective subsidy', *Journal of Urban Economics* **25**, 193–212.

Wilson, J.D. (1986), 'A theory of interregional tax competition', *Journal of Urban Economics* **19**, 296–315.

Wilson, J.D. (1999), 'Theories of tax competition', *National Tax Journal* **52**, 269–304.

Wilson, J.D. and E. Janeba (2005), 'Decentralization and international tax competition', *Journal of Public Economics* **89**, 1211–29.

Zodrow, G.R. and P. Mieszkowski (1986), 'Pigou, Tiebout, property taxation, and the underprovision of local public goods', *Journal of Urban Economics* **19**, 356–77.

14 Intergovernmental redistributive transfers: efficiency and equity

Robin Boadway[1]

Introduction

It can be argued that from the perspective of their fiscal policies, governments are primarily institutions for redistribution. Although some of their expenditures could be considered public goods or infrastructure, a large share of them serve redistributive purposes. A pervasive feature of countries with multiple levels of government is the decentralization of policy instruments for redistribution combined with the use of transfers from upper to lower levels of government to achieve redistributive objectives. Subnational governments – whether states or provinces with independent fiscal authority in federations, or regional or local governments in unitary-type countries – assume significant responsibility for providing public services in areas of health, education and welfare, but rely heavily on transfers from the center to finance their spending. The fact that many of these decentralized public services serve important redistributive functions gives these vertical transfers an important equity role *per se*. But more than that, transfers to subnational governments are also typically highly redistributive horizontally in the sense that they compensate for differences in fiscal capacity of the recipient jurisdictions. This chapter explores the economics of redistributive intergovernmental transfers, their rationale, their effects and their design.

Intergovernmental transfers come in a variety of forms. Some are explicitly redistributive in the sense that their amounts are contingent on some characteristic of the recipient jurisdiction, such as its needs for finance or the size of its tax bases. Others are only redistributive when taken together with their financing. Thus, transfers that are equal per capita to all jurisdictions are none the less implicitly redistributive if financed out of federal general revenues because the latter come disproportionately from jurisdictions with higher per capita tax bases. Some transfers may have a matching component, perhaps for incentive reasons or to reflect need. The extent to which conditions on the use of funds are imposed and enforced can differ as well. And, their aggregate size may be determined by federal discretion, by a formula-based escalator, or as part of a revenue-sharing arrangement. Yet, despite these differences, there are enough common features, and some well-enough established principles, to warrant studying redistributive transfers in generic terms.

The literature on the redistributive role of intergovernmental transfers is far from comprehensive, and there is nowhere near a consensus on their optimal design. It will serve as a useful set of caveats to state at the outset the sources from which the lack of consensus stem. The first and most obvious source of disagreement is the fact that when dealing with redistributive objectives, value judgments are required and rational people can disagree over those. The value judgments involve the usual equity criteria involved in redistribution, but the disagreements here may be less than for interpersonal redistribution policies because they tend to rely relatively more on horizontal as opposed to vertical equity arguments. The main arguments for intergovernmental fiscal equalization apply whatever the desired extent of vertical redistribution pursued in the interpersonal sphere. At the same time, equity arguments can become more clouded in a federal context to the extent that different subnational governments pursue different redistributive policies within their own jurisdictions. A major problem in the design of redistributive transfers is how to deal with that heterogeneity.

A second source of disagreement, one which applies to all policy problems, is that the effect of intergovernmental transfers on resource allocation is not readily predicted as an empirical matter. For example, we do not know how responsive labor and capital are to changes in intergovernmental transfers. This is relevant since some of the equity arguments for intergovernmental transfers depend on the extent to which there are real output consequences resulting from transfers. Indeed, there are parallel efficiency arguments for redistributive intergovernmental transfers that complement equity arguments, and that rely on the interregional mobility of economic activity.

Third, and perhaps the hardest to resolve, is the fact that economic decision makers in a federation include subnational governments themselves, and we are a long way from understanding their behavior. In particular, the case for intergovernmental transfers – and for the redistributive role of government more generally – depends upon one's view of the benevolence of governments. At one extreme, one might view governments as fully benevolent and acting faithfully in the interests of their constituents. At the other, governments may be viewed as self-serving and aggrandizing, unaffected by the disciplines of the political system.

Roughly speaking, those who put more weight on equity, who are more sanguine about the efficiency costs of redistribution, and who take a more benevolent view of government will take a more positive view of the role of intergovernmental transfers, and the vertical fiscal gap that they entail, as a means of achieving national equity and efficiency objectives. But, consensus is unlikely. Moreover, given the complicated nature of government decisions and of equity objectives themselves, there will be a distinct lack of precision about the appropriate design of intergovernmental transfers. Various practical considerations will turn out to be important. This implies that the role and design of intergovernmental transfers is as much an art as a science, although principles derived from theoretical models can certainly be informative.

Decentralization and intergovernmental transfers

Broadly speaking, there are two prevailing views of the primary purpose of decentralization. One, associated with Tiebout (1956) and Oates (1972), is that the primary function of local governments is to provide local public goods. Decentralization allows different localities to choose different tax-expenditure mixes that better reflect local preferences for public goods. Moreover, it allows households to migrate to the locality whose fiscal policies best suit them, thereby contributing to efficiency in the allocation of households across localities. Localities provide local public goods to reasonably homogeneous local populations, and finance them using taxes that approximate the benefit principle. In this Tiebout–Oates world, there is limited need for intergovernmental grants for redistributive or other purposes. To the extent that the Tiebout–Oates model has validity – especially its emphasis on interjurisdictional mobility – it can either temper or enhance the role of transfers, as we shall see.

The second view largely sets aside differences in preferences and in the mobility of households among states, and argues that decentralizing the provision of public services is beneficial because it enhances the efficiency with which these services can be targeted to those who need them and can be designed to accommodate local circumstances. The efficiency gains come from various sources, such as local informational advantages, accountability, a reduction in agency costs, political and yardstick competition, and incentives to innovate. It is this second view of the purpose of decentralization that provides the rationale for the use of intergovernmental transfers for equity purposes.

The argument is not a formal one, and can be put succinctly as follows.[2] In actual federations, the expenditures of subnational governments – what we shall from now on refer to as 'state governments' – are typically of the same order of magnitude as those of the national government, but the nature of the expenditures differs in important ways. The lion's share of state expenditures consists of public services in the areas of health, education and welfare, as well as targeted transfers. What one might think of as local public goods in the Tiebout–Oates tradition are much less significant. These public service and targeted transfer expenditures serve mainly equity purposes of one sort or another: equality of opportunity in the case of education, social insurance in the case of health care, and income redistribution in the case of welfare and targeted transfers. While the national government may also engage in redistributive fiscal policies through its tax-transfer and social protection systems, some of the most important policy instruments are devolved to the state level of government. Moreover, the mere fact that state public services are financed out of general revenues while being targeted to needy households implies that they are redistributive in effect: benefit taxation clearly does not apply at either the state or national levels of government. As mentioned, a case can be made for the decentralization of public service provision on efficiency grounds: states are better able to provide these services to their residents in a way that reflects the needs and circumstances of the state. At the same time, the efficiency case for decentralizing revenue-raising authority is less compelling. On the contrary, there are both administrative and efficiency gains from the national government dominating revenue raising for broad-based taxes.

These features of decentralization have important consequences for the system of intergovernmental fiscal arrangements. To the extent that it is desirable to provide comparable levels of public services throughout the federation, decentralization by itself will thwart that desire. Different states will inevitably have different needs for public services since the distributions of their populations by need groups will differ. They will also have different capacities to raise revenues. States with higher than average tax bases will be able to raise more revenues at given tax rates than other states. Moreover, these differences in revenue-raising capacity will be higher the more decentralized is revenue raising. As well, to the extent that redistribution is regarded as a national as opposed to a state objective, the federal government would want common standards of redistribution to apply: persons in comparable circumstances should have access to comparable public services in all states. This suggests that there should be some common standards of public services that should apply nationwide. How precise those common standards should be depends on how much weight one puts on the national versus the state dimension of redistribution.

The system of federal–state transfers is one instrument by which the federal government can ameliorate these consequences of decentralization for equity. Indeed, transfers may be the least intrusive way of ensuring that the benefits of decentralization are achieved without violating national equity objectives. Equalizing transfers can counter the tendency for decentralization of public service provision and taxes to cause disparities in need and fiscal capacity. Conditional transfers can be used to provide an incentive – the carrot and/or the stick – for states to design their public service programs to abide by national standards. In the following sections, we explore those roles of transfers in more detail.

Federal–state transfers serve more than redistributive roles. They might also be used to enhance the efficiency of the federal economy.[3] Matching grants can be used to provide an incentive for states to choose their expenditure programs in a way that takes account of any spillover benefits to residents of other states. Conditions imposed on grants can be used to induce provinces to design their programs so that they do not interfere with the efficiency of resource allocation across states. The size of the vertical gap can be chosen to minimize the ability or incentive of the states to engage in wasteful tax competition or to use tax bases that are not harmonized with those of other states. These efficiency factors will serve to enhance the need for federal–state transfers. Of most importance for our purposes, efficiency considerations will call for similar types of redistributive intergovernmental transfers as equity ones. Put simply, if different states have different fiscal capacities, then in the absence of corrective measures, states with above-average fiscal capacity will be able to provide any given level of public services at lower tax rates than states with below-average fiscal capacity. Otherwise similar households residing in the two states will obtain different fiscal benefits from their state governments. These differences will provide an incentive for households to migrate from one state to another based not on their productivity, but on differences in the fiscal capacity of the states. Such an incentive, which does not exist in a centralized nation, gives rise to inefficiencies in the allocation of resources among states. Correcting for this incentive will involve federal–state redistributive transfers of a similar pattern to those based on equity objectives. We shall consider this argument in more detail below.

Finally, the equity arguments for intergovernmental transfers become clouded once we take actual state decision making into account. A useful, though hypothetical, benchmark case is the so-called unitary nation outcome. If all states and their residents had common preferences, a system of intergovernmental transfers that offset differences in fiscal capacities and needs would replicate the outcome of a hypothetical unitary nation. Residents of a given type would incur the same taxes and receive the same benefits from public expenditures no matter where they resided, as if all public services were provided by a single national government. However, if state preferences for taxes and expenditures differ, perhaps because of differences in preferences across states, a unitary nation outcome will not be achieved by a system of transfers alone. Under these circumstances, the design of intergovernmental transfers necessarily becomes ambiguous. The desire to achieve national standards of redistribution must be traded off against the desire of state governments to exercise their discretion on behalf of their constituents, and some compromise must be reached. This kind of ambiguity will have to be taken into account when we consider the actual design of the system of intergovernmental transfers.

With this background, we now turn to the main arguments for intergovernmental transfers. These include three equity arguments and one efficiency argument. To make the equity arguments in the starkest way, we assume that households are immobile among states. The issue of mobility is taken up when we consider the efficiency argument.

First equity argument: fiscal equity

A consequence of fiscal decentralization is that households in otherwise identical circumstances are treated differently depending on their state of residence: horizontal equity is violated by the fiscal system.[4] There are two distinct sources of this violation. First, as emphasized above, the decentralization of public service provision and revenue-raising responsibilities results in differences in the states' ability to provide given levels of public services at comparable tax rates. Needs for public services differ as do taxing capacities. In a unitary nation, a common national tax system is used to finance a common public service program, implying some implicit cross-subsidization of public services among states. Second, states may choose different fiscal policies. The public services they provide and the progressivity of their tax structures will differ, so there will be different standards of redistributive equity implemented implying that persons in given circumstances are treated differently. One objective of the system of transfers might be to restore a degree of horizontal equity by undoing some of these consequences of fiscal decentralization.

The use of transfers to deal with horizontal inequities resulting from decentralization depends on the weight one attaches to horizontal equity across states as a national policy objective. In fact, horizontal inequity is not an innocuous assumption for various reasons. Even in a unitary nation setting, horizontal equity is an ambiguous objective at best since it involves being able to compare utility levels of households. As is well known, if persons have different preferences, this is not easy to do without making a strong value judgment.[5]

The issues that arise in a federalism setting are over and above that, and are somewhat different. The first is that horizontal equity may be violated by social welfare maximization applied to the federation as a whole, say, by a unitary national government. If there are state public goods whose benefit to each household depends on the size of the state population, social welfare maximization will result in otherwise identical households being treated differently in states with different populations.[6] Imposing horizontal equity would constrain the government from maximizing social welfare. By the same token, if the costs of providing public services differed from one location to another (for example, urban versus rural locations), it would not be socially optimal to treat likes in like ways. These conflicts of horizontal equity with social welfare maximization may lead one to abandon full horizontal equity as a policy objective in favor of a social welfare criterion. If so, one would not want to use federal–state transfers to compensate different states for differences in the ability to provide comparable levels of public services due to economies of scale either in the benefits of public services or in costs of provision. In what follows, we often assume these kinds of problems away by supposing that public services are private in nature and that the cost of providing them does not vary across states.[7]

Even assuming away these conflicts between horizontal equity and national social welfare maximization, horizontal equity applied to a federation poses some further difficult issues. One is that, even if they have the same fiscal capacities, states may well choose different tax-expenditure mixes, which will result in equals being treated unequally across states. In principle, this might be corrected by a complicated set of federal policies that treat households differently in different states. However, implementing such a policy – even if it were feasible – would violate an essential principle of federalism: the autonomy of decentralized decision making, an implication of which is that subnational governments should be able to choose policies that best suit their circumstances. One way out of this is to design a set of transfers that equalizes the capacity of different states to achieve horizontal equity for their citizens – that is, to replicate the policies that would be adopted by a unitary national government – without compelling them to do so. To distinguish this from full horizontal equity, we shall refer to it as 'fiscal equity'.

The objective of fiscal equity seems to represent a reasonable compromise between horizontal equity and the decentralized decision making that is a basic characteristic of federalism. But, a final difficult issue arises with applying even this weaker form of horizontal equity in a federal setting. A major source of horizontal inequity in a federation, as we have pointed out, is the difference in the ability of states to provide common levels of public services at comparable tax rates, as would be done in a unitary nation, and as would be required to satisfy horizontal (or fiscal) equity. Decentralization will imply that different states will have different revenue-raising capacity (for example, tax-base sizes) and different needs for public services. In these circumstances, insisting on the applicability of fiscal equity across states in a decentralized federation involves an underlying value judgment that may well not reflect the consensus in the federation. Put simply, fiscal equity involves an underlying judgment that households of a given type should be given equal weight from an equity point of view no matter where they reside. That is, 'solidarity' or 'social citizenship' should apply at the level of the nation rather than the state.

Accepting this judgment for fiscal equity implies that the differences in tax capacity and needs should be fully compensated by federal equalizing transfers, that is, resources from better-off states should be transferred to those of less well-off states so that comparable public services could potentially be delivered in all states using comparable tax systems. Whether or not such a level of national solidarity exists is a matter for societal consensus, and that consensus may be less robust the bigger are the differences in fiscal capacity across states, the more persistent they are, the less opportunity there is to migrate from one state to another, and the more heterogeneous are residents in different states with respect to culture, ethnicity, political culture and so on. To the extent that such a consensus does not exist, the fiscal equity case for inter-governmental transfers is reduced.

Implementing fiscal equity: a simple model

Assume that a consensus does exist for full fiscal equity to be applied nation-wide. To illustrate the type of equalizing transfers that fiscal equity might call for, consider a very simple model of a federation consisting of two states with given populations, n_i ($i = 1, 2$). In each state, there is a distribution of house-holds by personal income level. Let m_i^j be the income of a person of type j in state i, and $\bar{m}_i = \sum_j m_i^j / n_i$ be the average income in state i. Income as used here includes both earnings and asset income. Each state also has a stock of asset wealth, which can comprise both reproducible capital and natural resources, and can be owned at home or abroad. Suppose these assets generate total returns b_i in state i. For simplicity, assume that b_i is fixed, although the argu-ment does not require that. State i provides a public service, which is private in nature, and which accrues in equal amounts g_i to all households in the state. In the absence of federal transfers, the public service is financed by a state tax on residents' income at the proportional rate t_i and a state tax on asset returns at the rate θ_i. (Any after-tax returns from asset ownership are included in household income.) The former is typically referred to as a residence-based tax and the latter as a source-based tax. The budget constraint of state govern-ment i is therefore:

$$g_i = t_i \bar{m}_i + \theta_i b_i / n_i = t_i \bar{m}_i + \theta_i \bar{b}_i, \tag{14.1}$$

where $\bar{b}_i$ is per capita asset income generated in state i.

We can then define the *full income* of a household of type j in state i, y_i^j, as follows:

$$y_i^j \equiv (1 - t_i) m_i^j + g_i = m_i^j + \text{nfb}_i^j, \tag{14.2}$$

where $\text{nfb}_i^j = g_i - t_i m_i^j$ is the *net fiscal benefit* of a household of type j in state i. It represents the monetary value of public services received less state taxes paid for this household.

Horizontal equity requires that any two persons who are equally well-off in the absence of government continue to be so after government intervention. In the context of the above simple model, two persons with identical market incomes, $m_1^j = m_2^j = m^j$, should have identical full incomes, $y_1^j = y_2^j$.[8] This, in turn, requires that $\text{nfb}_1^j = \text{nfb}_2^j$. It is clear that this will not be satisfied in the absence of federal compensating transfers. To see this, note that from the definition of nfb_i^j in (14.2), for households of given income m^j, $\Delta nfb^j \equiv nfb_1^j - nfb_2^j$ $= g_1 - t_1 m_1^j - g_2 + t_2 m_2^j$, or using (14.1):

$$\Delta nfb^j = t_1 \bar{m}_1 - t_2 \bar{m}_2 - m^j(t_1 - t_2) + \theta_1 \bar{b}_1 - \theta_2 \bar{b}_2. \qquad (14.3)$$

In general, $\Delta nfb^j \neq 0$ in this simple model, and moreover $\Delta nfb^j \neq \Delta nfb^k$ for any two income types of households j and k. Three sources of nfb differences can be identified in (14.3). First, differences in average incomes between states gives rise to nfb differences: states with higher average incomes have a greater capacity to raise revenues. Similarly, differences in per capita assets, and therefore per capita asset returns, in the two states gives rise to differences in the ability to raise revenues using source-based taxes. And, finally, differences in tax rates t_i and θ_i give rise to differences in net fiscal benefits.

As (14.3) indicates, correcting for horizontal inequities arising from differences in revenue-raising capacity can be insuperably complicated. Since Δnfb^j differs not only between pairs of states but also across types of individuals, full horizontal equity would involve a complicated set of differential transfers between different types of individuals. However, matters can be simplified considerably if both states levy the same tax rates, $t_1 = t_2 = t$, $\theta_1 = \theta_2 = \theta$, since in that case (14.3) reduces to:

$$\Delta nfb = t(\bar{m}_1 - \bar{m}_2) + \theta(\bar{b}_1 - \bar{b}_2). \qquad (14.3')$$

Now, nfb differences, Δnfb^j, are the same for households of all income types j. In this case, a single intergovernmental per capita equalizing transfer between states can eliminate nfb differences among all households. The equalization transfer to state 1, denoted E_1, would take the following form:[9]

$$E_1 = \frac{n_1 n_2}{n_1 + n_2} [t(\bar{m}_2 - \bar{m}_1) + \theta(\bar{b}_2 - \bar{b}_1)], \qquad (14.4)$$

with an analogous expression applying for state 2. This equalization scheme effectively fully equalizes differences in per capita tax revenues between states. If such a scheme is in place, the level of public services and the tax rates in each state would replicate those that would be enacted in a unitary state (ignoring, of course, any differences in efficiency with which states may be able to provide public services).

The equalizing transfer characterized by (14.4) applies when the scheme is a so-called 'net equalization scheme'. That is, it is self-financing in the sense that transfers to the state with the low fiscal capacity is just offset by transfers *from* the other state. However, the same effective equalization can be achieved by a 'gross equalization scheme', which avoids making negative transfers to any state and which has the same real effect. Under a gross system, the federal government levies a nationwide tax and uses the proceeds to make differential transfers to each state based on their fiscal capacity. For example, the federal government could simply levy a tax of τ per person nationwide and use the proceeds to transfer an amount $E_i + n_i\tau$ to each state, where E_i satisfies (14.4). The federal tax τ can be chosen so that $E_i + n_i\tau \geq 0$ for all states, thereby avoiding the need for a negative transfer to any state. In practice, gross equalization schemes are the norm, although forms of net equalization have been used in Germany and Sweden.

Some complications

The above analysis generates an operational formula, but at the expense of assuming away various problems. The first of these is the likelihood that states will choose different fiscal policies. Beginning in the context of the above model, suppose that different states choose different tax rates, even in the presence of equalizing transfers. There are three reasons for not attempting to design equalization transfers to take account of that. The first is that it would be practically infeasible to do so since, as mentioned, the transfer would have to take into account the different nfb that accrues to each income group. But, even if such a scheme were feasible, there are two further reasons for not implementing it. One is that such a scheme would effectively undo the differences in fiscal policies that the states have independently chosen, and that would violate the spirit of federalism. The other is that if the federal government were to implement an equalization scheme that reflected the fiscal policies that the states had chosen, there would be strong incentives for states to manipulate their tax rates in order to obtain higher transfers. For example, by (14.3), a reduction in t_1 or θ_1 by state 1 would reduce nfb_1^j for households of type j in state 1 relative to those in state 2, thereby increasing equalization entitlements.

A reasonable way of addressing these problems in the context of the above model is to use the so-called 'representative tax system' (RTS) approach to equalization whereby a standard set of tax rates is used in the calculation of E_i rather than actual tax rates.[10] Let these standard tax rates be $\bar{t}$ and $\bar{\theta}$. A natural choice would be the nationwide average state tax rates applied to the two bases. The equalization entitlement would then be:

$$E_1 = \frac{n_1 n_2}{n_1 + n_2} [\bar{t}(\bar{m}_2 - \bar{m}_1) + \bar{\theta}(\bar{b}_2 - \bar{b}_1)]. \qquad (14.5)$$

This RTS approach can be interpreted as implementing fiscal equity rather than full horizontal equity. While it has superior incentive properties relative to a system that attempted to equalize nfb differences fully, not all incentive problems are avoided. In particular, two incentive problems remain.

The first is referred to as the 'rate tax-back problem', and results from the fact that individual states can influence the national average tax rates, $\bar{t}$ or $\bar{\theta}$, by changing their own tax rates, t_i or θ_i. There will be an incentive for states to reduce tax rates on tax bases with which they are relatively well endowed to enhance their equalization entitlements (Courchene 1984). This incentive problem is likely to be relatively insignificant in actual federations since the influence a given state has on the nationwide average state tax rate will be small unless it has a large share of the nationwide base.

A more serious problem is the 'base tax-back problem'. State tax bases – $\bar{m}_i$ and $\bar{b}_i$ in the above model – themselves can be influenced by state fiscal policies. The income and asset return bases may be elastic with respect to the tax rates. Moreover, the state may have direct control over resource development and therefore returns to natural resources. In these circumstances, there will be an incentive to undertake policies to reduce tax bases since any loss in tax revenue will be at least partly compensated by an increase in equalization entitlements. In a sense, this is a standard incentive problem that applies to any redistributive transfers, and can be used as an argument for tempering the transfer. At the same time, given that decentralization may lead to non-optimal choices of tax rates due to intergovernmental fiscal externalities – tax competition tending to make tax rates too low and vertical fiscal externalities tending to make them too high – equalization schemes can actually improve incentives for states to choose better fiscal policies (Smart 1998; Köthenbürger 2002; Bucovetsky and Smart 2006).

While the RTS approach is a suitable way of dealing with heterogeneous state behavior in the simple model outlined above, there are some other real-world considerations that complicate matters. One is that provinces may not only choose different tax rates, but they may also define their tax bases differently. In this case, not only must average tax rates be used, but so must representative tax bases, and these cannot be constructed by averaging as in the case of rate differences. Two approaches can be taken.[11] One is to define a representative base for each tax type that captures common features of actual state tax bases. The RTS system would then be applied to each base so defined. The other is to calculate equalization entitlements separately on the basis of each state's tax base, and aggregate these into a single equalization entitlement scheme. Obviously, the more heterogeneous are state tax bases, the less exact either of these schemes will be.

Further complications arise when one departs from the simple setting of the above model in which proportional taxes are used to finance equal per capita benefits. Suppose first that income taxes are progressive in the sense that tax rates as a proportion of income – average tax rates – rise with income levels. Then, the RTS approach in which a single national average tax rate $\bar{t}$ is used to calculate equalization entitlements will not eliminate nfb differentials arising from differences in average incomes. It is straightforward to show using numerical examples that per capita equalization entitlements under the RTS give by (14.5) above will be less than would be required to make Δnfb = 0.[12] However, a revised RTS approach can improve matters. If the state tax structures are piecewise linear with defined tax brackets and rates, the RTS approach will exactly offset nfb differences if each income bracket is treated as a separate tax base in the RTS formula. Of course, if different states adopt different tax structures, this stratified RTS approach cannot be exact. The same argument applies with respect to regressive tax structures. The standard RTS approach will tend to overequalize, and once again a stratified approach in which the RTS is applied separately within each tax bracket will be exact if all states adopt the same tax structure. In the limit, if the tax structure is equal per capita, the tax is a benefit tax and no nfb differences are created so no equalization is required. (Of course, equalization will still be needed if there are differences in source-based tax revenues.)

Next, suppose that public services are not provided in equal per capita amounts but are targeted to particular types of persons (those who are of school age, in poor health, unemployed, retired and so on). Given that states differ in the proportion of persons eligible for the various public service programs, there would be different needs for public service expenditures across states if similar levels of public services were provided (that is, if fiscal equity is to be satisfied). Similar arguments that were used to justify equalizing revenue-raising capacities can also be used to justify equalizing needs differences across states. Suppose that all states provide the same mix of public services to their residents, and finance them by proportional taxes on residents' incomes. Suppose also that average incomes are the same in both states to abstract from revenue equalization. Then, revenue requirements will differ systematically across states according to the expenditure needs. In the absence of federal–state equalizing transfers, tax rates will have to be higher in states with higher expenditure needs, and as a result there will be nfb differences across states. These nfb differences can be fully eliminated by a single system of equalizing transfers that compensates for differences in expenditure needs, provided all states choose the same fiscal policies in the presence of equalization. From a design point of view, a representative expenditure needs index can be calculated, similar to the RTS system. Each state's needs are its eligible population times the level of public services provided, aggregated over all public services.[13]

Similar implementation problems arise as in the case of revenue equalization. If states choose different expenditure mixes, some average level must be chosen as the basis for transfers. This can be complicated for public services since the type of service provided can vary as well as the level of service. Some representative measure of state public service levels must be chosen and weighted by the relevant eligible population for each service type, which may itself differ across states. An important consideration that arises in defining state expenditure needs concerns the treatment of different costs of providing the same public service across states. As mentioned earlier, when costs of provision differ by location, an equity–efficiency trade-off comes into play, and one in general may not want to provide the same level of services to high- as to low-cost states. This implies that one would not want to equalize fully for differences in costs across states. Indeed, given the difficulties in measuring costs, and the incentive problems that might arise if cost differences were equalized, a reasonable approach might instead be to apply a common cost of service provision in all states in determining equalization. Alternatively, one could incorporate costs indirectly by estimating the exogenous factors that give rise to cost differences, and basing equalization on differences in those factors across states.[14]

A further reason for constructing an index of needs rather than using actual state expenditures is to avoid adverse incentive effects. A needs-based equalization system that uses a set of standard costs per eligible recipient – analogous to the RTS system which uses national average tax rates – goes some way to preventing states from choosing their expenditure programs to exploit the equalization system. However, the system is not perfect. Just as states can manipulate tax bases, so they may be able to manipulate eligible populations. They may have discretion in deciding who is eligible for welfare payments or services, or for medical services, or for unemployment benefits.

This first equity argument for redistributive transfers calls for unconditional transfers. Although states may behave differently, there is no attempt on fiscal equity grounds to coerce them to enact common fiscal programs. Moreover, the amount of the transfer is essentially determined by the average fiscal behavior of the states themselves. If the states individually choose to increase their levels of public services, the ideal equalization system will accommodate the changes in net fiscal benefits to which such a change would give rise. The next argument goes beyond that by supposing that the federal government has an interest in the scope and magnitude of public services delivered by the states.

Second equity argument: national standards
As mentioned at the outset, efficient service delivery suggests that state governments have the responsibility for delivering major public services and targeted transfers to resident households. Some of these public services are

among the most important policy instruments for redistribution. To the extent that redistributive equity is national in dimension, the federal government will have an interest in the type of public services that the states choose to provide. There is obviously a conflict in objectives involved. The benefits of decentralizing public service provision – satisfying local needs, cost efficiency, accountability, innovation, administrative efficiency and so on – are better achieved the more discretion that state governments have over program design and financing. At the same time, to the extent that national equity objectives are involved in key public services, some oversight or intervention by the federal government seems necessary. The policy or constitutional problem involves balancing the benefits of decentralized decision making against the need to achieve national standards (Boadway 2001).

The issue is complicated by the fact that both equity objectives and public services are multifaceted. The former includes not only the redistribution of income obtained from the market economy, but also equality of opportunity, social insurance, and compensation for household characteristics such as health status, disability and special needs. Public services, which include in-kind transfers, transfers targeted by need, education, health insurance and so on, can vary along many dimensions of quality, quantity and eligibility. Even defining national equity standards, let alone enforcing them, can be a difficult task.

There are alternative approaches that can be taken to encouraging states to design their public service spending programs to conform with national equity standards (and national efficiency standards, for that matter). One approach is legislative oversight. The federal government can have the power to disallow state laws that are deemed to violate national standards, or more proactively to mandate that state legislation embody certain actions. This might be deemed to be fairly heavy-handed since it explicitly interferes with the autonomy of state decision making.

A second approach may be judicial. The courts may be empowered to determine whether state programs violate national standards that either are in the constitution or have been enacted by federal legislation. This approach has the disadvantage of putting in the hands of unelected judges the power to determine what are essentially economic and social policy issues.

Another approach is to seek a cooperative solution involving an agreement among federal and state governments, the notion being that national standards should have the consensus of all states. There are a number of problems with this approach. The unanimity required for such agreements would be difficult to achieve. Such an agreement would have to be formulated in explicit enough terms to be enforceable, and given the general nature of national standards, this may leave an undesirable lack of discretion. Perhaps most important, since national equity standards would likely involve some redistribution among states, that alone would make it difficult to achieve unanimity. Moreover, even with an intergovernmental agreement, some dispute settlement mechanism with bite would be necessary, and that would probably have to be outside the cooperative agreement process.

Given these difficulties, it is not surprising that federal–state transfers are commonly used as vehicles for inducing national standards in state spending programs.[15] The use of transfers to achieve national equity and efficiency objectives, referred to as the exercise of the federal *spending power*, is in fact one of the main arguments for a vertical fiscal gap in a federation, along with the equalization objective discussed above. Although the use of the spending power is widespread, there is little formal literature on the topic. We shall simply outline some of the issues that arise in its use.

The use of transfers to achieve national objectives can take various forms. On the one hand, there can be specific transfers applied to a limited policy area, where the federal control consists of determining eligibility for the transfer based on a set of defined conditions. Alternatively, they can be general, or bloc, conditional transfers applying to a broad class of expenditures. In this case, the conditions will typically be rather more general and will consist of general principles to which state programs must adhere. In addition to defining the conditions, conditional grants must also specify the funding allocations as well as the nature of the incentives that influence state program design. There are obvious advantages in terms of predictability and transparency for funding allocations to be formula based rather than discretionary. The formula should include both the allocation among states and the rate of growth over time, with the former obviously being related to equalization objectives discussed above. The financial influence can take the form of the carrot or the stick. In the former case, the federal grant has a matching component that encourages states to engage in spending, provided national standards are met. It has the additional possible advantage of relating the transfer to need, but has the disadvantage of encouraging overspending. The alternative is to provide a non-matching bloc conditional grant, but to impose financial penalties on states whose programs are deemed to violate national standards. In either case, the final arbiter of national standards is typically the federal government, although in principle other dispute settlement mechanisms could be used.

The use of federal–state transfers to achieve national standards of redistributive equity is as much an art as a science, and few general principles can be brought to bear. None the less, there are a number of issues and potential pitfalls that should be mentioned. First, there is no clear determinant of the size of the transfer needed to achieve national standards. The size will determine the proportion of state funding that is financed by the federal government, and therefore the strength of influence that the federal government is likely to have. On the other hand, a larger transfer may detract from accountability. The definition of national standards is fraught with ambiguity, and this ambiguity makes the exercise of financial penalties discretionary and possibly unpredictable for states. Presumably, the more negotiation and cooperation there is between federal and state governments, the clearer the rules will be. More generally, there is a delicate balance between the use of the spending power to achieve national standards and excessive intrusion of federal oversight into state decision making. This is a critical problem in any federation, and there are no clear criteria for resolving it. Ideally, the federation might strive for a system in which the minimal national standards required to achieve national equity goals are used as conditions. Examples of general conditions might include the absence of barriers to the use of public services by migrants, broad accessibility of all eligible citizens to public services and minimum standards of specified public services to which all citizens should be entitled. Within these general criteria, there is room for state discretion about levels and qualities of service and the financing of those services.

Third equity argument: interregional insurance

A final argument, one that is related to the equalization role, is that federal–state transfers serve as a means of insuring state governments against temporary shocks to their fiscal capacities. This is analogous to the role of private insurance markets for pooling risks of risk-averse households. In the literature, the state government is taken as personifying its representative resident for whom the risk of an adverse shock imposes a utility cost. A federal government that is able to pool risks across states can use its transfer system as a means of costlessly assuming the risk of the individual states. Indeed, a transfer system that equalizes fiscal capacities automatically insures against temporary shocks to states' tax bases as well as compensating for permanent differences in fiscal capacity.[16]

In assessing this interregional insurance argument for equalization, several observations are relevant. The first and most obvious question is why states cannot self-insure instead of relying on the federal government. To the extent that states are subject to idiosyncratic shocks, they should be able to use state borrowing to smooth out the shocks over time. The literature has by and large simply assumed that states do not self-insure. In principle, one reason is that state governments may be short-sighted, say, because of the election cycle. Alternatively, they may be rationally far-sighted and predict that if they do not self-insure, the federal government will bail them out of budgetary difficulties in the future.[17] This assumes that the federal government is unable to commit not to bail them out, an issue to which we return in the final section.

Second, if shocks to state tax bases in a given year are to some extent aggregate or correlated, so that all states are affected by them, an equalization system whose transfers are based on the fiscal capacities of all states will be pro-cyclical: equalization transfers will rise when the economy is booming and fall when it is in recession. This can actually cause the equalization system to increase the volatility of state revenues.[18] Of course, this would not be a problem either if states were able to self-insure.

Third, there are other ways that the fiscal system might adjust to idiosyncratic shocks (Asdrubali et al. 1996). The interpersonal tax-transfer system provides an implicit form of insurance. The movement of factors of production among states will do so as well. The latter, however, are likely to be slow to adjust to state-specific shocks.

Finally, as with private insurance schemes, interregional insurance may be subject to incentive and asymmetric information problems, which can be characterized as hidden action and hidden information problems. Hidden action problems occur when transfers recipients can influence either the probability of adverse outcomes occurring – *ex ante* moral hazard – or when they can influence the size of the loss in the event of an adverse outcome – *ex post* moral hazard. In the context of interregional insurance, *ex post* moral hazard is the more likely, and will occur when states have an influence on the fiscal capacity measure upon which transfers are based.[19] We have already encountered this in our discussion of the base tax-back problem of equalization. In principle, one might imagine designing a transfer system based on measures of fiscal capacity that states would find difficult to manipulate, for example, proven reserves whether they are developed or not in the case of resource assets. As well, one could use refinements to take account of moral hazard problems, like co-payments or non-linear schemes. Indeed, this is done to the extent that actual equalization transfer schemes equalize on the basis of less that 100 per cent of tax bases.

Hidden information problems in interregional insurance arise when the federal government cannot observe the underlying shocks that hit the different states, but can observe the fiscal actions that the states undertake. For example, the shock may affect the cost of providing public services, while the federal government can only observe the total spending on public goods. The situation is analogous to the well-known optimal income tax problem where the government cannot observe the productivities of households but can observe the incomes that they choose to earn based on those productivities (Mirrlees 1971; Stiglitz 1982). The progressivity of the income tax is constrained by incentive compatibility constraints that preclude persons of higher ability from mimicking those of lower ability.[20] A general approach to this problem has been formulated by Lockwood (1999). A federal government conditions redistributive interregional transfers on either the quantity of a public good each state chooses to supply or the total revenue it raises. States differ in the shocks to which they have been subject. Three separate types of shocks are considered: shocks to the cost of public goods, shocks to preferences for public goods, or shocks to the productivity of households.[21] In fact, these shocks could simply be regarded as unobserved differences in characteristics of states rather than temporal shocks *per se*. This interpretation makes the federal problem more of a redistribution one rather than an insurance one, and also accounts for the inability of states to self-insure. The basic result for all of these cases is that insurance – or redistribution – is incomplete in the sense that differences in characteristics are not fully compensated. As well, under the optimal interregional insurance scheme, states could under- or oversupply public goods compared with the first best.

The efficiency argument: fiscal efficiency

In the above discussion, we have assumed that households are immobile among states in order to focus on fiscal inequities arising from the different fiscal treatment afforded residents of different states when fiscal decisions are decentralized. With household mobility, these inequities are mitigated to the extent that households can migrate to states that offer them more favorable treatment. In a Tiebout-type model of local public goods where migration is costless, the horizontal equity arising from fiscal decentralization disappears completely. If otherwise identical persons are treated differently in different localities, free migration will undo those differences. But in this case, another problem arises. Even with free migration, there can be adverse consequences from fiscal decentralization. The same sort of differences in fiscal capacity that induce horizontal inequities without migration will result in an inefficient allocation of labor across localities with migration. Moreover, the policy prescriptions for dealing with inefficiencies of migration are similar to those for dealing with horizontal inequity, which is not surprising given that the source of the problem is the same.

The problem can be traced to the fact that there is a fundamental inefficiency of migration in decentralized economies. Even if state governments are behaving efficiently with respect to their expenditure and taxation decisions – that is, they are choosing the level of spending such that marginal costs of expenditures equal marginal benefits – there will typically be a fiscal externality arising from migration that potential migrants do not take into account.[22] Consider a simple federation consisting of a population of identical households each of which chooses a state of residence and supplies one unit of labor. Output in state i is generated by a strictly concave production function, $f_i(n_i)$, where n_i is the state population. Output can be divided between a private consumption good c_i and a public good G_i that yields per capita public services given by $g_i = G_i/n_i^\alpha$. The coefficient α, which satisfies $0 \le \alpha \le 1$, is an index of 'privateness' of G: if $\alpha = 1$, G is a private good, while if $\alpha = 0$ it is a pure public good. Suppose that t_i is the tax levied on each person in the state to finance the public good, and suppose further that the state government chooses G_i optimally (that is, to satisfy the modified Samuelson condition, which in this context is $n_i^{1-\alpha} \text{MRS}_{g,c} = \text{MRT}_{g,c}$ where MRS and MRT stand for the marginal rates of substitution and transformation, respectively). Then, the condition for an efficient allocation of labor between states 1 and 2 is (Buchanan and Goetz 1972):

$$t_1 - \frac{\alpha G_1}{n_1} = t_2 - \frac{\alpha G_2}{n_2}. \tag{14.6}$$

The terms on each side are the fiscal externalities of migration: a migrant into state i contributes t_i to the state in tax revenues but imposes a cost of $\alpha G_i / n_i$ on users of the public good G_i. The latter is just the increase in G_i required to keep the level of services g_i constant when an addition migrant enters. It is like a congestion cost. When G is a pure public good, this term disappears and we have as an optimality condition simply $t_1 = t_2$ (Flatters et al. 1974).

Optimality condition (14.6) will generally not be satisfied in decentralized economies, and this gives rise to an argument for equalization. In the context of this simple model with homogeneous labor, inefficiency can arise for two reasons depending on the nature of G and the manner of financing. Suppose that state revenue comes from a direct tax on households t_i, a tax at the rate θ_i on rents obtained from the production function denoted R_i, and an equalization transfer E_i. Then, the state budget constraint is $G_i = t_i n_i + \theta_i R_i + E_i$, where $n_1 E_1 + n_2 E_2 = 0$ for a federation consisting of two regions. The level of E_1 that ensures migration efficiency is satisfied can be obtained by substituting the state budget into (14.6) to obtain:[23]

$$E_1 = \frac{n_1 n_2}{n_1 + n_2} \left[\frac{(1-\alpha)G_1}{n_1} - \frac{(1-\alpha)G_2}{n_2} + \frac{\theta_2 R_2}{n_2} - \frac{\theta_1 R_1}{n_1} \right].$$

If state expenditures are on private goods, which is often assumed, this says that per capita source-based taxes should be fully equalized. This condition generalizes to any number of states, and is effectively equivalent to the condition that nfb differentials among states should be equalized.

If households are heterogeneous, matters become much more complicated since migration equilibrium must be satisfied for each household type. None the less, the principles are clear from our earlier discussion. Consider the case where G is private ($\alpha = 1$). Then the nfb differential for a household of type j is the same as (14.3) earlier. To obtain migration efficiency, this must be equalized across states. Thus, the same form of equalization that is required to achieve fiscal equity will also achieve fiscal efficiency. This is a remarkable result, for it says that, unlike in standard economic policy problems, there is no conflict between equity and efficiency considerations in this context. The case for full equalization of fiscal capacities applies whether households are mobile or immobile, and the previous discussion concerning the design of equalization systems also carries over.

The fiscal efficiency argument for equalization provides a further rationale for equalizing differences in the fiscal capacities of state governments, and as such, accords with the sorts of intergovernmental transfer schemes that one observes in practice. It is not the only efficiency argument for differential intergovernmental transfers. Dahlby and Wilson (1994) have argued that intergovernmental transfers can serve as a device for minimizing the efficiency costs associated with collecting taxes in a federation in which state governments rely on distorting taxes for their own-source revenues. They argue that transfers should be used to equate the so-called 'marginal cost of public funds' (MCPF) across states, where the MCPF refers to the social cost associated with the last increment of revenues raised. The MCPF includes both the value of resources transferred from the private to the public sector and the marginal deadweight loss incurred per unit of additional revenue raised. It will be larger the higher is the elasticity of the tax base from which the marginal revenues are drawn. In our above discussion of using redistributive transfers to equalize fiscal capacities across states, we neglected the distortionary effect of taxes and implicitly assumed that revenues can be raised in a lump-sum manner. Once distortionary taxes are used, this consideration of equalizing the MCPF in different states can be thought of as refining our earlier analysis. In practice, the direction of modification is not clear. One might expect that if one state has a higher fiscal capacity than another, it would also have a lower MCPF. Thus, the prescription for equalization would tend to be similar. Things would be more complicated if the mix of tax bases differed across states. If one state had a relative abundance of inelastic tax bases compared with another, the equalization of state MCPFs would involve transfers from it to the other state. Considerations of these sorts, although theoretically important, would be hard to implement with precision. For that reason, actual schemes tend to focus more on differences in fiscal capacities *per se*.

Finally, equalizing transfers may promote efficiency in the internal economic union that compromises the economy in the federation. It will do so to the extent that it reduces the tendency for state governments to use fiscal policies as devices to compete for mobile factors of production and business. To the extent that states' fiscal capacities are equalized so that comparable levels of public services can be supplied at comparable tax rates, that in itself may reduce the need to engage in such actions. At the same time, equalization schemes can reduce the advantages of tax competition by neutralizing the fiscal spillovers that have given rise to tax competition in the first place. The argument is that states tend to overestimate the true MCPF for taxes levied on mobile tax bases: part of the perceived cost of a rise in the tax rate consists of a loss in tax base to another state, which is an offsetting benefit from a social point of view. An RTS equalization system effectively compensates for that loss in tax base since equalization entitlements are inversely proportional to the state's tax base, a point made by Smart (1998) and referred to earlier. Against this must be set the possibility that there may also be vertical fiscal externalities acting in the opposite direction.[24] That is, states may underestimate the true MCPF as their tax bases overlap with those used by the federal government: an increase in a state tax rate will not only reduce its own tax base, it may also reduce the federal tax base and therefore the revenues of the federal government. In this case, equalization schemes could exacerbate the incentive for states to impose excessive tax rates.[25]

Other issues

The study of redistributive intergovernmental transfers remains a lively research area. In this concluding section, we touch on a few themes of the recent literature that can have significant consequences for the structure of intergovernmental transfers.

The first issue concerns the timing of decisions. In the standard literature, the federal government is assumed to set its policies first, followed by the state governments, and then households make their choices. However, given that household decisions can be long term in nature, while governments can change policies readily, this requires that governments can commit to the policies that they announce before households act. If such commitment is not possible, the policies that are feasible will generally be inferior from a social point of view compared with the commitment case.

One interesting possibility is a natural extension of the case we have focused on in which households are immobile. Suppose instead that they are mobile, but their migration decision is a long-term one. If neither federal nor state governments can commit to future policies, they must choose them after households have chosen their state of residence. In a subgame perfect equilibrium, households correctly anticipate that a benevolent federal government will implement equalizing transfers between states. Mitsui and Sato (2001) consider the simple case where states provide public goods that benefit their residents. In this context a utilitarian federal government will make transfers to equalize the marginal utility of consumption in all states *ex post*. Households anticipate this and will have an incentive to migrate to the more populous states: with the marginal utility of consumption equalized, their total benefit will be higher in the more populous state where more public goods are provided.[26] The result is an inefficient allocation of households across states.

Reversing the timing of federal and state government decisions may also cause a problem. If state governments choose their expenditure levels before the federal government chooses its transfer system, there is a soft budget constraint problem (Wildasin 2004). The states will choose g_i non-optimally anticipating that this will affect their federal transfer. The level of social welfare that can be attained in the federation will be inferior to that achieved when the federal government can commit.[27]

A second issue that can affect the role of redistributive intergovernmental transfers is the possibility of agglomeration. There may be economies of scale with respect to some dimension of economic activity in any state. This may take the form of scale economies in producing goods (Krugman 1993), economies in labor markets that enable skilled workers to more easily be matched with suitable employers (Boadway et al. 2004), or economies arising from public spending, including infrastructure (Bucovetsky 2005). In any case, agglomeration effects give rise to non-convexities in the allocation of productive activity across states, and equalizing transfers can potentially preclude those economies from being fully realized by preventing factors of production from moving to states where economies of scale can be realized.

A final issue concerns the political economy of transfers. As mentioned at the outset, our analysis has been largely normative in nature. There have, however, been some attempts to provide positive explanations for the pattern of fiscal transfers and of the constitutional arrangements that might best exploit them. An example of the former is Dixit and Londregan (1998), who use a party competition model to shed some light on federal grants and electoral outcomes in a federal setting. A version of their model was tested by Johansson (2003) for Sweden and was found to have some explanatory power. Persson and Tabellini (1996a) investigate the constitutional question. More generally, it might be argued that the case for transfers should be conditioned by the effect that they have on competition among states. Those who hold that such competition is important to the efficient functioning of federations might consider that to the extent that transfers diminish self-sufficiency, they might have a deleterious effect on such competition.[28]

Concluding remarks

Equalization transfers are the life-blood of federations. They facilitate the decentralization of fiscal responsibilities by addressing the inequities and inefficiencies that would result from decentralization of spending and revenue-raising responsibilities. Decentralization is typically seen as a good thing from the point of view of improving the effectiveness with which important public services are delivered to citizens in a federation. However, decentralization inevitably leaves different states with different abilities to raise revenues and different needs for expenditures required to provide comparable levels of public services. This will lead to horizontal inequities among otherwise comparable citizens in different states. It will also lead to purely fiscal incentives to migrate to states with favorable fiscal capacities. Equalization transfers can undo those inequities and inefficiencies, albeit imperfectly.

It is worth reiterating that the case for equalization transfers, like the case for all government policies that involve elements of redistribution, relies on some non-trivial judgments. These include first and foremost judgments about the equity basis for such transfers. There must be a consensus across the federation that horizontal equity is an accepted value, that is, that like persons ought to be treated alike no matter where they reside. Of course, this is not an absolute principle, but one that must be weighed against others, such as the desire to allow states maximum discretion in choosing the fiscal programs. In addition, the case for equalization also depends upon governments at all levels being to a considerable extent benevolent in the sense of taking decisions that are in the interests of their citizens. If this is not the case, the whole basis for fiscal federalism can be called into question.

Notes

1. The editors have provided helpful comments and advice on an earlier version.
2. This argument is recounted in more detail in Boadway (2001).
3. For an outline of the issues, see Dahlby (1996) and Boadway (2001).
4. This argument was originally made by Buchanan (1950). Some of the problems with applying the concept of horizontal equity as a normative criterion may be found in Feldstein (1976) and Musgrave (1976).
5. Indeed, the recent literature on equality of opportunity makes it clear that it is virtually impossible to treat persons with different preferences and identical skills neutrally while redistributing from the more- to the less-skilled groups. See Roemer (1998) and Fleurbaey and Maniquet (2002).
6. Mirrlees (1972) made this point in the context of a city area, while Boadway (2004) discusses its relevance for intergovernmental transfers.
7. We adopt the convention initiated by Bewley (1981) of referring to public spending that is private in nature as public services, as opposed to public goods, which benefit several persons simultaneously.
8. This, of course, assumes that these households attach the same weight in their preferences to public services relative to private goods. If not, a further difficulty applies to the principle of horizontal equity, whether or not in a federal setting.
9. This is obtained by revising state budgets to be $g_i = t_i \bar{m}_i + \theta_i b_i / n_i + E_i$, where federal budget balance requires $n_1 E_1 + n_2 E_2 = 0$. The equalizing transfers are then set so that Δnfb = 0. See Boadway and Flatters (1982). Note that for this result to apply, tax rates need only be equal after the equalization transfer is in place and not in its absence. For further discussion, see Mieszkowski and Musgrave (1999).
10. The RTS system has been used in Canada since the 1950s. For a summary of it, see Courchene (1984) and Boadway and Hobson (1998).
11. Actually, a rather more drastic approach may be taken, and that is to abandon the RTS approach altogether in favor of a simpler alternative. One such alternative, discussed in Barro (1986, 2002), is the macro approach whereby interstate redistribution would be based on a macro indicator such as state per capita income or production rather than the ability to raise revenues using actual state tax systems. Arguments for and against the RTS approach may be found in a symposium of the topic found on the website of the Institute of Intergovernmental Relations at Queen's University, Kingston, at www.iigr.ca/publication.
12. The following example, taken from Boadway (2004) illustrates this. There are two income

classes: H (m^H = 40,000) and L (m^L = 20,000). State 1 has two H persons for every L person, while state 2 has one H person for every two L persons. The first 20,000 of income is taxes at 10 per cent and the second 20,000 at 30 per cent. This yields g_1 = 6000 and g_2 = 4000, and Δnfb = 2000 for both H and L persons. Optimal equalization should then be 1000 per capita transferred from state 1 to state 2. Under the RTS system that national average tax rate (total tax revenues divided by the total tax base) will be $\bar{t}$ = 0.1667, and the equalization transfer calculated according to (14.5) will be 556 per person, which is less than required to eliminate the nfb differential.

13.   For a further discussion of needs-based equalization transfers, see Shah (1994) and Ahmad and Searle, Ch. 15 in this volume.
14.   This is effectively the procedure used in Australia to equalize expenditure needs.
15.   An extensive survey of the use of intergovernmental transfers for this and other purposes can be found in Watts (1999).
16.   There is a literature that has estimated the extent to which subnational governments in federations do face insurable shocks, and whether fiscal transfer systems do provide a risk-sharing service. Some examples include Asdrubali et al. (1996), von Hagen and Hammond (1998), Mélitz and Zumer (2002), Boadway and Hayashi (2004) and Smart (2004). Theoretical models of the risk-sharing role of central governments include Persson and Tabellini (1996a,b), Lockwood (1999), Bordignon et al. (2001) and Konrad and Seitz (2003).
17.   There is a literature on the so-called 'bailout problem' in fiscal federalism. For a general statement of the issues, see Wildasin (2004).
18.   Boadway and Hayashi (2004) and Smart (2004) found this to be the case for the Canadian equalization system. In response to this problem, the system was reformed so that equalization entitlements were calculated on the basis of a moving average of fiscal capacities, a change that reduces the ability to insure against idiosyncratic shocks.
19.   See Persson and Tabellini (1996b) for an analysis of this case.
20.   Note that this is different from the adverse selection problem in private insurance markets where the insurance companies can observe *ex post* outcomes but cannot observe the *ex ante* probabilities of good and bad outcomes for individual households. This form of asymmetric information is presumably regarded as not being relevant for the federalism context where the interregional insurance is modeled as an *ex post* redistribution problem.
21.   Lockwood's approach generalizes those of previous papers that had individually considered the same forms of shocks. Thus, Bucovetsky et al. (1998) considered federal redistributive transfers when states differed by unobservable preferences for providing public goods. In Boadway et al. (1999), states differ by the cost of providing public goods, while in Bordignon et al. (2001), states differ by the productivity of their states' residents.
22.   There is a large literature on inefficiency of migration in decentralized federations. It began with Buchanan (1952) and Buchanan and Goetz (1972), was formalized in Flatters et al. (1974) and Boadway and Flatters (1982), and was recently generalized by Boadway et al. (2002) and surveyed in Boadway (2004). On the empirical importance of the phenomenon, see Wilson (2003).
23.   In this context with identical households, Myers (1990) has pointed out that there would be no need for a central government to implement equalizing transfers: states would do so voluntarily. Unfortunately, the optimality of voluntary transfers no longer applies when there are migration costs and when equity becomes a criterion. See Boadway et al. (2002) for further discussion.
24.   See Keen (1998) for a survey of the concept of vertical fiscal externalities.
25.   Dahlby and Wilson (2003) have, however, shown that the effect of a vertical fiscal externality may be to cause the states to perceive the MCPF to be too high rather than too low for taxes that, like labor income taxes, are levied as a proportion of before-tax income. That is because an increase in state taxes will increase pre-tax income and therefore increase the size of the federal tax base.
26.   If the federal government abides by a horizontal equity constraint in choosing its interstate transfers, or if it adopts a maxi-min criterion, this adverse outcome will not occur (Boadway 2004).

27. For another example, see Köthenbürger (2004).
28. See the discussion of competing jurisdictions in Breton, Ch. 3 in this volume.

References

Asdrubali, P., Bent E. Sørenson and Oved Yosha (1996), 'Channels of interstate risk-sharing: United States, 1963–90', *Quarterly Journal of Economics* **111**, 1081–110.
Barro, Stephen M (1986), 'State fiscal capacity measures: a theoretical critique', in H. Clyde Reeves (ed.), *Measuring Fiscal Capacity*, Cambridge, MA: Oelgeschlager, Gunn & Hain, pp. 51–86.
Barro, Stephen M. (2002), 'Macroeconomic versus RTS measures of fiscal capacity: theoretical foundations and implication for Canada', Working Paper 2002 No. 7, Institute of Intergovernmental Relations, Queen's University, Kingston, Canada. www.iigr.ca/publication_detail.php?publication=131.
Bewley, Truman F. (1981), 'A critique of Tiebout's theory of local public expenditure', *Econometrica* **49**, 713–40.
Boadway, Robin (2001), 'Inter-governmental fiscal relations: the facilitator of fiscal decentralization', *Constitutional Political Economy* **12**, 93–121.
Boadway, Robin (2004), 'The theory and practice of equalization', *CESifo Economic Studies* **50**, 211–54.
Boadway, Robin, Katherine Cuff and Nicolas Marceau (2004), 'Agglomeration effects and the competition for firms', *International Tax and Public Finance* **11**, 623–45.
Boadway, Robin, Katherine Cuff and Maurice Marchand (2002), 'Equalization and the decentralization of revenue-raising in a federation', *Journal of Public Economic Theory* **5**, 201–28.
Boadway, Robin W. and Frank R. Flatters (1982), 'Efficiency and equalization payments in a federal system of government: a synthesis and extension of recent results', *Canadian Journal of Economics* **15**, 613–33.
Boadway, Robin and Masayoshi Hayashi (2004), 'An evaluation of the stabilization properties of equalization in Canada', *Canadian Public Policy* **30**, 91–109.
Boadway, Robin and Paul Hobson (1998), *Equalization: Its Contribution to Canada's Economic and Fiscal Progress*, Kingston, Canada: John Deutsch Institute for the Study of Economic Policy.
Boadway, Robin, Raghbendra Jha and Isao Horiba (1999), 'The provision of public services by government funded decentralized agencies', *Public Choice* **100**, 157–84.
Bordignon, Massimo, Paolo Manasse and Guido Tabellini (2001), 'Optimal regional redistribution under asymmetric information', *American Economic Review* **91**, 709–23.
Buchanan, James (1950), 'Federalism and fiscal equity', *American Economic Review* **40**, 583–99.
Buchanan, James (1952), 'Central grants and resource allocation', *Journal of Political Economy* **60**, 208–17.
Buchanan, James and Charles Goetz (1972), 'Efficiency limits of fiscal mobility: an assessment of the Tiebout model', *Journal of Public Economics* **1**, 25–43.
Bucovetsky, Sam (2005), 'Public input competition', *Journal of Public Economics* **89**, 1763–87.
Bucovetsky, Sam, Maurice Marchand and Pierre Pestieau (1998), 'Tax competition and revelation of preferences for public expenditure', *Journal of Urban Economics* **44**, 367–90.
Bucovetsky, Sam and Michael Smart (2006), 'The efficiency consequences of local revenue equalization: tax competition and tax distortions', *Journal of Public Economic Theory*, **8**, 119–44.
Courchene, Thomas J. (1984), *Equalization Payments: Past, Present, and Future*, Toronto: Ontario Economic Council.
Dahlby, Bev (1996), 'Fiscal externalities and the design of intergovernmental grants', *International Tax and Public Finance* **3**, 397–411.
Dahlby, Bev and Sam Wilson (1994), 'Fiscal capacity, tax effort and optimal equalization grants', *Canadian Journal of Economics* **27**, 657–72.
Dahlby, Bev and Sam Wilson (2003), 'Vertical fiscal externalities in a federation', *Journal of Public Economics* **86**, 917–30.
Dixit, Avinash and John Londregan (1998), 'Fiscal federalism and redistributive politics', *Journal of Public Economics* **68**, 153–80.

Feldstein, Martin (1976), 'On the theory of tax reform', *Journal of Public Economics* **6**, 77–104.
Flatters, Frank, Vernon Henderson and Peter Mieszkowski (1974), 'Public goods, efficiency, and regional fiscal equalisation', *Journal of Public Economics* **3**, 99–112.
Fleurbaey, Marc and François Maniquet (2002), 'Compensation and responsibility', in K. Arrow, A. Sen and K. Suzumura (eds), *Handbook of Social Choice and Welfare*, vol. 2, Amsterdam: North-Holland, forthcoming.
Johansson, Eva (2003), 'Intergovernmental grants as a tactical instrument: empirical evidence from Swedish municipalities', *Journal of Public Economics* **87**, 883–915.
Keen, Michael J. (1998), 'Vertical fiscal externalities in the theory of fiscal federalism', *International Monetary Fund Staff Papers* **45**, 454–85.
Konrad, Kai and H. Seitz (2003), 'Fiscal federalism and risksharing in Germany: the role of size difference', in Sijbren Cnossen and Hans-Werner Sinn (eds), *Public Finance and Public Policy in the New Century*, Cambridge, MA: MIT Press, pp. 469–89.
Köthenbürger, Marko (2002), 'Tax competition and fiscal equalization', *International Tax and Public Finance* **9**, 391–408.
Köthenbürger, Marko (2004), 'Federal commitment, externalities, and Pigouvian grants', CESifo, Munich, mimeo.
Krugman, Paul (1993), *Geography and Trade*, Cambridge, MA: MIT Press.
Lockwood, Ben (1999), 'Inter-regional insurance', *Journal of Public Economics* **72**, 1–37.
Mélitz, Jacques and Frédéric Zumer (2002), 'Regional redistribution and stabilization by the center in Canada, France, the UK and the US: a reassessment and new tests', *Journal of Public Economics* **86**, 263–86.
Mieszkowski, Peter M. and Richard A. Musgrave (1999), 'Federalism, grants, and fiscal equity', *National Tax Journal* **52**, 239–60.
Mirrlees, James A. (1971), 'An exploration in the theory of optimum income taxation', *Review of Economic Studies* **38**, 175–208.
Mirrlees, James A. (1972), 'The optimum town', *Swedish Journal of Economics* **74**, 114–36.
Mitsui, Kiyoshi and Motohiro Sato (2001), 'Ex ante free mobility, ex post immobility, and time-consistent policy in a federal system', *Journal of Public Economics* **82**, 445–60.
Musgrave, Richard A. (1976), 'ET, OT and SBT', *Journal of Public Economics* **6**, 3–16.
Myers, Gordon M. (1990), 'Optimality, free mobility and regional authority in a federation', *Journal of Public Economics* **43**, 107–21.
Oates, Wallace E. (1972), *Fiscal Federalism*, New York: Harcourt Brace Jovanovich.
Persson, Torsten and Guido Tabellini (1996a), 'Federal fiscal constitutions: risk sharing and redistribution', *Journal of Political Economy* **104**, 979–1009.
Persson, Torsten and Guido Tabellini (1996b), 'Federal fiscal constitutions: risk sharing and moral hazard', *Econometrica* **64**, 623–46.
Roemer, John (1998), *Equality of Opportunity*, Cambridge, MA: Harvard University Press.
Shah, Anwar (1994), 'A fiscal needs approach to equalization in a decentralized federation', Policy Research Working Paper No. 1289, World Bank, Washington, DC.
Smart, Michael (1998), 'Taxation and deadweight loss in a system of intergovernmental transfers', *Canadian Journal of Economics* **31**, 189–206.
Smart, Michael (2004), 'Equalization and stabilization', *Canadian Public Policy* **30**, 195–208.
Stiglitz, Joseph E. (1982), 'Self-selection and Pareto efficient taxation', *Journal of Public Economics* **17**, 213–40.
Tiebout, Charles M. (1956), 'A pure theory of local expenditures', *Journal of Political Economy* **64**, 416–24.
von Hagen, Jürgen and G.W. Hammond (1998), 'Regional insurance against asymmetric shocks: an empirical study for the European Community', *Manchester School* **66**, 331–53.
Watts, Ronald (1999), *The Spending Power in Federal Systems: A Comparative Study*, Kingston, Canada: Institute of Intergovernmental Relations.
Wildasin, David E. (2004), 'The institutions of federalism: toward an analytical approach', *National Tax Journal* **57**, 247–72.
Wilson, L. Sam (2003), 'Equalization, efficiency and migration – Watson revisited', *Canadian Public Policy* **29**, 385–95.

15 On the implementation of transfers to subnational governments
Ehtisham Ahmad and Bob Searle[1]

Objectives and context

A variety of grants instruments can be observed across the globe. The magnitude and type of grants depend considerably on the context – often on the extent to which subnational administrations have access to adequate own-source revenues in relation to their constitutional or assigned responsibilities. Grants may also serve to address the policy objectives of higher levels of government. And, as both revenue assignments and expenditure responsibilities are frequently reviewed or reformed, even in the developed countries, there needs to be a constant evaluation of the need for transfers and the mechanisms used to implement grants systems. While there are attempts to institutionalize the arrangements for the determination of grants, it is evident that political economy considerations play a significant role in the design of grants systems. However, poorly designed grants systems can have a negative impact on incentives for efficient management of public finances as well as on overall macroeconomic outcomes.

Grants to subnational governments are used to serve multiple goals. Often these goals are partially unrelated and they can be conflicting. They include:

- equity considerations and the reduction (or elimination) of vertical and horizontal imbalances;
- the correction of spillovers;
- the implementation of centrally determined standards for public services; and
- the enhancement of tax effort and expenditure efficiency.

To reconcile these goals, combinations of revenue sharing, and special-, and general-purpose grants tend to be used. Revenue sharing is often used to address vertical imbalances. General-purpose or unconditional grants are useful in the reduction of horizontal disparities. And special-purpose, or conditional grants, are used for fostering national priorities and to serve specific, efficiency-enhancing goals.[2]

This chapter focuses on transfer instruments and their implementation, and complements that by Boadway, which examines the efficiency and equity considerations underlying transfer design. We examine first a typology of grants, followed by greater details on an equalization framework. A final section examines practical issues of implementation of a general grants system, as well as the constraints on relying on different types of grants.

Equalization transfers or transfers to individuals?
Some argue that the objective of fiscal equalization through general-purpose grants should be to equalize personal incomes within and across regions. However, the equalization of personal incomes may be neither feasible nor desirable. Equalization of incomes did not work in the centrally planned economies, for instance in the former Soviet Union,[3] any more than it does in advanced market economies, most of which display relatively stable degrees of interpersonal inequality. Should governments target a certain level for the Gini coefficient and resulting distribution of income? It is difficult to make a case for this. At best, prevention of need and destitution might be at the center-piece of government objectives, and for which there might be more or less effective direct programs – pensions for the aged, assistance for families with children (family allowances in some countries), help for the unemployed and so on – while market forces determine the final outcomes. Some of these policy objectives could be met through special-purpose grants, if actual provision or implementation is by subnational governments. However, an excessive reliance on financing subnational spending through special-purpose transfers might conflict with or circumscribe subnational decision making.

A more defensible objective for fiscal equalization would be to facilitate the provision and access to public services, by subnational governments, at similar levels of tax effort (these are effectively the objectives of equalization systems in countries as diverse as Australia and Denmark).[4] This focus on potential access to services preserves a degree of autonomy for subnational jurisdictions.

Legal and institutional framework for transfers
The design of transfers or the context for the determination of transfers is often enshrined in constitutions or higher laws (where applicable, requiring more than a simple majority for amendments). Details that might be subject to frequent revision would typically be determined in regulations or pronouncements of special bodies that might be set up by a higher authority. The magnitude of the transfers, as well as the combination of instruments, might be specified in the higher legislation, or in annual budget laws reflecting changing macroeconomic considerations. Further, special-purpose grants are often associated with special laws defining specific programs, for example, in health care or education. Donors or international bodies might also be responsible for the introduction or diversification of special-purpose grants for basic services

(for example, to meet millennium development goals), or investments in the social sectors, or infrastructure.

Constitutions

Older constitutions mainly focused on separation, or concurrent access to distinct tax bases, or sharing of a pool or individual taxes, or specification of responsibilities.

Many modern constitutions refer to the principles and mechanisms of transfers. There are advantages for the main principles of a transfer system to be enshrined in constitutions or in higher-level legislation, in order to provide clarity in functions and roles, as well as financing mechanisms. However, several constitutions recognize that change is inevitable, and provide for periodic assessments (for example, the Indian and South African constitutions require quinquennial assessments by dedicated finance commissions).[5] Reassurance that adequate resources would be forthcoming for subnational levels of government, including a share of natural resources as well as transfers, as in Nigeria, have been seen as an ingredient in keeping the federation together.[6]

In other cases, particularly in some Latin American countries, detailed specification of formulae or floors on transfers in constitutions can generate undesirable rigidity that might considerably complicate macroeconomic adjustment. There is, however, a fine balance between reassurance to subnational administrations and flexibility for changing circumstances, refinements of data and methodology, and macroeconomic vicissitudes.

Specific legislation

Countries that have had a long or strong tradition of centralized operations (for example, Indonesia, France, and most recently, Peru) have sought to support a decentralization process through legislation that specifies both responsibilities and administrative arrangements, as well as the fiscal aspects, including the sharing of resources, the design and floor on transfers.

As subnational capacities are built up, it might become feasible to devolve functions gradually to lower levels without risking a negative impact on service delivery. Under these circumstances, the flexibility in the design of transfers might be useful – as countries are typically reluctant to amend constitutions, except in extreme crises – and the appropriate legal instrument may be a higher-level (where applicable) or specific legislation that might be easier to amend than a constitution, while at the same time providing assurance of continuity and a framework for the management of subnational public finances. Such 'framework' legislation would be supplemented by detailed appropriations in annual budget laws, or specific laws governing special-purpose programs, often with a multiyear impact.

As legal frameworks tend to vary, there is a tension between overspecification (for example, of details or floors in constitutions) providing assurance to the subnational levels of administration, and flexibility that might be needed for macroeconomic management and tailoring the intergovernmental arrangements to changing circumstances. In either case, the establishment of arm's-length coordination and dispute resolution bodies is important to establish a framework and parameters for discussion.

In many overdetermined legal frameworks, there have been attempts to instill macroeconomic discipline by placing constraints on subnational operations through fiscal responsibility legislations applying to all levels of government (see Ahmad, Albino-War and Singh, Ch. 16 in this volume). Depending on the political and legal context, if higher-level legislation (for example, the constitution) permits spending by lower-level administrations, regulations would not effectively constrain such spending. Introducing regulations, instead of tackling the lacunae in higher-level legislation, reflects the political weaknesses of the system, and the overall framework might not be defensible against a serious challenge by a lower-level administration. Under these circumstances, it might be safe to assume that subnational administrations will spend all their assigned revenue shares and other transfers, and the burden of adjustment would perforce fall on the central government.

Institutions

Under circumstances where the vertical imbalance in favor of the center is small, there is generally little that the central or federal government can do to redress horizontal imbalances. Institutions that facilitate transfers or redistribution across regions are thus likely to be important under such circumstances, and national identity, solidarity and traditions come into play, as in Germany. It is unusual to find such arrangements in countries with sharp ethnic, linguistic or other divisions.

The role of a central government in redistribution increases if there is a large vertical imbalance in its favor. Under these circumstances, checks and balances are generally needed to assure the subnational administrations that there will be fairness in the redistribution process, as well as predictability and certainty in the transfer design in order to finance the basic expenditures that are typically assigned to subnational administrations. We examine certain options for such institutions in the context of equalization transfers described in greater detail below.

Typology of transfers

There are a variety of transfers possible and each tends to have a different implication for incentives and distribution.

Gap-filling transfers

Transfers to finance deficits at the subnational level between own revenues and spending are commonly known as 'gap-filling'. If subnational governments have carte blanche in this respect, there is no effective budget constraint, hence no incentive to manage spending or raise revenues efficiently at the subnational level. Such transfers were common, for instance, in South Asia, and Govinda Rao (2002) has pointed to the deleterious effects of such 'fiscal dentistry'. Such arrangements are now increasingly rare.

Revenue sharing

Revenue sharing (for example, for value-added tax: VAT) is often used to partially offset vertical imbalances.[7] In Germany, VAT is shared on a per capita basis. Revenue sharing bears characteristics of transfers, as the subnational governments have little control over bases or rates.

In general, however, revenue sharing tends to be on the basis of the origin of the revenues, as in China, which may exacerbate horizontal inequalities. Similarly, the devolution of revenue bases to subnational jurisdictions does little for subnational governments with poorer bases or higher costs of service provision – thus horizontal equalization remains a problem to be addressed.

An extreme example is the case of Australia, which, in July 2000, introduced a national VAT – goods and services tax – to replace a range of inefficient state-level taxes (including sales taxes) and the Commonwealth wholesale sales tax. The political arrangement to facilitate this change was to place the entire amount of VAT revenue as the source of funds to be distributed back to the states through the equalization transfer system (see below).

Special-purpose grants

Reliance on special-purpose programs (SPPs) to further central government policy objectives and to correct for spillovers is universally recognized. The SPPs could be open-ended, reflecting continuing legislation, or close-ended, such as for specific projects.

Some conditional grants may have matching requirements from the recipient administrations (see Boadway and Hobson 1993 for a detailed exposition). While matching requirements might induce greater effort on the part of recipients, this could cause distortions leading to less spending elsewhere, with possibly deleterious effects on the overall welfare of the recipient populations. In other cases, such as in Denmark, matching grants have been criticized as leading to greater spending as well as additional taxation (Løtz 2005). In developing countries, limited revenue bases could restrict the take-up of the grant in poorer regions, and could widen horizontal disparities.

In practice, the excessive reliance on earmarked transfers, particularly in Latin American countries, has led to mixed outcomes and effectively reduced accountability on the part of subnational administrations. *In extremis*, such transfers could be construed as interference by the center often in areas of subnational competence. In developed countries, very detailed earmarking has generally been replaced by looser sectoral conditionality leading to an emphasis on block grants that require that the funds be used, say, for education, but with greater flexibility on the precise spending items to be determined by the recipient government.

Central governments in developing countries often lack the ability to monitor the use of conditional grants. If there is poor information on the implementation of the earmarked grants, then this could degenerate into additional finance for a subnational government, but without the local accountability that might be expected of local government's spending from own-source revenues or untied transfers. There may, however, be scope for inducing enhanced management and reporting on conditional grants, if these are designed as repeated games or contracts. This is an area for fruitful research.

Equalization transfers

Most large countries (many smaller ones as well, for example, Belgium and Denmark) practice forms of fiscal equalization. Indeed, much depends on the basic allocations of taxation functions and spending powers of specific jurisdictions, often specified in constitutional, legal or institutional arrangements. Given externalities in centralized tax administration, many countries assign the main tax heads to the center, including corporate and income taxes, customs and VAT. With an increasing pressure to decentralize expenditure responsibilities, the result is a greater vertical imbalance that generates a need for grants.

Equalization over revenues   Countries such as Canada have traditionally instituted equalization transfer systems based on revenue capacities. It had been argued that there were no significant differences between the service delivery levels across most Canadian provinces, hence it was sufficient to equalize across revenue capacity only (representative tax system: RTS).[8] However, more recently, it has been recognized that service delivery costs are higher in the Northwestern Territories than in the rest of Canada, and a special grant has been constituted for this purpose. Moreover, special-purpose grants, especially for health care and education – essentially meeting central government objectives – are based on needs criteria, and their magnitude outstrips that of equalization.[9]

Changing tax assignments and additional own-revenue powers for the Canadian provinces, which now have access to all the major tax bases available to the center, call into question the scope of any vertical imbalance, as the provinces should in principle be able to compensate for any loss of central revenues by raising their own taxes.

Further, the recent move to fix the amount of the equalization payments for a period of ten years effectively replaces the RTS. This has led to a decision to reconsider the formulation of the RTS and the overall equalization framework, including whether it should be based on a revenue-only equalization basis. The treatment of the center's significant 'individual-based' programs in an equalization framework might also be evaluated. In general, equalization over revenue capacities only might not be an appropriate option for large or disparate countries with significant differences in the cost of provision of public services.

Equalization over needs Some countries have chosen to equalize over expenditure needs alone for subnational governments. This could be ascribed more to the inadequate own-source revenues at the subnational level, rather than any other theoretical consideration. Expenditure needs in isolation from own-source revenues tend to weaken budget constraints. This is the case in South Africa[10] (although it could be argued that the 'economic output' variable in its calculation might be seen as a proxy for revenue capacity differences).[11]

The lack of provincial revenue-raising ability in South Africa constrains the design of the horizontal equalization program and also means that the national government cannot encourage efficient use of resources (for example, through the use of matching grants). The Financial and Fiscal Commission (FFC) has therefore suggested that a 'cost-based' approach should be developed that would force provinces to recognize the true opportunity cost of reallocating resources.[12] The cost-based approach, by providing a rational basis for a firm and binding provincial budget, should force these governments to take account of the reduction in other services implied by an increase in any given service. Thus, it argues that this approach is the best available instrument for encouraging provinces to make efficient budgetary decisions. Each provincial government would then have a strong incentive to find innovative, cost-saving ways to meet the social service goals specified by the national government. Because the basis for allocating nationally raised resources to each province is a measure of costs that reflects the underlying social conditions in each province, for example, the number of students and the rate of poverty, equitable share allocations to provinces that develop more efficient methods for delivering government services should not be reduced. However, existing spending patterns across the provinces reflect a combination of factors, including historical patterns of public service delivery, cost differences and inefficiencies in the delivery of services. For this reason, to the extent that the allocation of the equalization transfers in South Africa reflects current expenditure levels, the allocations may serve to reinforce both provincial government inefficiencies and historical patterns of public service provision, and may not lead to either fiscal equalization or equality in service provision. In Italy, there was little incentive for enhanced efficiency in the period when the government relied solely on expenditure needs – the introduction of revenue capacity considerations was important (see Brosio 1995).

In general, while the expenditure needs only approach is to be preferred to gap-filling transfers, the use of historical factors might not facilitate efficiencies, and the absence of reliance on own-source revenues at the margin reduces significantly the incentives for increased efficiency.

Equalization based on revenue capacities and expenditure needs   In an increasing number of countries, equalization systems take into account both revenue capacities and expenditure needs. This allows for moves towards equalizing the capacity of subnational administrations to provide access to public services at similar levels of revenue effort. This formulation addresses the difficulties associated with the abstraction from differential costs of services associated with a revenue-only approach, or the incentive problems or possible inefficiencies that might persist in an expenditure needs-only approach. This model has been adopted in many other countries, including those as diverse as Australia and Denmark, and more recently in China and Ethiopia. Yet the Australian system is also evolving, reflecting a political economy give and take between the center and the states of the control over resources.

An issue that might militate against application of the Australian model is the complexity of the estimation of relative costs.[13] The greater complexity currently reduces the transparency and attractiveness of the logic of the approach.

The political economy of the introduction of an equalization transfer system can also be seen in the case of China. In 1994, an equalization transfer system, based on the Australian model, but with relatively simple factors, was introduced to accompany a new revenue-sharing arrangement. While many of the objectives of the reform were met, including overall revenues and increasing the share of the central government, the equalization potential of the transfer system has still to be realized – given the needs and political power of the relatively well-to-do coastal provinces the central government did not realize the fiscal space to redistribute to a significant extent (see Ahmad et al. 2004a).

Impending tax reforms[14] and clarification in expenditure responsibilities will facilitate the reconsideration of the transfer system and its objectives, as well as design issues. The Chinese case illustrates that even with a well-coordinated process of policy reforms, there are evident interactions between policy instruments, and that it is neither desirable, nor indeed possible, to ignore political economy constraints and the interests of regions that are instrumental in generating growth and employment.

One issue that remains is whether the grant programs initiated by the central government to achieve its own policy aims should be taken into consideration in estimating the equalization transfers. In the extreme case, central governments might be better advised to use such special-purpose grants rather than equalization transfers to meet horizontal equalization objectives. In the Chinese context, the difficulties with the 'equalization' system have led the authorities to turn to regional development programs, as for the West China Development initiative. In general, the reliance on special-purpose transfers is limited by weak or absent capabilities to monitor the use of the special funds according to agreed objectives.

Mechanisms for the determination of equalization grants

A common goal in the use of unconditional grants is to allow beneficiary governments to provide access to equal – or at least comparable – levels of public services, taking account of the relative capacity of those governments to fund the provision of services.

The capacity to finance similar levels of services is not, however, only a function of the level of revenues. It also depends on the cost of producing the services, as well as on differences in the possible demand for those services (need). In other words, two local governments with the same per capita revenue capacity may not have the same capacity to satisfy the service needs of their population if their populations have different expenditure needs, resulting, for example, from differences in the proportions of young or elderly people and/or if they are confronted with different costs of providing these services, such as those arising from population density and climatic conditions.

The attenuation of the most blatant disparities between jurisdictions in levels of service provision requires filling any inequalities in infrastructure and capital stock. While in principle a single transfer scheme without distinction for recurrent and capital expenditure can be envisaged, the separation of recurrent from capital transfers may be more appropriate to the present conditions of many low- and middle-income countries. Scarcity of financial resources and popular pressure to use them for immediate current spending may leave little for capital formation. Under these circumstances, a separate capital transfer scheme is often beneficial.

The aim of instituting capital transfers, especially in poor countries, would be to start to fill backlogs in capital stock. This mechanism should also reduce the need for the central government to carry out projects in areas of subnational competence. Capital transfers may be allocated according to the difference between the actual stock or condition of infrastructure and an agreed minimum standard.

Other basic requirements of a well-designed grant system are that it be based on a transparent formula and that the indicators used in the assessment should not reflect discretionary policy choices made by the recipient governments. For example, the total amount of salaries paid to local employees should not be considered as an indicator of need because beneficiary governments would then be induced to increase their wage costs in order to get a larger share of the grant.

Many federal countries, such as Australia and Switzerland, and a growing number of advanced unitary countries, such as the Scandinavian countries and the United Kingdom, use a grants framework based on expenditure needs and revenue capacity to ensure that local governments have sufficient revenue to provide reasonably comparable levels of public services at comparable levels of taxation. The adoption of the expenditure-needs and revenue-capacity approach presents considerable advantages for most developing countries. It allocates the total amount of transfers among distinct subnational governments in a way that promotes efficiency and accountability; provides a known basis for the vertical allocation of national revenue among the different levels of government; and stimulates accountability by providing yardsticks against which subnational performance can be evaluated by the various stakeholders, namely citizens, auditing bodies, and upper levels of government that provide finance.

There are, however, a number of political and technical issues that have to be addressed for its implementation, and its financial sustainability has to be assessed against the amount of resources available.

Transfer design
One of the key questions for the operation of a system of equalization grants is whether it is to be based on both expenditure needs and revenue capacities. Decisions will also be needed in the design of the equalization system as to whether or not account should be taken of the interactions with any special-purpose grants.

The importance of an effective general transfer system based on an objective of fiscal capacity equalization could be described as 'the glue that holds the nation together'. It is based on the simple proposition that all people of a nation are entitled to a reasonably similar standard of government services so that people in remote regions can have access to, say, educational opportunities and health care at a standard not too dissimilar from those in the larger cities.

There are a number of important issues to be decided in designing such a transfer system.

One key question will be whether to assess *absolute or relative needs*. In many countries, the determination of general-purpose grants is a relative process. In Australia, for example, the capacities of the states are equalized to the average level (per capita) of service provision, assuming the application of average effort to raise revenue. It would, however, be possible if sufficient resources were available, to equalize to an absolute or minimum standard (such as the provision of nine years of education) which all regions should aspire to achieve, but it is usually more practical to use tied grants to raise standards where they fall short of national minima.

There is also a question of *accountability*. Most grants systems, particularly in larger, more diverse countries, operate through general-purpose (untied) grants. This enables different units of government at the same level to develop different methods of service provision to best suit their circumstances and the aspirations of their people. Questions about the applicability of a general-purpose grant system arise in countries where the accountability mechanisms, including information on what has been spent, are weak, and outputs or outcomes difficult to monitor. However, similar objections could be posed in relation to a grant system based on special-purpose grants, with limited information on what has actually transpired. Typically, special-purpose grants are more demanding of information and reporting mechanisms, and if these are weak, a simple equalization framework might be preferable.

In most countries, some degree of *flexibility* is considered necessary. For example, where the units of government to receive grants are small in terms of financial capacity, it may well be desirable to give them scope for cooperative efforts in service provision. A very small district is likely to find it more efficient to contract out some services to neighboring regions or to another level of government (or the non-government or private sector) rather than trying to provide everything itself.

The grants systems of many countries rely on the identification and estimation of *disabilities* (influences beyond a government's control that affect what it needs to spend on providing services or can raise from a particular kind of taxation). However, too many factors or indicators are likely to reduce the transparency of the system and could also erode general acceptability of a 'black box' approach, including in developed countries.

Most developing countries also lack the statistical base for more complex methods or models. However, the use of a few simple *indicators* (such as the proportions of relevant populations, for example, school-age children or the elderly) is likely to be all that is feasible, and can provide adequate redistributive transfers. Such systems can be elaborated over time with the development of databases, administrative capabilities and technical expertise.

Magnitude of grants

An overarching issue is how to decide on the quantum of funds to be devoted to general-purpose grants. In theory, 'full' equalization can be based on any level of services, but resource constraints ensure that few countries, and particularly developing countries, can achieve 'full' equalization at the standards of service to which they aspire. The overall budget constraints and other macro-economic considerations limit the ability of the central government to provide sufficient resources to close horizontal gaps.

A number of countries target less than full equalization, often with an absolute floor on the equalization transfer depending on what essential services are to be covered in the general grant formulation. This variation was introduced in the Indonesian legislation of 1999 that provides the lower-level governments, which have limited sources of own-source revenues, with an assurance that at least 25 per cent of total central government revenue will be distributed to them. The important issue here is whether the quantum of funds distributed through the unconditional grants pool is sufficient to fulfill the objectives of the unconditional grants. The pool size must therefore be related to the fiscal capacity inequalities in the recipient governments.

Minimum standards

Developing countries often face a choice concerning minimum levels of service delivery – this is so in Nigeria, South Africa, and many other developing countries. The method of estimating expenditure needs in terms of 'costed minimum standards' consists of estimating, for each unit of government, the resources needed to provide an agreed minimum standard of service level to the population (and is seen to be a special case of the general formulation).

In a federal or otherwise decentralized nation, the determination of the standards by the central government in isolation would be inappropriate, since the final outcome depends on effective participation of the other levels of government. Standards would need to be agreed among the concerned levels of government. This calls for consultation and agreements. Local governments might participate in consultative bodies, and the participation of representatives of every level of government in the decisions concerning them is widely practiced across the world. For example, many European Union member countries have consultative and/or participative bodies for the implementation of the 'Stability Pact'. Federal countries, such as Australia,[15] India and South Africa have similar intergovernmental bodies. Another issue relates to the choice of the appropriate instruments. Standards (and priorities) may be set up by using several instruments. The first mechanism for defining standards for service provisions is in terms of the inputs of the services. This is the most common method, and teacher/pupil ratios are a typical example. The main advantage of input-based standards is that they are easy to determine.

The second way of defining standards is in terms of outputs or outcomes.

For example, the water distribution service has to provide clean water to all connected households with a view to improving health standards. The output, clean water, is easier to quantify than the outcomes, although the latter more naturally reflects the objective of public policy. Output or outcome-based budgeting typically leaves the choice of inputs and their combination to the producing or providing governments. Output levels are, however, often difficult to define in a non-controversial way and are not easy to enforce. While many developing countries aspire to output-based decision making and budgeting, they lack the basic expenditure management tools and information flows, as well as audit and control mechanisms, which are needed to make such approaches viable. Outcome-based systems are even more difficult to implement.

Because of these considerations, input-based standards are applied in most cases. Issues involved in estimating costs are described in the following section.

A general model for equalization transfers

A general model to estimate equalization grants would involve an evaluation of both relative revenue capacities and relative expenditure needs. Special cases of this model would include equalization:

- in respect of revenues only, without reference to expenditure needs; and
- based on expenditure needs alone.

The general model may be written as:

$$G_i = E_i^s - R_i^s, \tag{15.1}$$

where E_i^s represents relative expenditure needs of region i; and R_i^s own-revenue-raising capacity relative to a 'standard'. In the Australian case, the issue of minimum standards is avoided within the equalization grant formulation and the standard is determined by the average expenditure levels across all states – the examples that follow reflect this formulation. In South Africa, a minimum expenditure standard is used. While there is some subjectivity in determining these minimum standards, this formulation may be meaningful in a developing country where the standard to which recipients are to be equalized may need to be higher than the level of service currently pertaining. While the absence of a revenue-capacities element reflects the existing revenue assignments, this may not matter if own-source revenue is insignificant, as in South Africa. It does, however, remain a constraint in moving towards greater accountability.

It is useful to decompose expenditure needs:

$$E_i^s = P_i \frac{E_s}{P_s}.v_i, \tag{15.2}$$

where P_i is the population of region i, E_s/P_s is the average expenditure standard in the country, and v_i represents a number of independent factors that might be relevant for region i, such as:

$$v_i = (u_i \cdot s_i \cdot d_i \cdot e_i - 1), \tag{15.3}$$

where, for example,

u_p = differential coverage of the population eligible for services relative to the total population;

i_s = differential costs arising out of 'scale' factors (that is, where larger size leads to reduced cost);

d_i = differential costs arising out of concentration or dispersion of the eligible population; and

e_i = differences in cost arising out of social, physical and economic factors (for example, higher costs in extremely cold or hot areas).

Whether positive or negative needs are assessed depends on whether u_i, s_i, d_i and e_i, which are all based around the average jurisdiction's experience, exceed or fall short of unity. Where it is judged that there are virtually no differences in public service delivery eligible demand or costs, this is equivalent to assuming that all regions face approximately the same costs in providing standard services (or that any such differences will be addressed through alternative means). In this case, the product of the items $(u_i,$ and so on) is about unity in all regions, and the expenditure term (15.2) goes to zero.

It is important to note that expenditure needs for equalization purposes must be attributable to unavoidable differences in costs of providing standard services, given different factors such as population size or density, and not to differences in policies or in the relative efficiencies with which services are provided. Recipient governments must not be able to influence the size of their assessed need.

Parallel to the assessment of expenditure needs, but requiring somewhat less in terms of data, is the estimation of own-revenue capacity in region i, R_{is},

$$R_i^s = P_i \frac{R_s}{P_s}.q_i, \tag{15.4}$$

where R_s/P_s reflects 'standard' per capita revenue collections, and q_i is the differential revenue-raising capacity of region i, $q_i = [(Y_i/P_i) - (Y_s/P_s)]$, where Y_i is the actual revenue base in region i. It is straightforward to relate q_i to the standard revenue base, Y_s, by expressing (15.4) as:

$$R_i^s = P_i \cdot \frac{R_s}{Y_s} \left(\frac{Y_i}{P_i} - \frac{Y_s}{P_s} \right). \tag{15.5}$$

Thus, the grants would relate a differential revenue-raising capacity relative to standard per capita revenue collection R_s/P_s.

The general formulation in equation (15.1) makes it clear that the capacity equalization grant depends on the magnitude of 'net of variations' from the standard per capita expenditures and revenues. Such variations will be positive where there is a shortfall in revenue-raising capacity, or regions face a higher per capita cost in providing standard services.

Treatment of special-purpose grants and tax-sharing arrangements Many countries use special-purpose grants and tax-sharing arrangements while also having an equalization grant mechanism. These forms of financing a vertical fiscal imbalance must be taken into account in the calculation of the horizontal imbalances because they are revenue sources designed to meet some of the assessed expenditure needs, and differential grants or tax shares can offset or augment the differential own-source revenues identified under the capacity equalization arrangements. For example, equation (15.1) can be expanded to:

$$G_i = P_i \cdot \frac{E_s}{P_s} \cdot v_i - P_i \cdot \frac{R_i}{P_s} q_i - \frac{O_s}{P_s} \cdot \sigma_i, \tag{15.6}$$

where $(O_s/P_s) \cdot \sigma_i$ is the differential special-purpose grant.

A decision to allow the regions to retain a share of the VAT collected on a derivation basis, for example, would provide sustained advantages to more developed regions. If the equalization objective was to be upheld, the VAT would be assessed as part of the each regions' 'own-revenue' resources, and an above-average fiscal revenue-raising capacity assessed in the more-developed regions. Alternatively, the assessment for equalization purposes could be restricted to own-source revenues and the shared taxes could be treated as a non-equalizing grant from the center. The shared revenue received would then be deducted from the total resources available to the region in assessing the overall fiscal capacity and the need for equalizing grants.

Within this framework, it would still be possible to make adjustments to permit local governments to retain all or a portion of the relative advantage they obtain from some central grants or tax shares. For example, it might not be appropriate to equalize all sources of own revenues, especially where these are related, say, to environmental costs of mining. Thus, the method allows regions to keep such revenues from an environmental transfer, charge or royalty flowing from certain natural resource projects within a specific region. However, the framework would seek to make such advantages explicit and quantifiable.

Special-purpose grants   Special-purpose grants that fall in the areas of competence of the subnational governments, hence helping the latter to meet part of their expenditure needs, might best be taken into account in the general grants scheme as a source of revenue. However, there is much less reason to take into account the spending by the center to meet its objectives in areas that do not overlap with those assigned to subnational governments – such as on defense, for example.

Other revenues   In developing countries, it may be necessary to consider donor inputs, and even activities of non-governmental organizations (NGOs), in exactly the same way as we have treated special-purpose grants. Any funds that flow to a recipient government and can be used to satisfy some of the assessed expenditure needs can upset the equalization-based distribution and thus need to be considered in the formulation of that distribution. It is often found that donor and NGO activities concentrate on the poorest of the poor regions in a nation and that the areas so selected can be 'double funded' if the activities of these agencies are not considered.

Including a fiscal effort adjustment   Although the fiscal capacity models set out above do not impose performance conditions on recipients, it is possible to insert an adjustment factor for fiscal effort to the grant entitlement calculation if that is judged to be appropriate. Such a fiscal effort adjustment factor will ensure that the grant entitlement for a recipient government will be reduced if the revenue actually collected by the recipient government from its own sources falls short of its capacity to raise revenue at standard rates, and commensurately increased if collections exceed the standard. These are legitimate objectives and actions of a grant-giving government but decisions to introduce them must be made in the full knowledge that they are in conflict with any equalization objective. Similarly, recipient governments must be able to see both objectives of the granting government and be able to identify the financial impact of each objective separately. If a recipient government's grant is increased, for example, it must be able to see how much of that increase was due to each policy.

A variant of this model, which would have the objective of imposing a penalty for below-standard revenue-raising effort, but not of rewarding above-standard effort, would restrict the fiscal effort adjustment to negative amounts.

Phasing in equalization arrangements   A full equalization of regional fiscal capacities, given the apparently large regional fiscal capacity differences that exist in most developing countries, may be difficult to achieve in the short term. Moreover, it may be inappropriate to seek to move rapidly in the direction of a historically determined standard, given the large shifts that may be occurring in the structure of the economy. Thus, an agreed 'indicative' standard, rather than a historically based standard, may need to be used during the period of rapid structural change. Where some localities are already above these indicative standards, they can be left at their actual standard rather than have funds taken from them, and the equalization arrangements phased in to reflect both how standards are increased and how 'well-off' localities are handled within the system.

Which government should pay the grant?   Although the discussion thus far has assumed that the central government has a favorable fiscal imbalance, there is a question as to who should pay the equalization grant. In Canada the 'equalizing grant' is paid by the central government, made possible by a vertical balance favoring the central government.[16] However, in Germany, where the vertical imbalances are smaller, *Länder* with above-average revenue capacity make equalization transfers directly to those with below-average revenue capacity. Such cooperative arrangements are difficult to achieve in developing countries, where the struggle over scarce resources is more intense, and divisions and schisms more clearly defined. The closing of horizontal gaps in most developing countries would require a vertical imbalance in favor of a central government, together with transparent and sustainable instruments and mechanisms for redistribution. These are examined next.

Institutional considerations

Institutional arrangements, organization and procedures
There are a variety of practical institutional arrangements that might be engaged to facilitate the implementation of a grants system. Any institutional system for the determination of grants to local government can work well, as long as it is accepted by the center as well as by the subnational governments involved. In this regard, it is highly advisable that the process is transparent and that subnational governments are involved in it.

As indicated above, countries with a British tradition have tended to adopt independent and arm's-length commissions to deal with the distribution of resources across levels of government – the CGC in Australia, and the finance commissions in India and Pakistan. However, a continental approach has been to rely on ministries of the interior for the administrative aspects of what initially was a deconcentration of responsibilities (for example, in Continental European, several Latin American countries, and Indonesia). In such countries, the role of the ministry of finance has become increasingly important in determining the basis and estimation of grants systems, and in ensuring that the financing is made available on a timely basis.

Going forward, the options essentially relate to whether an independent commission or the ministry of finance should be charged with the establishment of formulae and decisions on the amounts of funds to be allocated. Often there is a shared responsibility, and the pros and cons are examined below.

A separate independent agency works best if it is given wider powers within intergovernmental financial relations but few if any functions outside that field. Critical issues in making a separate agency work well include: (i) finding the right people to do the job – members should be beyond reproach and should not represent specific grant recipients or other interest groups; and (ii) that politicians should set the rules and principles by which the agency operates, but should have no power to change the recommended distribution simply to meet the expectations of specific interest groups. The main advantage of such an arrangement is that it could be seen as 'independent' and thus free of diktat by the center.

Some advantages of having the ministry of finance rather than an independent agency decide the relative needs for funding are the greater power of the ministry in getting cooperation and data, both from the local government and from central government line ministries; and in taking and implementing decisions. Its control over the macroeconomic parameters also predisposes it to be in a better position to come to a judgment on the extent to which decisions on transfers affect overall macroeconomic stability – though this advice could also be made known to an independent commission.

The main disadvantage of the ministry of finance being the arbiter of the grants system is that this may be seen as the central government taking decisions on behalf of the lower levels of government and in deciding on gainers and losers. This may accentuate political fissures and difficulties and make it harder to explain unpalatable decisions to the lower levels of government.

Intermediate options are also possible – with the ministry of finance deciding on the overall envelope for the amounts available for transfers, and an independent agency with representation from the lower levels of government deciding on the relative distribution of the resource. It would be hard to overstate the need to give recipient governments full opportunity to make their problems and views known or for transparency in both operations and outputs.

The experience of Australia's Grants Commission is worth noting. In its full-scale reviews (reports on which are made each five years or so), the Commission:

- provides discussion papers simultaneously to all state governments and the national treasury, and ensures that all responses and other submissions are distributed to all parties;
- provides for successive rounds of submissions from the states and the national treasury so that each has full opportunity to comment on the arguments of others;
- holds conferences on functional or more general issues, which allow state and national government experts in such areas as education and health to exchange views with each other and the Commission;
- visits each state in turn to conduct discussions with officials in their capital cities and in city and country areas (including, often, very remote areas) to talk with service providers at schools, hospitals, police stations and so on to get their 'on the ground' views on service provision and cost issues;
- makes shorter follow-up visits to state capitals later in the review cycle to allow states to provide supplementary views;
- sends out its reports simultaneously to all governments;
- supplements its reports, as soon as possible after their release, with extensive working papers providing full details of its decisions and the reasons for them, and software that enables those who are interested to make alternative calculations; and
- opens conferences to the public and provides reports and extracts of working papers free of charge to researchers.

Even in the preparation of its more routine annual update reports, the Commission provides an opportunity for the parties to comment on how it proposes to treat changes in state administrative structures and financial relations between the national government and the states (for example, the transfer of functions from one level to another).

A grants system will have little chance of acceptance if there is a belief that it has simply been imposed from the top. Clearly, it will take much time and much patient consultation to build up confidence in the system.

Information and data requirements

The assessments on which a grants commission might recommend a distribution can be as narrow or as extensive as the available data permit. In Australia, the assessments currently cover all recurrent expenditures and revenue sources of the states, but such a wide scope is not essential and is under review. In China, where the system is still being developed, the range of assessments is being expanded and is yet far from complete in its coverage. As long as the intention to expand is indicated and the assessments that are done are not thought to take the distribution away from what might be the end result, taking short cuts is an acceptable, and often necessary, procedure.

The data required of a grant distribution system are of two types – those relating to the accounts of the recipient units of government, and those relating to the assessments of expenditure needs and revenue capacities. Unless absolutely necessary, it is better if the accounting data of the recipient governments do not influence the assessments, except to the extent that they are inputs into decisions about current average levels of service or revenue raising. As noted earlier, it is important to avoid 'grant design inefficiencies' under which recipient governments can influence the size of their grant funding by changing their policies. The base data should be based on audited 'past period' data if possible, as this removes the natural tendencies to underestimate revenue collections and overestimate expenses when budgeting. The use of actual data avoids these biases within the standards against which assessments might be made.

Data used in assessments can be from any source as long as they can be used to measure differences in revenue bases, differences in the possible demand for services or differences in the unit costs of providing services, or are acceptable proxies for those variables. However, there are several attributes apart from their relevance to the assessments that make some data more appropriate than others for the task. These are:

- The data should be available for each unit of government. If not, it must be possible to use the data for one region as also being an appropriate indicator of need in others. This is sometimes possible when measuring differences in unit cost, but rarely otherwise.
- The data should be comparable across units of government. This is important to the end result and is usually a very time-consuming task. Lack of comparability and inaccuracies in the data can have major distributional consequences.
- The data should preferably be sourced to an independent authority. This is important to minimize 'grant design inefficiencies' and most countries use their central statistical agencies extensively as a source of these data.
- The data should be known to be updated annually or on some other known frequency such as at the time of a national population census, data from which will usually be a major source of information. It is important that the system not be subject to either constant changes as data become unavailable, or to rapid changes in distribution of funding because of changes in assessment methods. Stability of data sources usually gives greater stability of results.

The data used for revenue assessments will often need to be tailored to the legislative base of the revenue source being assessed. While GDP per capita, for example, might be thought to be an adequate measure of differences in the value of land being used for productive purposes, it is obviously better if the actual value of that land, based on a standard approach to valuing, can be collected. It might be acceptable in such cases to derive the data from the recipient governments if it is known to be sufficiently comparable and free of manipulation.

Such direct measures of a revenue base are not always available and general measures of economic activity, such as GDP per capita, household income, or value added by an industry sometimes need to be used. Such data are often unreliable at anything less than 'whole-of-nation' level and should be looked at closely for comparability before being used.

When looking at data on which to base expenditure needs assessments, those relating to differences in demand are much more likely to be available than those relating to unit cost differences. Data on where demand for services is emanating from is often used as a management tool, and similarities between regions in their management task will often create similarities in the data they collect.

Influences on regions' unit costs differ widely and are much more difficult to measure. Even on the demand side, however, it will be easier to get data on raw measures of demand such as the number of school-age children than it will be to get information on the extent to which different types of students in the appropriate age group might have different demand patterns. It is easy enough to show that old people use more hospital services per capita than the average, and to count the relative number of old people in each region's population, but much harder to decide what weighting to use when calculating their relative impact on demand for services.

Matching the use of actual financial standards, past period non-financial data in the expenditure and revenue assessments are generally used. This is a natural consequence of there rarely being forecasts of the range of data needed to make assessments based on the year for which the grants are being determined.

Before the assessments are finalized, it is beneficial to give them a 'reality' check to make sure they are sufficiently robust to be accepted in the regions. It is particularly important here to see that the assessments of those regions that are to be detrimentally affected can be justified. The best way to do this reality check is to have gathered policy information on at least the big issues in each function and know why a region's per capita expenditure or revenue might be expected to be greater or less than that in other regions. It is particularly important, where relevant, to be able to show that a region has a particularly low or high figure because of a different policy approach. Making such information available is part of the transparency of the system that we believe to be vital to its acceptance.

In Australia, the information on policy differences was originally collected by the Commission because no other government agency saw a need for it. However, it is now seen as critical to improving national public sector efficiency and is collected by the Productivity Commission, a central government authority charged with responsibility for recommending how this can be achieved. The states in Australia now habitually look at the comparable financial and non-financial data when setting their budgets, as do the central government agencies responsible for distributing special-purpose funds among the states.

Conclusions

The design of grant systems and the mix of instruments used reflect the constitutional framework, institutional and political constraints, and forces underlying the division of responsibilities and resources in a country. The magnitude of the grants should be determined by overall fiscal sustainability exercises for 'general government', but the distribution of resources across regions often reflects political economy considerations.

While special-purpose grants continue to be important in preserving the interests of the central government, there is a possibility of 'game playing' by subnational governments, possible limitations on monitoring the use of such grants (especially in developing countries), and likely adverse effects on horizontal disparities if matching conditions are used. Under these conditions, there is greater reliance on 'looser' block grants, coupled with contracts that can be monitored.

Given the extent of vertical imbalances, a central government is likely to have a role to play in horizontal equalization. Decisions are also needed as to whether the special-purpose grants might be taken into account in this assessment of equalization transfers. In order to enhance 'fairness' and incentives for more effective resource use, a combination of revenue capacities and expenditure needs might be used as the basis for the design of an equalization grants system. Thus, the first question faced by many designers of assessment-based grants distribution systems is whether the assessments are to cover both revenue capacities and expenditure needs. The question of the standard to which the regions are to be equalized is also very important.

There are several approaches that can be taken to measuring the differences between regions in revenue capacity and expenditure needs. The appropriateness of using these approaches changes as a grants system evolves and the data and other information systems improve. It is important to keep some flexibility in the design of the grants system, as fiscal policy evolves in response to changing circumstances in all cases.

In order to minimize arbitrariness, it is useful to place the administration of the grants system in as much of a cooperative arrangement as possible, with explicit involvement of subnational interests. Whether this is arranged under the aegis of a ministry of finance or an independent commission will depend on the circumstances of a particular country.

Notes

1. We are grateful to participants at the seminar on fiscal federalism held in Turin, 27–28 August 2004, and particularly to Giorgio Brosio for helpful comments.
2. See, for example, Shah (1995) and Boadway (Ch. 14 in this volume).
3. See Ahmad (1993).
4. See Ahmad (1997), and papers by Rye and Searle (1997) (on Australia) and Løtz (1997 and 2005) (on Denmark and the other Scandinavian countries).
5. In the Indian context, new finance commissions are constituted every five years, whereas the South African Fiscal and Financial Commission is a standing body.
6. The sharing of volatile revenues (for example, from petroleum and gas) can introduce considerable uncertainty in the budget process of lower levels of government that they are usually ill-equipped to handle, especially in less-developed countries (see Ahmad and Mottu 2003).
7. This is also an administratively neutral way of sharing VAT revenues – as separate subnational VATs pose administrative difficulties.
8. See Clark (1997). The exclusion of natural resource revenues accruing to the provinces under the five-province formulation of the RTS also weakens the conceptual basis for the system.
9. See Aubut and Sample (forthcoming).
10. Provincial governments raise only about 5 per cent of their revenues.
11. For local governments, which have access to own-source revenues, there is some fiscal capacity equalization.
12. See www.ffc.co.za for more details.
13. In its *Report on State Revenue Sharing Relativities, 2004 Review*, Australia's Commonwealth Grants Commission has recommended that there be work undertaken to simplify the determination of its equalization-based grants to state governments.
14. For instance, a rationalization and reassignment of the income tax or the likely reform of the investment VAT to a more standard consumption-based VAT, are policy measures that will have an impact on the share of revenues accruing to subnational governments in China, and cannot be achieved without a corresponding adjustment of the transfer system or rationalization of spending assignments (Ahmad, Lockwood and Singh 2004b).
15. Australia has a large number of ministerial councils that include the central government minister and all state ministers (and sometimes also the relevant minister from New Zealand). Each of these ministerial councils is supported by a committee of relevant officials.
16. The recent changes in assignments in Canada, where provinces have been given unrestricted access to all major revenue bases (see Aubut and Sample, forthcoming), make it difficult to establish the 'vertical imbalance'.

References

Ahmad, Ehtisham (1993), 'Poverty, demographic structure and social protection policy', in B. Wolfe (ed.), *On the Role of Budgetary Policy during Demographic Changes*, *Public Finance*, **48**, 366–79.

Ahmad, Ehtisham (ed.) (1997), *Financing Decentralized Expenditures: An International Comparison of Grants*, Cheltenham, UK and Lyme, USA: Edward Elgar.

Ahmad, Ehtisham, Gao Qiang and Vito Tanzi (eds) (1995), *Reforming China's Public Finances*, Washington, DC: International Monetary Fund.

Ahmad, Ehtisham and Vito Tanzi (eds) (2002), *Managing Fiscal Decentralization*, London: Routledge.

Ahmad, Ehtisham and Eric Mottu (2003), 'Oil revenue in federal systems: issues and country experience', in J. Davis, R. Ossowski, and A. Fedelino (eds), *Fiscal Policy Formulation and Implementation in Oil Producing Countries*, Washington, DC: International Monetary Fund, pp. 216–42.

Ahmad, Ehtisham, Mario Fortuna and Raju Singh (2004a), 'Towards more effective redistribution: reform options for intergovernmental fiscal relations in China', IMF Working Paper 04/98, Washington, DC: International Monetary Fund.

Ahmad, Ehtisham, Ben Lockwood and Raju Singh (2004b), 'Distributional constraints to the reform of the indirect tax system in China', IMF Working Paper 041125.

Aubut, Julie and Robert Sample (forthcoming), 'Decentralization: the Canadian experience', in Ehtisham Ahmad, Julie Aubut and Robert Sample, *Managing Subnational Fiscal Operations*, Washington, DC: International Monetary Fund.

Boadway, R. and P. Hobson (1993), *Intergovernmental Fiscal Relations in Canada*, Toronto: Canadian Tax Foundation.

Brosio, G. (1995), 'Local taxation in an international context', in Ahmad et al. (eds), pp. 178–93.

Clark, Douglas H. (1997), 'The fiscal transfer system in Canada', in Ahmad (ed.), pp. 70–102.

Commonwealth Grants Commission (2004a), *Report on State Revenue Sharing Relativities, 2004 Review*, Commonwealth of Australia.

Commonwealth Grants Commission (2004b), *Report on State Revenue Sharing Relativities, 2004 Review*, *Supporting Information*, Commonwealth of Australia.

Løtz, J. (1997), 'Denmark and other Scandinavian countries: equalization and grants', in Ahmad (ed.), pp. 184–203.

Løtz, J. (2005), *Danish Grant Policy: How Best to Influence Local Authority Behavior*, Copenhagen: Ministry of Finance.

Rao, Govinda (2002), 'Fiscal decentralization in Indian federalism', in Ahmad and Tanzi (eds), pp. 286–305.

Rye, C.R. and B. Searle (1997), 'The fiscal transfer system in Australia', in E. Ahmad (ed.), p. 144.

Shah, Anwar (1995), 'Theory and practice of international transfers,', in Ahmad et al. (eds), pp. 215–34.

16 Subnational public financial management: institutions and macroeconomic considerations

Ehtisham Ahmad, Maria Albino-War and Raju Singh[1]

Introduction

Practical issues relating to effective public financial management ultimately govern whether or not there is good governance at the subnational level – hence the success or failure of different policy options. Although there is a growing literature on 'fiscal rules' and subnational debt management,[2] less attention has been paid to the critical governance aspects of public financial management. Part of this neglect may be due to the presumption that decentralization, together with community-based decision making, would suffice in generating efficient and equitable spending decisions.

Indeed, the emphasis on community participation was a feature of development strategy in the 1950s, largely driven by the Ford Foundation and US foreign assistance programs.[3] Despite a lack of significant success at the time, there has been a resurgence of the policy in recent years due to the efforts of non-governmental organizations (NGOs). The emphasis on community-driven development was adopted as one of the cornerstones of the World Bank's Comprehensive Development Framework (World Bank 2001). However, there is increasing evidence that weak or absent public financial management functions and institutions are likely to negate any advantages that might be inherent in bringing public services 'closer' to local communities.

The underpinnings of public financial management relate to the basic institutional and procedural elements that might be enshrined in a constitution, or higher-level laws on the budget,[4] or laws or agreements governing subnational operations or levels of indebtedness. In some countries, such as South Africa, where the process has been nicely sequenced, there is a set of consistent and well-designed legislation covering all the areas mentioned above.[5]

In order for any level of government to take responsibility for its actions, there must be clarity in its functions, its spending prioritization, its mechanisms for appropriating funds and prioritizing and authorizing spending, and ensuring that the spending is actually carried out and accounted for. Another critical aspect relates to timely and accurate reporting to the respective legislature and any higher levels of administration. In short, questions would need to be posed concerning the transparency and accountability of a government and whether these meet minimum international standards.[6]

Quite often the consequences of subnational spending can be shifted to higher levels of government, or across generations, if there is no hard budget constraint at a junior level of government (Rodden et al. 2003). This generally translates into weak or non-existent control over borrowing. The borrowing might be explicit, for example, through issuance of debt or contracting of loans, or indirect, such as through the build-up of arrears or accounts payable. Under different constitutional arrangements, policy responses vary from enforced controls over subnational borrowing (generally in unitary states) to voluntary agreements or rules (in federations, as well as in supranational conglomerations of states, such as the EU), to sole reliance on the strictures of the market.[7]

In this chapter, we introduce the concepts and practices that would apply in the budget processes in unitary and federal states, and also mechanisms to manage overall indebtedness and sustainability of fiscal positions.

Community-based developments

The case for community-based governance depends on the possibilities of local information generation together with the networks of intercommunity interactions or social capital. The combination of these factors could, in principle, generate spending tailored to local needs, with substantive local interactions in order to ensure that funds are not diverted from expressed objectives. And as stated above, international and donor agencies have raised these possibilities in the design of assistance programs.[8] But, in practice, there are two substantive difficulties. The first relates to whether or not there might be elite capture,[9] and the second, that would serve to reinforce the first, relates to the type of information that is generated. In the final analysis, the case turns on the effectiveness of local service delivery and whether or not powerful local interest groups are able to garner a significant proportion of funds allocated to the localities.

Bardhan and Mookherjee (2005) discuss theoretical trade-offs between centralized and decentralized delivery of infrastructure services. Under conditions of considerable inequality, poorer and vulnerable sections of society might be disadvantaged by community-based development, as existing social and economic relations might be used by more influential groups to the disadvantage of the usual target groups (Platteau 2004). Platteau also emphasizes the risks of the outright embezzlement of funds, in addition to wasteful or misdirected spending. These tendencies are likely to be reinforced when, as described above, the public financial management (PFM) infrastructure, especially information flows and independent audit, are weak.

The evidence on community-based development is mixed, at best (see the survey by Mansuri and Rao 2004). An assessment of social investment funds suggests that these have been less than successful in generating 'ownership' among the local communities, with a mismatch between the preferences of the donors and recipients, despite a 'façade' of consultation between communities and donors through the PFM process.

A strong conclusion by Platteau (2004) is that electorates may not be willing or able to discipline corrupt local leaders, especially if there is some trickle-down and improvement regardless of the magnitude of funds diverted. And competition among donors may make matters worse. Platteau's proposals include a sequential disbursement of assistance, based on accurate information on the spending, together with an improved technology of fraud detection. Equally important are the effective mechanisms put in place to prevent and punish misuse of public funds. These translate into the infrastructure of budgeting and public spending, including adequate and effective control and audit mechanisms.

The public financial management processes
In order to meet the requirement of providing accurate and timely information to policy makers, the legislature and the broader public, there is increasing emphasis in organic budget laws around the world that the budget should comply with the principles of comprehensiveness, unity and internal consistency. Without the associated budgeting, reporting and audit infrastructure, it is unlikely that the good governance aspects of decentralized operations would be realized.

The principle of *comprehensiveness* requires that the budget cover all government agencies and institutions undertaking government operations, so that the budget presents a consolidated and complete view of these operations and is voted on, as a whole, by the body vested with national legislative authority. Unfortunately, in many cases, donors' demands to maintain donor funds in extrabudgetary or off-budget accounts have undermined the transparency and financial discipline of government operations (Premchand 1996), and often generated parallel and uncoordinated budget systems.

The principle of *unity* requires that the budget includes all revenues and expenditures of all government agencies undertaking government operations. This principle is important to ensure that the budget is an effective instrument to impose a constraint on total and sectoral government expenditure, and promote higher efficiency in the allocation of resources.

The principle of *internal consistency* between different components of the budget requires, in particular, that current expenditure needed for the maintenance and operation of past investments be fully reflected in the budget. Moreover, this principle implies that there should be no dual budget systems involving a split between current and capital (or development) spending.

The principles above translate in different ways in terms of information requirements for appropriations, accounting, controls and reporting, depending on the budgeting framework in use – and we distinguish here between a continuum based on traditional budgeting frameworks and those based on 'performance or outcomes'. These are discussed sequentially below.

Government accountability

Government accountability is an essential principle of democracy through which elected and unelected public officials are obligated to explain their decisions and actions to the legislature and the broader public to ensure an appropriate use of public resources. The framework for government accountability usually includes a combination of political, legal and administrative mechanisms designed to hold public officials responsible for their performance.[10]

Fixed terms of office and fair elections are key political mechanisms to hold policy makers accountable. With these mechanisms, the electorate could remove elected government officials if their performance is not in line with public expectations. Legal mechanisms of accountability for both elected and unelected officials include all legislation proscribing actions that public officials can and cannot take as well as sanctions against officials with unsatisfactory conduct. A precondition of legal accountability is an independent judicial system. Administrative accountability mechanisms entail independent auditors and ombudsmen, to ensure that public officials do not transgress mandates or misuse public monies.

A community-based scheme for government accountability combining political, legal and administrative mechanisms has received increasing attention from international agencies. Particularly important under this scheme are the legal instruments that require input from the communities on certain government decisions or provide access to the press or the broader public to information on government activities.

Traditional budgeting models

The traditional cycle of budget appropriations, execution, accounting, control and reporting are described for both unitary and federal states. The recent experiences of developing countries in meeting the expenditure accountability requirements of the heavily indebted poor country (HIPC) initiative are summarized in Dorotinsky and Floyd (2004).

Appropriations The typical stages of budgeting include decisions by the administration and authorized by the relative legislature on what to spend – this is the appropriation stage. This would increasingly be placed in a medium-term framework to fully capture the effects of decisions that last for multiple periods.

In a unitary state with deconcentrated subnational governments, all the budget decisions would be made by the central government and approved by the national legislature. Such an arrangement would be perfectly compatible with local communities reflecting their priorities to the agents of the center for incorporation in the national list of appropriations, as well as involvement with actual implementation.

In a federal system, the center would appropriate transfers for each level, which in turn would prepare their own budgets. There would then be a premium on ensuring that promised transfers – either special-purpose or general, 'equalization' transfers – are made in a timely manner.

Under either system, a fundamental rule for preventing rent seeking and ensuring accountability, throughout the entire budget process, is that there should be no spending without adequate appropriations and financing arrangements. In countries with the old Francophone PFM systems, funding could be provided to public entities without appropriations during the budget execution process, and 'legalized' as an *ex post* appropriation in the budget of the subsequent year. This practice clearly weakens the possibilities of ensuring government accountability.

In order to ensure macroeconomic stability, the central government has the responsibility of ensuring that overall risks, including debt, are kept within prudent limits. As discussed below, this places a responsibility on the center, even within federal systems, to ensure that prudential debt limits are not exceeded in aggregate – this poses difficult problems of determining the overall debt limit and then apportioning this among the different levels of government. This issue is reflected even in supranational administrations, such as the European Union's Stability and Growth Pact.[11] And considerable emphasis is needed on a standardized basis for budget appropriations and execution in order to ensure an orderly assessment of budgets and outcomes.[12]

Budget execution   The standardized budget classification is the basis for tracking and reporting expenditures, and for determining whether there have been any diversions of public monies for unauthorized purposes. This is essential even if there has been appropriation at a fairly aggregate level, in order to present consistent and comparable information to the policy makers or the public at large.

In some countries, especially in unitary ones, the central government is responsible for establishing standards for the accounting and reporting systems of all levels of governments and usually is also responsible for their enforcement. The development of sound budget, accounting and reporting systems is a complex and time-consuming process and it would not be efficient or cost-effective for subnational governments to develop their accounting and information reporting systems on their own.

While cash-based systems are generally deemed insufficient to cover all aspects of budget execution, relatively few developing countries have the capability to operate accrual accounting. None the less, many countries try to monitor the generation of arrears by registering commitments and recognition of liability. This usually entails the utilization of government financial information systems. These have been relatively expensive, but simpler versions are now becoming available for use in smaller jurisdictions – thus in principle permitting subnational administrations to also operate in an environment as conducive to overall accountability as the center – however, these systems require standardized generation of information (such as through the common budget classification described above).

This standardized generation of information was a major feature of the reform of subnational finances carried out in Brazil in the late 1990s, with substantial benefits for the management of the consolidated public finances. A Fiscal Responsibility Law for Brazil was approved in May 2000, which (i) introduced a golden rule provision; (ii) imposed new uniform accounting, planning and transparency requirements on all levels of government. States and municipalities are now required to submit multiyear plans and reports on the use of resources from privatization, social security funds and contingent liabilities; (iii) attempted to enhance the credibility of the central government's no-bailout commitment by prohibiting the central government from bailing out any member of the federation and the central bank from exchanging the debt securities of the states for federal public debt securities; and (iv) increased the role given to the judiciary and the penal system in the enforcement of certain of its provisions, mandating prison sentences for illegal efforts to issue bonds and stipulating the dismissal of a mayor or governor if debt limits or personnel expenditure ratios are exceeded. It is too early to assess whether the new legislation has improved the control of subnational borrowing, although the fiscal position of states seem to have improved significantly (Figure 16.1). Economic growth, improved tax administration, and privatization proceeds have increased states' resources and have contributed to an improvement in their fiscal positions. However, the fact that states have not spent all these windfall revenues may suggest a new pattern of behavior.

Other countries, such as China and Kazakhstan, have established treasury single accounts (TSAs) at the local level as a mechanism not only to enhance cash management and prevent diversion of government resources and accumulation of arrears but also to improve financial discipline and transparency of local government operations.[13]

Audit and control   Developing countries tend to place considerable importance on internal, *ex ante* controls, as the external controls exercised by

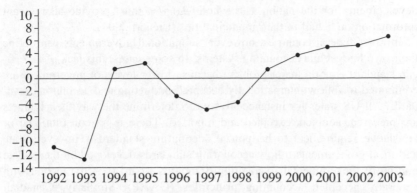

Figure 16.1   Brazil: subnational primary balance, 1992–2003 (in percent of revenues)

supreme audit agencies tends to be deficient or ill-defined – several state audit institutions (SAIs) in developing countries in Latin America and the Middle East are more engaged in *ex ante* vetting of operations than in external controls. Indeed this admixture leads to a conflict of interest, as the SAI would have to adjudicate in some cases on its own *ex ante* controls. The lack of independence from the administration is also often a factor that undermines the quality and effectiveness of external controls. As seen in the HIPC exercise, the control and audit mechanisms are a weak link in the spending chain and a major impediment to good governance and accountability (Dorotinsky and Floyd 2004).

Reporting and generation of information   Both unitary and federal states illustrate a mixture of standardization and some flexibility, but most have minimum requirements that periodic information must be presented in a common format. Where common reporting standards are absent, problems are faced in managing macroeconomic challenges.

In a unitary state, Denmark, municipalities and counties are required to use the standard budgeting and accounting systems defined by the center. However, local councils are free to adapt the accounting system to suit their local needs. Information based on the standard accounting system is collected by the central authorities to monitor development in local governments' expenditure and revenue (Juul forthcoming).

In Germany, a federal law governs budgetary management at all levels of government, mandating the use of a detailed budgetary classification, a uniform cash-based accounting system, as well as a multiannual financial planning. The law also obliges all levels of government to provide the Financial Planning Council with all necessary information to monitor fiscal developments for the nation as a whole. *Länder* must provide all relevant information on behalf of their municipalities (Lienert 2004).

In other federal countries, however, subnational governments can define their own budget and accounting systems. In some cases, this lack of an official standard is not a major problem because lower levels of government are committed to follow internationally accepted budgeting and accounting standards. All US states for instance are free to determine the way their budgets are prepared, adopted, executed and reported. There is no constitutional or legislative requirement to harmonize accounting standards. However, state and local governments follow accounting standards developed by the private non-profit Governmental Accounting Standards Board (GASB) in line with generally accepted accounting principles (GAAP). Similarly, Canadian provinces have voluntarily adhered to the standards of the Public Sector Accounting Board, the independent and authoritative standard-setting body for the public sector in Canada.

Belgium focuses on monitoring the budget execution of the different subsectors (federal government, the communities and the regions) and data on budget execution at all levels are now exchanged on a monthly basis. The interministerial conference is the driving force, serving as a forum for peer review and seeking to strengthen the accountability of subsectors (De Smet forthcoming). In Australia, Commonwealth States and Territories report a minimum amount of financial information in a uniform presentation framework (UPF). While many states and territories continue to prepare their budgets using different budget classification and accounting standards, each jurisdiction attaches data in the UPF format to their budgets (Robinson forthcoming).

In some other federations such as Mexico and Argentina, subnational governments are totally free to define their own budget and accounting systems. As a result, local fiscal data is characterized by large inconsistencies in terms of how revenues and expenditures are reported in public accounts. In addition, the lack of an agreed framework or guidelines for presenting state-level fiscal data makes it very difficult to consolidate fiscal accounts at the national level.[14] In the absence of uniform budget and accounting standards, at a minimum a uniform reporting system should be in place at the local level. Credible sanctions for either non-compliance or untimely reporting should be introduced. However, the increasing practice has usually been to reach agreements with lower levels of government on financial reporting requirements. Agreements which do not result in specific sanctions or penalties for breaches of the agreement are generally ineffective.

Poterba and von Hagen (1999) examined the experience in Europe and view the set of rules and regulations according to which budgets are drafted, approved and implemented as an important determinant of public sector deficits and debts. A similar result was found by von Hagen and Harden (1994): countries with more transparent budget procedures exhibited greater fiscal discipline in the 1980s and early 1990s.

Performance-based systems
In a number of countries, in particular, industrial countries such as the United Kingdom and New Zealand, there has been a sustained push to inculcate into the budgeting process greater accountability for results. This has been accompanied by a far-reaching reform of the state, including its functions in providing public services.

The most recent country attempting to follow this path is France, following on from the introduction of a new organic budget law in 2001, together with a restructuring of deconcentrated governments into decentralized levels of administration. The French reforms entail an overhaul of the appropriations system and the introduction of a new budget classification and reporting system, with adequate lead time for preparation (at least five years, and in practice longer).

Many developing countries (especially in Latin America and Africa) attempting to 'follow the lead' of the New Zealand reforms often lack the preconditions and necessary preparatory work in order to implement performance budgeting, especially at the subnational level where the public financial management systems are particularly weak.

Without mechanisms to effectively track spending (for example, on the basis of a consistent budget classification), it would be premature to rush into performance-based budgeting at the subnational level. Moreover, accounting and audit mechanisms would be critical in ensuring that funds are not misappropriated, and that the relevant officials are held responsible for funds received as well as the outcomes of such spending. There is typically greater need for good information systems, not only to track and monitor financial flows and public spending, but also to monitor physical targets and outcomes of the spending.

While performance-based budgeting systems are an attractive tool to generate accountability in spending agencies and levels of government, the preconditions for such an institutional change need to be carefully assessed and implemented before a major restructuring is introduced.

Macroeconomic stability and subnational debt management

Rationale for managing subnational debt
Macroeconomic stability for a country or supranational economic union depends on the overall aggregate exposure to risk – and a critical element of the latter is the borrowing of all the component jurisdictions in the relevant

country or economic union. It is important to distinguish between how the borrowing controls are defined and how they are enforced.

Local governments, as well as the center, could better face cyclical downturns and smooth delivery of public services if borrowing were permitted. The need for subnational borrowing could arise from the particular allocation of responsibilities, transfer system or revenue arrangements between the different levels of government. Subnational borrowing could be called for particularly when local governments are responsible for local infrastructure. Further, local borrowing could then be justified on the basis of the benefit principle. Investments that usually yield benefits over several years should be financed by borrowing, so that future generations enjoying the benefits would also share part of the financing. Further, such investment decisions are not subject to 'controls' from higher levels of administration. In line with this reasoning, many countries including Denmark, Germany, Italy and the United Kingdom have allowed subnational governments to borrow explicitly to finance investment expenditures.

Even if granting borrowing authority to local governments might be justified, handing them the power to borrow without limits may not be appropriate. Imposing borrowing controls at the local level may be needed to preserve macroeconomic stability as well as to safeguard local public finances.

In the absence of any limits on subnational borrowing, the central government faces the risk that local governments may try to free ride on its efforts to stabilize the economy – effectively passing the costs of excessive borrowing on to other jurisdictions or future generations. Larger subnational governments that are 'too big to be ignored' could hold the central government to ransom by bargaining for debt write-offs and other fiscal advantages.

Local governments' efforts to conduct anticyclical policies – if left unchecked – could also result in ratcheting up public spending. Policy makers are likely to borrow when the economy is slowing down, but may be reluctant to repay the debt when the economy is recovering. In addition, during recoveries voters and vested interest groups often put pressure on local authorities to increase the provision of public goods or decrease the tax burden, reducing any fiscal surpluses available for debt repayment (Buchanan, Rowley and Tollison 1987). Local politicians may even take advantage from the fact that taxpayers might not correctly discount their future tax liabilities and pursue increasing borrowing strategies to mitigate the current tax bill (Moesen 1993).

But above all, the need to control local borrowing arises from the common-pool problem and the soft budget constraint it implies. The common-pool problem stems from the separation of costs and benefits of public spending. If a certain public project predominantly benefits a particular jurisdiction but is financed through a common pool of taxes collected from all over the country, this jurisdiction will pay only a small fraction of the costs of the project while enjoying a large fraction of its benefits. This lack of full internalization of the costs of a project will result in excessive spending[15] and create a clear incentive for the regions to compete for federal transfers that enable them to finance region-specific projects out of a common pool. Ideally, regions would compete on the basis of the quality of their proposed spending projects. Alternatively, they could signal that they are in particular need of federal assistance by running large budget deficits or accumulating unsustainable debts, and hope that the central government grants will eventually bail them out.

The possibility of a bailout does not stem from the existence of a common pool *per se*, but from the way in which it is administered. When transfers are allocated on the basis of *ex post* financial needs rather than *ex ante* characteristics, regions experiencing financial difficulties could be bailed out by the central government. In this case the budget constraint faced by the subnational government becomes 'soft': if regional authorities undercollect taxes, overspend or default on the debt, they expect the federal government to cover the financing gap. Moreover, lenders also lose incentives to police regional governments as they view their investments as protected by a federal government guarantee.[16]

These problems would not exist, if central governments could credibly commit to never revising transfer allocations *ex post*, that is, to a no-bailout policy. Unfortunately, such a policy stance, arguably optimal in the long run, is difficult to commit to in the short run, especially if it involves a painful local default or a reduction in the provision of basic public services with schools being closed and pensions left unpaid. Persson and Tabellini (1996) and Bordignon et al. (2001) show formally that even a national government maximizing the federation's social welfare is likely to find it beneficial to bail out a financially distressed region. In addition, a default by one region can increase the cost of borrowing for all other regions in a federation, so neighbors themselves may be interested in providing the defaulting region with a bailout transfer.

A typology of borrowing controls

A typology of classification of borrowing controls described by Ter-Minassian and Craig (1997) refers to four broad 'stylized' categories: (i) market discipline; (ii) rules-based controls; (iii) administrative controls; and (iv) cooperation between different levels of government.

Market discipline   Some countries rely exclusively on capital markets to restrain subnational borrowing. In this case, the central government would not set any limits on subnational borrowing and local governments are free to decide amounts, sources and uses of borrowing. Provinces in Canada as well as US states have the right to borrow with no central review or control.

Similarly, in Argentina, all levels of government are permitted to borrow both domestically and abroad.[17]

Markets have been myopic, as in the case of Argentina, and in many parts of the world, capital markets at the local level are inadequately developed to conceive of extensive reliance on market-based borrowing, or the ability of markets to discipline subnational government. Moreover, it is increasingly becoming clear that the ratings agencies, where they operate at the subnational level, evaluate all the public financial management criteria described above, as well as the overall design of intergovernmental system.

Subnational governments may, however, decide independently to adopt a fiscal rule in an attempt to enhance their credit standing in the market. Such self-imposed rules are found for example in Canada, Switzerland and the United States. In these countries, subnational governments generally have direct access to financial markets to meet their borrowing requirements, and there are few precedents of bailouts of insolvent subnational governments by the central government; hence their desire to maintain a favorable credit rating in the markets. More recently, Argentina sought to follow this approach with the introduction of a fiscal responsibility law and the establishment of a Federal Council for Fiscal Responsibility.

Rules-based approach   In some cases, the central government might try to contain subnational borrowing by imposing a fiscal rule. Both federal and unitary states have relied on various standing rules, specified in the constitution or in laws to control subnational borrowing, in an effort to confer credibility for the conduct of macroeconomic policies. Such rules introduce a constraint on fiscal policy to guarantee that fundamentals will remain predictable and robust regardless of the government in charge.

Types of fiscal rules   Numeric fiscal rules can undermine a fiscal consolidation effort if poorly designed, not adequately enforced and easily reversible. We shall now discuss some categories of fiscal rules.

Ceilings on debt or borrowing are in general simple and relatively easy to monitor. However, they can be circumvented by asset sales, debt transfers to local public enterprises outside the governmental sector or by sale-and-lease-back operations. Debt ceilings should be defined in net terms to assess long-term fiscal sustainability, despite the uncertainty and volatility of the value of publicly held assets.

A *deficit target* has the advantage of simplicity and of being easily understood by the wider public, but could fail to prevent debt accumulation because of off-budget items. Fiscal rules targeting the overall budget deficit (for instance in Austria – within a domestic stability pact – Belgium, Spain, and most US states) or operating deficit (for instance in Norway) are the most frequent. However, such rules can be met with higher revenues and expenditures, with possible macroeconomic implications.

Expenditure rules place a ceiling on what governments can control most directly – the level of expenditure. These rules are conceptually simple, easy to monitor, and tackle the deficit problem at its source. Several studies have found that expenditure ceilings played a significant role in reducing spending in the United States (see Poterba 1997; Schick 2000). A common expenditure ceiling could be more difficult to implement at the subnational level than a deficit target and not necessarily prevent debt accumulation since spending could be pushed below the line.

The golden rule limits subnational governments' borrowing to investment purposes and is quite common in industrial countries. Intergenerational fairness provides the most forceful argument in favor of a golden rule. However, there is no guarantee that increased borrowing for infrastructure expenditure would be consistent with macroeconomic stability and debt sustainability. Moreover, it may not be desirable to allow borrowing for investments without an adequate rate of economic and social return. The German constitution defines a golden rule for the federal and subnational governments. More recently, the law on local finances in Spain introduced a golden rule in the late 1980s.

Rules related to debt repayment capacity seek to 'mimic' market discipline by linking limits on the indebtedness of subnational government to the projected debt service on the debt, or the other indicators of their debt-servicing capacity (such as past revenue or the tax base). These rules may be better suited to addressing considerations of long-term sustainability and intergenerational equity. In the mid-1990s, Colombia and Hungary established rules for subnational governments related to debt repayment capacity. These rules, however, might not be effective in containing debt accumulation if financial conditions are manipulated.

Effectiveness of fiscal rules Fiscal rules are attractive since they are generally transparent, and relatively easy to monitor. The main disadvantage of this approach is a subtle trade-off between ensuring compliance and preserving flexibility. Strict fiscal rules with universal coverage leave little room for maneuver in the case of unexpected economic downturns while more flexible fiscal rules with escape clauses lack credibility and, when easy to circumvent in practice, fail to impose sufficient discipline. In practice, the efficacy of fiscal rules for subnational governments (or for national governments in a supranational economic area, such as the EU) depends critically on the ability to measure and monitor the generation of debts and other liabilities.

Several studies have looked at the effectiveness of subnational government rules in the context of US states.[18] This sample provides a relatively large dataset and includes some variation in budget rules. Indeed, the nature and the scope of balanced budget requirements vary widely across US states. In most cases, limits apply only to part of the state budget, notably the operating budget (general fund), with the exclusion of special funds (such as capital-spending funds and social insurance trust funds). In some cases, the rule is included in the state constitution, in others it is contained in an ordinary law. The general results are that rules do enforce some budget discipline on US states, in terms of lower deficits and quicker reaction to negative fiscal shocks.

Administrative approach   In a number of countries, the central government is empowered with direct control over the borrowing of subnational governments. This control may take various forms, including the setting of annual (or more frequent) limits on the overall debt of individual subnational jurisdictions (or some of its components, such as external borrowing); the review and authorization of individual borrowing operations (including approval of the terms and conditions of the operation); and/or the centralization of all government borrowing, with on-lending to subnational governments. In India, for instance, any borrowing by state governments requires prior approval from the center whenever there are any loans outstanding from the latter (which is the case as all states are in debt to the center). Similarly in Spain, foreign debt as well as bond issuances by subnational governments are subject to the approval of the ministry of finance.

A major drawback of this approach is the moral hazard given the implicit or explicit guarantee that the central government's approval may confer to subnational borrowing. Administrative approval by the central government of individual borrowing operations of the subnational governments may well make it more difficult for the former to refuse financial support to the latter in the event of impending defaults. Detailed administrative controls may also involve the central government in microlevel decisions (for example, about the financing of individual investment projects) that would be best left to the relevant subnational jurisdictions.

Several considerations could argue, however, in favor of direct central government controls on the external borrowing of subnational governments. First, external debt policy is closely linked with other macroeconomic policies (monetary and exchange rate policies and foreign reserve management) that are the responsibility of central-level authorities (in particular, the central bank). Second, a coordinated approach to foreign markets for sovereign borrowing is likely to result in better terms and conditions than a fragmented one. Third, a deterioration of foreign ratings for one or more of the subnational borrowers may well spill-over to those of other borrowers, both public and private. Finally, foreign lenders often require an explicit central government guarantee for subnational borrowing or – at a minimum – expect an implicit guarantee.

Cooperative approach Under this approach, borrowing controls for subnational governments are designed through a negotiation process between the federal and the lower levels of government. Subnational governments are actively involved in formulating macroeconomic objectives and key fiscal parameters, making them co-responsible for their achievement. Through this process, agreement is reached on the overall deficit targets for the general government, as well as on the main items of revenue and expenditure. Specific limits are then agreed upon for the financing requirements of individual subnational jurisdictions. Variants of this approach may be found in some European countries and in Australia.

Austria, for example, introduced in 1996 a consultation mechanism between the different levels of government to ensure that the overall deficit fell below 3 per cent. Similarly, in Denmark annual borrowing ceilings for subnational governments are defined in (non-binding) negotiations between the central government and two associations of subnational governments in the context of the annual budget process. In Belgium, a Higher Finance Council (HFC), comprising members nominated by the federal, community and regional levels, and the Belgian National Bank, provide recommendations about the borrowing requirements of different levels of government. The federal government then concludes agreements with lower levels to achieve these targets (see De Smet forthcoming). In Australia, a fiscal institution – the Loan Council – was set up in 1929 to coordinate the borrowing of the Commonwealth and the states. The council is chaired by the Commonwealth treasurer and comprises the premier or treasurer of each state. In recent years, as greater reliance has been placed on market-based discipline, the role of the Loan Council has become one of establishing mandatory fiscal transparency requirements (see Robinson forthcoming).

The cooperative approach has clear advantages in promoting dialogue and exchange of information across various government levels. It also raises the awareness, at the subnational level, of the macroeconomic implications of their budgetary choices. However, this approach works best when the central government is strong and able to steer the intergovernmental negotiations effectively. This condition may not hold in many emerging markets.

Circumventing borrowing limits

There are a number of innovative mechanisms that have been used by subnational governments to circumvent borrowing limits.

Off-budget entities have been used in a number of cases, for instance in Germany to circumvent borrowing controls. Since the early 1990s, local governments have created independent administrative enterprises to which they outsourced a part of their fiscal activities. The newly created entities could take loans that did not appear in official statistics, since they were local enterprises under private law. In Saarbrucken, for example, while the local government debt declined from DM 658 million to DM 632 million from 1990 to 1994, the debt from administration-related enterprises increased from 0 to DM 227 million (Dafflon 2002).

Publicly owned enterprises have been used in disparate cases ranging from China to Australia for borrowing purposes. In response to the prospect of a resource-led boom in Australia in the late 1970s, the Commonwealth accepted the states' request for higher public sector borrowing for financing large infrastructure projects and established a separate category for such borrowing programs. In the early 1980s, the Loan Council decided to exempt from its approval domestic borrowings of large semi-government authorities and relaxed restrictions on foreign borrowing. As a result of the new opportunities, from 1977–78 to 1982–83, borrowing from state public enterprises tripled, reaching at its peak 2.8 per cent of GDP. In 1984, the Loan Council adopted a new global limit approach, abandoning the distinction between semi-government authorities and the rest of the government.

Sale-and-lease-back operations have been set up, for instance, in Denmark to avoid borrowing regulations. Local governments began converting fixed tangible assets such as schools and office buildings into liquidity reserves to avoid borrowing controls. The first reaction of the central government was to require local governments to deposit the cash in a bank account for a minimum of ten years. Local governments, however, were not deterred and even started to benefit financially from these arrangements by investing revenues in long-term bonds and providing the leasing company with short-term financing. The central government then expanded the definition of borrowing to include not only short- and long-term financing but also renting and leasing arrangements (Dafflon 2002).

Enforcing borrowing controls

Three basic mechanisms are used by countries to enforce borrowing controls at the subnational level: (i) market discipline; (ii) intergovernmental entities operating within a cooperative arrangement; and (iii) administrative procedures carried out by an entity of the public sector.

Market discipline   A well-functioning financial market enforces discipline and sound borrowing practices on subnational governments by imposing increasing borrowing costs or by denying access to financing. There is evidence in the US bond market that state and local governments with higher outstanding debt and lower incomes are faced with higher borrowing costs. Similarly, during the late 1980s on the Brazilian credit market, private investors demanded higher interest rates and shorter bond maturities from states with precarious finances. At some point, private markets even refused to hold state debt at any price.

The ballot box – electoral discipline – could also be viewed as an alternative form of market discipline. In Australia, in the early 1990s the political cost of relatively marginal downgrades in state credit ratings (for example, from AAA to A) was far greater than the financial cost. State governments which had presided over unsustainable deficits and growing debt were defeated at the polls (Robinson forthcoming).

A number of conditions should be satisfied, however, for financial markets to exert effective discipline over subnational borrowing (Lane 1993). First, markets should be free and open, with no regulations on financial intermediaries (such as portfolio composition requirements) that could place subnational governments in a privileged-borrower position. Second, adequate information on the borrower's outstanding debt and repayment capacity should be available to potential lenders. Third, there should be no perceived chance of bailout of the lenders by the central government in cases of impending defaults. Finally, the borrower should have institutional structures which ensure adequate policy responsiveness to market signals.

These are stringent conditions, unlikely to be realized in most countries. Typically, especially in developing countries, available information on subnational government finances still suffers from serious weaknesses in coverage, quality and timeliness. Many countries still use various forms of portfolio constraints on financial intermediaries to facilitate placement of government securities at reduced cost. Local governments, particularly in developing countries, maintain ownership or a controlling stake in financial institutions which provide a captive market for their borrowing. Furthermore, many countries have seen various forms of intervention by the central government (or the central bank) to prevent subnational government from defaulting and relatively short electoral cycles tend to make local politicians shortsighted and unresponsive to early warnings by the financial markets.

Moreover, an important shortcoming of market discipline is that it relies on instruments – most notably, interest rate risk premia and sovereign credit ratings – that do not react smoothly to fiscal developments. Instead, they often provide an abrupt response to particularly poor fiscal choices, and as such do not provide very much advance warning for the need to restore fiscal discipline.

The problems created by the buildup of state debts in Brazil illustrate the risks of overly relying on market discipline. Yet even in a country like Canada, with well-developed and relatively transparent financial markets and little history of bailouts by the federal government, market discipline has not proven fully effective. Despite a clear deterioration in ratings and sizeable increases in risk premia on provincial bonds, provincial debt has risen steadily over the

1990s and only in the last few years of that decade has the provincial government begun to design and implement fiscal retrenchment programs.

Cooperative arrangements   Because the conditions for effective market discipline are so stringent, few countries rely on sanctions and penalties imposed by the market or the electorate. Countries have usually relied on other enforcement mechanisms, based either on centrally organized administrative measures or on cooperative arrangements. In the latter framework, an agreement is sought among subnational governments to impose administrative as well as financial sanctions and penalties. An intergovernmental entity in charge of enforcing borrowing controls could promote the dialogue and enhance responsibility across different levels of government.

In this setting, peer pressure may play an important role. In Denmark, for example, the enforcement of subnational borrowing ceilings is carried out by two associations of local governments (one for regions and another for municipalities) in charge of negotiating agreements for such ceilings with the central government. The associations monitor the performance of their members through the budget process and put political and peer pressure on those deviating from the agreement. Peer pressure is to some extent effective, given the strong political position and credibility enjoyed by the associations and the collective nature of the financial sanctions applied to all members of an association.

Cooperative arrangements, however, could be a weak enforcement mechanism if the imposition of sanctions and penalties is subject to the unanimous decision of a body consisting of representatives from all government tiers. In Austria, sanctions for non-compliance are imposed on subnational governments after a long process and only in cases of major deviations. The National Statistical Office is responsible for reporting major cases of non-compliance to the National Coordination Committee. A conciliation committee is then set up to seek an expert assessment on the extent of the deviation. Based on the expert opinion, the conciliation committee decides which sanctions should be applied (Balassone et al. 2003).

Administrative procedures   Different public sector entities could also enforce borrowing controls on subnational governments through administrative procedures. This responsibility is often delegated to higher levels of government or to the national ministry of finance considering its role in ensuring a sustainable fiscal position for the region or the general public sector. In Belgium, the federal government as well as regional governments can impose sanctions and penalties on a subnational government that breaches borrowing limits. The action of the federal government focuses on limiting the borrowing capacity of a subnational government, while the regional government has the power to enforce, if necessary, expenditure reductions or tax increases.

Greater independence and credibility could be given to the enforcement process by delegating the monitoring as well as the imposition of sanctions and penalties to independent entities such as the national audit office or the judicial system. The national audit office could have the authority to fine institutions or persons, while the judicial system could impose prison sentences and loss of political immunity. In Brazil, the fiscal responsibility law has assigned to the judiciary the enforcement of certain of its provisions.

Dealing with subnational debt crises
Should borrowing controls fail to safeguard the soundness of subnational public finances, the institutional framework should include a clearly defined procedure for crisis resolution, if *ad hoc* bailouts are to be avoided. Several countries have thus strengthened their enforcement mechanisms by incorporating specific regulations to deal with subnational debt crises.

The resolution of such crises should comprise both short- as well as long-term measures. Short-term measures generally include some form of debt restructuring to alleviate the financial difficulties of the subnational government, but usually cannot ensure the sustainability of subnational finances unless they are supplemented with more structural measures. These could take the form of (i) subnational fiscal adjustments plans; (ii) administrative intervention by a higher level of government; or (iii) judicial procedures for insolvency and bankruptcy.

Subnational fiscal adjustment plans are usually linked to debt restructuring programs and thus are negotiated with the ministry of finance at the central level. The plans usually specify revenue or expenditure measures to be adopted by the subnational government to strengthen its fiscal position. In Brazil, for example, the fiscal adjustment plans negotiated in the context of the 1996 debt restructuring program committed states to debt reduction, higher revenue collection, and reduced payroll expenditure. In addition, the plan included tight conditions for new borrowing and mandated states to use as collateral their own revenue and transfers from the federal government. The plans also committed states to privatize their state-owned enterprises and use privatization receipts to reduce their debt.

Administrative intervention by higher levels of government could start by simply recommending that the subnational government strengthen its fiscal position. More direct administrative interventions imply specific measures to adjust the local fiscal positions. The most stringent administrative interventions consist of temporary takeovers of the local financial administration by a higher level of government, or by a council reporting to the higher-level government. The intervention of the US federal government in the finances of Washington, DC and the intervention approach of Ohio State are two cases in point.

In 1995, an act by Congress declared the District of Colombia (Washington, DC) in fiscal emergency, mandated that the District's budget be balanced by fiscal year 1999, and approved the temporary creation of a financial control board (FCB) to take over the District administration. The act also delegated the appointment of the five members of the FCB to the President of the United States and defined the main role of the FCB. The tasks of the FCB mandated by the act include the repayment of all borrowing by and on behalf of the District, assistance to the District in regaining adequate access to both short- and long-term credit markets at reasonable rates, and achieving a balanced budget for four consecutive fiscal years. The FCB also received power to reject any local legislation. The board ceased its operations in September 2001, once all its tasks had been achieved.

On the other hand, according to the Ohio State Code of Local Fiscal Emergency, administrative intervention takes a two-phase approach. In phase I, a 'Fiscal Watch Program' is announced by the state auditor when the fiscal position of a local government is close to default. During this phase, the state auditor could at the request of the local government recommend specific measures to improve local finances. In phase II, a 'Fiscal Planning and Advisory Commission' is established by the state to take over temporarily the administrative control of the subnational government in default and restore its debt service capacity. The commission has the power to freeze salaries and staff levels, raise additional revenues and build up reserves.

Finally, some countries have assigned the resolution of subnational debt crises to the judicial system, as a commitment to a no-bailout policy. The US introduced legislation on bankruptcy procedures for states and municipalities in 1937 and Hungary enacted legislation on local government bankruptcy in 1996. In such cases, a judicial court coordinates the interaction of debtors, creditors, citizens and government auditors. In particular, it receives, analyses and approves (or rejects) the request to declare a given subnational government bankrupt. Creditors negotiate with debtors conditions for payment or restructuring of subnational debt and government auditors monitor the financial activities of the insolvent government and impose the necessary penalties.

Conclusions

This chapter has focused on the institutional and procedural backbone of decentralized governance. It has illustrated that decentralization relying solely on community safeguards will generally be insufficient to ensure pro-poor spending, and that there needs to be concomitant emphasis on the generation of accurate and timely information on the actual spending, if not on the outcomes. This needs to be supplemented by effective mechanisms to detect, prevent and punish misuse of resources or diversion of funds.

Even with adequate monitoring of subnational spending, there has to be an emphasis on the effects of such spending, particularly the incurring of debt and other contingent liabilities, on overall macroeconomic aggregates. Again, the implementation of orderly macroeconomic adjustments will rely on the nature of the public financial management infrastructure at all levels of government.

Notes

1. Substantive inputs from Teresa Ter-Minassian were received on an earlier draft of the chapter, and helpful comments from participants at a seminar on fiscal federalism held in Turin, 27–28 August 2004, and from Giorgio Brosio are gratefully acknowledged, as were those received from Héctor Torres, Moises Schwartz and Stephane Rottier.
2. See, for example, reviews by Ter-Minassian and Craig (1997) and Kopits (2001).
3. See Platteau (2004), who reports that more than 60 countries were involved in this strategy. Mansuri and Rao (2004) provide a very comprehensive survey of this literature.
4. This may relate to organic budget laws – such as in France (see *Loi Organique*, 2001), or to ordinary legislation in other countries.
5. See also Republic of South Africa, The Constitution, Act 108 of 1996; the Public Finance Management Act, Act 1 of 1999; and the Municipal Finance Management Act, Act 56 of 2003.
6. For instance, the IMF's Code of Fiscal Transparency.
7. See Ter-Minassian and Craig (1997) for a typology, described in greater detail below.
8. For instance, the heavily indebted poor country (HIPC) debt relief program for Bolivia is designed to provide direct support to local governments to finance social investments.
9. See Bardhan (2002) and also Mansuri and Rao (2004) for a full review. See also Bardhan (Ch. 8 in this volume).
10. US Department of State (2004).
11. Indeed, as seen in the recent discussion of the debt limits in countries such as Germany, penalties under the pact must be implemented to be credible; and there should also be a corresponding capability to monitor the compliance with the stipulations (as has recently been illustrated in the case of Greece).
12. For example, this includes the economic classification as enunciated by the IMF's *Government Finance Statistics Manual* 2001, and the functional classification described by the UN's Classification of the Functions of Government.
13. The creation of a pure TSA implies that all government revenues must flow to the TSA and all spending must be made out of the TSA.
14. Mexico promoted higher transparency and publication of debt and fiscal statistics at the subnational level by states, by introducing in 2000 a requirement for states of holding credit ratings. Though to date, all states (with the exception of Campeche) have obtained at least two credit ratings from international credit rating agencies, the Mexican authorities recognize that more work remains to be done in the harmonization of accounting and reporting information by the states.
15. Also see Weingast et al. (1981) who show that bargaining in a legislature comprising regional representatives will lead to overprovision of spending programs with benefits concentrated in particular regions.
16. For more detailed discussion of soft budget constraints and their consequences, see Kornai et al. (2003).
17. Nevertheless, since the crisis of 2001–02, banking regulations have been strengthened to prohibit commercial banks from extending new loans to the provinces and the non-financial public sector, and bilateral agreements have been sought to enhance coordination between different levels of government.
18. See, for instance, Bohn and Inman (1996), Inman (1996) and Poterba (1997).

References

Ahmad, E. and M. Albino-War and T. Ter-Minassiun (eds) (forthcoming), *Issues in Managing Subnational Finances*.

Balassone, F., D. Franco and S. Zotteri (2003), 'Fiscal rules for subnational governments in the EMU context', Societa Italiana di Economia Pubblica, Pavia, Working Paper 196/2003.
Bardhan, Pranab (2002), 'Decentralization of governance and development', *Journal of Economic Perspectives*, Vol. 16, No. 4, pp. 185–205.
Bardhan, Pranab and Dilip Mookherjee (2005), 'Decentralizing antipoverty delivery in developing countries', *Journal of Public Economics*, Vol. 89, No. 4, pp. 675–704.
Bohn, H. and R. Inman (1996), 'Balanced-budget rules and public deficits: evidence from U.S. states', *Carnegie-Rochester Conference Series on Public Policy*, Vol. 45, pp. 13–76.
Bordignon, M., P. Manasse and G. Tabellini (2001), 'Optimal regional redistribution under asymmetric information', *American Economic Review*, Vol. 91, No. 3, pp. 709–23.
Buchanan, J., C.K. Rowley and R.D. Tollison (1987), *Deficits: The Political Economy of Budget Deficits*, Oxford and New York: Basil Blackwell.
Dafflon, B. (ed.) (2002), *Local Public Finance in Europe*, Cheltenham, UK and Northampton, MA, USA: Edward Elgar.
De Smet, G. (forthcoming), 'Fiscal federalism and the coordination of fiscal policy in Belgium', in E. Ahmad and M. Albino-War (eds), *Issues in Managing Subnational Finances*, Washington, DC: International Monetary Fund.
Dorotinsky, Bill and Rob Floyd (2004), 'Public expenditure accountability in Africa: progress, lessons and challenges', in Brian Levy and Sahr Kpundeh (eds), *Building State Capacity in Africa*, Washington, DC: World Bank.
Inman, R.P. (1996), 'Do balanced budget rules work? U.S. experience and possible lessons for the EMU', NBER Working Paper No. 5838, Cambridge, MA: National Bureau for Economic Research.
Juul, T. (forthcoming), 'Local and regional governments in Denmark', in Ehtisham Ahmad et al. (eds), *Issues in Managing Subnational Finances*, Washington, DC: International Monetary Fund.
Kopits, G. (2001), 'Fiscal rules: useful policy framework or unnecessary ornament?', IMF Working Paper 01/145, Washington, DC: International Monetary Fund.
Kornai, J., E. Maskin and G. Roland (2003), 'Understanding the soft budget constraint', *Journal of Economic Literature*, Vol. 41, No. 4, pp. 1095–136.
Lane, T.D. (1993), 'Market discipline', *Staff Papers*, International Monetary Fund, Vol. 40.
Lienert, I. (2004), 'The legal framework for budget systems: an international comparison', OECD Study, Paris: Organization for Economic Cooperation and Development.
Mansuri, G. and V. Rao (2004), 'Community-based and -driven development: a critical review', *The World Bank Research Observer*, Vol. 19, No. 1, pp. 1–39.
Moesen, W.A. (1993), 'The economics of community public finance', Office for Official Publications of the European Communities, pp. 167–90.
Persson, T. and G. Tabellini (1996), 'Federal fiscal constitutions: risk sharing and moral hazard', *Econometrica*, Vol. 64, No. 3, pp. 623–46.
Platteau, J.-P. (2004), 'Community-based development', in Francois Bourguignon and Boris Pleskovic (eds), *Accelerating Development*, Washington, DC: World Bank; Oxford and New York: Oxford University Press, pp. 241–70.
Poterba, J. (1997), 'Do budget rules work?', in Alan Auerbach (ed.), *Fiscal Policy: Lessons from Economic Research*, Cambridge, MA: MIT Press, pp. 53–86.
Poterba, J. and K.S. Reuben (1999), *Fiscal Rules and State Borrowing Costs: Evidence from California and other States*, San Francisco: Public Policy Institute of California.
Poterba, J. and J. von Hagen (eds) (1999), *Fiscal Institutions and Fiscal Performance*, Cambridge, MA: National Bureau of Economic Research.
Premchand, A. (1996), 'Erosion of expenditure management system: an unintended consequence of donor approaches', IMF Working Paper, Washington, DC: International Monetary Fund.
Robinson, M. (forthcoming), 'From central borrowing controls to market/electoral discipline', in Ahmad et al. (eds), *Issues in Managing Subnational Finances*, Washington, DC: International Monetary Fund.
Rodden, J. (2002), 'The dilemma of fiscal federalism: grants and fiscal performance around the world', *American Journal of Political Science*, Vol. 46, No. 3, pp. 670–87.

Rodden, J., G.S. Eskeland and J. Litvack (eds) (2003), *Fiscal Decentralization and the Challenge of Hard Budget Constraints*, Cambridge, MA: MIT Press.

Schick, A. (2000), 'A surplus, if we can keep it', *The Brookings Review*, Vol. 18, No. 1, pp. 36–9.

Ter-Minassian, T. (ed.) (1997), *Fiscal Federalism in Theory and Practice*, Washington, DC: International Monetary Fund.

Ter-Minassian, T. and J. Craig (1997), 'Control of subnational government borrowing', in T. Ter-Minassian (ed.), *Fiscal Federalism in Theory and Practice*, Washington, DC: International Monetary Fund.

US Department of State (2004), *Principles of Democracy*, Bureau of International Information Program, Washington, DC.

von Hagen, J. and I.J. Harden (1994), 'National budget processes and fiscal performance', *European Economy: Reports and Studies*, No. 3, pp. 331–418.

Weingast, B., K. Shepsle and C. Johnson (1981), 'The political economy of benefits and costs: a neoclassical approach to redistributive politics', *Journal of Political Economy*, Vol. 89, pp. 642–64.

World Bank (2001), *The World Development Report 2000/2001*, Washington, DC.

PART IV

EMERGING ISSUES

17 The assignment of revenue from natural resources

Giorgio Brosio

Introduction: the relevance of the problem

There is increasing pressure for recognizing the right of subnational governments and, in some cases, indigenous communities, to a share of natural resources. Rents from natural resources form an important share of subnational budgets in countries where such resources are found. Minerals, petroleum, forests, hydropower energy and fisheries, are the main types of natural resources that generate rents for local governments.

Other assets, such as cultural heritage and natural attractions, may be treated akin to natural resources, and generate rents. These assets share the main characteristics of natural resources, namely, limitations on their short-term supply and variation in their quality. For example, given the unique cultural heritage of the city of Venice, economic rents could be collected using the same tax and non-tax instruments that are used for extracting rents from natural resources.

The assignment of revenue from natural resources to subnational levels of government tends to generate rivalries between the constituent units of the same nation – between the central and local levels, and also across local governments. In developing countries with a large and unevenly distributed endowment of natural resources, the sharing of natural resource revenues often puts considerable strains on national unity. There are two reasons for this. First, the rent can be very substantial, as in the case of petroleum, natural gas, diamonds and other valuable minerals. Second, decentralization expands the role of subnational governments and makes them more vocal in pressing for a share of the rents originating within their jurisdiction.

The chapter is organized as follows. The next section presents the main instruments for extraction and sharing rent among different layers of government, as well as evidence showing the increasing access by subnational government units to this revenue. The third section reviews the arguments against and in favour of sharing the rent with subnational governments. It also presents innovations in the practice of intergovernmental relations and mechanisms and solutions, which can soften the political and economic impact of this assignment. The final section concludes and suggests that transfer mechanisms should be adjusted to accommodate disparities across regions arising from natural resource rents.

This chapter focuses largely on developing countries and on petroleum and gas, as these reflect much of the current theoretical discussions and political arguments.

Instruments for collecting rents from natural resources

Rent is the return to a resource that is fixed in total supply and is measured as the difference between the revenue derived from its sale and the economic cost of producing (exploring and extracting) the resource. Mines, petroleum fields and other deposits of natural resources vary in their quality and in proximity to the final market. Consequently, the amount of the rent per unit of resource extracted will vary inversely with the cost of extraction and directly with proximity to the final market. Rent could be described as a surplus value.

Figure 17.1 describes four mining companies that operate different 'grade' mines (or are located at different distances to the market). Firm D has the lowest grade and thus the highest average extraction cost. Given the aggregate demand curve, firm D gets no rent, and is the marginal producer. The other three firms, A, B and C (called 'infra marginal') have higher-grade resources (or are closer to the market) and consequently have lower production costs. P is the price line which is supposed to be constant over time. Firms have a rent illustrated by the dotted rectangles.[1]

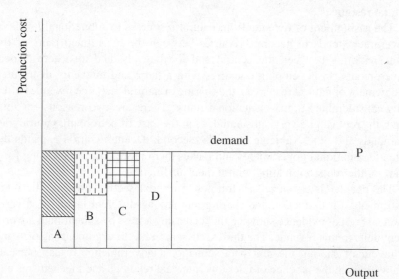

Figure 17.1   Natural resource rent

In most countries the ownership of natural resources, such as petroleum, is vested in the state. This could be central, or subnational governments. In a few countries private ownership is recognized. The owner, private individual or government, has the right to decide on the use of the resource; for example, it can lease a forest to a firm that will exploit it. In each case, the government aims to collect the maximum possible rent from the resource. A variety of instruments are available,[2] which can be grouped into two categories: *ex ante* and *ex post*. With *ex ante* instruments, the rent is collected by the government before the start of the exploration and the exploitation of the resource. Typical *ex ante* instruments are auctioning of rights, and payment of fixed fees for exploration and development. *Ex post* instruments are taxes and royalties, free acquisition of equity and production sharing agreements (Table 17.1). In other words, *ex ante* instruments are targeted to collect expected rent, while *ex post* instruments will collect realized, actual, rent. Obviously, expected rent will differ from the actual, either because after exploration the resources turn out to be lower (or higher) than expected, or because of moral hazard problems. For example, the government could renege on a contract, or the firm could cheat on production.

In terms of principal–agent theory, the government signs a contract with a firm to explore and develop the resource. Both the government and the firm are risk averse. To induce the firm to accept the contract, the project has to offer a minimum rate of return. This minimum return will have to be higher, the greater the risks faced by the project. Recognition of this fact has an important contractual consequence, namely, the government should avoid contractual instruments that increase the risk associated with the project, since this will increase the minimum return demanded by the investor and reduce the rent.

The best strategy for the government depends on its risk aversion and its intertemporal need for revenue. If the government were completely risk averse and completely cash strapped, its optimal strategy would be to ask an up-front payment from the investor, who would be given exclusive access to the natural resource. However, if the risk of the project is very high and/or the investor is highly risk averse, the amount of a possible up-front payment could be very minimal, since the investor will likely ask for a substantial risk premium. Thus, the optimal rent extraction strategy implies a sharing of risk between the government and the investor. This can be done by a combination of up-front payments and taxes conditional on actual rent.

There are four main sets of instruments for collecting resource rents. These are presented in Table 17.1. To a substantial extent they complement and substitute for one another other and combinations of these are used by governments in the real world.

Table 17.1 Main methods for collecting rent from natural resources

Method	Auctioning exploration and exploitation rights	Government equity in project	Production sharing	Taxation instruments
Advantages and problems	Allows, if properly done, the government to obtain a substantial up-front payment. Requires, however, a fully competitive setting, which might be different to ensure	Allows government to share any upside of the projects (e.g., transfers of technology). It is likely to be a source of conflict of interest: government as a shareholder versus government as regulator	Contracts for sharing of production can be relatively simple. If the rent has to be fully collected, permanent revision of their terms is, however, required, as the price of the shared resource changes	Neutrality and simplicity of tax instruments are negatively correlated

Non-tax instruments

Auctioning exploration and exploitation rights: cash payments bidding This is a development of the more traditional instrument consisting of imposing a fixed fee for exploration and/or exploitation. It consists of asking firms to submit cash payment bids[3] and choose the procedure for the selection of the best bid. Potential investors will determine their own value of the resource.

The literature[4] generally considers auctioning of rights as the potentially preferable system for capturing rent. It serves a dual function: (a) to allocate the right to the most efficient bidder; and (b) to efficiently capture the expected value of the rent. It is also neutral on extraction choices, since the winner's decision during the development of the resource will not be influenced by the up-front payment.

The literature (in particular, Mead 1994) points out that if there are enough bidders to ensure a fully competitive setting and if bidders are risk neutral and confident of their estimates of the value of the resource, the auction will allow the government to collect the entire expected value of the rent. Thus cash payments made at auctions are perfect substitutes for *ex post* tax payments.[5] Some authors (Garnaut and Ross 1975) raise doubts about the effectiveness of the instrument and consider it inferior to *ex post* instruments, particularly to a resource rent tax (see below). This is because of the risk aversion of investors, who have limited information on the value of the project and may be deterred from bidding because of sovereign risk. This is the risk that the government will renegotiate the terms, or take arbitrary action against the investor ('second bite of the cherry'). Moreover, in the case of large mineral/petroleum fields, the huge scale of costs and the large up-scale payment, that will be required to equal *ex post* taxes, will limit the number of real bidders.

Acquisition of equity in mining enterprises
The acquisition of equity is a system used in many developing and industrial economies. Its impact on rent collection depends on the terms under which the equity is acquired by the government. It can be as a share of the cost, or without charge.

In the first case, the government would pay a given share of the total cost of the investment in return for an equivalent share of the flow of revenues deriving from extraction. In this case, the revenue accruing to the government would include two distinct components: a share of the returns on its capital investment and an equivalent share of the resource rent.

In the second case, the government obtains a share of equity for free. This acquisition imposes a cost on the investor, which is similar to some forms of taxation. Through this acquisition the government is entitled to receive a certain share of the net revenues of the investor. This amounts to a tax on the investor's return to capital and a tax on the resource rent. For example, if the government acquires 50 per cent of the equity, it would appropriate 50 per cent of investment returns and 50 per cent of the resource rent.

In addition to the provision of revenue, acquisition of equity allows the government to control mining and extraction operations. It is also considered as an instrument to gain experience in running enterprises.[6] Further advantages include: (i) an element of government equity may reduce for private investors the perception of sovereign risk; and (ii) the provision by government of capital at cheaper terms than private investors, if the state enjoys a high creditworthiness in financial markets.

The equity element can thus increase the rent available to the public purse. There are also possible disadvantages. In particular, when the government holds an important equity, it can be tempted to use its power to influence corporate decisions according to its political needs and orientation (for example, to overstaff the company, or to accelerate the extraction rate beyond the optimal one).

Production-sharing arrangements
Under this arrangement, a company is contracted to extract the resource in exchange for a share of the production paid to the government. In its simplest form, which consists of paying a fixed proportional share of the physical output, the production-sharing agreement has virtually the same effects of a specific royalty (see below).

If the share is calculated on the value of output, the sharing agreement has the same effects as an *ad valorem* royalty. Frequently, less simple sharing contracts are used. For example, the contract could specify that the contractor retains a portion of the production to recover capital and exploration costs. The remaining product is shared between the government and the company. Very often, a limit is imposed on the share of production returned to the company to recover costs, to ensure that the government is able to collect its revenue as soon as production starts. The unrecovered costs are carried over to subsequent years with an interest factor. The simplicity of this instrument is more apparent than real. It may be difficult to determine allowable costs. Moreover, the real profitability of the project becomes totally known only after extraction commences, that is, after the signing of the agreement. This could induce renegotiation and strategic behaviour. Furthermore, the share of the production could be made to vary with the price of the resource or with changes in costs. In other words, production-sharing agreements can be devised in such a way as to approximate taxes on resource rents. They are, however, much more complicated because continuous changes are likely to be required (or the uncertainty might reduce the share accruing to the government).

Tax instruments
There are a number of tax instruments, as follows.

Fixed fees These consist in charging a fixed amount of money to the investor, independently of the outcome of the investment, or even of the making of the investment. Fixed fees are more appropriate when the government has no idea of the value of the actual rent and/or it is totally risk averse. Fixed fees are thus more suitable for the sale of exploration rights, rather than of exploitation rights. These are very easy to administer, but raise the difficult issue of determining their appropriate amount. This suggests that auctioning fees might be appropriate.

Royalties Specific, or *ad valorem*, royalties are the most popular form of taxation of natural resources. Specific royalties are levied at constant monetary value (for example, x dollars) per unit of output. *Ad valorem* royalties are determined as a constant percentage of the value of the output. By increasing the unit costs of extraction, royalties have distorting effects, which do not allow the maximization of revenue for the beneficiary government. In particular, specific royalties tend to restrict the production of 'lower-quality grades' (that is, of mines with lower percentages of mineral and of petroleum fields with lower-quality petroleum) and of higher-cost resources.

Ad valorem royalties do not discriminate against lower-quality grades, but do discriminate against high-cost deposits. Consider two projects which have the same expected rent. The first project requires much less investment than the second. The second will have a much higher flow of production that compensates the cost of investment. It will thus have to pay much greater royalties, which will reduce its profitability, making the project less desirable. Consequently, royalties tend to reduce the pace and the extent of extraction, inducing producers to leave in the ground deposits, although their price exceeds the social unit cost of extracting them.[7] To reduce the distortions they produce, the base of the royalties can be modified, for example, by deducting current costs from revenue. That would leave only capital costs taxed.

The main advantage of royalties, and the reason for their popularity, is simplicity of administration. It is easy to determine the volume of the output (for specific royalties). *Ad valorem* royalties require knowledge of the market price. This can be difficult and has to be approximated, for example, with the use of some formula. Of course, the advantage of simplicity disappears when, to reduce the shortcomings of the most simplified royalty schemes, the base is modified to include costs.

Income taxes Levying an income/profit tax with a higher-than-normal rate is less distorting than royalties. In countries where an income tax is already established, tax administration can build on this tax to impose an additional levy on natural resources. The higher-than-normal rate can be adapted, in principle, to the specificity of the project; thus, it can generate greater revenue than fees, or royalties. In practice, however, the determination of the rate raises problems. If it is too high, the tax rate will deter investments. If too low, the government will unnecessarily forgo revenue.

The progressive income/profit tax amounts to tax, at additional rates, on additional profits calculated as a percentage of the value of the accumulated investment. For example, a rate of 30 per cent is levied on taxable profits that amount to up to 20 per cent of the accumulated investment. Profits in excess of this threshold are taxed at a rate of 40 per cent. The burden of the progressive profit tax can be adapted to the profitability of the project better than with the previous instruments, thus generating larger revenue for the government. Also in this case the tax can be built superimposed on the existing profit tax, using the same rules for determining the taxable income and the existing tax administration. It requires, however, the definition of the accumulated investment.

Resource rent tax   This aims at capturing the total rent of project. There are different versions, proposed by scholars and implemented in the real world. For each period, the value of the current rent is the value of the production sold less all the opportunity costs incurred by the firm. Cost is both current and capital. Current costs refer to inputs that are used in the same period in which they are purchased. Capital costs refer to inputs that extend beyond the period of acquisition. While costing of current inputs presents relatively minor problems, capital inputs raise conceptual issues in attributing total capital costs to each period. Capital costs consist of three different sorts: depreciation, financing costs and capital losses. Some of these costs raise problems in the case of natural resources. To value depreciation one has to measure the present value of future rents, which requires specifying the time horizon and choosing a proper discount rate.

To solve the difficulties of costing capital inputs, the theory proposes a *cash-flow tax*. The structure of the tax can be better illustrated when the tax is assessed with reference to a single project, rather than to a firm. In each period of the project, the cash flow is the net value of all real transactions of the project and is calculated by subtracting from cash receipts from sales all expenses made for the purchase of inputs (both operating and capital). It means, for example, that all capital costs are deducted immediately from cash receipts in the period when the capital items are purchased. There is no need to calculate depreciation, cost of finance or capital losses.

If the resulting amount is positive, a tax is levied. If the cash flow is negative, the loss is carried forward to the next period at a rate of interest, until a cumulative positive value is attained. Positive cash flow is taxed at the specified tax rate. Should cash flows become negative in the future, losses are offset against future tax liability.

Since the present value of cash flow is equivalent to the present value of the rent, the two taxes are equal, but the time profile of their collections is different. Typically, with a cash flow tax there will be no tax liability for the project (or the firm) for several years after the commencement of the project, due to the necessary investment outlays. The cash-flow tax reduces the risk to investors, but it increases the revenue risk to government.

Equivalence of tax and non-tax instruments
Combinations of the above arrangements are often found in practice. The equivalence of tax and non-tax instruments is presented in Table 17.2.

Table 17.2   Equivalence of tax instruments with non-tax instruments

Production sharing	Tax instruments	Government equity	Auctioning exploration/exploitation rights
Share of physical output	Specific royalty		
Share of value of production	*Ad valorem* royalty		
Share of value of production after deduction of a proportion of operating and invest-ment costs	Income/profit tax	Equity at a cost	
Same as for previous line with a growing share for the government	Progressive income/profit tax		
Resource rent tax/cash flow tax		Free and at a cost equity	Cash payment bids

Sharing natural resource revenue among layers of government
At least five overlapping fiscal systems are available for sharing revenue from natural resources between distinct layers of government (Table 17.3). Revenue can also be shared through non-fiscal systems, such as bidding for the rights to exploit resources, production sharing and holding equity in mineral and/or petroleum companies. In these cases, the central government would conduct the bidding and share its results, or it would conclude a production sharing agreement, or acquire a share of equity in producing companies and then transfer part of it to subnational entities, or share systems in reversal. In this case, if subnational governments own the property rights to the resources, they would decide on their use or tax regime, sharing the revenue with the central government.

Separation of (own) taxes   With this system the national and the subnational governments are entitled to levy separate (own) natural resource taxes on firms or projects located within their jurisdiction. For example, royalties might be assigned to subnational governments, whereas profit or resource rent taxes are assigned to the central government. The revenue of an own tax can be represented, in the case of a royalty, as:

$$R_i = t_i B_i \tag{17.1}$$

Collection (or revenue), R_i, is equal to a locally determined share, t_i, of the locally determined tax base, B_i. In the usual case where the power of the subnational government to set the tax rate and to determine the tax base is constrained by the central government, we have:

$$R_i = (t + \Delta t_i)(B_{ni} + \Delta B_i), \tag{17.2}$$

where Δt_i is the local variation of the nationally determined tax rate, t, and ΔB_i is the local variation to the nationally determined tax base, B_{ni}, of the concerned jurisdiction.

Concurrence of taxes (tax-base sharing)   The difference between this instrument and the previous one is that in this case two, or more, levels of government use the same instrument. A typical case is local surcharges on royalties. In federal countries the tax bases and the tax rates of the surcharges may, usually, be determined freely, while in non-federal decentralized states the tax base is nationally determined, while subnational tax rates can be fixed within nationally determined brackets:

$$R_i = (t_i + l_i)B_i, \tag{17.3}$$

Table 17.3 Instruments for sharing rent from natural resources to subnational levels of government

Method	Separation of tax bases (own taxes)	Concurrence of taxes (sharing of tax bases)	Sharing of revenue	Sharing of revenue in kind	Intergovernmental transfers out of revenue from natural resources
Determination of the tax base	Subnational	National	National	Mostly national	National
Determination of the tax rates	Subnational	Subnational (within limits)	National	Mostly national	National
Administration	Subnational	Mostly national	National	By the producing firm	Mostly national
Criterion for determination of the beneficiary jurisdiction	Origin	Origin	Origin	Origin	Need, equity or other

where: R_i are the total collections in jurisdiction i of the shared tax; l_i is the locally determined tax rate applied to the nationally determined tax base, B_i. Local revenue is:

$$r_i = l_i B_i. \tag{17.4}$$

Tax revenue sharing In this system, the tax bases, the tax rates and the revenue shares are determined by the central government and the revenue is allocated according to the principle of origin:

$$R_i = \alpha t B_i \tag{17.5}$$

or

$$r_i = \alpha R_i. \tag{17.6}$$

that is, local revenue is a nationally determined share α of the total revenue of the tax collected in the jurisdiction.

In-kind revenue sharing (infrastructure tax credit schemes) According to this system, subnational governments have access to a share of natural resource revenue generated within their jurisdiction via the provision of infrastructure by the companies that exploit these resources, and on the basis of an explicit national regulation.[8] This is not to be confused with the common practice followed by producing companies of providing, on a voluntary basis, infrastructure and services to the areas affected by their operations. This is done to alleviate the problems created by their activity and to promote better relations with local communities and local governments.[9]

These schemes are suited to very small-size governments and local informal communities, with weak administrative capacity. Infrastructure credit schemes help to establish working relations between producing companies and local stakeholders. Higher levels of government could be involved in the decision making process and particularly in monitoring the execution of projects.

Intergovernmental transfers based on the revenue from natural resources revenue In a number of countries, such as Bolivia and Colombia, a share of revenue from natural resources goes to a national fund used for allocations to non-producing local jurisdictions. Specific systems for transfers of revenue from natural resources to indigenous communities have also been set up (see below for their illustration).

Rent extraction instruments for subnational governments

Ideally, all rent collecting instruments are available to any level of government. However, the central government is viewed as better equipped to use most of them than subnational government units. According to theory, natural resource taxes should be assigned to central government and (partly) reallocated to subnational government. In other words, revenue sharing or transfers are to be preferred over assignment of own taxes to subnational government and concurrence of taxes (sharing of tax bases).

There are two reasons against assignment of own taxes to subnational government. The first is administration. The principle is that, if a tax is collected by the more efficient government, its net revenue will be higher. Usually, the central government has more personnel and better organization. This can be particularly true for developing countries, where professional skills and organizational resources are generally scarce. Due to the complexity of administration, the resource rent tax, the most efficient tax for natural resource extraction, is out of reach for most subnational government tax administration offices.

Also natural resource tailored profit/income taxes present huge problems. The information required for taxing profits from natural resources is no more complex than that required for standard corporate taxation, but profit/income taxes are not recommended in general for subnational government. The more so as subnational governments, particularly in developing countries, do not have the sophisticated tax administration required for dealing with big petroleum, or mineral international companies,[10] while the size and variability of potential revenue presents additional problems.

Consideration of administrative problems restricts the range of tax instruments that might be assigned by subnational governments to production-based taxes, such as the royalties. Royalties are, in fact, the most common tax used in isolation by subnational government, or shared with the centre (Otto 2001). The weight of the administration argument is somewhat reduced when one considers that all governments can contract other governments and private firms, or can join efforts to acquire the capabilities that are required to use efficient/sophisticated rent extraction instruments. One can observe an increase in outsourcing of tax administration in the real world.[11]

The second reason advanced against local taxation of natural resources is delays and variability in revenue. This argument holds for cash flow taxes. As seen, their use implies that tax liabilities will be negative at the start of new projects and that collections will flow only after the project is operational. This is a burden that subnational administrations may find difficult to bear (particularly, after considering their need to build infrastructure before the start of production). In fact, the frequent use of royalties by subnational government is also explained by the fact that they ensure steadier revenue flows.

On the other hand, it has to be recognized that subnational governments may be ready to trade off less and/or delayed revenue with other advantages stemming from direct control and administration of their taxes, such as availability of taxing powers and control of revenue. In fact, in many (especially developing) countries, allocation to subnational governments of tax revenue collected on their behalf by the centre is often delayed and uncertain (McLure 2003).

The main reason against concurrency of natural resource taxes is vertical externalities. That is, the overall burden of a tax assigned concurrently to different layers of government is greater than the burden that would arise, if the tax instrument is assigned to one level of government only.[12]

The argument is valid mostly for royalties, which are levied jointly by the central and the subnational governments in a huge number of cases (see Otto 2001). It has less weight in the case of the resource rent tax, because of its neutrality and its structure. In principle, that is, ignoring the lack of inducements to control operating cost, the global tax rate – that is, the sum of the national and the local ones – could even exceed (in the case of sharing) 100 per cent, since the tax paid to every level of government is considered as an expense in the determination of this tax base. An overall consideration of vertical externalities – for example, the greater the royalties, the smaller the tax base of the resource rent tax, since the former are deductible from the latter – suggests the assignment to the same level of government of all taxes that apply to the same tax base.

Revenue sharing is one of the most frequent systems for sharing natural resource revenue between layers of government[13] (see also Ahmad and Mottu 2003). To be precise, revenue sharing is not an attractive general instrument for financing subnational governments, since it reduces their accountability. The reason is that, with revenue sharing, beneficiary governments are not responsible for the burden they impose on their citizens (as with revenue sharing, there is determination neither of the tax rates, nor of the tax base). When applied to taxes on natural resources, the drawbacks of revenue sharing lose most of their weight. In fact, most of the taxes on natural resources are exported, while tax rate setting and tax base determination are better left to the central government, considering the national dimension of most natural resource extraction policies.

The legal bases for assignment of ownership
The ownership of natural resources is determined by constitutions, mining laws and custom.

In countries with a civil law tradition, the ownership of natural resources is vested in the state (so-called 'regalian system'). Countries with a common law tradition recognize (partly) private ownership. In this case, the owner of the land is at the same time the owner of the subsoil. In practically all countries, non-iron minerals of a lesser value, such as sand and gravel, are left to private ownership. Offshore fields and mines are everywhere publicly owned.

In confederations natural resources are, on a strict legal basis, property of the members of the confederation and not of the confederation. The reason is that nothing is due to the confederation, which does not derive from a decision of each distinct confederated state. Federal and non-federal states offer a great variety of constitutional solutions concerning the level of government to which ownership of natural resources is recognized.

However, a somewhat clear historical pattern emerges. When subnational governments are institutionally strong, or are independent units within a federation or confederation and the existence of large quantities of natural resources is common knowledge, then constitution assigns full or partial ownership of natural resources to subnational levels of government.

The Canadian constitution (the British North America Act) states that ownership on minerals and other natural resources belongs to the provinces. Constitutional agreements have extended the same rights to the provinces, which later joined the federation. Mineral resources were already important in Australia at the time of the federation, but the constitution makes no specific reference to them. Since the Australian constitution specifies only the powers of the federal government and leaves every other responsibility to the states, the latter have retained the ownership on natural resources they had before the federation.

There is also no mention of natural resources in the recently written, and still to be adopted, EU constitution. The new European entity is, in fact, closer to a confederation than to a federation. It would have been quite unlikely that member states would have agreed to confer their property rights on natural resources to the European institutions. Latin American constitutions provide interesting examples of the evolution of constitutional assignments concerning natural resources, in particular petroleum. When the huge potentialities associated with new discoveries became common knowledge, but the actual distribution among regions remained unknown since no exploration had yet been made, constitutional provisions vested ownership and control of natural resources in the central government. However, when the veil of ignorance about the effective location of petroleum disappeared, as happened in the early 1990s, a shift took place towards the explicit recognition of subnational government entitlement to petroleum revenue. This is the case of the constitutions of Argentina and Colombia. Resource-rich jurisdictions exerted increasing pressures on the writers of those constitutions to see their property rights recognized.

Ownership may also be determined by constitutional interpretation. Canada and Nigeria provide a good illustrating example of the latitude of possible interpretations of constitutional arrangements and of the conflicting views about possible amendments. Canadian non-petroleum-producing provinces have traditionally adhered to the principle that Canada is a single nation and a single community. If so, natural resources belong to the federal government and should be shared among all provinces, and/or used for country-building purposes.

Petroleum-producing provinces held the opposite view, stressing the primacy of provincial communities and that national majorities are not entitled to take natural resources away from where they are produced. Provinces situated on the Atlantic coast shifted gradually from the nation- to the province-building approach, when the prospects of off-shore petroleum discoveries became brighter (Simeon 1980; McMillan 1981).

Interregional conflicts regarding access to petroleum, for example, in Nigeria, have generated secession, civil war and the frequent demise of democracy. Petroleum-producing federated states have traditionally taken the view that 'equitable federalism' implies the adoption of the derivation principle (resources stay where they are produced). Non-producing states have brought forward the principle that equitable federalism means redistribution (Ikein and Briggs-Anigboh 1998).

The influence of resource-rich local jurisdictions is evidenced by the recent trend in the allocation of revenue from off-shore petroleum. This resource, which is generally the property of the central government, is presently shared among neighbouring subnational governments in a number of countries, such as Canada, Australia, Brazil and Italy. Since there are much lower infrastructure costs and almost no externalities from offshore exploration and production, the sharing with subnational government shows the intensity of their pressures and the difficulty of resisting them.

As mentioned at the beginning of this section, custom is important in assigning ownership of natural resources, in particular in old nations in Europe and in India. For example, ownership of forests provides an important source of revenue to municipalities located in mountainous areas in Switzerland, Italy and Austria. Water used for irrigation and generation of electricity is also traditionally a source of considerable royalties to subnational government units situated in the same areas.

Characteristics of natural resource exploitation that impact on the assignment of revenue
A few features concerning the exploitation of natural resources have to be borne in mind in assessing assignments of revenue. The most important characteristic is the frequent, huge geographic concentration of production. This is a pure geological hazard, but it is the most common case in large and medium-sized countries.[14]

The same hazard ensures that in a number of countries petroleum and mineral resources are discovered and exploited in sparsely populated areas. Russia shows, possibly, the most striking case, with the *oblast* of Tyumen producing two-thirds of Russian petroleum but having only 1 per cent of the Russian population. When natural resource, especially petroleum, rents are assigned exclusively, or mainly, to subnational governments, they tend to produce huge horizontal imbalances; that is, large disparities in per capita revenue of distinct subnational governments. For example, in 1981 Alaska collected US$3.3 billion in petroleum revenue, which corresponded to approximately $8000 per capita.

Obviously, big imbalances across subnational jurisdictions stimulate political pressures and provide theoretical grounds for national equalization of these resources. At the same time, sparsely populated regions exercise a very small weight in national politics, particularly in weak democracies with few mechanisms of checks and balances. This increases their perceived risks of having to bear the costs of exploitation without reaping the benefits, if entitlements to national resource revenue are transferred to the national government. In general, when local jurisdictions have little power at the central level, they make increased demand for decentralization of powers and resources.

Minerals, petroleum and natural gas are rapidly depleting resources, creating the typical 'boomtowns' phenomenon. Exploration and production attract individuals and capital, but reserves can be rapidly exhausted. Large-scale projects require huge investments and impact geographically on small areas. Even when local governments do not benefit from petroleum revenue, the economic impact of exploration and exploitation on local communities is large and difficult to regulate.

When inflow of workers and the population are large, risks of social disruption and of environmental damage are only too real and substantial. In addition, natural resource exploration, and to a lesser extent production, entail huge pecuniary externalities, such as higher land rents and increases in the cost of living in the nearby communities. Potentially, those risks could be compensated by generation of local development from the natural resource sector and by construction of infrastructure in transport and communications. However, pecuniary externalities impacting on the price of inputs and factors can seriously distort or hamper development. Involvement of local governments in controlling damage, providing infrastructure and diversifying growth can hardly be denied but it requires resources.

The price of most natural resources, especially of petroleum, shows large but unpredictable fluctuations. According to empirical evidence (see Davis et al. 2001) the price of petroleum does not seem to have a well-defined time invariant average. In other words, there is no notion of 'normal' price towards which actual price approximates at the end of boom or slump periods.

Volatility of revenue from natural resource rents is much higher than for other sources of fiscal revenue. This compromises the fiscal management and the efficiency of spending, particularly in countries whose revenue base is highly dependent on natural resources. It is typically more difficult to handle such variance at the subnational than national level (see below).

Arguments against assignment of revenue from natural resources to subnational government

The access of subnational governments to rents is in question here, and not the way the resources are collected. Hence, possible distortions derive from the way the revenue is spent. Unless beneficiary subnational governments spend these revenues for 'country-building projects' – such as the provision of purely national public goods, the construction of truly national infrastructure, or portfolio investments in financial assets made according to the same principles followed by private investors – labour and capital allocation distortions are inevitable. In this sense, revenue from natural resources is similar to that from any other tax. It is the unequal access to revenue that allows governments, which benefit most from it, to spend it in distortionary ways.

Efficiency and mobility of factors   The main argument in the literature against the assignment of economic rent to subnational governments is the inefficiency in the geographical allocation of factors of production, which derives from the concentration of the rent. A simple illustration (drawn from Boadway and Flatters 1982) refers to inefficient migration of labour. Take a country with two local jurisdictions: A and B. The population of the country is fixed and, for the sake of simplicity, it is entirely composed of persons of working age, homogeneous in skills and preferences and perfectly mobile between A and B. Mobility is induced only by economic considerations. More specifically, people maximize their comprehensive income, *CI*, which is salary, minus the taxes paid to the local jurisdiction, plus the value of the goods and services locally provided. Individuals will migrate to the jurisdiction where *CI* is, for any reason, higher.

Initially, no rent from natural resources is collected. Local jurisdictions provide goods and finance them with benefit taxes; that is, with taxes determined for each individual on the basis of the benefit she/he receives from the locally provided goods. The net fiscal benefit, equal to the difference between the value of the locally provided good and the taxes paid to finance them, does not vary across jurisdictions. In this situation, there is no fiscal inducement to migrate and the location of individuals is determined only by the wage they receive. In turn, the wage is determined by the value of the marginal product of labour. Individuals will thus distribute themselves between the two jurisdictions as to equalize the marginal value of product, as illustrated in Figure 17.2.

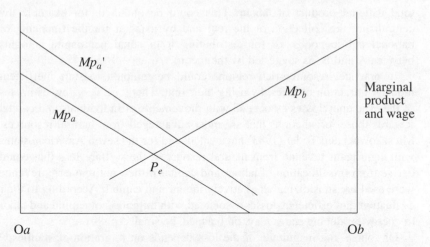

Figure 17.2   Location choices of individuals and rent

The horizontal axis measures the total population. Any point on this axis shows the distribution of the population between the jurisdictions. The distance from Oa to the right shows the population of A, while the distance from Ob to the left shows the population of B. There are two vertical axes, one for each jurisdiction, which show the wage paid (and thus the marginal product of labour). The two lines, Mp_a and Mp_b represent the demand for labour in each jurisdiction. Their intersection, corresponding to point P_e on the horizontal axis, determines the efficient distribution of the population (and of labour) between the jurisdictions. In fact, individuals move from one to the other until no further gains can be obtained. That is, they move until wages and marginal products are equalized.

Now consider natural resources. These are discovered and exploited in A, which collects them. The amount of the taxed rent can be used to enhance the quality of the publicly provided goods, or to reduce the taxes paid for them. This use increases CI in A above its previous level, as shown in the figure by the line Mp_a'. Its per capita incidence is shown in the figure by the distance between Mp_a and Mp_a'.[15] The net fiscal benefit will now be higher in A, thus increasing CI_a. Individuals will move from B to A, attracted by the gap between CI_a and CI_b. Under the pressure of new migrants, wages will diminish until equality is restored between CI_a and CI_b, as happens in P_i. This point represents an inefficient distribution of labour, since the marginal product is lower in A than in B. In fact, to accommodate more migrants, jobs with lower marginal product have been provided.

This means that redistributing individuals from A to B could increase the total national product of labour. This could be obtained, for example, by centralizing the collection of the rent and by using it for the financing of national public goods, or for distributing it in equal per capita amounts between A and B, as suggested by the theory.

In practice, resource-rich regions could be tempted to start inefficient industry attraction policies, by using their rent. There are very few estimates of the efficiency losses associated with movements of individuals and capital towards those jurisdictions that are most advantaged from natural resources. Mieszkowski and Toder (1983) have calculated for the seven American states with significant revenue from natural resources, the welfare loss that could derive from misallocation of labour and capital if their entire energy revenue were used for subsidizing alternatively labour and capital. According to their evaluation the 'efficiency losses associated with migration of capital and labor to energy producing states may, on balance, be small' (p. 89).

Of course, the magnitude of the loss depends on migration elasticities,[16] which depend, on region-specific factors. For example, migration elasticities in Alaska are surely much lower than in the other American states. They can, however, be substantial in developing countries with very few employment opportunities nationwide, especially when minerals and petroleum are discovered in non-remote and non-inhospitable areas. However, the picture should be completed with the inclusion of other factors impacting on the marginal productivity of factors.[17]

Inefficiency and misspending of rent   Substantial efficiency losses can also derive from misspending of rent in natural resource-rich jurisdictions. In turn, misspending can derive from insufficient absorption capacity and/or from corruption. The geographical concentration of rent makes its amount disproportionate to the absorption capacity of subnational government units (sometimes, it is even disproportionate to the absorption capacity of the national government). Non-economic investments can be made, subnational bureaucracies may indulge in slack and the capacity of controlling costs may decline. While these problems are usually context specific, meaning that the central government is not inherently superior in administering funds, the sheer size of revenue constitutes a greater challenge for smaller governments. This is especially true in developing countries with generally weak or incipient traditions of local administration.[18]

Similar arguments can be replicated concerning the evaluation of the likely impact of corruption. Prevalence of corruption at either the national, or the local level is context specific. It depends, among other things, on the level of information, on the peculiarities of the political system, on administrative traditions, on the homogeneity of local jurisdictions, and on the sectoral composition of expenditure at the national and local levels.

However, concentration of resources within a small jurisdiction may endanger rent-seeking or corrupt behaviour. In a number of countries, access to natural resource revenue has produced corruption and a generalized weakening of public institutions.

Volatility of revenue constitutes one of the strongest arguments against assignment of natural resource revenue to subnational governments. The reason is that the central government is better equipped than its subnational units to face revenue fluctuations, considering its access to a wider range of financial instruments. When revenue diminishes abruptly, subnational units can only resort to expenditure cuts, thus endangering even the provision of minimum levels of essential services, such as education and health, where these are decentralized. During upturns in prices, subnational jurisdictions would be literally awash with funds they are unable to spend efficiently, or enter into spending commitments that might not be sustainable in the longer term, especially if prices fall.

Arguments for assigning some natural resource rents to subnational levels

Additional costs of investment in infrastructure Although most investment for the exploitation of petroleum and other natural resources is made directly by the producing companies, additional investment in local infrastructure is usually required. Roads to the producing mines and fields have to be built, airports and ports may have to be upgraded, schools, health and social services have to be expanded to serve the growing population attracted to the area.

To the extent to which the demand for these services exceeds the demand that would have prevailed in the absence of petroleum and natural resource extraction, there is no doubt that the governments of the producing jurisdictions are entitled to have these additional costs funded. Since the natural resource rent is the income in excess of that required to cover the costs of all inputs necessary for the production to take place, both efficiency and equity considerations suggest that the costs faced by subnational governments are refunded before this rent is distributed. In other words, only the net rent should to be allocated among levels of government.

In a way, this amounts to applying the peak load pricing principle (McLure 1983). Natural resource exploration and production require an expansion of the capacity that has to be funded by those who make use of it. Effective implementation of this principle is far from easy, since one has to determine who is the effective beneficiary of the expansion, that is, firms or the local population.

Environmental protection Natural resource exploration and extraction entail the use of substantial environmental services in addition to the use of other inputs that are needed for extracting rent. In other words, they produce environmental damages, which have to be taken into account in determining the total rent generated by a project.

Government intervention is needed to determine the socially efficient level of natural resource use. In an intergovernmental framework this requires a decision concerning the appropriate level of government to which environmental protection is to be assigned. The problem is compounded by the decision concerning the allocation of the rent.

A simple example clarifies the issue. Consider the leasing of a mine. M is the expected value of production and C is the private cost of exploration and exploitation. However, exploration and exploitation of the mine require the use of environmental services. Their cost C_e has to be added to the private cost to determine the value of the rent: $M - C - C_e$. Suppose also that most of the environmental costs are localized around the mine. As we know, there is a wide latitude in the determination of the cost of mining as demonstrated by conflicts between pure conservationists and those who maintain that the environment is capable of providing a determined amount of services indefinitely. In other words, standards and the corresponding costs of implementing them can absorb a variable share of the rent.

If the rent is allocated to the central government and if the latter is also responsible for the protection of the environment – through the determination of environmental standards – then the central government will have few incentives to impose strict standards and enforce them. C_e would be minimal and the rent would be quite high. An example is the environmental degradation in the petroleum-producing areas of Nigeria, where natural gas is burned at the wellhead, and petroleum spills and installations have spoilt the quality of the environment to a massive degree. The case of Nigeria is not unique among both developed and developing countries, especially in remote and sparsely populated jurisdictions that hold little sway with the central government. In these cases, equity and efficiency require that local jurisdictions receive full compensation for environmental damages.

If environmental protection is assigned to the local level, but the rent is totally centralized, local governments are induced to impose strict limits on natural resource exploitation. In fact, they perceive no advantages from mining. The opposite would apply if rents were totally decentralized and environmental protection centralized. This suggests, prima facie, that environmental protection should be shared between the central and the local levels, with the latter able to impose and or enforce stricter than national limits. It suggests also, prima facie, that some sharing of rent between levels of government is necessary to have efficient levels of environmental protection.

Obviously when no environmental regulation exists and no standards are enforced, as in the case of Nigeria, the concerned areas are entitled to receive compensation for the damages done to them. Mining and petroleum companies should finance rehabilitation, that is, restoration of areas disturbed by mining to make them compatible with surrounding areas. This is a once-and-for-all payment that should concern mining sites and petroleum fields which have already been abandoned. Only in the case where there is no regulation and/or standards are not enforced and thus ongoing exploitation of natural resources uses environmental services on a permanent basis, are concerned jurisdictions entitled to receive permanently a share of the rent – for example, through payment of royalties – as compensation for the damage caused.

Asymmetric and contract federalism Negotiation between central and natural resource-rich jurisdictions can solve some of the problems from excessive concentration. In fact, contract federalism – see Spahn, Ch. 7 in this volume – is one of the most important recent developments in intergovernmental fiscal relations. It is increasingly used, among other things, for the reassignment of expenditure and revenue responsibilities, when the existing legal framework is obsolete, and/or too rigid to accommodate cases of potential conflict. This can be the case when the legal framework assigns the ownership of natural resources to subnational levels of government. When concentration is huge and divisive among the various areas of the country, the central government, which represents the interests of all areas, could propose the assignment of additional responsibilities to the rich areas, for example, the construction of infrastructure of national interest in their area. In other words, larger availability of resources for the rich subnational government is exchanged with an enhanced role in the assignment of expenditure.

Sharing of rents with all levels of governments to foster competition Resource rents may be shared by all levels of government, as in many non-federal countries and in non-classical federal countries. Rent may be shared among wide-area (states/provinces) and small-area (municipalities) subnational government units. One could imagine that this distribution is conducive to a larger allocation of rent, compared with the case where only one level of subnational government benefits. But this is not always granted. In fact, the central government can apply the divide and rule precept. This is quite important in combating secessionist tendencies, which come to the fore frequently when the sharing of natural resource rent is disputed. A secessionist front is hard to create and to sustain, when government units situated at different levels in the same area have access to negotiation and to sharing of resources. This is simply because different units may have different political orientations and strategies. This is usually the case between the government of a state, or region, and the government of the capital or main city of the state/region.

Furthermore, some splitting of natural resources between layers could, when appropriate financial control mechanisms are in place, reduce the overall level of misspending. The reason is that the very sharing could induce competition between beneficiary layers. In other words, citizens can more or less easily compare what they receive from the central and their local government in terms of infrastructure and services and check whether it broadly corresponds to the money assigned to each of them, while in the case of assignment to one layer only this comparison might not be so easy.

Use by the central government of intersecting policy instruments   When the constitution assigns ownership of natural resources to subnational governments, its actual use for the collection of the rent can be controlled by the central government by using other constitutional regulations. The reverse case can also be possible, although it seems more unlikely.

In fact, all constitutions provide the central government with the power to control and circumscribe the power by subnational governments to collect the rent and to alleviate some of its non-desirable effects. The most typical instrument is what, with reference to the American constitution, is known as the 'commerce clause'. This clause has its own equivalent in other constitutions.

In fact, every modern constitution mandates the central government to ensure the smooth working of the domestic market. Subnational government units are not allowed to introduce fiscal or regulatory instruments that reduce competition within their own jurisdiction or, more generally, that reduce competition on the national/domestic market.

Moreover, the central government can use other policy instruments that intersect with rent extraction. For example, the Australian constitution confers on the federal government the power to regulate 'trade and commerce with other countries, and among the States'. Since Australia exports a large share of its mineral production, this constitutional provision has empowered the federal government to control the industry and the collection of the rents by the states. The case of the iron embargo illustrates the problem quite well. This embargo was introduced in 1938 and maintained until 1960, thus eliminating the collection of royalties by states on the output that could have been exported.

The importance of intersecting instruments to counteract the effects of assignment of natural resource rent to subnational government is also shown by the moves of the federal government in Canada after the first petroleum shock (McLure 1983). To counteract the excessive shift of resources in favour of Alberta, it resorted to a few but quite effective decisions such as: (i) holding domestic prices below market prices: this is a system for benefiting consumers, but has little impact if petroleum is mainly exported; (ii) levying of export taxes on foreign sales of petroleum: this will reduce the opportunity for subnational taxes; (iii) eliminating deductions for subnational taxes and royalties in the calculation of central income (company) tax liability; and (iv) modifying the formula used for equalization in a way that penalizes producing and too tax-prone subnational governments.

Conclusion and the need for equalization mechanisms

This chapter has presented the pros and cons for assigning some natural resource rents to subnational levels of government. It has also illustrated an array of potential instruments that might be used in this regard, and possible interactions across instruments.

Clearly, political economy considerations play an important role in the decision on whether or not to share natural resource revenues with subnational governments, and the form that these arrangements might take. However, it should be recognized that disparities in revenues from natural resources, and problems arising from them, can be alleviated through equalization mechanisms. This is what central governments do, especially when the constitution, or previous agreements that are not easily renegotiable, grant a large share of revenues to producing jurisdictions. Equalization can be done for efficiency reasons, as explained above, and also for equity reasons. Boadway, Ch. 14 in this volume, details these reasons and Ahmad and Searle (Ch. 15) examine implementation mechanisms that should be borne in mind in the formulation of joint policies regarding natural resources and transfers.

Clearly, present-day political orientations and redistribution policies are in most countries in favour of redistribution of wealth, but not for total equalization. That translates into equalization transfers that reduce the gap, *ceteris paribus*, between natural resource-rich and natural resource-poor jurisdictions. In addition to efficiency and equity reasons, the intensity of the equalization may be dictated by political convenience, and for keeping countries together and for nation building.

Notes

1. It is possible, however, that at a given moment not all the firms will be in operation. Suppose, for example, that only mines B and C are operated. In that case all operating mines will enjoy a rent.
2. When private ownership is recognized, the government choice concerning instruments is restricted to taxation.
3. In fact bids may refer, in addition to cash payments, to work programmes, royalties and shares of profits. See Sunnevåg (2000).
4. The main contributions are: Garnaut and Ross (1975, 1983); Heaps and Helliwell (1985); Nellor (1987); Boadway and Flatters (1993); Garnaut (1995); Otto (1995); Emerson (2000); Sunley and Baunsgaard (2001); Sunley et al. (2003).
5. This is easily illustrated. Suppose that all bidders agree that the chances of finding a mineral are such that it will have a value of M. The expected cost of exploration is C. The expected value of the lease is $M - C$. This is exactly the value of the rent. If there is enough competition, the highest bid would be $B = M - C$. To see the equivalence, suppose the bid is combined with cash flow tax. As we will see, the cash flow tax base is exactly the rent. If the tax rate is t and the cash bid is not deductible from the cash flow tax, then the highest

bidder will offer $(M - C)(1 - t)$, that is the after-tax value of the bid. If $t = 1$, that is, if the government wants to extract the entire rent, then the highest bidder would offer $(M \quad C)$ $(t - 1) = 0$. If the cash bid is entirely deductible from the tax base, then the highest bidder will offer, whatever the tax rate: $(M - C) - t [M - C - (M - C)] = M - C$.

6. It can be objected, however, that to exercise control, professional skills and experience have to be previously acquired.

7. Moreover, specific royalties tend to delay extraction, while *ad valorem* royalties induce firms to delay, to leave unchanged or to delay extraction, as the price of the resource grows faster, equal to or less than the interest rate. This derives from the assumption that firms choose the extraction path so as to maximize the present discounted value of the profits from the project. The rule to reach this result is to choose a time profile for extraction so that the present discounted value of the profit generated by the extraction of one more physical unit of output is the same over all periods. In the case of specific royalties, the rate of increase of the tax on an incremental unit of output is zero. Thus the discounted value of the tax declines over time, inducing the firm to delay extraction. In the case of *ad valorem* royalties the rate of variation of the tax over time is equal to the rate of variation of the price of the output. Thus, if the growth rate in the price of output is higher than the discount rate (the interest rate) used by the firm, the present value of the royalties will increase over time and the firm will accelerate it extraction path. The opposite applies for the case where the price grows more slowly than the interest rate.

8. The most quoted example is the Infrastructure Tax Credit Scheme of Papua New Guinea, whereby up to 2 per cent of a developer's total tax obligation can be spent on infrastructure within the province in a given year, providing the infrastructure is approved by the Department of Mining and Petroleum, the Provincial Government and the Taxation Office (Andrews-Speed and Rogers 1999).

9. Illustrations are provided by Filer (1995), and Labonne (1995) and Davy and McPhail (1998).

10. Consider, for example, how apportioning of collections among distinct jurisdictions may be difficult, when the same company operates across different areas.

11. For example, indigenous people, rich in energy resources, in the US have set up an organization, namely the Council of Energy Resource Tribes (CERT) to share information and specialist expertise. This allowed individual groups to expand the range of taxation instruments actually utilized (see O'Faircheallaigh, 1998, p. 191).

12. These externalities are analysed in detail by Wilson, Ch. 13 in this volume.

13. Examples are provided, in the case of petroleum, both by federal countries, such as Australia, Brazil, Argentina, Russia and Canada (in the case of the 'Atlantic Accord' concerning the Newfoundland and Labrador provincial governments) and by non-federal countries, such as Colombia, Bolivia, Papua New Guinea and Italy.

14. Petroleum production in Colombia is located in only two provinces; the Siberian *oblast* of Tyumen produces almost two-thirds of total Russian petroleum. In Argentina a single province, Nequén, produces more than one-third of the total. The province of Katanga in the Democratic Republic of Congo possesses most of the mineral wealth of the country. This has fostered secessionist tendencies since the independence of the country (with strong external interference).

15. The distance between the two lines diminishes as population in A increases, since there is surely some lumpiness in the availability of rent from natural resources.

16. More specifically, the welfare loss stemming from using energy resources to subsidize capital would amount to slightly under 9 per cent of energy revenue, while the percentage loss deriving from entirely subsidizing labour would decrease to no more than 2 per cent, because of the lower migration elasticity of labour.

17. In a recent study, Day and Winer (2001) provide evidence for Canada about the impact from public policies on migration flows. They conclude that: 'The average impact of the public policies considered here on the volume of migration . . . is small . . . Even the simultaneous elimination of regional variation in all the policy variables included in the analysis (unemployment insurance, personal income taxes, social assistance and provincial and federal spending on goods and services) is predicted to raise the volume of migration by at most

5%, or by less than half a percentage point' (p. 38). The main determinant of migration seems to be the moving costs.

18. A World Bank study on Casanare, one of the two Colombian petroleum-producing departments, illustrates the risk of wasting fiscal funds when they reach huge levels in a short period of time. Casanare, created in 1991, is one of the newest departments in Colombia. Petroleum royalties were negligible until 1994, then came to represent 73 per cent of the department total income by 1997. According to the law, local governments must invest 100 per cent of royalties in high priority projects in the sectors of education, public health, sewage systems and water supply. However, in 1996, expenditure in these sectors financed out of petroleum royalty income amounted to less than 40 per cent (Davy et al. 1999).

References

Ahmad, Ehtisham and Eric Mottu (2003), 'Petroleum assignments: country experiences and issues; revenue from the petroleum and the gas sector: issues and country experience', in J.M. Davis, R. Ossowski and A. Fedelino (eds), *Fiscal Policy Formulation and Implementation in Petroleum-Producing Countries*, Washington, DC: International Monetary Fund, pp. 216–42.

Andrews-Speed, Philip and Christopher D. Rogers (1999), 'Mining taxation issues for the future', *Resource Policy*, **25**, 221–27.

Boadway, Robin and Frank Flatters (1982), 'Equalization in a federal state', Ottawa: Economic Council of Canada.

Boadway, Robin and Frank Flatters (1982), 'The taxation of natural resources. Principles and policy issues', World Bank Working Papers, 1210, Washington, DC.

Davis, Jeffrey, Rolando Ossowski, James Daniel and Steven Carnet (2001), 'Stabilization and savings funds for nonrenewable resources. Experience and fiscal policy implications', IMF Occasional Papers, Washington, DC.

Davy, Aidan and Kathryn McPhail (1998), 'Integrating social concerns into private sector decisionmaking. A review of corporate practices in the mining, oil and gas sector', World Bank Discussion Paper No. 384, Washington, DC.

Davy, Aidan, Kathryn McPhail and Favian Sandoval Moreno (1999), 'BPXC's operations in Casanare, Colombia: factoring social concerns into development decision making', World Bank Social Development Papers, **31**, Washington, DC.

Day, Kathleen and Stanley Winer (2001), 'Policy-induced migration in Canada: an empirical study', Carleton Economic Papers 01–08, Carleton University, Canada.

Emerson, Craig (2000), 'Mineral taxation and mineral processing policies', in Terry Dwyer (ed.), *Resource Tax Policy in Countries of the Asia Pacific Region*, Canberra: Australian National University Press.

Filer, Colin (1995), 'Participation, governance and social impact: the planning of the Lihir gold mine', in D. Denoon, C. Ballard, G. Banks and P. Hancock (eds), *Mining and Mineral Resource Policy Issues in Asia-Pacific. Prospects for the 21st Century*, Canberra: Australian National University Press, pp. 65–75.

Garnaut, Ross (1995), 'Mining: dilemmas of governance', in D. Denoon, C. Ballard, G. Banks and P. Hancock (eds), *Mining and Mineral Resource Policy Issues in Asia-Pacific. Prospects for the 21st Century*, Canberra: Australian National University Press, pp. 61–8.

Garnaut, Ross and A. Clunies Ross (1975), 'Uncertainty, risk aversion and the taxing of natural resource projects', *Economic Journal*, **85**, 278–87.

Garnaut, Ross and A. Clunies Ross (1983), *Taxation of Mineral Rents*, Oxford: Clarendon.

Heaps, Terry and John Helliwell (1985), 'The taxation of natural resources', in A.J. Auerbach and M. Feldstein (eds), *Handbook of Public Economics*, Vol. I, Amsterdam: North-Holland, pp. 449–67.

Ikein, A. and C. Briggs-Anigboh (1998), *Oil and Fiscal Federalism in Nigeria*, Aldershot: Ashgate.

Labonne, Beatrice (1995), 'Community and mineral resources: from adversarial confrontation to social development through participation, accountability and sustainability', in D. Denoon, C. Ballard, G. Banks and P. Hancock (eds), *Mining and Mineral Resource Policy Issues in Asia-Pacific. Prospects for the 21st Century*, Canberra: Australian National University Press, pp. 111–16.

McLure, Charles E. (1983), 'Fiscal federalism and the taxation of economic rents', in George Break (ed.), *State and Local Finance: The Pressure of the 1980's*, Madison, WI: The University of Wisconsin Press, pp. 133–60.

McLure, Charles E. (2003), 'The assignment of oil tax revenue', in J.M. Davis, R. Ossowski and A. Fedelino (eds), *Fiscal Policy Formulation and Implementation in Oil-Producing Countries*, Washington, DC: International Monetary Fund, pp. 204–15.

McMillan, Melville (1981), *Natural Resource Prosperity: Boon or Burden for Canadian Federalism*, Canberra: ANU Press.

Mead, W.J. (1994), 'Toward an optimal petroleum and gas leasing system', *Energy Journal*, **15**, 1–18.

Mieszkowski, Peter and Eric Toder (1983), 'Taxation of energy resources', in Charles McLure and Peter Mieszkowki (eds), *Fiscal Federalism and the Taxation of Natural Resources*, Lexington, MA: Lexington Books, pp. 65–91.

Nellor, David (1987), 'Sovereignty and natural resource taxation in developing countries', *Economic Development and Cultural Change*, **35**(2), 367–92.

O'Faircheallaigh (1998), 'Indigenous people and mineral taxation regimes', *Resource Policy*, **24**, 187–94.

Otto, James (ed.) (1995), *Taxation of Mineral Enterprises*, Dordrecht: Kluwer.

Otto, James M. (2001), 'Fiscal decentralization and mining taxation', World Bank Group Mining Department, Washington, DC.

Simeon, Richard (1980), 'Natural resource revenues and Canadian federalism: a survey of the issues', *Canadian Public Policy, Supplement*, pp. 182–91.

Sunley, Emil and Thomas Baunsgaard (2001), 'The tax treatment of the mining sector: an IMF perspective', Background paper prepared for the World Bank workshop on the taxation of the mining sector.

Sunley, Emil, Thomas Baunsgaard and Dominique Simard (2003), 'Revenue from the petroleum and the gas sector: issues and country experience', in J.M. Davis, R. Ossowski and A. Fedelins (eds), *Fiscal Policy Formulation and Implementation in Petroleum-Producing Countries*, Washington, DC: International Monetary Fund, pp. 153–83.

Sunnevåg, K. (2000), 'Designing auctions for offshore petroleum lease allocation', *Resources Policy*, **26**, 3–16.

18 Decentralization and the environment
Silvana Dalmazzone[1]

Introduction

The issue of how to allocate powers over environmental policies at different levels of government has received attention, so far, mainly within the framework of the literature on fiscal federalism. The grounds for arguing in favour of the decentralization of public sector responsibilities include the fact that most public goods are local, that their production does not exhibit important economies of scale, and that there is a possibility of tailoring the supply of public goods to citizen preferences that are heterogeneous across jurisdictions, and of avoiding the inefficiency of imposing a uniform national standard in the face of locally different marginal costs of provision. These grounds are applicable directly to the regulation of activities that affect the environment. However, there has been little interchange between these studies and the considerable body of literature dealing specifically with the interactions between economic activities and environmental resources. This chapter focuses largely on the issues relating to pollution control, the area with which most of the environmental federalism literature has been concerned. To some extent the considerations stemming from analyses of optimal jurisdiction over air and water quality are applicable also to issues pertaining more generally to natural resources, such as forest management, wildlife conservation, and the exploitation of oil, gas and fisheries. Wildlife populations with large territories that cross jurisdictional boundaries pose problems that are in some ways similar to transboundary pollution. The implications of an economic analysis of global pollution may have a bearing also for policies about endangered species and other global commons for which the public good aspect weighs heavily. There are, however, also important differences – the relationship between landownership and property rights over the resident natural resources, for instance – which have led to the development of a distinct stream of literature dealing specifically with the allocation of powers over natural resources, and which for space reasons will not be the main object of this chapter.

In conventional environmental economics (as in the welfare economics literature from which it descends), governments are depicted as carrying the responsibility for much of the desired environmental protection. That literature tends to ignore that fact that environmental policy making does not emanate from a single unitary authority but is the outcome of a multilayered structure designed to deal with the large number of different and conflicting demands that citizens place on their governments. Decentralization is a way of dealing effectively with a large number of objectives, increasing flexibility in policy-making, and permitting the use of a broader range of policy instruments.

In addition, the complexity of ecological systems implies that economic decisions concerning a specific natural resource generally affect more than one ecological component, although the impact is often lagged and difficult to predict. In multilevel governmental systems, the interdependence between environmental impacts caused by economic activities that take place at different points in space and time poses problems that have a bearing on the assignment of environmental powers.

A knowledge of the specificity of environmental policy within the more general problem of public goods provision, an adequate scientific specification of environmental issues, and a correct understanding of the decentralization of governmental systems, are all essential and possibly inseparable components for the design of environmental policies. There is in this field an important need for integration between different strands of economic and scientific enquiry.

Environmental federalism: who should do what?
A considerable share of the literature on environmental federalism is linked to the work of Wallace Oates. The basic idea that runs through his several contributions to the subject (in particular Oates and Schwab 1996; Oates 1998b, 2002a, 2002b; Oates and Portney 2001) is the general one that the responsibility of decision making over a particular environmental issue should be given to the smallest jurisdiction that spatially encompasses all (or nearly all) the benefits and costs associated with it. Following this rule, the provision of environmental protection can be tailored to the preferences of citizens, the costs of production and other local conditions, and this would allow the attainment of a higher social welfare compared to the provision of a uniform standard of environmental protection across all jurisdictions.

Setting pollution standards
Environmental policy in this literature refers exclusively to pollution control. The fundamental responsibility of environmental decision making is therefore, in that framework, setting pollution standards. Oates (2002a) identifies three benchmark cases: a first in which environmental quality is a pure public good, a second in which it is a local public good, and a third in which there are local spillover effects.

- *Case 1. Pure public good*   Environmental protection can be thought of as a pure public good within a given country in those cases when environmental quality (Q), although varying across different locations, still is a function of the aggregate level of emissions (P): $Q_i = f(P)$. This case corresponds to that of global (or uniformly mixing) pollutants such as greenhouse gases[2] and ozone-depleting substances:[3] the impact citizens may suffer from climate change or from a reduced ozone layer, for example, may vary across regions but depends on the aggregate, not on the local, emissions. The location of the emission source is irrelevant as far as the vector of damages in the different jurisdictions is concerned.

This is the only case in which the environmental federalism literature univocally recognizes a need for the central government to set standards, since decentralized decision makers have no control over the level of environmental quality within their jurisdiction. In fact, policies aimed at dealing with global environmental issues probably require a standard-setting authority at a tier higher than central governments: the international coordination required to allocate the abatement effort efficiently and limit free riding in many cases has been shown to require supranational institutions.

The efficient level of pollution would have to be established by equalizing marginal benefits of emission reductions, summed over all citizens, to marginal abatement cost. A cost-effective implementation would then require use of economic instruments (such as emission taxes or tradable permits) capable of equalizing marginal abatement costs across all sources.

• *Case 2. Local public good*   Environmental protection is a local public good when environmental quality in each jurisdiction is a function only of the quantity of pollution emitted in that jurisdiction: $Q_i = f(p_i)$. This is the case for local, or non-uniformly mixing pollutants such as particulate emissions from diesel engines, trace metal emissions, ozone accumulation in the lower atmosphere, and some cases of water and ground pollution.

It is in this case that the argument for decentralized standard setting is strongest: the efficient level of environmental protection should equalize marginal benefits summed over the residents of the jurisdiction with marginal abatement costs. If either abatement costs or preferences vary across jurisdictions, then decentralized choices will be superior to a uniform policy designed at the central level: the magnitude of the gains from decentralization will depend on the differences in costs across jurisdictions and on the price elasticity of demand for environmental protection (Oates 1997).

Schoenbrod (1996) adds democratic accountability to the benefits of decentralized standard setting: the massive job of controlling the nation's environment from the centre would induce the central government to delegate its decision-making responsibilities to experts and bureaucrats in functional agencies (such as the US Environmental Protection Agency: EPA) established at the national level but away from officials who are directly responsible to voters. The argument has not gained much following, however. The same US EPA, rather than a monolithic structure operating through uniform regulations, is a reasonably decentralized organization articulated into ten regional offices working closely with the states.

*   *Case 3. Local spillovers*   Most types of pollution cause damages that do depend on the location of the source of emissions, and their impact is felt both locally and in neighbouring jurisdictions. The level of environmental quality in each jurisdiction would then depend on the particular pattern of emissions in each of the others: $Q_i = f(p_1, p_2, \ldots, p_n)$. This category comprises regional, non-uniformly mixing pollutants such as sulphur oxides from power stations and industrial plants, unburned hydrocarbons and nitrogenous air pollutants from vehicle exhausts, but also agricultural emissions of nitrogen species, such as nitric oxide, ammonia, pesticides and their derivatives which can be both airborne and waterborne for long distances across the border of jurisdictions.

    When environmental impacts are felt in different political units from those where the emissions occur, so that the benefits of pollution control also accrue to people in jurisdictions other than those in which the control is exercised, environmental protection will usually be underprovided. Inter-jurisdictional externalities, in a setting of a decentralized allocation of powers, will lead to an inefficiently low level of control. Some authors here highlight the conditions under which Coasian bargaining may bring about efficient solutions; others recommend differentiated taxes or subsidies designed by the central level so as to induce local governments to internalize the damage caused by pollution spillovers.

In summary, the message of the fiscal federalism literature is pretty straightforward: those forms of environmental protection that tend to generate benefits contained within the boundaries of local jurisdictions would present a strong case for decentralized environmental management, whereas environmental issues that tend to spill over such boundaries – and all the more global environmental problems – would require some form of central government intervention.

Straightforwardness notwithstanding, environmental economists have substantially ignored interjurisdictional externalities as a motive behind the assignment of powers over the environment. One reason may be that the impact of most environmental policies has a limited geographical span, so that it is relatively rare that significant benefits of pollution control actually accrue to people in other jurisdictions (Scott 2000). Another explanation is that many interjurisdictional externalities can be dealt with by coordination – a theme which has received attention in the literature on decentralization, for example, by Breton and Scott (1978) and Inman and Rubinfeld (1997). Integrated management of multijurisdictional river basins offers many examples of coordination in federal countries as well as across national boundaries.[4] More generally, international environmental agreements coordinating national policies on sulphur, CFCs, CO_2 emissions and a number of other issues, are all attempts (a few of which reasonably successful) to internalize transboundary externalities in the absence of a centralized authority.

Furthermore, underlying the fiscal federalism literature there seems to be a sharp dichotomy between the centralized and the decentralized mode of organizing environmental governance. Oates's decentralization theorem, for instance, equates the allocation of environmental powers to higher-level governments with the setting of uniform standards.[5] On the other hand, it places decentralized decisions that will be tailored to the local circumstances. It assumes, in other words, a rigid constraint on the capacity of the central government to respond to local differences in costs and preferences. Reality is probably less clear-cut. Some standardization of services provided by central governments does seem to be observed in practice (Walsh 1992). In the case of environmental governance, however, in several countries a tendency has been observed for the policies of the central government not to be imposed by a command system but to be implemented unevenly and flexibly through a process of negotiation (Breton and Salmon forthcoming). The *modus operandi* of EU directives to the European member states, again, is not one of top-down imposition of uniform standards, but a complex decision making system where member states influence the Union's policy formation in the Council (the official institution where they can defend their interests) as well as at many other levels in the policy process. When mechanisms of this sort are at work, they probably create wide margins for central policies to reflect local variations across jurisdictions. The institutional devices by which a governance system can build up the capacity of higher levels of government to tailor their policies to suit local heterogeneity is a subject that deserves further attention.[6]

Policy design and implementation

The task of ensuring the implementation of rules or norms established on a national level is normally allocated to subcentral authorities.

The allocation of powers over implementation can take quite different forms. To simplify, one could identify a structured and an adaptive approach as benchmark cases, with real-world situations fitting along the continuum between the two extremes. In structured implementation (the US Clean Air Act, most of the German environmental law, many EU directives) legislation from the centre regulates the behaviour of local authorities in detail, for example, through the establishment of binding standards, deadlines and procedures. This is most frequently observed in federal systems. In adaptive implementation (for example, the Danish systems), national legislation establishes just the framework for the activities of local authorities, leaving the latter with the responsibility for filling in the details according to local conditions (Berman 1980; Andersen forthcoming).

In general, the economic literature on environmental federalism does not devote as much attention as it should to the issues of implementation and enforcement.[7] For instance, establishing the objectives is not a question completely disjoint from the level at which policy design and implementation – the actual provision of the environmental public good – then takes place. The conventional condition for an efficient provision of public goods says, in fact, that an efficient standard should be set where the sum of all individuals' willingness to pay for increases in environmental quality (the marginal rate of substitution between private and public good, X and Q, respectively) equals the cost of providing Q. If we add a term to recognize the eventual welfare losses due to distortionary effects of the taxes needed to finance environmental policies (often referred to as the marginal cost of public funds, $MCPF$), we get:

$$\sum_i MRS^i_{XQ} = MRT_{XQ} + MCPF. \qquad (18.1)$$

The costs of provision (the properties of the MRT term), however, are in all likelihood influenced by the level at which implementation occurs – with factors such as technology, economies of scale, and size of the jurisdiction sometimes playing a relevant role. Ease or efficiency in collecting the required taxes (which would impact the $MCPF$ term) may also vary at different levels of government.[8]

Whereas a few of these factors – economies of scale and heterogeneity *across jurisdictions* in the costs of provision or in preferences (the MRS term) – have often been considered as elements that can determine the desirable degree of decentralization, the comparative advantages *across levels of government* that these and other factors may determine in implementing environmental policies still require further study, both in empirical and theoretical terms.

Generating and diffusing scientific information
Beside standard setting, the environmental federalism literature frequently cites the generation and diffusion of information on environmental problems

as a task that is generally assigned, in theory as in the real world, to the central level of government. Research and collection of data are activities that benefit everyone and that tend to be subject to important economies of scale. In most countries these tasks are assigned to environmental protection agencies that function at the federal or national level.

The environment is a policy area that relies heavily on scientific and technical information. A problem of scale may act as a constraint on the extent of feasible decentralization: below a given size of a jurisdiction there may be a capacity problem on the part of local authorities even to process the existing information and data for use in the ongoing administration of national legislation. The capacity problem is a function of the resources and specializations of the local environmental administrations' personnel (Andersen forthcoming).

Decentralization of the standard-setting authority may therefore require an active central environmental agency that, in addition to carrying out research on the environment, offers guidance in the form of recommended standards and best-available technology, so as to lay out the menu of choices at the local governments' disposal (Oates and Portney 2001).

Environmental policy and interjurisdictional competition
Even in the strongest case for decentralized decision making over environmental standards, the one of local pollutants, a large body of literature has argued that assigning the power at the local level may result in suboptimal outcomes. One reason relates to the potential trade distortions that may arise from locally differentiated environmental standards. A second, linked, reason arises if local governments lowered their environmental standards in order to hold down the costs of compliance for existing and prospective firms. The resulting dynamic instability, in the absence of countervailing forces, could set in motion a competitive 'race to the bottom' leading to inefficiently high levels of pollution.

Trade distortions
The harmonization of safety, health and environmental standards with the objective of preventing or eliminating distortions of competition in international trade has been, in the real word, a strong motive behind the centralization of environmental standard setting, particularly in the European Union.[9]

From the point of view of economic theory, however, it is not obvious that differences in environmental regulation across countries should induce a distortion of competition, defined as any measure that reduces the efficiency of international trade. The environment, in its function as a sink for emissions, is one of the scarce inputs of which different countries have different initial allocations. Environmental regulations create an artificial price for such input, depending on its relative abundance and on national preferences. Common markets are created to ensure the welfare gains of international specialization based on competitive advantage; uniform environmental standards across member states, besides overwriting local preferences, could hinder efficiency by reducing the scope for such gains (Oates 1998a).

In actual policy-making (particularly in the European Union) as well as in the economic literature, the harmonization of environmental standards finds none the less many supporters. The case for international coordination rests on three main arguments. The first and most obvious are transboundary spillovers, which require agreements and negotiations on reciprocal reductions of emissions in order to contain inefficiency. International coordination, however, does not necessarily mean harmonization to a uniform standard.

The second is the possibility that countries will make strategic use of national environmental policies to improve their position on the international markets. One way this can be done is by using environmental regulation as a substitute for tariffs and quotas, for example using domestic standards to influence the international price of a product. A lax standard would work as an import subsidy, whereas a strict standard as an export tax, and countries could increase their welfare by choosing the most favourable policy depending on whether they are a net importer or a net exporter of that good. This can happen when the industry at home is perfectly competitive (firms are price takers) but the domestic industry has a large enough share of the world market to influence the international price (Ulph 1997; Van Der Laan and Nentjes 2001).

Another way of making strategic use of national environmental policy, depending on the degree and kind of competition in the international market, is setting lax standards in order to keep one's export industries competitive. A number of studies (Barrett 1994; Ulph 1998, among others) have shown, usually assuming Cournot oligopolies and either standards or emission taxes as policy instruments, that in theory at least this can generate a race towards inefficiently low environmental protection – the race to the bottom discussed in more detail in the next subsection.

The third argument for harmonization is that locally differentiated environmental regulations in some cases may translate themselves in differences in product standards and in a consequent fragmentation of the market, which interferes with specialization and competition (Nentjes 1993).

According to Van Der Laan and Nentjes (2001) the concept of 'distortion of competition' has sometimes received a slightly different interpretation, focusing on considerations of fairness rather than on the efficiency of results. That interpretation would have played some role, for example, in EU decisions regarding harmonization versus subsidiarity in environmental legislation. The use of uniform standards in that case would serve the purpose of guaranteeing a level playing field to producers in the common market, on grounds analogous to those behind uniform national legislations on health, safety and labour conditions.

Race to the bottom
The issue of a race to the bottom in environmental standards in a context of interjurisdictional competition has received wide attention. Wilson (1996) provides a detailed survey of this literature up to the mid-1990s. Oates and Portney (2001) also include some more recent works.

One stream of literature develops a set of models describing a world in which competition among governments for mobile firms also leads to efficient choices in terms of levels of local environmental protection. With local governments free to set their own environmental standards, intergovernmental competition would not only not generate a race to the bottom but even be welfare enhancing (Oates and Schwab 1988, 1996).

These models, however, are based on fairly restrictive necessary conditions: governments must be price takers on the capital market and not engage in strategic behaviour in response to policies of other competing governments; they must be in conditions to avail themselves of the best suited among expenditure, tax and environmental policy instruments; and their policies should have no external effects on other jurisdictions.

In more realistic settings, the efficiency properties of these models may no longer hold. If, for instance, the financial weight of government choices may impact on the price of capital, interjurisdictional competition may result in allocative distortions. The same can happen as a result of capacity or institutional constraints on the part of governments in the choice of policy instruments (for example, restrictions on the allowable revenue-raising mechanisms for local governments), or of strategic considerations in the design of policies (for example, public agencies responding also to objectives of budget maximization). Both may result in an inefficiently low level of provision of environmental protection if tight environmental measures have a potentially negative impact on the local tax base (Zodrow and Mieszkowski 1986; Oates and Schwab 1988; Wildasin 1989; Wilson 1996).

Kanbur et al. (1995) take into account the dimension of the country and show that small countries will reduce their environmental standards to be able to attract foreign investors. Marsiliani et al. (2004) present a model of environmental tax competition where saving behaviour is taken into account, since one cannot consider the capital stock being invariant with respect to the fiscal regimes. Uncoordinated policy making (tax competition) will induce a lower capital tax than coordinated policy making. Individuals will therefore save more (if savings respond positively to the after-tax return), and the uncoordinated regime will have larger capital stocks. If the environment is a normal good, a larger capital stock makes a country choose larger environmental consumption (that is, a more stringent standard). On the other hand, in the uncoordinated regime, countries do not internalize international spillovers. This implies that if the international externalities are small, the uncoordinated equilibrium would result in higher environmental quality, whereas if they are large the opposite would hold.

A number of studies looking for evidence of a race to the bottom in environmental matters appear to conclude that, at least at the intergovernmental level, it is not a phenomenon of significant empirical importance (among others, Revesz 1996; Dinan et al. 1999; List and Gerking 2000).[10] Scott (2000) argues that the feared downward instability is rare because, first, industrialization also implies costs for a jurisdiction in terms of infrastructure, health services and so on, that can set fairly high limits to the competitive cut in standards; and second, abatement costs may not be a major element in many firms' location decision − location in a clean environment may have a positive value for firms and their workers as well.

The evidence, in other words, remains mixed, as argued by Wilson (1996) in his survey of the various analytical models which have dealt with the theoretical case of a race to the bottom in environmental standards in a world with free trade and capital mobility. The race to the bottom may arise when there are domestic distortions and constraints on tax and subsidy instruments that leave governments with the option of lowering standards as a last resort (Lal 1998). Outside the world of first-best outcomes, it is the case-by-case magnitude of the distortions that would allow us to say more on how best to allocate powers over environmental regulation.

Heterogeneous preferences over environmental policy

A central point in the argument in favour of decentralized standard setting to maximize social welfare is that heterogeneous preferences across jurisdictions over environmental and health standards must be respected.

When the US EPA, in 2001, issued a new standard for the permissible level of arsenic (a contaminant with certain carcinogenic risks) in drinking water, reducing allowable concentrations by 80 per cent from 50 to 10 parts per billion, it was argued that the new rule would violate efficiency conditions (see for example, Oates 2002a). Treatment of drinking water is an activity that exhibits large economies of scale, so the standard would be most expensive for small districts. Differences in marginal costs alone could provide the case for some form of government transfer aimed at allowing residents in small districts to benefit from the same reduction in health risk as the rest of the country. However, it was argued that a uniform, national standard would also fail to consider the differences in preferences across various communities, and that subsidies would even amplify the resulting inefficiency.

But are preferences over the environment really subject to significant variability across jurisdictions? The issue deserves further attention. Whereas the argument probably holds for a number of publicly provided public goods, the same may not necessarily be true for environmental standards – particularly those involving high risks and/or effects on human health. It would make intuitive sense, in particular, if in matters of risk over human health most of the variation in choices were determined more by the ability of individuals to pay for the relevant policies – their budget constraints and consequent trade-offs – than by a difference in preferences. It is obviously an empirical matter. Elliot et al. (1997) for example, find that both socio-demographic and economic factors have a significant impact on individual support on environmental spending in the United States. Kahn and Matsusaka (1997), in an empirical study of California, find that most of the variation in voting on environmental policies is explained by individual income and the price of the environmental good.

Looking for a theoretical explanation, Marsiliani and Renström (2000, 2002) find that non-inferiority of consumption goods and of the environmental good are sufficient conditions in a wide class of models (from static to overlapping generations models) to obtain a negative relationship between income inequality and the stringency of environmental policy. Since environmental regulations come at the expense of production possibilities, poorer individuals (with a higher marginal utility of consumption and, if the environment is a normal good, a lower marginal rate of substitution between environmental quality and private consumption) will prefer lower pollution taxes or laxer standards: the endowment of the decisive individual in relation to the average influences his/her preferences with respect to the stringency of environmental policies.

Much more investigation is needed to reach conclusions on the matter, but in the meantime it is not defensible to argue in favour of decentralizing choices in the matter of environmental standards with health implications only on the ground of differences in preferences across jurisdictions.

Ecological constraints to the decentralization problem

The environmental federalism literature aims at providing normative prescriptions to deal with the general problem of assigning responsibilities over environmental policy at different levels of government. It is, however, possible to identify some limitations that affect the generality of some of its most widely accepted results.

As discussed above, regional and global spillovers – spatial interconnection in the consequences of emissions from economic activities – have generally been recognized as a potential limit to environmental decentralization. Even some of the literature that more cogently makes the case for maximum decentralization and for market solutions to most environmental issues (for example,

Anderson and Hill 1996; Butler and Macey 1996) recognizes the existence of environmental limits to the extent of sustainable devolution in this regard. The guiding principle is that to minimize the costs of monitoring regulatory agencies, authority should be devolved to the lowest level of government that also allows for control of pollution or other spillover effects.

The environment, however, is not just a sink which passively receives pollution, as it may appear from the economic literature dealing with environmental federalism. The discharge of waste, particularly on the scale implied by modern industrial economies, sets in motion feedbacks and indirect effects. Besides the assimilation of emissions, the impacted environmental resources supply a multiplicity of other services that are essential to the ecosystem and to human activities: the fixation of solar energy into biomass, regulation of the gas composition of the atmosphere, regulation of local, regional and global climate (including the redistribution of humidity), soil formation and stabilization, fixation of nitrogen, decomposition and recycling of organic waste, biological control of organisms that can be deleterious to agriculture and other economic activities, biological control of human and animal disease, pollination, regulation of the water cycle and so on. The biological resources that provide these services are integral parts of ecosystems characterized by complex interrelationships of many species with each other and with the environment in which they live.

The complexity of ecological systems implies that policy decisions concerning, for example, the regulation of a specific kind of pollution in a given jurisdiction generally indirectly affects more than one ecological component, although the impact is sometimes lagged and difficult to predict. The functions performed by environmental resources inhabit different hierarchical levels within an ecosystem as well as different spatial domains. Nature may therefore act as a limit to the extent of decentralization that can retain the capacity to design and implement environmental policies capable of encompassing these multiple and overlapping spatial dimensions.

On the other hand, economic efficiency conditions for the use of environmental resources are based on a view of an environment made of unconnected components, so that only the direct (and often only the local) impacts are considered: the assimilative capacity of pesticides or nutrients by a watershed, or of CO_2 by the atmosphere, the ozone layer, fisheries and so on as fragments whose management and regulation can be considered serially and in isolation.

This is partly a consequence of the fact that efficiency conditions for the use of all environmental resources have been developed as extensions of theoretical constructs originally concerned with non-renewable resources – oil, gas and other mineral deposits – whose depletion has indeed had little impact on the stock of other resources and on the rest of the ecosystem. The capacity of the environment to assimilate waste and pollution – one among the fundamental services provided by the environment – is a renewable resource. As for all renewable resources, a rate of use in excess of its natural regenerative rate can lead to collapse of the assimilative capacity of a given medium.

A further limitation in conventional models of environmental federalism lies in a set of assumptions on both individual preferences and on the processes associated with the supply of environmental policies. The typical prescriptions in terms of desirable decentralization implicitly assume separability of the level of provision of the public good 'environmental quality' from the taxation used to finance environmental policies. But changes in environmental quality Q are generally attained through regulation of private economic activities; we should therefore expect environmental regulation to induce modifications in the behaviour of firms producing the private goods X, and hence in the *MRT* term in equation (18.1). Smith et al. (1999) examine in detail the implications of such an assumption. In partial equilibrium terms, the change in the *MRT* term would reflect changes in the marginal cost of both Q and of other private goods whose production is responsible for deterioration in Q. These effects in turn have general equilibrium consequences: the level of Q will also depend on natural services impacted by the production of other commodities. The effect of regulation on Q will therefore depend on the interconnections within both the environmental and the economic system. The net benefit of pollution control for the citizens in one jurisdiction will generally depend on regulatory and private production activities both within and outside the jurisdiction: the general equilibrium effects will impact both the distribution of benefits and the nature of the costs. Similarly, the services provided by protected and wilderness areas are affected by the external activities taking place in zones of influence around these reserves: again the two sides of equation (18.1) are not separable.

The point that the spatial dimension of the environmental media linking economic activities and environmental quality matters is not a new one: it was already developed in detail in the work of Kneese and Haefele (1974), Kneese and Bower (1979) and others who advocated issue-specific environmental agencies with authority over regions defined on the ground of the spatial dimension of the environmental resource to be managed rather than on political jurisdictions. More recently, this point has been taken into account in empirical analyses of the social cost of environmental regulation (see, for example, Hazilla and Kopp 1990). With the exception of some works on functional overlapping jurisdictions (Casella and Frey 1992; Frey and Eichenberger 1999), this is mostly ignored in the literature on environmental federalism. Relaxing the separability restrictions, however, implies losing the generality of the simplified normative judgements expressed in that literature.

In addition to a spatial component, the ecological and economic values of environmental resources also possess a temporal dimension. Ecological functions have different temporal cycles: for some the cycle is seasonal; for others, it may be of longer duration. When ecological functions are disrupted or variability suppressed through, let us say, regional policies and programmes, some of the damage may consequently be manifest with a lag of a season, of years, perhaps of decades. Furthermore, the damage resulting from subjecting a particular cycle to duress may inflict damage to the ecological productivity of other functions that have temporal cycles of varying lengths.

The existence of a positive discount rate implies that damage that is more distant in time will be imputed a lower present value than that that is less distant. If governments at different levels use different intertemporal discount rates, this would have to be taken into account. Should there be evidence, for example, that higher-level governments use lower discount rates in making their decisions, decentralized solutions would then lead to an allocation nearer to efficiency for environmental resources whose ecological functions have shorter temporal cycles, and vice versa. This too is largely an empirical matter and further enquiry is needed, but the intertemporal dimension of many environmental policies may well impose further constraints on the extent of desirable decentralization.

An additional aspect that may influence the judgement on a desirable degree of decentralization concerns the demand side of environmental policy. The dominant logic, following Oates's work, has been to evaluate the welfare gains or losses from allocating powers at a given level on the grounds of the heterogeneity in individual preferences across jurisdictions, and of the price elasticity of their demands. This approach, as Smith et al. (1997) note, implicitly assumes that the environmental goods can be reproduced at different locations, so that all citizens will access the same goods within their own jurisdictions. If this holds for several dimensions of environmental quality, such as clean air and water, it may not hold for other dimensions such as biodiversity, wilderness areas, national parks and other natural assets, which may be intrinsically available only in some jurisdictions and not be reproduceable elsewhere. In these cases, the question of who should be counted in the sum of the *MRS* in the left-hand side of equation (18.1) is not a trivial one, and may crucially affect the amount of environmental public good to be provided. If people outside the decision-making jurisdictional unit also have a stake but are not counted, then decentralization would lead to welfare losses.

Most of the arguments above appear to point to constraints on the desirable extent of environmental decentralization. Environmental interdependences, for instance, would seem to dictate the necessity of a highly centralized regulatory structure for the protection of the different interconnected components. More than reversing the conventional results, however, this section is aimed at pointing out a few aspects generally overlooked in the mainstream literature and that deserve further analysis. A normative prescription in favour of centralization, for example, would hold only in the presence of extremely high costs of coordination between governments located at different jurisdictional levels. If coordination costs allow, decentralization can bring about potential benefits such as a more direct access to local information, as well as initiative and creativity on the part of the citizenry and of more junior governments. Moreover decentralization, by fostering competition among units of governmental systems, allows these to adjust automatically, to a degree at least, to exogenous changes. This capacity to adjust is particularly important for decision-making structures dealing with environmental issues, where there is a need to be adaptive and flexible to be able to cope with high levels of uncertainty and respond to a continuing flow of new evidence and scientific information.

Future research directions

Several issues, in this field, remain open for further research, and a few are outlined below.

The existing literature mainly deals with the allocation of the standard-setting authority or, in a few cases, with the power of implementing policies. An interesting subject for further enquiry is that of the monitoring and enforcement of environmental policies. Do the same limits to decentralizing the powers discussed in the previous section apply also to decentralizing tasks such as monitoring and enforcement? Intuition suggests that they probably do not and that there may be efficiency gains from allocating such tasks to levels of government different from those that make the decisions. A number of issues would, however, have to be considered. Setting the standards at the central level and allocating monitoring and enforcement to local authorities, as is generally the case in the real world, may open up a large discretionary power for local government in deciding the level of implementation.

A further issue is that of regulatory capture. Coordination between levels of government, both in setting the standards and in defining the details of implementation, would allow for more decentralization than could otherwise take place. This, however, opens up the risk of capture of the regulatory authorities by lobbies that may exercise a stronger influence at the local level. Precisely in the attempt to avoid capture, in the US Clean Air Act, Congress has described the legislation in minute detail and in fact prohibited the EPA from negotiating with interested parties.

The existing research work on the division of powers that pertain to environmental issues in decentralized governance structures is set in a framework that takes for granted that the relevant governance structure is federal. Two points must be made about this research strategy. The first is that there may be mechanisms at work in federal states that are absent in decentralized unitary states; if so, then there would be a gap in the literature regarding environmental policy-making in the latter. The second is that there may be supranational structures such as the EU, which are neither federal nor unitary. This case also would benefit from further analysis rather than being subject to a mechanical application of the existing models dealing with environmental policy-making in federal countries.

A few important recent developments in the theory of decentralized governmental systems have not, as yet, been integrated into the theoretical and policy discussions of how policy-making regarding the environment should be assigned to different levels of government. A number of models have been constructed, considering the benefits and costs of decentralization, to arrive at some notion of an equilibrium assignment. Breton (1987, 1996) argued that intergovernmental competition could serve to articulate a mechanism that could execute an initial assignment and that would change an assignment should it no longer be appropriate. There is now a considerable body of research available (see, for example, Oates 1999; Bird 2000; Breton and Salmon 2001; Breton and Fraschini 2003) supporting the idea that an automatic mechanism based on intergovernmental competition operates to determine equilibrium decentralized assignments in federal and in some unitary states (again, the case of structures like the EU has not been investigated). On the part of the legal–political institutions that preside over assignments and reassignments, failing to take into account intergovernmental competition would probably mean failing to minimize the costs of adjustments. These developments too could possibly provide useful insights if incorporated into the study of environmental governance.

Notes

1. I thank Massimo Bordignon, Pierre Salmon, Bob Searle, Bernd Spahn and the other participants in the Seminar on Fiscal Federalism (Turin, 27–28 August 2004) for helpful comments, and Albert Breton for his invaluable advice.
2. Such as carbon dioxide (CO_2), methane, water vapour and nitrous oxide.
3. Chlorofluorocarbons (CFCs), halons and other chlorine- or bromine-containing compounds used mainly as industrial chemicals, solvents and fire-extinguishing agents.
4. In Germany, the *Länder* agreed among themselves to unify their regulations for the water of their common rivers. The most important institution of cooperation between regions is the LAWA (Länder Arbeitsgemeinschaft Wasser), which brings together all the ministers of the environment of the various *Länder*. See, for example, French Académie de l'Eau (2002) for worldwide case studies of joint water management in federal countries as well as between countries.
5. See, for example, Oates (1972, pp. 11, 36).
6. See Breton and Salmon forthcoming) for a detailed discussion of a few such institutional devices (for example, *cumul des mandats* whereby political actors at the centre also have important responsibilities at the subcentral level) at work in the French political system.
7. More is to be found in the political science literature on policy analysis and environmental governance; see, for example, Ingram and Mann (1980).
8. If a tax is a pure benefit tax – such as a user charge – the marginal cost of public funds is zero. If the tax is greater or smaller than the marginal utility citizens derive from the supplied good, then the benefit tax is imperfect. The size of the *MCPF* term is therefore also affected

by citizens' preferences over environmental quality: the more citizens have a real demand for Q and derive utility from it, the smaller the *MCPF*. On the relationship between environmental policy, public consumption and the marginal cost of public funds, see also van der Ploeg and Bovenberg (1994).

9. In the case of the EU, article 100 of the EEC Treaty (now article 94 of the Amsterdam Treaty), on the approximation of laws for the internal market, has been used to harmonize emission norms from stationary sources across member states.

10. A different issue is that pertaining to international races to the bottom in environmental regulation due to the competition for the allocation of globally mobile capital. The role played by the need to attract foreign investment in locking industrializing countries into lax environmental measures – a 'trap in the bottom' – still requires serious investigation. Whereas there seems to be little empirical evidence of environmental races to the bottom among countries which already have high standards and strong institutions, or between the industrialized and the developing part of the world (Porter 1999; Wheeler 1999; Ahlering 2004), it is between countries with low standards and weak institutions that competition for market shares and foreign investments appear to produce a downward pressure on standards. This could lead to a polarization of international environmental conditions with third-world countries specializing in pollution-intensive productions (Tannenwald 1997; Muradian and Martinez-Alier 2001).

References

Ahlering, Beth (2004), 'The impact of regulatory stringency on the foreign direct investment of global pharmaceutical firms', Working paper, ESRC Centre for Business Research, Cambridge, UK.

Andersen, Michael Skou (forthcoming), 'The Danish communes: capacities and constraints in environmental policy implementation', in Albert Breton, Giorgio Brosio, Silvana Dalmazzone and Giovanna Garrone (eds), *Environmental Governance and Decentralization: Country Studies*, Cheltenham, UK and Northampton, MA: Edward Elgar.

Anderson, Terry L. and Peter J. Hill (1996), 'Environmental federalism: thinking smaller', PERC Policy Series PS-8, Bozeman, MT: Political Economy Research Center, December, www.perc.org/publications/policyseries.

Barrett, Scott (1994), 'Strategic environmental policy and international trade', *Journal of Public Economics*, **54**, 325–38.

Berman, Paul (1980), 'Thinking about programmed and adaptive implementation', in Helen M. Ingram and Dean E. Mann (eds), *Why Policies Succeed or Fail*, Beverly Hills, CA: Sage, 205–37.

Bird, Richard M. (2000), 'Fiscal decentralization and competitive governments', in Gianluigi Galeotti, Pierre Salmon and Ronald Wintrobe (eds), *Competition and Structure: Essays in Honor of Albert Breton*, Cambridge and New York: Cambridge University Press, 129–49.

Breton, Albert (1987), 'Towards an economic theory of competitive federalism', *European Journal of Political Economy*, **3**(1–2), 263–329.

Breton, Albert (1996), *Competitive Governments. An Economic Theory of Politics and Public Finance*, Cambridge and New York: Cambridge University Press.

Breton, Albert and Angela Fraschini (2003), 'Vertical competition in unitary states: the case of Italy', *Public Choice*, **114**(1–2), 57–77.

Breton, Albert and Pierre Salmon (2001), 'External effects of domestic regulations: comparing internal and international barriers to trade', *International Review of Law and Economics*, **21**, 135–55.

Breton, Albert and Pierre Salmon (forthcoming), 'Environmental governance in France: forces shaping centralization and decentralization', in Albert Breton, Giorgio Brosio, Silvana Dalmazzone and Giovanna Garrone (eds), *Environmental Governance and Decentralization: Country Studies*, Cheltenham, UK and Northampton, MA: Edward Elgar

Breton, Albert and Anthony Scott (1978), *The Economic Constitution of Federal States*, Toronto, ON: University of Toronto Press.

Butler, Henry N. and Jonathan R. Macey (1996), *Using Federalism to Improve Environmental Policy*, Washington, DC: AEI Press.

Casella, Alessandra and Bruno Frey (1992), 'Federalism and clubs: towards an economic theory of overlapping political jurisdictions', *European Economic Review*, **36**(2–3), 639–46.

Dinan, Terry, Maureen Cropper and Paul Portney (1999), 'Environmental federalism: welfare losses from uniform national drinking water standards', in A. Panagariya, P. Portney and R.M. Schwab (eds), *Environmental and Public Economics: Essays in Honor of Wallace E. Oates*, Cheltenham, UK and Northampton, MA, USA: Edward Elgar, 13–31.

Elliott, E., B.J. Seldon and J.L. Regens (1997), 'Political and economic determinants of individuals' support for environmental spending', *Journal of Environmental Management*, **51**(1), 15–27.

French Académie de l'Eau (2002), 'Proposal for a strategic guide to assist in the constitution of international inter-state commissions for shared water resources', Technical report, www.inbo-news.org/ag2002/GuideStrategiqueAcademieGb.PDF.

Frey, Bruno and Reiner Eichenberger (1999), *The New Democratic Federalism for Europe: Functional Overlapping and Competing Jurisdictions*, Cheltenham, UK and Northampton, MA, USA: Edward Elgar.

Hazilla, Michael and Raymond J. Kopp (1990), 'Social cost of environmental quality regulations: a general equilibrium analysis', *Journal of Political Economy*, **98**, 853–73.

Inman, Robert P. and Daniel L. Rubinfeld (1997), 'The political economy of federalism', in Dennis C. Mueller (ed.), *Perspectives on Public Choice: A Handbook*, Cambridge and New York: Cambridge University Press, 73–105.

Kahn, M.E. and J.G. Matsusaka (1997), 'Demand for environmental goods: evidence from voting patterns on California initiatives', *Journal of Law and Economics*, **40**(1), 137–73.

Kanbur, R., M. Keen and S. van Wijnbergen (1995), 'Industrial competitiveness, environmental regulation and direct foreign investment', in Ian Goldin and L. Alan Winters (eds), *The Economics of Sustainable Development*, Cambridge and New York: Cambridge University Press, 289–302.

Kneese, Allen V. and Blair T. Bower (1979), *Environmental Quality and Residual Management*, Baltimore, MD: Johns Hopkins University Press.

Kneese, Allen V. and Edwin T. Haefele (1974), 'Environmental quality and the optimal jurisdiction', in Allen V. Kneese (ed.) (1995), *Natural Resource Economics: Selected Papers of Allen V. Kneese*, Aldershot, UK: Edward Elgar, 94–113.

Lal, Deepak (1998), 'Social standards and social dumping', in Herbert Giersch (ed.), *Merits and Limits of Markets*, Heidelberg and New York: Springer, 255–74.

List, John A. and S. Gerking (2000), 'Regulatory federalism and U.S. environmental policies', *Journal of Regional Science*, **40**, 453–71.

Marsiliani, Laura and Thomas I. Renström (2000), 'Inequality, environmental protection and growth', CentER Discussion Paper 34/2000, Tilburg, the Netherlands.

Marsiliani, Laura and Thomas I. Renström (2002), 'On income inequality and green preferences', Working Paper No. 30, October, W. Allen Wallis Institute of Political Economy, University of Rochester, Rochester, NY.

Marsiliani, Laura, Thomas I. Renström and Cees Withagen (2004), 'Environmental policy and interjurisdictional competition in a second-best world', Working Paper in Economics and Finance, 04109, September, University of Durham, UK.

Muradian, Roldan and Joan Martinez-Alier (2001), 'Trade and the environment: from a "southern" perspective', *Ecological Economics*, **36**(2), 281–97.

Oates, Wallace E. (1972), *Fiscal Federalism*, New York: Harcourt Brace.

Oates, Wallace E. (1997), 'On the welfare gains from fiscal decentralization', *Journal of Public Finance and Public Choice*, **2**(3), 83–92.

Oates, Wallace E. (1998a), 'Environmental policy in the European Community: harmonization or national standards?', *Empirica*, **25**, 1–13.

Oates, Wallace E. (1998b), 'Thinking about environmental federalism', *Resources*, **130**, 14–16.

Oates, Wallace E. (1999), 'An essay on fiscal federalism', *Journal of Economic Literature*, **37**(3), 1120–49.

Oates, Wallace E. (2002a), 'The arsenic rule: a case for decentralized standard setting?', *Resources*, **147**, 16–18.

Oates, Wallace E. (2002b), 'A reconsideration of environmental federalism', in John A. List and

Aart de Zeeuw (eds), *Recent Advances in Environmental Economics*, Cheltenham, UK and Northampton, MA, USA: Edward Elgar, 1–32.

Oates, Wallace E. and Paul R. Portney (2001), 'The political economy of environmental policy', Discussion Paper 01-55, November, Resources for the Future, Washington, DC, www.rff.org.

Oates, Wallace E. and Robert M. Schwab (1988), 'Economic competition among jurisdictions: efficiency enhancing or distortion inducing?', *Journal of Public Economics*, **35**, 333–54.

Oates, Wallace E. and Robert M. Schwab (1996), 'The theory of regulatory federalism: the case of environmental management', in Wallace E. Oates (ed.), *The Economics of Environmental Regulation*, Cheltenham, UK and Brookfield, USA: Edward Elgar, 319–31.

Panagariya, Arvind, Paul R. Portney and Robert M. Schwab (eds) (1999), *Essays in Honor of Wallace E. Oates*, Cheltenham, UK and Northampton, MA, USA: Edward Elgar.

Porter, Gareth (1999), 'Trade competition and pollution standards: "Race to the Bottom" or "Stuck at the Bottom?"', *Journal of Environment and Development*, **8**(2), 133–51.

Revesz, Richard L. (1996), 'Federalism and interstate environmental externalities', *University of Pennsylvania Law Review*, **144**(6), 2341–416.

Schoenbrod, David (1996), 'Why states, not EPA, should set pollution standards', *Regulation*, **19**(4), 18–26.

Scott, Anthony D. (2000), 'Assigning powers over the Canadian environment', in Gianluigi Galeotti, Pierre Salmon and Ronald Wintrobe (eds), *Competition and Structure: Essays in Honor of Albert Breton*, Cambridge and New York: Cambridge University Press, 174–219.

Smith, V. Kerry, Kurt A. Schwabe and Carol Mansfield (1999), 'Does nature limit environmental federalism?', in A Panagariya, P.R. Portney and R.M. Schwab (eds), 126–48.

Tannenwald, Robert (1997), 'State regulatory policy and economic development', *New England Economic Review*, March/April, 83–103.

Ulph, Alistair (1997), 'International trade and the environment: a survey of recent economic analysis', in Henk Folmer and Tom Tietenberg (eds), *The International Yearbook of Environmental and Resource Economics 1997/1998*, Cheltenham, UK and Lyme, USA: Edward Elgar, 205–42.

Ulph, Alistair (1998), 'Political institutions and the design of environmental policy in a federal system with asymmetric information', *European Economic Review*, **42**, 583–92.

Van Der Laan, Rob and Andries Nentjes (2001), 'Competitive distortions in EU environmental legislation: inefficiency versus inequity', *European Journal of Law and Economics*, **11**(2), 131–52.

van der Ploeg, Frederick and A. Lans Bovenberg (1994), 'Environmental policy, public goods and the marginal cost of public funds', *Economic Journal*, **104**(423), 444–54.

Walsh, Cliff (1992), 'Fiscal federalism. An overview of issues and a discussion of their relevance to the European Community', Discussion Paper 12, February, Federalism Research Centre, Australian National University.

Wheeler, David (1999), 'Racing to the bottom? Foreign investment and air pollution in developing countries', Policy Research Working Paper Series 2524, World Bank, Washington, DC.

Wildasin, David (1989), 'Interjurisdictional capital mobility: fiscal externality and a corrective subsidy', *Journal of Urban Economics*, **25**, 192–212.

Wilson, John Douglas (1996), 'Capital mobility and environmental standards: is there a theoretical basis for a race to the bottom?', in J. Bhagwati and R. Hudec (eds), *Fair Trade and Harmonization: Prerequisites for Free Trade?*, Cambridge, MA: MIT Press, 393–427.

Zodrow, George R. and Peter Mieszkowski (1986), 'Pigou, Tiebout, property taxation, and the underprovision of public goods', *Journal of Urban Economics*, **19**, 356–70.

19 Corruption and decentralized public governance
Anwar Shah

Introduction

In their quest for responsive, responsible and accountable public governance a large number of countries have recently taken steps to re-examine the roles of their various levels of government. This re-examination has resulted in a silent revolution sweeping the globe, slowly but gradually bringing about rearrangements that embody diverse features of supra-nationalization, confederalization, centralization, provincialization and localization. Note that localization implies home rule, that is, decision making and accountability for local services at the local level. Fundamental elements of home rule are: local political autonomy with elected officials accountable to local residents; local administrative autonomy – ability for local officials to hire and fire local government employees; and local fiscal autonomy – discretionary ability to raise revenues and authority and flexibility in the use of local resources. The vision of a governance structure that is slowly taking hold through this silent revolution is the one that indicates either a gradual shift from unitary constitutional structures to federal or confederal form of governance for the large majority of people or strengthening local governance under a unitary form of government (25 federal and 20 decentralized unitary countries with a combined total of 60.4 per cent of the world's population).[1] This trend is a current source of concern among certain academic and policy circles that are worried that localization may adversely affect the quality of public governance through an increase in the incidence of corruption.

This chapter examines the conceptual and empirical basis of these concerns. The next section defines corruption and governance and discusses the importance of current concerns about corruption. The third section provides analytical perspectives on corruption. This is followed by a discussion in the subsequent two sections of special concerns about corruption under decentralized governance and a synthesis of empirical evidence on this subject. A final section presents some conclusions.

Corruption and governance: fundamental concepts and concerns

Corruption is defined as the exercise of official powers against public interest or the abuse of public office for private gains. Public sector corruption is a symptom of failed governance. Here, we define 'governance' as the norms, traditions and institutions by which power and authority in a country is exercised – including the institutions of participation and accountability in governance and mechanisms of citizens' voice and exit and norms and networks of civic engagement; the constitutional–legal framework and the nature of the accountability relationship among citizens and governments, the process by which governments are selected, monitored, held accountable and renewed or replaced; and the legitimacy, credibility and efficacy of the institutions that govern political, economic, cultural and social interactions among citizens themselves and their governments.

Concern about corruption – the abuse of public office for private gain – is as old as the history of government. In 350 BC, Aristotle suggested in *Politics* that 'to protect the treasury from being defrauded, let all money be issued openly in front of the whole city, and let copies of the accounts be deposited in various wards'.

In recent years, concerns about corruption have mounted in tandem with growing evidence of its detrimental impact on development (see World Bank 2004). Corruption is shown to adversely affect GDP growth (Mauro 1995; Abed and Davoodi 2000), to lower the quality of (Gupta et al. 2000) public infrastructure (Tanzi and Davoodi 1997) and health services (Tomaszewska and Shah 2000; Triesman 2000), and to adversely affect capital accumulation. It reduces the effectiveness of development aid and increases income inequality and poverty (Gupta et al. 1998). Bribery, often the most visible manifestation of public sector corruption, harms the reputation of and erodes trust in the state. As well, poor governance and corruption have made it more difficult for the poor and other disadvantaged groups, such as women and minorities, to obtain public services. Macroeconomic stability may also suffer when, for example, the allocation of debt guarantees based on cronyism, or fraud in financial institutions, leads to a loss of confidence by savers, investors and foreign exchange markets. For example, the Bank of Credit and Commerce International (BCCI) scandal, uncovered in 1991, led to the financial ruin of Gabon's pension system and the corrupt practices at Mehran Bank in the Sindh Province of Pakistan in the mid-1990s led to a loss of confidence in the national banking system in Pakistan.

Although statistics on corruption are often questionable, the available data suggest that it accounts for a significant proportion of economic activity. For example, in Kenya, 'questionable' public expenditures noted by the controller and auditor general in 1997 amounted to 7.6 per cent of GDP. In Latvia, a World Bank survey (World Bank 2004) found that more than 40 per cent of Latvian households and enterprises agreed that 'corruption is a natural part of our lives and helps solve many problems'. In Tanzania, service delivery survey data suggests that bribes paid to officials in the police, courts, tax services, and land offices amounted to 62 per cent of official public expenditures in these areas. In the Philippines, the Audit Commission estimates that $4 billion is diverted annually because of public sector corruption. Moreover, a study by Tomaszewska and Shah (2000) on the ramifications of corruption for service delivery concludes that an improvement of one standard deviation in the ICRG corruption index leads to a 29 per cent decrease in infant mortality rates, a 52 per cent increase in satisfaction among recipients of public health care, and a 30–60 per cent increase in public satisfaction stemming from improved road conditions.

As a result of this growing concern, there has been universal condemnation of corrupt practices, leading to the removal of some country leaders. Moreover, many governments and development agencies have devoted substantial resources and energy to fighting corruption in recent years. Even so, it is not yet clear that the incidence of corruption has declined perceptibly, especially in highly corrupt countries. The lack of significant progress can be attributed to the fact that many programs are simply folk remedies or 'one-size-fits-all' approaches and offer little chance of success. For programs to work, they must identify the type of corruption they are targeting and tackle the underlying, country-specific causes, or 'drivers', of dysfunctional governance.

Corruption is not manifested in one single form; indeed it typically takes at least four broad forms:

1. *Petty, administrative or bureaucratic corruption*   Many corrupt acts are isolated transactions by individual public officials who abuse their office, for example, by demanding bribes and kickbacks, diverting public funds, or awarding favors in return for personal considerations. Such acts are often referred to as petty corruption even though, in the aggregate, a substantial amount of public resources may be involved.

2. *Grand corruption*   The theft or misuse of vast amounts of public resources by state officials – usually members of, or associated with, the political or administrative elite – constitutes grand corruption.

3. *State or regulatory capture and influence peddling*   Collusion by private actors with public officials or politicians for their mutual, private benefit is referred to as state capture. That is, the private sector 'captures' the state legislative, executive and judicial apparatus for its own purposes. State capture coexists with the conventional (and opposite) view of corruption, in which public officials extort or otherwise exploit the private sector for private ends.

4. *Patronage/paternalism and being a 'team player'*   Using an official position to provide assistance to clients having the same geographic,

ethnic and cultural origin so that they receive preferential treatment in their dealings with the public sector including public sector employment. Also providing the same assistance on a *quid pro quo* basis to colleagues belonging to an informal network of friends and allies.

It is also known that corruption is country specific; thus, approaches that apply common policies and tools (that is, one-size-fits-all approaches) to countries in which acts of corruption and the quality of governance vary widely are likely to fail. One needs to understand the local circumstances that encourage or permit public and private actors to be corrupt.

Finally, we know that if corruption is about governance and governance is about the exercise of state power, then efforts to combat corruption demand strong local leadership and ownership if they are to be successful and sustainable.

What drives corruption?

Public sector corruption, as a symptom of failed governance, depends on a multitude of factors such as the quality of public sector management, the nature of accountability relations between the government and citizens, the legal framework and the degree to which public sector processes are accompanied by transparency and dissemination of information. Efforts to address corruption that fail to adequately account for these underlying 'drivers' are unlikely to generate profound and sustainable results. To understand these drivers, a conceptual and empirical perspective is needed to understand why corruption persists and what can be a useful antidote. At the conceptual level, a number of interesting ideas have been put forward.[2] These ideas can be broadly grouped together into three categories: (a) principal–agent or agency models; (b) new public management perspectives; and (c) neo-institutional economics frameworks.

Conceptual perspectives

Principal–agent models This is the most widely used modeling strategy. A common thread in these models is that the government is led by a benevolent dictator, the principal, who aims to motivate government officials (agents) to act with integrity in the use of public resources (see Becker 1968; Becker and Stigler 1974; Banfield 1975; Rose Ackerman 1975, 1978; Klitgaard 1988, 1991; Becker 1983). One such view, the so-called 'crime and punishment' model by Gary Becker (1968), states that self-interested public officials seek out or accept bribes so long as the expected gains from corruption exceed the expected costs (detection and punishment) associated with corrupt acts. Thus, according to this view, corruption could be reduced by (a) reducing the number of transactions over which public officials have discretion; (b) reducing the scope of gains from each transaction; (c) increasing the probability for detection; and (d) increasing the penalties for corrupt activities. Klitgaard (1988) restates this model to emphasize the unrestrained monopoly power and discretionary authority of government officials. According to him, corruption equals monopoly plus discretion minus accountability. To curtail corruption under this framework, one has to have a rules-driven government with strong internal controls and with little discretion given to public officials. This model gained wide acceptance in public policy circles and served as a foundation for empirical research and policy design to combat administrative bureaucratic or petty corruption. Experience in highly corrupt countries contradicts the effectiveness of such an approach as the rules enforcers themselves add an extra burden of corruption and lack of discretion is also thwarted by the collusive behavior of the corruptors. In fact, lack of discretion is often cited as a defense by corrupt officials who partake in corruption as part of a vertically well-knit network enjoying immunity from prosecution.

Another variant of principal–agent models integrates the role of legislators and elected officials in the analysis. In this variant, high-level government officials – represented by legislators or elected public officials – institute or manipulate existing policy and legislation in favor of particular interest groups – representing private sector interests and entities or individual units of public bureaucracy competing for higher budgets – in exchange for rents or side payments. In this framework, legislators weigh the personal monetary gains from corrupt practices and improved chances of re-election against the chance of being caught, punished and losing the election with a tarnished reputation. Factors affecting this decision include campaign financing mechanisms, information access by voters, the ability of citizens to vote out corrupt legislators, the degree of political contestability, electoral systems, democratic institutions and traditions and institutions of accountability in governance. Examples of such analyses include Rose-Ackerman (1978), Andvig and Moene (1990), Grossman and Helpman (1994), Flatters and Macleod (1995), Chand and Moene (1997), Van Rijckeghem and Weder (1998), and Acconcia D'Amato and Marina (2003). This conceptual framework is useful in analysing political corruption or state capture.

There is a fine line dividing theoretical models that focus on the effects of localization on corruption and those that analyse the decentralization of corruption within a multi-tier hierarchy from an 'industrial organization of corruption' type of framework. In the latter group, a distinction is made between 'top-down corruption' – where corrupt high levels buy lower levels by sharing a portion of gains – and 'bottom-up corruption' – where low-level officials share their own collected bribes with superior-level officials to avoid detection or punishment. The former phenomenon is more likely to exist in a federal system of governance where powers may be shared among various orders of government and the latter is more likely to prevail under unitary or centralized forms of governance or dictatorial regimes. The impact of governance on the corruption networks is an interesting yet unresearched topic. Tirole (1986) analysed one aspect of this network by means of a three-tier principal–supervisor–agent model (see also Guriev 1999). This extension of a conventional principal–agent model assists in drawing inferences regarding the type of corrupt relations that could evolve under a three-tier unitary government structure. These inferences are highly sensitive to underlying assumptions regarding principal–agent relationships under a multi-tiered system of governance (four-tier hierarchies are modeled by Carillo 2000 and Bac and Bag 1998). In Guriev's three-tier hierarchy model, the mid-level bureaucrat supervises the agent and reports to the principal. In comparing the characteristics of equilibria with top–bottom and all-level corruption, Guriev concludes that top-level corruption 'is not efficient, as it redistribute rents in favor of agents, and therefore makes it more attractive for potential entrants' (1999, p. 2) and thereby leading to higher total corruption.

Shleifer and Vishny (1993) utilize the conventional industrial organization theory model and conclude that decentralization is likely to increase corruption. In this model, government bureaucracies and agencies act as monopolists selling complimentary government-produced goods which are legally required for private sector activity. The main idea behind the model is that under centralized corruption bureaucracies act like a joint monopoly, whereas under decentralized corruption bureaucracies behave as independent monopolies. When bureaucracies act as independent monopolies, they ignore the effects of higher prices on the overall demand for a good and hence drive up the cumulative bribe burden.

Waller, Verdier and Gardner (2002) define decentralized corruption as a system in which higher-level officials collect a fixed amount of bribe income from each of the bureaucrats that take bribes, without mandating on the bribe size that the bureaucrats charge. On a centralized system, on the contrary, bribe size is determined by the higher level of government which collects and redistributes it among the bureaucrats after keeping a share. Waller et al. posit that decentralized corruption leads to lower levels of total corruption in the economy (lower spread), higher levels of bribe per entrepreneur (higher depth), and a smaller formal sector *vis-à-vis* a centralized corruption equilibrium. Yet, these results vary widely for specific 'regimes' in the model – when given parameters satisfy key conditions – for instance, for high-enough wages and monitoring systems, centralized corruption may reduce total corruption and expand the formal economy.

While previously discussed studies centered on the organizational structure of corruption, Ahlin (2001) differs by concentrating on the alternative effects of different types of decentralization, and doing so from a horizontal, as opposed to hierarchical, perspective. In this model, a country is divided into regions, each with a given number of independent power groups. *Bureaucratic decentralization* affects the political organization in a region by increasing the number of power groups or bureaucracies, while the number of jurisdictions captures the degree of *regional decentralization* (that is, having a single region and bureaucracy would reflect the maximum degree of centralization). Ahlin's theoretical results suggest that corruption is determined by the mobility of economic agents across regions. Under the assumption of no interregional mobility, corruption increases with the degree of bureaucratic decentralization but is independent of the degree of regional decentralization, whereas for perfect interregional mobility corruption decreases with regional decentralization and is independent of bureaucratic decentralization. A key intuition of the model is that corrupt bureaucrats fail to internalize the costs of increases in bribe-charges imposed on other bureaucrats.

Arikan (2004) uses a tax competition framework to examine localization–corruption links. In his model, corruption is measured as the proportion of tax revenue appropriate by bureaucrats, whereas decentralization is captured by the number of jurisdictions competing for a mobile tax base. Local governments decide on the levels of tax rates and corrupt earnings in order to maximize a weighted sum of corrupt earnings and citizen's utility. In this framework, a higher degree of decentralization is expected to lead to lower levels of corruption.

Bardhan and Mookherjee (2000a) shed light upon the determinants of capture of the democratic process. Not surprisingly, they conclude that the extent of relative capture is ambiguous and context specific. Bardhan and Mookherjee find that the extent of capture at the local level depends on the degree of voter awareness, interest group cohesiveness, electoral uncertainty, electoral competition and the heterogeneity of inter-district income inequality. A key assumption of this model is that the degree of political awareness is correlated to education and socioeconomic position; in particular, that the fraction of informed voters in the middle-income class is lower than or equal to that of the rich, and higher than that of the poor. Uninformed voters are swayed by campaign financing, whereas informed voters favor the party platform that maximizes their own class utility. The outcome of local and national elections in terms of policy platforms will coincide under four assumptions: (i) all districts have the same socioeconomic composition, and swings among districts (particular district-specific preferences for one of two political parties) are perfectly correlated; (ii) national elections are majoritarian; (iii) there is an equal proportion of informed voters in local and national elections; and (iv) the proportion of rich who contribute to their lobby is equal at the national and local levels – rich are as well organized nationally as locally.

Alternatively, capture will be higher at the local level if conditions (iii) and (iv) fail. That is, if the proportion of informed voters is lower at the national level and the rich are less organized nationally than they are locally. On the contrary, greater electoral uncertainty at the local level due to differences in the electoral competition imply lower capture at the local level. This would be the case if, for example, swings are not identical but rather drawn from the same distribution across districts – assuming this distribution satisfies a regularity condition – and heterogeneity on swings will favor different parties implying less capture of the nationally dominant party.

In conclusion, no definitive conclusions can be drawn regarding corruption and the centralization–decentralization nexus from the agency type conceptual models. These models simply reaffirm that the incidence of corruption is context-dependent and therefore cannot be uncovered by generalized models.

New public management frameworks The new public management (NPM) literature, on the other hand, points to a more fundamental discordance among public sector mandate, its authorizing environment and the operational culture and capacity. According to NPM, this discordance contributes to government acting like a runaway train and government officials indulging in rent-seeking behaviors with little opportunity for citizens to constrain government behavior. This viewpoint calls for fundamental civil service and political reforms to create a government under contract and accountable for results. Public officials will no longer have permanent rotating appointments but instead they could keep their jobs as long as they fulfilled their contractual obligations (see Shah 1999, 2005).

The NPM paradigms have clear implications for the study of localization and corruption as it argues for contractual arrangements in provision of public services. Such a contractual framework may encourage competitive service delivery through outsourcing and a purchaser–provider split under a decentralized structure of governance. The NPM goals are harmonious with localization as greater accountability for results reinforces government accountability to citizens through voice and exit mechanisms. Conceptually, therefore, the NPM is expected to reduce opportunities for corruption (see Shah 1999, 2005; Von Maravic 2003). Andrews and Shah (2005) integrate these two ideas in a common framework of citizen-centered governance. They argue that citizen empowerment holds the key to enhanced accountability and reduced opportunities for corruption.

Others disagree with such conclusions and argue that that NPM could lead to higher corruption as opposed to greater accountability. This may happen because the tendering for service delivery and separation of purchasers from providers may lead to increased rent-seeking behaviors and enhanced possibilities for corruption (Batley 1999; Von Maravic, 2003). Furthermore some argue that decentralized management leads to weaker vertical supervision from higher levels and the inadequacy of mechanisms to exert controls over decentralized agencies (Scharpf, 1997). This loss in vertical accountability is seen as a source of enhanced opportunities for corruption. Of course, this viewpoint simply neglects potential gains from higher horizontal accountability.

Neo-institutional economics frameworks   Finally, neo-institutional economics (NIE) presents a refreshing perspective on the causes and cures of corruption. The NIE approach argues that corruption results from the opportunistic behavior of public officials, as citizens are either not empowered or face a high transaction cost to hold public officials accountable for their corrupt acts. The NIE treats citizens as principals and public officials as agents. The principals have bounded rationality – they act rationally based upon the incomplete information they have. In order to have a more informed perspective on public sector operations, they face high transaction costs in acquiring and processing the information. On the other hand, agents (public officials) are better informed. This asymmetry of information allows agents to indulge in opportunistic behavior, which goes unchecked due to high *transactions costs* faced by the principals and a lack of or inadequacy of countervailing institutions to enforce accountable governance.[3] Thus, corrupt countries have inadequate mechanisms for contract enforcement, weak judicial systems and inadequate provision for public safety. This raises the transactions costs in the economy further, raising the cost of private capital as well as the cost of public service provision. The problem is further compounded by path dependency (that is, a major break with the past is difficult to achieve as any major reforms are likely to be blocked by influential interest groups), cultural and historical factors and mental models where those who are victimized by corruption feel that attempts to deal with corruption will lead to further victimization, with little hope of corrupt actors being brought to justice. These considerations lead principals to the conclusion that any attempt on their part to constrain corrupt behaviors will invite strong retaliation from powerful interests. Therefore, citizen empowerment (for example, through devolution, a citizens' charter, a bill of rights, elections and other forms of civic engagement) assumes critical importance in combating corruption because it may have a significant impact on the incentives faced by public officials to be responsive to public interest.

Empirical perspectives
The empirical literature on this subject lends support to the NIE perspective elaborated above but goes beyond to identify some key drivers based on in-depth country studies – including a recent World Bank look at Guatemala,

Kenya, Latvia, Pakistan, the Philippines and Tanzania – and econometric studies of developing, transition and industrial countries (see World Bank 2004; Shah and Schacter 2004; Gurgur and Shah 2002; Huther and Shah 2000). The six country case studies examined the root causes of corruption and evaluated the impact of World Bank efforts to reduce corruption in each country. The key corruption drivers identified by these studies are summarized below.

The legitimacy of the state as the guardian of the 'public interest' is contested In highly corrupt countries, there is little public acceptance of the notion that the role of the state is to rise above private interests to protect the broader public interest. 'Clientelism' – public office holders focusing on serving particular client groups linked to them by ethnic, geographic or other ties – shapes the public landscape and creates conditions that are ripe for corruption. The line between what is 'public' and what is 'private' is blurred so that abuse of public office for private gain is a routine occurrence.

The rule of law is weakly embedded Public sector corruption thrives where laws apply to some but not to others, and where enforcement of the law is often used as a device for furthering private interests rather than protecting the public interest. A common symbol of the breakdown of the rule of law in highly corrupt countries is the police acting as law breakers rather than law enforcers – for example, stopping motorists for invented traffic violations as an excuse for extracting bribes. As well, the independence of the judiciary – a pillar of the rule of law – is usually deeply compromised in highly corrupt countries.

Institutions of participation and accountability are ineffective In societies where the level of public sector corruption is relatively low, one normally finds strong institutions of participation and accountability that control abuses of power by public officials. These institutions either are created by the state itself (for example, electoral process, citizens' charter, bill of rights, auditors-general, the judiciary, the legislature) or arise outside of formal state structures (for example, the news media and organized civic groups). There are glaring weaknesses in institutions of participation and accountability in highly corrupt countries.

The commitment of national leaders to combating corruption is weak Widespread corruption endures in the public sector when national authorities are either unwilling or unable to address it forcefully. In societies where public sector corruption is endemic, it is reasonable to suspect that it touches the highest levels of government, and that many senior office-holders will not be motivated to work against it.

How to formulate a strategy

So what can policy makers do to combat corruption? Experience strongly suggests that the answer lies in taking an indirect approach and starting with the root causes. To understand why, it is helpful to look at a model that divides developing countries into three broad categories – 'high', 'medium' and 'low' – reflecting the incidence of corruption. The model also assumes that countries with 'high' corruption have a 'low' quality of governance, those with 'medium' corruption have 'fair' governance, and those with 'low' corruption have 'good' governance (see Table 19.1).

What this model reveals is that because corruption is itself a symptom of fundamental governance failure, the higher the incidence of corruption, the *less* an anti-corruption strategy should include tactics that are narrowly targeted to corrupt behaviors and the *more* it should focus on the broad under-lying features of the governance environment. For example, support for anti-corruption agencies and public awareness campaigns is likely to meet with limited success in environments where corruption is rampant and the governance environment deeply flawed. In fact, in environments where governance is weak, anti-corruption agencies are prone to being misused as a tools of political victimization. These types of intervention are more appropriate to a 'low' corruption setting, where one can take for granted (more or less) that the governance fundamentals are reasonably sound and that corruption is a relatively marginal phenomenon.

Table 19.1   One size does not fit all: effective anti-corruption policies and reforms

Incidence of corruption	Quality of governance	Priorities of anti-corruption efforts
High	Poor	Establish rule of law, strengthen institutions of participation and accountability; establish citizens' charter, limit government intervention, implement economic policy reforms
Medium	Fair	Decentralize and reform economic policies and public management and introduce accountability for results
Low	Good	Establish anti-corruption agencies; strengthen financial accountability; raise public and official awareness; anti-bribery pledges, conduct high-profile prosecutions

The model also suggests that where corruption is high (and the quality of governance is correspondingly low), it makes more sense to focus on the underlying drivers of malfeasance in the public sector – for example, by building the rule of law and strengthening institutions of accountability. Indeed, a lack of democratic institutions (a key component of accountability) has been shown to be one of the most important determinants of corruption (Gurgur and Shah 2002). When Malaysia adopted a 'client's charter' in the early 1990s that specified service standards and citizens' recourse in the event of non-compliance by government agencies, it helped reorient the public sector toward service delivery and transform the culture of governance (Shah 1999, 2005).

In societies where the level of corruption lies somewhere in between the high and low cases, it may be advisable to attempt reforms that assume a modicum of governance capacity – such as trying to make civil servants more accountable for results, bringing government decision making closer to citizens through decentralization, simplifying administrative procedures, and reducing discretion for simple government tasks such as the distribution of licenses and permits.

Insights into past failures

With this model in mind, it is not hard to understand why so many anti-corruption initiatives have met with so little success. Take, for example, the almost universal failure of wide-ranging media awareness campaigns, and of seminars and workshops on corruption targeted at parliamentarians and journalists. As the model shows, this outcome would be expected in countries with weak governance, where corruption is openly practiced but neither the general public nor honest public officials feel empowered to take a stand against it and even fear being victimized (see Table 19.1). On the other hand, awareness campaigns would be expected to have a positive impact in countries where governance is fair or good and the incidence of corruption is low.

Decentralization provides a further illustration of the importance of understanding the circumstances in which corruption occurs. There is indeed evidence that decentralization can be an effective antidote to corruption because it increases the accountability of public authorities to citizens (for additional references and evidence, see Gurgur and Shah 2002; Shah et al. 2004). On the other hand, decentralization creates hundreds of new public authorities, each having powers to tax, spend and regulate that are liable to being abused in environments where governance is weak. As the World Bank's analysis of the Philippines in the 1990s has shown, decentralization may multiply rather than limit opportunities for corruption if it is implemented under the wrong circumstances. This issue is the central theme of this chapter and it is analysed further in the following sections.

As for raising civil service salaries and reducing wage compression – the ratio between the salaries of the highest- and lowest-paid civil servants in a given country – again, the model provides some insights. The evidence suggests that in environments where governance is weak, wage-based strategies are not likely to have a significant impact on civil service corruption (see Huther and Shah 2000 for references). Moreover, reducing wage compression may even encourage corruption if public sector positions are viewed as a lucrative career option. For instance, in corrupt societies, public positions are often purchased by borrowing money from family and friends. Raising public sector wages simply raises the purchase price and subsequent corruption efforts to repay loans.

How about the establishment of 'watchdog' agencies – something most developing countries have done – with a mandate to detect and prosecute corrupt acts? Here, too, the governance–corruption nexus is key. Watchdog agencies have achieved success only in countries where governance is generally good, such as Australia and Chile. In weak governance environments, however, these agencies often lack credibility and may even extort rents. In Kenya, Malawi, Sierra Leone, Tanzania, Uganda and Nigeria, for example, anti-corruption agencies have been ineffective. In Tanzania, the government's Prevention of Corruption Bureau produces only about six convictions a year, mostly against low-level functionaries, in a public sector environment rife with corruption. In Pakistan, the National Accountability Bureau does not even have a mandate to investigate corruption in the powerful and influential military. Ethics offices and ombudsmen have had no more success than anti-corruption agencies in countries where governance is poor.

Revisiting the debate on localization and corruption
A brief review of the corruption literature presented above serves as a useful background to the debate on corruption and decentralization. In the following sections, we briefly review the arguments and the evidence on both sides of the debate and then draw some conclusions based upon the simple analytical model presented earlier.

Localization breeds corruption
A number of arguments have been advanced to support the notion that corruption increases with localization. A few of these are summarized below.

Personalism Vito Tanzi (1995) argued that localization brings officials in close contact with citizens. This promotes personalism and reduces professionalism and arm's length relationships. Personalism in his view breeds corruption as officials pay greater attention to individual citizen needs and disregard public interest. Further, a higher degree of discretion at the local level and a long tenure of local officials make it easier to establish unethical relationships (Prud'homme 1995).

Weak monitoring and vertical controls　Impediments to corrupt practices also decrease as local politicians and bureaucrats collude to advance narrow self-interests while the effectiveness of auditing agencies and monitoring from the central level wanes (Prud'homme 1994). Localization may increase the motivation for corruption among public officials by creating an impression that they are subject to lower monitoring, control and supervision.

Fiscal decentralization and overgrazing　Triesman argues that decentralized federal systems tend to have higher corruption ratings due to (a) their larger size; (b) they are more likely to have separate police forces at both central and subnational levels (which increases corruption due to overgrazing) and their greater propensity to have a regionally elected upper house of parliament with veto power (which also may increase corruption as regional governments may buy off these veto players or have greater leverage to protect their ill-gotten gains).

Using cross-country regression analysis, Triesman (1999, 2000, 2002) presents empirical evidence that support the existence of this negative relationship. Triesman's empirical results, however, are sensitive to the inclusion of other variables in the equation and may have omitted variables bias in view of a lack of underlying framework for corruption.

Political decentralization and lack of discipline　Political decentralization is seen as a cascading system of bribes by Shleifer and Vishny (1993). They note that 'to invest in a Russian company, a foreigner must bribe every agency involved in foreign investment including the foreign investment office, the relevant industrial ministry, the finance ministry, the executive branch of the local government, the legislative branch, the central bank, the state property bureau, and so on' (1993, p. 615). In the same vain, Bardhan (1997) and Blanchard and Shleifer (2000) have argued that political centralization leads to lower levels of corruption. Blanchard and Schleifer sustain that political decentralization is seen as a source of corruption in Russia but not China. This conclusion emerges from the contrasting role of local governments in their relations with local enterprises observed in China and Russia. In China, local governments have provided a supporting role whereas in Russia, local governments have stymied the growth of new firms through taxation, regulation and corruption. The authors note that the behavior of Russian local governments can be explained by (a) state capture by old firms, leading local governments to protect them from competition and (b) rent-seeking behavior of local officials discouraging new firms to enter. The authors attribute this contrasting experience to the presence of political decentralization in Russia and its absence in China. They argue that political centralization in China contributes to party discipline, which in turn reduces the risk of local capture and corruption. However, the Blanchard and Shleifer analysis does not pay sufficient attention to local-enterprise relations in the two countries. Local enterprises in China are owned and run by local governments and even deliver local services such as education, health and transportation in addition to their economic functions. Thus, local enterprises are part and parcel of the local government. In Russia, on the other hand, a mixed pattern of these relationships has begun to emerge. Therefore, the contrasting experience of the local governments may be better explained by agency problems rather than by political decentralization. In fact, the weakening of party discipline through the emergence of powerful local leaders may be contributing to the growth of local industry as the strong arm of central planning is held at bay by these leaders.

Interest group capture   Opportunities for corruption increase due to a greater influence of interest groups at the local level (Prud'homme 1994). In this regard, Bardhan and Mookherjee (2000a) argue that the probability of capture by local interest groups could be greater at the local level if, for example, interest group cohesiveness (fraction of the richest class that contribute to lobby) is higher, or the proportion of informed voters is lower at the local level. Lower levels of political awareness at the local level and less coverage of local elections by media may also impair local democracy and lead to higher capture. The notion of capture at the local levels due to weaknesses of the democratic system has also been raised by Shah (1998). Concerns about risks of local capture are also expressed in a recent World Bank Study (World Bank 2004). The study argues that decentralization may increase opportunities for corruption in some developing countries where interference in public administration is the norm, merit culture and management systems in the civil service are weak and institutions of participation and accountability are ineffective.

The issue is significant, for example, in Pakistan and Philippines, and also relevant to Guatemala and Tanzania where more limited decentralization is underway. Pakistan has launched a decentralization program involving the creation of 7000 local and subnational governments. Given systemic politicization of public services in Pakistan, decentralization may intensify rather than reduce pressures for political/bureaucratic collusion, although this may be further mitigated by further administrative decentralization, giving elected local officials the power to hire, fire and set terms of employment of civil servants in their jurisdiction. Note that administration decentralization in areas under feudal influence is likely to exacerbate the corruption concerns. Identical concerns are pertinent in the Philippines, where legislation in 1991 devolved to regions and localities powers to provide services and raise revenues. A study of local government procurement in the Philippines revealed that (see Tapales 2001, p. 21):

> Contractors admit to paying mayors of the towns where they have projects, because,

they say, the officials can delay the work by withholding necessary permits or harassing the workers. Municipal mayors get seven percent while the barangay (village) captain is given three percent. The heads of implementing agencies – usually the district, municipal or city engineer – get about 10 per cent.

The World Bank study (2004) is concerned with the effect of decentralized on corruption when there is a local capture by political and bureaucratic elites. There is little disagreement in the literature that is such a situation, localization without fundamental electoral and land reforms is likely to increase corruption. On the contrary, the perception of localization as a breeding ground for corruption in the presence of democratic participation and accountability, is neither grounded in theory nor in evidence.

Localization limits opportunities for corruption
Localization's ability to curtail corruption opportunities has been commonly based on the potential for greater accountability when the decision making is closer to the people. This line of thought is supported from the following perspectives:

* *Competition among local governments* for mobile factors of production re-enforces the accountability culture. Such enhanced accountability has the potential to reduce corruption (Weingast 1995; Arikan 2004).
* *Exit and voice mechanisms at the local level* There is a general agreement in the literature that localization can open up greater opportunities for voice and choice thereby making the public sector more responsive and accountable to citizen-voters. Furthermore, due to regional heterogeneity of political preferences, localization may reduce the range of potential capture by a unique nationally dominant party.
* *Higher levels of information* Seabright (1996) argues that accountability is always better at the local level, since local citizens who are better informed about government performance can vote these governments out of office. Under centralization, people vote for parties or candidates partly on the basis of performance in other regions and on issues of national interest. As a result, accountability is defused and potential for corruption increases. Bardhan and Mookherjee (2000b) also argue that decentralization of the delivery of anti-poverty programs in developing countries promotes cost-effectiveness and reduces corruption, owing to the superior access of local governments to information on local costs and needs.
* *Lower expected gains from corruption but greater probability of detection and punishment* Administrative decentralization causes a loss in control to higher levels, thus curbing their incentives to monitor and detect corrupt activities. However, it also lowers the expected gains from

corruption as, following decentralization, the number of individuals who are in charge of a single decision is reduced. It is then more likely that corrupt agents are called to bear the consequences of their actions. This line of thought complements those put forward by Carbonara (1999), who concludes that decentralization, although creating agency problems inside an organization, can help in controlling corruption, and Wildasin (1995), who argues that local officials with limited powers have little scope to engage in massive corruption.

*   *Political decentralization*   Ahlin (2000) has argued that deconcentration has the potential to increase corruption, whereas political decentralization has the potential to contain it due to interjurisdictional competition. This may result from a reduction in the information asymmetry between the bureaucrats and politicians that appoint them *vis à vis* a politically centralized system. Crook and Manor (2000) examined the process of political decentralization in India (Karnatka state), Bangladesh, Cote d'Ivoire and Ghana and found that such decentralization leads to enhanced transparency. With this enhanced transparency, ordinary citizens become better aware of government's successes and failures and they may perceive the government institutions to be more corrupt than they perceived before. Crook and Manor observed that in Karnatka, India, political decentralization substantially reduced the amount of public funds diverted by powerful individuals. However, since citizens were not aware of these diversions, they concluded that corruption has increased. From the evidence from Karnatka, they conclude that political decentralization reduces grand theft but increases petty corruption in the short run, but in the long run, both may go down. Olowu (1993) also considers political centralization as a root cause of endemic corruption in Africa. Fiszbein (1997), based upon a review of political decentralization in Colombia, concludes that competition for political office opened the door for responsible and innovative leadership, which in turn became the driving force behind capacity building, improved service delivery and reduced corruption at the local level.

*   *Administrative decentralization*   A few studies show that administrative decentralization reduces corruption. Wade (1997) finds that over-centralized top-down management, accompanied by weak communication and monitoring systems, contributes to corruption and poor-delivery performance for canal irrigation in India. Kuncoro (2000) finds that with administrative decentralization in Indonesia, firms relocated to areas with lower bribes.

*   *Fiscal decentralization*   Huther and Shah (1998), using international cross-section and time series data, find that fiscal decentralization is associated with enhanced quality of governance as measured by citizen

participation, political and bureaucratic accountability, social justice, improved economic management and reduced corruption. Arikan (2004) reconfirms the same result. De Mello and Barenstein (2001), based upon cross-country data, conclude that tax decentralization is positively associated with improved quality of governance. Fisman and Gatti (2002) find a negative relation between fiscal decentralization and corruption. Gurgur and Shah (2002) is the only study providing a comprehensive theoretical and empirical framework on the root causes of corruption. They identify major drivers of corruption in order to isolate the effect of decentralization. In a sample of industrial and non-industrial countries, lack of service orientation in the public sector, weak democratic institutions, economic isolation (closed economy), colonial past, internal bureaucratic controls and centralized decision making are identified as the major causes of corruption. For a non-industrial countries sample, drivers for corruption are lack of service orientation in the public sector, weak democratic institutions and closed economy. Decentralization reduces corruption but has a greater negative impact on corruption in unitary countries than in federal countries. Gurgur and Shah conclude that decentralization is confirmed to support greater accountability in the public sector and reduced corruption.

In all, a small yet growing body of theoretical and empirical literature confirms that localization offers significant potential in bringing greater accountability and responsiveness to the public sector at the local level and reducing the incidence of grand corruption.

Corruption and decentralization: some conclusions
Power corrupts and absolute power corrupts absolutely. Localization helps to break the monopoly of power at the national level by bringing decision making closer to the people. Localization strengthens government accountability to citizens by involving citizens in monitoring government performance and demanding corrective actions. Localization as a means of making government responsive and accountable to the people can help reduce corruption and improve service delivery. Efforts to improve service delivery usually force the authorities to address corruption and its causes. However, one must pay attention to the institutional environment and the risk of local capture by elites. In the institutional environments typical of some developing countries, when in a geographical area, feudal industrial interests dominate and institutions of participation and accountability are weak or ineffective and political interference in local affairs is rampant, thus localization may increase opportunities for corruption. This suggests a pecking order of anti-corruption policies and programs as highlighted in Table 19.1. Thus rule of law and citizen empowerment should be

the first priority in any reform efforts. Localization in the absence of rule of law may not prove to be a potent remedy for combating corruption.

Notes

1. The total number of countries has risen from 140 in 1975 to over 200 in 2004. In 2001, there were 24 federal countries with 25.4 per cent of the world's population, with another 20 decentralized unitary countries with some federal features comprising 35 per cent of the world's population.
2. For comprehensive surveys on corruption, see Jain (2001) and Aidt (2003).
3. Following this line of thought, Lambsdorff et al. note that in fighting corruption from an NIE perspective, policy makers should aim to 'encourage betrayal among corrupt parties, to destabilize corrupt agreements, to disallow corrupt contracts to be legally enforced, to hinder the operation of corrupt middlemen and to find clearer ways of regulating conflicts of interest.'

References

Abed, George T. and Hamid Davoodi (2000), 'Corruption, structural reforms, and economic performance in the transition economies', International Monetary Fund Working Paper 00/132.

Acconcia, Antonio, Marcello D'Amato and Riccardo Martina (2003), 'Corruption and tax evasion with competitive bribes', CSEF Working Paper 112, University of Salerno, Italy: Centre for Studies in Economics and Finance.

Ades, Alberto and Rafael Di Tella (1997), 'National champions and corruption: some unpleasant interventionist arithmetic', *The Economic Journal*, **107**: 1023–42.

Advig, Jens Chr. and Karl O. Moene (1990), 'How corruption may corrupt', *Journal of Economic Behavior and Organization*, **13**, 63–76.

Ahlin, Christian (2000), 'Corruption, aggregate economic activity and political organization', manuscript, University of Chicago.

Ahlin, Christian (2001), 'Corruption: political determinants and macroeconomic effect', Working Paper 01-W26, Vanderbilt University: Department of Economics.

Andrews, Matthew and Anwar Shah (2005), 'Towards citizen-centered local budgets in developing countries', in A. Shah (ed.), *Public Expenditure Analysis*, Washington DC: World Bank.

Arikan, Gulsun (2004), 'Fiscal decentralization: a remedy for corruption?', *International Tax and Public Finance*, **11**: 175–95.

Bac, Mehmet and Parimal K. Bag (1998), 'Corruption, collusion and implementation: a hierarchical design', mimeo, University of Liverpool.

Banfield, Edward (1975), 'Corruption as feature of government organization', *Journal of Law and Economics*, **18**: 587–695.

Bardhan, Pranab (1997), 'Corruption and development: a review of issues', *Journal of Economic Literature*, **35**(September): 1320–46.

Bardhan, Pranab and Dilip Mookherjee (2000), 'Decentralizing anti-poverty program delivery in developing countries', Working Paper, University of California, Berkeley.

Batley, R. (1999), 'The role of government in adjusting economies: an overview of findings', research paper, International Development Department, University of Birmingham, Alabama.

Becker, Gary Stanley (1968), 'Crime and punishment: an economic approach', *Journal of Political Economy*, **76**(2): 169–217.

Becker, Gary Stanley (1983), 'A theory of competition among pressure groups for political influence', *Quarterly Journal of Economics*, **XCVII**(3), 371–400.

Becker, Gary Stanley and George Stigler (1974), 'Law enforcement, malfeasance and the compensation of enforcers', *Journal of Legal Studies*, **3**: 1–19.

Blanchard, Olivier and Andrei Shleifer (2000), 'Federalism with and without political centralization: China versus Russia', Working Paper 7616, National Bureau of Economic Research, March: 1–14.

Carbonara Emanuela (1999), 'Bureaucracy, corruption and decentralization', Working Paper 342/33, Department of Economics, University of Bologna, Italy.

Carillo, Juan D. (2000), 'Corruption in hierarchies', Annales d'Economie et de Statistique/ Institut National de la Statistique et des Etudes Economiques (France) **59**: 37–61.

Chand, Sheetal K. and Karl O. Moene (1997), 'Controlling fiscal corruption', International Monetary Fund Working Paper WP/97/100.

Crook, Richard and James Manor (2000), 'Democratic dentralization', OECD Working Paper Series No. 11, Summer, Washington, DC: World Bank.

De Mello, Luis and Matias Barenstein (2001), 'Fiscal decentralization and governance – a cross-country analysis', IMF Working Paper 01/71.

Fisman, Raymond and Roberta Gatti (2002), 'Decentralization and corruption: evidence across countries', *Journal of Public Economics*, **83**: 325–45.

Fiszbein, Ariel (1997), 'Emergence of local capacity: lessons from Colombia', *World Development*, **25**(7): 1029–43.

Flatters, Frank and W. Bentley Macleod (1995), 'Administrative corruption and taxation', *International Tax and Public Finance*, **2**: 397–417.

Grossman, Gene M. and Elhanan Helpman (1994), 'Protection for sale', *American Economic Review*, **84**(4): 833–50.

Gupta, Sanjeev, Hamid Davoodi and Rosa Alosno-Terme (1998), 'Does corruption affect income inequality and poverty?', International Monetary Fund Working Paper 98/76.

Gupta, Sanjeev, Hamid Davoodi and Erwin Tiongson (2000), 'Corruption and the provision of health care and education services', International Monetary Fund Working Paper 00/116.

Gurgur, Tugrul and Anwar Shah (2002), 'Localizational and corruption: panacea or Pandora's box?', in E. Ahmad and V. Tanzi (eds), *Managing Fiscal Decentralization*, London and New York: Routledge, pp. 46–67.

Guriev, Sergei (1999), 'A theory of informative red tape with an application to top-level corruption', Working Paper 99/007, New Economic School, Moscow.

Guriev, Sergei (2003), 'Red tape and corruption', Discussion Paper 3972, Centre for Economic Policy Research: 1–27.

Huther, Jeff and Anwar Shah (1998), 'Applying a simple measure of good governance to the debate on fiscal decentralization', Policy Research Working Paper 1894, Washington, DC: World Bank.

Huther, Jeff and Anwar Shah (2000), 'Anti-corruption policies and programs: a framework for evaluation', Policy Research Working Paper 2501, Washington, DC: World Bank.

Klitgaard, Robert E. (1991), 'Gifts and bribes', in Richard Zeckhauser (ed.), *Strategy and Choice*, Cambridge, MA: MIT Press.

Klitgaard, Robert E. (1988), *Controlling Corruption*, Berkeley: University of California Press.

Kuncoro, Ari (2000), 'The impact of licensing decentralization on firm location choice: the case of Indonesia', manuscript, Faculty of Economics, University of Indonesia.

Lambsdorff, Johann (1999), 'Corruption in empirical research – a review', Transparency International Working Paper.

Mauro, Paola (1995), 'Corruption and growth', *Quarterly Journal of Economics*, **110**(3): 681–713.

Olowu, Dele (1993), 'Roots and remedies of government corruption in Africa', *Corruption and Reform*, **7**(3): 227–36.

Prud'homme, Remy (1994), 'On the dangers of decentralization', World Bank Policy Research Working Paper 1252, Washington, DC: World Bank.

Rose-Ackerman, S. (1975), 'The economics of corruption', *Journal of Public Economics*, **4**(February): 187–203.

Rose-Ackerman, S. (1978), *Corruption: a Study in Political Economy*, New York, San Francisco, London: Academic Press.

Scharpf, Fritz W. (1997), *Games Real Actors Play – Actor-Centered Institutionalism in Policy Research*, Boulder, CO: Westview Print.

Seabright, Paul (1996), 'Accountability and decentralization in government: an incomplete contracts model', *European Economic Review*, **40**(1): 61–89.

Shah, Anwar (1998), 'Balance, accountability, and responsiveness: lessons about decentralization', World Bank Policy Research Working Paper 2021 (December).

Shah, Anwar (1999), 'Governing for results in a globalized and localized world', *The Pakistan Development Review*, **38**(4), Part I: 385–431.

Shah, Anwar (2005), 'On getting the giant to kneel: approaches to a change in the bureaucratic culture', in A. Shah (ed.), *Fiscal Management*, Public Sector Governance and Accountability Series, Washington, DC: World Bank, pp. 211–29.

Shah, Anwar and Mark Schacter (2004), 'Combating corruption. Look before you leap', *Finance and Development*, **41**(4), December, 40–43.

Shah, Anwar, Theresa Thompson and Heng-fu Zou (2004), 'The impact of decentralization on service delivery, corruption, fiscal management and growth in developing and emerging market economics: a synthesis of empirical evidence', *CESifo Dice Report, a Quarterly Journal for Institutional Comparisons*, **2**(Spring): 10–14.

Shleifer, Andrei and Robert W. Vishny (1993), 'Corruption', *Quarterly Journal of Economics*, **108**: 599–617.

Tanzi, Vito (1995), 'Fiscal federalism and decentralization: a review of some efficiency and microeconomic aspects', Annual Work Bank Conference on Development Economics; reprinted in V. Tazi (2000), *Policies, Institutions and the Dark Side of Economics*, Cheltenham, UK and Northampton, MA, USA: Edward Elgar, pp. 231–63.

Tanzi, Vito and Hamid Davoodi (1997), 'Corruption, public investment and growth', International Monetary Fund Working Paper 97/139.

Tirole, Jean (1986), 'Hierarchies and bureaucracies: on the role of collusion in organizations', *Journal of Law Economics and Organization*, **2**: 181–214.

Tirole, Jean and Jean-Jacques Laffont (1988), 'Politics of government decision-making: a theory of regulatory capture', Working Paper 506, Department of Economics, Massachusetts Institute of Technology: 1–48.

Tomaszewska, Ewa and Anwar Shah (2000), 'Phantom hospitals, ghost schools and roads to nowhere: the impact of corruption on public services delivery performance in developing countries', Working Paper, Operations Evaluation Department, World Bank, Washington, DC.

Treisman, Daniel (1999), *After the Deluge: Regional Crises and Political Consolidation in Russia*, Ann Arbor, MI: University of Michigan Press.

Treisman, Daniel S. (2000), 'The causes of corruption: a cross national study', *Journal of Public Economics*, **76**(3), June: 399–457.

Treisman, Daniel S. and Andrei Shleifer (2002), 'A normal country', Working Paper 10057, National Bureau of Economic Research, October: 1–46.

Van Rijckeghem, Caroline and Beatrice Weder (2001), 'Bureaucratic corruption and the rate of temptation: do low wages in civil service cause corruption?', *Journal of Development Economics*, **65**: 307–31.

Wade, Robert (1997), 'How infrastructure agencies motivate staff: canal irrigation in India and the Republic of Korea', in A. Mody (ed.), *Infrastructure Strategies in East Asia*, Washington, DC: World Bank.

Waller, Christopher J., Thierry A. Verdier and Roy Gardner (2002), 'Corruption: top-down or bottom-up', *Economic Inquiry*, **40**(4): 688–703.

Weinsgast, Barry (1995), 'The economic role of political institutions: market preserving federalism and economic growth', *Journal of Law, Economics, and Organization*, **11**: 1–31.

Wildasin, David (1995), 'Comment on "Fiscal federalism and decentralization"', Annual World Bank Conference on Development Economics, pp. 323–8.

World Bank (2004), *Mainstreaming Anti-Corruption Activities in World Bank Assistance – A Review of Progress Since 1997*, Washington, DC: World Bank.

Van Rijckeghem and Beatrice Weder (1997), 'Corruption and the role of temptation: do low wages in civil service cause corruption?', IMF Working Paper WP/97/73.

Von Maravic, Patrick (2003), 'How to analyse corruption in the context of public management reform?', paper presented at the first meeting of the Study Group on Ethics and Integrity of Governance EGPA Conference, September, Portugal.

20 Fiscal federalism and national unity
Richard M. Bird and Robert D. Ebel

Introduction

Belgium, Bosnia–Herzegovina, Canada, the People's Republic of China, Germany, India, Indonesia, Iraq, the Philippines, Russia, Spain, Sudan, Switzerland – what can this diverse set of countries possibly have in common? One important answer is that each contains within its boundaries a significant territorially-based group of people who are, or who consider themselves to be, distinct and different in ethnicity, in language, in religion, or just in history (ancient or recent) from the majority of the population. Indeed, contrary to the common view – one might say mythology – that the most 'natural' nation state is a unified and homogeneous entity, such 'fragmented' countries (Bird and Stauffer 2001)[1] – are found throughout the world. Homogeneous nations are more the exception than the rule. Indeed, heterogeneity, whether ethnic or economic, is a more common feature of most countries than homogeneity.[2] A second important characteristic of many countries is that they exhibit, to greater or lesser degrees, some 'asymmetry' in the way in which different regions are treated by their intergovernmental fiscal systems. While such asymmetry is often most obvious in formal federal countries, it comes up, sometimes in surprising ways, in almost every instance. This chapter explores the varied extent and manner in which asymmetrical treatment helps (or hinders) the maintenance of an effective nation state.

'Effectiveness' in this context may be understood in two ways. The first relates to the normal focus of economic analysis of public sector activities: how effectively, efficiently, and (perhaps) equitably are public services provided throughout the national territory? The second meaning, however, lies well outside the normal field of expertise of economists: what are the connections between how a country's public finances are structured and how a nation state that is fragmented holds together in the first place? This question has risen to the forefront of public policy analysis in an especially important way when it comes to creating 'new' countries out of regions torn by civil conflicts, such as those in Bosnia–Herzegovina and Sudan. But it is also much on the minds of those concerned with public policy in such long-established countries as Belgium, Canada and Spain.

In many fragmented countries, it is not surprising that the majority group dominates politically. Sometimes, a particular minority exerts more influence, perhaps because of its wealth and power, perhaps owing to historical factors. Occasionally, as may be argued to be the case, even in such large federal countries as the United States and Brazil, important overriding factors may suppress much or all of the potential political influence of ethnicity.[3] Even in countries such as Argentina, Brazil and Germany, in which most people are ethnically and linguistically homogeneous, the economic situation of different regions may be extreme, ranging from large, rich metropolitan areas to remote, impoverished settlements, or to regions rich in petroleum or other highly-valued natural resources versus others with little but an expanse of barren lands. Such problems may become more pronounced when regions are dominated by people of a different ethnicity from the majority of the population, and may become bitterly contested when ethnic and economic factors combine, but such problems are by no means confined to countries with this combination of characteristics.

Some potentially fragmented countries have – often through a prolonged historical process, sometimes including civil wars – reached an equilibrium in which their political, fiscal and institutional structure balances the diverse forces and sustains the maintenance of an effective national state.[4] Switzerland, the UK and the US in different ways provide examples. Others, however, remained in turmoil and then fell apart under such pressures, for example, the 'formers' – Czechoslovakia, Yugoslavia and the Union of Soviet Socialist Republics. And the integrity and effectiveness of other countries, even such long-established and prosperous countries as Belgium, Canada and Spain, remain under constant threat. In recent years such pressures have increased in many such countries, in part because of globalization and the related (but not fully consistent) phenomenon of new regional economic unions – the European Union (EU) and the North American Free Trade Agreement (NAFTA) – that have upset the established balance of wealth and power and hence called into question the desirability and sustainability of some established nation states.

In part in response to such factors, decentralization is on the leading edge of policy. Developed countries, developing countries, transitional countries federal countries and unitary countries – wherever one looks some kind of decentralization is taking place, or is at least being discussed. But what, exactly, is going on? And why is it going on? A variety of rationales and institutional arrangements can be, and are, encompassed under the label 'decentralization'.

What is decentralization?

Some of the confusion that prevails about decentralization arises because this term can, and does, mean very different things to different people.[5] Sorting out these differences is important to framing the discussion of the potentially reinforcing relationship between nation state solidarity, subsidiarity and intergovernmental asymmetry.[6]

Political decentralization in the sense of devolving decision making power to locally elected officials, for example, is not the same as, or necessarily associated with, *administrative decentralization* – and the reverse is also true. Administrative decentralization may simply redistribute responsibilities among different ministries of the central government, up to and including the creation of moderately autonomous field administrations. This process is sometimes referred to as 'deconcentration'. Deconcentration does not place any political decision making power in the hands of locally representative bodies and hence is unlikely to give rise to serious intergovernmental conflicts. Similarly, if the full administrative responsibility for particular functions has been fully devolved to local governments, such conflict should not arise in principle. The same might even be true with apparently full political devolution if regional and local governments as a rule remain dependent to a large extent on central financing. Even allegedly independent subnational governments are often subject to a certain degree of central influence, monitoring and, in some instances, control. It can thus be hard in practice to distinguish some forms of devolution from *delegation* in which the major feature is that the system of subnational government can be characterized as that of a principal–agent relationship.[7]

To add to the prevailing confusion in most countries, decentralization, whatever form it takes – including that of substantial devolution whereby subnational governments are independently established and have responsibility for the authority to impose taxes and finance services – need not, and indeed usually does not, occur evenly across the board. Some activities, or parts of some activities, may be deconcentrated, delegated or devolved to some degree or another. Others may not. Expenditures may be more decentralized than revenues, or the reverse may hold. Some transfers may be much more heavily 'conditioned' by central government than others. Borrowing may, or may not, be tightly controlled. Understanding, measuring and analysing the extent and nature of decentralization in any country is far from simple (Ebel and Yilmaz 2003).

Why is decentralization occurring?

However decentralization may be defined or understood, why is it occurring? The evidence is mixed with respect to all of the traditional rationales for decentralization found in the conventional economic literature on fiscal federalism: for example, efficiency and responsiveness, 'place' equity between rich and poor, growth and stability.[8] There are different degrees of merit to each of these, and once the initial political decision is made to adopt a policy of sorting out fiscal roles and responsibilities among governments, accomplishing these economic goals matters very much.[9]

But for fragmented societies, the political aspect may be all that matters, at least in the initial stages of change. Chechnya, East Timor, Kosovo, Moldova, Sri Lanka, Macedonia and Sudan – the list of territorially based ethnic minorities taking up arms against the nation state (and/or each other) is long. It is thus not surprising that some countries have tried to preempt such pressures in part by decentralizing some activities.[10] When a country finds itself deeply divided, especially along geographic or ethnic lines, decentralization provides an institutional mechanism for bringing opposition groups into a formal, rule-bound bargaining process. Thus, decentralization may (i) sometimes serve as a path to national unity (for example, Canada, South Africa, Switzerland and Uganda);[11] (ii) it may be seen to offer a political solution to civil war (Bosnia–Herzegovina, Sri Lanka, Sudan);[12] (iii) it may serve as an instrument for deflating secessionist tendencies (Bosnia–Herzegovina, Ethiopia, Spain), or formally forestalling the decision as to whether or not to secede (Sudan);[13] (iv) it may attempt to achieve a similar aim by conceding enough power to regional interests to forestall their departure from the republic (Canada, Russia, Spain;[14] or (v) it may be used, in effect, to co-opt 'grassroots support' for central policies (Colombia, maybe China).[15]

The trade-offs of decentralization

Whatever one thinks of these particular arguments, whether decentralization in any of its myriad forms helps or hurts political stability is clearly a key question in many countries. It seems unlikely, however, that anyone can answer that question in the abstract. As in the case of the economic arguments for and against decentralization, something like the Scottish legal decision of 'Not Proven' is perhaps the best that can be offered at present with respect to such political arguments. None the less, it is clearly political factors that are leading even long-centralized countries like the United Kingdom to decentralize (particularly with respect to Scotland). Similar decentralization to varying degrees can be seen in many other countries – for example, Italy (South Tyrol), Finland (Aland Islands) and even France (Corsica). Ethnic groups in countries as different and distant as China (Tibetans and Uighurs), Iraq (Kurds), Turkey (Kurds), Nigeria (Ogoni) and Georgia (Abkhaz and Ossetians) are seeking similar (or greater) territorial autonomy.

Whether the result of greater decentralization in response to such pressures is likely to be political stability or increased instability is far from clear. Certainly there are many past examples of instability and then dissolution, such as the (once) Federation of the West Indies, Rhodesia and Nyasaland, Yugoslavia, Pakistan, Czechoslovakia and the USSR (Watts 1999; Saunders 2002). None the less, there are also counterexamples where decentralizing policies may be argued to be one factor holding together countries that might otherwise have fragmented: Belgium, Canada, India and Malaysia.[16] Annett

(2000), who focuses on countries in which he concludes that budgetary institutions are too weak to support increased intergovernmental transfers, suggests that how successful such attempts are may in the end depend upon the ability of such nations to deliver higher levels of public goods and services. As yet, however, the empirical evidence in support of such propositions remains tenuous.

An additional important political concern is that decentralization may unduly restrict the ability of a country to take decisive action in the face of crisis. While most commonly manifested in the form of concerns about stabilization policy (Tanzi 1996), the problem is more general. There is, some argue, a fundamental trade-off in any country between the extent to which its political system represents different local points of view and its capacity for effective political action in the face of economic crisis. In the same circumstances, some degree of decentralization may be needed to maintain the nation state, but, then, too much decentralization might render that state ineffective in coping with crisis. While it may be argued that such apocalyptic conclusions seldom pay sufficient attention to the all-important details of precisely how decentralization institutions are designed and implemented, the effect of fiscal decentralization on stabilization policy remains unresolved.[17]

Another concern is the fact that the trade-off between effectiveness and decentralization also manifests itself with respect to redistributive policy, whether interregional or interpersonal. It is not by chance that the welfare state was a centralized state because only at the national level could the interests of the disadvantaged receive sufficient weight to overcome the influence of local elites (Wilensky 1975). To the extent that effective decentralization implies local autonomy in revenue and expenditure policy, there may be an inherent conflict between subsidiarity and solidarity, between local autonomy and national redistribution. Yet the precise terms of any such trade-off, and the related question of whether there is a 'breakpoint' beyond which a country can have both a high degree of local political autonomy and at the same time an effective social net, depend upon too many details of local institutions and circumstances to permit easy generalizations.

The incorporation of the much poorer eastern regions may, for instance, have pushed Germany closer to this breakpoint (Spahn and Werner 2005). If even a country as essentially homogeneous as Germany has a point beyond which those in richer regions are not prepared to expand their 'span of concern' (Breton and Scott 1978; Spahn 2005) to encompass those in poorer regions within their distributive concerns, other countries – in Europe, the case of Belgium comes to mind[18] – may perhaps reach such a point at considerably lower levels of redistribution. The redistributive question is particularly difficult because it encompasses both interpersonal and interregional redistribution. Canada has to some extent bypassed this problem at the provincial level by carrying out most interpersonal redistribution at the federal level, but it too faces the problem of group versus individual redistribution with respect to its large aboriginal population (as does Australia).[19]

Fiscal decentralization: glue or solvent?

Whatever its rationale or form, decentralization has often changed the fiscal structure of the state and hence may be expected to affect the nature and scope of state activities. Often, the most disputed questions with respect to decentralization are fiscal: who gets what, and who pays for it? Such fiscal changes may feed back upon and strengthen – or weaken – the political and economic pressures leading to decentralization in the first place. A key question is thus the nature and strength of the interactions in fragmented countries between changes in intergovernmental fiscal relations in response to changing economic and political factors and the continued maintenance of (or the creation of) an effective public sector. Under what conditions does increased subsidiarity foster solidarity, and under what conditions might increasing the autonomy of subnational governments have the opposite result of fostering not national integration but perhaps the disintegration of a nation? When, that is, is decentralization the glue that holds countries together, and when is it a solvent that may result in their disintegration?

These are five key fiscal aspects of decentralization: (i) Who determines who gets what revenues? (ii) Who is responsible for what expenditures? (iii) How do intergovernmental transfers work? (iv) What degree of freedom do subnational governments have with respect to borrowing? and (v) Who determines the institutional setting within which the preceding questions are answered?

The fiscal rules that the literature on this subject suggests should bind the various players in the intergovernmental game – if the outcome is to be the efficient and responsible provision of public services in an equitable and stable way – include such things as clear expenditure assignments, giving responsibility for determining the *rates* of some major revenues to subnational governments, and distributing transfers by a predetermined formula (see, for example, Bird 2001; Bahl 2002; Ebel and Taliercio 2005). Properly designed, an intergovernmental fiscal regime set up along these lines in effect imposes a hard budget constraint on subnational governments and hence provides the appropriate structure of incentives to ensure economically efficient outcomes.

The transfer system may also provide a combined sense of national solidarity and 'place equity' through a well-designed system of central–subnational transfers. Thus conditional grants can address projects that confer benefits that are national and or regional in scope, and unconditional grants can address issues of both vertical and locational equity (Ahmad 1997). In addition, to ensure macroeconomic stability, subnational borrowing may initially have to be constrained by hierarchical controls, although in the longer run it should ideally become subject primarily to the discipline of the capital markets (Rodden et al. 2003; Petersen et al. 2004).[20] And finally, to make the whole system work, not only must the central government itself keep to the rules, but there should be an adequate institutional structure to ensure the development of sufficient local capacity, provide for periodic adjustments to meet changing circumstances, and serve as a forum for the resolution of the disputes that inevitably arise in any functioning intergovernmental system (Bird 2001).

Such rules do not, however, describe the reality in most countries. Moreover, the relation of such institutional rules to the political issues that appear to motivate much of the current concern with decentralization seems to be, at best, remote. How may this gap be closed?

Asymmetric decentralization

One way to close the gap between theoretical prescriptions and institutional reality is by taking into account some important aspects of the decentralization story that are not encompassed in such simple rules and then considering how in practice the rules have often been bent to varying degrees to accommodate such deviations (Agranoff 1999; Hayson 2002). Rules such as those found in much of the economic literature explicitly recognize only one element of the heterogeneity that characterizes most countries in the real world, namely, that some territorial units are richer than others. They neglect the important role played by ethnic, linguistic and cultural differences in explaining the nature of political institutions in many countries. Some of these differences –such as language-specific investment in human capital – can be readily placed in a purely rational economic framework (Vaillancourt 1992), but others, such as the different perceptions of history and current reality held by different groups, cannot.

None the less, countries containing diverse groups, particularly those that are territorially concentrated, need to find some way to work together if they are to provide public services effectively. In this connection, the extent and nature of tolerable or necessary asymmetry becomes a key issue.

Traditionally, in part perhaps because symmetrical constitutional status for all basic territorial units was the norm in such 'classic' federations as the United States, Switzerland and Australia, most discussion of federalism – and indeed often of decentralization more generally – has implicitly assumed that symmetry was the rule. In fact, even in the most classical federal countries there has always been some formal asymmetry (the District of Columbia and the territories in the US, for example, and the Northern Territory in Australia). In many other federations, as Watts (2000) emphasizes, there has been a degree of formal constitutional asymmetry from the beginning – for example in Canada, India, Malaysia, Spain, Belgium and Russia.[21] Indeed, even such traditionally unitary countries as the United Kingdom, which has always included distinctly different regimes for Northern Ireland, the Isle of Man and the Channel Islands, have moved in the direction of still greater asymmetry in recent years.

When examined closely, virtually every country, federal or unitary, large or small, appears to offer some evidence of asymmetry in practice – between rich and poor, urban and non-urban, capital cities and frontier territories, and territorial or non-territorial groupings based on race, religion or language. In this manner, asymmetrical decentralization illustrates the adaptive nature of political institutions: it may be imposed from above, agreed to by all parties, or optionally chosen by particular communities.

Such asymmetrical arrangements may arise (i) for political reasons to diffuse ethnic or regional tensions; (ii) for efficiency reasons so as to achieve better macroeconomic management and administrative cohesion; and/or (iii) to enable subnational governments with differing capacities to exercise the full range of their functions and powers (Wehner 2000; Chapter 5, this volume). The first type of asymmetry, *political asymmetry*, is clearly driven by non-economic concerns, while the last two are consistent with an administrative 'top-down' approach to decentralization and might, for example, be implemented bilaterally through a staged (or contract) approach under which those units that met certain standards (size, budget, institutional development) would be granted greater autonomy than others.[22]

Such *administrative asymmetry* might be applied either on a discretionary basis or, more desirably (to reduce the scope for short-run political maneuvering), in accordance with some predetermined rules. Either type of asymmetry might be transitional or permanent in nature and might have functional as well as financial manifestations. Asymmetry might be established constitutionally or by statute (*de jure*) or simply by administrative practice or political agreement (*de facto*). It may be manifested through different degrees of autonomy or powers, through different degrees of representation in federal (or central) institutions, or through differential application of central laws (the January 2005 Sudan Peace Accord reflects all three of these manifestations). Asymmetry might be confined to peripheral units (such as the various types of territories in the United States) or it might apply to some of the principal constituent units of the country, as in Canada and Spain, for example.[23]

In fiscal terms, asymmetry may be manifested in differential direct central spending patterns, in differential central taxes, in differential subnational functional or revenue responsibilities, or in differential transfers. It may result in more or less equal treatment in certain respects. It may improve or worsen the efficiency and effectiveness of the public sector as a whole, for example, improving or worsening the uniformity of service delivery or macroeconomic balance. And, critically, it may sometimes strengthen, and sometimes weaken, the allegiance of differentially treated communities to the nation state as a whole. Outcomes may vary with the relative size and strength of the units affected, the precise nature and extent of their fiscal autonomy, the structure of intergovernmental transfers, the manner in which regional interests are represented in both central and intergovernmental political institutions, exactly how the regional and national party systems work, and many other factors.

For example, consider the important role played by linguistic and cultural differences in explaining the nature of Canadian fiscal federalism. To some extent Canadians may perhaps be thought of as two peoples divided by a misunderstood word – 'sovereignty' (Simeon 2000). To English Canadians, sovereignty tends to be interpreted in its classical sense of a fully independent state. To many Quebeckers, on the other hand, the term evokes not a black-or-white, or in-or-out meaning, but rather a fluid concept of a sense of national identity, and a sense that this is a community with a right to make a choice. Such differences in perception are dangerous and may result in outcomes not really desired by either group. Canada is by no means the only country suffering from such communication difficulties.

Of course, fragmented societies will not necessarily become more coherent simply by ensuring that everyone really understands what everyone else wants. There may be real and fundamental conflicts that are not resolvable without major political concessions by one side, or perhaps by both. Improved information and communication, like any other possible solution to the perceived problems of fragmented societies, may help. Or it may hurt. Once again, it depends. As the tortured recent history of the Balkans shows clearly, bygones are never bygones if (some version of) history, however distorted, remains alive in the minds of significant groups of the population and motivates them to political action.[24] As much recent analysis suggests, and contrary to a key assumption in much economic discussion, ethnic identities and loyalties are not constants, but are rather subject to dynamic formation (and reformation) and may often be as much 'state-cued' – that is, developed in response to policies and pressures – as they are in any sense 'given' or inherent (Esman and Herring 2001).

In the face of emotionally laden symbolism, fiscal rationality may seem an irrelevant concern. None the less, though communication alone cannot do the job of achieving the consensus or trust that is the essential ingredient of any democratic polity, it is clear that unless all major players in the political game communicate in the sense of getting the right information to the right people at the right time, outcomes that will be both politically relevant and administratively feasible are unlikely to emerge. One important role of fiscal institutions is to deliver the message of transparency and accountability (Kopits and

Craig 1998). But whether the message will be received and acted upon will, as always, depend upon whether other institutions allow the message to be heard (Addison 2005).

Thus, as a minimum condition for operating an effective nation state, it seems clear that countries containing diverse groups, particularly those that are territorially concentrated, need to find some way for these groups to work together if they are to provide public services effectively. Again, consider Canada where, over the years, several approaches have been employed for this purpose, ranging from formal constitutional amendments through changing judicial interpretation of the constitution, so-called 'executive federalism' and formal intergovernmental agreements, to, of course, the use of federal funds for both direct spending and intergovernmental transfers. At some points, each of these approaches seems sometimes to have helped; at others, each appears to have exacerbated matters. On the whole, by changing the mix of instruments and policies employed, Canada has up to now managed quite well, although it is not at all clear that it will be able to continue to muddle through without considering more fundamental political changes (Bird and Vaillancourt 2005).

For instance, an important question that has constantly emerged, and which appears to resonate much more widely, relates to the underlying rationale and acceptability of asymmetry.[25] Thus, Quebec is not a province *comme les autres* in a number of important ways. Over time, this difference has been recognized by the creation of a number of asymmetries in Canadian political and fiscal institutions. None the less, as in other countries there remains an inherent tension between the common view, namely, that all provinces should be treated equally before the law, and such asymmetrical arrangements.[26] Such tension exists even if asymmetry can be argued to be necessary not only to maintain the integrity of the nation state but also to ensure that the intended results of national policies are in fact achieved in the different circumstances of different regions.

Whether viewed in political or economic terms, the nature and effects of asymmetrical fiscal policies can best be understood in terms of the concrete and specific circumstances of each country. Only then can it be seen whether such differentiation has made maintenance of the nation state and the effective provision of public services more feasible – that is, has, as it were, acted as glue to hold the state together, or whether on the contrary regions that are treated differently decide to go further and opt out completely so that the intended glue has become a solvent. The most important questions about asymmetrical decentralization thus relate to its effect on the dynamics of political equilibrium, something that appears to be very context-dependent and not easily reducible to simple generalizations. A particular concern in this respect in recent years in a number of countries relates to the much discussed reinforcing relationship between decentralization (localization) and globalization (World Bank 2000).

Regionalization, institutions and globalization

Asymmetrical policies may sometimes be required to elicit uniform responses to central policies from differently advantaged regions.[27] Similarly, differentiation may seem needed to soothe disaffected regions sufficiently to maintain political stability, even if doing so risks increasing the disaffection of those regions that see themselves as paying the price of such special treatment. The economic and political factors giving rise to such policies have been accentuated in recent years by the phenomenon of globalization in many countries.

While just what globalization means and the extent to which it has increased remains in much more dispute among scholars than casual readers might expect, the fact that the world has changed enormously over the last century is clear. Empires have risen and fallen. New countries have been created. Old countries have disintegrated. Wars have been fought. Population has soared. Living standards have risen enormously for many and technology has changed the world in many respects. Much has been said and written recently about the resulting 'new economy'. However, much less has been said about the 'new polity'.

It is true, of course, that in the political sphere life has changed in many respects over the last century. Many more people around the world now live in some kind of democracy and have, at least occasionally, some limited say in how they are governed. As in the nineteenth century, however, the most important political institution everywhere continues to be the nation state. Moreover, although at first glance, surprisingly little has changed in the basic structure of political democracies, closer examination reveals that there are many variants in democratic institutions around the world – different voting systems, different legislative structures, different types of party organization, different roles for different levels of governments, different relations among legislature, executive and judiciary, and very different levels of popular participation in the political process.

The world thus offers a potentially rich laboratory of experiments in different governance structures that may be associated with different policy outcomes. Sorting out what differences in political institutions matter, how, and how much, in affecting such outcomes as economic growth and the distribution of income and wealth is a complex analytical task that social scientists have only recently begun to untangle.[28] The relevant point here is that pressures from above on the nation state may, at least in some instances, increase pressures from below and thus bring to the fore the latent interregional tensions that lie below the surface in many countries. Such tensions are most obviously politically explosive when they reflect ethnic, linguistic or other potentially fragmenting characteristics – that is, when more than one 'nation' is contained within a single country.[29] Similar tensions may arise even in ethnically homogenous countries, when, for example, one result of increasing openness to the world economy is to exacerbate (or even create) existing regional economic inequalities.

For example, to return to the case of Canada, such pressures, and their political and economic consequences, have clearly been manifested in that country. Although intranational trade remains vastly more important than international trade (Helliwell 1998), the increasing integration of both the Canadian industrial heartland (Quebec and especially Ontario) and its raw-material-rich West (British Columbia and especially Alberta) with the United States has profoundly altered the character of Canadian federalism. Quebec's disenchantment with some aspects of the existing political system is of course well known, as is the role that the internationalization – or, better, 'Americanization' – of Canada's economy has played in strengthening the hand of those who argue that Quebec is as economically viable on its own as it is as part of Canada. Similarly, the rise of the western region as a separate and important player in the federal game, has been well documented. But what has really marked the key change in Canada is the increasing self-definition of an 'Ontario' interest as separate from that of 'Canada' in contrast to the long-standing view that Ontario's interests were a reflection of all of Canada (Courchène and Telmer 1998).

Regionalism and equalization   A problem in any federation is to explain why rich regions are willing to support poor regions, whether such support is instituted through formal equalization systems, favorable treatment in federal investment and other policies, the tolerance of discriminatory barriers or whatever. In the absence of monetary, exchange and tariff policies, regions within a country are severely constrained to the extent to which they can achieve the 'core of Swiss "cooperative federalism" . . . of equalizing policies for cantons and regions' (Linder 1994, p. 62). Regional regulatory barriers, discriminatory federal expenditures and regulations, and differential tax and spending policies are the principal instruments open to regions that wish to make their mark – for good or for ill – on economic decisions. The richer regions, those that are expected to be the source of redistribution, may in effect be given more 'sovereignty' (autonomy) as partial compensation in order to keep them in a country. Sometimes, however, centralizing pressures are exerted through both the economic (factor mobility) and political (for example, harmonization in the name of a common economic union) markets in order to discourage such 'disintegrating' policies. Alternatively, as appears to occur especially with small natural resource-rich regions, they may be explicitly exempted from making their 'full' contribution to regionally redistributive policy.[30]

Viewed from the recipient's side, what interregional transfers may lead to is a moral hazard – for example, implementing beggar-my-neighbor policies without paying the full economic penalty for such actions. Conversely, however, such economic efficiencies might be considered to some extent a necessary cost of political stability. Indeed, at the extreme the total 'rents' created and distributed through economically inefficient policies may perhaps be used as a measure of the stock of political capital that has been created (Wintrobe 1998). One author (Treisman 1998) has, for example, rationalized the inequality characterizing Russian interregional transfers in this context: the larger transfers went to those regions (notably excluding Chechnya) that could most credibly threaten to damage the nation state by secession and/or withholding revenues. One could extend this logic to the view that the sum of such inefficient transfers is an investment by the central government in securing the loyalty of recalcitrant regions.

To the extent that regional transfers can be thought of as constituting payments in exchange either for yielding constitutionally entrenched authority or for adhering to the existing framework of the nation state, globalization may have an important impact. If the result of growing connections between foreign interests and local economies is to strengthen the latter in relative terms, centrifugal forces may be strengthened.

But if the resulting strengthening of the national economy as a whole results in increasing central revenues, the central government may none the less be able to increase its 'buyout' package and maintain political stability, a task that will obviously be easier if the economic incentives are not strengthened by more fundamental political forces such as linguistic distinctiveness. Of course, if the major new revenues accruing to the state from globalization accrue to provincial governments – whether because they own natural resources (Alberta in Canada or Alaska in the United States) or simply have the first administrative access to central revenues – centrifugal pressures may be exacerbated rather than alleviated (Russia, and to some extent, Canada).[31] Regional differences are accentuated while at the same time the capacity of the central government to level them out – whether through transfers or repression – is diminished.

Generally, if increasing openness to the world economy exacerbates regional economic disparities, poor regions in which exportable resources are located may be expected increasingly to assert their claim to a larger share of the increasing rents yielded by such resources. Aceh in Indonesia and the new regional government of South Sudan are examples.[32] At the same time, rich regions – although they may themselves benefit disproportionately from increased trade – may become decreasingly inclined to support their poorer neighbors through interregional transfers. The bonds of common nationhood that were previously strengthened by the market dependency of the rich on the poor – in most countries most transfers probably quickly flow right back to the so-called 'donor' provinces through trade patterns – may be weakened. If so, the income dependency of the poor on the rich may thus be eroded from both sides as globalization increasingly makes the world the relevant market.

Institutional sustainability   Broadly speaking, there are only three ways for political institutions to be sustainable – so that people not only believe in their credibility but are willing to act on this belief. First, most people may simply share the underlying values, that is, they are pre-committed to the maintenance of the institution through a common ideology or belief system. If such a system does not exist, efforts may be made to create it, through such means as the heavy use of such political symbolism (for example, the flag in the US or perhaps in some countries the role of political parties and associated ideologies).

A second way to further political sustainability is to put into place a series of checks and balances – for example, through a constitution that is not easy to amend and is interpreted by a credibly independent judiciary (US) or can be changed only by a very 'direct' democratic process (Switzerland). Such checks and balances need not be governmental. Thus a different approach is to limit the power of government through such devices as a free press that can not only criticize the actions of those in political power but also, and equally importantly, serve as an important means of informing them of what citizens really want.[33] Combined with the existence of a credible constitutional means of removing leaders from power, such information systems may both enable commitments to be more credible and serve as an important signal transmitter between citizens and leaders. Indeed, as Wintrobe (1998) argues, such considerations suggest that no matter how inadequate democratic systems may sometimes seem in practice, they are theoretically always superior to dictatorial alternatives. Alternatively, the integrity of the nation state may be maintained by fear of the consequences of the failure of the institution. While most obviously at play in non-democratic systems, the 'fear card' of adverse economic consequences is certainly not unknown elsewhere. In Canada, for example, fear of adverse economic consequences is thought by some to be the main deterrent to Quebec separatism.

And, third, the loyalty of potential territorial dissidents may simply be bought, at least for a time. Examples range from 'pork-barrel politics', as this process has been labeled in the United States, to granting monopoly privileges or rent to one's supporters in a manner that not only pays for political support but also tends to deter 'shirking' since what has been given can be taken back. On the other hand, sometimes those who feel that their support has been bought may actually be reinforced in their dissident views.[34] Similarly, those who feel that they are paying may become increasingly resentful of the burden over time – indeed, perhaps within a very short time, as seems to have occurred in Germany.[35] To the extent that a country is seen by significant groups as being worthwhile only so long as it is profitable in some sense for them, increased global pressures may have serious implications for the continued existence of some countries. Increased pressure may turn glue into solvent.

Globalization   The World Development Report, *Entering the 21st Century* finds that policy makers during the twenty-first century will face two main trends that will 'shape the world in which development policy will be defined and implemented: globalization (the continuing integration of the world's economies) and localization (the desire of self determination and the devolution of power' (World Bank 2000, p. 31). The report goes on to argue that while at first glance these two trends may seem countervailing, they often stem from the same sources such as advances in information and communications technology and, thus, are reinforcing. However, at the same time that globalization is 'gathering the world's economies together, the forces of localization are tilting the balance of power within them' as local groups can now often bypass the central authority with respect to once nationally dominated activities such as access developing international political alliances and development financing.

But globalization may also strengthen the center at the expense of the regions. For example, if the revenue base of the central government is improved as a result, it may be able to increase transfers and strengthen the effectiveness of the state as a whole.[36] On the other hand, if the result is to give new economic and fiscal strength to the regions, while weakening the central treasury, centrifugal pressures may be exacerbated rather than alleviated as some regions will feel more able to stand alone.[37] At the extreme, globalization weakens the domestic political bargains that have, over time, been struck in order to enable different groups to live together, the result may be an unhealthy tension that may be alleviated in part by directing anger at some foreign entity (Barber 1996).

Concluding comment
To sum up, if the result of globalization is increased economic growth concentrated in a certain region, the effects will vary from country to country depending upon a variety of factors, such as: whether the region that benefits most was previously rich or poor; whether it is large or small; whether it is actually or potentially disaffected (for instance, on historical or ethnic grounds); what the effects are on fiscal revenues at both the regional and central levels; the nature of the intergovernmental fiscal system in place and how it is affected; and, of course, the ability and willingness of all parties to adjust to the new

circumstances in a timely fashion. Listing such factors simply sets up a research agenda: it is far too soon to say how important particular factors may be in different countries or how any problems that may emerge as a result may be resolved in any country, let alone whether the result will be the introduction of more asymmetrical policies than those already in place.

One can, however, say that no reward comes without risk. Increased economic openness may raise income levels, but it also often increases volatility. Considering the downward side of increased economic volatility suggests a quite different way of looking at the potential impact of globalization on regionalization. Some form of fiscal decentralization – used here loosely as a generic term for some degree of power division and separation – may be a sensible means of coping with downside risk by achieving a certain degree of risk pooling (von Hagen 2003). Decentralization within a national framework may thus be viewed to some extent as a defensive maneuver to protect regional and national interests, which are congruent to this extent at least.

All in all, both general considerations and the detailed examination of very diverse national experiences to be found around the world suggest that we should all perhaps remember, to paraphrase Charles Darwin, that it is not always the strongest species that survive, or the most intelligent, but the ones most responsive to change.[38] With respect to asymmetry in particular and decentralized political and fiscal institutions more generally the interaction of globalization and decentralization may put this view of evolution to another test.

Notes

1. Bird and Stauffer (2001) contains the proceedings of a conference held in February 2000 in Murten, Switzerland on this topic, organized by the World Bank Institut in collaboration with the Institut du Federalisme of the University of Fribourg.
2. Alesina et al. (2002) develop a parallel concept of 'fractionalization', which is an index that measures a country's ethnic, linguistic and religious mix. Fragmentation emphasizes the territorial dimension of ethnic or other differentiation.
3. Even with respect to the United States (broadly conceived) there are many 'asymmetrical' relationships: for example, Puerto Rico. Indeed, Elazar (1957) identified two '*federacies*', three 'associated states', three 'home-rule territories', three 'unincorporated territories', and 130 distinct First Nations with asymmetrical relations to the US federal government (Zeilo 2005).
    For a brief overview of the racial and economic diversity of Brazil, see Avelar (1999); Affonso (2001) provides a useful recent review of decentralization and reform in Brazil. Watts (1999) provides a useful categorization of different forms of 'association' between territories.
4. For a discussion of the role played by fiscal factors in sustaining political equilibrium (with particular reference to Latin America), see Bird (2003). Winik (2002) in his brilliant account of the resolution of the American Civil War provides an excellent reminder of how precarious the political balance may be at critical moments in a country's history.
5. The present discussion focuses on fiscal decentralization. While we note the relation between fiscal, administrative and political decentralization, this subject is not discussed in detail here: for further discussion, see, for example, Rondinelli et al. (1983) and Bird et al. (1995).

6. The term 'subsidiarity' is drawn from the *European Charter of Local Self-Government*, which provides that 'public responsibilities shall generally be exercised, in preference, by those authorities which are closest to the citizen. Allocation of responsibility to another authority should weigh up the extent and nature of the task and requirements of efficiency and economy', Council of Europe Committee of Ministers, *European Charter of Local Self-Government*, Recommendation No. R(95)19, On the Implementation of the Principle of Subsidiarity, Adopted by the Committee of Ministers on 12 October 1995 at the 545th meeting of the Ministers' Deputies'.

7. Bird and Chen (1998), however, note the sharp contrast between delegation (provincial–local) and devolution (federal–provincial) in Canada.

8. Some assert that the literature can be characterized as a 'curious combination of strong preconceived beliefs and limited empirical information' (Litvack et al. 1998: 3).

9. See World Bank (2000) for citations to the relevant literature, much of which is also reviewed in Bird and Vaillancourt (1998).

10. See Esman and Herring (2001) for detailed consideration of the role that development assistance may play in exacerbating or alleviating such pressures.

11. The South African case is discussed in Ahmad (1998), Simeon and Murray (2000) and Bahl and Smoke (2003).

12. Welikala (2003) provides a recent consideration of the fiscal aspects of decentralization in Sri Lanka.

13. The Machakos Protocol of 10 July 2002, which is embedded in the Final Peace Protocol of 16 January, establishes a half year 'Pre-interim' period following the peace signing, followed by a six (6) year 'Interim Period' after which the people of South Sudan shall participate in an internationally monitored referenced, to 'confirm the unity of the Sudan by voting to adopt the system of government established under the Peace Agreement; or to vote for Secession'.

    For another, very different, case of attempting to construct a new government from a scattered (though not ethnically diverse) population, see Ford and Litvack (2001) on West Bank–Gaza. On Ethiopia, see World Bank (1999).

14. See also Treisman (1998) and Martinez-Vazquez and Boex (2001).

15. This list, and most of the country examples, come from World Bank (2000, 207–8). For a quite different version of the Colombian case, see Bird and Fiszbein (1998) and Acosta and Bird (2005).

16. For a discussion of Belgium, Canada and India, see Bird and Ebel (2006). For some discussion of the Malaysian case, see Holzhausen (1974) and Mahbob et al. (1997).

17. For a book-length review focusing on the macroeconomic aspects of decentralization, see Rodden et al. (2003).

18. See Bayenet and de Bruycker (2006).

19. The aboriginal question in Canada is discussed extensively, from very different perspectives, in Cairns (2000) and Flanagan (2000). For Australia, see Lane (2003).

20. While there might be some asymmetrical aspects with respect to macroeconomic equilibrium, it is not clear either analytically or empirically whether small or large subnational governments are most likely to breach macroeconomic balance. The case for the former is that they are more susceptible to external shocks and are cheaper to bail out (Pisauro 2001), while the case for the latter is that they are 'too big to fail' in the sense of the negative externalities if they do so, with the result that they may thus be able to expect to be bailed out and hence able to get away with worse behavior (Wildasin 1997).

21. As Dafflon (2006) shows, even the Swiss have, in their usual deliberate and pragmatic way, gradually introduced many asymmetrical elements into their system of fiscal federalism. See also Basta and Fleiner (1996) and Stauffer (2001).

22. For an example of such an approach in Colombia with respect to education, see Bird and Fiszbein (1998).

23. See Watts (2000) for extensive discussion of all these possible classifications, with examples. The Spanish case is particularly interesting: see Castells (2001), Vinuela (2001), Ruiz Almendar (2002) and Garcia-Mila and McGuire (2006), for recent discussions.

24. There can be few more telling political slogans in this respect than that displayed on every

automobile license place in the province of Quebec: the motto of what was once 'la belle province' has, since the rise of separatist sentiment, become 'je me souviens'. For an idiosyncratic but telling consideration of this and many other relevant issues, see Saul (1997).

25.   In the context of the European Union, essentially the same issue is often discussed under the label of 'variable geometry', or the extent to which and the time span within which different member states take part in different aspects of EU policy (for example, monetary union or defense).

26.   A recent example relates to the regulation of financial markets, as discussed in Vaillancourt and Bird (2006).

27.   Feldstein (1975) provides a classic illustration of this proposition.

28.   Persson and Tabellini (2000) provide a useful overview of what economists are up to in this regard, and Alesina and Spolaore (2003) a number of illuminating illustrations.

29.   A theme well illustrated with respect to Bosnia–Herzegovina in Fox and Wallich (2005).

30.   For an interesting early attempt to analyse some of these conflicting choices, see Milanovic (1996).

31.   Alesina and Spolaore (2003) provide a useful review of the empirical and theoretical literature on the trade-offs between political heterogeneity and the economic gains of market size: they conclude that globalization on the whole fosters political separatism.

32.   See Bahl and Tumennasan (2002) for discussion of the Aceh case.

33.   Islam (2002).

34.   As Hirschman (1971) noted with respect to foreign aid, for example, people may take your money, explicitly given for purposes with which they are not in agreement, rationalize in some way the apparent betrayal of their beliefs by doing so, and continue to hold their beliefs.

35.   Spahn 2006.

36.   Wildavsky (1977) makes an argument along these lines.

37.   The most dramatic instances relate to sudden infusions of mineral wealth: what this means fiscally in a variety of different countries, and how it has been handled, is discussed in Davis et al. (2003).

38.   This thought is developed by Katzenstein (1985).

References

Acosta, Olga Lucia and Richard M. Bird (2005), 'The dilemma of decentralization in Colombia', in Richard M. Bird, James Poterba and Joel Slemrod (eds), *Fiscal Reform in Colombia*, Cambridge, MA: MIT Press.

Addison, Tony (2005), *From Conflict to Recovery*, Oxford: Oxford University Press.

Affonso, Rui de Britto Alvares (2001) 'Decentralization and reform of the state: the Brazilian federation at the crossroads', in Bird and Stauffer (eds).

Agranoff, Robert (ed.) (1999), *Accommodating Diversity: Asymmetry in Federal States*, European Center for Federalism Series 10, Baden-Baden, Germany: NOMOS.

Ahmad, Ehtisham (1997), 'Intergovernmental transfers: an international perspective', in Ehtisham Ahmad (ed.), *Financing Decentralized Expenditures; An International Comparison of Grants*, Cheltenham, UK and Northampton, MA, USA: Edward Elgar.

Ahmad, Junaid (1998), 'South Africa: an intergovernmental fiscal system in transition', in Bird and Vaillancourt (eds).

Alesina, Alberto and Enrico Spolaore (2003), *The Size of Nations*, Cambridge, MA: MIT Press.

Alesina, Alberto, Arnaud Devleeschauwer, William Easterly, Sergio Kurlat and Romain Wacziarg (2002), 'Fractionalization', NBER Working Paper 9411, December, Cambridge, MA.

Annett, Anthony (2000), 'Social fractionalization, political instability, and the size of government', IMF Working Paper WP/00/82, International Monetary Fund, April.

Avelar, Lucia (1999), 'Citizenship and social diversity: the aspect of regional diversity', Background Paper for Forum of Federations, International Conference on Federalism, Ottawa.

Bahl, Roy W. (2002), 'Implementation rules for fiscal decentralization', in M. Govinda Rao (ed.), *Development, Poverty, and Fiscal Policy: Decentralization of Institutions*, Oxford and New Delhi: Oxford University Press.

Bahl, Roy W. and Paul Smoke (eds) (2003), *Restructuring Local Government Finance in Developing Countries: Lessons from South Africa*, Cheltenham, UK and Northampton, MA, USA: Edward Elgar.

Bahl, Roy W. and Bayar Tumennsan (2002), 'How should revenues from natural resources be shared?', Working Paper 02-14, International Studies Program, Andrew Young School of Policy Studies, Georgia State University, May.

Barber, Benjamin (1996), *Jihad vs. McWorld: How Globalism and Tribalism are Reshaping the World*, New York: Ballantine.

Basta, Lidja R. and Thomas Fleiner (1996), *Federalism and Multiethnic States: The Case of Switzerland*, Fribourg: Institut du Federalisme, Université de Fribourg.

Bayenet, Benoit and Philippe de Bruycker (2006), 'Belgium: a unique evolving federalism', in Bird and Ebel (eds).

Bell, Michael E. and John H. Bowman (2002), *Property Taxes in South Africa: Challenges in the Post-Apartheid Era*, Cambridge, MA: Lincoln Institute of Land Policy.

Bird, Richard M. (2001), *Intergovernmental Fiscal Relations in Latin America: Policy Design and Policy Outcomes*, Washington, DC: Inter-American Development Bank.

Bird, Richard M. (2003) 'Taxation in Latin America: reflections on sustainability and the balance between efficiency and equity', ITP Paper 0306, International Tax Program, Rotman School of Management, University of Toronto, June.

Bird, Richard M. and Duanjie Chen (1998) 'Federal finance and fiscal federalism: the two worlds of Canadian public finance', *Canadian Public Administration*, **43**(1), 51–74.

Bird, Richard M. and Robert Ebel (eds) (2006), *Fiscal Fragmentation in Decentralized Countries: Subsidiarity, Solidarity and Asymmetry*, Cheltenham, UK and Northampton, MA, USA: Edward Elgar, forthcoming.

Bird, Richard M., Robert D. Ebel and Christine Wallich (eds) (1995), *Decentralization of the Socialist State*, Washington, DC: World Bank.

Bird, Richard M. and Ariel Fiszbein (1998), 'The central role of central government in decentralization: Colombia', in Bird and Vaillancourt (eds).

Bird, Richard M. and Thomas Stauffer (eds) (2001), *Intergovernmental Fiscal Relations in Fragmented Societies*, Fribourg: Institut du Federalisme.

Bird, Richard M. and Francois Vaillancourt (eds) (1998), *Fiscal Decentralization in Developing Countries*, Cambridge: Cambridge University Press.

Bird, Richard M. and Francois Vaillancourt (2005), 'Reconciling diversity with equality: the role of intergovernmental fiscal arrangements in maintaining an effective state in Canada', in Bird and Ebel (eds).

Breton, Albert and Anthony Scott (1978), *The Economic Constitution of Federal States*, Toronto: University of Toronto Press.

Cairns, Alan (2000), *Citizens Plus: Aboriginal Peoples and the Canadian State*, Vancouver: UBC Press.

Castells, Antoni (2001) 'The role of intergovernmental finance in achieving diversity and cohesion: the case of Spain', *Environment and Planning C: Government and Policy*, **19** (April): 189–206.

Courchène, Thomas J. and Colin R. Telmer (1998), *From Heartland to North American Region State: The Social, Fiscal and Federal Evolution of Ontario*, Toronto: Centre for Public Management, Faculty of Management, University of Toronto.

Dafflon, Bernard (2006) 'Accommodating asymmetry through pragmatism: an overview of Swiss fiscal federalism', in Bird and Ebel (eds).

Davis, Jeffrey, Rolando J. Ossowski and Annalisa Fedolina (eds) (2003), *Fiscal Policy Formulation and Implementation in Oil-Producing Countries*, Washington, DC: International Monetary Fund.

Ebel, Robert D. and Robert Taliercio (2005), 'Subnational tax policy and administration in developing economies', *Tax Notes International*, 7 March, 919–36.

Ebel, Robert D. and Serdar Yilmaz (2003), 'On the measurement and impact of fiscal decentralization', in James Alm and Jorge Martinez-Vazquez (eds), *Public Finance in Developing and Transitional Countries: Essays in Honor of Richard M. Bird*, Cheltenham, UK and Northampton, MA, USA: Edward Elgar.

Elazar, Daniel J. (1957), *Exploring Federalism*, Tuscaloosa, AL: University of Alabama Press.

Esman, Milton J. and Ronald J. Herring (2001), *Carrots, Sticks, and Ethnic Conflict: Rethinking Development Assistance*, Ann Arbor, MI: University of Michigan Press.

Faguet, Jean-Paul (2001), 'Does decentralization increase responsiveness to local needs? Evidence from Bolivia', Centre for Economic Performance and Development Studies Institute, London School of Economics.

Feldstein, Martin (1975), 'Wealth neutrality and local choice in public education', *American Economic Review*, **65**: 75–89.

Flanagan, Tom (2000), *First Nations? Second Thoughts*, Montreal: McGill–Queen's University Press.

Ford, James Fitz and Jennie Litvack (2001), 'Intergovernmental fiscal relations and nation duilding: West Bank–Gaza case study', in Bird and Stauffer (eds).

Fox, William and Christine Wallich (2006), 'Fiscal Federalism in Bosnia–Herzegovina: subsidiarity and solidarity in a three-nation state', in Bird and Ebel (eds).

Garcia-Mila, Teresa and Therese J. McGuire (2006), 'Fiscal decentralization in Spain: an asymmetric transition to democracy', in Bird and Ebel (eds).

Haysom, Nicholas R.L. (2002), 'Constitution making and nation building', in Raoul Blindenbacher and Arnold Koller (eds), *Federalism In a Changing World – Learning from Each Other*, Montreal & Kingston: McGill–Queen's University Press.

Helliwell, John (1998), *How Much Do National Borders Matter?*, Washington, DC: The Brookings Institution.

Hirschman, Albert O. (1971), *A Bias for Hope*, New Haven, CT: Yale University Press.

Holzhausen, Walter (1974), *Federal Finance in Malaysia*, Kuala Lumpur: Penerbit Universiti Malaya.

Islam, Roumeen (2002), 'Into the looking glass: what the media tell and why – an overview', in Roumeen Islam, Simeon Djankov and Caralee McLeish (eds), *The Right to Tell: The Role of Mass Media in Economic Development*, Washington, DC: World Bank.

Katzenstein, Peter J. (1985), *Small States in World Markets*, Ithaca, NY: Cornell University Press.

Kopits, George and Jon Craig (1998), *Transparency in Government Operations*, Occasional Paper No. 158, Washington, DC: International Monetary Fund.

Lane, Patricia (2003), 'Land law and communal title in Australia', Presentation to Parties and Observers, Sudan Peace Conference, Machakos, Kenya, May.

Linder, Wolf (1994), *Swiss Democracy: Possible Solutions to Conflict in Multicultural Societies*, London: Macmillan.

Litvack, Jennie, Junaid Ahmad and Richard Bird (1998), *Rethinking Decentralization*, Washington, DC: World Bank.

Mahbob, Sulaiman, Frank Flatters, Robin Boadway, Sam Wilson and Elayne Yee Siew Lin (eds) (1997), *Malaysia's Public Sector in the Twenty-First Century: Planning for 2020 and Beyond*, Kingston, Canada: John Deutsch Institute for the Study of Economic Policy, Queen's University.

Martinez-Vazquez, Jorge and Jamie Boex (2001), *Russia's Transition to a New Federalism*, Washington, DC: World Bank.

Milanovic, Branko (1996), 'Nations, conglomerates, and empires: the tradeoff between income and sovereignty', Policy Research Working Paper 1675, World Bank, Washington, DC, October.

Persson, Torsten and Guido Tabellini (2000), *Political Economics: Explaining Economic Policy*, Cambridge, MA: MIT Press.

Petersen, John, Mila Freire, Marcela Huertas and Miguel Valadez (2004), *Subnational Capital Markets in Developing Countries: From Theory to Practice*, Oxford: Oxford University Press and World Bank.

Pisauro, Giuseppe (2001), 'Intergovernmental relations and fiscal discipline: between commons and soft budget constraints', IMF Working Paper WP/01/65, International Monetary Fund, Washington, DC, May.

Rodden, Jonathan, Gunnar S. Eskeland and Jennie Litvack (eds) (2003), *Fiscal Decentralization and the Challenge of Hard Budget Constraints*, Cambridge, MA: MIT Press.

Rondinelli, Dennis, J. Nellis and G. Cheema (1983), 'Decentralization in developing countries', Staff Working Paper 581, World Bank, Washington, DC.

Ruiz Almendar, Violet (2002), 'Fiscal federalism in Spain: the assignment of taxation powers to the autonomous communities', *European Taxation*, November, 467–75.

Saul, John Ralston (1997), *Reflections of a Slamese Twin: Canada at the End of the Twentieth Century*, Toronto: Penguin Books.

Saunders, Cheryl (2002), 'Federalism, decentralization and conflict management in multicultural societies', in Raoul Blindenbacher and Arnold Koller (eds), (2002), *Federalism in a Changing World: Learning from Each Other*, Montreal and Kingston: McGill–Queen's University Press.

Simeon, Richard (2000), 'Let's get at the basic question indirectly', *Policy Options*, **21** (January/February), 11–16.

Simeon, Richard and Christina Murray (2000), 'Multi-level governance in South Africa: an interim assessment', University of Toronto.

Spahn, Paul Bernd (2005), 'Public finances and federalism: autonomy, coordination and solidarity', *Proceedings of the Third International Conference on Federalism*, Brussels, March.

Spahn, Paul Bernd and Jan Werner (2006), 'Germany at the junction between solidarity and subsidiarity', in Bird and Ebel (eds).

Stauffer, Thomas P. (2001), 'Intergovernmental relations in fragmented societies – the case of Switzerland', *Environment and Planning C: Government and Policy*, **19** (April), 207–22.

Tanzi, Vito (1996), 'Fiscal federalism and decentralization: a review of some efficiency and macroeconomic aspects', in Michael Bruno and Boris Pleskovic (eds), *Annual World Bank Conference on Development Economics 1995*, Washington, DC: World Bank.

Treisman, Daniel (1998), *After the Deluge: Regional Crisis and Political Consolidation in Russia*, Ann Arbor, MI: University of Michigan Press.

Vaillancourt, Francois (1992) 'English and Anglophones in Quebec: an economic perspective', in J. Richards, F. Vaillancourt and W.G. Watson, *Survival – Official Language Rights in Canada*, The Canada Round.

Vaillancourt, Francois and Richard M. Bird (2006), 'Changing with the times: success, failure, and inertia in Canadian federal arrangements, 1945–2001', in T.N. Srinivasan and Jessica Wallack (eds), *The Dynamics of Federalism*, Cambridge: Cambridge University Press.

Vinuela, Julio (2001), 'Fiscal decentralization in Spain', International Monetary Fund, Washington, DC.

Von Hagen, Jurgen (2003), 'Fiscal federalism and political decision structures', in Raoul Blindenbacher and Arnold Koller (eds), *Federalism in a Changing World*, Montreal: McGill–Queen's University Press.

Watts, Ronald (1999), *Comparing Federal Systems*, 2nd edn, Montreal and Kingston: McGill–Queen's University Press.

Watts, Ronald L. (2000), 'Asymmetrical decentralization: functional or dysfunctional', Queen's University, Kingston.

Wehner, Joachim H.-G. (2000), 'Asymmetrical devolution', *Development Southern Africa*, 17 (June), 249–62.

Welikala, Asanga (2003), 'Fiscal and financial arrangements in a federal Sri Lanka: some issues for discussion', Centre for Policy Alternatives, Colombo.

Wildasin, David (1997), 'Externalities and bailouts: hard and soft budget constraints in intergovernmental fiscal relations', Policy Research Working Paper No. 1843, World Bank, November.

Wildavsky, Aaron (1977), *Budgeting*, New Brunswick, NJ: Transaction.

Wilensky, Harold (1975), *The Welfare State and Equality*, Berkeley, CA: University of California Press.

Winik, Jay (2002), *April 1865: The Month that Saved America*, New York: Harper.

Wintrobe, Ronald (1998), *The Political Economy of Dictatorship*, Cambridge: Cambridge University Press.

World Bank (1999), *Regionalization in Ethiopia*, Washington, DC: World Bank.
World Bank (2000), *Entering the 21st Century. World Development Report 1999/2000*, Oxford: Published for the World Bank by Oxford University Press.
Zelio, Judy (2005), 'Tribal taxation', in Joseph J. Cordes, Robert D. Ebel and Jane G. Gravelle (eds), *The Encyclopedia of Taxation and Tax Policy*, Washington, DC: Urban Institute Press.

21 Institutions of federalism and decentralized government
Brian Galligan

Introduction

Twentieth-century concerns with nationalism and state sovereignty tended to buttress unitary systems of government, and especially after the Second World War established federations became more centralized, while some federations thrown together by retreating colonial powers often failed (Franck 1961). Harold Laski (1939) pronounced '[t]he obsolescence of federalism', and his prognostication was echoed by a generation of post-war scholars in established federations like Australia (Greenwood 1976). Despite these tendencies and warnings, established federations like the United States, Canada, Australia and Switzerland flourished, and federal systems were successfully established in India, and re-established in Germany and Austria. There has been renewed interest in decentralization in general and federalism in particular as ways of organizing government for complex societies in the modern world. The twin waves of democratization and marketization have eroded centralized rule and national planning in countries as diverse as Russia, South Africa and Brazil. At the same time, globalization has internationalized aspects of governance, especially rule making and standard setting in policy areas that have international dimensions. The formation of regional associations of nations such as the European Union has further restricted the traditional sovereignty of the nation state.

Twenty-first century processes of globalization and supranational associations, however, are producing a 'paradigm shift from a world of sovereign nation states to a world of diminished state sovereignty and increased interstate linkages of a constitutionally federal character' (Watts 1999, ix). In many countries this is accompanied by popular pressure for the downward devolution of power to regions. These two trends are most prominent in contemporary Europe, which Peter Russell calls 'the epicenter of federalism', with the 'federalizing tendency' being a worldwide phenomenon (Russell 2005, 13). The 'changing faces of federalism' are evident in the institutional reconfiguration of Europe into an association of member states that has as many differences as similarities with traditional federal forms (Filippov et al. 2004). Although not so well developed as in Europe, regional trade associations in other parts of the world are eroding the economic sovereignty of national governments in quasi-federal ways. Building upon their Closer Economic Relations (CER) Treaty, closer political association between Australia and New Zealand is bringing those two Australasian countries with similar cultures together in an asymmetric association that has elements of federal as well as joint national structures (Galligan and Mulgan 1999). The North American Free Trade Agreement between the United States, Canada and Mexico is standardizing aspects of domestic economic management in the member states.

Decentralization comes in many shapes and forms, and is advocated and adopted for a variety of political, economic and policy reasons. Federalism is a special case of decentralized government that has been more or less standardized in commonly agreed institutional arrangements that are examined in the body of this chapter. Federalism, however, is not one shape that fits all. As we shall see, established Anglo and European federal countries like the United States, Switzerland, Canada, Germany, Austria and Australia all have variations of the core institutions that are considered to make up federalism, as do autonomous regional communities, and Belgium in accommodating its distinct French- and Dutch-speaking peoples. Federalism becomes more diverse in the broader spectrum of Asian, most notably India but also Malaysia, and Latin American countries, Argentina, Brazil and Venezuela. In Africa, it remains an essential part of the Nigerian constitution as it does in Ethiopia, while South Africa has adopted some federal features in its new constitution. Federal and quasi-federal features are found in many more countries, such as Mexico, Russia, and even China (Davis 1999) despite its unitary constitution.

Watts (1999, 8–10) identifies 24 federations (now 23 with the breakup of Yugoslavia) where about 40 per cent of the world's population lives, although the bulk of these are in India. Included in Watts's list, however, are quasi-federations or hybrids that are 'predominantly federations in their constitutions and operation but which have some overriding federal government powers more typical of a unitary system'. Examples of such quasi-federations are India, Pakistan and Malaysia because of their overriding central emergency powers, and South Africa which retains some of its pre-1996 unitary features (Dollery 1998; Simeon and Murray 2001). Watts's 1999 list is longer than Elazar's earlier one (1987, 43–4) of 19 because of the addition of Belgium and Spain, as well as South Africa, even though the last two countries have not formally adopted the term 'federal' in their constitutions. In addition, Watts lists two tiny island federations of St. Kitts and Nevis and of Micronesia, and also Ethiopia. Even without Watts's additions, the list includes different clusters of major countries with different political cultures and at different stages of development. For example the older European federations of Germany, Austria and Switzerland have sufficient in common among themselves and also with the Anglo federations of the United States, Canada and Australia to ground fruitful comparison. But the developing Latin American federations of Argentina, Brazil, Venezuela and Mexico are quite different, and India is distinctive in its scale and history (Khan 1992; Jenkins 2003; Verney 2003).

Decentralization in government serves a number of political, economic and policy purposes and countries adopt decentralization measures for one or all of these reasons. The traditional purposes of federalism were to strengthen national government while also protecting established subnational or state governments, and at the same time to limit the power of government in order to protect individual and property rights. In its classic American form, federalism was also intended to both strengthen democracy and enable its practice in large states – previously it was assumed that democracy was only possible in small states and that large states would require centralized government. Variations of these reasons still provide the basic rationale for federalism and decentralization, with satisfying democratic demands and preserving markets and property rights being to the fore. These dual purposes of federalism might be summarized as 'rights preserving' and 'market preserving'.

Decentralization and federalism have broader application than to developed liberal democratic countries, and can serve additional purposes. Countries that are geographically large, or culturally diverse, or with developing economies or large disparities in resource endowments of regions often adopt decentralized institutional arrangements. Despite bouts of centralized military power, Nigerian federalism remains grounded in its quite disparate regions and peoples (Elaigwu 2002). In a somewhat different way, Brazilian federalism 'has always been a means of accommodating deep-rooted regional disparities' (Souza 2002, 23). We might sum up these additional purposes of decentralization and federalism as 'government facilitating' and 'responding to regionally based diversity'. These two are often interlinked: large and regionally diverse countries like India, China, Nigeria and Brazil could hardly be governed effectively through a centralized system. One of the most intriguing issues regarding federalism, explored by Alfred Stepan in explaining Brazil's system, is the way in which it affects democratization and decentralization by bringing government closer to citizens (Stepan 2000).

Even without regional diversity, centralized government is a blunt instrument for dealing with complex policy in large countries. Some policy issues have primarily local or regional domains and are best dealt with at subnational levels of government, while others have multiple dimensions that require attention at various levels of government. Education, health care and environmental protection all have major local components, but also regional and national aspects as well. As Ahmad et al. (1994, 25–6) have pointed out, dealing with these 'mixed goods' is best done through a mixed regime with 'some degree of decentralization coupled with some centralized coordination of policy'. Matching jurisdictional powers and responsibilities with appropriate policy domains and fiscal arrangements for levels of government is one of the great tasks of intergovernmental design and management.

The focus of this chapter is the institutions of decentralization, and in particular those of federalism. Such institutions are not peculiar to federalism, however, and can be found in non-federal countries serving various purposes including decentralization. While most established federations are found in countries with strong liberal democratic traditions and relatively sophisticated political elites and citizenry, a range of centralized and developing countries have adopted versions of federalism or certain federal institutions. In this chapter we concentrate upon the well-established federal systems and their common institutional components that make up the usual federal paradigm. That is not to deny the rich diversity of the growing spectrum of quasi-federal and decentralized countries, or the international associations and arrangements that have extended federal-type arrangements. Indeed, an important reason for studying federal systems is offered by Louis Imbeau: 'we can view federal systems as historical experiments at sharing policy responsibilities and look at them as working models of a new global order' (Imbeau 2004, 13). Assessing whether and to what extent federalism does give us insights into the new global order is beyond the scope of this chapter, although in the last section we argue that federalism and decentralized government are broadly compatible with globalization.

Federalism and federal countries
Political decentralization is essential to federalism[1] which is characterized by two spheres of government, national and state, operating in the one political entity according to defined arrangements for sharing powers so that neither is sovereign over the other. This is captured in William Riker's definition that 'the activities of government are divided between regional governments and a central government in such a way that each kind of government has some activities on which it makes final decisions' (Riker 1975, 101). Daniel Elazar identifies the constitutional diffusion of power as the essence of federalism: 'the constituting elements in a federal arrangement share in the processes of common policy making and administration by right, while the activities of the common government are conducted in such a way as to maintain their respective integrities'. For Elazar, who takes the viewpoint of the constituting elements, this is a system of '*self-rule plus shared rule*' (Elazar 1987, 12, italics in original).

Federalism is the antithesis of unitary government by an all-powerful sovereign or Leviathan, to use Thomas Hobbes's famous metaphor. An early theoretical exposition is found in Johannes Althusius's notion of an association of associations (Carney 1965), and earlier quasi-federal forms existed in confederations and leagues of member states. The anchor of modern federalism, pioneered by the American constitutional founders and explained in the *Federalist Papers*, is its foundation in republican democracy (Beer 1993). Popular sovereignty provides a vital and legitimating basis for federalism and its institutions, including the constitution that specifies and controls both spheres of government and the institutions of government in each of those federal spheres. Dual citizenship and the political culture that supports such allegiance to two spheres of government, each for specific but limited purposes, underpins modern federalism.

There has been debate over the meaning, significance and defining institutions of federalism. Sceptics like Ivo Duchacek have claimed that federalism has no accepted theory or consensus as to what it is (Duchacek 1987). While this goes too far and presupposes too narrow notions of political and institutional theory, the sceptical view highlights the variety of applications and spectrum of possibilities for federal systems. At the other extreme is the recent work by Filippov et al., *Designing Federalism*, which purports to give 'a theory of federal design that is universal and complete' (2004, 17). While the authors find this in the 'properly developed' political party system that channels political behaviour of elites (2004, 39–40), the explanation is too simple because the structure and functioning of parties in stable federal systems are endogenous to those systems and partly shaped by them and their supporting political culture.

Others like William Livingston maintained a sociological view that '[f]ederalism was a function not of constitutions but of societies' (Livingston 1956, 4). Hence one would need to look to societal factors such as ethnically distinct regions and their interests to find explanations for federalism. Riker's earlier reflections on federalism were based on this sociological rationale: he wondered why Australia, without regional differences to appease, persisted with federalism (1964), and argued that federalism was trivial in the absence of such differences (1970). This view that federalism should serve regionally based diversity captures only one of the four purposes identified earlier, and neglects the other three of rights preserving and market preserving in liberal democratic polities, and government facilitating in large countries whether they have regionally diverse cultures or not. Riker was to change his mind about federalism (1975, 1993), reverting to the more classical view that it was primarily a system of decentralized government that limited central power. In recent years, the 'new institutionalism' (Goodin 1996) of political scientists and public choice economists has promoted a renewed interest in the institutions of federalism in various country settings.

The diverse examples of federal countries show the different and multiple purposes that federalism serves. Probably the most common purpose is government facilitating especially in larger countries with diverse geographic regions such as India, the United States, Canada, Germany, South Africa, Nigeria, Australia and Brazil. Often federalism serves the combined purposes of facilitating government in large countries and responding to regionally based cultural diversity, as is the case for India, Canada and Nigeria among the established federations. This latter purpose is also significant for smaller federations like Belgium and Switzerland. The United States is the paradigm case for federalism's liberal purposes of rights preserving and market preserving, but these purposes are also of primary significance in many other federations including Canada, Australia, Germany and Switzerland. Indeed, they are inherent in the anti-Leviathan features of federalism that will tend to have liberalizing effects, depending on the political culture of the country and the push and pull of counter forces. Because of these multiple purposes, federalism or quasi-federal arrangements have obvious suitability for most large and diverse countries, including China, Russia and Indonesia, even if some continue to maintain unitary constitutions.

Any discussion of the institutions of federalism is complicated by a number of factors: one is the variability of federal forms; the second is the complexity of federal systems and institutions in particular countries; and a third is the reflexivity of institutions. The first point is concerned with the definition of federalism, or the basic institutions required before a country can be considered to be truly federal. Even when this is done, there is the second complicating factor that in any particular federal country there exists a wide variety of institutions and practices that are interdependent with other non-federal institutions and traditions. Sorting out what is peculiarly federal in a particular country, or due to federal institutions is a difficult task. And, as the third point indicates, political institutions are worked by human agents who can operate them in different ways to produce similar outcomes or vice versa. As a consequence of these factors, it is common among federal scholars to first sort out the federal countries from others that might have some partial federal features, and then to refine the group to a handful of those that have sufficiently similar systems to justify comparative analysis.

Faced with a heterogeneous bunch of federal countries, scholars typically group them in manageable clusters and concentrate upon the older and more stable Anglo and European federations. This is done by Obinger et al. (2005) in *Federalism and the Welfare State* who restrict their study to the established Anglo and European federations: Australia, Austria, Canada, Germany, Switzerland and the United States. This selection is appropriate because, as their subtitle suggests, the 'New World and European Experiences' have sufficient in common to merit comparative analysis of the complex ways in which federal institutions have interacted with post-war welfare policies. Focusing on the older Anglo and European federations is also sufficient for our purposes because the main institutions of federalism are most evident in well-established and functioning federations. These countries score highest on Arend Lijphart's 'Index of federalism' for democratic countries, based on quantifying variables of federal–unitary dimensions on a scale of 1 to 5 (Lijphart 1999, Appendix A, 312–13). Whereas unitary countries like Great Britain, New Zealand and Greece score 1, the five well-established federations Australia, Canada, Germany, Switzerland and the United States all score 5. The other federal countries that score highly are Austria and India with scores of 4.5, and Venezuela with 4. Belgium and Spain are lower with scores of 3.2 and 3, respectively, although these scores may have increased with recent developments. Lijphart's index of federalism shows a spectrum of countries with varying degrees of decentralization; variability also characterizes the institutional arrangements for embodying federalism that are considered in the next section.

Federal institutions
As outlined above, federalism consists essentially of two spheres of government with powers divided between them so that each has its own primary jurisdiction and neither is sovereign over the other. Federalism is a spatial or territorial arrangement with the component states being discreet, contiguous regions, although there can be major asymmetry in the size and significance of member states as is the case with California and Wyoming in the United States, or Ontario and Prince Edward Island in Canada. Federal thinking often uses or assumes a cartwheel or pyramid metaphor with the national government at the centre or apex and the states at the periphery or base. Instead, Elazar (1987, 36–8) has championed a matrix model of power distribution among multiple centres of government, which gives less prominence to the national government. The additional democratic feature that accounts for the strength of modern federations is that each sphere of government acts directly upon its citizens, so that in effect they have dual loyalties and divided citizenship as members of both state and national polities.

These essential features of federalism are embodied in institutions of government that are sufficiently common to be considered characteristic of federalism. Lijphart (1999, 4, 187) lists three key ones: a bicameral legislature with a strong federal chamber to represent the constituent regions, a written constitution that is difficult to amend, and a supreme or constitutional court to protect the constitution through the power of judicial review. There is an essential fourth one that Watts (1999, 7) includes: intergovernmental institutions and processes to facilitate collaboration in areas of shared or overlapping jurisdiction. We discuss these four institutional features of federalism, beginning with the most significant one, the written constitution that sets up the two spheres of government and divides powers between them, and is difficult to amend. It should be emphasized, however, that none of these particular institutions is peculiarly federal – unitary countries often have one or some of them. Rather it is the combination of institutions and the purpose they serve that makes them federal.

Written constitution   The written constitution is the institutional foundation of federalism and has three basic characteristics: (i) it is superior to both spheres of government and draws its legitimacy from the people; (ii) it establishes or acknowledges the two spheres of government, national and state; (iii) it specifies the division of powers between them. The first attribute needs some explanation because only the Swiss and Australian constitutions have the obvious institutional embodiment of popular sovereignty in their amendment procedures. The US constitution, however, is the classic model of a republican federation based squarely upon popular sovereignty as Samuel Beer (1993, 137) points out: the 'principle that made possible the distinctively American form of constitutionalism and so of federalism was popular sovereignty'. As Donald Lutz (1994, 355) affirms, American political writing predated John Locke in using the language of popular sovereignty, and earlier state constitutions such as those of Massachusetts and New Hampshire as well as the US federal constitution were based squarely on popular sovereignty. Switzerland has an alternative long tradition of popular sovereignty but of a more communal than individualistic kind.

Ideally, popular sovereignty would require the constitution to be written by a popularly elected convention and not the legislature, and be adopted through popular referendum. This has not always been the case, with legislatures often serving as proxies for the popular will but usually with special majority requirements. The US constitution was drafted by a convention of delegates from the states and ratified by state conventions. For amendment it requires both two-thirds majorities in both houses of the national legislature as well as approval from three-quarters of the states. Being drafted in the 1890s with the American and Swiss models before them, Australia's founders used both popularly elected conventions to draft the constitution and popular referendums in the states to ratify it, before sending it to the Westminster Imperial parliament for formal ratification. Whereas Australia had this dual popular and Westminster foundation, Canada settled for Westminster ratification only in 1867 and has suffered from not constituting itself as a sovereign people (Russell 2004). Germany has a long federal tradition that predates democracy in that country, and its modern Basic Law is based upon popular sovereignty, and its amending procedure upon special majorities of two-thirds in both houses of the national legislature. The practical lesson to be drawn from this variety of practice is that various institutional arrangements can work in linking the people with their federal constitution.

Federal constitutions need to affirm the dual spheres of government. The way in which this is done varies among federal constitutions and reflects their historical origins. The Anglo constitutions are bottom-up in the sense of being formed from existing smaller states and provinces that had been quasi-independent colonies within the British Empire. Hence their federal constitutions serve the dual functions of both creating the national institutions of government and specifying its powers *vis-à-vis* the states and provinces. Since the latter already existed with their own establishing acts or constitutions, they receive relatively scant attention. The US and Australian constitutions affirm the states' continuing existence and powers in so far as these are not modified by the constitution. The Canadian constitution gives more attention to the provinces in accommodating the English–French divide and because of the more fluid colonial configuration of Canada at the time. Germany's Basic Law, adopted in 1949 and so termed to leave open the possibility of reunification, sets out the interdependent roles of federal and *Land* governments (Jeffery 1999). The Swiss constitution is the most decentralized in securing the powers of the cantons and constraining the central government. This reflects its long-standing regionally based linguistic diversity.

The division of power or competencies is central to federal systems and invariably linked to ways in which the spheres of government are constituted and operate. K.C. Wheare (1963) focused on the legal distribution of powers. Prominent was the difference between the US model of enumerating Congress's heads of power and guaranteeing the residual to the states, also followed by Australia, and the Canadian model of enumerating both sets of powers. In effect, the difference was blurred because of the broad categories of definition and the ingenuity of judges in interpreting them. Nevertheless, Canada's enumeration of provincial power provided Privy Council judges with a ready basis for expanding provincial powers in sanctioning that country's evolution from a centralized to a decentralized federation. Some Australian critics of centralization have championed the Canadian model as a way of arresting its High Court's centralist bent in constitutional jurisprudence.

A more dynamic organizing distinction from European scholarship is that between *interstate* and *intrastate* federalism, which takes account of both the distribution of legislative power and the implementation. Dietmar Braun (2004, 47) defines these two types of federal division of powers as follows. In the interstate model 'jurisdictional authority is separated between territorial actors and competition and bipolarity predominate', whereas in intrastate federalism 'most of the decisions are taken at the federal level where subgovernments and the federal government have their say' and 'implementation is almost completely in the hands of subgovernments'. Canada epitomizes the former type and Germany the latter. The Canadian provinces have no direct say in federal legislation or its implementation but are relatively autonomous in using their own legislative powers and carry out out their own policies. In contrast, the German *Länder* have a direct say in legislation that is predominantly national through the Bundesrat, and also have the main responsibility for its implementation.

Difficult to amend   As Giovanni Sartori reminds us, 'constitutions are, first and above all, instruments of government which limit, restrain and allow for the control of the exercise of political power' (1994, 198). Since a federal constitution creates two spheres of government and divides powers between them so that each has limited powers, it is a powerful instrument of limiting and controlling political power. Australia, Canada, Germany, Switzerland and the United States all come within Lijphart's (1999, 220–21) hardest category of constitutional amendment, requiring 'super-majorities' greater than two-thirds approval of both houses of the national legislature, and scoring a maximum of 4 on his scale of 1 to 4. By way of contrast, New Zealand, the United Kingdom and Sweden score only 1, while the mean index of constitutional rigidity is 2.6 and the median 3. Germany is included in the super-majorities category even though it scores 3.5 on the grounds that as well as the two-thirds majorities in both houses of the national legislature, the composition of the Bundesrat and the Bundestag are significantly different. The only other country in this hardest-to-amend category is non-federal Japan, which requires a referendum in addition to a two-thirds majority in both houses of its legislature.

Constitutional amendment procedures vary significantly among federal countries. Australia and Switzerland have popular referendum procedures that are also federally weighted: majorities of voters overall, and majorities in a majority of the states and cantons. In Australia, for example, where this means majorities in four of the six states as well as an overall majority nationwide, five amendments have been lost because of the additional requirement of a majority of states. This is important given Australia's slim record of only eight amendments from 44 proposals put, especially as the five that failed the double majority test included substantial additional Commonwealth powers – over aviation in 1936 and marketing and industrial relations in 1946, as well as simultaneous elections for both houses of the Commonwealth parliament that would have curtailed the independence of the Senate in 1977 and again in 1984 (Galligan 2001). The United States has ratification by three-quarters of the states in addition to a two-thirds majority in both houses of Congress. Canada has a range of measures depending on the constitutional section, but the normal one is a weighted federal formula that takes account of both numbers of provinces and population – assent of the national parliament and of two-thirds of the provincial legislatures for provinces containing at least half the total population. There is a harder unanimity rule for a select number of areas concerning basic language rights. Germany has only the two-thirds rule for a majority in both houses, but these are differently constituted with the Bundesrat representing the *Länder*.

Is difficulty of amendment a constitutional virtue? And has it been an undue break on change in federal countries? These are debated questions whose answers in part depend upon the higher law character of a constitution that controls the other institutions of government. According to Donald Lutz (1994, 357), amendment procedures should be 'neither too easy nor too diffi- cult' but strike a balance between preserving a high-level order of deliberation on constitutional matters and fixing up human mistakes. He defines a success- ful constitutional system as one that has 'a moderate amendment rate'. Lutz finds that variance in amendment rate is largely explained by the interaction of length of the constitution and difficulty of the amendment process. The more that is put into a constitution, the longer it gets and the more it needs to be altered. And if the amendment process is easy, there will be more amend- ments. The rate of amendment also depends on whether there are alternative avenues for change, namely judicial review. Applying this sort of analysis to the older federations, we would expect them to have higher amendment rates because of their age; lower rates because of the difficulty of the amendment process; lower rates because of their relative shortness; and lower rates because of alternative means of amendment via judicial review. Overall we should expect relatively low rates of amendment in established federations because of the predominance of lower factors.

That is the case with Australia and the United States having exceptionally low rates of 0.09 and 0.13, respectively, Switzerland being higher at 0.78 and Germany having 2.91. These are extremely low except for Germany – the average for 32 countries was 2.54 (Lutz 1994, 369). Canada is omitted, presumably because it could not agree on an amending formula so continued to rely upon Britain's Westminster parliament until Pierre Trudeau's patriation of the constitution in the 1980s replete with complex amendment procedures and a Charter of Rights. Since then Canada has been engaged in a largely fruit- less discussion of 'mega-constitutional' change that proposed to move an enormous range of political matters into the constitution.

The matter is more complex, however, when we take account of political factors. One is intergovernmental politics which, given institutional reflexiv- ity, allows political actors to make federal systems work flexibly and adapt to changing circumstances without formal amendment. The other crucial factors that influence the rate of successful amendment are political ones: who controls the process of putting proposals, who decides their outcome, and who benefits from the outcomes. If governments control the process we would expect them to put up proposals that are for their benefit. Moreover, if only one sphere of government has the right of proposal, the pattern of proposals would likely be skewed in its favour. Outcomes depend on who has the final say on amendment and who the proposals benefit. If the national government controls the calling and wording of referendum proposals, we would expect centralist proposals. If the people decide on amendments, we would expect support for popular measures; also opposition to centralist power grabs, given their attachment to state and local government. Australia provides a copybook case of hegemonic national government control of the process, with the Commonwealth government of the day proposing and drafting amendment legislation that has to be passed by both houses of parliament and then voted upon by popular referendum. This explains why most of the 44 amendment proposals put to the people over 100 years have failed (only eight have succeeded): most have been to increase Commonwealth powers *via-à-vis* the states or curtail the independent electoral cycle of the Senate. If Australia had the Swiss system of popular initiative of referendum proposals, or if the states could propose constitutional amendments, there would have been a different pattern of proposals and, most probably, of outcomes.

Judicial review   Judicial review provides an ongoing routine channel for constitutional adjustment that takes the pressure off formal amendment in most federations. The United States Supreme Court pioneered this crucial role in the famous *Marbury v Madison* (1803) decision when its chief justice, John Marshall, asserted the right of a superior court to interpret and apply the higher law of the constitution over a lower law congressional act. While Marshall's logic was impeccable, he asserted rather than established from any constitutional basis that this vital role should be assumed by the Court. While sparingly used earlier on, judicial review became a major instrument of American constitutional development and has been copied in most federations.

As Watts points out (1999, 100), there are two types of constitutional court in the major federations: one is a general court serving as final adjudicator for all laws including the constitution; the other is a constitutional court specializing in constitutional interpretation. As well as the United States, Australia, Canada, India, Malaysia and Austria have the general court type, while Germany, Belgium and Spain have specialized constitutional courts. Switzerland has a more limited Federal Tribunal to decide the validity of cantonal laws, but uses popular referendums for federal laws. The type of court affects the character of the appointees: specialists in various branches of the law are required for general supreme courts where constitutional adjudication is only a part of the workload; whereas constitutional experts are appointed to constitutional courts. For example, the seven judges of the

Australian High Court are typically leading barristers and judges from lower courts who will likely have only incidental constitutional experience, and are appointed by the Commonwealth government after consultation with the states. By way of contrast, the Bundesrat and the *Länder* each appoint half of Germany's 16 constitutional judges using special majority arrangements. Federations with linguistic diversity such as Canada and Switzerland have arrangements for ensuring proportional representation of judges from those linguistic groups.

Constitutional adjudication and interpretation is highly sensitive because it affects government powers as well as individual rights and group interests. At times, courts make bold and innovative constitutional decisions but they are constrained by the cases that come to them and by the need for continuing legitimacy. Supreme courts might have the final say in constitutional matters, but they cannot get too far out of step with the mainstream of political consensus. Governments can change the direction of courts through the appointment process in the longer term, and in the shorter term can often work around their decisions.

The expansive interpretation of national powers in federations such as the United States, Canada and Australia has reduced the role of supreme courts as arbiters of those federal systems. The main focus of constitutional adjudication in Canada and the United States has shifted to rights protection in interpreting charters and bills of rights. In Australia, which does not have a bill of rights, the expansive interpretation of Commonwealth powers combined with the broad expenditure power of the Commonwealth have left few areas of formal restraint upon the Commonwealth. That leaves the balance of national and state roles and responsibilities to be sorted out largely through the institutions and processes of intergovernmental relations. In most modern federations this is also the case to a greater or lesser extent.

Nevertheless courts and judicial review remain a significant part of the institutions of federalism in evolving policy areas such as environmental protection (Holland et al. 1996). The judiciary can play a balancing role because of its opportunities to referee conflicts between development, which is localized and often supported by state governments, and environment protection, which has broader support of public opinion and national governments. The significance of supreme courts in environmental and other major policy areas varies among federations and from time to time. In the United States the federal judiciary has become a major player in environmental decision making, whereas in the Australian and Canadian parliamentary federations their role has been less significant.

Legislative bicameralism   Although not peculiar to federal countries, legislative bicameralism is considered integral to federalism and decentralized government. Bicameralism increases the number of veto players and hence policy stability (Tsebelis 2002, 136–60), and in federal systems is part of the diffuse power arrangements that check and restrain government. Historically, bicameralism was a key part of the Connecticut compromise between large and small states that underpinned the US constitution. To alleviate fears that direct representation of the people in proportion to state populations would jeopardize the smaller states, the American founders agreed to a bicameral congress with the Senate based on equal state representation. Since they expected the legislature to be the most powerful branch of government in a democratic republic, this was a means both of introducing the federal principle into the legislature and dividing its power between two houses that were differently constituted. The Senate was not intended to be simply a states' house; indeed, the American founders intended it to be the premier house of the national legislature whose fewer members (two per state) would be elite politicians free of petty local interests that would dominate concerns of members of the House of Representatives. The earlier selection process of direct election by the state legislatures was in keeping with this view of the enhanced status and role of senators. The switch to direct election by the people of the states in 1913 signalled that democratic election has become a more powerful legitimating force. The Senate has full legislative powers and hence an absolute veto over all legislation.

Australia follows most closely the American model in both the powers and equal state representation of its Senate. The Australian Senate has virtually co-equal powers with the House of Representatives. The only limits are that it cannot propose or amend money bills, but has the larger power of passing or refusing to pass any money bill or any amendment proposed by the lower House. The first restriction it shares with the US constitution, and the second is to respect the monetary prerogative of the responsible government executive based in the House of Representatives. The number of senators per state is equal, originally set at six but now 12 per state plus two for each of the two territories, with the total number fixed to half the size of the House of Representatives, which has been increased from time to time. Party discipline almost invariably overrides state representation by senators, although senators take state concerns into parliamentary party caucus forums. The adoption of proportional representation for Senate voting in 1948 has given minor parties and independents a significant, and often controlling, influence in the Australian Senate.

Germany has quite a different bicameral arrangement that is more directly federal in its purpose with its Bundesrat comprising delegates appointed by *Land* governments and voting on the instructions of those governments. The *Länder* quota of members is proportional to relative population size and can be from three to six. The Burdesrat has veto power over all federal legislation that involves *Länder* administration, which in practice is between 50 and 60 per cent. This bicameral structure gives German federalism its highly integrative, or intrastate character. At the same time German bicameralism provides a substantial check on legislative power because of the representation it gives different national and regional, as well as popular and party interests. Switzerland has its own peculiar Council of States in which members are chosen by direct election of the people of the cantons. There are two representatives for each of the 20 larger cantons and one each for six smaller ones. Copied from the American Senate, this is a strong house with full legislative powers and a veto over all legislation.

Canada stands out because of its ineffectual bicameralism. The basic flaw in its design is appointment by the national government which ensures that it is stocked with patronage appointees or people with little independent political standing or legitimacy in their regions. So, although there is the requirement of regional representation for groups of provinces, those selected by the centre have little provincial credibility. This makes the Canadian a tame chamber despite its considerable formal powers of having to pass, and being in theory able to reject, any bills. Ineffectual bicameralism has exacerbated problems in Canadian governance, especially the incorporation of the western provinces in national decision making. While western reformers advocate a Triple-E Senate – elected, equal and effective – on the Australian model, national governments dominated by the most populous central provinces, Ontario and Quebec, have been reluctant to address the issue.

Bicameral systems vary because of their different institutional structures, as described above, but also because of their interaction with other parts of the political system of which they are part, especially political parties. While it is customary to emphasize that federal second chambers represent the interests of state or regional electorates (Watts 1999, 95), this is often only the minor part of the story. In Australia where parties are dominant, state senators mainly represent party interests and those of state party branches that will likely have at most only secondary concern with local or regional matters. To the extent that they do, they take these into their party caucuses. US senators do have state constituencies, but party and national allegiances and concerns are often more significant, depending on the issues at stake. In Germany, because the parties in government in the *Länder* choose the delegates to the Bundesrat, the party provides an additional overlay to *Länder* representation (Strum 1999). In Switzerland as well, the party is a significant overlay on the regional representation role of Council of States members.

Intergovernmental relations and fiscal federalism
There was little scope for intergovernmental relations in the classic writings of earlier scholars of federalism, because they viewed the two spheres of

government as having separate and distinct, or coordinate powers. According to James Bryce, American federalism was like a great factory with two sets of machinery crisscrossing without ever touching or hampering each other's functioning. The aim was 'to keep the two mechanisms as distinct and independent of each other as was compatible with the still higher need of subordinating, for national purposes, the State to the Central government' (Bryce 1888, vol. 1, 425). Wheare (1963, 93) argued: 'The federal principle requires that the general and regional governments of a country shall be independent each of the other within its sphere, shall be not subordinate one to another but co-ordinate with each other'. Wheare, too, invoked the principle of paramountcy that in cases of conflict the central government should be authoritative.

With the expansion of modern government and multiple dimensions of major policy areas being addressed by both spheres of government, it became obvious to American political scientists that federal reality was much more complex and messy. Federalism was more like a marble than a layered cake, Grodzens (1966) commented, where there was a mixing and blending of government activities rather than separate and distinct operation. For Elazar, federalism was a non-hierarchical policy matrix – 'polycentric by design', like 'a communications network that establishes the linkages that create the whole' (1987, 13). Rather than attempting to re-establish neat categories of coordinate powers, the focus of federal scholarship shifted to exploring institutions and processes of intergovernmental relations. Understanding and managing this complexity of interdependent and interacting governments provided a rich field for public policy scholars (Wright 1998), especially as the field was expanding into most major policy areas. As Agranoff points out, 'a steady demand for governmental services in health, education, housing, income maintenance, employment and training, and personal social services has forced governments at all levels to become more interdependent' (Agranoff 1986, 1) – so much so that 'public administration and the processes of federalism have merged to a nearly indistinguishable point' (Agranoff and McGuire 2001, 671).

At the same time there has been renewed effort to sort out the institutional logic and propensities of intergovernmental arrangements, especially in the area of federal financial relations where ambitious claims have been made for the significance of such work. Introducing a recent set of studies on deficits and surpluses in federal states, Louis Imbeau (2004, 13) claims 'we can view federal systems as historical experiments at sharing policy responsibilities and look at them as working models of a new global order'. How systems of multiple governments interact in interdependent ways and how fiscal decentralization affects the size of overall government are big issues that the study of federal systems allows us to address, even if these claims are contentious.

An earlier fillip to the study of fiscal federalism was the anti-Leviathan thesis of Geoffrey Brennan and James Buchanan (1980, 15), claiming that decentralization of taxes and expenditures produced smaller government. This was because people and corporations could vote with their feet, and hence governments would have to compete for mobile sources of revenue. Fiscal decentralization does not necessarily produce smaller government, however; it depends on the nature of fiscal federalism, according to a recent study by Jonathan Rodden (2003). That is because the institutional incentives created by different fiscal arrangements can be quite different. Where increases in state and local expenditures are funded by grants or other revenue arrangements controlled by central governments, which tends to have been the case in recent decades, Rodden finds that expenditure decentralization is associated with faster growth in overall government spending. That is because, as he explains, 'mere expenditure decentralization might turn the public sector's resources into a common pool that competing governments will attempt to overfish'. Only where decentralized expenditure is funded by decentralized or 'own-source' taxes is there slower government growth (2003, 697–8).

Rodden's findings for federations need qualification in several respects. The first one, concerning expenditure decentralization funded by sharing of centrally collected taxes, is based on a large sample of mainly unitary countries in which, as he notes, the highly decentralized federations, Canada, Switzerland and the United States, are in a class by themselves, having the smallest public sectors. This might seem to support the Brennan–Buchanan thesis. However, Germany, along with Austria and Belgium, support his broader finding, and Australia is not included in his analysis. Rodden's second finding that 'own-source' revenues are associated with smaller government relies on the much smaller sample of the three decentralized federations, Canada, Switzerland and the United States. This complements their being exceptions in the first finding and suggests that there might be something distinctive about these three particular federations or, as Rodden (2003, 723) intimates, something else driving both tax decentralization and smaller government. Had Australia been included, it would have stood out as something of an exception to both of Rodden's theses – the Australian states rely on the centre for half their revenue but are also constrained by market discipline.

As Bahl and Linn point out in their study of fiscal decentralization in less-developed countries: 'Theory cannot lead to firm conclusions about the best division of fiscal responsibilities between national, state, and local governments' (1994, 2). There is no 'best' system, but a wide variety of subsidies, grants and tax sharing arrangement depending on what the country is trying to achieve (1994, 19). Nor does it follow that the particular arrangements that are put in place by a particular country will work very well and achieve their purpose, as for example with the deteriorating fiscal performance of India's states (Rao 2003). Nor can theory provide a model template that applies to decentralization more generally. From his study of Argentina, Brazil, Mexico and Spain, Alfred Montero concludes that explanations of decentralization must go beyond the usual party and legislative explanations to dynamic models of 'intergovernmental coordination games' played in multiple arenas (2001, 65–6). To find out what is going on in decentralization, whether for developed or less-developed countries, we need fine-grained institutional and political analysis that takes account of the dynamic interactions of players as well as the institutional arrangements in place. This is why country studies remain so important: to understand Canadian 'executive federalism', for example, one needs detailed knowledge of its particular institutions, politics and policy processes (Bakvis and Skogstad 2002).

One generalization that seems incontrovertible is that political and institutional factors are both important, as is their combination. According to Louis Imbeau and Francois Petry (2004) and their team of contributors, political–institutional variables – the proximity of elections, the ideology of incumbent governments, and the severity of formal rules limiting deficits – all have significant effect on budgetary outcomes (Petry 2004, 222). This conclusion is based upon pooled evidence over the past couple of decades for the five federations that we have been considering. Canada and Germany stand out as high-deficit countries, while Australia, Switzerland and the United States are low-deficit countries.

Dietmar Braun (2003, 2004) shows how different types of intergovernmental institutions affect federal fiscal policy making using case studies of Canada, Germany, Belgium and Switzerland. He identifies Canada and Germany as opposite federal types – interstate and intrastate, respectively – and explains how their institutional differences are played out in fiscal policy processes and outcomes. Canada's national government has extensive scope for fiscal policy making without provincial interference, but weak implementation because provinces are independent. It can gain leverage through negotiation and provision of incentives such as contributing to shared cost programmes, but more recently the strategy has been to withdraw from such programmes and leave market forces to impose financial discipline on the provinces. Germany is quite different with its intrastate type of federalism that gives the *Länder* a direct say in, and veto power over, national fiscal policy via the Bundesrat. This ensures negotiation and consensus in the whole process of shaping of fiscal policy that is then readily implemented because everyone has agreed but, because of the process, inclines towards the status quo (Braun 2004, 25–8). Whereas Canada has a competition tax system, albeit with a shared collection arrangement for income tax, Germany's has a cooperative one. On the expenditure side, the Canadian national government can move quickly to cut expenditure, whereas the German government is constrained by consensus (Braun 2003, 118). Switzerland is like Germany in having a cooperative system, but with weak governments constrained by the additional strong democratic check of popular referendums.

Social welfare is another major policy area in which federalism has been considered to have a significant effect on outcomes, mainly retarding their adoption and growth in the post-war decades. Obinger et al. (2005) find that the effects of federalism on welfare state development are multiple and complex, variable over time, and contingent on particular institutional configurations, political actors and pressure groups and broader historical and cultural contexts. Federalism, through its institutional decentralization and fragmentation of political power, can retard new policy developments or facilitate them. Federalism provides multiple veto points but also multiple entry points for new initiatives. Federalism can help slow down the adoption of welfare policies, for which it was much blamed in the immediate post-war decades, or it can slow down their dismantling which is more of a current issue. The study by Obinger et al. shows the complexity of federalism's interaction on social policy in 'new world', Australia, Canada and the United States, and European federations, Austria, Germany and Switzerland. Using historical case studies, they find that time periods are crucial for establishing whether federalism impedes social welfare policy or not: early on that was the case but after consolidation in mature systems other cross-national differences explain differences among countries.

Globalization and the future of federalism
The world of the twenty-first century is likely to be one of increasing globalization and transnational regionalism that is antithetical to national sovereignty and centralized government. Although recognized by international law and diplomacy, international legal sovereignty is often a legal fiction that distorts the real state of interdependent nations (Krasner 1999). The post-sovereignty world of the twenty-first century will likely be 'a world characterized by shifting allegiances, new forms of identity and overlapping tiers of jurisdiction' (Camilleri and Falk 1992, 256). In European nations, power has moved downwards to subnational regions and upwards to the European Union. Britain, the home of the Hobbesian sovereignty doctrine and parliamentary sovereignty discourse, has embraced devolution to Scotland and Wales and joined the European Union. According to Andrew Linklater: 'the subnational revolt, the internationalization of decision making and emergent transnational loyalties in Western Europe reveal that the processes which created and sustained sovereign states in this region are being reversed' (Linklater 1998, 113). Recent post-sovereignty writing draws upon the earlier work of Hedley Bull (1977) who argued that the world was moving towards

a form of 'neo-medievalism' of overlapping structures and cross-cutting loyalties.

For many federal countries, including new world ones like Australia and Canada as well as old European ones like Germany, the post-sovereignty world of the future is in some part a return to the past. The sweep of political history includes long periods of sprawling empire when nations became states with varying degrees of autonomy. The British Empire is a case in point, with Australia, along with Canada, South Africa, India and many other countries becoming nations without sovereignty through the nineteenth and twentieth centuries (Galligan et al. 2001). Europe and Asia, and India in particular, have long histories of complex state arrangements not characterized by sovereign nation states. The European Union gives space for subnations like Scotland and regions with distinctive cultures and histories, such as in northern Italy and Barcelona in Spain. Multiple spheres of governance, international as well as national and subnational including state or provincial and metropolitan, regional and local, are becoming more prevalent.

As we have seen, federalism is a complex system of multiple governments with divided but invariably overlapping jurisdictions and extensive interaction, both vertical and horizontal, among the various governments' departments and agencies. No one government is sovereign or supreme in its powers, but a part of a non-hierarchical system. Understood in this way, federalism is quite compatible with regionalism and globalization. Adding another sphere of governance where some norms and standards are formulated and collective decisions are made that impinge on a nation's domestic affairs does complicate things (Lazar et al. 2003), but in ways that are consistent with the operation of federalism.

Federalism is a more formalized version of political decentralization that is found in a broader range of countries, especially those that are geographically large, and regionally or culturally diverse. In its classic form, federalism was designed to secure democratic government and protect citizen and property rights through limiting central government powers. But federalism has also been adopted to address regionally based diversity and to facilitate government in complex policy areas through providing multiple government spheres. Many countries have some federal or quasi-federal features in order to provide a measure of decentralization, and prescriptions for better governance in large and diverse unitary states often entail some form of greater decentralization or arrangements that mimic federations. While federalism seems compatible with globalization, and established federal systems are likely to endure, the future will probably see greater diversity and asymmetry in multiple governance structures. Even if that is the case, the lessons of institutional and intergovernmental design and management from federal systems will remain relevant.

Note

1. Federalism is used here as a generic term for federal systems. Some contemporary scholars like Ron Watts want to distinguish 'federalism', taken to be a normative term referring to the advocacy of multilevel government, from 'federal systems' or 'federations' that are said to be descriptive of actual federations (Watts 1999, 6–7). While federalism might well be used by some of its advocates in a normative way, in normal usage it is simply the general term for federations and federal systems.

References

Agranoff, Robert J. (1986), *Intergovernmental Management: Human Services Problem-Solving in Six Metropolitan Areas*, Albany, NY: State University of New York Press.

Agranoff, Robert J. and Michael McGuire (2001), 'American federalism and the search for models of management', *Public Administration Review*, **6**(6): 671–81.

Ahmad, Ehtisham, Daniel Hewitt and Edgardo Ruggiero (1994), 'Assigning expenditure responsibilities', in Teresa Ter-Minassian (ed.), *Fiscal Federalism in Theory and Practice*, Washington, DC: International Monetary Fund: 25–48.

Bahl, Roy and Johannes Linn (1994), 'Fiscal decentralization and intergovernmental transfers in less developed countries', *Publius: The Journal of Federalism*, **24**(1): 1–19.

Bakvis, Herman and Grace Skogstad (eds) (2002), *Canadian Federalism: Performance, Effectiveness, and Legitimacy*, Oxford and Toronto: Oxford University Press.

Beer, Samuel H. (1993), *To Make a Nation: The Rediscovery of American Federalism*, Cambridge, MA: Harvard University Press.

Braun, Dietmar (2003), *Fiscal Policies in Federal States*, Aldershot: Ashgate.

Braun, Dietmar (2004), 'Intergovernmental relationships and fiscal policymaking in federal countries', in Imbeau and Petry (eds): 21–48.

Brennan, Geoffrey and James Buchanan (1980), *The Power to Tax: Analytic Foundations of a Fiscal Constitution*, Cambridge: Cambridge University Press.

Bryce, James (1888), *The American Commonwealth*, Vols 1–3, London: Macmillan.

Bull, Hedley (1977), *The Anarchical Society: A Study of Order in World Politics*, London: Macmillan.

Camilleri, J.A. and J. Falk (1992), *The End of Sovereignty? The Politics of a Shrinking and Fragmented World*, Aldershot, UK and Brookfield, US: Edward Elgar.

Carney, F.S. (ed.) (1965), *The Politics of Johannes Althusius*, London: Eyre & Spottiswoode.

Davis, Michael C. (1999), 'The case for Chinese federalism', *Journal of Democracy*, **10**(2): 124–37.

Dollery, Brian (1998), 'An initial evaluation of revenue-sharing arrangements in the New South African fiscal federalism', *Publius: The Journal of Federalism*, **28**(2): 129–49.

Duchacek, Ivo D. (1987), *Comparative Federalism: The Territorial Dimension of Politics*, Lanham/London: University Press of America.

Elaigwu, J. Isawa (2002), 'Federalism in Nigeria'a new democratic polity', *Publius: The Journal of Federalism*, **32**(2): 73–97.

Elazar, Daniel J. (1987), *Exploring Federalism*, Tuscaloosa: University of Alabama Press.

Federalist Papers ([1787] 1961), Alexander Hamilton, James Madison and John Jay, *The Federalist Papers*, New York: Mentor.

Filippov, Mikhail, Peter C. Ordeshook and Olga Shvetsova (2004), *Designing Federalism: A Theory of Self-Sustainable Federal Institutions*, Cambridge: Cambridge University Press.

Franck, T.M. (ed.) (1968), *Why Federations Fail*, New York: New York University Press.

Galligan, Brian (2001), 'Amending constitutions through the referendum device', in M. Mendelsohn, and A. Parkin (eds), *Referendum Democracy: Citizens, Elites, and Deliberation in Referendum Campaigns*, London: Palgrave: 109–24.

Galligan, Brian and Richard Mulgan (1999), 'Asymmetric political association: the Australasian experiment', in Robert Agranoff (ed.), *Accommodating Diversity: Asymmetry in Federal States*, Baden-Baden, Germany: Nomos Verlagsgesellschaft: 57–72.

Galligan, Brian, Winsome Roberts and Gabriella Trifiletti (2001), *Australians and Globalisation*, Cambridge: Cambridge University Press.

Goodin, Robert E. (1996), *The Theory of Institutional Design*, Cambridge: Cambridge University Press.

Greenwood, Gordon (1976; first published 1946), *The Future of Australian Federalism*, 2nd edn, St. Lucia, Queensland: University of Queensland Press.

Grodzins, Morton (1966), *The American System: A New View of Government in the United States*, Ed. Daniel Elazar, New Brunswick, NJ: Transaction Books.

Holland, Kenneth M., F.L. Morton and Brian Galligan (eds) (1996), *Federalism and the Environment: Environmental Policymaking in Australia, Canada, and the United States*, Westport, CT: Greenwood Press.

Imbeau, Louis M. (2004), 'The political-economy of public deficits', in Imbeau and Petry (eds): 1–20.

Imbeau, Louis M. and Francois Petry (eds) (2004), *Politics, Institutions, and Fiscal Policy: Deficits and Surpluses in Federated States*, London: Lexington Books.

Jeffery, Charlie (ed.) (1999), *Recasting German Federalism: The Legacies of Unification*, London: Pinter.

Jenkins, Rob (2003), 'India's states and the making of foreign economic policy: the limits of the constituent diplomacy paradigm', *Publius: The Journal of Federalism*, 33(4): 63–82.

Khan, Rasheeduddin (1992), *Federal India: A Design for Change*, New Delhi: Vikas Publishing House.

Krasner, Stephen (1999), *Sovereignty: Organized Hypocrisy*, Princeton, NJ: Princeton University Press.

Laski, Harold J. (1939), 'The obsolescence of federalism', *New Republic*, 3, May: 367–9.

Lazar, Harvey, Hamish Telford and Ronald L. Watts (eds) (2003), *The Impact of Global and Regional Integration on Federal Systems: A Comparative Analysis*, Montreal: McGill–Queen's University Press.

Lijphart, Arend (1999), *Patterns of Democracy: Government Forms and Performance in Thirty-Six Countries*, New Haven, CT: Yale University Press.

Linklater, Andrew (1998), 'Citizenship and sovereignty in the post-Westphalian state', in D. Archibugi, D. Held and M. Kohler (eds), *Re-imagining Political Community: Studies in Cosmopolitan Democracy*, Stanford, CA: Stanford University Press: 113–37.

Livingston, William S. (1956), *Federalism and Constitutional Change*, Oxford: Clarendon.

Lutz, Donald S. (1994), 'Towards a theory of constitutional amendment', *American Political Science Review*, 88(2): 355–70.

Montero, Alfred P. (2001), 'After decentralization: patterns of intergovernmental conflict in Argentina, Brazil, Spain, and Mexico', *Publius: The Journal of Federalism*, 31(4): 43–66.

Obinger, Herbert, Stephan Leibfried and Francis G. Castles (eds) (2005), *Federalism and the Welfare State: New World and European Experiences*, Cambridge: Cambridge University Press.

Ortino, Sergio, Mitja Zagar and Vojtech Mastny (eds) (2005), *The Changing Faces of Federalism: Institutional Reconfiguration in Europe from East to West*, Manchester: Manchester University Press.

Petry, Francois (2004), 'Deficits and surpluses in federated states: a pooled analysis', in Imbeau and Petry (eds): 203–24.

Rao, M. Govinda (2003), 'Incentivizing fiscal transfers in the Indian federation', *Publius: The Journal of Federalism*, 33(4): 43–63.

Riker, William H. (1964), *Federalism: Origin, Operation, Significance*, Boston, MA: Little, Brown.

Riker, William H. (1970), 'The triviality of federalism', *Politics* [now the *Australian Journal of Political Science*], 5: 239–41.

Riker, William H. (1975), 'Federalism', in Fred I. Greenstein and Nelson W. Polsby (eds), *Handbook of Political Science*, vol. 5: *Governmental Institutions and Processes*, Reading, MA: Addison-Wesley: 93–172.

Riker, William H. (1993), 'Federalism', in Robert E. Goodin and Phillip Pettit (eds), *A Companion to Contemporary Political Philosophy*, Oxford: Basil Blackwell: 508–14.

Rodden, Jonathan (2003), 'Reviving Leviathan: fiscal federalism and the growth of government', *International Organization*. 57, fall: 695–729.

Russell, Peter H. (2004), *Constitutional Odyssey: Can Canadians Become a Sovereign People?*, 3rd edn, Toronto: University of Toronto Press.

Russell, Peter H. (2005), 'The future of Europe in an era of federalism', in Ortino et al. (eds): 4–20.

Sartori, Giovanni (1994), *Comparative Constitutional Engineering*, London: Macmillan.

Simeon, Richard and Christina Murray (2001), 'Multi-sphere governance in South Africa: an interim assessment', *Publius: The Journal of Federalism*, **31**(4): 65–95.

Souza, Celina (2002). 'Brazil: the prospects of a center-constraining federation in a fragmented polity', *Publius: The Journal of Federalism*, **32**(2): 23–49.

Stepan, Alfred (2000), 'Brazil's decentralized federalism: bringing government closer to the citizens?', *Daedalus*, **129**, spring: 145–69.

Strum, Roland (1999), 'Party competition and the federal system: the Lehmbruck hypothesis revisited', in Jeffery (ed.): 107–216.

Tsebelis, George (2002), *Veto Players: How Political Institutions Work*, Princeton, NJ: Princeton University Press.

Verney, Douglas V. (2003), 'From quasi-federation to quasi-confederacy? The transformation of India's party system', *Publius: The Journal of Federalism*, **33**(4): 153–72.

Watts, Ronald L. (1999), *Comparing Federal Systems*, 2nd edn, Montreal: McGill–Queen's University Press.

Wheare, K.C. (1963; first published 1946), *Federal Government*, 4th edn, Oxford: Oxford University Press.

Wright, Deal S. (1998), *Understanding Intergovernmental Relations*, 3rd edn, Pacific Grove, CA: Brooks/Cole.

Index

absenteeism 209, 241, 263
accountability
    and anti-corruption 488, 493–5, 496
    in centralization 46–8, 207, 244–51
    and contracts 485
    in decentralization 33, 155, 287,
        485–6
    and decentralized pollution control
        standards 461–2
    in decentralized public goods and
        service provision (*see*
        accountability in decentralized
        public goods and service
        provision)
    defining 6, 45
    and democracy 408
    and exit 485, 493
    and fiscal federalism 507–8
    in governance 479
    and intergovernmental transfers
        247–8, 369–70, 386, 390, 391,
        393
    in planned economies 231
    in political economy of
        decentralization 34, 44–5
        decentralization and competition
            48–50
        decentralization and lobbying
            50–51
        decentralization and rent diversion
            45, 46–8
        electoral accountability models
            45–6, 207
    in public financial management
        405–6, 408, 409, 412, 413
    and revenue sharing 444
    in standard model of costs and
        benefits of decentralization 34
    and voice 485, 493
    and yardstick competition 77, 207,
        390
    see also local accountability; political
        accountability

accountability in decentralized public
        goods and service provision
    between central and local policy
        makers and providers
    administrative responsibilities and
        capacity building
        250–251
    financing 248–50
    fiscal issues 245–8
    and poor persons 243–4
    of subnational governments to local
        citizens 251
    information, participation and
        monitoring 252, 253–5
    political institutions 258–9
    political markets 252–3
    politician credibility 252–3, 256–8
    public expenditure misallocation
        251–2
    social polarization and elite
        capture 252, 253, 255–6
accounting and reporting standards 406,
        409, 412
accounting systems 409–10, 411, 412
ad valorem royalties 436, 437, 439
administration
    in Breton–Scott assignment model 91
    decentralized public goods and
        service provision 242,
        250–251
    natural resource revenue 443, 444,
        450–451
    subnational public debt control and
        enforcement 418–19, 422–3
    taxation 330–332, 410, 443, 444
administrative asymmetry 506
administrative capacity 205, 206, 242,
        250–251, 294, 331
administrative decentralization 501
agency problems 90–91, 206–7, 208,
        492
    see also principal–agent theories
Ahlin, Christian 483–4, 494